DATE DUE

DEMCO 38-296

Entertainment Awards

To my wonderful wife Dana

Entertainment Awards

A Music, Cinema, Theatre and
Broadcasting Reference,
1928 through 1993

by
DON FRANKS

McFarland & Company, Inc., Publishers
Jefferson, North Carolina, and London

British Library Cataloguing-in-Publication data are available

Library of Congress Cataloguing-in-Publication Data

Franks, Don, 1945–
 Entertainment awards : a music, cinema, theatre and broadcasting
reference, 1928 through 1993 / by Don Franks
  p. cm.
  Includes indexes.
  ISBN 0-7864-0031-5 (lib. bdg. : 50# alk. paper) ∞
  1. Performing arts — United States — Awards. I. Title.
PN2270.A93F68 1996
792′.079′73 — dc20   94-24192
                                                            CIP

Manufactured in the United States of America

McFarland & Company, Inc., Publishers
 Box 611, Jefferson, North Carolina 28640

Preface

I wish to acknowledge the help I received in putting this book together: from the Academy of Motion Picture Arts and Sciences (Oscar Awards), from the Hollywood Foreign Press Association (Golden Globe Awards both for film and television), from the National Academy of Recording Arts & Sciences (Grammy Awards), from the New York Film Critics' Circle, from the Country Music Association (CMA Awards), from Columbia University in New York City (Pulitzer Prizes for both music and theater), from the American Theater Wing (Tony Awards), from *The Village Voice* in New York City (Obie Awards), from the New York Drama Critics' Circle, from the National Academy of Television Arts and Sciences, the Academy of Television Arts and Sciences (Emmy Awards), the University of Georgia (Peabody Awards), Robert Goodman, and finally the staff and research facilities of the Seattle Public Library.

This book is not an official publication of nor is it endorsed by the Academy of Motion Picture Arts and Sciences, the Hollywood Foreign Press Association, the National Academy of Recording Arts & Sciences, the New York Film Critics' Circle, the Country Music Association, Columbia University, the American Theater Wing, *The Village Voice*, the New York Drama Critics' Circle, the National Academy of Television Arts and Sciences, the Academy of Television Arts and Sciences, or the University of Georgia.

My first book for McFarland was published in 1986. The book was titled *Tony, Grammy, Emmy, Country: A Broadway, Television and Record Awards Reference*. The book contained complete listings of the winners of the Tony Awards (Broadway), Grammy Awards (records), CMA Awards (country music) and Emmy Awards (television). Critical reviews of the book questioned why the book was limited to only those four awards. The current book expands the number of awards to thirteen. In addition to theatre, music and broadcasting awards, others have been added for cinema. The list of winners of each of the thirteen awards is complete from the beginning of the award through 1993.

Table of Contents

Introduction

Most fields of endeavor enjoy the prestige of reward and recognition. Many of these recognitions take the form of awards. Many people find awards for achievement in front of or behind the scenes in broadcasting, on stage or on film interesting. In fact you may even cheer for a specific person to win. There are many of these performance awards. This book contains both big and small awards in four main categories. Section One contains awards given for broadcasting; Two deals with music awards; Three is for awards in cinema, and Section Four concentrates on awards given in theatre. The awards are not limited to performances before an audience. People working behind the scenes often make the difference between an award-winning performance and one which is only average. The awarding agencies are:

Oscar Awards
Academy of Motion Picture Arts and
  Sciences
Beverly Hills, California

Golden Globe Awards
Hollywood Foreign Press Association
Beverly Hills, California

Grammy Awards
National Academy of Recording Arts
  & Sciences
Burbank, California

New York Film Critics' Circle Awards
New York Film Critics' Circle
New York, New York

Pulitzer Prize Awards
Columbia University
New York, New York

Tony Awards
American Theater Wing
New York, New York

Obie Awards
The Village Voice
New York, New York

New York Drama Critics' Circle Awards
New York Drama Critics' Circle
New York, New York

Prime-Time Emmy Awards
Academy of Television Arts and
  Sciences
North Hollywood, California

Daytime Emmy Awards
National Academy of Television Arts
  and Sciences
New York, New York

Peabody Awards
University of Georgia
Athens, Georgia

1

Part One

BROADCASTING

Emmy Awards

The National Academy of Television Arts & Sciences was formed in 1946. NATAS was organized similarly to the Association of Motion Picture Arts & Sciences which presents the Oscar Awards. Only six awards were given at the first ceremonies held January 25, 1949, at the Hollywood Athletic Club. This award was named for an Image Orthicon tube used in early television cameras. Technicians called the tube an "immy," hence "emmy."

The Seventh Annual Emmy Awards Ceremony, held March 7, 1955, was the first televised coast-to-coast. NBC carried the ceremonies through 1966. Since then, a rotating system of coverage has been in effect.

Television has always had a difficult time deciding on the categories for the awards. Partially because of the ever-changing categories and methods of determining winners, the first major defection among the broadcasters occurred in May 1964. CBS News withdrew from the ceremonies and ABC followed shortly after. To try and overcome the problem, a multiple award system was tried in 1965. The new system was not very popular and the Emmy Awards returned to the original method of presentation the next year.

Things went smoothly for several years. Everyone in the Academy voted for all awards. But most of the prime-time programs were made in Hollywood. So in 1976, the Hollywood Chapter boycotted the ceremonies.

A new organization was formed out of the old Hollywood Chapter. The new organization was called the Academy of Television Arts & Sciences. ATAS gained control over the prime-time Emmies and NATAS awarded the Emmies for daytime television.

A labor dispute at the 1980 ceremonies caused the most recent disruption. The 32nd Annual Emmy Awards were handed out September 7, 1980. The Emmy boycott was called by members of the Screen Actor's Guild and the American Federation of Television and Radio Artists.

Although this labor dispute was not about the Emmy Awards, pressure exerted by the strike of the Emmy ceremonies helped gain increased recognition for actors whether they were represented by the Screen Actors Guild (SAG) or the American Federation of Television and Radio Artists (AFTRA).

----------- **1 9 4 8** -----------

1 **Most Outstanding Television Personality:** Shirley Dinsdale and her puppet Judy Splinters (KTLA)
2 **Most Popular Television Program:** *Pantomime Quiz Time* (KTLA)
3 **Best Film Made for Television:** *The Necklace*
4 **Station Award for Outstanding Overall Achievement:** KTLA (Los Angeles)
5 **Technical Award:** Charles Mesak for the Phase-fader
6 **Special Award:** Louis McManus for original design of the Emmy statuette

----------- **1 9 4 9** -----------

7 **Most Outstanding Live Personality:** Ed Wynn (KTTV)
8 **Most Outstanding Kinescope Personality:** Milton Berle (KTTV)
9 **Best Live Show:** *Ed Wynn* (KTTV)
10 **Best Kinescope Show:** *Texaco Star Theatre* (KNBH/NBC)
11 **Best Children's Show:** *Time for Beany* (KTLA)
12 **Best Film Made for and Viewed on Television:** *Life of Riley* (KNBH)
13 **Best Sports Coverage:** Wrestling (KTLA)
14 **Station Achievement:** KTLA (Los Angeles)
15 **Best Public Service, Cultural or Educational Program:** *Crusade in Europe* (KECA-TV/KTTV)
16 **Best Commercial Made for Television:** Lucky Strike/N.W. Ayer
17 **Technical Award:** Harold W. Jury

----------- **1 9 5 0** -----------

18 **Most Outstanding Personality:** Groucho Marx (KNBH/NBC)
19 **Best Actor:** Alan Young (KTTV/CBS)
20 **Best Actress:** Gertrude Berg (KTTV/CBS)
21 **Best Public Service:** *City at Night* (KTLA)
22 **Best Children's Show:** *Time for Beany* (KTLA)
23 **Best Dramatic Show:** *Pulitzer Prize Playhouse* (KECA-TV)

24 **Best Sports Program:** Rams Football (KNBH)
25 **Station Achievement:** KTLA (Los Angeles)
26 **Best Cultural Show:** *Campus Chorus and Orchestra* (KTSL)
27 **Special Events:** Departure of Marines for Korea (KFMB and KTLA)
28 **Best News Program:** *KTLA Newsreel*
29 **Best Educational Show:** *KFI-TV University*
30 **Best Variety Show:** *The Alan Young Show* (KTTV/CBS)
31 **Best Game and Audience Participation Show:** *Truth or Consequences* (KTTV/CBS)
32 **Technical Award:** KNBH/NBC for Orthogram T.V.

----------- **1 9 5 1** -----------

33 **Best Comedian or Comedienne:** Red Skelton (NBC)
34 **Best Comedy Show:** *Red Skelton Show* (NBC)
35 **Best Dramatic Show:** *Studio One* (CBS)
36 **Best Actor:** Sid Caesar
37 **Best Actress:** Imogene Coca
38 **Best Variety Show:** *Your Show of Shows* (NBC)
39 **Special Achievement Award:** U.S. Senator Estes Kefauver

----------- **1 9 5 2** -----------

40 **Best Comedian:** Jimmy Durante
41 **Best Comedienne:** Lucille Ball
42 **Best Situation Comedy:** *I Love Lucy* (CBS)
43 **Best Dramatic Show:** *Robert Montgomery Presents* (NBC)
44 **Best Actor:** Thomas Mitchell
45 **Best Actress:** Helen Hayes
46 **Best Variety Show:** *Your Show of Shows* (NBC)
47 **Best Public Affairs Program:** *See It Now* (CBS)
48 **Best Children's Program:** *Time for Beany* (KTLA)
49 **Best Audience Participation, Quiz or Panel Show:** *What's My Line?* (CBS)
50 **Best Mystery, Action or Adventure Program:** *Dragnet* (NBC)

51 **Most Outstanding Personality:** Bishop Fulton J. Sheen

──────── **1 9 5 3** ────────

52 **Best Dramatic Show:** *U.S. Steel Hour* (ABC)
53 **Best Situation Comedy:** *I Love Lucy* (CBS)
54 **Best Variety Program:** *Omnibus* (CBS)
55 **Best Male Star of a Regular Series:** Donald O'Connor on the *Colgate Comedy Hour* (NBC)
56 **Best Female Star of a Regular Series:** Eve Arden on *Our Miss Brooks* (CBS)
57 **Best Series Supporting Actor:** Art Carney on *The Jackie Gleason Show* (CBS)
58 **Most Outstanding Personality:** Edward R. Murrow (CBS)
59 **Best Public Affairs Program:** *Victory at Sea* (NBC)
60 **Best Children's Program:** *Kukla, Fran and Ollie* (NBC)
61 **Best Audience Participation, Quiz or Panel Programs:** *What's My Line?* (CBS), and *This Is Your Life* (NBC)
62 **Best Mystery, Action or Adventure Program:** *Dragnet* (NBC)
63 **Best Program of News or Sports:** *See It Now* (CBS)
64 **Best New Programs:** *Make Room for Daddy* (ABC), and *U.S. Steel Hour* (ABC)

──────── **1 9 5 4** ────────

65 **Best Dramatic Series:** *U.S. Steel Hour* (ABC)
66 **Best Situation Comedy Series:** *Make Room for Daddy* (ABC)
67 **Best Variety Series Including Musical Varieties:** *Disneyland* (ABC)
68 **Best Male Star of a Regular Series:** Danny Thomas in *Make Room for Daddy* (ABC)
69 **Best Female Star of a Regular Series:** Loretta Young in *The Loretta Young Show* (NBC)
70 **Best Series Supporting Actor:** Art Carney on *The Jackie Gleason Show* (CBS)
71 **Best Series Supporting Actress:** Audrey Meadows on *The Jackie Gleason Show* (CBS)
72 **Most Outstanding New Personality:** George Gobel (NBC)
73 **Best Cultural, Religious or Educational Program:** *Omnibus* (CBS)
74 **Best Sports Program:** *Gillette Cavalcade of Sports* (NBC)
75 **Best Audience Participation, Quiz or Panel Programs:** *This Is Your Life* (NBC)
76 **Best Mystery or Intrigue Series:** *Dragnet* (NBC)
77 **Best Children's Program:** *Lassie* (CBS)
78 **Best Daytime Program:** *Art Linkletter's House Party* (CBS)
79 **Best Male Singer:** Perry Como (CBS)
80 **Best Female Singer:** Dinah Shore (NBC)
81 **Best Actor for Single Performance:** Robert Cummings in "Twelve Angry Men" on *Studio One* (CBS)
82 **Best Actress for Single Performance:** Judith Anderson in "Macbeth" on *Hallmark Hall of Fame* (NBC)
83 **Best News Reporter or Commentator:** John Daly (ABC)
84 **Best Western or Adventure Series:** *Stories of the Century* (syndicated)
85 **Best Individual Program of the Year:** "Operation Undersea" on *Disneyland* (ABC)
86 **Best Written Dramatic Material:** Reginald Rose for "Twelve Angry Men" on *Studio One* (CBS)
87 **Best Written Comedy Material:** James Allardice, Hal Kanter, Harry Winkler and Jack Douglas for *The George Gobel Show* (NBC)
88 **Best Art Direction of a Live Show:** Bob Markel for *Mallory's Tragedy on Mt. Everest* (CBS)
89 **Best Direction of Photography:** Lester Schorr for "I Climb the Stairs" on *Medic* (NBC)
90 **Best Sound Editing:** George Nicholson for *Dragnet* (NBC)
91 **Best Television Film Editing:** Grant Smith and Lynn Harrison for "Operation Undersea" on *Disneyland* (ABC)
92 **Best Direction:** Franklin Schaffner for "Twelve Angry Men" on *Studio One* (CBS)

93 **Best Art Direction of a Filmed Show:** Ralph Berger and Albert Pyke for "A Christmas Carol" on *Shower of Stars* (CBS)

94 **Best Choreographer:** June Taylor for *The Jackie Gleason Show* (CBS)

95 **Best Original Music Composed for TV:** Walter Schumann for *Dragnet* (NBC)

96 **Best Scoring of a Dramatic or Variety Program:** Victor Young for *Diamond Jubilee of Lights* (four networks)

97 **Best Engineering Effects:** Robert Shelby for four quadrant screen for National Election Coverage (NBC)

98 **Best Technical Achievements for Color TV Policy:** John West (NBC)

————— **1955** —————

99 **Best Dramatic Series:** *Producer's Showcase* (NBC)

100 **Best Situation Comedy Series:** *You'll Never Get Rich* (CBS)

101 **Best Variety Series:** *The Ed Sullivan Show* (CBS)

102 **Best Male Star of a Regular Series:** Phil Silvers on *You'll Never Get Rich* (CBS)

103 **Best Female Star of a Regular Series:** Lucille Ball on *I Love Lucy* (CBS)

104 **Best Series Supporting Actor:** Art Carney on *The Jackie Gleason Show* (CBS)

105 **Best Series Supporting Actress:** Nanette Fabray in *Caesar's Hour* (NBC)

106 **Best Actor Single Performance:** Lloyd Nolan for "Caine Mutiny Court Martial" on *Ford Star Jubilee* (CBS)

107 **Best Actress Single Performance:** Mary Martin for "Peter Pan" on *Producer's Showcase* (NBC)

108 **Best Comedian:** Phil Silvers (CBS)

109 **Best Comedienne:** Nanette Fabray (NBC)

110 **Best Special Event or News Program:** *A-Bomb Coverage* (CBS)

111 **Best Documentary Program:** *Omnibus* (CBS)

112 **Best Contribution to Daytime Program:** *Matinee Theatre* (NBC)

113 **Best Audience Participation, Quiz or Panel Program:** *$64,000 Question* (CBS)

114 **Best News Commentator or Reporter:** Edward R. Murrow (CBS)

115 **Best Children's Program:** *Lassie* (CBS)

116 **Best M.C. or Program Host:** Perry Como (NBC)

117 **Best Male Singer:** Perry Como (CBS)

118 **Best Female Singer:** Dinah Shore (NBC)

119 **Best Specialty Act:** Marcel Marceau (NBC)

120 **Best Comedy Writing:** Nat Hiken, Barry Blister, Arnold Aurbach, Harry Orkin, Vincent Bogert, Arnold Rosen, Tony Webster, Terry Ryan and Coleman Jacoby for *You'll Never Get Rich* (CBS)

121 **Best Musical Contribution:** "Love and Marriage" from "Our Town" on *Producer's Showcase* (NBC)

122 **Best Television Adaptation:** Paul Gregory and Franklin Schaffner for "Caine Mutiny Court Martial" on *Ford Star Jubilee* (CBS)

123 **Best Live Series Director:** Franklin Schaffner for "Caine Mutiny Court Martial" on *Ford Star Jubilee* (CBS)

124 **Best Film Series Director:** Nat Hiken for *You'll Never Get Rich* (CBS)

125 **Best Original Teleplay Writing:** Rod Serling for *Kraft Television Theatre* (NBC)

126 **Best Live Series Producer:** Fred Coe for *Producer's Showcase* (NBC)

127 **Best Film Series Producer:** Walt Disney for *Disneyland* (ABC)

128 **Best Editing of a Television Film:** Edward Williams for "Breakdown" on *Alfred Hitchcock Presents* (CBS)

129 **Best Cinematography for Television:** William Sickner for "Black Friday" on *Medic* (NBC)

130 **Best Live Show Camerawork:** T. Miller for *Studio One* (CBS)

131 **Best Live Series Art Direction:** Otis Riggs for *Playwrights' '56* and *Producer's Showcase* (NBC)

132 **Best Film Series Art Direction:** William Ferrari for *You Are There* (CBS)

133 **Best Choreographer:** Tony Charmoli for "Show Biz" on *Your Hit Parade* (NBC)

134 **Best Commercial Campaign:** Ford Motor Company

135 **Best Technical Achievement:** RCA tricolor picture tube

136 **Governor's Award:** President Dwight D. Eisenhower for his use and continuing encouragement of television

———————— **1 9 5 6** ————————

137 **Best Series of One Hour or Longer:** *Caesar's Hour* (NBC)
138 **Best Series of One Half Hour:** *Phil Silvers Show* (CBS)
139 **Best Single Program:** "Requiem for a Heavyweight" on *Playhouse 90* (CBS)
140 **Best New Program Series:** *Playhouse 90* (CBS)
141 **Best Public Service Series:** *See It Now* (CBS)
142 **Best Coverage of a Newsworthy Event:** Edward R. Murrow for *Years of Crisis* (CBS)
143 **Best Dramatic Actor in a Regular Series:** Robert Young for *Father Knows Best* (NBC)
144 **Best Dramatic Actor in a Regular Series:** Loretta Young for *The Loretta Young Show* (NBC)
145 **Best Comic Actor in a Regular Series:** Sid Caesar in *Caesar's Hour* (NBC)
146 **Best Comedienne in a Regular Series:** Nanette Fabray in *Caesar's Hour* (NBC)
147 **Best Supporting Actor:** Carl Reiner for *Caesar's Hour* (NBC)
148 **Best Supporting Actress:** Pat Carroll for *Caesar's Hour* (NBC)
149 **Best Single Performance by an Actor:** Jack Palance for "Requiem for a Heavyweight" on *Playhouse 90* (CBS)
150 **Best Single Performance by an Actress:** Claire Trevor for "Dodsworth" on *Producer's Showcase* (NBC)
151 **Best Continuing Performance by an Actor:** Perry Como (NBC)
152 **Best Continuing Performance by an Actress:** Dinah Shore (NBC)
153 **Best News Commentator:** Edward R. Murrow (CBS)
154 **Best Hour or Longer Teleplay Writing:** Rod Serling for "Requiem for a Heavyweight" on *Playhouse 90* (CBS)
155 **Best Half Hour Teleplay Writing:** James P. Cavanaugh for "Fog Closing In" on *Alfred Hitchcock Presents* (CBS)
156 **Best Comedy Writing:** Nat Hiken, Tony Webster, Coleman Jacoby, Arnold Rosen, Billy Friedberg and Leonard Stern for *The Phil Silvers Show* (CBS)
157 **Best One Hour or Longer Direction:** Ralph Nelson for "Requiem for a Heavyweight" on *Playhouse 90* (CBS)
158 **Best Half Hour Direction:** Sheldon Leonard for "Danny's Comeback" on *The Danny Thomas Show* (ABC)
159 **Best Editing of a Television Film:** Frank Keller for "Our Mr. Sun" on *A.T.&T. Science Series* (CBS)
160 **Best Cinematography for Television:** Norbert Brodine for "The Pearl" on *The Loretta Young Show* (NBC)
161 **Best Live Show Camerawork:** "A Night to Remember" on *Kraft Television Theatre* (NBC)
162 **Best One Hour or Longer Art Direction:** Albert Hershong for "Requiem for a Heavyweight" on *Playhouse 90* (CBS)
163 **Best Half Hour Art Direction:** Paul Barnes for *Your Hit Parade* (NBC)
164 **Best Musical Contribution for Television:** Leonard Bernstein, composing and conducting on *Omnibus* (CBS)
165 **Best Engineering or Technical Development:** Ampex and CBS for videotape development and applications

———————— **1 9 5 7** ————————

166 **Best Dramatic Anthology Series:** *Playhouse 90* (CBS)
167 **Best Dramatic Series with Continuing Characters:** *Gunsmoke* (CBS)
168 **Best Single Program:** "The Comedian" on *Playhouse 90* (CBS)
169 **Best New Program Series:** *Seven Lively Arts* (CBS)
170 **Best Comedy:** *The Phil Silvers Show* (CBS)
171 **Best Coverage of an Unscheduled Newsworthy Event:** "Riker's Island Plane Crash" on *World News Roundup* (CBS)
172 **Best Musical Variety, Audience Participation or Quiz Series:** *Dinah Shore Chevy Show* (NBC)
173 **Best Public Service Program or Series:** *Omnibus* (ABC and NBC)
174 **Best Performance by an Actor in a Series:** Robert Young for *Father Knows Best* (NBC)

175 **Best Performance by an Actress in a Series:** Jane Wyatt for *Father Knows Best* (NBC)

176 **Best Single Performance by an Actor:** Peter Ustinov for "The Life of Samuel Johnson" on *Omnibus* (NBC)

177 **Best Single Performance by an Actress:** Polly Bergen for "The Helen Morgan Story" on *Playhouse 90* (CBS)

178 **Best Continuing Support Performance by an Actor:** Carl Reiner for *Caesar's Hour* (NBC)

179 **Best Continuing Support Performance by an Actress:** Ann B. Davis for *The Bob Cummings Show* (CBS and NBC)

180 **Best Continuing Performance by an Actor Essentially Playing Himself:** Jack Benny (CBS)

181 **Best Continuing Performance by an Actress Essentially Playing Herself:** Dinah Shore (NBC)

182 **Best News Commentary:** Edward R. Murrow for *See It Now* (CBS)

183 **Best Hour or Longer Teleplay Writing:** Rod Serling for "The Comedian" on *Playhouse 90* (CBS)

184 **Best Half Hour Teleplay Writing:** Paul Monash for "The Lonely Wizard" on *Schlitz Playhouse of Stars* (CBS)

185 **Best Comedy Writing:** Nat Hiken, Tony Webster, Coleman Jacoby, Billy Friedberg, Terry Ryan and Phil Sharp for *The Phil Silvers Show* (CBS)

186 **Best One Hour or Longer Direction:** Bob Banner for *The Dinah Shore Chevy Show* (NBC)

187 **Best Half Hour Direction:** Robert Stevens for "The Glass Eye" on *Alfred Hitchcock Presents* (CBS)

188 **Best Editing of a Television Film:** Moke Pozen for "How to Kill a Woman" on *Gunsmoke* (CBS)

189 **Best Cinematography for Television:** Harold E. Wellman for "Hemo the Magnificent" on *The Bell Telephone Science Series* (CBS)

190 **Best Live Show Camerawork:** *Playhouse 90* (CBS)

191 **Best Art Direction:** Rouben Ter-Arutunian for "Twelfth Night" on *Hallmark Hall of Fame* (NBC)

192 **Best Half Hour Art Direction:** Paul Barnes for *Your Hit Parade* (NBC)

193 **Best Musical Contribution for Television:** Leonard Bernstein conducting and analyzing the music of Johann Sebastian Bach on *Omnibus* (ABC)

194 **Best Engineering or Technical Achievement:** *Wide, Wide World* (NBC)

──────── **1958** ────────

195 **Best One Hour or Longer Dramatic Series:** *Playhouse 90* (CBS)

196 **Best Half Hour Dramatic Series:** *Alcoa-Goodyear Theatre* (NBC)

197 **Best Single Program:** *An Evening with Fred Astaire* (NBC)

198 **Best Comedy Series:** *The Jack Benny Show* (CBS)

199 **Best Western Series:** *Maverick* (ABC)

200 **Best News Reporting Series:** *The Huntley-Brinkley Report* (NBC)

201 **Best Special News Program:** *The Face of Red China* (CBS)

202 **Best Public Service Program or Series:** *Omnibus* (NBC)

203 **Best Musical or Variety Series:** *Dinah Shore Chevy Show* (NBC)

204 **Best Panel, Quiz or Audience Participation Series:** *What's My Line?* (CBS)

205 **Best One Hour or Longer Dramatic Program:** "Little Moon of Alban" on *Hallmark Hall of Fame* (NBC)

206 **Best Continuing Leading Performance by an Actress in a Comedy Series:** Jane Wyatt for *Father Knows Best* (NBC and CBS)

207 **Best Continuing Leading Performance by an Actor in a Comedy Series:** Jack Benny for *The Jack Benny Show* (CBS)

208 **Best Actress in a Leading Role in a Dramatic Series:** Loretta Young in *The Loretta Young Show* (NBC)

209 **Best Actor in a Leading Role in a Dramatic Series:** Raymond Burr in *Perry Mason* (CBS)

210 **Best Supporting Actress in a Dramatic Series:** Barbara Hale in *Perry Mason* (CBS)

211 **Best Supporting Actor in a Dramatic Series:** Dennis Weaver in *Gunsmoke* (CBS)

212 **Best Supporting Actress in a Comedy Series:** Ann B. Davis in *The Bob Cummings Show* (NBC)

213 **Best Supporting Actor in a Comedy Series:** Tom Poston in *The Steve Allen Show* (NBC)

214 **Best Performance by an Actor in a Musical or Variety Series:** Perry Como (CBS)

215 **Best Performance by an Actress in a Musical or Variety Series:** Dinah Shore (NBC)

216 **Best Single Performance by an Actor:** Fred Astaire in *An Evening with Fred Astaire* (NBC)

217 **Best Single Performance by an Actress:** Julie Harris in "Little Moon of Alban" on *Hallmark Hall of Fame* (NBC)

218 **Best News Commentator or Analyst:** Edward R. Murrow (CBS)

219 **Best One Hour or Longer Direction from a Dramatic Series:** George Schaefer for "Little Moon of Alban" on *Hallmark Hall of Fame* (NBC)

220 **Best Half Hour Direction from a Dramatic Series:** Jack Smight for "Eddie" on *Alcoa-Goodyear Theatre* (NBC)

221 **Best Direction of a Single Musical or Variety Program:** Bud Yorkin for *An Evening with Fred Astaire* (NBC)

222 **Best Direction of a Single Program from a Comedy Series:** Peter Tewksbury for "Medal for Margaret" on *Father Knows Best* (CBS)

223 **Best One Hour or Longer Writing of a Single Dramatic Program:** James Costigan for "Little Moon of Alban" on *Hallmark Hall of Fame* (NBC)

224 **Best Half Hour Writing of a Single Dramatic Program of a Dramatic Series:** Alfred Brenner and Ken Hughes for "Eddie" on *Alcoa-Goodyear Theatre* (NBC)

225 **Best Writing of a Single Program of a Comedy Series:** Sam Perin, Hal Goodman, George Balzer and Al Gordon for "With Ernie Kovacs" on *The Jack Benny Show* (CBS)

226 **Best Editing of a Television Film:** Silvio d'Alisera for "Meet Mr. Lincoln" on *Project 20* (NBC)

227 **Best Cinematography for Television:** Ellis W. Carter for "Alphabet Conspiracy" on *The Bell Telephone Special* (NBC)

228 **Best Live Show Camerawork:** *An Evening with Fred Astaire* (NBC)

229 **Best Art Direction in a Television Film:** Claudio Guzman for "Bernadette" on *Westinghouse Desilu Playhouse* (CBS)

230 **Best Art Direction of a Live Program:** Edward Stephenson for *An Evening with Fred Astaire* (NBC)

231 **Best Musical Contribution for Television:** David Rose for *An Evening with Fred Astaire* (NBC)

232 **Best Choreography:** Hermes Pan for *An Evening with Fred Astaire* (NBC)

233 **Best Spot Coverage of a News Event:** *Cuban Revolution* (CBS)

234 **Best Engineering or Technical Achievement:** Industrywide improvement of editing (ABC, CBS and NBC)

235 **Trustees Award:** Bob Hope

——— **1959** ———

236 **Outstanding Achievement in Drama:** *Playhouse 90* (CBS)

237 **Outstanding Achievement in Variety:** *Fabulous Fifties* (CBS)

238 **Outstanding Achievement in Humor:** *Art Carney Special* (NBC)

239 **Outstanding Achievement in News:** *Huntley-Brinkley Report* (NBC)

240 **Outstanding Achievement in Public Affairs and Education:** *Twentieth Century* (CBS)

241 **Outstanding Achievement in Children's Programming:** *Huckleberry Hound* (syndicated)

242 **Outstanding Achievement by a Series Actor:** Robert Stack for *The Untouchables* (ABC)

243 **Outstanding Achievement by a Series Actress:** Jane Wyatt for *Father Knows Best* (CBS)

244 **Outstanding Single Performance by an Actor:** Laurence Olivier in *The Moon and Sixpence* (NBC)

245 **Outstanding Single Performance by an Actress:** Ingrid Bergman in "The Turn of the Screw" on *Ford Startime* (NBC)

246 **Outstanding Performance in a Variety or Musical Program Series:** Harry Belafonte in "Tonight with Belafonte" on *Revlon Revue* (CBS)

247 **Outstanding Achievement in Direction of Drama:** Robert Mulligan for *The Moon and Sixpence* (NBC)

248 **Outstanding Achievement in Direction of Comedy:** Ralph Levy and Bud Yorkin for *The Jack Benny Hour Specials* (CBS)

249 **Outstanding Writing Achievement in Drama:** Rod Serling for *Twilight Zone* (CBS)

250 **Outstanding Writing Achievement in Comedy:** Sam Perin, George Balzer, Al Gordon and Hal Goldman for *The Jack Benny Show* (CBS)

251 **Outstanding Writing Achievement in Documentary:** Howard K. Smith and Av Westin for *The Population Explosion* (CBS)

252 **Best Editing of a Television Film:** Ben H. Ray and Robert L. Swanson for *The Untouchables* (ABC)

253 **Best Cinematography for Television:** Charles Straumer for "The Untouchables" on *Westinghouse Desilu Playhouse* (CBS)

254 **Best Live Show Camerawork:** Winter Olympics (CBS)

255 **Best Art Direction and Scenic Design:** Ralph Berger and Frank Smith for "The Untouchables" on *Westinghouse Desilu Playhouse* (CBS)

256 **Outstanding Achievement in Music:** *Leonard Bernstein and the New York Philharmonic* (CBS)

257 **Best Engineering or Technical Achievement:** General Electric super sensitive camera tube

258 **Trustees' Award:** Frank Stanton

259 **Trustees' Citation:** Michael R. Gargiulo, Richard Gillaspy, Ampex Corporation and the Radio Corporation of America for the Nixon-Khrushchev Debates in Moscow

────── **1 9 6 0** ──────

260 **Outstanding Achievement in Drama:** "Macbeth" on *Hallmark Hall of Fame* (NBC)

261 **Outstanding Achievement in Variety:** *Astaire Time* (NBC)

262 **Outstanding Achievement in Humor:** *Jack Benny Show* (CBS)

263 **Outstanding Achievement in News:** *Huntley-Brinkley Report* (NBC)

264 **Outstanding Achievement in Public Affairs and Education:** *Twentieth Century* (CBS)

265 **Outstanding Achievement in Children's Programming:** "Aaron Copland's Birthday Party" on *Young People's Concert* (CBS)

266 **Outstanding Program of the Year:** "Macbeth" on *Hallmark Hall of Fame* (NBC)

267 **Outstanding Achievement by a Series Actor:** Raymond Burr on *Perry Mason* (CBS)

268 **Outstanding Achievement by a Series Actress:** Barbara Stanwyck on *The Barbara Stanwyck Show* (NBC)

269 **Outstanding Single Performance by an Actor:** Maurice Evans in "Macbeth" on *Hallmark Hall of Fame* (NBC)

270 **Outstanding Single Performance by an Actress:** Judith Anderson in "Macbeth" on *Hallmark Hall of Fame* (NBC)

271 **Outstanding Performance in a Variety or Musical Program Series:** Fred Astaire on *Astaire Time* (NBC)

272 **Outstanding Performance in a Series Supporting Role:** Don Knotts on *The Andy Griffith Show* (CBS)

273 **Outstanding Performance in a Supporting Role:** Roddy McDowall in "Not Without Honor" on *Equitable's American Heritage* (NBC)

274 **Outstanding Achievement in Direction of Drama:** George Schaefer for "Macbeth" on *Hallmark Hall of Fame* (NBC)

275 **Outstanding Achievement in Direction of Comedy:** Sheldon Leonard for *The Danny Thomas Show* (CBS)

276 **Outstanding Writing Achievement in Drama:** Rod Serling for *Twilight Zone* (CBS)

277 **Outstanding Writing Achievement in Comedy:** Sherwood Schwartz, Dave O'Brien, Al Schwartz, Martin Ragaway and Red Skelton for *The Red Skelton Show* (CBS)

278 **Outstanding Writing Achievement in a Documentary:** Victor Wolfson for *Winston Churchill, the Valiant Years* (ABC)

279 **Best Editing of a Television Film:** Harry Coswick, Aaron Nibley and Milton Schifman for *Naked City* (ABC)

280 **Best Cinematography for Television:** George Clemens for *Twilight Zone* (CBS)

281 **Outstanding Achievement in Electronic Camera Work:** "Sounds of America" on *Bell Telephone Hour* (NBC)

282 **Outstanding Achievement in Art Direction and Scenic Design:** John J. Lloyd for *Checkmate* (CBS)

283 **Outstanding Achievement in Music:** *Leonard Bernstein and the New York Philharmonic* (CBS)

284 **Outstanding Engineering or Technical Achievement:** Marconi's Wireless Telegraph Company and the Radio Corporation of America for independent development of the 4½ inch image orthicon tube.

285 **Trustees' Award:** Joyce C. Hall, National Educational Television and Radio Center and its affiliated stations

———— **1 9 6 1** ————

286 **Outstanding Achievement in Drama:** *The Defenders* (CBS)

287 **Outstanding Achievement in Variety:** *Gary Moore Show* (CBS)

288 **Outstanding Achievement in Humor:** *Bob Newhart Show* (CBS)

289 **Outstanding Achievement in News:** *Huntley-Brinkley Report* (NBC)

290 **Outstanding Achievement in Public Affairs and Education:** *David Brinkley's Journal* (NBC)

291 **Outstanding Achievement in Children's Programming:** *New York Philharmonic Young People's Concerts with Leonard Bernstein* (CBS)

292 **Outstanding Program of the Year:** "Victoria Regina" on *Hallmark Hall of Fame* (NBC)

293 **Outstanding Achievement by a Series Actor:** E.G. Marshall in *The Defenders* (CBS)

294 **Outstanding Achievement by a Series Actress:** Shirley Booth in *Hazel* (NBC)

295 **Outstanding Single Performance by an Actor:** Peter Falk in "The Price of Tomatoes" on *The Dick Powell Show* (NBC)

296 **Outstanding Single Performance by an Actress:** Julie Harris in "Victoria Regina" on *Hallmark Hall of Fame* (NBC)

297 **Outstanding Performance in a Variety or Musical Program Series:** Carol Burnett on *The Gary Moore Show* (CBS)

298 **Outstanding Performance in a Series Supporting Role by an Actor:** Don Knotts on *The Andy Griffith Show* (CBS)

299 **Outstanding Performance in a Supporting Role by an Actress:** Pamela Brown in "Victoria Regina" on *Hallmark Hall of Fame* (NBC)

300 **Outstanding Achievement in Direction of Drama:** Franklin Schaffner in *The Defenders* (CBS)

301 **Outstanding Achievement in Direction of Comedy:** Nat Hiken for *Car 54, Where Are You?* (NBC)

302 **Outstanding Writing Achievement in Drama:** Reginald Rose for *The Defenders* (CBS)

303 **Outstanding Writing Achievement in Comedy:** Carl Reiner for *Dick Van Dyke Show* (CBS)

304 **Outstanding Writing Achievement in a Documentary:** Lou Hazam for *Vincent Van Gogh: A Self Portrait* (NBC)

305 **Best Editing of a Television Film:** Aaron Nibley, Charles L. Freeman and Hugh Chaloupka for *Naked City* (ABC)

306 **Best Cinematography for Television:** John S. Priestly for *Naked City* (ABC)

307 **Outstanding Achievement in Electronic Camera Work:** Ernie Kovacs (ABC)

308 **Outstanding Achievement in Art Direction and Scenic Design:** Gary Smith for *Perry Como's Kraft Music Hall* (NBC)

309 **Outstanding Achievement in Music:** *Leonard Bernstein and the New York Philharmonic in Japan* (CBS)

310 **Outstanding Achievement in Music Composed for Television:** Richard Rodgers for *Winston Churchill, the Valiant Years* (NBC)

311 **Outstanding Daytime Program:** *Purex Specials for Women* (NBC)

312 **Outstanding Engineering or Technical Achievement:** ABC Videotape Expander, slow motion tape developed by Albert Malang

313 **Trustees' Awards:** CBS, NBC and ABC News Department heads, CBS News and Jacqueline Kennedy for *A Tour of the White House*, and General David Sarnoff

─────────── **1962** ───────────

314 **Outstanding Achievement in Drama:** *The Defenders* (CBS)
315 **Outstanding Achievement in Variety:** *Andy Williams Show* (NBC)
316 **Outstanding Achievement in Humor:** *Dick Van Dyke Show* (CBS)
317 **Outstanding Achievement in News:** *Huntley-Brinkley Report* (NBC)
318 **Outstanding Achievement in News Commentary or Public Affairs:** *David Brinkley's Journal* (NBC)
319 **Outstanding Achievement in Children's Programming:** *Walt Disney's Wonderful World of Color* (CBS)
320 **Outstanding Program of the Year:** *The Tunnel* (NBC)
321 **Outstanding Achievement of Documentary Programs:** *The Tunnel* (NBC)
322 **Outstanding Achievement for International Reporting or Commentary:** Piers Anderton on *The Tunnel* (NBC)
323 **Outstanding Achievement of Panel, Quiz or Audience Participation:** *G.E. College Bowl* (CBS)
324 **Outstanding Achievement by a Series Actor:** E.G. Marshall in *The Defenders* (CBS)
325 **Outstanding Achievement by a Series Actress:** Shirley Booth in *Hazel* (NBC)
326 **Outstanding Single Performance by an Actor:** Trevor Howard in "The Invincible Mr. Disraeli" on *Hallmark Hall of Fame* (NBC)
327 **Outstanding Single Performance by an Actress:** Kim Stanley in "A Cardinal Act of Mercy" on *Ben Casey* (ABC)
328 **Outstanding Performance in a Variety or Musical Program or Series:** Carol Burnett on *Julie and Carol at Carnegie Hall* (CBS)
329 **Outstanding Performance by an Actor in a Series Supporting Role:** Don Knotts on *The Andy Griffith Show* (CBS)
330 **Outstanding Performance in a Supporting Role by an Actress:** Glenda Farrell for "A Cardinal Act of Mercy" on *Ben Casey* (ABC)
331 **Outstanding Achievement in Direction of Drama:** Stuart Rosenberg for "The Madman" on *The Defenders* (CBS)

332 **Outstanding Achievement in Direction of Comedy:** John Rich for *Dick Van Dyke Show* (CBS)
333 **Outstanding Writing Achievement in Drama:** Robert Thom and Reginald Rose for "The Madman" on *The Defenders* (CBS)
334 **Outstanding Writing Achievement in Comedy:** Carl Reiner for *Dick Van Dyke Show* (CBS)
335 **Outstanding Program Achievement in Music:** *Julie and Carol at Carnegie Hall* (CBS)
336 **Outstanding Achievement for Original Music:** Robert Russell Bennett for "He Is Risen" on *Project 20* (NBC)
337 **Best Editing of a Television Film:** Sid Katz for *The Defenders* (CBS)
338 **Best Cinematography for Television:** John S. Priestly for *Naked City* (ABC)
339 **Outstanding Achievement in Electronic Camera Work:** "The Invincible Mr. Disraeli" on *Hallmark Hall of Fame* (NBC)
340 **Outstanding Achievement in Art Direction and Scenic Design:** Carroll Clark and Marvin Aubrey Davis for *Walt Disney's World of Color* (NBC)
341 **International Award:** *War and Peace* on England's Granada Network
342 **Station Award:** WCBS-TV, New York for *Superfluous People*
343 **Trustees' Award:** Dick Powell, the American Telephone and Telegraph Company and President John F. Kennedy

─────────── **1963** ───────────

344 **Outstanding Achievement in Drama:** *The Defenders* (CBS)
345 **Outstanding Achievement in Variety:** *The Danny Kaye Show* (CBS)
346 **Outstanding Achievement in Humor:** *Dick Van Dyke Show* (CBS)
347 **Outstanding Achievement in News:** *Huntley-Brinkley Report* (NBC)
348 **Outstanding Achievement in News Commentary or Public Affairs:** *David Brinkley's Journal* (NBC)
349 **Outstanding Achievement in Children's Programming:** *Discovery '63-'64* (ABC)

350 **Outstanding Program of the Year:** *Making of the President 1960* (ABC)

351 **Outstanding Achievement of Documentary Programs:** *Making of the President 1960* (ABC)

352 **Outstanding Achievement for News Commentary or Public Affairs:** Cuba Parts I & II, *The Bay of Pigs* and *The Missile Crisis* (NBC)

353 **Outstanding Achievement in Music:** *Bell Telephone Hour* (NBC)

354 **Outstanding Achievement by a Series Actor:** Dick Van Dyke for *Dick Van Dyke Show* (CBS)

355 **Outstanding Achievement by a Series Actress:** Mary Tyler Moore for *Dick Van Dyke Show* (CBS)

356 **Outstanding Single Performance by an Actor:** Jack Klugman for "Blacklist" on *The Defenders* (CBS)

357 **Outstanding Single Performance by an Actress:** Shelley Winters for "Two Is the Number" on *Bob Hope Presents the Chrysler Theatre* (NBC)

358 **Outstanding Performance in a Variety or Musical Program or Series:** Danny Kaye for *The Danny Kaye Show* (CBS)

359 **Outstanding Performance by an Actor in a Supporting Role:** Albert Paulson for "One Day in the Life of Ivan Denisovich" on *Bob Hope Presents the Chrysler Theatre* (NBC)

360 **Outstanding Performance in a Supporting Role by an Actress:** Ruth White for "Little Moon of Alban" on *Hallmark Hall of Fame* (NBC)

361 **Outstanding Writing Achievement in Drama Adaptation:** Rod Serling for "It's Mental Work" on *Bob Hope Presents the Chrysler Theatre* (NBC)

362 **Outstanding Writing Achievement in Original Drama:** Ernest Kinoy for "Blacklist" on *The Defenders* (CBS)

363 **Outstanding Writing Achievement in Comedy or Variety:** Carl Reiner, Sam Denoff and Bill Persky for *Dick Van Dyke Show* (CBS)

364 **Outstanding Achievement in Direction for Drama:** Tom Gries for "Who Do You Kill?" on *East Side/West Side* (CBS)

365 **Outstanding Achievement in Direction for Comedy:** Jerry Paris for *Dick Van Dyke Show* (CBS)

366 **Outstanding Achievement in Direction for Variety or Music:** Robert Sheerer for *The Danny Kaye Show* (CBS)

367 **Outstanding Achievement for Original Music:** Elmer Bernstein for *The Making of the President 1960* (ABC)

368 **Best Editing of a Television Film:** William T. Cartwright for *The Making of the President 1960* (ABC)

369 **Best Cinematography for Television:** J. Baxter Peters for *The Kremlin* (ABC)

370 **Outstanding Achievement in Electronic Camera Work:** *The Danny Kaye Show* (CBS)

371 **Outstanding Achievement in Art Direction and Scenic Design:** Warren Clymer for *Hallmark Hall of Fame* (NBC)

372 **International Award:** *Les Raisins Verts* Radiodiffusion Télévision Français

373 **Station Award:** KPIX, San Francisco for *Operation Challenge—A Study in Hope*

———————— **1964** ————————

374 **Outstanding Program Achievement in Entertainment:** *Dick Van Dyke Show* (CBS)

375 **Outstanding Program Achievement in Entertainment:** "The Magnificent Yankee" on *Hallmark Hall of Fame* (NBC)

376 **Outstanding Program Achievement in Entertainment:** *My Name Is Barbra* (CBS)

377 **Outstanding Program Achievement in Entertainment:** "What Is Sonata Form?" on *New York Philharmonic Young People's Concert with Leonard Bernstein* (CBS)

378 **Outstanding Individual Achievement of an Actor or Performer in Entertainment:** Leonard Bernstein for *New York Philharmonic Young People's Concert with Leonard Bernstein* (CBS)

379 **Outstanding Individual Achievement of an Actor or Performer in Entertainment:** Lynn Fontanne in "The Magnificent Yankee" on *Hallmark Hall of Fame* (NBC)

380 **Outstanding Individual Achievement of an Actor or Performer in Entertainment:** Alfred Lunt in "The Magnificent Yankee" on *Hallmark Hall of Fame* (NBC)

381 Outstanding Individual Achievement of an Actor or Performer in Entertainment: Barbra Streisand for *My Name Is Barbra* (CBS)
382 Outstanding Individual Achievement of an Actor or Performer in Entertainment: Dick Van Dyke for *Dick Van Dyke Show* (CBS)
383 Outstanding Program Achievement in News, Documentaries or Sports: "I, Leonardo" on *Saga of Western Man* (ABC)
384 Outstanding Program Achievement in News, Documentaries or Sports: *The Louvre* (NBC)
385 Outstanding Individual Achievement in News, Documentaries or Sports: Richard Basehart for *Let My People Go* (syndicated)
386 Outstanding Individual Writing Achievement in News, Documentaries or Sports: Sidney Carroll for *The Louvre* (NBC)
387 Outstanding Individual Film Editing Achievement in News, Documentaries or Sports: Aram Boyajian for *The Louvre* (NBC)
388 Outstanding Individual Directing Achievement in News, Documentaries or Sports: John J. Sughrue for *The Louvre* (NBC)
389 Outstanding Individual Achievement in Cinematography in News, Documentaries or Sports: Tom Priestly for *The Louvre* (NBC)
390 Outstanding Individual Achievement in Music for News, Documentaries or Sports: Norman Dello Joio for *The Louvre* (NBC)
391 Outstanding Individual Achievement in Cinematography in Entertainment: William Spencer for *Twelve O'Clock High* (ABC)
392 Outstanding Individual Music Achievement in Entertainment: Peter Matz for *My Name Is Barbra* (CBS)
393 Outstanding Individual Achievement in Directing Entertainment: Paul Bogert for "The 700 Year Old Gang" on *The Defenders* (CBS)
394 Outstanding Individual Writing Achievement in Entertainment: David Karp for "The 700 Year Old Gang" on *The Defenders* (CBS)
395 Outstanding Individual Achievement in Costume Design in Entertainment:

Noel Taylor for "The Magnificent Yankee" on *Hallmark Hall of Fame* (NBC)
396 Outstanding Individual Achievement in Lighting Direction in Entertainment: Henry Berman, Joseph Dervin and Will Glock for *The Man from U.N.C.L.E.* (NBC)
397 Outstanding Individual Achievement in Lighting Direction in Entertainment: Phil Hymes for "The Magnificent Yankee" on *Hallmark Hall of Fame* (NBC)
398 Outstanding Individual Achievement in Choreography in Entertainment: Joe Layton for *My Name Is Barbra* (CBS)
399 Outstanding Individual Achievement in Set Decoration in Entertainment: Warren Clymer for "The Holy Terror" on *Hallmark Hall of Fame* (NBC)
400 Outstanding Individual Achievement in Art and Set Direction in Entertainment: Bill Harp and Tom John for *My Name Is Barbra* (CBS)
401 Outstanding Individual Achievement in Make-Up in Entertainment: Robert O'Bradovich for "The Magnificent Yankee" on *Hallmark Hall of Fame* (NBC)
402 Outstanding Individual Achievement in Special Photographic Effects in Entertainment: L.B. Abbott for *Voyage to the Bottom of the Sea* (ABC)
403 Outstanding Individual Achievement in Special Effects in Entertainment: Production Team from *Man from U.N.C.L.E.* (NBC)
404 Outstanding Individual Achievement in Color Consulting in Entertainment: Edward Acona for *Bonanza* (NBC)
405 Outstanding Individual Achievement in Technical Directing in Entertainment: Clair McCoy for *The Wonderful World of Burlesque* (NBC)
406 International Award: *Le Barber de Seville* Canadian Broadcasting Company
407 Station Award: WDSU-TV, New Orleans for *Ku Klux Klan*

———— 1 9 6 5 ————

408 Outstanding Comedy Series: *The Dick Van Dyke Show* (CBS)

409 **Outstanding Variety Series:** *The Andy Williams Show* (NBC)
410 **Outstanding Dramatic Series:** *The Fugitive* (ABC)
411 **Outstanding Children's Program:** *A Charlie Brown Christmas* (CBS)
412 **Outstanding Musical Program:** *Frank Sinatra: A Man and His Music* (NBC)
413 **Outstanding Variety Special:** *Chrysler Presents the Bob Hope Christmas Special* (NBC)
414 **Outstanding Dramatic Program:** *Ages of Man* (CBS)
415 **Outstanding Single Performance by a Dramatic Actor:** Cliff Robertson in "The Game" on *Bob Hope Presents the Chrysler Theatre* (NBC)
416 **Outstanding Single Performance by a Dramatic Actress:** Simone Signoret in "A Small Rebellion" on *Bob Hope Presents the Chrysler Theatre* (NBC)
417 **Outstanding Continuing Performance by a Dramatic Actor:** Bill Cosby in *I Spy* (NBC)
418 **Outstanding Continuing Performance by a Dramatic Actress:** Barbara Stanwyck in *The Big Valley* (ABC)
419 **Outstanding Supporting Performance by a Dramatic Actor:** James Daly on "Eagle in a Cage" on *Hallmark Hall of Fame* (NBC)
420 **Outstanding Supporting Performance by a Dramatic Actress:** Lee Grant on *Peyton Place* (ABC)
421 **Outstanding Continuing Performance by a Comic Actor:** Dick Van Dyke on *Dick Van Dyke Show* (CBS)
422 **Outstanding Continuing Performance by a Comic Actress:** Mary Tyler Moore on *Dick Van Dyke Show* (CBS)
423 **Outstanding Supporting Performance by a Comic Actor:** Don Knotts on *The Andy Griffith Show* (CBS)
424 **Outstanding Supporting Performance by a Comic Actress:** Alice Pearce on *Bewitched* (ABC)
425 **Outstanding Directing of Drama:** Sydney Pollack for "The Game" on *Bob Hope Presents the Chrysler Theatre* (NBC)
426 **Outstanding Directing of Comedy:** William Asher for *Bewitched* (ABC)
427 **Outstanding Directing of Music or Variety:** Alan Handley for *The Julie Andrews Show* (NBC)

428 **Outstanding Writing in Drama:** Millard Lampell for "Eagle in a Cage" on *Hallmark Hall of Fame* (NBC)
429 **Outstanding Writing in Comedy:** Bill Persky and Sam Denoff for "Coast to Coast Big Mouth" on *Dick Van Dyke Show* (CBS)
430 **Outstanding Writing on Variety:** Al Gordon, Hal Goodman and Sheldon Keller for *An Evening with Carol Channing* (CBS)
431 **Outstanding Individual Achievement in Film Editing:** David Blewitt and William T. Cartwright for *The Making of the President 1964* (CBS)
432 **Outstanding Individual Achievement in Film Editing:** Marvin Coil, Everett Douglass and Ellsworth Hoagland for *Bonanza* (NBC)
433 **Outstanding Individual Achievement in Videotape Editing:** Craig Curtis and Art Schneider for *The Julie Andrews Show* (NBC)
434 **Outstanding Achievement in News and Documentaries:** *American White Paper: United States Foreign Policy* (NBC)
435 **Outstanding Achievement in News and Documentaries:** *KKK—The Invisible Empire* (CBS)
436 **Outstanding Achievement in News and Documentaries:** *Senate Hearings on Vietnam* (CBS)
437 **Outstanding Achievement in Daytime Programs:** *Camera Three* (CBS)
438 **Outstanding Achievement in Daytime Programs:** *Mutual of Omaha's Wild Kingdom* (NBC)
439 **Outstanding Achievement in Sports:** *CBS Golf Classic* (CBS)
440 **Outstanding Achievement in Sports:** *ABC Wide World of Sports* (ABC)
441 **Outstanding Achievement in Sports:** *Shell's Wonderful World of Golf* (NBC)
442 **Outstanding Individual Achievement in Educational Television:** Julia Child in *The French Chef* (NET)
443 **Outstanding Individual Achievement in Music:** Laurence Rosenthal for *Michelangelo: The Last Giant* (NBC)
444 **Outstanding Individual Achievement in Technical Directing:** O. Tamburri for "Inherit the Wind" on *Hallmark Hall of Fame* (NBC)

445 **Outstanding Individual Achievement in Lighting:** Lon Stucky for *Frank Sinatra: A Man and His Music* (NBC)

446 **Outstanding Individual Achievement in Art Direction:** James W. Trittipo for *The Hollywood Palace* (ABC)

447 **Outstanding Individual Achievement in Special Photographic Effects:** L.B. Abbott and Howard Lydecker in *Voyage to the Bottom of the Sea* (ABC)

448 **Outstanding Individual Achievement in Cinematography:** Winton C. Hoch for *Voyage to the Bottom of the Sea* (ABC)

449 **Outstanding Individual Achievement in Audio Engineering:** Laurence Schneider for "Seventh Annual Young Performer's Concert" on *The New York Philharmonic with Leonard Bernstein* (CBS)

450 **Outstanding Individual Achievement in Engineering:** Hughes Aircraft Corporation and Communications Satellite Corporation for the Early Bird Satellite

451 **Outstanding Individual Achievement in Engineering:** MVR Corporation and CBS for Stop Action Playback

452 **Outstanding Individual Achievement in Engineering:** Burr Tillstrom for "Berlin Wall" on *That Was the Week That Was* (NBC)

453 **International Award:** "Breakout" on *Wyvern at War No. 2* (Westwood Television Limited, Plymouth, England)

454 **Station Award:** WBBM, Chicago for *I See Chicago*

455 **Trustees' Awards:** Edward R. Murrow and the Xerox Corporation

———————— **1966** ————————

456 **Outstanding Comedy Series:** *The Monkees* (NBC)

457 **Outstanding Variety Series:** *The Andy Williams Show* (NBC)

458 **Outstanding Dramatic Series:** *Mission: Impossible* (CBS)

459 **Outstanding Children's Program:** *Jack and the Beanstalk* (CBS)

460 **Outstanding Musical Program:** *Brigadoon* (ABC)

461 **Outstanding Variety Special:** *The Sid Caesar, Imogene Coca, Carl Reiner, Howard Morris Special* (NBC)

462 **Outstanding Program Achievement in News and Documentaries:** *Hall of Kings* (ABC)

463 **Outstanding Program Achievement in News and Documentaries:** *The Italians* (CBS)

464 **Outstanding Program Achievement in News and Documentaries:** *China: The Roots of Madness* (syndicated)

465 **Outstanding Program Achievement in Daytime Programming:** *Mutual of Omaha's Wild Kingdom* (NBC)

466 **Outstanding Individual Achievement in Daytime Programming:** *The Mike Douglas Show* (syndicated)

467 **Outstanding Achievement in Sports Programming:** *ABC's Wide World of Sports* (ABC)

468 **Outstanding Single Performance by a Dramatic Actor:** Peter Ustinov in "Barefoot in Athens" on *Hallmark Hall of Fame* (NBC)

469 **Outstanding Single Performance by a Dramatic Actress:** Geraldine Page in "A Christmas Memory" on *ABC Stage 67* (ABC)

470 **Outstanding Continuing Performance by a Dramatic Actor:** Bill Cosby on *I Spy* (NBC)

471 **Outstanding Continuing Performance by a Dramatic Actress:** Barbara Bain on *Mission: Impossible* (CBS)

472 **Outstanding Continuing Performance by a Comic Actor:** Don Adams for *Get Smart* (NBC)

473 **Outstanding Continuing Performance by a Comic Actress:** Lucille Ball in *The Lucy Show* (CBS)

474 **Outstanding Supporting Performance by a Comic Actor:** Don Knotts on *The Andy Griffith Show* (CBS)

475 **Outstanding Supporting Performance by a Comic Actress:** Frances Bavier on *The Andy Griffith Show* (CBS)

476 **Outstanding Supporting Performance by a Dramatic Actor:** Eli Wallach on "The Poppy Is Also a Flower" on *Xerox Special* (ABC)

477 **Outstanding Supporting Performance by a Dramatic Actress:** Agnes Moorehead for "Night of the Vicious Valentine" on *Wild, Wild West* (CBS)

478 **Outstanding Achievement in Directing of Drama:** Alex Segal for *Death of a Salesman* (CBS)

479 Outstanding Achievement in Directing of Comedy: James Frawley for "Royal Flush" on *The Monkees* (NBC)

480 Outstanding Directing of Music or Variety: Fielder Cook for *Brigadoon* (ABC)

481 Outstanding Writing in Drama: Bruce Geller for *Mission: Impossible* (CBS)

482 Outstanding Writing in Comedy: Buck Henry and Leonard Stern for "Ship of Spies" on *Get Smart* (NBC)

483 Outstanding Writing on Variety: Mel Brooks, Sam Denoff, Carl Reiner, Bill Persky and Mel Tonkin for *The Sid Caesar, Imogene Coca, Carl Reiner, Howard Morris Special* (CBS)

484 Outstanding Individual Achievement in Film Editing: Paul Krasny and Robert Watts for *Mission: Impossible* (CBS)

485 Outstanding Individual Achievement in Sound Editing: Don Hall, Dick Legrand, Daniel Mandell for *Voyage to the Bottom of the Sea* (ABC)

486 Outstanding Costume Design: Ray Aghayan for *Alice Through the Looking Glass* (NBC)

487 Outstanding Make-Up: Dick Smith for *Mark Twain Tonight!* (CBS)

488 Outstanding Lighting Direction: Leard Davis for *Brigadoon* (ABC)

489 Outstanding Audio Engineering: Bill Cole for *Frank Sinatra: A Man and His Music, Part II* (CBS)

490 Outstanding Individual Achievement in Photographic Special Effects: L.B. Abbott for *The Time Tunnel* (ABC)

491 Outstanding Achievement in News or Documentaries: Theodore H. White for *China: The Roots of Madness* (syndicated)

492 Outstanding Individual Achievement in Technical Directing: A.J. Cunningham for *Brigadoon* (ABC)

493 Outstanding Achievement in Electronic Camerawork: Robert Dunn, Gorm Erickson, Ben Wolf and Nick Demos for *Brigadoon* (ABC)

494 Outstanding Achievement in Engineering Development: Ampex Company for High-Band Videotape Recorder

495 Outstanding Achievement in Engineering Development: A.C. Philips Gloelampenfabrieken for the Plumbicon Tube

496 Special Award: Truman Capote and Eleanor Perry for "A Christmas Memory" on *ABC Stage 67* (ABC)

497 Special Award: Arthur Miller for *Death of a Salesman* (CBS)

498 Special Award: Art Carney for *The Jackie Gleason Show* (CBS)

499 International Award: *Big Deal at Gothenburg* (Tyne Tees Television Limited, Newcastle-upon-Tyne, England)

500 Station Award: KLZ-TV, Denver for *The Road to Nowhere*

501 Trustees' Award: Sylvester L. "Pat" Weaver, Jr.

──────── **1 9 6 7** ────────

502 Outstanding Comedy Series: *Get Smart* (NBC)

503 Outstanding Variety or Music Series: *Rowan and Martin's Laugh-In* (NBC)

504 Outstanding Variety or Music Program: *Rowan and Martin's Laugh-In Special* (NBC)

505 Outstanding Dramatic Series: *Mission: Impossible* (CBS)

506 Outstanding Dramatic Program: "Elizabeth the Queen" on *Hallmark Hall of Fame* (NBC)

507 Outstanding News Documentary Program: *Africa* (ABC)

508 Outstanding News Documentary Program: *Crisis in the Cities* (NET)

509 Outstanding News Documentary Program: *Summer 67: What We Learned* (NBC)

510 Outstanding Cultural Documentary: *Eric Hoffer: The Passionate State of Mind* (CBS)

511 Outstanding Cultural Documentary: *John Steinbeck's America and Americans* (NBC)

512 Outstanding Cultural Documentary: *Gauguin in Tahiti: The Search for Paradise* (CBS)

513 Outstanding Cultural Documentary: *Dylan Thomas: The World I Breathe* (NET)

514 Other News Documentary Program: *The 21st Century* (CBS)

515 Other News Documentary Program: *Science and Religion: Who Will Play God?* (CBS)

516 **Outstanding Sports Program:** *ABC's Wide World of Sports* (ABC)

517 **Outstanding Daytime Program:** *Today* (NBC)

518 **Outstanding Dramatic Actor in a Single Performance:** Melvyn Douglas in "Do Not Go Gentle Into That Good Night" on *CBS Playhouse* (CBS)

519 **Outstanding Dramatic Actress in a Single Performance:** Maureen Stapleton in "Among the Paths to Eden" on *Xerox Special* (ABC)

520 **Outstanding Dramatic Actor in a Series:** Bill Cosby in *I Spy* (NBC)

521 **Outstanding Dramatic Actress in a Series:** Barbara Bain in *Mission: Impossible* (CBS)

522 **Outstanding Supporting Dramatic Actor:** Milburn Stone in *Gunsmoke* (CBS)

523 **Outstanding Supporting Dramatic Actress:** Barbara Anderson in *Ironside* (NBC)

524 **Outstanding Comic Actor in a Series:** Don Adams in *Get Smart* (NBC)

525 **Outstanding Comic Actress in a Series:** Lucille Ball in *The Lucy Show* (CBS)

526 **Outstanding Supporting Comic Actor:** Werner Klemperer in *Hogan's Heroes* (CBS)

527 **Outstanding Supporting Comic Actress:** Marion Lorne in *Bewitched* (ABC)

528 **Outstanding Individual Achievement in Sports Programming:** Jim McKay in *ABC's Wide World of Sports* (ABC)

529 **Special Individual Achievement:** Pat Paulsen on *The Smothers Brothers Comedy Hour* (CBS)

530 **Special Individual Achievement:** Art Carney on *The Jackie Gleason Show*

531 **Outstanding Individual Achievement in News and Documentaries:** Harry Reasoner for "What About Ronald Reagan" on *CBS Reports* (CBS)

532 **Outstanding Individual Achievement in News and Documentaries:** John Laurence and Keith Kay, correspondent and cameraman for "Con Thien," "1st Cavalry" and other stories on *CBS Evening News with Walter Cronkite* (CBS)

533 **Outstanding Individual Achievement in Special Events:** Frank McGee for satellite coverage of Konrad Adenauer's funeral (NBC)

534 **Outstanding Dramatic Writing:** Loring Mandell for "Do Not Go Gentle Into That Good Night" on *CBS Playhouse* (CBS)

535 **Outstanding Comic Writing:** Allan Burns and Chris Hayward for "The Coming Out Party" on *He and She* (CBS)

536 **Outstanding Music or Variety Writing:** Chris Beard, Phil Hahn, Jack Hanrahan, Paul Keyes, Marc London, Hugh Wedlock, Digby Wolf, David Panich, Coslough Johnson and Allan Mannings for *Rowan and Martin's Laugh-In* (NBC)

537 **Outstanding Writing for Cultural Documentaries:** Harry Morgan for *Who, What, When, Where, Why with Harry Reasoner* (CBS)

538 **Outstanding Comedy Director:** Bruce Billson for "Maxwell Smart, Private Eye" on *Get Smart* (NBC)

539 **Outstanding Dramatic Director:** Paul Bogert for "Dear Friends" on *CBS Playhouse* (CBS)

540 **Outstanding Music or Variety Director:** Jack Haley, Jr., for *Movin' with Nancy* (NBC)

541 **Outstanding Film Editing:** Peter Johnson for "The Sounds of Chicago" on *Bell Telephone Hour* (NBC)

542 **Outstanding Individual Achievement in Electronic Production:** Arthur Schneider, videotape editor for *Rowan and Martin's Laugh-In Special* (NBC)

543 **Outstanding Achievement Cultural Documentaries:** Thomas A. Priestly and Robert Loweree, director of photography and editor for *John Steinbeck's America and Americans* (NBC)

544 **Outstanding Cinematography:** Ralph Woolsey for "A Thief Is a Thief" on *It Takes a Thief* (ABC)

545 **Outstanding Electronic Camerawork:** Edward Chaney, Robert Fonorow, Harry Tatarian and Ben Wolf (cameramen) and A.J. Cunningham (technical director) for "Do Not Go Gentle Into That Good Night" on *CBS Playhouse* (CBS)

546 **Outstanding Camerawork for News and Documentaries:** Vo Huynh for *Same Mud, Same Blood* (NBC)

547 **Outstanding Art Photography for Cultural Documentaries:** Nathaniel Dorsky for *Gauguin in Tahiti: The Search for Paradise* (CBS)

548 **Outstanding Music Composition:** Earle Hagen for "Laya" on *I Spy* (NBC)

549 **Outstanding Music Composition for News and Documentaries:** Georges Delerue for *Our World* (NET)

550 **Outstanding Art Direction and Scenic Design:** James W. Trittipo for *The Fred Astaire Show* (NBC)

551 **Outstanding Achievement in Engineering Development:** British Broadcasting Corporation for electronic field/store colour television standards concerter

552 **Trustees' Award:** Donald McGannon

553 **Station Award:** WCAU-TV, Philadelphia for *Now Is the Time*

554 **Special Citation:** WRC-TV, Washington for *The Other Washington*

555 **Special Citation:** WWL-TV, New Orleans for *The Other Side of the Shadow*

556 **International Award (Documentary):** *La Section Anderson* (Office de Radiodiffusion Télévision Français, O.R.T.F., Paris, France)

557 **International Award (Entertainment):** "Call Me Daddy" on *Armchair Theatre* (ABC Television Limited, Middlesex, Great Britain)

———————— **1 9 6 8** ————————

558 **Outstanding Comedy Series:** *Get Smart* (NBC)

559 **Outstanding Variety or Music Series:** *Rowan and Martin's Laugh-In* (NBC)

560 **Outstanding Variety or Music Program:** *The Bill Cosby Special* (NBC)

561 **Outstanding Dramatic Series:** *NET Playhouse* (NET)

562 **Outstanding Dramatic Program:** "Teacher, Teacher" on *Hallmark Hall of Fame* (NBC)

563 **Outstanding Series Comic Actor:** Don Adams for *Get Smart* (NBC)

564 **Outstanding Series Comic Actress:** Hope Lange for *The Ghost and Mrs. Muir* (NBC)

565 **Outstanding Series Dramatic Actor:** Carl Betz for *Judd for the Defense* (ABC)

566 **Outstanding Series Dramatic Actress:** Barbara Bain for *Mission: Impossible* (CBS)

567 **Outstanding Individual Performance by a Dramatic Actor:** Paul Scofield in "Male of the Species" on *Prudential's on Stage* (NBC)

568 **Outstanding Individual Performance by a Dramatic Actress:** Geraldine Page in *The Thanksgiving Visitor* (ABC)

569 **Outstanding Continuing Performance by a Supporting Actor:** Werner Klemperer in *Hogan's Heroes* (CBS)

570 **Outstanding Individual Performance by a Supporting Actress:** Anna Calder-Marshall in "The Male of the Species" on *Prudential's on Stage* (NBC)

571 **Outstanding Continuing Performance by a Supporting Actress:** Susan St. James in *The Name of the Game* (NBC)

572 **Outstanding Daytime Program:** *The Dick Cavett Show* (ABC)

573 **Outstanding Sports Program:** *19th Summer Olympic Games* (ABC)

574 **Outstanding Individual Achievement in Sports Programming:** Robert Ringer, Bill Bennington, Mike Freedman, Mac Memion, Andy Sidaris, Marv Schenkler, Lou Volpicelli and Doug Wilson for *19th Summer Olympic Games* (ABC)

575 **Outstanding News Documentary Program:** *CBS Reports: Hunger in America* (CBS)

576 **Outstanding News Documentary Program:** *Law and Order* (NET)

577 **Outstanding Special Event Coverage:** Coverage of Martin Luther King's assassination and aftermath (CBS)

578 **Outstanding Achievement Within Regularly Scheduled News Program:** James Wilson, Charles Kuralt and Robert Funk for "On the Road" series on *CBS Evening News* (CBS)

579 **Outstanding Achievement Within Regularly Scheduled News Program:** Coverage of hunger in America on *The Huntley-Brinkley Report* (NBC)

580 **Outstanding News Documentary Individual Achievement:** Andy Rooney and Perry Wolff for "Black History: Lost, Stolen or Strayed" on *CBS News Hour* (CBS)

581 **Outstanding Cultural Documentary and Magazine-type Program:** "Don't Count the Candles" on *CBS News Hour* (CBS)

582 **Outstanding Cultural Documentary and Magazine-type Program:** "The Great American Novel" on *CBS News Hour* (CBS)

583 **Outstanding Cultural Documentary and Magazine-type Program:** "Man Who Dances: Edward Villella" on *Bell Telephone Hour* (NBC)

584 **Outstanding Cultural Documentary and Magazine-type Program:** "Justice Black and the Bill of Rights" on *CBS News Hour* (CBS)

585 **Outstanding Cultural Documentary and Magazine-type Program:** Walter Dombrow and Jerry Sims, cinematographers for "The Great American Novel" on *CBS News Hour* (CBS)

586 **Outstanding Cultural Documentary and Magazine-type Program:** Lord Snowdon, cinematographer for "Don't Count the Candles" on *CBS News Hour* (CBS)

587 **Outstanding Cultural Documentary and Magazine-type Program:** Tom Pettit, producer for "CBW: The Secrets of Secrecy" on *First Tuesday* (NBC)

588 **Outstanding Achievement in Film Editing:** Bill Mosher for "An Elephant in a Cigar Box" on *Judd for the Defense* (ABC)

589 **Outstanding Dramatic Director:** David Green for "The People Next Door" on *CBS Playhouse* (CBS)

590 **Outstanding Dramatic Writer:** J.P. Miller for "The People Next Door" on *CBS Playhouse* (CBS)

591 **Outstanding Comedy Writing:** Mason Williams, Allan Blye, Bob Einstein, Murray Roman, Carl Gottlieb, Steve Martin, Jerry Music, Cecil Tuck, Paul Wayne and Cy Howard for *The Smothers Brothers Comedy Hour* (CBS)

592 **Outstanding Cinematography:** George Folsey for *Here's Peggy Fleming* (NBC)

593 **Outstanding Electronic Camerawork:** Nick Demos, Bob Fonorow, Fred Gough, Jack Jennings, Dick Nelson, Rick Tanzi and Ben Wolf; A.J. Cunningham, technical director for "The People Next Door" for *CBS Playhouse* (CBS)

594 **Outstanding Achievement in Art Direction and Scenic Design:** William P. Ross and Lou Hafley for "The Bunker" on *Mission: Impossible* (CBS)

595 **Outstanding Achievement in Musical Composition:** John T. Williams for *Heidi* (NBC)

596 **Outstanding Individual Achievement in Music:** Mort Lindsey for *Barbra Streisand: A Happening in Central Park* (CBS)

597 **Special Classification Program Achievement:** *Firing Line with William F. Buckley, Jr.* (syndicated)

598 **Special Classification Program Achievement:** *Mutual of Omaha's Wild Kingdom* (NBC)

599 **Special Variety Performance Classification:** Harvey Korman in *The Carol Burnett Show* (CBS)

600 **Special Variety Performance Classification:** Arte Johnson in *Rowan and Martin's Laugh-In* (NBC)

601 **Trustees' Awards:** William R. McAndrew and the *Apollo VII, VIII, IX* and *X* astronauts

602 **Special Citations:** The Columbia Broadcasting System, Billy Schulman and WFIL-TV, Philadelphia for *Assignment: The Young Greats*

603 **Station Award:** WHA-TV, Madison, Wisconsin for *Pretty Soon Runs Out*

604 **International Documentary Award:** *The Last Campaign of Robert Kennedy* (Swiss Broadcasting and Television, Zurich)

605 **International Entertainment Award:** *A Scent of Flowers* (Canadian Broadcasting Corporation, Ontario)

———————— **1 9 6 9** ————————

606 **Outstanding Comedy Series:** *My World and Welcome to It* (NBC)

607 **Outstanding Variety or Music Series:** *The David Frost Program* (syndicated)

608 **Outstanding Variety or Music Program:** *Annie, the Women in the Life of a Man* (CBS)

609 **Outstanding Classical Variety or Music Program:** *Cinderella* (NET)

610 **Outstanding Dramatic Series:** *Marcus Welby, M.D.* (ABC)

611 **Outstanding Dramatic Program:** "A Storm in Summer" in *Hallmark Hall of Fame* (NBC)

612 **Outstanding New Series:** *Room 222* (ABC)

613 **Outstanding Series Comic Actor:** William Windom for *My World and Welcome to It* (NBC)

614 **Outstanding Series Comic Actress:** Hope Lange for *The Ghost and Mrs. Muir* (NBC)

615 **Outstanding Series Dramatic Actor:** Robert Young for *Marcus Welby, M.D.* (ABC)

616 **Outstanding Series Dramatic Actress:** Susan Hampshire in *The Forsyte Saga* (NET)

617 **Outstanding Individual Performance by a Dramatic Actor:** Peter Ustinov in "A Storm in Summer" on *Hallmark Hall of Fame* (NBC)

618 **Outstanding Individual Performance by a Dramatic Actress:** Patty Duke in "My Sweet Charlie" on *World Premiere* (NBC)

619 **Outstanding Continuing Dramatic Performance by a Supporting Actor:** James Brolin in *Marcus Welby, M.D.* (ABC)

620 **Outstanding Continuing Dramatic Performance by a Supporting Actress:** Gail Fisher in *Mannix* (CBS)

621 **Outstanding Continuing Comic Performance by a Supporting Actor:** Michael Constantine in *Room 222* (ABC)

622 **Outstanding Continuing Comic Performance by a Supporting Actress:** Karen Valentine in *Room 222* (ABC)

623 **Outstanding Daytime Program:** *Today* (NBC)

624 **Outstanding Sports Programs:** *The NFL Games* (CBS), and *ABC's Wide Wide World of Sports* (ABC)

625 **Special Classification of Outstanding Program Achievement:** *Mutual of Omaha's Wild Kingdom* (NBC)

626 **Outstanding Children's Program:** *Sesame Street* (NET)

627 **Outstanding Program Achievement in News Documentary Programming:** *Hospital* (NET)

628 **Outstanding Program Achievement in Magazine-type Programming:** *Black Journal* (NET)

629 **Outstanding Program Achievement in Cultural Documentary Programming:** "The Japanese" on *CBS News Hour* (CBS)

630 **Outstanding Program Achievements Within Regularly Scheduled News Programs:** "An Investigation of Teenage Drug Addiction: Odyssey House" on *The Huntley-Brinkley Report* (NBC), and "Can the World Be Saved?" on *CBS Evening News with Walter Cronkite* (CBS)

631 **Outstanding Program Achievements in Coverage of Special Events:** "Apollo: A Journey to the Moon" on *Apollo X, XI and XII* (NBC), and *Solar Eclipse: A Darkness at Noon* (NBC)

632 **Outstanding Individual Achievement in Special Events Coverage:** Walter Cronkite for *Man on the Moon: The Epic Journey of Apollo XI* (CBS)

633 **Outstanding Individual Achievement in News Documentary Programming:** Frederick Wiseman, director of *Hospital* (NET)

634 **Outstanding Program Achievement in Cultural Documentary Programming:** Arthur Rubinstein (NBC)

635 **Outstanding Individual Achievements in Cultural Documentary Programming:** Arthur Rubinstein for *Arthur Rubinstein* (NBC), and Edwin O. Reischauer for "The Japanese" on *CBS News Hour* (CBS)

636 **Outstanding Individual Achievement in Magazine-type Programming:** Tom Pettit for "Some Footnotes to 25 Nuclear Years" on *First Tuesday* (NBC)

637 **Outstanding Drama Director:** Paul Bogert for "Shadow Game" on *CBS Playhouse* (CBS)

638 **Outstanding Comedy, Variety or Music Director:** Dwight A. Hemion for "The Sound of Burt Bacharach" on *Kraft Music Hall* (NBC)

639/640 **Outstanding Achievement in Film Editing for Entertainment Program in a Series:** Bill Mosher for "Sweet Smell of Failure" on *Bracken's World* (NBC)

641 **Outstanding Achievement in Film Editing for Entertainment Program Specially Made for Television:** Edward R. Abroms for "My Sweet Charlie" on *World Premiere* (NBC)

642 Outstanding Achievement in Film Editing for Individual News and Documentary Programming: Michael C. Shugrue for "The High School Profile" on *The Huntley-Brinkley Report* (NBC)

643 Outstanding Achievement in Film Editing for Magazine-type or Documentary Program: John Soh for "The Desert Whales" on *The Undersea World of Jacques Cousteau* (ABC)

644 Outstanding Individual Achievement in Sports Programming: Robert R. Forte, film editor for *Pre-Game Program* (CBS)

645 Outstanding Achievement in Film/Sound Editing: Richard E. Raderman and Norman Karlin for "Charlie Noon" on *Gunsmoke* (CBS)

646 Outstanding Achievement in Film/Sound Mixing: Gordon L. Day and Dominick Gaffney for "The Submarine" on *Mission: Impossible* (CBS)

647 Outstanding Achievement in Film/Sound Editing: Douglas H. Grindstaff, Alex Bamattre, Michael Colgan, Bill Lee, Joe Kavigan and Josef von Stroheim for "The Immortal" on *Movie of the Week* (ABC)

648 Outstanding Achievement in Videotape Editing: John Shultis for "The Sound of Burt Bacharach" on *Kraft Music Hall* (NBC)

649 Outstanding Achievement in Live or Tape Sound Mixing: Bill Cole and Dave Williams for *The Switched-on Symphony* (NBC)

650 Outstanding Achievement in Entertainment Series Cinematography: Walter Strenge for "Hello, Goodbye, Hello" on *Marcus Welby, M.D.* (ABC)

651 Outstanding Achievement in Entertainment Cinematography of Made for Television Program: Lionel Lindon for "Ritual of Evil" on *NBC Monday Night at the Movies* (NBC)

652 Outstanding Achievement Within Regularly Scheduled News and Documentary Cinematography: Edward Winkle for "Model Hippie" on *The Huntley-Brinkley Report* (NBC)

653 Outstanding Achievement in Documentary or Magazine-type Cinematography: Thomas A. Priestly for *Sahara: La Caravanne du Sel* (NBC)

654 Outstanding Achievement in Technical Direction and Electronic Camerawork: Heino Ripp, Al Camoin, Gene Martin, Donald Mulvaney and Cal Shadwell for "The Sound of Burt Bacharach" on *Kraft Music Hall* (NBC)

655 Outstanding Dramatic Writing Achievement: Richard Levinson and William Link for "My Sweet Charlie" on *World Premiere* (NBC)

656 Outstanding Comedy, Variety or Music Writing: Gary Belkin, Peter Bellwood, Herb Sargent, Thomas Meehan and Judith Viorst for *Annie, the Women in the Life of a Man* (CBS)

657 Outstanding Achievement in Music, Lyrics and Special Material: Arnold Margolin and Charles Fox for *Love, American Style* (ABC)

658 Outstanding Music Direction of a Variety, Musical or Dramatic Program: Peter Matz for "The Sound of Burt Bacharach" on *Kraft Music Hall* (NBC)

659 Outstanding Special Program Musical Composition: Pete Rugolo for "The Challengers" on *CBS Friday Night Movies* (CBS)

660 Outstanding First Year Series Musical Composition: Morton Stevens for "A Thousand Pardons, You're Dead" on *Hawaii Five-O* (CBS)

661 Outstanding Choreography: Norman Maen for *This Is Tom Jones* (ABC)

662 Outstanding Dramatic Art Direction or Scenic Design: Jan Scott and Earl Carlson for "Shadow Game" on *CBS Playhouse* (CBS)

663 Outstanding Music or Variety Art Direction or Scenic Design: E. Jay Krause for *Mitzi's 2nd Special* (NBC)

664 Outstanding Achievement in Costume Design: Bob Mackie for *Diana Ross and the Supremes and the Temptations on Broadway* (NBC)

665 Outstanding Achievement in Lighting Direction: Leard Davis and Ed Hill for "Appalachian Autumn" on *CBS Playhouse* (CBS)

666 Outstanding Achievement in Make-Up: Louis A. Phillippi and Ray Sebastian for *The Don Adams Special: Hooray for Hollywood* (CBS)

667 **Outstanding Individual Achievements in Children's Programming:** Joe Raposo and Jeffrey Moss for "This Way to Sesame Street" (NBC), and Jon Stone, Jeffrey Moss, Ray Sipherd, Jerry Juhl, Dan Wilcox, Dave Connell, Bruce Hart, Carole Hart and Virginia Schone for "Sally Sees Sesame Street" on *Sesame Street* (NET)

668 **Outstanding Engineering Development:** Video Communications Division of NASA and Westinghouse Corporation for Apollo color television from space

669 **Citation:** Ampex Corporation for development of HS-200 color television production system

670 **Trustees' Awards:** Presidents of the three network news divisions, NASA and 3M Company

671 **Station Award:** KNBC-TV, Los Angeles for *The Slow Guillotine*

672 **Special Citation:** WJZ-TV, Baltimore, Maryland for *The Other Americans*

──────── **1 9 7 0** ────────

673 **Outstanding Comedy Series:** *All in the Family* (CBS)

674 **Outstanding Musical Variety Series:** *The Flip Wilson Show* (NBC)

675 **Outstanding Talk Variety Series:** *The David Frost Show* (syndicated)

676 **Outstanding Variety or Music Program:** *Singer Presents Burt Bacharach* (CBS)

677 **Outstanding Classical Variety or Music Program:** *Leopold Stokowski* (PBS)

678 **Outstanding New Series:** *All in the Family* (CBS)

679 **Outstanding Dramatic Series:** *The Senator – The Bold Ones* (NBC)

680 **Outstanding Drama or Comedy Program:** *The Andersonville Trial* (PBS)

681 **Outstanding Series Comic Actor:** Jack Klugman for *The Odd Couple* (ABC)

682 **Outstanding Series Comic Actress:** Jean Stapleton for *All in the Family* (CBS)

683 **Outstanding Series Dramatic Actor:** Hal Holbrook for *The Senator – The Bold Ones* (NBC)

684 **Outstanding Series Dramatic Actress:** Susan Hampshire in "The First Churchills" on *Masterpiece Theatre* (PBS)

685 **Outstanding Individual Performance by a Dramatic Actor:** George C. Scott in "The Price" on *Hallmark Hall of Fame* (NBC)

686 **Outstanding Individual Performance by a Dramatic Actress:** Lee Grant in "The Neon Ceiling" on *World Premiere NBC Monday Night at the Movies* (NBC)

687 **Outstanding Dramatic Performance by a Supporting Actor:** David Burns in "The Price" on *Hallmark Hall of Fame* (NBC)

688 **Outstanding Dramatic Performance by a Supporting Actress:** Margaret Leighton in "Hamlet" on *Hallmark Hall of Fame* (NBC)

689 **Outstanding Continuing Comic Performance by a Supporting Actor:** Edward Asner in *The Mary Tyler Moore Show* (CBS)

690 **Outstanding Continuing Comic Performance by a Supporting Actress:** Valerie Harper in *The Mary Tyler Moore Show* (CBS)

691 **Outstanding Daytime Program:** *Today* (NBC)

692 **Outstanding Sports Program:** *ABC's Wide World of Sports* (ABC)

693 **Outstanding Children's Program:** *Sesame Street* (PBS)

694 **Outstanding Program Achievement in News Documentary Programming:** "The World of Charlie Company," correspondent John Laurence on "The World of Charlie Company," "The Selling of the Pentagon" on *CBS News* (CBS)

695 **Outstanding Program Achievement in News Documentary Programming:** "Pollution Is a Matter of Choice," and writer Fred Freed for "Pollution Is a Matter of Choice" on *NBC White Paper* (NBC)

696 **Outstanding Program Achievement in Magazine-type Programming:** *The Great American Dream Machine* (PBS)

697 **Outstanding Program Achievement in Magazine-type Programming:** "Gulf of Tonkin" segment on *60 Minutes* (CBS)

698 Outstanding Program Achievement in Magazine-type Programming: Correspondent Mike Wallace for *60 Minutes* (CBS)

699 Outstanding Program Achievement in Cultural Documentary Programming: *The Everglades* and *The Making of "Butch Cassidy and the Sundance Kid"* (NBC)

700 Outstanding Individual Achievements in Cultural Documentary Programming: Narrator Nana Mahomo for *A Black View of South Africa* (CBS); writers Robert Guenette and Theodore H. Strauss for *They've Killed President Lincoln* (NBC); and director Robert Young for *The Eskimo: Fight for Life* (CBS)

701 Outstanding Program Achievement in Special Event Coverage: "CBS News Space Coverage for 1970-71," and correspondent Walter Cronkite for "CBS News Space Coverage for 1970-71" (CBS)

702 Outstanding Program Achievement Within Regularly Scheduled News Programs: "Five Part Investigation of Welfare" on *NBC Nightly News* (NBC)

703 Outstanding Individual Achievement Within Regularly Scheduled News Programs: Correspondent Bruce Morton for "Reports from the Lt. Calley Trial" on *CBS Evening News with Walter Cronkite* (CBS)

704 Outstanding Director of Comedy Series Program: Jay Sandrich for "Toulouse Lautrec Is One of My Favorite Artists" on *The Mary Tyler Moore Show* (CBS)

705 Outstanding Achievement as Director of Comedy, Variety or Music Special Program: Sterling Johnson for *Timex Presents Peggy Fleming at Sun Valley* (NBC)

706 Outstanding Director of Drama Series Program: Daryl Duke for "The Day the Lion Died" on *The Bold Ones — The Senator* (NBC)

707 Outstanding Achievement as Director of Single Drama: Fielder Cook for "The Price" on *Hallmark Hall of Fame* (NBC)

708 Outstanding Achievement as Director of Series Variety or Music Program: Mark Warren for *Rowan and Martin's Laugh-In* (NBC)

709 Outstanding Achievement in Film Editing for Entertainment Series Programming: Michael Economou for "A Continual Roar of Musketry" on *The Bold Ones — The Senator* (NBC)

710 Outstanding Achievement in Film Editing for Special or Feature Made for Television: George J. Nicholson for "Longstreet" on *ABC Movie of the Week* (ABC)

711 Outstanding Achievement in Film Editing for News or Documentary Program or Program Segment: George L. Johnson for "Prisons Parts I Through IV" on *NBC Nightly News* (NBC)

712 Outstanding Achievement in Film Editing for Magazine-type or Mini-Documentary News and Documentary Programming: Robert B. Loweree and Henry J. Grennon for *Cry Help! An NBC White Paper on Mentally Disturbed Youth* (NBC)

713 Outstanding Achievement in Film Sound Editing: Don Hall, Jack Johnson, Bob Weatherford and Dick Jensen for "Tribes" on *Movie of the Week* (ABC)

714 Outstanding Achievement in Videotape Editing: Marco Zappia for *Hee Haw* (CBS)

715 Outstanding Achievement in Film Sound Mixing: Theodore Sonderberg for "Tribes" on *Movie of the Week* (ABC)

716 Outstanding Achievement in Live or Tape Sound Mixing: Henry Bird for "Hamlet" on *Hallmark Hall of Fame* (NBC)

717 Outstanding Achievement in Choreography: Ernest O. Flatt for *The Carol Burnett Show* (CBS)

718 Outstanding Achievement in Dramatic Writing for Single Program in Series: Joel Oliansky for "To Taste of Death but Once" on *The Bold Ones — The Senator* (NBC)

719 Outstanding Achievement in Original Teleplay Writing: Tracy Keenan Wynn and Marvin Schwartz for "Tribes" on *Movie of the Week* (ABC)

720 Outstanding Achievement in Drama Adaptation Writing: Saul Levitt for "The Andersonville Trial" on *Hollywood Television Theatre* (PBS)

721 Outstanding Achievement in Writing for Program in Comedy Series: James L. Brooks and Allan Burns for "Support Your Local Mother" on *The Mary Tyler Moore Show* (CBS)

722 **Outstanding Achievement in Writing for Program in Variety or Music:** Herbert Baker, Hal Goodman, Larry Klein, Bob Weiskopf, Norman Steinberg, Bob Schiller and Flip Wilson for *The Flip Wilson Show* (NBC)

723 **Outstanding Achievement in Special Program Comedy, Variety or Music:** Bob Ellison and Marty Farrell for *Singer Presents Burt Bacharach* (CBS)

724 **Outstanding Individual Achievement in Children's Programming:** Burr Tillstrom on *Kukla, Fran and Ollie* (PBS)

725 **Outstanding Individual Achievements in Sports Programming:** Jim McKay for *Wide World of Sports* (ABC), and Don Meredith for *NFL Monday Night Football* (ABC)

726 **Outstanding Achievement in Lighting Direction:** John Rook for "Hamlet" on *Hallmark Hall of Fame* (NBC)

727 **Outstanding Achievement in Technical Direction and Electronic Camerawork:** Gordon Baird, Tom Ancell, Rick Bennewitz, Larry Bentley and Jack Reader for "The Andersonville Trial" on *Hollywood Television Theatre* (PBS)

728 **Outstanding Achievement in Series Entertainment Cinematography:** Jack Marta for "Cynthia Is Alive and Living in Avalon" on *The Name of the Game* (NBC)

729 **Outstanding Achievements in Special Entertainment Cinematography:** Lionel Lindon for "Vanished Parts I and II" on *Movie of the Week* (ABC), and Bob Collins for *Timex Presents Peggy Fleming at Sun Valley* (NBC)

730 **Outstanding Achievement in Regularly Scheduled News Cinematography:** Larry Travis for "Los Angeles—Earthquake" on *CBS Evening News with Walter Cronkite* (CBS)

731 **Outstanding Achievement in News and Documentary Cinematography:** Jacques Renoir for "Tragedy of the Red Salmon" on *The Undersea World of Jacques Cousteau* (ABC)

732 **Outstanding Achievements in Any Area of Creative Technical Crafts:** Lenwood B. Abbott and John C. Caldwell for "City Beneath the Sea" on *World Premiere NBC Monday Night at the Movies* (NBC), and Gene Widhoff for courtroom sketches at the Manson trial on *The Huntley-Brinkley Report* (NBC)

733 **Outstanding Achievement in Dramatic Program Art Direction or Scenic Design:** Peter Roden for "Hamlet" on *Hallmark Hall of Fame* (NBC)

734 **Outstanding Achievement in Music or Variety Art Direction or Scenic Design:** James W. Trittipo and George Gaines for *Robert Young the Family* (CBS)

735 **Outstanding Achievement in Make-Up:** Robert Down for "Catafalque" on *Mission: Impossible* (CBS)

736 **Outstanding Achievement in Costume Design:** Martin Baugh and David Walker for "Hamlet" on *Hallmark Hall of Fame* (NBC)

737 **Outstanding Achievement in Series Music Composition:** David Rose for "The Love Child" on *Bonanza* (CBS)

738 **Outstanding Achievement in Special Program Music Composition:** Walter Scharf for "Tragedy of the Red Salmon" on *The Undersea World of Jacques Cousteau* (ABC)

739 **Outstanding Achievement in Music Direction for Drama, Variety or Music:** Dominic Frontiere for *Swing Out, Sweet Land* (NBC)

740 **Outstanding Achievement in Music, Lyrics or Special Material:** Ray Charles for *The First Months Are the Hardest* (NBC)

741 **Outstanding Achievement in Engineering Developments:** Columbia Broadcasting System for the Color Corrector and American Broadcasting Company for open-loop synchronizing system

742 **Trustees' Award:** Ed Sullivan, first president of Academy

743 **Citations:** General Electric for Portable Earth Station Transmitter, and Stefan Kudelski for design of NAGRA IV recorder

744 **Station Award:** KNXT, Los Angeles for *If You Turn On*

———————— **1971** ————————

745 **Outstanding Comedy Series:** *All in the Family* (CBS)

746 **Outstanding Musical Variety Series:** *The Carol Burnett Show* (CBS)

747 **Outstanding Talk Variety Series:** *The Dick Cavett Show* (ABC)

748 **Outstanding Variety or Music Program:** "Jack Lemmon in 'S Wonderful, 'S Marvelous, 'S Gershwin" on *Bell System Family Theatre* (NBC)

749 **Outstanding Classical Variety or Music Program:** *Beethoven's Birthday: A Celebration in Vienna with Leonard Bernstein* (CBS)

750 **Outstanding New Series:** *Elizabeth R* (PBS)

751 **Outstanding Dramatic Series:** *Elizabeth R* (PBS)

752 **Outstanding Drama or Comedy Program:** *Brian's Song* (ABC)

753 **Outstanding Series Comic Actor:** Carroll O'Connor in *All in the Family* (CBS)

754 **Outstanding Series Comic Actress:** Jean Stapleton for *All in the Family* (CBS)

755 **Outstanding Series Dramatic Actor:** Peter Falk in "Columbo" on *NBC Mystery Movie* (NBC)

756 **Outstanding Series Dramatic Actress:** Glenda Jackson in "Elizabeth R" on *Masterpiece Theatre* (PBS)

757 **Outstanding Individual Performance by a Dramatic Actor:** Keith Mitchell in "Catherina Howard" on *The Six Wives of Henry VIII* (PBS)

758 **Outstanding Dramatic Performance by a Supporting Actor:** Jack Warden in "Brian's Song" on *Movie of the Week* (ABC)

759 **Outstanding Dramatic Performance by a Supporting Actress:** Jenny Agutter in "The Snow Goose" on *Hallmark Hall of Fame* (NBC)

760 **Outstanding Continuing Comic Performance by a Supporting Actor:** Edward Asner in *The Mary Tyler Moore Show* (CBS)

761 **Outstanding Continuing Comic Performance by a Supporting Actress:** Valerie Harper in *The Mary Tyler Moore Show* (CBS)

762 **Outstanding Comic Performance by a Supporting Actress:** Sally Struthers in *All in the Family* (CBS)

763 **Outstanding Performance in Music or Variety:** Harvey Korman on *The Carol Burnett Show* (CBS)

764 **Outstanding Daytime Drama:** *The Doctors* (NBC)

765 **Outstanding Sports Program:** *ABC's Wide World of Sports* (ABC)

766 **Outstanding Children's Program:** *Sesame Street* (PBS)

767 **Outstanding Cultural Achievements in Documentary Programming:** "Hollywood: The Dream Factory" on *The Monday Night Special* (ABC); "A Sound of Dolphins" on *The Undersea World of Jacques Cousteau* (ABC); and "The Unsinkable Sea Otter" on *The Undersea World of Jacques Cousteau* (ABC)

768 **Outstanding Program Achievement Currently Significant Documentary Programming:** *A Night in Jail, a Day in Court* (CBS), and *This Child Is Rated X: An NBC News White Paper on Juvenile Justice* (NBC)

769 **Outstanding Achievement in a Special Event Coverage:** *The China Trip* (ABC); *A Ride on the Moon: The Flight of Apollo 15* (CBS); and *June 30, 1971, a Day in History: The Supreme Court and the Pentagon Papers* (NBC)

770 **Outstanding Program Achievements in Magazine-type Programming:** *Chronolog* (NBC), and *The Great American Dream Machine* (PBS)

771 **Outstanding Individual Achievement in Magazine-type Programming:** Mike Wallace, reporter on *60 Minutes* (CBS)

772 **Outstanding Program Achievement Within Regularly Scheduled News Programs:** "Defeat at Dacca" on *NBC Nightly News* (NBC)

773 **Outstanding Individual Achievements Within Regularly Scheduled News:** Phil Brady, reporter on "Defeat at Dacca" on *NBC Nightly News* (NBC), and Bob Schieffer, Phil Jones, Don Webster and Bill Plante for "The Air War" on *CBS Evening News with Walter Cronkite* (CBS)

774 **Outstanding Individual Achievements in Documentary Programming:** Louise J. Hazam, writer for *Venice Be Damned* (NBC), and Robert Northshield, writer for *Suffer the Little Children—An NBC News White Paper on Northern Ireland* (NBC)

775 **Outstanding Direction of Single Program in a Series:** Alexander Singer for "The Invasion of Kevin Ireland" on *The Bold Ones—The Lawyers* (NBC)

776 Outstanding Direction of Single Program: Tom Gries for "The Glass House" on *The CBS Friday Night Movies* (CBS)

777 Outstanding Direction in Series Comedy: John Rich for "Sammy's Visit" on *All in the Family* (CBS)

778 Outstanding Series Music or Variety Direction: Art Fisher for *The Sonny and Cher Comedy Hour* (CBS)

779 Outstanding Special Comedy, Variety or Music Direction: Walter C. Miller and Martin Charnin for "Jack Lemmon in 'S Wonderful, 'S Marvelous, 'S Gershwin" on *Bell System Family Theatre* (NBC)

780 Outstanding Entertainment Series Film Editing: Edward R. Abroms for "Death Lends a Hand" on *Columbo* (NBC)

781 Outstanding Entertainment Special Film Editing: Bud S. Isaacs for "Brian's Song" on *Movie of the Week* (ABC)

782 Outstanding Documentary Film Editing: Spencer David Saxon for "Monkeys, Apes and Man" on *National Geographic Special* (CBS)

783 Outstanding Regularly Scheduled News Program Film Editing: Darold Murray for "War Song" on *NBC Nightly News* (NBC)

784 Outstanding Achievement in Videotape Editing: Pat McKenna for "Hogan's Goat" on *Special of the Week* (PBS)

785 Outstanding Achievement in Film Sound Editing: Jerry Christian, James Troutman, Ronald LaVine, Sidney Lubow, Richard Raderman, Dale Johnston, Sam Caylor, John Stacy and Jack Kirschner for "Duel" on *Movie of the Week* (ABC)

786 Outstanding Achievement in Live or Tape Sound Mixing: Norman H. Dewes for "The Elevator Story" on *All in the Family* (CBS)

787 Outstanding Achievement in Film Sound Mixing: Theodore Soderberg and Richard Overton for "Fireball Forward" on *The ABC Sunday Night Movie* (ABC)

788 Outstanding Achievement in Technical Direction and Electronic Camerawork: Heino Ripp, Albert Camoin, Frank Gaeta, Gene Martin and Donald Mulvaney for "Jack Lemmon in 'S Wonderful, 'S Marvelous, 'S Gershwin" on *Bell System Family Theatre* (NBC)

789 Outstanding Achievement in Series Entertainment Cinematography: Lloyd Ahern for "Blueprint for Murder" on *Columbo* (NBC)

790 Outstanding Achievement in Special Entertainment Programming: Joseph Biroc for "Brian's Song" on *Movie of the Week* (ABC)

791 Outstanding Achievement in Regularly Scheduled News Cinematography: Peter McIntyre and Lim Youn Choul for "Defeat at Dacca" on *NBC Nightly News* (NBC)

792 Outstanding Achievement in Documentary Cinematography: Thomas Priestly for *Venice Be Damned* (NBC)

793 Outstanding Achievement in Lighting Direction: John Freschi for "Gideon" on *Hallmark Hall of Fame* (NBC)

794 Special Classification of Outstanding Docu-Drama Programming: *The Search for the Nile, Parts I–IV* (NBC)

795 Special Classification of Outstanding General Programming: *The Pentagon Papers* (PBS)

796 Outstanding Choreography: Alan Johnson for "Jack Lemmon in 'S Wonderful, 'S Marvelous, 'S Gershwin" on *Bell System Family Theatre* (NBC)

797 Outstanding Achievement in Musical or Variety Art Direction or Scenic Design: E. Jay Krause for *Diana* (ABC)

798 Outstanding Achievement in Feature Length Art Direction or Scenic Design: Jan Scott for "Scarecrow" on *Hollywood Television Theatre* (PBS)

799 Outstanding Costume Design: Elizabeth Waller for "Lion's Club" on *Elizabeth R* (PBS)

800 Outstanding Make-Up: Frank Westmore for "Kung Fu" on *Movie of the Week* (ABC)

801 Outstanding Individual Achievements in Sports Programming: William P. Kelley, Jim Culley, Jack Bennett, Buddy Joseph, Mario Ciarlo, Frank Manfredi, Corey Leible, Gene Martin, Cal Shadwell, Billy Barnes and Ron Charbonneau for *The AFC Championship* (NBC)

802 Outstanding Achievement in Dramatic Writing for Single Program in a Series: Richard Levinson and William Link for "Death Lends a Hand" on *Columbo* (NBC)

803 Outstanding Achievement in Original Teleplay Writing: Allan Sloane for *To All My Friends on Shore* (CBS)

804 Outstanding Achievement in Drama Adaptation Writing: William Blinn for "Brian's Song" on *Movie of the Week* (ABC)

805 Outstanding Achievement in Writing for Program in Comedy Series: Burt Styler for "Edith's Problem" on *All in the Family* (CBS)

806 Outstanding Achievement in Writing for Series Program in Variety or Music: Don Hinkley, Stan Hart, Larry Siegel, Woody Kling, Art Baer, Robert Beatty, Ben Joelson, Stan Burns, Mike Marmer and Arnie Rosen for *The Carol Burnett Show* (CBS)

807 Outstanding Achievement in Writing for Special Program in Variety or Music: Anne Howard Bailey for "The Trial of Mary Lincoln" on *NET Opera Theatre* (PBS)

808 Special Classification for Outstanding Individual Achievement: Michael Hastings and Derek Marlow, writers for *Search for the Nile, Parts I–IV* (NBC)

809 Outstanding Achievement in Series Music: Peter Rugolo for "In Defense of Ellen McKay" on *The Bold Ones — The Lawyers* (NBC)

810 Outstanding Achievement in Special Music: John T. Williams for "Jane Eyre" on *Bell System Family Theatre* (NBC)

811 Outstanding Musical Direction for Musical, Variety or Dramatic Program: Elliott Lawrence for "Jack Lemmon in 'S Wonderful, 'S Marvelous, 'S Gershwin" on *Bell System Family Theatre* (NBC)

812 Outstanding Achievement in Music, Lyrics and Special Material: Ray Charles for *The Funny Side of Marriage* (NBC)

813 Outstanding Individual Achievements in Religious Programming: Alfredo Antonini, music director for *And David Wept* (CBS), and Lon Stuckey, lighting director for *A City of the King* (syndicated)

814 Outstanding Achievements in Any Area of Creative Technical Crafts: Pierre Goupil, Michael Deloire and Yves Omer for underwater camerawork on "Secrets of the Sunken Caves" on *The Undersea World of Jacques Cousteau* (ABC)

815 Trustees' Awards: William H. (Bill) Lawrence, national affairs editor of ABC News and Frank Stanton, president of CBS

816 Outstanding Achievement for Engineering Development: Lee Harrison for Scanimate Electronic Animation

817 Citations: National Broadcasting Company for Hum Bucker means of correcting remote pickup transmission defects and Richard E. Hill and the Electronic Engineering Company of California for editing equipment for videotape editing

818 Station Award: WZZM-TV, Grand Rapids for *Sickle Cell Disease: Paradox of Neglect*

──────── **1972** ────────

819 Outstanding Comedy Series: *All in the Family* (CBS)

820 Outstanding Musical Variety Series: *The Julie Andrews Hour* (ABC)

821 Outstanding Variety or Popular Music Program: *Singer Presents Liza with a Z* (NBC)

822 Outstanding Classical Music Program: *The Sleeping Beauty* (PBS)

823 Outstanding New Series: *America* (NBC)

824 Outstanding Continuing Dramatic Series: *The Waltons* (CBS)

825 Outstanding Limited Episode Dramatic Series: *Tom Brown's Schooldays, Parts I–V* (PBS)

826 Outstanding Drama or Comedy Program: "A War of Children" on *The New CBS Tuesday Night Movie* (CBS)

827 Outstanding Daytime Drama: *The Edge of Night* (CBS)

828 Outstanding Daytime Program: *Dinah's Place* (NBC)

829 Outstanding Children's Entertainment/Fictional Programming: *Sesame Street* (PBS), *Zoom* (PBS), Tom Whedon, John Boni, Sara Compton, Tom Dunsmuir, Thad Mumford, Jeremy Stevens and Jim Thurman writers for *The Electric Company* (PBS)

830 **Outstanding Children's Informational/Factual Programming:** "Last of the Curlews" on *The ABC Afterschool Special* (ABC); and Shari Lewis, performer in "A Picture of Us" on *NBC Children's Theatre* (NBC)

831 **Outstanding Sports Programming:** *ABC's Wide World of Sports* (ABC), and *1972 Summer Olympic Games* (ABC)

832 **Outstanding Series Comic Actor:** Jack Klugman in *The Odd Couple* (ABC)

833 **Outstanding Religious Program:** *Duty Bound* (NBC)

834 **Special Classification of Outstanding Program:** *The Advocates* (PBS), and *VD Blues* (PBS)

835 **Outstanding Series Comic Actress:** Mary Tyler Moore in *The Mary Tyler Moore Show* (CBS)

836 **Outstanding Series Dramatic Actor:** Richard Thomas in *The Waltons* (CBS)

837 **Outstanding Series Dramatic Actress:** Michael Learned in *The Waltons* (CBS)

838 **Outstanding Individual Performance by Actor:** Laurence Olivier in *Long Day's Journey Into Night* (ABC)

839 **Outstanding Individual Performance by Actress:** Cloris Leachman in "A Brand New Life" on *Movie of the Week* (ABC)

840 **Outstanding Limited Episode Leading Actor in a Comic or Dramatic Performance:** Anthony Murphy in *Tom Brown's Schooldays, Parts I-V* (PBS)

841 **Outstanding Limited Episode Leading Actress in a Comic or Dramatic Performance:** Susan Hampshire in "Vanity Fair, Parts I-V" on *Masterpiece Theatre* (PBS)

842 **Outstanding Continuing Comic Performance by a Supporting Actress:** Valerie Harper in *The Mary Tyler Moore Show* (CBS)

843 **Outstanding Continuing Comic Performance by a Supporting Actor:** Ted Knight in *The Mary Tyler Moore Show* (CBS)

844 **Outstanding Dramatic Performance by a Supporting Actor:** Scott Jacoby in "That Certain Summer" on *Wednesday Night Movie of the Week* (ABC)

845 **Outstanding Dramatic Performance by a Supporting Actress:** Ellen Corby in *The Waltons* (CBS)

846 **Outstanding Performance in Music or Variety:** Tim Conway on *The Carol Burnett Show* (CBS)

847 **Outstanding Daytime Performer:** Mary Fickett in *All My Children* (ABC)

848 **Outstanding Dramatic Series Director:** Jerry Thorpe for "An Eye for an Eye" on *Kung Fu* (ABC)

849 **Outstanding Single Program Director:** Joseph Sargent for "The Marcus-Nelson Murders" on *The CBS Thursday Night Movies* (CBS)

850 **Outstanding Comedy Series Director:** Jay Sandrich for "It's Whether You Win or Lose" on *The Mary Tyler Moore Show* (CBS)

851 **Outstanding Series Variety or Music Director:** Bill Davis for *The Julie Andrews Hour* (ABC)

852 **Outstanding Single Program Variety or Music Director:** Bob Fosse for *Singer Presents Liza with a Z* (NBC)

853 **Outstanding Entertainment Series Film Editing:** Gene Fowler, Jr., Marjorie Fowler and Anthony Wollner for "The Literary Man" on *The Waltons* (CBS)

854 **Outstanding Single Program Entertainment Film Editing:** Peter C. Johnson and Ed Spiegel for *Surrender at Appomattox: Appointment with Destiny* (CBS)

855 **Outstanding Videotape Editing:** Nick Giordano and Arthur Schneider for *The Julie Andrews Hour* (ABC)

856 **Outstanding News Film Editing:** Patrick Minerva, Martin Sheppard, George Johnson, William J. Freeda, Miguel E. Portillo, Albert J. Helias, Irwin Graf, Jean Venable, Rick Hessel, Loren Berry, Nick Wilkins, Gerry Breese, Michael Shugrue, K. Su, Edwin Einarsen, Thomas Dunphy, Russell Moore and Albert Mole for *NBC Nightly News* (NBC)

857 **Outstanding Documentary Film Editing:** Les Parry for *The Incredible Flight of the Snow Geese* (NBC)

858 **Outstanding Sports Programming:** John Croak, Charles Gardner, Jacob Hierl, Conrad Kraus, Edward McCarthy, Nick Mazur, Alex Moscovic, James Parker, Louis Rende, Ross Skipper,

Robert Steinbeck, John de Lisa, George Boettcher, Merritt Roesser, Leo Scharf, Randy Cohen, Vito Geraldi, Harold Byers, Winfield Gross, Paul Scoskie, Peter Fritz, Leo Stephan, Gerber McBeath, Louis Torino, Michael Wenig, Tom Wight and James Kelly, videotape editors for *The 1972 Summer Olympic Games* (ABC)

859 **Outstanding Film Sound Editing:** Ross Taylor, Fred Brown and David Marshall for "The Red Pony" on *Bell System Family Theatre* (NBC)

860 **Outstanding Film Sound Mixing:** Richard Wagner, George E. Porte, Eddie Nelson and Fred Leroy Granville for *Surrender at Appomattox: Appointment with Destiny* (CBS)

861 **Outstanding Live or Tape Sound Mixing:** Al Gramaglia and Mahlon Fox for *Much Ado About Nothing* (CBS)

862 **Outstanding Series Entertainment Cinematography:** Jack Wolf for "An Eye for an Eye" on *Kung Fu* (ABC)

863 **Outstanding Single Program Entertainment Cinematography:** Howard Schwartz for "Night of Terror" on *Tuesday Movie of the Week* (ABC)

864 **Outstanding Documentary Cinematography:** Des and Jen Bartlett for *The Incredible Flight of the Snow Geese* (NBC)

865 **Outstanding News and Special Event Cinematography:** Laurens Pierce for coverage of the shooting of Governor George Wallace on *The CBS Evening News with Walter Cronkite* (CBS)

866 **Outstanding Technical Direction and Electronic Camerawork:** Ernie Buttelman, Robert A. Kemp, James Angel, James Balden and David Hilmer for *The Julie Andrews Hour* (ABC)

867 **Outstanding Lighting Direction:** John Freschi and John Casagrande for *The 44th Oscar Awards* (NBC) and Trucke Krone for *The Julie Andrews Christmas Hour* (ABC)

868 **Outstanding Costume Design:** Jack Bear for *The Julie Andrews Hour* (ABC)

869 **Outstanding Make-Up:** Del Armstrong, Ellis Burman and Stan Winston for "Jayoupes" on *The New CBS Tuesday Night Movie* (CBS)

870 **Outstanding Original Dramatic Teleplay:** Abby Mann for "The Marcus-Nelson Murders" on *The CBS Thursday Night Movies* (CBS)

871 **Outstanding Dramatic Adaptation:** Eleanor Perry for *The House Without a Christmas Tree* (CBS)

872 **Outstanding Choreography:** Bob Fosse for *Singer Presents Liza with a Z* (NBC)

873 **Outstanding Series Music Composition:** Charles Fox for *Love, American Style* (ABC)

874 **Outstanding Single Program Musical Composition:** Jerry Goldsmith for "The Red Pony" on *Bell System Family Theatre* (NBC)

875 **Outstanding Variety, Dramatic or Musical Program Music Direction:** Peter Matz for *The Carol Burnett Show* (CBS)

876 **Outstanding Music, Lyrics and Special Material:** Fred Ebb and John Kander for *Singer Presents Liza with a Z* (NBC)

877 **Outstanding Dramatic Program Art Direction or Scenic Direction:** Tom John for *Much Ado About Nothing* (CBS)

878 **Outstanding Music or Variety Series Art Direction or Scenic Design:** Brian Bartholomew and Keaton S. Walker for *The Julie Andrews Hour* (ABC)

879 **Outstanding Series Comedy Writing:** Michael Ross, Bernie West and Lee Kalcheim for "The Bunkers and the Swingers" on *All in the Family* (CBS)

880 **Outstanding Special Program Writing in Comedy, Variety or Music:** Renee Taylor and Joseph Bologna for *Acts of Love and Other Comedies* (ABC)

881 **Outstanding Series Writing in Comedy, Variety or Music:** Stan Hart, Larry Siegel, Gail Parent, Woody Kling, Robert Beatty, Tom Patchett, Jay Tarses, Robert Hilliard, Arnie Kogen, Bill Angelos and Buz Kohan for *The Carol Burnett Show* (CBS)

882 **Outstanding Cultural Achievements in Documentary Programming:** *America* (NBC), and *Jane Goodall and the World of Animal Behavior* (ABC)

883 **Outstanding Program Achievement Currently Significant Documentary**

Programming: "The Blue Collar Trap" in *NBC White Paper*, "The Mexican Connection" on *CBS Reports* (CBS), and *One Billion Dollar Weapon; And Now the War Is Over, the American Military in the '70s* (NBC)

884 Outstanding Program Achievement in Special Event Coverage: Jim McKay commentator and ABC for coverage of the Munich Olympic tragedy (ABC)

885 Outstanding Program Achievements in Magazine-type Programming: *60 Minutes* (CBS), "The Selling of Colonel Herbert" on *60 Minutes* (CBS); and "The Poppy Fields in Turkey – The Heroin Labs of Marseilles – The New York Connection" on *60 Minutes* (CBS)

886 Outstanding Individual Achievement in Magazine-type Programming: Mike Wallace, reporter on "The Selling of Colonel Herbert" on *60 Minutes* (CBS), and Mike Wallace for correspondent for *60 Minutes* (CBS)

887 Outstanding Program Achievement Within Regularly Scheduled News Programs: "The U.S./Soviet Wheat Deal" on *CBS Evening News with Walter Cronkite* (CBS)

888 Outstanding Individual Achievements Within Regularly Scheduled News: Eric Sevareid, correspondent for "L.B.J. the Man and the President" on *CBS Evening News with Walter Cronkite* (CBS); Joel Blocker, Walter Cronkite, Dan Rather and Daniel Schorr correspondents for "The Watergate Affair" on *CBS Evening News with Walter Cronkite* (CBS); and David Dick, Dan Rather, Roger Mudd and Walter Cronkite correspondents for the coverage of the shooting of Governor George Wallace on *CBS Evening News with Walter Cronkite* (CBS)

889 Outstanding Individual Achievements in Documentary Programming: Alistair Cooke, narrator for *America* (NBC); Alistair Cooke, writer for "A Fireball in the Night" on *America* (NBC); and Hugo Van Lawick, director for *Jane Goodall and the World of Animal Behavior* (ABC)

890 Outstanding Achievements in Any Area of Creative Technical Crafts: Donald Feldstein, Robert Fontana and Joe Zuckerman for the animation layout of Leonardo da Vinci art for *Leonardo: To Know How to See* (NBC)

891 Outstanding Engineering Development: Sony for trinitron picture tube and CBS Systems for computer videotape editing system

892 National Community Service Award: KDIN-TV, Des Moines, Iowa for *Take Des Moines . . . Please*

———— **1973** ————

893 Outstanding Comedy Series: *M*A*S*H* (CBS)

894 Outstanding Musical Variety Series: *The Carol Burnett Show* (CBS)

895 Outstanding Variety or Popular Music Program: *Lily* (CBS)

896 Outstanding Limited Series: *Columbo* (NBC)

897 Outstanding Dramatic Series: "Upstairs, Downstairs" on *Masterpiece Theatre* (PBS)

898 Outstanding Drama or Comedy Special: *The Autobiography of Miss Jane Pittman* (CBS)

899 Outstanding Daytime Drama: *The Doctors* (NBC)

900 Outstanding Drama Special: *The Other Woman* (ABC)

901 Outstanding Game Show: *Password* (ABC)

902 Outstanding Talk, Service or Variety Series: *The Merv Griffin Show* (syndicated)

903 Outstanding Children's Entertainment Series: *Zoom* (PBS)

904 Outstanding Children's Entertainment Special: "Rookie of the Year" on *The ABC Afterschool Special* (ABC)

905 Outstanding Children's Informational Series: *Make a Wish* (ABC)

906 Outstanding Children's Informational Special: *The Runaways* (ABC)

907 Outstanding Children's Instructional Programming: *Inside/Out* (syndicated)

908 Outstanding Children's Special: *Marlo Thomas and Friends in Free to Be – You and Me* (ABC)

909 Outstanding Sports Program: *ABC's Wide World of Sports* (ABC)

910 Special Award for Outstanding Program and Individual Achievement: Tom Snyder for *Tomorrow* (NBC) and *The Dick Cavett Show* (ABC)

911 Outstanding Series Comic Actor: Alan Alda in *M*A *S*H* (CBS)
912 Outstanding Series Comic Actress: Mary Tyler Moore in *The Mary Tyler Moore Show* (CBS)
913 Outstanding Series Dramatic Actor: Telly Savalas in *Kojak* (CBS)
914 Outstanding Series Dramatic Actress: Michael Learned in *The Waltons* (CBS)
915 Outstanding Limited Series Actor: William Holden in *The Blue Knight* (NBC)
916 Outstanding Limited Series Actress: Mildred Natwick in "The Snoop Sisters" on *NBC Tuesday Night Mystery Movie* (NBC)
917 Outstanding Special Dramatic Actor: Hal Holbrook in "Pueblo" on *ABC Theatre* (ABC)
918 Outstanding Special Dramatic Actress: Cicely Tyson in *The Autobiography of Miss Jane Pittman* (CBS)
919 Series Actor of the Year: Alan Alda in *M*A *S*H* (CBS)
920 Series Actress of the Year: Mary Tyler Moore in *The Mary Tyler Moore Show* (CBS)
921 Special Actor of the Year: Hal Holbrook in "Pueblo" on *ABC Theatre* (ABC)
922 Special Actress of the Year: Cicely Tyson in *The Autobiography of Miss Jane Pittman* (CBS)
923 Best Supporting Comedy Actor: Rob Reiner in *All in the Family* (CBS)
924 Best Supporting Comedy Actress: Cloris Leachman in "The Lars Affair" on *The Mary Tyler Moore Show* (CBS)
925 Best Supporting Dramatic Actor: Michael Moriarty in *The Glass Menagerie* (ABC)
926 Best Supporting Dramatic Actress: Joanna Miles in *The Glass Menagerie* (ABC)
927 Best Supporting Variety Actor: Harvey Korman in *The Carol Burnett Show* (CBS)
928 Best Supporting Variety or Music Actress: Brenda Vaccaro in *The Shape of Things* (CBS)
929 Supporting Actor of the Year: Michael Moriarty in *The Glass Menagerie* (ABC)
930 Supporting Actress of the Year: Joanna Miles in *The Glass Menagerie* (ABC)
931 Best Daytime Dramatic Series Actor: MacDonald Carey in *Days of Our Lives* (NBC)
932 Best Daytime Dramatic Series Actress: Elizabeth Hubbard in *The Doctors* (NBC)
933 Best Daytime Dramatic Special Actor: Pat O'Brien in *The Other Woman* (ABC)
934 Best Daytime Dramatic Special Actress: Cathleen Nesbitt in "The Mask of Love" on *ABC Matinee Today* (ABC)
935 Daytime Actor of the Year: Pat O'Brien in "The Other Woman" on *ABC Matinee Today* (ABC)
936 Daytime Actress of the Year: Cathleen Nesbitt in "The Mask of Love" on *ABC Matinee Today* (ABC)
937 Best Game Show Host or Hostess: Peter Marshall in *The Hollywood Squares* (NBC)
938 Best Variety Host or Hostess: Dinah Shore in *Dinah's Place* (NBC)
939 Daytime Host of the Year: Peter Marshall in *The Hollywood Squares* (NBC)
940 Outstanding Comedy Series Director: Jackie Cooper for "Carry On, Hawkeye" on *M*A *S*H* (CBS)
941 Outstanding Series Variety or Music Director: Dave Powers for "The Australia Show" on *The Carol Burnett Show* (CBS)
942 Outstanding Single Program Variety or Music Director: Dwight Hemion for *Barbra Streisand . . . And Other Musical Instruments* (CBS)
943 Best Series Dramatic Director: Robert Butler for *The Blue Knight, Part III* (NBC)
944 Best Special Dramatic Director: John Korty for *The Autobiography of Miss Jane Pittman* (CBS)
945 Best Daytime Drama Series Director: H. Wesley Kenney for *Days of Our Lives* (NBC)
946 Best Game Show Director: Mike Gargiulo for *Jackpot!* (NBC)
947 Best Special Director: H. Wesley Kenney for *Miss Kline, We Love You* (ABC)
948 Best Variety Director: Dick Carson

for *The Merv Griffin Show* (syndicated)

949 Daytime Director of the Year: H. Wesley Kenney for *Miss Kline, We Love You* (ABC)

950 Series Director of the Year: Robert Butler for *The Blue Knight* (NBC)

951 Special Director of the Year: Dwight Hemion for *Barbra Streisand . . . And Other Musical Instruments* (CBS)

952 Outstanding Entertainment Series Film Editing: Gene Fowler, Jr., Marjorie Fowler and Samuel E. Beetley for *The Blue Knight* (NBC)

953 Outstanding Single Program Entertainment Film Editing: Frank Morris for "The Execution of Private Slovak" on *NBC Wednesday Night at the Movies* (NBC)

954 Film Editor of the Year: Frank Morris for "The Execution of Private Slovak" on *NBC Wednesday Night at the Movies* (NBC)

955 Outstanding Special Videotape Editing: Alfred Muller for "Pueblo" on *ABC Theatre* (ABC)

956 Best Videotape Editing: Gary Anderson for *Paramount Presents . . . ABC Wide World of Entertainment* (ABC)

957 Outstanding Daytime Editing: Gary Anderson for *Miss Kline, We Love You* (ABC)

958 Outstanding News Film Editing: William J. Freeda for "Profile of Poverty in Appalachia" on *NBC Nightly News* (NBC)

959 Outstanding Documentary Film Editing: Ann Chegwidden for "The Baboons of Gombe" on *Jane Goodall and the World of Animal Behavior* (ABC)

960 Outstanding Film Sound Editing: Bud Nolan for "Pueblo" on *ABC Theatre* (ABC)

961 Outstanding Film or Tape Sound Mixing: Robert A. Gramaglia and Michael Schindler for "Pueblo" on *ABC Theatre* (ABC)

962 Best Film or Tape Sound Editing: Charles L. Campbell, Robert Cornett, Larry Caron, Larry Kaufman, Colin Moria, Don Warner and Frank R. White for "The Baboons of Gombe" on *Jane Goodall and the World of Animal Behavior* (ABC)

963 Best Film or Tape Sound Mixing: Peter Pilafian, George R. Porter, Eddie J. Nelson and Robert L. Harman for "Journey to the Outer Limits" on *National Geographic Special* (ABC)

964 Outstanding Daytime Sound Mixing: Ernest Dellutri for *Days of Our Lives* (NBC)

965 Best Series Entertainment Cinematography: Harry Wolf in "Any Old Port in a Storm" on *Columbo* (NBC)

966 Best Special Entertainment Cinematography: Ted Voigtlander for "It's Good to Be Alive" on *GE Theatre* (CBS)

967 Cinematographer of the Year: Ted Voigtlander for "It's Good to Be Alive" on *GE Theatre* (CBS)

968 Outstanding Technical Direction and Electronic Camerawork: Gerry Bucci, Kenneth Tamburri, Dave Hilmer, Dave Smith, Jim Balden and Ron Brooks for "In Concert with Cat Stevens" on *ABC Wide World of Entertainment* (ABC)

969 Outstanding Daytime Technical Direction and Electronic Camerawork: Lou Marchand, Gerald M. Dowd, Frank Melchiorre and John Morrow for *One Life to Live* (ABC)

970 Outstanding Achievement in Sports Programming: Jim McKay, host for *ABC's Wide World of Sports* (ABC)

971 Best Series Dramatic Writing: Joanna Lee for "The Thanksgiving Story" on *The Waltons* (CBS)

972 Best Original Teleplay Dramatic Writing: Fay Kanin for "Tell Me Where It Hurts" on *GE Theatre* (CBS)

973 Best Adaptation Dramatic Writing: Tracy Keenan Wynn for *The Autobiography of Miss Jane Pittman* (CBS)

974 Best Series Comedy Writing: Treva Silverman for "The Lou and Edie Story" on *The Mary Tyler Moore Show* (CBS)

975 Best Series Variety Writing: Ed Simmons, Gary Belkin, Robert Beatty, Arnie Kogen, Bill Richmond, Gene Perret, Rudy de Luca, Barry Levinson, Dick Clair, Jenna McMahon and Barry Harmon for *The Carol Burnett Show* (CBS)

976 Best Special Variety Writing: Herb Sargent, Rosalyn Drexler, Lorne Michaels, Richard Pryor, Jim Rusk, James R. Stein, Robert Illes, Lily Tomlin, George Yanok, Jane Wagner, Rod Warren, Ann Elder and Karyl Geld for *Lily* (CBS)

977 Series Writer of the Year: Treva Silverman for *The Mary Tyler Moore Show* (CBS)

978 Special Writer of the Year: Fay Kanin for "Tell Me Where It Hurts" on *GE Theatre* (CBS)

979 Best Daytime Dramatic Writing: Henry Slesar for *The Edge of Night* (CBS)

980 Best Daytime Special Dramatic Writing: Lila Garrett and Sandy Krinski for "Mother of the Bride" on *ABC Afternoon Playbreak* (ABC)

981 Best Daytime Game Show Writing: Jay Reack, Harry Friedman, Harold Schneider, Gary Johnson, Steve Levitch, Rick Kellard and Rowby Goren for *The Hollywood Squares* (NBC)

982 Best Daytime Variety Writing: Tony Grafalo, Bob Murphy and Merv Griffin for *The Merv Griffin Show* (syndicated)

983 Best Daytime Writer of the Year: Lila Garrett and Sandy Krinski for "Mother of the Bride" on *ABC Afternoon Playbreak* (ABC)

984 Outstanding Choreography: Tony Charmoli for *Mitzi . . . A Tribute to the American Housewife* (CBS)

985 Best Series Music Composition: Morton Stevens for "Hookman" on *Hawaii Five-O* (CBS)

986 Best Special Music Composition: Fred Karlin for *The Autobiography of Miss Jane Pittman* (CBS)

987 Best Song or Theme: Marty Paich and David Paich for "Light the Way" on *Ironside* (NBC)

988 Best Music Direction of Musical Program: Jack Parnell, Ken Welch and Mitzi Welch for *Barbra Streisand . . . And Other Musical Instruments* (CBS)

989 Musician of the Year: Jack Parnell, Ken Welch and Mitzi Welch for *Barbra Streisand—And Other Musical Instruments* (CBS)

990 Outstanding Daytime Musical Direction: Richard Clements for "A Special Act of Love" on *ABC Afternoon Playbreak* (ABC)

991 Outstanding Lighting Direction: William M. Klages for "The Lie" on *CBS Playhouse* (CBS)

992 Outstanding Daytime Lighting Direction: Richard Holbrook for *The Young and the Restless* (CBS)

993 Outstanding Individual Achievement in Children's Programming: Charles M. Schulz, writer for *A Charlie Brown Thanksgiving* (CBS), and William Zaharuk and Peter Razmofski for "The Borrowers" on *Hallmark Hall of Fame* (NBC)

994 Best Series Dramatic Art Direction or Scenic Design: Jan Scott and Charles Kreiner for "The Lie" on *CBS Playhouse* (CBS)

995 Best Special Musical Art Direction or Scenic Design: Brian C. Bartholomew for *Barbra Streisand . . . and Other Musical Instruments* (CBS)

996 Art Director and Set Decorator of the Year: Jan Scott and Charles Kreiner for "The Lie" on *CBS Playhouse* (CBS)

997 Outstanding Daytime Art Direction or Scenic Design: Tom Trimble and Brock Broughton for *The Young and the Restless* (CBS)

998 Outstanding Costume Design: Bruce Walkup and Sandy Stewart for *The Autobiography of Miss Jane Pittman* (CBS)

999 Outstanding Daytime Costume Design: Bill Jobe for "The Mask of Love" on *ABC Matinee Today* (ABC)

1000 Outstanding Make-Up: Stan Winston and Rick Baker for *The Autobiography of Miss Jane Pittman* (CBS)

1001 Outstanding Daytime Make-Up: Douglas C. Kelly for "The Mask of Love" on *ABC Matinee Today* (ABC)

1002 Outstanding Achievement in Any Area of Creative Technical Craft: Lynda Gurasich, hairstylist for *The Autobiography of Miss Jane Pittman* (CBS)

1003 Outstanding Segment Within Regularly Scheduled News Program: "The Agnew Resignation" on *CBS Evening News with Walter Cronkite* (CBS); "The Key Biscayne Bank Charter Struggle" on *CBS Evening News with Walter Cronkite* (CBS); "Reports on World Hunger" on

NBC Nightly News (NBC); and coverage of the October War from Israel's Northern Front on *CBS Evening News with Walter Cronkite* (CBS)

1004 Outstanding Achievement in Magazine-type Programming: "America's Nerve Gas Arsenal" on *First Tuesday* (NBC); "A Question of Impeachment" on *Bill Moyers' Journal* (PBS); and "The Adversaries" on *Behind the Lines* (PBS)

1005 Outstanding Special Event Coverage: *Watergate Coverage* (PBS), and *Watergate: The White House Transcripts* (CBS)

1006 Outstanding Current Interest Documentary: "Fire!" on *ABC News Closeup* (ABC) and *CBS News Special Report: The Senate and the Watergate Affair* (CBS)

1007 Outstanding Artistic, Cultural or Historic Documentary: "Journey to the Outer Limits" on *National Geographic Special* (ABC); *CBS Reports: The Rockefellers* (CBS); and *The World at War* (syndicated)

1008 Outstanding Interview Program: "Henry Steele Commager" on *Bill Moyers' Journal* (PBS), and "Solzhenitsyn" on *CBS News Special* (CBS)

1009 Outstanding News Broadcaster: Harry Reasoner on *ABC News* (ABC), and Bill Moyers on "Essay on Watergate" on *Bill Moyers' Journal* (PBS)

1010 Outstanding News and Documentary Direction: Pamela Hill for "Fire!" on *ABC News Closeup* (ABC)

1011 Best Magazine-type Program Cinematography: Walter Dumbrow for "Ballerina" on *60 Minutes* (CBS)

1012 Best Technical Direction and Electronic Camerawork: Carl Schutzman, Joseph Schwartz and William Bell for *60 Minutes* (CBS)

1013 Best Regularly Scheduled News Cinematography: Delos Hall for "Clanking Savannah Blacksmith" on *The CBS Evening News with Walter Cronkite* (CBS)

1014 Outstanding Achievement in Any Area of Creative Technical Crafts: Philippe Cousteau, underwater camerawork on "Beneath the Frozen World" on *The Undersea World of Jacques Cousteau* (ABC); Aggie Whelan, courtroom artist on the Mitchell-Stans Trial on *The*

CBS Evening News (CBS); and John Chambers and Tom Burman, make-up for *Struggle for Survival: Primal Man* (ABC)

1015 Best Art Direction or Scenic Design: William Sunshine for *60 Minutes* (CBS)

1016 Best Music Composition: Walter Scharf for "Beneath the Frozen World" on *The Undersea World of Jacques Cousteau* (ABC)

1017 Outstanding Achievement in Children's Programming: Jon Stone, Joseph A. Bailey, Jerry Juhl, Emily Perl, Jeffrey Moss, Ray Sipherd and Norman Stiles, writers for *Sesame Street* (PBS), and the Muppets, performers on *Sesame Street* (PBS)

1018 Outstanding Set Decorating and Art Direction in Children's Programming: Ronald Baldwin and Nat Mongioi for *The Electric Company* (PBS)

1019 Outstanding Religious Program: Kan Lamkin, Sam Drummy, Garry Stanton and Robert Hatfield for "Gift of Tears" on *This Is the Life* (syndicated)

1020 National Award for Community Service: *Through the Looking Glass Darkly* (WKY-TV, Oklahoma City)

1021 Outstanding Achievement in Engineering Achievement: Consolidated Video Systems, Inc. for portable videotape equipment and RCA for quadraplex videotape cartridge equipment

1022 International Non-fiction Award: *Horizon: The Making of a Natural History Film* (British Broadcasting Corporation, London)

1023 International Fiction Award: *La Cabina* (Television Española, Madrid)

1024 International Directorate Emmy Award: Charles Curran, president of the European Broadcasting Union and director general of the British Broadcasting Corporation

─────── **1974** ───────

1025 Outstanding Comedy Series: *The Mary Tyler Moore Show* (CBS)

1026 Outstanding Musical Variety Series: *The Carol Burnett Show* (CBS)

1027 Outstanding Variety or Popular Music Program: *An Evening with John Denver* (ABC)

1028 **Outstanding Limited Series:** *Benjamin Franklin* (CBS)

1029 **Outstanding Dramatic Series:** *Benjamin Franklin* (CBS)

1030 **Outstanding Drama or Comedy Special:** "The Law" on *NBC World Premiere Movie* (NBC)

1031 **Outstanding Classical Music Program:** *Profile in Music: Beverly Sills* (PBS)

1032 **Outstanding Daytime Drama:** *The Young and the Restless* (CBS)

1033 **Outstanding Drama Special:** *The Girl Who Couldn't Lose* (ABC)

1034 **Outstanding Game Show:** *Hollywood Squares* (NBC)

1035 **Outstanding Talk, Service or Variety Series:** *Dinah!* (syndicated)

1036 **Outstanding Children's Entertainment Series:** *Star Trek* (NBC)

1037 **Outstanding Children's Entertainment Special:** "Harlequin" on *The CBS Festival of Lively Arts for Young People* (CBS)

1038 **Outstanding Children's Special:** *Yes, Virginia, There Is a Santa Claus* (ABC)

1039 **Outstanding Sports Program:** *Wide World of Sports* (ABC)

1040 **Outstanding Sports Event:** *Jimmy Connors vs. Rod Laver Tennis Challenge* (CBS)

1041 **National Award for Community Service:** *The Willowbrook Case: The People vs. The State of New York* (WABC-TV, New York)

1042 **International Non-fiction Award:** *Aquarius: Hello Dali!* on London Weekend Television (London), and *Inside Story: Marek* on British Broadcasting Corporation (London)

1043 **International Fiction Award:** *Mr. Axelford's Angel* on Yorkshire Television Limited (London), and *The Evacuees* on British Broadcasting Corporation (London)

1044 **Outstanding Series Comic Actor:** Tony Randall in *The Odd Couple* (ABC)

1045 **Outstanding Series Comic Actress:** Valerie Harper in *Rhoda* (CBS)

1046 **Outstanding Series Dramatic Actor:** Robert Blake in *Baretta* (ABC)

1047 **Outstanding Series Dramatic Actress:** Jean Marsh in "Upstairs, Downstairs" on *Masterpiece Theatre* (PBS)

1048 **Outstanding Limited Series Actor:** Peter Falk in "Columbo" on *NBC Sunday Mystery Movie* (NBC)

1049 **Outstanding Limited Series Actress:** Jessica Walter in "Amy Prentiss" on *NBC Sunday Mystery Movie* (NBC)

1050 **Outstanding Special Dramatic Actor:** Laurence Olivier in "Love Among the Ruins" on *ABC Theatre* (ABC)

1051 **Outstanding Special Dramatic Actress:** Katharine Hepburn in "Love Among the Ruins" on *ABC Theatre* (ABC)

1052 **Outstanding Continuing Supporting Actor in a Comedy Series:** Ed Asner in *The Mary Tyler Moore Show* (CBS)

1053 **Outstanding Continuing Supporting Actress in a Comedy Series:** Betty White in *The Mary Tyler Moore Show* (CBS)

1054 **Outstanding Continuing Supporting Actor in a Drama Series:** Will Geer in *The Waltons* (CBS)

1055 **Outstanding Continuing Supporting Actress in a Drama Series:** Ellen Corby in *The Waltons* (CBS)

1056 **Outstanding Supporting Actor in Comedy or Drama Special:** Jack Albertson in *Cher* (CBS)

1057 **Outstanding Supporting Actor in Comedy or Drama:** Anthony Quayle in "QB VII, Parts 1 and 2" on *ABC Movie Special* (ABC)

1058 **Outstanding Supporting Actor in Comedy or Drama Series:** Patrick McGoohan in "By the Dawn's Early Light" on *Columbo* (NBC)

1059 **Outstanding Supporting Actress in Variety or Music Special:** Cloris Leachman in *Cher* (CBS)

1060 **Outstanding Supporting Actress in Comedy or Drama:** Juliet Mills in "QB VII, Parts 1 and 2" on *ABC Movie Special* (ABC)

1061 **Outstanding Supporting Actress in Comedy or Drama Series:** Cloris Leachman in "Phyllis Whips Inflation" on *The Mary Tyler Moore Show* (CBS)

1062 **Outstanding Single Performance by Supporting Actress in Comedy or Drama:** Zohra Lampert in "Queen of the Gypsies" on *Kojak* (CBS)

1063 **Outstanding Sports Broadcaster:** Jim McKay on *Wide World of Sports* (ABC)

1064 **Outstanding Actor in Daytime Drama Series:** MacDonald Carey in *Days of Our Lives* (NBC)

1065 **Outstanding Actress in Daytime Drama Series:** Susan Flannery in *Days of Our Lives* (NBC)

1066 **Outstanding Actor in Daytime Drama Special:** Bradford Dillmann in "The Last Bride of Salem" on *ABC Afternoon Playbreak* (ABC)

1067 **Outstanding Actress in Daytime Drama Special:** Kay Lenz in "Heart in Hiding" on *ABC Afternoon Playbreak* (ABC)

1068 **Outstanding Host or Hostess in Talk, Service or Variety Series:** Barbara Walters in *Today* (NBC)

1069 **Outstanding Host in Quiz or Audience Participation Show:** Peter Marshall in *The Hollywood Squares* (NBC)

1070 **Special Classification of Outstanding Individual Achievement:** Alistair Cooke in *Masterpiece Theatre* (PBS)

1071 **Outstanding Directing in a Drama Series:** Bill Bain for *Upstairs, Downstairs* (PBS)

1072 **Outstanding Directing in a Comedy Series:** Gene Reynolds for *M*A*S*H* (CBS)

1073 **Outstanding Directing in a Comedy/Variety or Music Series:** Dave Powers for *The Carol Burnett Show* (CBS)

1074 **Outstanding Directing in a Comedy/Variety or Music Special:** Bill Davis for *An Evening with John Denver* (ABC)

1075 **Outstanding Directing in a Comedy or Variety Special:** George Cukor for "Love Among the Ruins" on *ABC Theatre* (ABC)

1076 **Outstanding Directing in a Daytime Drama Series:** Richard Dunlap for *The Young and the Restless* (CBS)

1077 **Outstanding Directing in a Daytime Special Program:** Mort Lachman for *The Girl Who Couldn't Lose* (ABC)

1078 **Outstanding Directing in a Daytime Variety Program:** Glen Swanson for "Dinah Salutes Broadway" on *Dinah!* (syndicated)

1079 **Outstanding Directing in a Game or Audience Participation Show:** Jerome Shaw for *The Hollywood Squares* (NBC)

1080 **Outstanding Comedy Series Film Editing:** Douglas Hines for "An Affair to Forget" on *The Mary Tyler Moore Show* (CBS)

1081 **Outstanding Drama Series Film Editing:** Donald R. Rode for "Mirror, Mirror on the Wall" on *Petrocelli* (NBC)

1082 **Outstanding Special Film Editing:** John A. Martinelli for "The Legend of Lizzie Borden" on *ABC Monday Night Movie* (ABC)

1083 **Outstanding Individual Achievement in Sports Programming:** Herb Altman, film editor for *The Baseball World of Joe Garagiola* (NBC)

1084 **Outstanding Achievement in Videotape Editing:** Gary Anderson and Jim McElroy for *Judgment: The Court Martial of Lt. William Calley* (ABC)

1085 **Outstanding Achievement in Film Sound Editing:** Marvin I. Kosberg, Richard Burrow, Milton C. Burrow, Jack Milner, Ronald Ashcroft, James Ballas, Josef von Stroheim, Jerry Rosenthal, William Andrews, Edward Sandlin, David Horton, Alvin Kajita, Tony Garber and Jeremy Hoenack for "QB VII, Parts 1 and 2" on *ABC Movie Special* (ABC)

1086 **Outstanding Achievement in Film or Tape Sound Mixing:** Marshall King for *The American Film Institute Salute to James Cagney* (CBS)

1087 **Outstanding Drama Series Writing:** Howard Fast for "The Ambassador" on *Benjamin Franklin* (CBS)

1088 **Outstanding Comedy Series Writing:** Ed Weinberger and Stan Daniels for "Mary Richards Goes to Jail" on *The Mary Tyler Moore Show* (CBS)

1089 **Outstanding Writing in a Comedy/Variety or Music Series:** Gary Belkin, Robert Beatty, Ed Simmons, Arnie Kogen, Bill Richmond, Gene Perret, Rudy de Luca, Barry Levinson, Dick Clair and Jenna McMahon for *The Carol Burnett Show* (CBS)

1090 **Outstanding Writing in a Comedy/Variety or Music Special:** Bob Wells, John Bradford and Cy Coleman for *Shirley MacLaine: If They Could See Me Now* (CBS)

1091 **Outstanding Writing in a Drama or Comedy Special Program Original Teleplay:** James Costigan for "Love Among the Ruins" on *ABC Theatre* (ABC)

1092 **Outstanding Writing in a Drama or Comedy Special Program Adaptation:** David W. Rintels for *IBM Presents Clarence Darrow* (NBC)

1093 **Outstanding Writing for a Daytime Drama Series:** Harding Lemay, Tom King, Charles Kozloff, Jan Merlin and Douglas Marland for *Another World* (NBC)

1094 **Outstanding Writing for a Daytime Special:** Audrey Davis Levin for "Heart in Hiding" on *ABC Afternoon Playbreak* (ABC)

1095 **Outstanding Series Cinematography:** Richard Glouner for *Columbo* (NBC)

1096 **Outstanding Special Cinematography:** David M. Walsh for *Queen of the Stardust Ballroom* (CBS)

1097 **Outstanding Technical Direction and Electronic Camerawork:** Ernie Buttleman, technical director and Jim Angel, Jim Balden, Ron Brooks and Art Lacombe, cameramen for "The Missiles of October" on *ABC Theatre* (ABC)

1098 **Outstanding Choreography:** Marge Champion for *Queen of the Stardust Ballroom* (CBS)

1099 **Outstanding Series Musical Composition:** Billy Goldenberg for "The Rebel" on *Benjamin Franklin* (CBS)

1100 **Outstanding Special Musical Composition:** Jerry Goldsmith for "QB VII, Parts 1 and 2" on *ABC Movie Special* (ABC)

1101 **Outstanding Lighting Direction:** John Freschi for *The Perry Como Christmas Show* (CBS)

1102 **Outstanding Art Direction or Scenic Design from Comedy/Variety or Music Series:** Robert Kelly, art director and Robert Checchi, set decorator for *Cher* (CBS)

1103 **Outstanding Art Direction or Scenic Design from Dramatic Special or Feature-Length Television Production:** Carmen Dillon, art director and Tess Davis, set director for "Love Among the Ruins" on *ABC Theatre* (ABC)

1104 **Outstanding Art Direction or Scenic Design from Single Episode of Comedy or Drama Series:** Charles Lisanby, art director and Robert Checchi for "The Ambassador" on *Benjamin Franklin* (CBS)

1105 **Outstanding Graphic Design and Title Sequences:** Phil Norman for "QB VII, Parts 1 and 2" on *ABC Movie Special* (ABC)

1106 **Outstanding Costume Design:** Guy Verhille for "The Legend of Lizzie Borden" on *ABC Monday Night Movie* (ABC), and Margaret Furse for "Love Among the Ruins" on *ABC Theatre* (ABC)

1107 **Outstanding Individual Achievement in Sports Programming:** Gene Schwarz, technical director for *The 1974 World Series* (NBC); Corey Leible, Ben Basile, Jack Bennett, Lou Gerard and Ray Figelski, electronic cameramen for *The 1974 Stanley Cup Playoffs* (NBC); John Pumo, Charles D'Onofrio and Frank Florio, technical directors and George Klimcsak, Robert Kania, Harold Hoffmann, Herman Lang, George Drago, Walt Deniear, Stan Gould, Al Diamond, Charles Armstrong, Al Brantley, Sig Meyers, Frank McSpedon, George F. Naeder, Gordon Sweeney, Joseph Sidlo, William Hathaway, Gene Pescalek and Curly Fonorow, cameramen for *Masters Tournament* (CBS)

1108 **Outstanding Individual Achievement in Children's Programming:** Elinor Bunin, graphic design and title sequences for *Funshine Saturday and Sunday* (ABC)

1109 **Outstanding Achievement in Any Area of Television Creative Crafts:** Edie Panda, hair stylist for "The Ambassador" on *Benjamin Franklin* (CBS), and Doug Nelson and Norm Schwartz for double-system sound editing and synchronization for stereo broadcasting on *Wide World Concert* (ABC)

1110 **Outstanding Achievement in Engineering Development:** Columbia Broadcasting System for development of Electronic News Gathering System and Nippon Electronic Company for television digital frame synchronizers

1111 **Special Classification for Outstanding Program Achievement:** *American Film Institute Salute to James Cagney* (CBS)

1112 **International Directorate Award:** Junzo Imamichi, chairman of the board of Tokyo Broadcasting Company

1113 **Trustees' Award:** Elmer Lower

of American Broadcasting Company and Peter Goldmark of Goldmark Laboratories

———————— **1 9 7 5** ————————

1114 Outstanding Comedy Series: *The Mary Tyler Moore Show* (CBS)
1115 Outstanding Comedy/Variety or Music Series: *NBC's Saturday Night Live* (NBC)
1116 Outstanding Drama Series: *Police Story* (NBC)
1117 Outstanding Limited Series: "Upstairs, Downstairs" on *Masterpiece Theatre* (PBS)
1118 Outstanding Classical Music Program: *Bernstein and the New York Philharmonic* (PBS)
1119 Outstanding Drama or Comedy Special: "Eleanor and Franklin" on *ABC Theatre* (ABC)
1120 Outstanding Comedy/Variety or Music Special: *Gypsy in My Soul* (CBS)
1121 Special Classification of Outstanding Program Achievement: *The Tonight Show Starring Johnny Carson* (NBC), and *Bicentennial Minutes* (CBS)
1122 Outstanding Daytime Drama: *Another World* (NBC)
1123 Outstanding Daytime Drama Special: *First Ladies' Diaries: Edith Wilson* (NBC)
1124 Outstanding Daytime Game or Audience Participation Show: *The $20,000 Pyramid* (ABC)
1125 Outstanding Children's Entertainment Series: *Big Blue Marble* (syndicated)
1126 Outstanding Children's Informational Series: *Go* (NBC)
1127 Outstanding Children's Entertainment Special: "Danny Kaye's Look-in at the Metropolitan Opera" on *The CBS Festival of Lively Arts for Young People* (CBS)
1128 Outstanding Informational Children's Program: *Happy Anniversary, Charlie Brown* (CBS)
1129 Outstanding Children's Instructional Series or Special: *Grammar Rock* (ABC)
1130 Outstanding Daytime Talk, Service or Variety Series: *Dinah!* (syndicated)

1131 Outstanding Children's Special: *You're a Good Sport, Charlie Brown* (CBS)
1132 Outstanding Live Sports Special: *1975 World Series* (NBC)
1133 Outstanding Live Sports Special: *NFL Monday Night Football* (ABC)
1134 Outstanding Edited Sports Special: *XII Winter Olympic Games* (ABC)
1135 Outstanding Edited Sports Series: *ABC's Wide World of Sports* (ABC)
1136 Outstanding Series Lead Comedy Actress: Mary Tyler Moore in *The Mary Tyler Moore Show* (CBS)
1137 Outstanding Series Lead Comedy Actor: Jack Albertson in *Chico and the Man* (NBC)
1138 Outstanding Series Lead Dramatic Actress: Michael Learned in *The Waltons* (CBS)
1139 Outstanding Series Lead Dramatic Actor: Peter Falk in *Columbo* (NBC)
1140 Outstanding Limited Series Lead Actress: Rosemary Harris in "Notorious Woman" on *Masterpiece Theatre* (PBS)
1141 Outstanding Limited Series Lead Actor: Hal Holbrook in *Sandburg's Lincoln* (NBC)
1142 Outstanding Lead Actress in Comedy or Drama Special: Susan Clark in *Babe* (CBS)
1143 Outstanding Lead Actor in Comedy or Drama Special: Anthony Hopkins in "The Lindbergh Kidnapping Case" on *NBC World Premiere Movie* (NBC)
1144 Outstanding Lead Actress in a Single Performance in a Drama or Comedy Series: Kathryn Walker in "John Adams, Lawyer" on *The Adams Chronicles* (PBS)
1145 Outstanding Lead Actor in a Single Performance in a Drama or Comedy Series: Edward Asner in *Rich Man, Poor Man* (ABC)
1146 Outstanding Supporting Actress in a Comedy Series: Betty White in *The Mary Tyler Moore Show* (CBS)
1147 Outstanding Supporting Actor in a Comedy Series: Ted Knight in *The Mary Tyler Moore Show* (CBS)
1148 Outstanding Supporting Actress in a Drama Series: Ellen Corby in *The Waltons* (CBS)

1149 **Outstanding Supporting Actor in a Drama Series:** Anthony Zerbe in *Harry O* (ABC)

1150 **Outstanding Supporting Actress in Variety or Music:** Vicki Lawrence in *The Carol Burnett Show* (CBS)

1151 **Outstanding Supporting Actor in Variety or Music:** Chevy Chase in *NBC's Saturday Night Live* (NBC)

1152 **Outstanding Supporting Actress in a Comedy or Drama Special:** Rosemary Murphy in "Eleanor and Franklin" on *ABC Theatre* (ABC)

1153 **Outstanding Supporting Actor in a Comedy or Drama Special:** Ed Flanders in *A Moon for the Misbegotten* (ABC)

1154 **Outstanding Comedy or Drama Single Performance by a Supporting Actress:** Fionnula Flanagan in *Rich Man, Poor Man* (ABC)

1155 **Outstanding Actor in Daytime Drama Series:** Larry Haines in *Search for Tomorrow* (CBS)

1156 **Outstanding Actress in Daytime Drama Series:** Helen Gallagher in *Ryan's Hope* (ABC)

1157 **Outstanding Actor in Daytime Drama Special:** Gerald Gordon in *First Ladies' Diaries: Martha Washington* (NBC), and James Luisi in *First Ladies' Diaries: Martha Washington* (NBC)

1158 **Outstanding Actress in Daytime Drama Special:** Elizabeth Hubbard in *First Ladies' Diaries: Edith Wilson* (NBC)

1159 **Outstanding Host or Hostess in a Game or Audience Participation Show:** Allen Ludden in *Password* (ABC)

1160 **Outstanding Host or Hostess in a Talk, Service or Variety Show:** Dinah Shore in *Dinah!* (syndicated)

1161 **Outstanding Sports Personality:** Jim McKay in *ABC's Wide World of Sports* (ABC)

1162 **Outstanding Directing in a Drama Series:** David Greene for *Rich Man, Poor Man* (ABC)

1163 **Outstanding Directing in a Comedy Series:** Gene Reynolds for *M*A*S*H* (CBS)

1164 **Outstanding Directing in a Comedy, Variety or Music Special:** Dwight Hemion for *Steve and Eydie: Our Love Is Here to Stay* (CBS)

1165 **Outstanding Directing in a Comedy, Variety or Music Series:** Dave Wilson for *NBC's Saturday Night Live* (NBC)

1166 **Outstanding Directing in a Drama or Comedy Special:** Daniel Petrie for "Eleanor and Franklin" on *ABC Theatre* (ABC)

1167 **Outstanding Directing in a Daytime Variety Program:** Glen Swanson for *Dinah!* (syndicated)

1168 **Outstanding Directing in a Game or Audience Participation Show:** Mike Gargiulo for *The $20,000 Pyramid* (ABC)

1169 **Outstanding Directing in a Daytime Drama Series:** David Pressman for *One Life to Live* (ABC)

1170 **Outstanding Directing in a Daytime Special:** Nicholas Havinga for *First Ladies' Diaries: Edith Wilson* (NBC)

1171 **Outstanding Individual Achievement in Sports Programming:** Andy Sidaris, Don Ohlmeyer, Larry Kamm, Roger Goodman, Ronnie Hawkins and Ralph Melanby, directors for *XII Winter Olympic Games* (ABC)

1172 **Outstanding Film Editing in a Comedy Series:** Stanford Tischler and Fred W. Berger for "Welcome to Korea" on *M*A*S*H* (CBS)

1173 **Outstanding Film Editing in Dramatic or Limited Series:** Samuel Beetley and Ken Zemke for "The Quality of Mercy" on *Medical Story* (NBC)

1174 **Outstanding Film Editing in Special Program:** Michael Kahn for "Eleanor and Franklin" on *ABC Theatre* (ABC)

1175 **Outstanding Achievement in Series Videotape Editing:** Girish Bhargava and Manfred Schorn for *The Adams Chronicles* (PBS)

1176 **Outstanding Videotape Editing in a Special:** Nick V. Giordano for "Alice Cooper—The Nightmare" on *Wide, Wide World: In Concert* (ABC)

1177 **Outstanding Individual Achievement in Sports Program:** Jeff Cohan, Joe Aceti, John de Lisa, Lou Frederick, Jack Gallivan, Jim Jennett, Carol Lehti, Howard Fritz, Eddie C. Joseph, Ken Klingbeil, Leo Stephan, Michael Wenig, Ted Summers, Ron Ackerman, Michael Bonifazio, Barbara Bowman, Charlie Burnham, John Croak, Charles Gardner, Marvin Gench, Victor Gonzales, Jacob Hierl, Nick Mazur, Ed McCarthy, Alex Moscovic, Arthur Nace, Lou Rende, Erskin Roberts, Merritt Roesser, Arthur Volk, Roger Haenelt, Curt Brand, Phil Mollica, Herb Ohlandt and George Boettcher, videotape editors for *XII Winter Olympic Games* (ABC)

1178 Outstanding Film Sound Editing: Marvin I. Kosberg, Douglas H. Grindstaff, Al Kajita, Hans Mewman, Leon Selditz, Dick Friedman, Stan Gilbert, Hank Salerno, Larry Singer and William Andrews for "The Quality of Mercy" on *Medical Story* (NBC)

1179 Outstanding Film Sound Mixing: Don Bassman and Don Johnson for "Eleanor and Franklin" on *ABC Theatre* (ABC)

1180 Outstanding Videotape Sound Mixing: Dave Williams for the anniversary show of *The Tonight Show Starring Johnny Carson* (NBC)

1181 Outstanding Individual Achievement in Sports Program: Dick Roes, Jack Kelly, Bill Sandreuter, Frank Bailey and Jack Kestenbaum, videotape sound mixers for *XII Winter Olympic Games* (ABC)

1182 Outstanding Individual Achievement in Children's Program: Bud Nolan and Jim Cookman, film sound editors for *Sound of Freedom* (NBC)

1183 Outstanding Entertainment Series Cinematography: Harry L. Wolf for "Keep Your Eye on the Sparrow" on *Baretta* (ABC)

1184 Outstanding Entertainment Special Cinematography: Paul Lohmann and Edward R. Brown for *Eleanor and Franklin* (ABC)

1185 Outstanding Technical Direction and Electronic Camerawork: Leonard Chumbley, technical director, and Walter Edel, John Fehler and Steve Zink, cameramen for *The Adams Chronicles* (PBS)

1186 Outstanding Drama Series Writing: Sherman Yellen for *The Adams Chronicles* (PBS)

1187 Outstanding Comedy Series Writing: David Lloyd for *The Mary Tyler Moore Show* (CBS)

1188 Outstanding Comedy/Variety or Music Series Writing: Anne Beatts, Chevy Chase, Al Franken, Tom Davis, Lorne Michaels, Marilyn Suzanne Miller, Michael O'Donoghue, Herb Sargent, Tom Schiller, Rosie Schuster and Alan Zweibel for *NBC's Saturday Night Live* (NBC)

1189 Outstanding Writing Adaptation for Comedy or Drama: David W. Rintels for *Fear on Trial* (CBS)

1190 Outstanding Original Teleplay Writing for Comedy or Drama: James Costigan for "Eleanor and Franklin" on *ABC Theatre* (ABC)

1191 Outstanding Writing for Comedy/Variety or Music Special: Jane Wagner, Lorne Michaels, Ann Elder, Christopher Guest, Earl Pomerantz, Jim Rusk, Lily Tomlin, Rod Warren and George Yanok for *Lily Tomlin* (ABC)

1192 Outstanding Daytime Drama Series Writing: Kay Lenard, Pat Falken Smith, William J. Bell, Margaret Stewart, Bill Rega, Sheri Anderson and Wanda Coleman for *Days of Our Lives* (NBC)

1193 Outstanding Daytime Special Writing: Audrey Davis Levin for *First Ladies' Diaries: Edith Wilson* (NBC)

1194 Outstanding Special Classification of Program Achievement: Ann Marcus, Jerry Adelman and Daniel Gregory Brown, writers for *Mary Hartman, Mary Hartman* (syndicated)

1195 Outstanding Lighting Direction: William Krages and Lon Stuckey for *Mitzi and the Hundred Guys* (CBS), and John Freschi for *Mitzi . . . Roarin' in the 20's* (CBS)

1196 Outstanding Achievement in Choreography: Tony Charmoli for *Gypsy in My Soul* (CBS)

1197 Outstanding Series Musical Composition: Alex North for *Rich Man, Poor Man* (ABC)

1198 Outstanding Special Musical Composition: Jerry Goldsmith for *Babe* (CBS)

1199 Outstanding Achievement Musical Direction: Seiji Ozawa for "Central Park in the Dark/A Hero's Life" on *Evening at the Symphony* (PBS)

1200 Special Achievement in Special Musical Material: Ken Welch, Mitzi Welch and Artie Malvin for *The Carol Burnett Show* (CBS)

1201 **Outstanding Comedy or Drama Art Direction or Scenic Design:** Tom John, art direction, and John Wendell and Wes Laws, set decorators, for pilot of *Beacon Hill* (CBS)

1202 **Outstanding Comedy/Variety or Music Series Scenic Design and Art Direction:** Raymond Klausen, art director, and Robert Checchi, set decorator for *Cher* (CBS)

1203 **Outstanding Dramatic Special Art Direction and Scenic Design:** Jan Scott, art direction, and Anthony Mondello, set decorator for *Eleanor and Franklin* (ABC)

1204 **Outstanding Individual Achievement in Daytime Program:** Rene Lagler, art director, and Richard Harvey, set decorator for *Dinah!* (syndicated)

1205 **Outstanding Make-Up:** Del Armstrong and Mike Westmore for *Eleanor and Franklin* (ABC)

1206 **Outstanding Drama or Comedy Series Costume Design:** Jane Robinson and Jill Silverside for "Recover," "Jenny" and "Lady Randolph Churchill" on *Great Performances* (PBS)

1207 **Outstanding Music and Variety Costume Design:** Bob Mackie for *Mitzi . . . Roarin' in the 20's* (CBS)

1208 **Outstanding Hairstylists:** Jean Burt Reilly and Billy Laughridge for *Eleanor and Franklin* (ABC)

1209 **Outstanding Achievement in Any Area of Creative Technical Crafts:** Donald Sahlin, Kermit Love, Caroly Wilcox, John Lovelady and Rollie Krewson, costumes and props for the Muppets on *Sesame Street* (PBS)

1210 **Outstanding Individual Achievement in Children's Programming:** The Muppets, Jim Henson, Frank Oz, Jerry Nelson, Carroll Spinney and Richard Hunt on *Sesame Street* (PBS)

1211 **Outstanding Graphic Design and Title Sequences:** Norman Sunshine for *Addie and the King of Hearts* (CBS)

1212 **Outstanding Drama Special Costume Design:** Joe I. Tompkins for *Eleanor and Franklin* (ABC)

1213 **Outstanding Achievement in Religious Programming:** Joseph J.H. Valdala, cinematographer for *A Determining Force* (NBC)

1214 **National Award for Community Service:** WBBM-TV, Chicago for *Forgotten Children*

1215 **Outstanding Engineering Development:** Eastman Kodak for Eastman Ektachrome Video News Film, and Sony Corporation for U-Matic Video Cassette Concept

——————— **1976** ———————

1216 **Outstanding Comedy Series:** *The Mary Tyler Moore Show* (CBS)

1217 **Outstanding Comedy/Variety or Music Series:** *Dick Van Dyke and Company* (NBC)

1218 **Outstanding Drama Series:** "Upstairs, Downstairs" on *Masterpiece Theatre* (PBS)

1219 **Outstanding Limited Series:** *Roots* (ABC)

1220 **Special Classification of Outstanding Program Achievement:** *The Tonight Show Starring Johnny Carson* (NBC)

1221 **Outstanding Comedy, Variety or Music Special:** *The Barry Manilow Special* (ABC)

1222 **Outstanding Drama or Comedy Special:** "Eleanor and Franklin: The White House Years" on *ABC Theatre* (ABC), and "Sybil" on *NBC World Premiere Movie: The Big Event* (NBC)

1223 **Outstanding Lead Comedy Actor:** Carroll O'Connor in *All in the Family* (CBS)

1224 **Outstanding Lead Comedy Actress:** Beatrice Arthur in *Maude* (CBS)

1225 **Outstanding Continuing Performance by a Supporting Actor in Comedy Series:** Gary Burghoff in *M*A*S*H* (CBS)

1226 **Outstanding Continuing Performance by a Supporting Actress in Comedy Series:** Mary Kay Place in *Mary Hartman, Mary Hartman* (syndicated)

1227 **Outstanding Lead Dramatic Actor:** James Garner in *The Rockford Files* (NBC)

1228 **Outstanding Lead Dramatic Actress:** Lindsay Wagner in *The Bionic Woman* (ABC)

1229 **Outstanding Continuing Performance by a Supporting Actor in a Drama Series:** Gary Frank in *Family* (ABC)

1230 Outstanding Continuing Performance by a Supporting Actress in a Drama Series: Kristy McNichol in *Family* (ABC)

1231 Outstanding Single Performance by a Supporting Actor in a Comedy or Drama Series: Edward Asner in *Roots, Part 1* (ABC)

1232 Outstanding Single Performance by a Supporting Actress in a Comedy or Drama Series: Olivia Cole in *Roots, Part 8* (ABC)

1233 Outstanding Lead Actor for Single Appearance in a Drama or Comedy Series: Louis Gossett, Jr., in *Roots, Part 2* (ABC)

1234 Outstanding Lead Actress for Single Appearance in a Drama or Comedy Series: Beulah Bondi in "The Pony Cart" on *The Waltons* (CBS)

1235 Outstanding Continuing or Single Performance by a Supporting Actor in Variety or Music: Tim Conway in *The Carol Burnett Show* (CBS)

1236 Outstanding Continuing or Single Performance by a Supporting Actress in Variety or Music: Rita Moreno in *The Muppet Show* (syndicated)

1237 Outstanding Lead Actor in a Drama or Comedy Special: Ed Flanders in *Harry S Truman: Plain Speaking* (PBS)

1238 Outstanding Lead Actress in a Drama or Comedy Series: Sally Field in "Sybil" on *The Big Event* (NBC)

1239 Outstanding Lead Actor in a Limited Series: Christopher Plummer in "The Moneychangers" on *NBC World Premiere: The Big Event* (NBC)

1240 Outstanding Lead Actress in a Limited Series: Patty Duke Astin in "Captains and the Kings" on *NBC's Best Seller* (NBC)

1241 Outstanding Performance by a Supporting Actor in a Drama or Comedy Special: Burgess Meredith in "Tail Gunner Joe" on *The Big Event* (NBC)

1242 Outstanding Performance by a Supporting Actress in a Drama or Comedy Special: Diana Hyland in "The Boy in the Plastic Bubble" on *The ABC Friday Night Movie* (ABC)

1243 Outstanding Comedy Directing: Alan Alda for *M*A*S*H* (CBS)

1244 Outstanding Directing in a Comedy or Drama Special: Daniel Petrie for "Eleanor and Franklin: The White House Years" on *ABC Theatre* (ABC)

1245 Outstanding Drama Series Direction: David Greene for *Roots, Part 1* (ABC)

1246 Outstanding Comedy, Variety or Music Special Directing: Dwight Hemion for *America Salutes Richard Rodgers: The Sound of His Music* (CBS)

1247 Outstanding Comedy, Variety or Music Series Directing: Dave Powers for *The Carol Burnett Show* (CBS)

1248 Outstanding Individual Achievement in Coverage of Special Events: John C. Moffitt, director of *The 28th Annual Emmy Awards* (ABC)

1249 Outstanding Children's Special: "Ballet Shoes, Parts I and II" on *Piccadilly Circus* (PBS)

1250 Outstanding Performing Arts Classical Program: "American Ballet Theatre: Swan Lake" on *Live from Lincoln Center, Great Performances* (PBS)

1251 Outstanding Comedy Series Film Editing: Douglas Hines for *The Mary Tyler Moore Show* (CBS)

1252 Outstanding Drama Series Film Editing: Neil Travis and James Heckert for *Roots, Part 2* (ABC)

1253 Outstanding Special Program Film Editing: Rita Roland and Michael S. McLean for "Eleanor and Franklin: The White House Years" on *ABC Theatre* (ABC)

1254 Special Classification of Outstanding Individual Achievement: Allen Brewster, Bob Roethle, William Lorenz, Manuel Martinez, Ron Fleury, Mike Welch, Jerry Burling, Walter Balderson and Chuck Droege, videotape editors for "The First Fifty Years" on *The Big Event* (NBC), and George Pitts and Clay Cassell, film editors for "The First Fifty Years" on *The Big Event* (NBC)

1255 Outstanding Series Videotape Editing: Roy Stewart for "The War Window" on *Visions* (PBS)

1256 Outstanding Special Program Videotape Editing: Gary H. Anderson for *American Bandstand's 25th Anniversary* (ABC)

1257 Outstanding Series Film Sound Editing: Larry Carow, Larry Neiman, Don Warner, Colin Mouat, George Fredrick, Dave Pettijohn and Paul Bruce Richardson for *Roots, Part 2* (ABC)

1258 Outstanding Special Program Film Sound Editing: Bernard F. Pincus, Milton C. Burrow, Gene Eliot, Don Ernst, Tony Garber, Don V. Isaacs, Larry Kaufman, William L. Manger, David Marshall, Richard Oswald, Edward L. Sandlin and Rusty Tinsley for "Raid on Entebbe" on *The Big Event* (NBC)

1259 Outstanding Film Sound Mixing: Alan Bernard, George R. Porter, Eddie J. Nelson and Robert L. Harman for "The Savage Bees" on *NBC Monday Night at the Movies* (NBC)

1260 Outstanding Tape Sound Mixing: Doug Nelson for *John Denver and Friend* (ABC)

1261 Outstanding Entertainment Series Cinematography: Ric Waite for "Captains and Kings, Chapter 1" on *NBC's Best Seller* (NBC)

1262 Outstanding Entertainment Special Cinematography: Wilmer C. Butler for "Raid on Entebbe" on *The Big Event* (NBC)

1263 Outstanding Technical Direction and Electronic Camerawork: Karl Messerschmidt, technical director, and Jon Olson, Bruce Gray, John Guiterrez, Jim Dodge and Wayne McDonald, cameramen, for *Doug Henning's World of Magic* (NBC)

1264 Outstanding Individual Achievement in Children's Programming: Jean de Joux and Elizabeth Savel, videoanimation on "Peter Pan" on *Hallmark Hall of Fame: The Big Event* (NBC), Bill Hargate, costume designer, and Jerry Greene, videotape editor, for "Peter Pan" on *Hallmark Hall of Fame: The Big Event* (NBC)

1265 Outstanding Comedy Series Writing: Allan Burns, James L. Brooks, Ed Weinberger, Stan Daniels, David Lloyd and Bob Ellison for "Ted's Change of Heart" on *The Mary Tyler Moore Show* (CBS)

1266 Outstanding Drama Series Writing: Ernest Kinoy and William Blinn for *Roots, Part 2* (ABC)

1267 Outstanding Comedy, Variety or Music Series Writing: Anne Beatts, Dan Aykroyd, Al Franken, Tom Davis, James Downey, Lorne Michaels, Marilyn Suzanne Miller, Michael O'Donoghue, Herb Sargent, Tom Schiller, Rosie Schuster, Alan Zweibel, John Belushi and Bill Murray for *NBC's Saturday Night Live* (NBC)

1268 Outstanding Writing Adaptation in a Drama or Comedy Special: Stewart Stern for "Sybil" on *The Big Event* (NBC)

1269 Outstanding Original Teleplay Writing for Drama or Comedy: Lane Slate for "Tail Gunner Joe" on *The Big Event* (NBC)

1270 Outstanding Writing for Comedy, Variety or Music Special: Alan Buz Kohan and Ted Strauss for *America Salutes Richard Rodgers: The Sound of His Music* (CBS)

1271 Outstanding Comedy Series Art Direction or Scenic Design: Thomas E. Azzari, art director for *Fish* (ABC)

1272 Outstanding Drama Series Art Direction or Scenic Design: Tim Harvey, scenic designer for *The Pallisers, Episode 1* (PBS)

1273 Outstanding Art Direction or Scenic Design for Comedy, Variety or Music Series: Romain Johnston, art director, for *The Mac Davis Show* (NBC)

1274 Outstanding Dramatic Special Art Direction or Scenic Design: Jan Scott, art director, and Anne D. McCully, set decorator, for "Eleanor and Franklin: The White House Years" on *ABC Theatre* (ABC)

1275 Outstanding Art Direction or Scenic Design for Comedy, Variety or Music Special: Robert Kelly, art director, for *America Salutes Richard Rodgers: The Sound of His Music* (CBS)

1276 Outstanding Series Music Composition: Quincy Jones and Gerald Fried for *Roots, Part 1* (ABC)

1277 Outstanding Special Program Music Composition: Alan Bergman, Marilyn Bergman and Leonard Rosenman for "Sybil" on *The Big Event* (NBC)

1278 Outstanding Musical Direction: Ian Fraser for *America Salutes Richard Rodgers: The Sound of His Music* (CBS)

1279 **Outstanding Graphic Design and Title Sequences:** Stu Bernstein and Eytan Keller for *Bell Telephone Jubilee* (NBC)

1280 **Outstanding Drama Special Costume Design:** Joe I. Tompkins for "Eleanor and Franklin: The White House Years" on *ABC Theatre* (ABC)

1281 **Outstanding Music/Variety Costume Design:** Jan Skalicky for "The Barber of Seville" on *Live from Lincoln Center, Great Performances* (PBS)

1282 **Outstanding Drama or Comedy Series Costume Design:** Raymond Hughes for *The Pallisers, Episode 1* (PBS)

1283 **Outstanding Make-Up:** Ken Chase, make-up design, and Joe DiBella, make-up artist, for "Eleanor and Franklin: The White House Years" on *ABC Theatre* (ABC)

1284 **Outstanding Choreography:** Ron Field for *America Salutes Richard Rodgers: The Sound of His Music* (CBS)

1285 **Outstanding Lighting Direction:** William M. Klages and Peter Edwards for *The Dorothy Hamill Special* (ABC)

1286 **Outstanding Achievement in Any Area of Creative Technical Crafts:** Emma di Vittorio and Vivienne Walker, hairstylists, for "Eleanor and Franklin: The White House Years" on *ABC Theatre* (ABC)

1287 **Outstanding Individual Achievement in Special Event Coverage:** Brian C. Bartholomew and Keaton S. Walker, Walter Edel, John Fehler and Steve Zink, cameramen, art directors, for *The 28th Annual Emmy Awards* (ABC)

1288 **Special Award for Leadership in Establishing Circularly Polarized Transmission to Improve Television Reception:** American Broadcasting Company

1289 **Special Citation for Improving the Efficiency of UHF Klystrons:** Varian Associates

1290 **Outstanding Achievement in Broadcast Journalism:** *The MacNeil-Lehrer Report,* Eric Sevareid, League of Women Voters, *60 Minutes*

1291 **Outstanding Daytime Drama Series:** *Ryan's Hope* (ABC)

1292 **Outstanding Daytime Talk, Service or Variety Show:** *The Merv Griffin Show* (syndicated)

1293 **Outstanding Game or Audience Participation Show:** *The Family Feud* (ABC)

1294 **Outstanding Children's Entertainment Series:** *Zoom* (PBS)

1295 **Outstanding Children's Informational Series:** *The Electric Company* (PBS)

1296 **Outstanding Children's Instructional Programming:** *Sesame Street* (PBS)

1297 **Outstanding Children's Entertainment Special:** "Big Henry and the Polka Dot Kid" on *Special Treat* (NBC)

1298 **Outstanding Children's Informational Special:** "My Mom's Having a Baby" on *ABC Afterschool Specials* (ABC)

1299 **Outstanding Program and Individual Achievement in Daytime Drama Specials:** Gaby Monet and Anne Grant, writers, and Lois Nettleton, performer, for *The American Woman: Portraits of Courage* (ABC)

1300 **Outstanding Daytime Dramatic Actor:** Val Dufor in *Search for Tomorrow* (CBS)

1301 **Outstanding Daytime Dramatic Actress:** Helen Gallagher in *Ryan's Hope* (ABC)

1302 **Outstanding Host or Hostess in a Talk, Service or Variety Series:** Phil Donahue in *Donahue* (syndicated)

1303 **Outstanding Host or Hostess in a Game or Audience Participation Series:** Bert Convy in *Tattletales* (CBS)

1304 **Outstanding Daytime Drama Series Director:** Lela Swift for February 8 program of *Ryan's Hope* (ABC)

1305 **Outstanding Single Episode Director for Daytime Variety Program:** Donald R. King for "Mike in Hollywood with Ray Charles and Michel Legrand" on *The Mike Douglas Show* (syndicated)

1306 **Outstanding Single Episode Director for Game or Audience Participation Show:** Mike Gargiulo for August 10 program of *The $20,000 Pyramid* (ABC)

1307 **Outstanding Writing for Daytime Drama Series:** Claire Labine, Paul Avila Mayer and Mary Munisteri for *Ryan's Hope* (ABC)

1308 **Original Teleplay Writing for Drama or Comedy Special Program:** Lane Slate for "Tail Gunner Joe" on *The Big Event* (NBC)

1309 **Outstanding Live Sports Special:** Roone Arledge, Chuck Howard, Don Ohlmeyer, Chet Forte, Dennis Lewin, Bob Goodrich, Geoffrey Mason, Terry Lastrow, Eleanor Riger, Ted Steckel, Bruce Weisman, John Wilcox and Doug Wilson for *1976 Olympic Games* (ABC)

1310 **Outstanding Live Sports Series:** Michael Pearl, Hal Classen and Sid Kaufman for *The NFL Today/NFL Football on CBS* (CBS)

1311 **Outstanding Sports Personality:** Frank Gifford

1312 **Outstanding Directing in Sports Directing:** Chet Forte for *NFL Monday Night Football* (ABC)

1313 **Outstanding Edited Sports Series:** Bud Greenspan and Cappy Petrash Greenspan for *The Olympiad* (PBS)

1314 **Outstanding Edited Sports Special:** Roone Arledge, Chuck Howard, Don Ohlmeyer, Chet Forte, Dennis Lewin, Bob Goodrich, Geoffrey Mason, Terry Lastrow, Eleanor Riger, Ted Steckel, Bruce Weisman, John Wilcox and Doug Wilson for *A Special Preview of the 1976 Olympic Games from Montreal, Canada* (ABC)

1315 **Outstanding Individual Achievement in Sports Film Editing:** John Petersen, Angelo Bernarducci, Irwin Krechaf, Margaret Murphy, Vincent Reda and Anthony Zaccaro for *1976 Winter Olympic Games* (ABC)

1316 **Outstanding Individual Achievement in Sports Cinematography:** Peter Henning, Harvey Harrison, Harry Hart, D'Arcy March, Don Shapiro, Don Shoemaker and Joe Valentine for *1976 Winter Olympic Games* (ABC)

1317 **National Award for Community Service:** WGBH-TV, Boston, Massachusetts for *Rape*

─────────── **1 9 7 7** ───────────

1318 **Outstanding Comedy Series:** *All in the Family* (CBS)

1319 **Outstanding Drama Series:** *The Rockford Files* (NBC)

1320 **Outstanding Comedy/Variety or Music Series:** *The Muppet Show* (ITC syndication)

1321 **Outstanding Children's Special:** *Halloween Is Grinch Night* (ABC)

1322 **Outstanding Program Achievement:** *The Tonight Show Starring Johnny Carson* (NBC)

1323 **Outstanding Comedy, Variety or Music Special:** *Bette Midler — Ole Red Hair Is Back* (NBC)

1324 **Outstanding Limited Series:** *Holocaust* (NBC)

1325 **Outstanding Informational Series:** *The Body Human* (CBS)

1326 **Outstanding Classical Program in the Performing Arts:** American Ballet Theatre's "Giselle" on *Live from Lincoln Center* (PBS)

1327 **Outstanding Informational Special:** "The Great Whales" on *National Geographic Special* (PBS)

1328 **Outstanding Drama or Comedy Special:** *The Gathering* (ABC)

1329 **Outstanding Special Classification Program Achievement:** *Live from Lincoln Center: Recital of Tenor Luciano Pavarotti from the Met* (PBS)

1330 **Outstanding Lead Comedy Actress:** Jean Stapleton in *All in the Family* (CBS)

1331 **Outstanding Lead Comedy Actor:** Carroll O'Connor in *All in the Family* (CBS)

1332 **Outstanding Continuing Performance by a Supporting Actress in a Comedy Series:** Julie Kavner in *Rhoda* (CBS)

1333 **Outstanding Continuing Performance by a Supporting Actor in a Comedy Series:** Rob Reiner in *All in the Family* (CBS)

1334 **Outstanding Lead Actress in a Drama Series:** Sada Thompson in *Family* (ABC)

1335 **Outstanding Lead Actor in a Drama Series:** Edward Asner in *Lou Grant* (CBS)

1336 **Outstanding Continuing Performance by a Supporting Actress in a Drama Series:** Nancy Marchand in *Lou Grant* (CBS)

1337 **Outstanding Continuing Performance by a Supporting Actor in a Drama Series:** Robert Vaughn in *Washington: Behind Closed Doors* (ABC)

1338 **Outstanding Lead Actress in a Limited Series:** Meryl Streep in *Holocaust* (NBC)

1339 **Outstanding Lead Actor in a Limited Series:** Michael Moriarty in *Holocaust* (NBC)

1340 **Outstanding Continuing or Single Performance by a Supporting Actress in Variety or Music:** Gilda Radner in *NBC's Saturday Night Live* (NBC)

1341 **Outstanding Continuing or Single Performance by a Supporting Actor in Variety or Music:** Tim Conway in *The Carol Burnett Show* (CBS)

1342 **Outstanding Single Performance by a Supporting Actress in a Comedy or Drama Series:** Blanche Baker in *Holocaust* (NBC)

1343 **Outstanding Single Performance by a Supporting Actor in a Comedy or Drama Series:** Ricardo Montalban in *How the West Was Won, Part Two* (ABC)

1344 **Outstanding Lead Actress for a Single Appearance in a Drama or Comedy Series:** Rita Moreno in "The Paper Palace" on *The Rockford Files* (NBC)

1345 **Outstanding Lead Actor for a Single Appearance in a Drama or Comedy Series:** Barnard Hughes in "Judge" on *Lou Grant* (CBS)

1346 **Outstanding Performance by a Supporting Actress in a Comedy or Drama Special:** Eva Le Gallienne in *The Royal Family* (PBS)

1347 **Outstanding Performance by a Supporting Actor in a Comedy or Drama Special:** Howard Da Silva in "Verna: USO Girl" on *Great Performances* (PBS)

1348 **Outstanding Lead Actress in a Drama or Comedy Special:** Joanne Woodward in "See How She Runs" on *GE Theatre* (CBS)

1349 **Outstanding Lead Actor in a Drama or Comedy Special:** Fred Astaire in *A Family Upside Down* (NBC)

1350 **Outstanding Directing in a Comedy Series:** Paul Bogert for "Edith's 50th Birthday" on *All in the Family* (CBS)

1351 **Outstanding Directing in a Drama Series:** Marvin J. Chomsky for *Holocaust* (NBC)

1352 **Outstanding Directing in a Comedy/Variety or Music Series:** Dave Powers for *The Carol Burnett Show* (CBS)

1353 **Outstanding Directing in a Comedy/Variety or Music Special:** Dwight Hemion for *The Sentry Collection Presents Ben Vereen—His Roots* (ABC)

1354 **Outstanding Directing in a Special Drama or Comedy Program:** David Lowell Rich for *The Defection of Simas Kudirka* (CBS)

1355 **Outstanding Writing in a Comedy Series:** Bob Weiskopf, Harve Brosten, Barry Harman and Bob Schiller for "Cousin Liz" on *All in the Family* (CBS)

1356 **Outstanding Writing in a Drama Series:** Gerald Green for *Holocaust* (NBC)

1357 **Outstanding Writing in a Comedy/Variety or Music Series:** Robert Beatty, Tim Conway, Dick Clair, Elias Davis, Rick Hawkins, Jenna McMahon, Gene Perret, Bill Richmond, Liz Sage, David Pollock, Adele Styler, Ed Simmons and Burt Styler for *The Carol Burnett Show* (CBS)

1358 **Outstanding Writing in a Comedy/Variety or Music Special:** Chevy Chase, Al Franken, Tom Davis, Charles Grodin, Lorne Michaels, Lily Tomlin, Paul Simon and Alan Zweibel for *The Paul Simon Special* (NBC)

1359 **Outstanding Writing in a Special Program, Adaptation:** Caryl Ledner for *Mary White* (ABC)

1360 **Outstanding Writing in a Comedy or Drama Special Program, Original Teleplay:** George Rubino for *The Last Tenant*

1361 **First Annual ATAS Governor's Award:** William S. Paley, Chairman (CBS)

1362 **Outstanding Comedy Series Film Editing:** Ed Cotter for "Richie Almost Dies" on *Happy Days* (ABC)

1363 **Outstanding Drama Series Film Editing:** Alan Heim, Craig McKay, Robert M. Reitano, Stephen A. Rotter and Brian Smedley-Aston for *Holocaust* (NBC)

1364 **Outstanding Special Film Editing:** John A. Martinelli for *The Defection of Simas Kudirka* (CBS)

1365 **Outstanding Special Film Sound Editing:** James Yant, Donald Higgins, Michael Corrigan, William Jackson, John Strauss, Richard Le Grand, Jerry Pirozzi, John Kline and Jerry Rosenthal for *The Amazing Howard Hughes* (CBS)

1366 **Outstanding Series or Special Film Sound Mixing:** Robert L. Harman, Eddie J. Nelson, George E. Porter and William Teague for *Young Joe, the Forgotten Kennedy* (ABC)

1367 **Outstanding Series Videotape Editing:** Tucker Wiard for *The Carol Burnett Show* (CBS)

1368 **Outstanding Special Videotape Editing:** Pam Marshall and Andy Zall for *The Sentry Collection Presents Ben Vereen—His Roots* (ABC)

1369 **Outstanding Entertainment Series Cinematography:** Ted Voigtlander for "The Fighter" on *Little House on the Prairie* (NBC)

1370 **Outstanding Entertainment Special Cinematography:** Gerald Perry Finnerman for *Ziegfeld: The Man and His Women* (NBC)

1371 **Outstanding Series Technical Direction and Electronic Camerawork:** Gene Crowe, Larry Heider, Dave Hilmer, Bob Keys and Wayne Orr for *The Sentry Collection Presents Ben Vereen—His Roots* (ABC)

1372 **Outstanding Series Music Composition:** Billy Goldenberg for *King* (NBC)

1373 **Outstanding Special Music Composition:** Jimmie Haskell for "See How She Runs" on *GE Theatre* (CBS)

1374 **Outstanding Series or Special Music Direction:** Ian Fraser for *The Sentry Collection Presents Ben Vereen—His Roots* (ABC)

1375 **Outstanding Series or Special Tape Sound Mixing:** Ron Bryan, Edward J. Greene and Thomas J. Huth for *Bette Midler—Ole Red Hair Is Back* (NBC)

1376 **Outstanding Series or Special Lighting Direction:** Greg Brunton for *Cher* (CBS)

1377 **Outstanding Special Music Material:** Stan Freeman and Arthur Malvin for "High Hat" on *The Carol Burnett Show* (CBS)

1378 **Outstanding Sound Effects:** William F. Brownell and John H. Kantrowe for *Our Town* (NBC)

1379 **Outstanding Special or Series Choreography:** Ron Field for *The Sentry Collection Presents Ben Vereen—His Roots* (ABC)

1380 **Outstanding Special or Series Graphic Design and Title Sequence:** Bill Davis, Bob Fletcher and Bill Melendez for *NBC: The First 50 Years—A Closer Look* (NBC)

1381 **Outstanding Drama Special Costume Design:** Noel Taylor for "Actor" on *Hollywood Television Theatre* (PBS)

1382 **Outstanding Music/Variety Series or Special Costume Design:** Bob Mackie and Ret Turner for *Mitzi . . . Zings Into Spring* (CBS)

1383 **Outstanding Drama or Comedy Series Costume Design:** Edith Almoslino and Peggy Farrell for *Holocaust* (NBC)

1384 **Outstanding Individual Achievement in Costume Design:** William Pitkin for *Romeo and Juliet* (PBS)

1385 **Outstanding Series or Special Make-Up:** Richard Cobos and Walter Schenck for *How the West Was Won, Part Two* (ABC)

1386 **Outstanding Individual Achievement in Children's Programming:** Robert Checchi (set design), Bill Hargate (costume design) and Ken Johnson (art direction) for *Once Upon a Brothers Grimm* (CBS)

1387 **Outstanding Comedy Series Art Direction:** Robert Checchi and Edward Stephenson for *Soap, Episode One* (ABC)

1388 **Outstanding Drama Series Art Direction:** Tim Harvey for "I, Claudius, Episode One" on *Masterpiece Theatre* (PBS); Derek Rodd for "Anna Karenina" on *Masterpiece Theatre* (PBS); Wilfred J. Shingleton, Theo Harish, Jurgen Kiebach and Max Hareiter for *Holocaust* (NBC)

1389 **Outstanding Comedy/Variety or Music Series Art Direction:** Roy Christopher for *The Richard Pryor Show* (NBC)

1390 **Outstanding Dramatic Special Art Direction:** John de Cuir and Richard C. Goddard for *Ziegfeld: The Man and His Women* (NBC)

1391 **Outstanding Comedy/Variety or Music Special Art Direction:** Romain Johnston for *The Sentry Collection Presents Ben Vereen—His Roots* (ABC)

1392 **Outstanding Series Film Sound Editing:** H. Lee Chaney, Mark Dennis, Douglas H. Grindstaff, Don V. Isaacs, Dick Raderman, Hank Salerno, Christopher Chulack, Don Crosby, Donald V. Isaacs and Larry Singer for "River of Promises" on *Police Story* (NBC)

1393 Outstanding Achievement in Broadcast Journalism: Charles Kuralt, Bill Moyers, *The Fire Next Door, Exploding Gas Tanks*

1394 Outstanding Achievement in Engineering Development: Vlahos-Gottschalk Research Corporation for invention and development of Ultimatte video matting device

1395 Governor's Medallion: Frederick Wolcott for 30 years of service on the ATAS Engineering Awards Panel

1396 Outstanding Daytime Drama Series: *Days of Our Lives* (NBC)

1397 Outstanding Children's Entertainment Series: *Captain Kangaroo* (CBS)

1398 Outstanding Children's Informational Series: *Animals* (ABC)

1399 Outstanding Children's Instructional Series: *Schoolhouse Rock* (ABC)

1400 Outstanding Children's Entertainment Special: "Hewitt's Just Different" on *ABC Afterschool Special* (ABC)

1401 Outstanding Children's Information Special: "Very Good Friends" on *ABC Afterschool Special* (ABC)

1402 Outstanding Daytime Talk, Service or Variety Series: *Donahue* (syndicated)

1403 Outstanding Game or Audience Participation Series: *Hollywood Squares* (NBC)

1404 Outstanding Daytime Dramatic Actor: James Pritchett in *The Doctors* (NBC)

1405 Outstanding Daytime Dramatic Actress: Laurie Heineman for *Another World* (NBC)

1406 Outstanding Host or Hostess in a Talk, Service or Variety Series: Phil Donahue in *Donahue* (syndicated)

1407 Outstanding Host or Hostess in a Game or Audience Participation Show: Richard Dawson in *The Family Feud* (ABC)

1408 Outstanding Single Program Directing of a Daytime Drama Series: Richard Dunlap for March 3 program of *The Young and the Restless* (CBS)

1409 Outstanding Single Program Directing of a Daytime Variety Series: Martin Haig Mackey for March 20 program of *Over Easy* (PBS)

1410 Outstanding Single Program Directing of a Daytime Game or Audience Participation Show: Mike Gargiulo for June 20 program of *The $20,000 Pyramid* (ABC)

1411 Outstanding Writing in a Daytime Drama Series: Claire Labine, Paul Avila Mayer, Mary Munisteri, Allan Leicht and Judith Pinsker for *Ryan's Hope* (ABC)

1412 Outstanding Special Event Coverage: *The Great English Garden Party— Peter Ustinov Looks at 100 Years of Wimbledon* (NBC)

1413 Outstanding Individual Achievement in Children's Programming: Tony Di Girolamo and Tom Aldredge in "Henry Winkler Meets William Shakespeare" on *CBS Festival of Lively Arts for Young People* (CBS); Jan Hartman for "Hewitt's Just Different" on *ABC Afterschool Special* (ABC); David Wolf for "The Magic Hat" on *Unicorn Tales* (syndicated); Bonnie Karrin for "Big Apple Birthday" on *Unicorn Tales* (syndicated); and Brianne Murphy for "Five Finger Discount" on *Special Treat* (NBC)

1414 Outstanding Daytime Programming Individual Achievement: Connie Wexler for *Search for Tomorrow* (CBS); Steve Cunningham, Hector Ramirez, Sheldon Mooney, Martin Wagner and David Finch for *After Hours: Singin', Swingin' & All That Jazz* (CBS); Steve Cunningham, Fred Gough, Mike Stitch and Joe Vicens for *The Young and the Restless* (CBS); David M. Clark for "The New York Remotes" on *The Mike Douglas Show* (syndicated); and Joyce Tamara Grossman for "Valentine's Day Special" on *The Family Feud* (ABC)

1415 Outstanding Religious Programming Individual Achievement: Carolee Campbell for *This Is My Son* (NBC), and Douglas Watson and Joseph Vadala for *Continuing Creations* (NBC)

1416 Outstanding Live Sports Special: *World Championship Boxing (Ali/Spinks)* (CBS)

1417 Outstanding Live Sports Series: *The NFL Today/NFL Football on CBS* (CBS)

1418 Outstanding Edited Sports Special: *The Impossible Dream: Ballooning Across the Atlantic* (CBS)

1419 Outstanding Edited Sports Series: *The Way It Was* (syndicated)

1420 Outstanding Sports Personaliity: Jack Whitaker

1421 Outstanding Sports Directing: Ted Nathanson for *AFC Championship* (NBC)

1422 Outstanding Individual Achievement in Sports: Steve Sabol for "Joe and the Magic Bean: The Story of Superbowl III" on *NFL Today* (CBS); Steve Sabol for "Skateboard Fever" on *Sportsworld* (NBC); Arthur Tinn for *Superbowl Today/Superbowl XII* (CBS); Bob Levy, Jerome Haggert, Richard Leible, Charles Liotta, John Olszewski, Matthew F. McCarthy and Peter Caesar for *Sportsworld* (NBC)

1423 Outstanding Achievement in Religious Programming: Doc Siegel for "The Healer" on *This Is the Life* (syndicated), and *Marshall Efron's Illustrated, Simplified and Painless Sunday School* (CBS)

1424 Outstanding Award for Community Service: KOOL-TV, Phoenix Arizona for *Water*

1425 International Fiction Award: Granada Television Ltd., London for *The Collection*

1426 Outstanding Non-Fiction Award: Canadian Broadcasting Corporation for *Henry Ford's America*, and Yorkshire Television Ltd., England for *The Good, the Bad and Indifferent*

––––––––––– **1978** –––––––––––

1427 Outstanding Comedy Series: *Taxi* (ABC)

1428 Outstanding Drama Series: *Lou Grant* (CBS)

1429 Outstanding Limited Series: *Roots: The Next Generation* (ABC)

1430 Outstanding Comedy/Variety or Music Program: *Steve and Eydie Celebrate Irving Berlin* (NBC)

1431 Outstanding Animated Program: *The Lion, the Witch and the Wardrobe* (CBS)

1432 Outstanding Children's Program: *Christmas Eve on Sesame Street* (PBS)

1433 Outstanding Comedy or Drama Special: *Friendly Fire* (ABC)

1434 Outstanding Information Program: *Scared Straight* (syndicated)

1435 Outstanding Program in the Performing Arts: "Balanchine IV – Dance in America" on *Great Performances* (PBS)

1436 Outstanding Special Classification Program Achievement: *Lifeline* (NBC) and *The Tonight Show Starring Johnny Carson* (NBC)

1437 Outstanding Special Events Program Achievement: *51st Annual Academy Awards Ceremonies* (ABC)

1438 Outstanding Comedy Series Lead Actress, Episode: Ruth Gordon in "Sugar Mama" on *Taxi* (ABC)

1439 Outstanding Comedy Series Lead Actor: Carroll O'Connor in *All in the Family* (CBS)

1440 Outstanding Comedy/Variety or Music Series Supporting Actress: Sally Struthers in "California Here We Come" on *All in the Family* (CBS)

1441 Outstanding Comedy/Variety or Music Series Supporting Actor: Robert Guillaume in *Soap* (ABC)

1442 Outstanding Limited Series or Special Lead Actress: Bette Davis in *Strangers: The Story of a Mother & Daughter* (CBS)

1443 Outstanding Limited Series or Special Lead Actor: Peter Strauss in *The Jericho Mile* (ABC)

1444 Outstanding Limited Series or Special Supporting Actress: Esther Rolle in *Summer of My German Soldier* (NBC)

1445 Outstanding Limited Series or Special Supporting Actor: Marlon Brando in *Roots: The Next Generation* (ABC)

1446 Outstanding Drama Series Lead Actress: Mariette Hartley in "Married" on *The Incredible Hulk* (CBS)

1447 Outstanding Drama Series Lead Actor: Ron Liebman in *Kaz* (CBS)

1448 Outstanding Drama Series Supporting Actress: Kristy McNichol in *Family* (ABC)

1449 Outstanding Drama Series Supporting Actor: Stuart Margolin in *The Rockford Files* (NBC)

1450 Outstanding Comedy, Comedy/Variety or Music Series Director: Noam Pitlik for "The Harris Incident" on *Barney Miller* (ABC)

1451 **Outstanding Limited Series or Special Director:** David Greene for *Friendly Fire* (ABC)

1452 **Outstanding Drama Series Director:** Jackie Cooper for *White Shadow* pilot (CBS)

1453 **Outstanding Information Program Individual Achievement Director:** John Korty for *Who Are the DeBolts & Where Did They Get 19 Kids?* (ABC)

1454 **Outstanding Comedy, Comedy/Variety or Music Series Writer:** Alan Alda for "Inga" on *M*A*S*H* (CBS)

1455 **Outstanding Limited Series or Special Writer:** Patrick Nolan & Michael Mann for *The Jericho Mile* (ABC)

1456 **Outstanding Drama Series Writer:** Michele Gallery for "Dying" on *Lou Grant* (CBS)

1457 **Outstanding Special Events Individual Achievement:** Mikhail Baryshnikov in *Baryshnikov at the White House* (PBS)

1458 **Outstanding Single Episode Film Editing of a Series:** M. Pam Blumenthal for "Paper Marriage" on *Taxi* (ABC)

1459 **Outstanding Limited Series or Special Film Editing:** Arthur Schmidt for *The Jericho Mile* (ABC)

1460 **Outstanding Film Sound Editing:** William H. Wistrom for *Friendly Fire* (ABC)

1461 **Outstanding Film Sound Mixing:** Bill Teague, George R. Porter, Eddie J. Nelson and Ray West for *The Winds of Kitty Hawk* (NBC)

1462 **Outstanding Single Episode Cinematography of a Series:** Ted Voigtlander for "The Craftsman" on *Little House on the Prairie* (NBC)

1463 **Outstanding Limited Series or Special Cinematography:** Howard Schwartz for *Rainbow* (NBC)

1464 **Outstanding Limited Series or Special Videotape Editing:** Ken Denisoff, Tucker Wiard and Janet McFadden for *The Scarlet Letter, Part Two* (PBS)

1465 **Outstanding Technical Direction and Electronic Camerawork:** Jerry Weiss, Don Barker, Peggy Mahoney, Reed Howard, Kurt Tonnesson, Bill Landers, Lou Cywinski, George Loomis and Brian Sherriffe for *Dick Clark's Live Wednesday, Program One* (NBC)

1466 **Outstanding Series Art Direction:** Richard C. Goddard and Howard E. Johnson for *Little Women, Part One* (NBC)

1467 **Outstanding Limited Series or Special Art Direction:** Jan Scott and Bill Harp for *Studs Lonigan, Part Three* (NBC)

1468 **Outstanding Choreography:** Kevin Carlisle for *The Third Barry Manilow Special* (ABC)

1469 **Outstanding Series Costume Design:** Jean-Pierre Dorleac for "Furlon" on *Battlestar Galactica* (ABC)

1470 **Outstanding Limited Series or Special Costume Design:** Ann Hollowood, Sue Le Cash and Christine Wilson for "King at Last" on *Edward the King* (syndicated)

1471 **Outstanding Series Music Composition:** David Rose for "The Craftsman" on *Little House on the Prairie* (NBC)

1472 **Outstanding Limited Series or Special Music Composition:** Leonard Rosenman for *Friendly Fire* (ABC)

1473 **Outstanding Graphic Design and Title Sequence:** Eytan Keller and Stu Bernstein for *Cinderella at the Palace* (CBS)

1474 **Outstanding Lighting Direction:** Roy A. Barnett and George Riesenberger for *You Can't Take It with You* (CBS)

1475 **Outstanding Tape Sound Mixing:** Ed Greene, Phillip J. Seretti, Dennis S. Sands and Gary Ulmer for *Steve and Eydie Celebrate Irving Berlin* (NBC)

1476 **Outstanding Make-up:** Tommy Cole, Mark Bussan and Ron Walters for *Backstage at the White House, Book Four* (NBC)

1477 **Outstanding Hairstyling:** Janice D. Brandow for *The Triangle Factory Fire Scandal* (NBC)

1478 **Outstanding Informational Program Individual Achievement:** Robert Niemack for *Scared Straight* (syndicated)

1479 **Outstanding Creative Technical Crafts Individual Achievement:** John Dykstra, Richard Edlund and Joseph Gross for "Saga of a Star World" on *Battlestar Galactica* (ABC), and Tom Ancell for *Giulini's Beethoven's Ninth Live: A Gift from Los Angeles* (PBS)

1480 **ATAS Governor's Award:** Walter Cronkite

1481 **Special Presentation:** Milton Berle

1482 **Outstanding Series Videotape Editing:** Andy Zall for "Stockard Channing in Just Friends" (Pilot) (CBS)

1483 **Outstanding Engineering Development:** SONY Video Products Company, the Society of Motion Picture and Television Engineers, and Ampex Corporation for development of Automatic Scan Tracking System for helical videotape equipment

1484 **Outstanding Children's Entertainment Series:** *Kids Are People Too* (ABC)

1485 **Outstanding Children's Informational Series:** *Big Blue Marble* (syndicated)

1486 **Outstanding Children's Instructional Series:** "Science Rock" on *Schoolhouse Rock* (ABC)

1487 **Outstanding Children's Entertainment Special:** "The Tap Dance Kid" on *Special Treat* (NBC)

1488 **Outstanding Children's Informational Special:** February 1 program of *Razzmatazz* (CBS)

1489 **Outstanding Daytime Drama Series:** *Ryan's Hope* (ABC)

1490 **Outstanding Talk, Service or Variety Program:** *Donahue* (syndicated)

1491 **Outstanding Game or Audience Participation Show:** *Hollywood Squares* (NBC)

1492 **Outstanding Achievement Daytime Drama Technical Excellence:** William Edwards, Joanne Goodhart, Paul York, Edward R. Atchison, William Hughes, Arie Hefter, Jay Millard, Barbara Miller, Robert Saxon and Roman Spinner for *The Edge of Night* (CBS)

1493 **Outstanding Program Coverage of Special Events:** *Horowitz: Live!* (NBC), and *Leontyne Price at the White House* (PBS)

1494 **Outstanding Special Classification Program Achievement:** *Camera* (CBS)

1495 **Outstanding Daytime Dramatic Actor:** Al Freeman, Jr., in *One Life to Live* (ABC)

1496 **Outstanding Daytime Dramatic Actress:** Irene Dailey in *Another World* (NBC)

1497 **Outstanding Daytime Supporting Dramatic Actor:** Peter Hansen in *General Hospital* (ABC)

1498 **Outstanding Daytime Supporting Dramatic Actress:** Suzanne Rogers in *Days of Our Lives* (NBC)

1499 **Outstanding Host or Hostess in a Talk, Service or Variety Series:** Phil Donahue in *Donahue* (syndicated)

1500 **Outstanding Host or Hostess in a Game or Audience Participation Show:** Dick Clark in *The $20,000 Pyramid* (ABC)

1501 **Outstanding Direction of a Daytime Drama Series:** Jerry Evans and Lela Swift for *Ryan's Hope* (ABC)

1502 **Outstanding Direction for a Variety Program:** Ron Wiener for "Nazis and the Klan" on *Donahue* (syndicated)

1503 **Outstanding Single Program Direction for Game or Audience Participation Show:** Jerome Shaw for June 20 program of *Hollywood Squares* (NBC)

1504 **Outstanding Director for Children's Programming:** Larry Elikann for "Mom and Dad Can't Hear Me" on *ABC Afterschool Special* (ABC)

1505 **Outstanding Daytime Drama Series Writing:** Claire Labine, Paul Avila Mayer, Mary Munisteri, Judith Pinsker and Jeffrey Lane for *Ryan's Hope* (ABC)

1506 **Outstanding Children's Program Performers:** Jack Gilford in "Hello in There" on *Big Blue Marble* (syndicated); Geraldine Fitzgerald in "Rodeo Red and the Runaway" on *NBC Special Treat* (NBC); and Frank Oz, Jim Henson, Carroll Spinney, Jerry Nelson and Richard Hunt in "The Muppets of Sesame Street" on *Sesame Street* (PBS)

1507 **Outstanding Performers in Special Event Coverage:** Vladimir Horowitz in *Horowitz: Live!* (NBC), and Leontyne Price in *Leontyne Price at the White House* (PBS)

1508 **Outstanding Individual Achievement in Religious Programming:** Martin Hoade, director, and Rolanda Mendels, performer, for *Interrogation at Budapest* (NBC), and Joseph J. Vadala for *This Other Eden* (NBC)

1509 **Outstanding Special Classification of Individual Achievement:** Paul Lynde, panelist on May 18 *Hollywood Squares* (NBC), and Bill Walker, Jay Burton, Tom Perew, Mark Davidson and Fred Tatashore, writers for *Dinah!* (syndicated)

1510 **Outstanding Achievement in Daytime Drama Design Excellence:** Lloyd R. Evans, Wesley Laws, Dean Nelson, Bob Anton, Lee Halls, Phyllis Sagnelli and Lou Dorfsman for *Love of Life* (CBS)

1511 **Outstanding Live Sports Special:** *Superbowl XIII* (NBC)

1512 **Outstanding Edited Sports Special:** *Spirit of '78 — The Flight of the Double Eagle II* (ABC)

1513 **Outstanding Live Sports Series:** *ABC's Monday Night Football* (ABC)

1514 **Outstanding Edited Sports Series:** *The American Sportsman* (ABC)

1515 **Outstanding Sports Directing:** Harry Coyle for *1978 World Series* (NBC)

1516 **Outstanding Individual Achievement in Sports:** Bob Angelo, Ernie Ernst, Jay Gerber, Stan Leshner, Hank McElwee, Howard Neef, Jack Newman, Steve Sabol, Bob Smith, Art Spieller and Phil Tuckett for *NFL Game of the Week* (syndicated); Horace Ruiz, Dick Roecker, Ray Figelski, Robert McKearnin, Jack Bennett, Ernest Thiel, Jerry Ireland, Bob Brown, Leonard G. Basile, Mario J. Ciarlo, Roy Ratliff, George Loomis, Bernard Joseph, Louis Gerard, Steve Cimino, Mike Stramsky, Roger Harbaugh, Al Rice, Jr., William M. Goetz, Jim Johnson, Brian Cherrifie, Phil Cantrell, Steven H. Gonzalez, Russ K. Ross, Art Parker, Bill Landers, Jim Bragg, James Culley, Corey Lieble and Len Stucker for *1978 World Series* (NBC); Horace Ruiz, Joe Commare, Bob McKearnin, Jack Bennett, George Loomis, Roger Harbaugh, William W. Landers, Michael C. Stramsky, Rov V. Ratliff, Leonard Basile, Mario J. Ciarlo, Tom C. Dezondorf, Steve Cimino, William M. Goetz, Louis Gerard, Len Stucker, Steven H. Gonzalez, Jim Johnson, Corey Lieble, Don Mulvaney, Al Rice, Jr., and Russ K. Ross for *Super Bowl XIII* (NBC); Sandy Bell, Bob Brown, Ralph Savignano, Art Tinn, Barry Drago, Jim McCarthy, Joe Sakota, George Rothweiler, George Naeder, John Lincoln, Tom McCarthy, Hans Singer, Keeth Lawrence, Jim Murphy, Neil McCaffrey, Herman Lang, Sig Meyers, Frank McSpedon, Anthony Hlavaty, Wayne Wright, Johnny Morris, Ed Ambrosini, Frank Florio and Tom Spalding for *Daytona 500* (CBS); and James M. Grau for "Closing Logo" for *CBS Sports Programs* (CBS)

1517 **Outstanding Sports Personality:** Jim McKay

1518 **Outstanding Individual Achievement in Children's Programming:** Charles Gross, Dorothy Weaver and Ian Maitland for "Rodeo Red and the Runaway" on *Special Treat* (NBC); John Morris and Norman Gay for "The Tap Dance Kid" on *Special Treat* (NBC); Jack Regas, Harvey Berger and Ron Hays for *Krofft Superstar Hour Starring the Bay City Rollers* (NBC); Michael Baugh for "Todos Los Ninos Del Mundo" on *Villa Alegre* (PBS); Dick Maitland and Roy Carch for *Sesame Street* (PBS); Gene Piatrowsky for "A Special Day in the Year of the Child" on *CBS Festival of Lively Arts for Young People* (CBS); Rene Verxier for *Big Blue Marble* (syndicated); Dick Young for "Day of the Jouster" on *Big Blue Marble* (syndicated); Vince Humphrey for *Gaucho* (ABC); Ken Gutstein for "The Secret of Charles Dickens" on *CBS Festival of Lively Arts for Young People* (CBS); and Roy Stewart for "Flat" on *Freestyle!* (PBS)

1519 **National Community Service Award:** WBBM-TV, Chicago for *Agent Orange: The Human Harvest*

1520 **International Fiction Award:** Televise Radio Omroep Stichting, the Netherlands for *The Fly*

1521 **International Non-Fiction Award:** Canadian Broadcasting Corporation for *Four Women*

─────────── **1979** ───────────

1522 **Outstanding Comedy Series:** *Taxi* (ABC)

1523 **Outstanding Drama Series:** *Lou Grant* (CBS)

1524 **Outstanding Drama or Comedy Special:** *The Miracle Worker* (NBC)

1525 **Outstanding Variety/Music Program:** *IBM Presents Baryshnikov on Broadway* (ABC)

1526 **Outstanding Informational Program:** *The Body Human: The Magic Sense* (CBS)

1527 **Outstanding Limited Series:** *Edward and Mrs. Simpson* (syndicated)

1528 **Outstanding Animated Program:** *Carlton Your Doorman* (CBS)

1529 **Outstanding Children's Program:** *The Halloween That Almost Wasn't* (ABC)

1530 **Outstanding Classical Program in the Performing Arts:** *Live from Studio 8H: A Tribute to Toscanini* (NBC)

1531 **Outstanding Special Classification Program Achievement:** *Fred Astaire: Change Partners and Dance* (PBS)

1532 **Outstanding Special Events Program Achievement:** *The 34th Annual Tony Awards* (CBS)

1533 **Outstanding Comedy Series Lead Actress:** Cathryn Damon in *Soap* (ABC)

1534 **Outstanding Comedy Series Lead Actor:** Richard Mulligan in *Soap* (ABC)

1535 **Outstanding Drama Series Lead Actress:** Barbara Bel Geddes in *Dallas* (CBS)

1536 **Outstanding Drama Series Lead Actor:** Ed Asner in *Lou Grant* (CBS)

1537 **Outstanding Drama Series Supporting Actress:** Nancy Marchand in *Lou Grant* (CBS)

1538 **Outstanding Drama Series Supporting Actor:** Stuart Margolin in *The Rockford Files* (NBC)

1539 **Outstanding Comedy Series Supporting Actor:** Harry Morgan in *M*A*S*H* (CBS)

1540 **Outstanding Comedy Series Supporting Actress:** Loretta Swit in *M*A*S*H* (CBS)

1541 **Outstanding Limited Series or Special Supporting Actor:** George Grizzard in *The Oldest Living Graduate* (NBC)

1542 **Outstanding Limited Series or Special Supporting Actress:** Mare Winningham in *Amber Waves* (ABC)

1543 **Outstanding Limited Series or Special Lead Actress:** Patty Duke Astin in *The Miracle Worker* (NBC)

1544 **Outstanding Limited Series or Special Lead Actor:** Powers Boothe in *Guyana Tragedy: The Story of Jim Jones* (CBS)

1545 **Outstanding Comedy Series Director:** James Burrows for "Louie and the Nice Girl" on *Taxi* (ABC)

1546 **Outstanding Drama Series Director:** Roger Young for "Cop" on *Lou Grant* (CBS)

1547 **Outstanding Limited Series or Special Director:** Marvin J. Chomsky for *Attica* (ABC)

1548 **Outstanding Variety or Music Program Director:** Dwight Hemion for *IBM Presents Baryshnikov on Broadway* (ABC)

1549 **Outstanding Comedy Series Writing:** Bob Colleary for "Photographer" on *Barney Miller* (ABC)

1550 **Outstanding Drama Series Writing:** Seth Freeman for "Cop" on *Lou Grant* (CBS)

1551 **Outstanding Variety or Music Program Writing:** Buz Kohan for *Shirley MacLaine . . . Every Little Movement* (CBS)

1552 **Outstanding Limited Series or Special Writing:** David Chase for *Off the Minnesota Strip* (ABC)

1553 **Outstanding Series Videotape Editing:** John Hawkins for *The Muppet Show with Liza Minnelli* (syndicated)

1554 **Outstanding Limited Series or Special Videotape Editing:** Danny White for *Olivia Newton-John—Hollywood Nights* (ABC)

1555 **Outstanding Informational Program Film Editing:** Robert Eisenhardt, Hank O'Karma and Jane Kurson for *The Body Human: The Body Beautiful* (CBS)

1556 **Outstanding Tape Sound Mixing:** Bruce Burns and Jerry Clemans for *Sinatra: The First 40 Years* (NBC)

1557 **Outstanding Film Sound Mixing:** Ray Barons, David Campbell, Bob Pettis and John Reitz for *The Ordeal of Dr. Mudd* (CBS)

1558 **Outstanding Informational Program Film Sound Mixers:** David Clark, Joel Fein, Robert L. Harman and George E. Porter for "Dive to the Edge of Creation" on *National Geographic Special* (PBS)

1559 **Outstanding Series Cinematography:** Enzo A. Martinelli for "Breakthrough" on *The Contender* (CBS)

1560 **Outstanding Informational Program Cinematography:** Bryan Anderson, Bob Elfstrom and Al Giddings for *Mysteries of the Sea* (ABC)

1561 **Outstanding Series Music Composition:** Patrick Williams for "Hollywood" on *Lou Grant* (CBS)

1562 Outstanding Limited Series or Special Music Composition: Jerry Fielding for *High Midnight* (CBS)

1563 Outstanding Graphic Design and Title Sequence: Phil Norman for *The French Atlantic Affair, Part One* (ABC)

1564 Outstanding Children's Program Individual Achievement: Robert O'Bradovich for makeup for *The Halloween That Almost Wasn't* (ABC)

1565 Outstanding Individual Achievement in Creative Technical Crafts: Scott Schachter for Live Audio Mixing for *Live from Studio 8H: A Tribute to Toscanini* (NBC)

1566 Outstanding Individual Achievement in Creative Technical Crafts: Mark Schubin for Live Stereo Simulcast for *Luciano Pavarotti and the New York Philharmonic* (PBS)

1567 Outstanding Individual Achievement in Special Classification: Geof Bartz for film editing for "Dr. James 'Red' Duke, Trauma Surgeon" on *Operation Lifeline* (NBC)

1568 Outstanding Music Direction: Ian Fraser, Ralph Burns and Billy Byers for *IBM Presents Baryshnikov on Broadway* (ABC)

1569 Outstanding Lighting Direction: Peter S. Edwards, William Knight and Peter S. Passas for *FDR the Last Year* (NBC)

1570 Outstanding Limited Series Cinematography: Gayne Rescher for "The Silent Lovers" on *Moviola* (NBC)

1571 Outstanding Limited Series or Special Film Editing: Bill Blunden and Alan Pattillo for *All Quiet on the Western Front* (CBS)

1572 Outstanding Variety/Music Program Art Direction: Charles Lisanby and Dwight Jackson for *IBM Presents Baryshnikov on Broadway* (ABC)

1573 Outstanding Choreography: Alan Johnson for *Shirley MacLaine . . . Every Little Movement* (CBS)

1574 Outstanding Technical Direction and Electronic Camerawork: Wayne Parsons, Tom Green, Dean Hall, Bob Highton, William Landers and Ron Sheldon for *The Oldest Living Graduate* (NBC)

1575 Outstanding Series Art Direction: James D. Bissell and William Webb for "The Old Sister" on *Palmerstown, U.S.A.* (CBS)

1576 Outstanding Limited Series or Special Art Direction: Wilfred Shingleton, Juliann Sacks, Jean Taillander, Robert Christides and Cheryal Kearney for *Gauguin the Savage* (CBS)

1577 Outstanding Limited Series or Special Costume Design: Travilla for "The Scarlet O'Hara War" on *Moviola* (NBC)

1578 Outstanding Make-Up: Richard Blair for "The Scarlet O'Hara War" on *Moviola* (NBC)

1579 Outstanding Hairstyling: Larry Germain and Donna Gilbert for *The Miracle Worker* (NBC)

1580 Outstanding Series Film Editing: M. Pam Blumenthal for "Louie and the Nice Girl" on *Taxi* (ABC)

1581 Outstanding Film Sound Editing: Don Crosby, Mark Dennis, Tony Garber, Doug Grindstaff, Don V. Isaacs, Hank Salerno and Larry Singer for *Power, Part One* (NBC)

1582 Governor's Award: Johnny Carson

1583 Outstanding Series Costume Design: Pete Menefee for *The Big Show with Tony Randall and Herve Villechaize* (NBC)

1584 Outstanding Achievement in Engineering Development: National Bureau of Standards, Public Broadcasting Service and American Broadcasting Company for their development of Closed Captioning for the deaf

1585 Outstanding Daytime Drama Series: *Guiding Light* (CBS)

1586 Outstanding Talk, Service or Variety Series: *Donahue* (syndicated)

1587 Outstanding Game or Audience Participation Show: *The Hollywood Squares* (NBC), and *The $20,000 Pyramid* (ABC)

1588 Outstanding Children's Entertainment Special: "The Late, Great Me: Story of a Teenage Alcoholic" on *ABC Afterschool Special* (ABC)

1589 Outstanding Children's Informational/Instructional Short Format Programming: *ABC Schoolhouse Rock* (ABC); *Ask NBC News* (NBC); *H.E.L.P. (Dr. Henry's Emergency Lessons for People)* (ABC); and *In the News* (CBS)

1590 Outstanding Children's Entertainment Series: *Hot Hero Sandwich* (NBC)

1591 Outstanding Children's Informational/Instructional Series or Special: *Sesame Street* (PBS), *30 Minutes* (CBS), and "Why a Conductor" on *CBS Festival of Lively Arts for Young People* (CBS)

1592 Outstanding Children's Anthology/Dramatic Programming: "Animal Talk" on *CBS Library* (CBS); "The Gold Bug" on *ABC Weekend Special* (ABC); "Leatherstocking Tales" on *Once Upon a Classic* (PBS); and "Once Upon a Midnight Dreary" on *CBS Library* (CBS)

1593 Outstanding Series or Special Religious Programming: *Directions* (ABC), and *For Our Times* (CBS)

1594 Outstanding Special Events Coverage: *La Gioconda* (PBS), and *Macy's 53rd Annual Thanksgiving Parade* (NBC)

1595 Outstanding Special Classification of Program Achievement: *FYI* (ABC)

1596 Outstanding Daytime Dramatic Actor: Douglas Watson in *Another World* (NBC)

1597 Outstanding Daytime Dramatic Actress: Judith Light in *One Life to Live* (ABC)

1598 Outstanding Daytime Supporting Dramatic Actor: Warren Burton in *All My Children* (ABC)

1599 Outstanding Daytime Supporting Dramatic Actress: Francesca James in *All My Children* (ABC)

1600 Outstanding Daytime Drama Guest or Cameo Appearance: Hugh McPhillips in *Days of Our Lives* (NBC)

1601 Outstanding Host or Hostess in a Talk, Service or Variety Series: Phil Donahue in *Donahue* (syndicated)

1602 Outstanding Host or Hostess in a Game or Audience Participation Show: Peter Marshall in *The Hollywood Squares* (NBC)

1603 Outstanding Daytime Drama Series Direction: Lela Swift and Jerry Evans for *Ryan's Hope* (ABC)

1604 Outstanding Talk, Service or Variety Series Direction: Duke Struck for "Henry Fonda Tribute" on *Good Morning America* (ABC)

1605 Outstanding Individual Game or Audience Participation Show Direction: Jerome Shaw for the June 14 program *The Hollywood Squares* (NBC)

1606 Outstanding Daytime Drama Series Writing: Claire Labine, Paul Avila Mayer, Mary Munisteri, Judith Pinsker and Jeffrey Lane for *Ryan's Hope* (ABC)

1607 Outstanding Individual Achievement in Religious Programming: Dean Jagger in "Independence and '76" on *This Is the Life* (syndicated); Richard F. Morean, writer of "If No Birds Sang" on *This Is the Life* (syndicated); Justus Taylor for "Seeds of Revolution" on *Directions* (ABC); John Duffy for *A Talent for Life: Jews of the Italian Renaissance* (NBC); and Thomas E. Azzari for "Stable Boy's Christmas" on *This Is the Life* (syndicated)

1608 Outstanding Individual Achievement in Special Event Coverage: Kirk Browning, director, and Luciano Pavarotti and Renata Scotti, performers, in *La Gioconda* (PBS)

1609 Outstanding Individual Achievement in Children's Programming: Arthur Allen Seidelman, director, and Melissa Sue Anderson, performer for "Which Mother Is Mine" on *ABC Afterschool Special* (ABC); Jan Hartman, writer, Anthony Lover, director, Vincent Sklena, film editor and Maia Danziger, performer in "The Late Great Me: Story of a Teenage Alcoholic" on *ABC Afterschool Special* (ABC); Butterfly McQueen, performer in "The Seven Wishes of a Rich Kid" on *ABC Afterschool Special* (ABC); Fred Rogers, performer on "Mister Rogers Goes to School" on *Mister Rogers' Neighborhood* (PBS); David Axlerod, Joseph A. Bailey, Andy Breckman, Bruce Hart, Richard Camp, Sherry Coben, Carole Hart and Marianne Mayer, writers for December 8 program of *Hot Hero Sandwich* (NBC); Alex Thompson and Steven Atha for "The Gold Bug" on *ABC Weekend Special* (ABC); Steven Zink for *Sesame Street* (PBS); John Gonzales, Charles Liotta, John A. Servidio and George A. Magda for *Time Out* (NBC); George Alch for "A Special Gift" on *ABC Afterschool Special* (ABC); Lee Dichter for *Big Blue Marble* (syndicated); John Beymer and

Mike Fash for "Movie Star's Daughter" on *ABC Afterschool Special* (ABC); David Sanderson for "Once Upon a Midnight Dreary" on *CBS Library* (CBS); Jack Sholder for "Noisy/Quiet Hearing" on *3-2-1 Contact* (PBS); Merle Worth for "Fast/Slow/Speed Up/Slow Down" on *3-2-1 Contact* (PBS); Ronald Baldwin for "Growth/Decay" on *3-2-1 Contact* (PBS); and Michael Baugh for "I Can Sing a Rainbow" on *Villa Alegre* (PBS)

1610 Outstanding Daytime Drama Technical Achievement: Joseph Solomito, Howard Zweig, Lawrence Hammond, Robert Ambrico, Dianne Cates-Cantrell, Christopher N. Mauro, Larry Strack, Vincent Senatore, Albin S. Lemanski, Len Walas, Diana Wenman, Jean Dadario, Roger Haenelt, John L. Grella, Irving Robbin, Jim Reichert and Teri Smith for *All My Children* (ABC)

1611 Outstanding Daytime Drama Design Excellence: William Mickley, William Itkin, Donna Larson, Mel Handelsman, Carol Luiken, Sylvia Lawrence, Michael Huddle and Hy Bley for *All My Children* (ABC)

1612 Outstanding Achievement for Special Classification: Danny Seagren for "The Annual Thanksgiving Turkey Day Raffle" on *Miss Peach and the Kelly School* (syndicated)

1613 Outstanding Special Event Individual Achievement: Ron Craft, Kenneth Patterson, Gary Emrick, Luis A. Fuerte, Daniel J. Webb, Jack Reader, Thomas Tucker, William Kelsey, Greg Harms, Tom Ancell, Val Riolo, Roy Stewart, Zack Brown, Ken Dettling and Luciano Pavarotti for *La Gioconda* (PBS)

1614 Outstanding News Program Achievement: *Showdown in Iran – CBS Reports* (CBS), and *The Boat People – CBS Reports* (CBS)

1615 Outstanding Individual Achievement in News Film Editing: Maurice Murad for *The Boston Goes to China – CBS Reports* (CBS); Joseph Muriania for "Baryshnikov" on *60 Minutes* (CBS); and Mili Bonsignori for *But What About the Children – CBS Reports* (CBS)

1616 Outstanding Individual Achievement in News Videotape Editing: Susan Raymond for *The Police Tapes – ABC News Close-Up* (ABC)

1617 Outstanding Individual Achievement in News Writing: George Crile, III and Bill Moyers for *Battle for South Africa – CBS Reports* (CBS); Andrew A. Rooney for "Who Won What in America, a Few Minutes with Andy Rooney" on *60 Minutes* (CBS); Tom Spain for *Anyplace but Here – CBS Reports* (CBS); and Perry Wolff for *1968 – CBS News Special* (CBS)

1618 Outstanding Individual Achievement in News Directing: Tom Priestly for *The Killing Ground – ABC News Close-Up* (ABC); Howard Stringer for *The Boston Goes to China – CBS Reports* (CBS); Andrew Lack for *The Boat People – CBS Reports* (CBS); and Maurice Murad for *Anyplace but Here – CBS Reports* (CBS)

1619 Outstanding Individual Achievement in News Camerawork: Tom Spain for *Anyplace but Here – CBS Reports* (CBS)

1620 Outstanding Individual Achievement in News Audio: James R. Camery and Philip Gleason for *The Boston Goes to China – CBS Reports* (CBS)

1621 Outstanding Achievement in News Writing: *Anyplace but Here – CBS Reports* (CBS); *The Police Tapes – ABC News Close-Up* (ABC); *Is Anyone Out There Learning – CBS Report Card on American Education* (CBS); and "The Rating Game" on *60 Minutes* (CBS)

1622 Outstanding Achievement in News Film Editing: *The Killing Ground – ABC News Close-Up* (ABC); *Migrants – NBC Nightly News* (NBC); *Children of Hope – NBC Weekend* (NBC); *Erasing Vietnam – NBC Nightly News* (NBC); *Mission Mind Control* (ABC); and *Paul Jacobs and the Nuclear Gang* (PBS)

1623 Outstanding Achievement in News Music: "Misha" on *60 Minutes* (CBS); "Teddy Kolleck's Jerusalem" on *60 Minutes* (CBS); "Pops" on *60 Minutes* (CBS); "Noah" on *60 Minutes* (CBS); *1968 – CBS News Special* (CBS); *Incest: The Best Kept Secret* (CBS); *The Boston Goes to China – CBS Reports* (CBS); *A Very, Very Special Place – NBC Weekend* (NBC); and *Palestine* (PBS, Thames Television, London)

1624 Outstanding Live Sports Special: *1980 Winter Olympic Games* (ABC)

1625 **Outstanding Edited Sports Special:** *Gossamer Albatross—Flight of Imagination* (CBS)
1626 **Outstanding Live Sports Series:** *NCAA College Football* (ABC)
1627 **Outstanding Edited Sports Series:** *NFL Game of the Week* (syndicated)
1628 **Outstanding Sports Directing:** Sandy Grossman for *Superbowl XIV* (CBS)
1629 **Outstanding Sports Film Editing:** Jon Day, Sam Fine, Angelo Bernarducci, John Petersen, Vincent Reda, Anthony Scandiffio, Wayne Weiss and Ted Winterburn for "Up Close and Personal" on *1980 Winter Olympic Games* (ABC)
1630 **Outstanding Sports Audio:** Trevor Carless, George Hause, Jim Lynch, Dennis Fierman and Jan Schulte for "Up Close and Personal" on *1980 Winter Olympic Games* (ABC)
1631 **Outstanding Sports Cinematography:** Bob Angelo, Ernie Ernst, Jay Gerber, Stan Leshner, Don Marx, Hank McElwee, Howard Neef, Jack Newman, Steve Sabol, Bob Smith, Art Spieller and Phil Tuckett for *NFL Game of the Week* (syndicated), and Harvey Harrison, Harry Hart and Don Shapiro for "Up Close and Personal" on *1980 Winter Oympic Games* (ABC)
1632 **Outstanding Sports Music Composition:** Chuck Mangione for *1980 Winter Olympic Games* (ABC)
1633 **Outstanding Sports Associate Direction/Videotape Editing:** Barbara Bowman, Paul Fanelli, Charles Gardner, Marvin Gench, Roger Haenelt, Conrad Kraus, Ann Stone, Alex Moscovic, Lou Rende, Nathan Rogers, Erskin Roberts, Mario Schencman, Arthur Volk, Francis Guigliano, Ronald Ackerman, Michael Altieri, Tom Capace, John Croak, Jacob Hierl, Tony Jutchenko, Hector Kicelian, Ken Klingbeil, Pete Murphy, Hiorshi Nakamoto, Carl Pollack, Merritt Roesser, Winston Sadoo, Fausto Sanchez, Leo Stephan, Richard Velasco and Ed Zlotnik for *1980 Winter Olympic Games* (ABC)
1634 **Outstanding Sports Engineering Supervision/Technical Direction/Electronic Camerawork:** Julius Barnathan, Bill Stone, Joseph Debonis, Joseph A.

Maltz, Charles Baldour, David E. Eschelbacher, David Linick, Eric Rosenthal, Abdelnour Tadros, Tony Uttendaele, Dick Horan, Robert Armbruster, Bill Blummel, Loren Coltran, Geoffrey Felger, Mike Jochim, Jacques Lesgards, Bill Maier, Gary Larkins, Joseph Polito, Elliott R. Reed, Martin Sandberg, Tony Versley, Mike Fisher, Joseph Kresnicka, Bud Untiedt, Les Weiss, Werner Gunther, Chester Mazurek, William Morris, Joseph Schiavo, Joe Nesi, Ernie Buttelman, J. Allen, Gerry Bucci, H. Falk, David Smith, Dianne Cates-Cantrell, Gary Donatelli, Danny La Mothe, Charles Mitchell, Steve Nikifor, William Sullivan, Don Farnham, Rick Knipe, Morton Lipow and Joseph Montesano for *1980 Winter Olympic Games* (ABC)
1635 **Outstanding Sports Personality:** Jim McKay
1636 **Outstanding Sports Individual Achievement:** Jerry P. Caruso and Harry Smith, creators and developers of the Radio Frequency Golf Cup Mike

—————— **1 9 8 0** ——————

1637 **Outstanding Comedy Series:** *Taxi* (ABC)
1638 **Outstanding Drama Series:** *Hill Street Blues* (NBC)
1639 **Outstanding Limited Series:** *Shogun* (NBC)
1640 **Outstanding Variety/Music Comedy Program:** *Lily: Sold Out* (CBS)
1641 **Outstanding Drama Special:** *Playing for Time* (CBS)
1642 **Outstanding Classical Program:** "Jerome Robbins Ballets" on *Live from Studio 8H* (NBC)
1643 **Outstanding Informational Special:** *The Body Human: The Bionic Breakthrough* (CBS)
1644 **Outstanding Informational Series:** *Steve Allen's Meeting of the Minds* (PBS)
1645 **Outstanding Animated Program:** *Life Is a Circus, Charlie Brown* (CBS)
1646 **Outstanding Children's Program:** "Donahue and Kids" on *Project Peacock* (NBC)
1647 **Outstanding Limited Series or Special Lead Actress:** Vanessa Redgrave in *Playing for Time* (CBS)

1648 Outstanding Limited Series or Special Lead Actor: Anthony Hopkins in *The Bunker* (CBS)

1649 Outstanding Limited Series or Special Supporting Actress: Jane Alexander in *Playing for Time* (CBS)

1650 Outstanding Comedy Series Lead Actress: Isabel Sanford in *The Jeffersons* (CBS)

1651 Outstanding Comedy Series Lead Actor: Judd Hirsch in *Taxi* (ABC)

1652 Outstanding Comedy Series Supporting Actress: Eileen Brennan in *Private Benjamin* (CBS)

1653 Outstanding Comedy Series Supporting Actor: Danny De Vito in *Taxi* (ABC)

1654 Outstanding Drama Series Lead Actor: Daniel J. Travanti in *Hill Street Blues* (NBC)

1655 Outstanding Drama Series Lead Actress: Barbara Babcock for "Fecund Hand Rose" on *Hill Street Blues* (NBC)

1656 Outstanding Drama Series Supporting Actress: Nancy Marchand in *Lou Grant* (CBS)

1657 Outstanding Variety/Music or Comedy Special Director: Don Mischer for *The Kennedy Center Honors* (CBS)

1658 Outstanding Comedy Series Directing: James Burrows for "Elaine's Strange Triangle" on *Taxi* (ABC)

1659 Outstanding Drama Series Direction: Robert Butler for "Hill Street Station" on *Hill Street Blues* (NBC)

1660 Outstanding Limited Series or Special Direction: James Goldstone for *Kent State* (NBC)

1661 Outstanding Drama Series Writers: Steven Bochco and Michael Kozoll for *Hill Street Blues* (NBC)

1662 Outstanding Comedy Series Writing: Michael Leeson for "Tony's Sister and Jim" on *Taxi* (ABC)

1663 Outstanding Variety/Music or Comedy Program Writers: Jerry Juhl, David Odell and Chris Langham for *The Muppet Show,* Episode with Carol Burnett (syndicated)

1664 Outstanding Limited Series or Special Writing: Arthur Miller for *Playing for Time* (CBS)

1665 Outstanding Music and Lyrics: Ken Welch and Mitzi Welch for "This Is My Night" on *Lynda in Wonderland* (CBS)

1666 Outstanding Comedy Series Film Editing: M. Pam Blumenthal and Jack Michon for "Elaine's Strange Triangle" on *Taxi* (ABC)

1667 Outstanding Drama Series Film Sound Editing: Samuel Horta, Robert Cornett, Denise Horta and Eileen Horta for "Hill Street Station" on *Hill Street Blues* (NBC)

1668 Outstanding Series Videotape Editing: Andy Ackerman for "Bah, Humbug" on *WKRP in Cincinnati* (CBS)

1669 Outstanding Drama Series Cinematography: William H. Cronjager for "Hill Street Station" on *Hill Street Blues* (NBC)

1670 Outstanding Limited Series or Special Cinematography: Arthur F. Ibbetson for *Little Lord Fauntleroy* (CBS)

1671 Outstanding Choreography: Walter Painter for "Lynda Carter's Celebration" on *Lynda in Wonderland* (CBS)

1672 Outstanding Make-Up: Albert Paul Jeyte and James Kail for *Peter and Paul* (CBS)

1673 Outstanding Music Direction: Ian Fraser, Billy Byers, Chris Boardman and Bob Florence for "Lynda Carter's Celebration" on *Lynda in Wonderland* (CBS)

1674 Special Award: Lawrence Welk

1675 Special Award: Max Liebman, producer

1676 Special Award: Lucille Ball

1677 Special Award: Sarah Vaughan

1678 Outstanding Technical Achievement: Rank Precision Industries, Ltd. for development of Mark III Flying Spot Telecine

1679 Governor's Award: Elton H. Rule, ABC Network president

1680 Outstanding Drama Series Supporting Actor: Michael Conrad in *Hill Street Blues* (NBC)

1681 Outstanding Supporting Actor in a Limited Series or Special: David Warner in *Masada* (ABC)

1682 Outstanding Series Art Direction: Howard E. Johnson, John M. Dwyer and Robert C. Freer for *The Gangster Chronicles* (NBC)

1683 Outstanding Limited Series or Special Videotape Editing: Marco Zappia and Branda S. Miller for *Perry Como's Christmas in the Holy Land* (ABC)

1684 **Outstanding Film Sound Mixing:** William R. Teague, Robert L. Harman, William L. McCaughey and Howard Wollman for *Evita Peron, Part One* (NBC)

1685 **Outstanding Tape Sound Mixing:** Jerry Clemans, Doug Nelson and Donald Worsham for *John Denver with His Special Guest George Burns: Two of a Kind* (ABC)

1686 **Outstanding Technical Direction and Electronic Camerawork:** Heino Ripp, Peter Basil, Al Camoin, Tom Dezondorf, Vince Di Pietro and Gene Martin for "An Evening with Jerome Robbins" on *Live from Studio 8H* (NBC)

1687 **Outstanding Lighting Direction:** Ralph Holmes for "Nureyev and the Joffrey Ballet/In Tribute to Nijinsky" on *Dance in America* (PBS)

1688 **Outstanding Special Classification of Individual Achievement:** Sarah Vaughan for *Rhapsody and Song—A Tribute to George Gershwin* (PBS)

1689 **Outstanding Creative Technical Crafts Individual Achievement:** John Allison, Adolf Schaller, Don Davis, Rick Sternbach, Jon Lomberg, Anne Norica and Ernie Norica for "The Shores of the Cosmic Ocean" on *Cosmos* (PBS), and Carey Melcher, Bob Bruckner, Steve Burum, Jim Dow, John Gale, Larry Heider, Mike Johnson, Robert C. King, Cleve Landsberg, Joseph Matza, George C. Reilly and Joe Wolcott for "The Shores of the Cosmic Ocean" on *Cosmos* (PBS)

1690 **Outstanding Limited Series or Special Art Direction:** Ray Storey, Dennis Peeples and David Love for *John Steinbeck's "East of Eden," Episode Three* (ABC)

1691 **Outstanding Music or Variety Art Direction:** Roy Christopher for *53rd Annual Academy Awards* (ABC)

1692 **Outstanding Drama Series Music Composition:** Bruce Broughton for "The Satyr" on *Buck Rogers* (NBC)

1693 **Outstanding Limited Series or Special Music Composition:** Jerry Goldsmith for *Masada, Episode 2* (ABC)

1694 **Outstanding Series Costume Design:** Shin Nishida for *Shogun* (NBC)

1695 **Outstanding Special Costume Design:** Willa Kim for "The Tempest

Live with the San Francisco Ballet" on *Dance in America* (PBS)

1696 **Outstanding Hairstyling:** Shirley Padgett for *Madame X* (NBC)

1697 **Outstanding Graphic Design and Title Sequences:** Phil Norman for *Shogun, Episode One* (NBC)

1698 **Outstanding Limited Series or Special Film Editing:** John A. Martinelli for *Murder in Texas* (NBC)

1699 **Outstanding Informational Programming Individual Achievement:** Kent Gibson and Gerald Zelinger for "Blues for a Red Planet" on *Cosmos* (PBS), and Chuck White, Gary Bourgeois, Dave Dockendorf and John Mack for "Gorilla" on *National Geographic Special* (PBS)

1700 **Outstanding Daytime Drama:** *General Hospital* (ABC)

1701 **Outstanding Children's Entertainment Series:** *Captain Kangaroo* (CBS), and "A Tale of Two Cities" on *Once Upon a Classic* (PBS)

1702 **Outstanding Children's Entertainment Special:** "A Matter of Time" on *ABC Afterschool Special* (ABC)

1703 **Outstanding Children's Informational/Instructional Series:** *30 Minutes* (CBS)

1704 **Outstanding Children's Informational/Instructional Special:** "Julie Andrews' Invitation to the Dance with Rudolf Nureyev" on *CBS Festival of Lively Arts for Young People* (CBS)

1705 **Outstanding Short Form Children's Instructional/Informational Programming:** *In the News* (CBS)

1706 **Outstanding Achievement in Religious Programming:** *Directions* (ABC), and *Insight* (syndicated)

1707 **Outstanding Achievement in Special Classification:** *FYI* (ABC)

1708 **Outstanding Talk or Service Series:** *Donahue* (syndicated)

1709 **Outstanding Variety Series:** *The Merv Griffin Show* (syndicated)

1710 **Outstanding Game or Audience Participation Series:** *The $20,000 Pyramid* (ABC)

1711 **Outstanding Daytime Dramatic Actor:** Douglas Watson in *Another World* (NBC)

1712 **Outstanding Daytime Dramatic Actress:** Judith Light in *One Life to Live* (ABC)

1713 **Outstanding Daytime Supporting Dramatic Actor:** Larry Haines in *Search for Tomorrow* (CBS)

1714 **Outstanding Daytime Supporting Dramatic Actress:** Jane Elliot in *General Hospital* (ABC)

1715 **Outstanding Host or Hostess in a Talk or Service Series:** Hugh Downs for *Over Easy* (PBS)

1716 **Outstanding Host or Hostess in a Variety Series:** David Letterman for *The David Letterman Show* (NBC)

1717 **Outstanding Host or Hostess in a Game or Audience Participation Series:** Peter Marshall in *The Hollywood Squares* (NBC)

1718 **Outstanding Daytime Drama Series Direction:** Marlena Laird, Alan Pultz and Philip Sogard for *General Hospital* (ABC)

1719 **Outstanding Individual Direction for a Talk or Service Series:** Jerry Kupcinet for the March 13 program of *The Richard Simmons Show* (syndicated)

1720 **Outstanding Variety Series Direction:** Sterling Johnson for *Dinah & Friends in Israel* (syndicated)

1721 **Outstanding Individual Direction for a Game or Audience Participation Show:** Mike Gargiulo for the May 15 program *The $20,000 Pyramid* (ABC)

1722 **Outstanding Special Classification of Outstanding Individual Achievement:** Merrill Markoe, Rich Hall, David Letterman, Gerard Mulligan, Paul Raley and Ron Richards, writers for *The David Letterman Show* (NBC), Caroly Wilcox, Cheryl Blalock and Edward G. Christie for *Sesame Street* (PBS)

1723 **Outstanding Daytime Drama Series Writing:** Douglas Marland, Robert Dwyer, Nancy Franklin and Harding Lemay for *The Guiding Light* (CBS)

1724 **Outstanding Individual Achievement in Children's Programming:** Robert E. Fuisz, M.D., writer and Marlo Thomas, performer in *The Body Human: Facts of Life for Girls* (CBS); Robert Elfstrom and Ken Howard in *The Body Human: Facts of Life for Boys* (CBS); Bill Cosby in "The Secret" on *The New Fat Albert Show* (CBS); Danny Aiello in "Family of Strangers" on *ABC Afterschool Special* (ABC); John Herzfeld, director for "Stoned" on *ABC After-*

school Special (ABC); Blossom Elfman, writer for "I Think I'm Having a Baby" on *The CBS Afternoon Playhouse* (CBS); Mary Munisteri, writer for *Mandy's Grandmother* (syndicated); Eric Van Haren Norman for "Egyptian Weavers" on *Big Blue Marble* (syndicated); Joe Consentino for "Globetrotter" on *Big Blue Marble* (syndicated); Peter Hammer for "Do Me a Favor ... Don't Vote for My Mom" on *Big Blue Marble* (syndicated); Allen Kirkpatrick for "Bike Racing" on *Big Blue Marble* (syndicated); Dick Maitland for "Tuning the Engine" on *Sesame Street* (PBS); Dick Hyman and Steven Atha for "Sunshine's on the Way" on *Special Treat* (NBC); Dorothy Weaver for "Family of Strangers" on *ABC Afterschool Special* (ABC); and Lewis Gifford, Paul Kim and Tom Yohe for *Drawing Power* (NBC)

1725 **Outstanding Individual Achievement in Religious Programming:** Dahl Delu, C. Murawski, Scott Heineman and Martin Sheen in "Long Road Home" on *Insight* (syndicated)

1726 **Outstanding Daytime Creative Technical Craft Individual Achievement:** Donald Spangolia, Thomas Burton and Claudio Zeitlin Burtin for *The John Davidson Show* (syndicated); Michael Gass for *Good Morning America* (ABC); Dayton Anderson for *The Mike Douglas Show* (syndicated); and Robert Hoffman, Anthony Gambino and Lawrence Hammond for *All My Children* (ABC)

1727 **Outstanding Daytime Drama Technical Excellence:** *All My Children* (ABC)

1728 **Outstanding Daytime Drama Design Excellence:** *Ryan's Hope* (ABC)

1729 **Outstanding News Programs and Program Segments:** *Pope John Paul II in Poland* (NBC); *Fishing Boat Sinks* (NBC); *CBS Reports: Miami — The Trial That Sparked the Riots* (CBS); *CBS Reports: On the Road* (CBS); *Too Little, Too Late?* (CBS); "Bette Davis" on *60 Minutes* (CBS); *Post Election Special Edition* (ABC); "Onward Christian Voters" on *60 Minutes* (CBS); "Here's Johnny!" on *60 Minutes* (CBS); "George Burns: An Update" on *20/20* (ABC); "VW Beetle: The Hidden Danger" on *20/20* (ABC); "The Invisible World" on *National*

Geographic Special (PBS); "Heart Transplant" on *Prime Time Sunday* (NBC); *Murder of a Correspondent* (ABC); "Arson for Profit—Parts I and II" on *20/20* (ABC); "Mysteries of the Mind" on *National Geographic Special* (PBS); *CBS Reports: Teddy* (CBS); *Lights, Camera . . . Politics* (ABC); "Who Killed Georgi Markov?" on *World* (PBS); "Urethane" on *Prime Time Saturday* (NBC); and "Nicaragua" on *20/20* (ABC)

1730 Outstanding News Individual Achievement: Morton Silverstein and Chris Wallace for *NBC Reports: The Migrants* (NBC); Mike Edwards and Steve Sheppard for "Inside Afghanistan" on *60 Minutes* (CBS); Jack Clark and Jim Cefalo for *Shooting of Bill Stewart* (ABC); John Godfrey, Jon Alpert and Keiko Tsuno for *Third Avenue: Only the Strong Survive* (PBS); Nils Rassmussen, Kenneth E. Werner and Patrick M. Cook for *Death in a Southwest Prison* (ABC); Marlene Sanders and Judy Towers Reemtsma for *CBS Reports: What Shall We Do About Mother?* (CBS); Bill Moyers for "Our Times" on *Bill Moyers' Journal* (PBS); Irwin Rosten for "Mysteries of the Mind" on *National Geographic Special* (PBS); Perry Wolff for *American Dream, American Nightmare* (CBS); Ray Lockart for *NBC White Paper: If Japan Can, Why Can't We?* (NBC); Roger Phenix for *NBC Reports: To Be a Doctor* (NBC); Alan Raymond for *To Die for Ireland* (ABC); Ruth Neuwald for *CBS Reports: Miami—The Trial That Sparked the Riots* (CBS); Maurice Murad for *CBS Reports: The Saudis* (CBS); Robert Rogow and Joel Dulberg for "Pavarotti" on *60 Minutes* (CBS); and Lionel Hampton for *No Maps on My Taps* (PBS)

1731 Outstanding Live Sports Special: *Kentucky Derby* (ABC)

1732 Outstanding Edited Sports Special: *ABC's Wide World of Sports 20th Anniversary Show* (ABC)

1733 Outstanding Live Sports Series: *PGA Tour on CBS* (CBS)

1734 Outstanding Edited Sports Series: *The American Sportsman* (ABC)

1735 Outstanding Sports Program Individual Achievement: Ray Savignano,

Jesse Rineer, Sandy Bell, Robert Brown, Edward Ambrosini, Robert Squittieri, Donald Resch, James Murphy, Neil McCaffrey, Herman Lang, Frank McSpedon, Thomas McCarthy, Barry Drago, Joseph Sokota, Stephen Gorsuch, George Rothweiler, George Naeder, David Graham, Jeffrey Pollack, James McCarthy, Hans Singer and Sigmund Meyers for *Daytona 500* (CBS); Louis Scannapieco, Arthur Tinn, Charles D'Onofrio, Sandy Bell, Edward Ambrosini, Robert Hanford, Robert Pieringer, Frank Florio, George Klimcsak, George Naeder, James McCarthy, George Rothweiler, Al Loreto, Herman Lang, Hans Singer, Nicholas Lauria, James Murphy, Harry Haigood, Michael English, John Lincoln, Frank McSpedon, Dennis McBride, Stan Gould, Joseph Sokota, Barry Drago, Neil McCaffrey, David Graham, Walter Soucy, Robert Welch, David Finch, Richard E. Kearney, Joseph Sidlo and W. Haigood for *The Masters* (CBS); Tony Tocci, Ken Brown and Gary Bradley for *The Baseball Bunch* (syndicated); Rob Beiner, Dick Buffington, Jeff Cohan, Vince Dedario, Kathy Cook, John de Lisa, Joel Feld, Ben Harvey, Bob Hersh, Jack Graham, Bob Lanning, Peter Lasser, Carol Lehti, Brian McCullough, Dennis Mazzocco, Bob Rosburg, Norm Samet, Ned Simon, Toni Slotkin, Larry Carolina and Bob Dekas for *ABC's Wide World of Sports* (ABC); Jim McQueen, Jeff U'Ren, Matthew McCarthy, Mark Jankeloff and Richard Leible for *NBC Sportsworld* (NBC); Mike Adams, Bob Ryan and Phil Tuckett for *NFL Symfunny* (syndicated); Cathy Barreto, Joel Arnowitz, Jack Black, Bob Coffey, Joe D'Ornellas, Stanley Faer, Bob Halper, Beth Hermelin, Howard N. Miller, Gady Reinhold, Roni Scherman, Steve Dellapietra, Barry Hicks, George Palmisano, John Wells, Jim Alkins, Curtis Campbell, Bob Clark, Ted Demers, Joe Drake, Tom Durkin, Bob Foster, Harve Gilman, Al Golly, Sigmund Gordon, Elliott Greenblatt, Bob Hickson, Frank Hodnett, George Joanitis, Andy Klein, Gary Kozak, Ed Knudholt, Pete La Corte, Marvin Lee, George Magee, Mario Marino, John Mayer, Walter

Matwichuk, Henry Menusan, Jeff Ringel, Jesse Michnick, Charlotte Robinson, Allan Segal, Bill Vandernort, Irv Villafana, Hank Wolf and Bill Zizza for *NFL Today* (CBS); Angelo Bernarducci, Vincent Reda, Richard Rossi, Anthony Scandiffio, Norman Smith, Chris Riger, Ted Winterburn and Anthony Zaccaro for *The American Sportsman* (ABC); Robert Brown, Frank Florio, Edward Kushner, Robert Hanford, Rick Blane, Stan Gould, Stephen Gorsuch, John Lincoln, George Klimcsak, Robert Jamieson, David Graham, James Murphy, Frank McSpedon, Jeffrey Pollack, Joseph Vincens and David Finch for *NFC Championship Game* (CBS); Joe Schavio, Joseph Lee, Drew Derosa, Jim Heneghan, Andrew Armentani, Jessel Kohn, Gary Donatelli, Jack Dorfman, Jack Savoy, Steve Nikifor, Tom O'Connell, Joe Cotugno and Roy Hitchings for *NFL Football* (ABC); Gilbert A. Miller, Donald Resch, Emanuel Kaufman, John Curtin, Thomas McCarthy, James McCarthy, Neil McCaffrey, Stephen Gorsuch and Michael English for *NFL Today* (CBS); and James M. Grau for NFL and U.S. Open closing logos (CBS)

1736 **Outstanding Special Sports Program:** *The Baseball Bunch* (syndicated), and "The Arlberg Kandahar Downhill from St. Anton" on *NBC Sportsworld* (NBC)

1737 **Outstanding Special Sports Individual:** Steve Gonzalez for *Superbowl XV* (NBC), and Don Ohlmeyer and Ted Nathanson for *Friday Night Fights* (NBC)

1738 **Outstanding Sports Host:** Dick Enberg

1739 **Outstanding Sports Analyst:** Dick Button

1740 **International Documentary:** Canadian Broadcasting Corporation for *Fighting Back*

1741 **International Popular Arts:** British Broadcasting Corporation for *Not the Last of the Nine O'Clock News*

1742 **International Drama:** Yorkshire Television Limited, England for *A Rod of Iron*

1743 **International Performing Arts:** Société Radio, Canada for *L'Oiseau de Feu (The Firebird)*

1744 **Outstanding Drama Special:** "A Woman Named Golda" on *Operation Prime Time* (syndicated)

1745 **Outstanding Drama Series:** *Hill Street Blues* (NBC)

1746 **Outstanding Comedy Series:** *Barney Miller* (ABC)

1747 **Outstanding Music/Variety or Comedy Program:** *Night of 100 Stars* (ABC)

1748 **Outstanding Lead Actress in a Limited Series or a Special:** Ingrid Bergman for "A Woman Named Golda" on *Operation Prime Time* (syndicated)

1749 **Outstanding Lead Actor in a Limited Series or a Special:** Laurence Olivier in *Brideshead Revisited* (PBS)

1750 **Outstanding Series Comedy Lead Actor:** Alan Alda in *M*A*S*H* (CBS)

1751 **Outstanding Series Comedy Supporting Actress:** Loretta Swit in *M*A*S*H* (CBS)

1752 **Outstanding Drama Series Lead Actor:** Daniel J. Travanti in *Hill Street Blues* (NBC)

1753 **Outstanding Drama Series Supporting Actor:** Michael Conrad in *Hill Street Blues* (NBC)

1754 **Outstanding Drama Series Lead Actress:** Michael Learned in *Nurse* (CBS)

1755 **Outstanding Drama Series Supporting Actress:** Nancy Marchand in *Lou Grant* (CBS)

1756 **Outstanding Comedy Lead Actress:** Carol Kane in "Simka Returns" on *Taxi* (ABC)

1757 **Outstanding Comedy Supporting Actor:** Christopher Lloyd in *Taxi* (ABC)

1758 **Outstanding Comedy Series Director:** Alan Rafkin for "Barbara's Crisis" on *One Day at a Time* (CBS)

1759 **Outstanding Drama Series Director:** Harry Harris for "To Soar and Never Falter" on *Fame* (NBC)

1760 **Outstanding Drama Special Director:** Marvin J. Chomsky for *Inside the Third Reich* (ABC)

1761 **Outstanding Children's Program Director:** Dwight Hemion for *Goldie & Kids ... Listen to Us* (ABC)

1762 **Outstanding Limited Series or Special Film Editing:** Robert F. Shugrue for "A Woman Named Golda" on *Operation Prime Time* (syndicated)

1763 **Outstanding Limited Series:** *Marco Polo* (NBC)

1764 **Outstanding Informational Special:** *Making of "Raiders of the Lost Ark"* (PBS)

1765 **Outstanding Children's Program:** *The Wave* (ABC)

1766 **Outstanding Classical Program in the Performing Arts:** *La Bohème, Live from the Met* (PBS)

1767 **Outstanding Information Series:** *Creativity with Bill Moyers* (PBS)

1768 **Outstanding Animated Program:** *The Grinch Grinches the Cat in the Hat* (ABC)

1769 **Outstanding Limited Series or Special Lead Actor:** Mickey Rooney in *Bill* (CBS)

1770 **Outstanding Limited Series or Special Supporting Actress:** Penny Fuller in *The Elephant Man* (ABC)

1771 **Outstanding Series Film Editing:** Andrew Chulack for "Of Mouse and Man" on *Hill Street Blues* (NBC)

1772 **Outstanding Videotape Series Editing:** Ken Denisoff for *Barbara Mandrell and the Mandrell Sisters* (NBC)

1773 **Outstanding Limited Series or Special Videotape Editing:** William H. Breshears, Sr., Pam Marshall and Tucker Wiard for *American Bandstand's 30th Anniversary Special* (ABC)

1774 **Outstanding Comedy Series Writing:** Ken Estin for "Elegant Iggy" on *Taxi* (ABC)

1775 **Outstanding Drama Series Writing:** Steven Bochco, Anthony Yerkovich, Jeffrey Lewis, Michael Wagner and Michael Kozoll for "Freedom's Last Stand" on *Hill Street Blues* (NBC)

1776 **Outstanding Limited Series or Special Writing:** Corey Blechman and Barry Morrow for *Bill* (CBS)

1777 **Outstanding Variety or Music Writing:** John Candy, Joe Flaherty, Eugene Levy, Andrea Martin, Catherine O'Hara, Rick Moranis, Dave Thomas, Dick Blasucci, Paul Flaherty, Bob Dolman, John McAndrew, Doug Steckler, Mert Rich, Jeffrey Barron, Michael Short, Chris Cluess, Stuart Kreisman and Brian McConnachie for "Moral Majority Show" on *SCTV Network* (NBC)

1778 **Outstanding Series Cinematography:** William W. Spencer for "Alone in a Crowd" on *Fame* (NBC)

1779 **Outstanding Limited Series or Special Cinematography:** James Crabe for *The Letter* (ABC)

1780 **Outstanding Special Creative Individual Achievement:** Andy Zall, videotape editor for *Shirley MacLaine ... Illusions* (CBS)

1781 **Outstanding Film Sound Editing:** William H. Wistrom, Rusty Tinsley, Peter Bond, Tom Cornwell, David Elliott, Tony Garber, Peter Harrison, Charles W. McCann, Joseph Mayer, Joseph Melody, R. William, and A. Thiederman for *Inside the Third Reich* (ABC)

1782 **Outstanding Drama Series Music Composition:** David Rose for "He Was Only Twelve – Part 2" on *Little House on the Prairie* (NBC)

1783 **Outstanding Limited Series or Drama Special Music Composition:** Patrick Williams for *The Princess and the Cabbie* (CBS)

1784 **Outstanding Music Direction:** Elliott Lawrence, Bill Elton, Tommy Newsom, Torrie Zito, Jonathan Tunick and Lanny Meyers for *Night of 100 Stars* (ABC)

1785 **Outstanding Music and Lyrics:** Larry Grossman and Alan Buz Kohan for "On the Outside Looking In" on *Shirley MacLaine ... Illusions* (CBS)

1786 **Outstanding Film Sound Mixing:** Robert W. Glass, Jr., William Marky, William M. Nicholson and Howard Wilmarth for "Personal Foul" on *Hill Street Blues* (NBC)

1787 **Outstanding Tape Sound Mixing:** Christopher L. Haire, Richard J. Masci and Doug Nelson for *Perry Como's Easter in Guadalajara* (ABC)

1788 **Outstanding Series Art Direction:** Ira Diamond and Joseph Stone for "Tomorrow's Farewell" on *Fame* (NBC)

1789 **Outstanding Limited Series or Special Art Direction:** James Hulsey and Jerry Adams for *The Letter* (ABC)

1790 **Outstanding Variety or Music Art Direction:** Ray Klausen for *The Fifty-Fourth Annual Academy Awards* (ABC)

1791 Outstanding Technical Direction and Electronic Camerawork: Jerry Weiss, Bruce Bottone, Dean Hall, Ken Dahlquist, James Herring, Royden Holm, Wayne Nostaja, David Nowell and Tom Munshower for *The Magic of David Copperfield* (CBS)

1792 Outstanding Regular or Limited Series Costume Design: Enrico Sabbatini for *Marco Polo, Part 3* (NBC)

1793 Outstanding Special Costume Design: Donald Brooks for *The Letter* (ABC)

1794 Outstanding Make-Up: Paul Stanhope for *World War III* (NBC)

1795 Outstanding Hairstyling: Hazel Catmull for *Eleanor, First Lady of the World* (CBS)

1796 Outstanding Electronic Lighting Direction: Ken Dettling and George W. Reisenberger for "Working" on *American Playhouse* (PBS)

1797 Outstanding Choreography: Debbie Allen for "Come One, Come All" on *Fame* (NBC)

1798 Outstanding Individual Achievement in Children's Programming: Ralph Holmes for "Alice at the Palace" on *Project Peacock* (NBC)

1799 Outstanding Individual Achievement in Animated Programming: Bill Perez for *The Grinch Grinches the Cat in the Hat* (ABC)

1800 Outstanding Special Classification of Individual Achievement: Nell Carter and Andre DeShields, performers for *Ain't Misbehavin'* (NBC), and Marilyn Matthews, costume supervisor for "The Strike" on *Fame* (NBC)

1801 Outstanding Engineering Development: American Broadcasting Company and Dubner Computer Systems, Inc. for the Dubner CBG-2 electronic and background character generator and Hal Collins for his contributions to the art and development of videotape editing

1802 ATAS Governor's Award: Hallmark Cards, Inc. for *Hallmark Hall of Fame*

1803 Outstanding Daytime Drama Series: *Guiding Light* (CBS)

1804 Outstanding Children's Entertainment Series: *Captain Kangaroo* (CBS)

1805 Outstanding Children's Entertainment Special: "Starstruck" on *ABC Afterschool Special* (ABC)

1806 Outstanding Children's Informational/Instructional Programming: *30 Minutes* (CBS)

1807 Outstanding Short Format Informational/Instructional Programming: *In the News* (CBS)

1808 Outstanding Children's Informational/Instructional Special: *Kathy* (PBS)

1809 Outstanding Achievement in Religious Programming: *Insight* (syndicated)

1810 Outstanding Special Classification of Program Achievement: *FYI*

1811 Outstanding Talk or Service Series: *The Richard Simmons Show* (syndicated)

1812 Outstanding Variety Series: *The Regis Philbin Show* (NBC)

1813 Outstanding Game or Audience Participation Show: *Password Plus* (NBC)

1814 Outstanding Daytime Dramatic Actor: Anthony Geary on *General Hospital* (ABC)

1815 Outstanding Daytime Dramatic Actress: Robin Strasser in *One Life to Live* (ABC)

1816 Outstanding Daytime Supporting Dramatic Actor: David Lewis in *General Hospital* (ABC)

1817 Outstanding Daytime Supporting Dramatic Actress: Dorothy Lyman in *All My Children* (ABC)

1818 Outstanding Host or Hostess in a Talk or Service Series: Phil Donahue in *Donahue* (syndicated)

1819 Outstanding Host or Hostess in a Game or Audience Participation Show: Bob Barker in *The Price Is Right* (CBS)

1820 Outstanding Host or Hostess in a Variety Series: Merv Griffin in *The Merv Griffin Show* (syndicated)

1821 Outstanding Performer in Children's Programming: Bob Keeshan in *Captain Kangaroo* (CBS)

1822 Outstanding Daytime Drama Series Direction: Marlena Laird, Alan Pultz and Philip Sogard for *General Hospital* (ABC)

1823 Outstanding Variety Series Direction: Ron Wiener for the January 21 program of *Donahue* (syndicated)

1824 **Outstanding Individual Direction of a Variety Series:** Barry Glazer for the April 18 program of *American Bandstand* (ABC)

1825 **Outstanding Individual Direction of a Game Show:** Paul Alter for the May 29 program of *Family Feud* (ABC)

1826 **Outstanding Individual Direction of a Children's Program:** Arthur Allen Seidelman for "She Drinks a Little" on *ABC Afterschool Special* (ABC)

1827 **Outstanding Individual Achievement in Direction for Special Classification:** Alfred R. Kelman for *The Body Human: The Loving Process — Women* (CBS)

1828 **Outstanding Daytime Drama Series Writing:** Douglas Marland, Nancy Franklin, Patrick Mulcahey, Gene Palumbo and Frank Salisbury for *Guiding Light* (CBS)

1829 **Outstanding Children's Writing:** Paul W. Cooper for "She Drinks a Little" on *ABC Afterschool Special* (ABC)

1830 **Outstanding Individual Achievement Writing for Special Classification:** Elaine Meryl Brown, Betty Cornfeld, Mary Ann Donahue, Joe Gustaitis and Robin Westin for *FYI* (ABC)

1831 **Outstanding Children's Cinematography:** Tom Hurwitz for "Horseman of Inner Mongolia" on *Big Blue Marble* (syndicated)

1832 **Outstanding Children's Film Editing:** Peter Hammer and Allen Kirkpatrick for "Horseman of Inner Mongolia" on *Big Blue Marble* (syndicated)

1833 **Outstanding Daytime Drama Design Excellence:** James Ellingwood, Mercer Barrows, Grant Velie, Thomas Markle, John Zak, Jim O'Daniel, P.K. Cole, Vikki McCarter, Diane Lewis, Katherine Kotarakos, Debbie Holmes, Jill Farren Phelps, Dominic Messinger and Charles Paul for *General Hospital* (ABC)

1834 **Outstanding Children's Music Composition:** Elliott Lawrence for "The Unforgivable Secret" on *ABC Afterschool Special* (ABC)

1835 **Outstanding Daytime Drama Technical Excellence:** Joseph Solomito, Howard Zweig, Diana Wenman, Jean Dadario, Barbara Martin Simmons, Lawrence Hammond, Robert Ambrico, Larry Strack, Vincent Senatore, Jay Kenn, Trevor Thompson, Len Walas, Al Lemanski, Charles Eisen, Roger Haenelt and Barbara Wood for *All My Children* (ABC)

1836 **Outstanding Daytime Technical Directing/Electronic Camerawork:** Sanford Bell and Hal Classen for *The Guiding Light* (CBS)

1837 **Outstanding Daytime Art Direction/Scenic Design/Set Decoration:** Bob Keene and Griff Lambert for *The Richard Simmons Show* (syndicated)

1838 **Outstanding Daytime Lighting Direction:** Everett Melosh for *One Life to Live* (ABC)

1839 **Outstanding Daytime Costume Design:** Nancy Simmons for *The Richard Simmons Show* (syndicated)

1840 **Outstanding Children's Art Direction/Scenic Design/Set Decoration:** Claude Bonniere for "My Mother Was Never a Kid" on *ABC Afterschool Special* (ABC)

1841 **Outstanding Children's Audio:** Steven J. Palecek for "An Orchestra Is a Team, Too!" on *CBS Festival of Lively Arts for Young People* (CBS)

1842 **Outstanding Children's Make-Up and Hair Design:** Judy Cooper Sealy for "My Mother Was Never a Kid" on *ABC Afterschool Special* (ABC)

1843 **Outstanding Children's Graphic Design:** Ray Favita and Michael J. Smollin for *The Great Space Coaster* (syndicated)

1844 **National Community Service:** WTHR-TV, Indianapolis, Indiana, for *Klan*

1845 **International Documentary:** Société Nationale de Télévision Française — 1, France for *Charters Pour L'Enfer (Charters to Hell)*

1846 **International Drama:** Mariner Films and Channel 7, Australia for *A Town Like Alice*

1847 **International Performing Arts:** London Weekend Television, Ltd., United Kingdom for *Sweeney Todd: Scenes from the Making of a Musical*

1848 **International Popular Arts:** Treve Globo, Ltd., Brazil for *Vinicus Para Criancas or Arca De Noe (Noah's Ark)*

1849 **Founders Award:** Roone Arledge and Shaun Sutton
1850 **Directorate Award:** Sir Huw Wheldon
1851 **Trustee Award:** Agnes E. Nixon

——————— **1 9 8 2** ———————

1852 **Outstanding Drama Series:** *Hill Street Blues* (NBC)
1853 **Outstanding Drama Special:** *Special Bulletin* (NBC)
1854 **Outstanding Comedy Series:** *Cheers* (NBC)
1855 **Outstanding Limited Series:** *Nicholas Nickelby* (syndicated)
1856 **Outstanding Children's Program:** *Big Bird in China* (NBC)
1857 **Outstanding Variety/Music or Comedy Special:** *Motown 25: Yesterday, Today, Forever* (NBC)
1858 **Outstanding Animated Program:** *Ziggy's Gift* (ABC)
1859 **Outstanding Informational Series:** *The Barbara Walters Special* (ABC)
1860 **Outstanding Classical Program in the Performing Arts:** *Pavarotti in Philadelphia: La Bohème* (PBS)
1861 **Outstanding Informational Special:** *The Body Human: The Living Code* (CBS)
1862 **Outstanding Lead Actress in a Comedy Series:** Shelley Long in *Cheers* (NBC)
1863 **Outstanding Lead Actor in a Comedy Series:** Judd Hirsch in *Taxi* (NBC)
1864 **Outstanding Lead Actress in a Drama Series:** Tyne Daly in *Cagney & Lacey* (CBS)
1865 **Outstanding Lead Actor in a Drama Series:** Ed Flanders in *St. Elsewhere* (NBC)
1866 **Outstanding Lead Actress in a Limited Series or Special:** Barbara Stanwyck in *The Thorn Birds, Part One* (ABC)
1867 **Outstanding Lead Actor in a Limited Series or Special:** Tommy Lee Jones in *The Executioner's Song* (NBC)
1868 **Outstanding Dramatic Series Supporting Actress:** Doris Roberts in "Cora and Arnie" on *St. Elsewhere* (NBC)
1869 **Outstanding Dramatic Series Supporting Actor:** James Coco in "Cora and Arnie" on *St. Elsewhere* (NBC)
1870 **Outstanding Comedy Series Supporting Actress:** Carol Kane in *Taxi* (NBC)
1871 **Outstanding Comedy Series Supporting Actor:** Christopher Lloyd in *Taxi* (NBC)
1872 **Outstanding Limited Series or Special Supporting Actress:** Jean Simmons in *The Thorn Birds* (ABC)
1873 **Outstanding Limited Series or Special Supporting Actor:** Richard Kiley in *The Thorn Birds* (ABC)
1874 **Outstanding Individual Performance in Variety or Music Program:** Leontyne Price in *Live from Lincoln Center: Leontyne Price, Zubin Mehta and the New York Philharmonic* (PBS)
1875 **Outstanding Drama Series Directing:** Jeff Bleckner for "Life in the Minors" on *Hill Street Blues* (NBC)
1876 **Outstanding Comedy Series Directing:** James Burrows for "Sundown — Part 2" on *Cheers* (NBC)
1877 **Outstanding Variety or Music Program Directing:** Dwight Hemion for *Sheena Easton — Act 1* (NBC)
1878 **Outstanding Limited Series or Special Directing:** John Erman for *Who Will Love My Children?* (ABC)
1879 **Outstanding Informational Program Individual Achievement:** Alfred R. Kelman and Charles Bangert, directors and Louis H. Gorfain and Robert E. Fuisz, writers for *The Body Human: The Living Code* (CBS)
1880 **Outstanding Series Film Editing:** Ray Daniels for "Phantom of the Hill" on *Hill Street Blues* (NBC)
1881 **Outstanding Limited Series or Special Film Editing:** C. Timothy O'Meara for *The Thorn Birds* (ABC)
1882 **Outstanding Series Videotape Editing:** Larry M. Harris for "Change of a Dollar" on *The Jeffersons* (CBS)
1883 **Outstanding Limited Series or Special Videotape Editing:** Arden Rynew for *Special Bulletin* (NBC)
1884 **Outstanding Series Cinematography:** Joseph Biroc for "The Masterbuilder's Woman" on *Casablanca* (NBC)
1885 **Outstanding Limited Series or Special Cinematography:** Charles Correll and Steven Larner for "Into the Maelstrom" on *The Winds of War* (ABC)

1886 Outstanding Comedy Series Writing: Glen Charles and Les Charles for "Give Me a Ring Sometime" on *Cheers* (NBC)

1887 Outstanding Drama Series Writing: David Milch for "Trial by Fury" on *Hill Street Blues* (NBC)

1888 Outstanding Limited Series or Special Writing: Marshall Herskovitz and Edward Zwick for *Special Bulletin* (NBC)

1889 Outstanding Variety or Music Writing: John Candy, Joe Flaherty, Eugene Levy, Andrea Martin, Martin Short, Paul Flaherty, Dick Blasucci, John McAndrew, Doug Steckler, Bob Dolman, Michael Short and Mary Charlotte Wilcox for "The Energy Ball/Sweeps Week" on *SCTV Network* (CBS)

1890 Outstanding Individual Achievement in Informational Programming Writing: Louis H. Gorfain and Robert E. Fulaz for *The Body Human: The Living Code* (CBS)

1891 Outstanding Limited Series or Special Art Direction: Robert Mac-Kichan and Jerry Adams for *The Thorn Birds, Part One* (ABC)

1892 Outstanding Series Art Direction: John W. Corso, Frank Grieco, Jr. and Robert G. Freer for *Tales of the Gold Monkey* (ABC)

1893 Outstanding Variety or Music Program Art Direction: Ray Klausen and Michael Corenblith for *55th Annual Academy Awards Presentation* (ABC)

1894 Outstanding Series Technical Direction and Electronic Camerawork: Heino Ripp, Mike Bennett, Al Camoin, Jan Kasoff, John Pinto and Maurey Verschore for *Saturday Night Live* (NBC)

1895 Outstanding Limited Series or Special Technical Direction and Electronic Camerawork: Hank Geving for *Special Bulletin* (NBC)

1896 Outstanding Series Costume Design: Theodora Van Runkle for "Dungeon of Death" on *Wizards and Warriors* (CBS)

1897 Outstanding Limited Series or Special Costume Design: Phyllis Dalton for *The Scarlet Pimpernel* (CBS)

1898 Outstanding Individual Costumers Achievement: Tommy Welsh, Paul Vachon, Johannes Nilmark and

John Napolitana for "The Storm Breaks" on *The Winds of War* (ABC)

1899 Outstanding Make-Up: Del Acevedo for *The Thorn Birds* (ABC)

1900 Outstanding Hairstyling: Edie Panda for *Rosie: The Rosemary Clooney Story* (CBS)

1901 Outstanding Series Electronic Lighting Direction: Robert A. Dickinson and C. Frank Olivas for *Solid Gold* (syndicated)

1902 Outstanding Limited Series or Special Electronic Lighting Direction: John Rook, Ken Wilcox and Bob Pohle for *Sheena Easton ... Act 1* (ABC)

1903 Outstanding Series Music Composition: Bruce Broughton for "The Ewing Blues" on *Dallas* (CBS)

1904 Outstanding Limited Series or Special Music Composition: Billy Goldenberg for *Rage of Angels* (NBC)

1905 Outstanding Musical Direction: Dick Hyman for *Eubie Blake: A Century of Music* (PBS)

1906 Outstanding Music and Lyrics: James Di Pasquale and Dory Previn for "We'll Win This World" on *Two of a Kind* (CBS)

1907 Outstanding Graphic Design and Title Sequences: James Castle and Bruce Bryant for "Showdown" on *Cheers* (NBC)

1908 Outstanding Series Film Sound Editing: Sam Horta, Don Ernst, Avram Gold, Eileen Horta, Constance A. Kazmer and Gary Krivacek for "Stan the Man" on *Hill Street Blues* (NBC)

1909 Outstanding Limited Series or Special Film Sound Editing: James Troutman, Dave Caldwell, Paul Clay, Paul Laune, Tony Magro, Richard Raderman, Karen Rasch, Jeff Sandler, William Shenberg, Dan Thomas and Ascher Yates for *The Executioner's Song* (NBC)

1910 Outstanding Series Film Sound Mixing: William B. Marky, John B. Asman, William Nicholson and Ken S. Polk for "Trial by Fury" on *Hill Street Blues* (NBC)

1911 Outstanding Limited Series or Special Film Sound Mixing: John Mitchell, Gordon L. Day, Stanley A. Wetzel and Howard Wilmarth for *The Scarlet and the Black* (CBS)

1912 **Outstanding Series Tape Sound Mixing:** Frank Kulaga and Ken Hahn for "The Magic Flute" on *Dance in America* (PBS)

1913 **Outstanding Limited Series or Special Tape Sound Mixing:** Edward J. Greene, Ron Estes and Carroll Pratt for *Sheena Easton . . . Act 1* (NBC)

1914 **Outstanding Choreography:** Debbie Allen for "Class Act" on *Fame* (NBC)

1915/1916 **Outstanding Special Visual Effects:** Gene Warren, Jr., Michael Milner, Jackson De Govia, Peter Kleinow and Leslie Huntley for "Defiance" on *The Winds of War* (ABC)

1917 **Citation:** Ikegami Electronics and CBS for the engineering and development of the EC-35 Electronic Camera

1918 **Emmy:** Eastman Kodak Company for engineering development for high speed color film 5294/7294

1919 **Governor's Award:** Sylvester L. (Pat) Weaver, former NBC president who revolutionized network programming in the late 1940's and early 1950's

1920 **Citation:** Ampex Corporation for development of the ADO, a digital effects unit displaying unique capabilities with improved picture quality

1921 **Outstanding Daytime Drama Series:** *The Young and the Restless* (CBS)

1922 **Outstanding Children's Entertainment Series:** *Captain Kangaroo* (CBS), and *Smurfs* (NBC)

1923 **Outstanding Children's Informational/Instructional Series:** *Sesame Street* (PBS)

1924 **Outstanding Children's Entertainment Special:** "The Woman Who Willed a Miracle" on *ABC Afterschool Special* (ABC)

1925 **Outstanding Children's Informational/Instructional Special:** *Winners* (syndicated)

1926 **Outstanding Achievement in Series Religious Programming:** *Insight* (syndicated)

1927 **Outstanding Achievement in Special Religious Programming:** *The Juggler of Notre Dame* (syndicated), and *The Land of Fear, the Land of Courage* (NBC)

1928 **Outstanding Program Achievement in the Performing Arts:** *Hansel and Gretel: Live from the Met* (PBS), and *Zubin and the I.P.O.* (NBC)

1929 **Outstanding Achievement in Coverage of a Special Event:** *Macy's Thanksgiving Day Parade* (NBC)

1930 **Outstanding Short Form Instructional/Informational Program:** *In the News* (CBS)

1931 **Outstanding Program Achievement in a Special Classification:** *American Bandstand* (ABC)

1932 **Outstanding Talk/Service Series:** *This Old House* (PBS)

1933 **Outstanding Variety Series:** *The Merv Griffin Show* (syndicated)

1934 **Outstanding Game or Audience Participation Show:** *The $25,000 Pyramid* (CBS)

1935 **Outstanding Daytime Dramatic Actor:** Robert Woods in *One Life to Live* (ABC)

1936 **Outstanding Daytime Dramatic Actress:** Dorothy Lyman in *All My Children* (ABC)

1937 **Outstanding Daytime Supporting Dramatic Actor:** Darnell Williams in *All My Children* (ABC)

1938 **Outstanding Daytime Supporting Dramatic Actress:** Louise Shaffer in *Ryan's Hope* (ABC)

1939 **Outstanding Performer in Children's Programming:** Cloris Leachman in "The Woman Who Willed a Miracle" on *ABC Afterschool Special* (ABC)

1940 **Outstanding Individual Achievement in Religious Programming:** Lois Nettleton in "A Gun for Mandy" on *Insight* (syndicated), and Edwin Newman, moderator in *Kids, Drugs and Alcohol* (NBC)

1941 **Outstanding Host or Hostess in a Variety Series:** Leslie Uggams in *Fantasy* (NBC)

1942 **Outstanding Host or Hostess in a Talk or Service Program:** Phil Donahue in *Donahue* (syndicated)

1943 **Outstanding Host or Hostess in a Game or Audience Participation Show:** Betty White in *Just Men!* (NBC)

1944 **Outstanding Individual Achievement in Performing Arts:** Zubin Mehta, conductor in *Zubin and the I.P.O.* (NBC)

1945 **Outstanding Individual Achieve-**

ment in a Special Classification: Hal Linden, host in *FYI* (ABC)

1946 Outstanding Daytime Drama Direction: Allen Fristoe, Norman Hall, Peter Miner and David Pressman for *One Life to Live* (ABC)

1947 Outstanding Children's Programming Directing: Sharon Miller for "The Woman Who Willed a Miracle" on *ABC Afterschool Special* (ABC)

1948 Outstanding Episode Direction for a Variety Series: Dick Carson for the September 17 program of *The Merv Griffin Show* (syndicated)

1949 Outstanding Episode Direction for a Talk/Service Series: Glen Swanson for November 10 program of *Hour Magazine* (syndicated)

1950 Outstanding Episode Direction for a Game or Audience Participation Show: Mark Breslow for the December 30 program of *The Price Is Right* (CBS)

1951 Outstanding Daytime Drama Series Writing: Claire Labine, Paul Avila Mayer, Mary Ryan Munisteri, Eugene Price, Judith Pinsker, Nancy Ford, B.K. Perlman, Rory Metcalf and Trent Jones for *Ryan's Hope* (ABC)

1952 Outstanding Writing for Children's Programming: Arthur Heinemann for "The Woman Who Willed a Miracle" on *ABC Afterschool Special* (ABC)

1953 Trustees' Award: Robert E. Short, daytime programmer for Proctor and Gamble

1954 Outstanding Daytime Drama Design Excellence: Sid Ramin, Teri Smith, Robert Chui, Richard Greene, Scott Hersh, Sylvia Lawrence, Carol Luiken, Robert Griffin, Donald Gavitt, Donna Larson, William Itkin and William Mickley for *All My Children* (ABC)

1955 Outstanding Daytime Drama Technical Excellence: Howard Zweig, Henry Enrico Ferro, Diana Wenman, Jean Dadario, Lawrence Hammond, Robert Ambrico, Trevor Thompson, Vincent Senatore, Robert Bellairs, Thomas French and Richard Westlein for *All My Children* (ABC)

1956 Outstanding Children's Music: Elliott Lawrence for "Sometimes I Don't Like My Mother" on *ABC Afterschool Special* (ABC)

1957 Outstanding Children's Cinematography: Terry Meade for "The Shooting" on *CBS Afternoon Playhouse* (CBS)

1958 Outstanding Children's Film Editing: Scott McKinsey for "The Shooting" on *CBS Afternoon Playhouse* (CBS)

1959 Outstanding Daytime Special Event Technical Direction/Electronic Camerawork: Eric Eisenstein, Terry Rohnke, Carl Eckert, Mike Bennett, Barry Frischer, Bill Boetz, Steve Gonzalez, Dave Hagen, John Hillyer, Gene Martin, Don Mulvaney and John Pinto for *Macy's Thanksgiving Day Parade* (NBC)

1960 Outstanding Children's Associate Director/Videotape Editing: Ilie Agopian for *Young People's Specials* (syndicated)

1961 Outstanding Achievement in a Daytime Technical Craft: Robert Ryan, Les Brown and Jack Urbont for *Lorne Greene's New Wilderness* (syndicated); Victor Di Napoli and Gerri Brioso for *Sesame Street* (PBS); Jay David Saks for *Hansel and Gretel: Live from the Met* (PBS); John N. Castaldo for *Donahue* (syndicated); and Nicholas Hutak for "Franconia Notch" on *The Guiding Light* (CBS)

1962 Outstanding Religious Film Editing: Scott McKinsey for *Insight* (syndicated), and Ed Williams for *The Land of Fear, the Land of Courage* (NBC)

1963 Outstanding Live Sports Series: *NFL Football* (CBS)

1964 Outstanding Edited Sports Series: *The American Sportsman* (ABC)

1965 Outstanding Live Sports Special: *NCAA Basketball Championship Final* (CBS)

1966 Outstanding Edited Sports Special: *Indianapolis 500* (ABC)

1967 Outstanding Sports Personality/Analyst: John Madden

1968 Outstanding Sports Personality/Host: Jim McKay

1969 Outstanding Breaking News Program: "Disaster on the Potomac" on *ABC World News Tonight* (ABC)

1970 Outstanding Breaking News Segment: "Personal Note/Beirut" on *ABC World News Tonight* (ABC); "New Mexico's Yates Oil Company" on *CBS Evening News with Dan Rather* (CBS); and "Linda Down's Marathon" on *World News This Morning* (ABC)

1971 Outstanding Current News Analysis Program: *Chrysler: Once Upon a Time ... And Now* (PBS); *From the Ashes ... Nicaragua Today* (PBS); and "Guatemala" on *CBS Reports* (CBS)

1972 Outstanding Current News Analysis Segment: "Tanks" on *A Few Minutes with Andy Rooney* (CBS), and "Welcome to Palermo" on *60 Minutes* (CBS)

1973 Outstanding Investigative Program: *Frank Terpil: Confessions of a Dangerous Man* (PBS)

1974 Outstanding Investigative Segments: "Air Force Surgeon" and "The Nazi Connection" on *60 Minutes* (CBS)

1975 Outstanding Interview/Interviewers Program: Ted Koppel and Bob Jordan for "The Palestinian Viewpoint" on *Nightline* (ABC), and Barbara Walters and Beth Polson for *The Barbara Walters Special* (ABC)

1976 Outstanding Interview/Interviewers Segment: Ed Bradley and Monika Jensen for "In the Belly of the Beast" on *60 Minutes* (CBS)

1977 Outstanding Continuing News Story Program: Howard Husock and Scott Simon for *The Peterson Project* (PBS)

1978 Outstanding Continuing News Story Segment: Rita Braver, David Browning, Quentin Neufeld, Terry Martin, David Gelber, Bruce Morton, Jerry Bowen, Ed Rabel, Terry Drinkwater and Ray Brady for "Coverage of American Unemployment" on *CBS Evening News with Dan Rather* (CBS)

1979 Outstanding Informational, Cultural or Historical Program: James M. Messenger and Stuart Sillery for *The Taj Mahal* (PBS), and Andrew McGuire for *Here's Looking at You, Kid* (PBS)

1980 Outstanding Informational, Cultural or Historical Segment: Dick Schaap and Betsy Osha for "Sid Caesar" on *20/20* (ABC); Brett Alexander and Billy Taylor for "Eclectic: A Profile of Quincy" on *Sunday Morning* (CBS); and Jeanne Solomon and Ed Bradley for "Lena" on *60 Minutes* (CBS)

1981 Outstanding Special Classification Program Achievement: *Vietnam Requiem* (ABC)

1982 Outstanding Special Classification Segment Achievement: "It Didn't Have to Happen" on *60 Minutes* (CBS)

1983 Outstanding News Writing Individual Achievement: Sharon Blair Brysac and Perry Wolff for *Juilliard and Beyond: A Life in Music* (CBS), Charles Kuralt for "Cicada Invasion" on *CBS Evening News with Dan Rather* (CBS)

1984 Outstanding News Direction Individual Achievement: Jonas McCord and William Couturie for *Vietnam Requiem* (ABC), and Bill Jersey for *Children of Violence* (PBS)

1985 Outstanding News Camerawork Individual Achievement: James Deckard and James Lipscomb for "Polar Bear Alert" on *National Geographic Special* (PBS); Norris Brock for "Egypt: Quest for Eternity" on *National Geographic Special* (PBS); Arnie Serlin for *The Taj Mahal* (PBS); and Bill Bacon for *Alaska: Story of a Dream* (syndicated)

1986 Outstanding News Electronic Videographers: David Green for "Guerillas in Usulatan" on *CBS Evening News with Dan Rather* (CBS), and George Fredrick for *Along Route 30* (NBC)

1987 Outstanding News Sound Individual Achievement: Larry Loewinger, Francis Daniel, Michael Lonsdale, Peter Miller and David Moshlak for *Juilliard and Beyond: A Life in Music* (CBS); Tim Cohen for *The Campaign* (PBS); and Simon Jones, Mike Lonsdale, Kim Ornitz and David Moshlak for *FDR* (ABC)

1988 Outstanding News Associate Directors Individual Achievement: Consuelo Gonzalez and Neill Phillipson for *FDR* (ABC)

1989 Outstanding News Videotape Editors Individual Achievement: Cathy Black, Catherine Isabella, Dean Irwin, Carla Morgenstern, Edward Bude, Ruth Iwano, Chris Von Benge and Mike Seigal for *FDR* (ABC); Anthony Ciccimarro, Kathy Hardigan, Don Orrico and Matty Powers for *The Man Who Shot the Pope: A Study in Terrorism* (NBC); and Thomas Micklas for "Ice Sculptor" on *CBS Evening News with Dan Rather* (CBS)

1990 Outstanding News Film Editors Individual Achievement: James Flanagan,

Nils Rassmussen, William Longo and Walter Essenfeld for *FDR* (ABC); Nobuko Oganesoff for *Juilliard and Beyond: A Life in Music* (CBS); and Bob Brady for *The Campaign* (PBS)
1991 Outstanding News Graphic Designers Individual Achievement: Rebecca Allen for *Walter Cronkite's Universe* (CBS), and David Millman for "The Cuban Missile Crisis" on *Nightline* (ABC)
1992 Outstanding News Music Composition Individual Achievement: James G. Pirie for *Alaska: Story of a Dream* (syndicated)
1993 Community Service Award: WCCO-TV, Minneapolis, Minnesota, for *Sexual Abuse of Children*
1994 International Documentary: Radio Telefis Eireann, Ireland for *Is There One Who Understands Me? – The World of James Joyce*
1995 International Drama: Thames Television, United Kingdom for *A Voyage Round My Father*
1996 International Performing Arts: Grenada Television Ltd., United Kingdom for *A Lot of Happiness*
1997 Outstanding Popular Arts: TV Globo, Brazil for *Death and Life Severinian*

————— **1 9 8 3** —————

1998 Outstanding Drama Series: *Hill Street Blues* (NBC)
1999 Outstanding Drama/Comedy Special: "Something About Amelia" on *An ABC Theatre Presentation* (ABC)
2000 Outstanding Comedy Series: *Cheers* (NBC)
2001 Outstanding Limited Series: "Concealed Enemies" on *American Playhouse* (PBS)
2002 Outstanding Animated Program: *Garfield on the Town* (CBS)
2003 Outstanding Variety/Music or Comedy Program: *The 6th Annual Kennedy Center Honors: A Celebration of the Performing Arts* (CBS)
2004 Outstanding Children's Program: *He Makes Me Feel Like Dancin'* (NBC)
2005 Outstanding Classical Program in the Performing Arts: "Placido Domingo

Celebrates Seville" on *Great Performances* (PBS)
2006 Outstanding Informational Special: *America Remembers John F. Kennedy* (syndicated)
2007 Outstanding Informational Series: *A Walk Through the 20th Century with Bill Moyers* (PBS)
2008 Outstanding Lead Actress in a Limited Series or a Special: Jane Fonda in "The Dollmaker" on *An ABC Theatre Presentation* (ABC)
2009 Outstanding Lead Actor in a Limited Series or a Special: Laurence Olivier in *King Lear* (syndicated)
2010 Outstanding Lead Actress in a Dramatic Series: Tyne Daly in *Cagney & Lacey* (CBS)
2011 Outstanding Lead Actor in a Dramatic Series: Tom Selleck in *Magnum, P.I.* (CBS)
2012 Outstanding Lead Actress in a Comedy Series: Jane Curtin in *Kate & Allie* (CBS)
2013 Outstanding Lead Actor in a Comedy Series: John Ritter in *Three's Company* (ABC)
2014 Outstanding Supporting Actor in a Comedy Series: Pat Harrington, Jr., in *One Day at a Time* (CBS)
2015 Outstanding Supporting Actor in a Limited Series or Special: Art Carney in "Terrible Joe Moran" on *An ITT Theatre Special* (CBS)
2016 Outstanding Supporting Actress in a Limited Series or Special: Roxana Zal in "Something About Amelia" on *An ABC Theatre Presentation* (ABC)
2017 Outstanding Supporting Dramatic Actress: Alfre Woodard in "Doris in Wonderland" on *Hill Street Blues* (NBC)
2018 Outstanding Supporting Dramatic Actor: Bruce Weitz in *Hill Street Blues* (NBC)
2019 Outstanding Supporting Actress in a Comedy Series: Rhea Perlman in *Cheers* (NBC)
2020 Outstanding Individual Performance in a Variety or Music Program: Cloris Leachman in *Screen Actors Guild 50th Anniversary Celebration* (CBS)
2021 Outstanding Limited Series or Special Direction: Jeff Bleckner for "Concealed Enemies" on *American Playhouse* (PBS)

2022 Outstanding Drama Series Directing: Corey Allen for "Goodbye, Mr. Scripps" on *Hill Street Blues* (NBC)

2023 Outstanding Comedy Series Directing: Bill Persky for "A Very Loud Family" on *Kate & Allie* (CBS)

2024 Outstanding Variety or Music Program Directing: Dwight Hemion for *Here's Television Entertainment* (NBC)

2025 Outstanding Series Film Editing: Andrew Chulack for "Old Flames" on *Cheers* (NBC)

2026 Outstanding Limited Series or Special Film Editing: Jerrold L. Ludwig for "A Streetcar Named Desire" on *An ABC Theatre Presentation* (ABC)

2027 Outstanding Series Videotape Editing: Howard Brock for "Gonna Learn How to Fly" on *Fame* (syndicated)

2028 Outstanding Limited Series or Special Videotape Editing: Jim McQueen and Catherine Shields for *American Film Institute Salute to Lillian Gish* (CBS)

2029 Outstanding Series Film Sound Editing: Sam Shaw, Michael Ford, Donlee Jorgensen, Mark Roberts, Breck Warwick, Bob Weatherford, Michael Wilhoit, Nicholas Korda and Gene Gillette for *Airwolf* (CBS)

2030 Outstanding Limited Series or Special Film Sound Editing: Christopher T. Welch, Brian Courcier, Greg Dillon, David R. Elliott, Michael Hilkene, Fred Judkins, Carl Mahakian, Joseph Mayer, Joseph Melody, Catherine Shorr, Richard Shorr, Jill Taggart and Roy Prendergast for "The Day After" on *An ABC Theatre Presentation* (ABC)

2031 Outstanding Series Film Sound Mixing: John B. Asman, David Schneiderman, William M. Nicholson and Ken S. Polk for "Parting Is Such Sweep Sorrow" on *Hill Street Blues* (NBC)

2032 Outstanding Limited Series or Special Film Sound Mixing: Richard Raguse, William L. McCaughey, Mel Metcalfe and Terry Porter for "A Streetcar Named Desire" on *An ABC Theatre Presentation* (ABC)

2033 Outstanding Limited Series or Special Writing: William Hanley for "Something About Amelia" on *An ABC Theatre Presentation* (ABC)

2034 Outstanding Drama Series Writing: Tom Fontana, John Masius and John Ford Noonan for "The Women" on *St. Elsewhere* (NBC)

2035 Outstanding Comedy Series Writing: David Angell for "Old Flames" on *Cheers* (NBC)

2036 Outstanding Variety or Music Program Writing: Steve O'Donnell, Gerard Mulligan, Sanford Frank, Joseph E. Toplyn, Christopher Elliott, Matt Wickline, Jeff Martin, Ted Greenberg, David Yazbek, Merrill Markoe and David Letterman for "Show Number 312" on *Late Night with David Letterman* (NBC)

2037 Outstanding Limited Series or Special Cinematography: Bill Butler for "A Streetcar Named Desire" on *An ABC Theatre Presentation* (ABC)

2038 Outstanding Series Cinematography: James Crabe for "More Than Murder" on *Mickey Spillane's Mike Hammer* (CBS)

2039 Outstanding Series Technical Direction/Camerawork: Gene Crowe, Sam Drummy, Larry Heider, Dave Levisohn, Wayne Orr, Ron Sheldon and Mark Sanford for *On Stage America, Number Five* (syndicated)

2040 Outstanding Limited Series or Special Technical Direction/Camerawork: Lou Fusari, Les Atkinson, Bruce Bottone, George Falardeau, Dean Hall, Dave Hilmer, Roy Holm, David Nowell and Jerry R. Smith for *The Magic of David Copperfield VI* (CBS)

2041 Outstanding Special Visual Effects: William M. Klages for *The 26th Annual Grammy Awards* (CBS), and Robert Blalack, Nancy Rushlow, Dan Pinkham, Chris Regan, Larry Stevens, Dan Nosenchuck and Chris Dierdorff for "The Day After" (ABC)

2042 Outstanding Graphic Design and Title Sequence: Ted Woolery and Gerry Woolery for "Filling Buddy's Shoes" on *The Duck Factory* (NBC)

2043 Outstanding Individual Achievement in Animated Programming: R.O. Blechman for *The Soldier's Tale* (PBS)

2044 Outstanding Individual Achievement in Informational Programming: Emile Ardolino for *He Makes Me Feel Like Dancin'* (NBC), and Bill Moyers for *Marshall, Texas* (PBS)

2045 Outstanding Series Art Direction: James Hulsey and Bruce Kay for *The Duck Factory* (NBC)

2046 Outstanding Limited Series or Special Art Direction: James Hulsey and George R. Nelson for "A Streetcar Named Desire" on *An ABC Theatre Presentation* (ABC)

2047 Outstanding Variety or Music Program Art Direction: Roy Christopher for *56th Annual Academy Awards* (ABC)

2048 Outstanding Series Lighting Direction: Robert A. Dickinson and C. Frank Olivas for *Solid Gold* (syndicated)

2049 Outstanding Limited Series or Special Art Direction: William M. Klages for *The 6th Annual Kennedy Center Honors: A Celebration of the Performing Arts* (CBS)

2050 Outstanding Choreography: Michael Smuin for "A Song for Dead Warriors" on *Dance in America* (PBS)

2051 Outstanding Music Direction: Ian Fraser, Billy Byers, Chris Boardman, J. Hill and Lenny Stack for *The Screen Actors Guild 50th Anniversary Celebration* (CBS)

2052 Outstanding Series Music Composition: Bruce Broughton for "The Letter" on *Dallas* (CBS)

2053 Outstanding Limited Series or Special Music Composition: Bruce Broughton for *The First Olympics — Athens 1896, Part One* (NBC)

2054 Outstanding Music and Lyrics: Larry Grossman and Buz Kohan for "Gone Too Soon" from *Here's Television Entertainment* (NBC)

2055 Outstanding Limited Series or Special Live and Tape Sound Mixing: Edward J. Greene and Carroll Pratt for *Anne Murray's Winter Carnival . . . From Quebec* (CBS)

2056 Outstanding Series Live and Tape Sound Mixing: Mark Hanes, Stu Fox, Dean Okrand and Ed Suski for "The Hawaii Show — Sarah's Wedding" on *Real People* (NBC)

2057 Outstanding Series Costume Design: Bob Mackie and Ret Turner for "Mama's Birthday" on *Mama's Family* (NBC)

2058 Outstanding Limited Series or Special Costume Design: Julie Weiss for "The Dollmaker" on *An ABC Theatre Presentation* (ABC)

2059 Outstanding Make-Up: Michael Westmore for *Why Me?* (ABC)

2060 Outstanding Hairstyling: Dino Ganziano for *The Mystic Warrior* (ABC)

2061 Outstanding Individual Achievement in Classical Music/Dance Programming: Merrill Brockway for "A Song for Dead Warriors" on *Dance in America* (PBS); James Levine for "Centennial Gala, Part Two" on *Live from the Met* (PBS); and Leontyne Price for *In Performance at the White House — An Evening of Spirituals and Gospel Music* (PBS)

2062 Governor's Award: Bob Hope

2063 Special Award: David L. Wolper for the ceremonies at the Olympics

2064 Outstanding Achievement in Engineering Development: Corporate Communications Consultants, Inc., for the 60XL Color Correction System

2065 Outstanding Edited Sports Special: *Wimbledon '83* (NBC)

2066 Outstanding Sports Associate Directing: Angelo Bernarducci and Jean MacLean for "Triumph on Mt. Everest" on *The American Sportsman* (ABC)

2067 Outstanding Sports Graphic Designers: Douglas E. Towey and Bill Feigenbaum for *NBA World Championship Series* (CBS)

2068 Outstanding Sports Special Classification, Journalism: Michael Marley, Ed Silverman, Howard Cosell, Maury Rubin, Noubar Stone and Rob Beiner for *ABC Sportsbeat* (ABC)

2069 Outstanding Sports Special Classification, Music: John Tresh for *World University Games* (CBS)

2070 Outstanding Edited Sports Series: *The American Sportsman* (ABC)

2071 Outstanding Sports Special Classification, Film Editor: Yale Nelson for *The 79th World Series* (NBC)

2072 Outstanding Sports Special Classification, Writing: Steve Sabol and Phil Tuckett for *Wake Up the Echoes: The History of Notre Dame Football* (Independent), and George Bell, Jr., for "A Retrospective of William Holden's Africa" on *The American Sportsman* (ABC)

2073 Outstanding Sports Personality, Analyst: John Madden

2074 **Outstanding Sports Engineering/Technical Supervisors:** Walter Pile and John Pumo for *Daytona 500* (CBS)

2075 **Outstanding Live Sports Series:** *CBS Sports Presents the National Football League* (CBS)

2076 **Outstanding Sports Lighting Director:** Joe Crookham for *NCAA Football on CBS* (CBS)

2077 **Outstanding Sports Cinematographers:** Peter Henning and Bill Philbin for *The Iditarod Dog Sled Race* (CBS), and Kurt Diemburger and David Breshears for "The Mt. Everest East Face" on *The American Sportsman* (ABC)

2078 **Outstanding Sports Program Special Achievement:** Roone Arledge, Dennis Lewin, Larry Kamm and Peter Lasser for "Great American Bike Race" on *ABC's Wide World of Sports* (ABC); John Wilcox for "Triumph on Mt. Everest" on *The American Sportsman* (ABC); and Robert Carmichael for *Football in America* (PBS)

2079 **Outstanding Sports Videotape Editors:** Mike Kostel, Rick Reed, Rich Domich and John Servideo for *NBC Baseball Pre-Game/Major League Baseball: An Inside Look* (NBC); Bob Hickson, George Joanitis and Lito Magpayo for *Closing Segment—NCAA Basketball Championship Game* (CBS); and Sandy Bell, Bob Brown, Anthony Filippi, Bob Siderman, Tom Jimenez, Robert Pieringer, Tom Delilla, Bill Berridge, Donald S. Resch, Jim Murphy, Neil McCaffrey, Tom McCarthy, Herman Lang, Barry Drago, Joe Sokota, Jim McCarthy, Jeff Pollack, Frank McSpedon, George Rothweiler, Ray Christe, George Naeder, George Graffeo, Hans Singer, Sig Meyers and Walt Soucy for *Daytona 500* (CBS)

2080 **Outstanding Live Sports Special:** *The 79th World Series* (NBC)

2081 **Outstanding Sports Personality, Host:** Dick Enberg

2082 **Outstanding International Drama:** Granada Television Limited, United Kingdom for *King Lear*

2083 **Outstanding International Documentary:** Swedish Television, Sweden for *The Miracle of Life*

2084 **Outstanding International Popular Arts:** British Broadcasting System, United Kingdom for *The Black Adder: The Archbishop*

2085 **International Children's Programming:** Canadian Broadcasting Corporation, Canada for *Fraggle Rock*

———————— **1 9 8 4** ————————

2086 **Outstanding Drama Series:** *Cagney & Lacey* (CBS)

2087 **Outstanding Comedy Series:** *The Cosby Show* (NBC)

2088 **Outstanding Lead Actor in a Drama Series:** William Daniels in *St. Elsewhere* (NBC)

2089 **Outstanding Lead Actress in a Drama Series:** Tyne Daly in *Cagney & Lacey* (CBS)

2090 **Outstanding Lead Actor in a Comedy Series:** Robert Guillaume in *Benson* (ABC)

2091 **Outstanding Lead Actress in a Comedy Series:** Jane Curtin in *Kate & Allie* (CBS)

2092 **Outstanding Supporting Actor in a Drama Series:** Edward James Olmos in *Miami Vice* (NBC)

2093 **Outstanding Supporting Actress in a Drama Series:** Betty Thomas in *Hill Street Blues* (NBC)

2094 **Outstanding Supporting Actor in a Comedy Series:** John Larroquette in *Night Court* (NBC)

2095 **Outstanding Supporting Actress in a Comedy Series:** Rhea Perlman in *Cheers* (NBC)

2096 **Outstanding Writing in a Drama Series:** Patricia Green for *Cagney & Lacey* episode "Who Said It's Fair?, Part II" (CBS)

2097 **Outstanding Writing in a Comedy Series:** Ed Weinberger and Michael Leeson for the premier episode of *The Cosby Show* (NBC)

2098 **Outstanding Directing in a Drama Series:** Karen Arthur for *Cagney & Lacey* episode "Heat" (CBS)

2099 **Outstanding Directing in a Variety or Music Program:** Terry Hughes for "Sweeny Todd" on *Great Performances* (PBS)

2100 **Outstanding Classical Program in the Performing Arts:** *Tosca, Live from*

the Met producer Samuel J. Paul, executive producer Michael Bronson (PBS)
2101 Outstanding Live and Tape Sound Mixing and Sound Effects for a Series: Douglas Gray, pre-production; Michael Ballin, production; Thomas Huth, post-production; Sam Black, sound effects for *Cheers* episode "The Executive's Executioner" (NBC)
2102 Outstanding Cinematography for a Series: Robert E. Collins for the pilot of *Miami Vice* (NBC)
2103 Outstanding Film Sound Mixing for a Limited Series or Special: Clark David King, production; David J. Hudson, Mel Metcalfe, Terry Porter, CAS, re-recording for *Space Part 5* (CBS)
2104 Outstanding Art Direction for a Variety or Music Program: Rene Lagler, production designer; Jeremy Railton, art director for *The 57th Annual Academy Awards* (ABC)
2105 Outstanding Achievement in Make-Up: Michael G. Westmore; special makeup designed and created by Bob Norin, makeup supervisor; Jamie Brown, Sandy Cooper, makeup artists for *The Three Wishes of Billy Grier* (ABC)
2106 Outstanding Film Sound Editing for a Limited Series or Special: Jeff Clark, supervisor; Paul Carden, Nick Eliopoulos, Jim Koford, Don Malouf, Dick Raderman, Greg Stacy, Dan Thomas, James Troutman, Mike Virnig, editors; Tally Paulos, ADR; John Lasalandra, music for *Wallenberg: A Hero's Story* (NBC)
2107 Outstanding Children's Program: *American Playhouse* episode "Displaced Person" (PBS)
2108 Outstanding Achievement in Music Direction: Ian Fraser, music director; Ian Fraser, Bill Byers, Angela Morley, principal arrangers for *Christmas in Washington* (NBC)
2109 Outstanding Film Sound Mixing for a Series: Maury Harris, production; John B. Asman, William Nicholson, Ken S. Polk, CAS, re-recording for *Cagney & Lacey* episode "Heat" (CBS)
2110 Outstanding Costume Design for a Limited Series or a Special: Barbara Lane for *Ellis Island, Part 1* (PBS)

2111 Outstanding Film Editing for a Series: Jim Gross for *Cagney & Lacey* episode "Who Said It's Fair?, Part II" (CBS)
2112 Outstanding Art Direction for a Series: Jeffrey Howard, art director; Robert Lacey, Jr., set decorator for *Miami Vice* episode "No Exit" (NBC)
2113 Outstanding Individual Achievement for Directing Classical Music/Dance Programming: Don Mischer and Twyla Tharp for *Dance in America* episode "Baryshnikov by Tharp with American Ballet Theatre" (PBS) and Franco Zeffirelli for *Great Performances* episode "I Pagliacci" (PBS)
2114 Outstanding Individual Achievement for Performing Classical Music/Dance Programming: Luciano Pavarotti for *Great Performances* episode "Duke of Mantus: Rigoletto" (PBS)
2115 Outstanding Individual Achievement for Writing Informational Programming: Howard Enders, John G. Fox, Michael Joseloff, Marc Siegel for *Heritage: Civilization and the Jews* episode "The Crucible of Europe" (PBS) and Brian Winston for *Heritage: Civilization and the Jews* episode "Out of the Ashes" (PBS)
2116 Outstanding Videotape Editing for a Limited Series or Special: Jimmy B. Frazier, editor for *Great Performances* episode "Sweeny Todd" (PBS)
2117 Outstanding Achievement in Engineering Development: Ron and Richard Grant for the development of the Auricle Time Processor, a computer system that enables the music composer to score a program with speed and accuracy previously unattainable.
2118 Outstanding Videotape Editing for a Series: Jim McElroy for *Fame* episode "Reflections" (syndicated)
2119 Outstanding Special Visual Effects: Albert Whitlock, special effects supervisor and matte artist; Syd Dutton, matte artist; Bill Taylor, matte photography; Dennis Glouner, matte photography; Lynn Ledgerwood, *Special Rigging, A.D.* (NBC); John Allison, director, designer and supervisor for *The Brain* (5-part series) (PBS); Michael Pangrazio, visual effects supervisor; Dennis Muren, post-production effects supervisor;

Phil Tippett, stop-motion supervisor; John Berg, creative supervisor; Harley Jessup, art director; John Ellis, optical photography supervisor; Chris Evans, matte painting supervisor for *The Ewok Adventure* (ABC); Bill Mesa, introvision visual effects director and director of photography; Mike Hanan, introvision art director; Tim Donahue, introvision stage-matte artist; Gene Rizzardi, model shop supervisor for *The Huggs Bunch* (syndicated)

2120 Outstanding Achievement in Music Composition for a Limited Series or Special (Dramatic Underscore): Allyn Ferguson, "Camille" for *Hallmark Hall of Fame* (CBS)

2121 Outstanding Informational Series: *The Living Planet: A Portrait of Earth* executive producer Richard Brack, producers Adrian Warren, Ned Kelly, Andrew Neal, Richard Brock (PBS)

2122 Outstanding Achievement in Choreography: Twyla Tharp for *Dance in America* "Baryshnikov by Tharp with the American Ballet Theatre" (PBS)

2123 Outstanding Achievement in Costuming: USA costume supervisor Tommy Welsh, USA costumer Bob E. Horn, Yugoslavian costumer Marko Cerovec for *Wallenberg: A Hero's Story* (NBC)

2124 Outstanding Achievement in Music and Lyrics: composer James D. Pasquale, lyricist Douglas Brayfield for *Love Lives On* (ABC)

2125 Outstanding Cinematography for a Limited Series or a Special: Philip Lathrop, ASC for *Malice in Wonderland* (CBS)

2126 Outstanding Achievement in Hairstyling: Robert L. Stevenson for *The Jesse Owens Story* (OPT)

2127 Outstanding Achievement in Music Composition for a Series (Dramatic Underscore): John Addison for *Murder, She Wrote* episode "The Murder of Sherlock Holmes" (CBS)

2128 Outstanding Art Direction for a Limited Series or a Special: production designer Jan Scott; art directors Charles C. Bennett, David Davis; set decorators Robert Lee Drumheller, Jacques Bradette for *Evergreen, Part I* (NBC)

2129 Outstanding Technical Direction/Electronic Camera/Video Control for a Limited Series or a Special: technical director Louis Fusari; camerapersons Les Atkinson, Jim Herring, Mike Higuera, Roy Holm, Dave Levisohn, Dana Martin, Mike Straminsky; senior video control Jerry Smith for *The Magic of David Copperfield VII* (CBS)

2130 Outstanding Electronic Lighting Direction for a Limited Series or Special: Bill Klages, Arnie Smith for *Dance in America* "Baryshnikov by Tharp with the American Ballet Theatre" (PBS)

2131 Outstanding Live and Tape Sound Mixing and Sound Effects for a Limited Series or Special: pre-production Robert Liftin; production Edward J. Greene; post-production Russ Terrana; sound effects Carroll Pratt for *Motown Returns to the Apollo* (NBC)

2132 Outstanding Technical Direction/Electronic Camerawork/Video Control for a Series: technical director Herm Falk; camerapersons Randall Baer, Stephen Jones, Bill McCloud, Donna Quante; senior video control Victor Bagdadi for *Benson* "Home for Christmas" (ABC)

2133 Outstanding Writing in a Variety or Music Program: Gerard Mulligan, Sandy Frank, Joe Toplyn, Chris Elliott, Matt Wickline, Jeff Martin, Kevin Curran, Eddie Gorodetsky, Randy Cohen, Larry Jacobson, Fred Graver, Merrill Markoe, David Letterman for *Late Night with David Letterman* episode "Christmas with the Lettermans" (NBC)

2134 Outstanding Individual Performance in a Variety or Music Program: George Hearn in *Great Performances* episode "Sweeny Todd" (PBS)

2135 Outstanding Variety, Music or Comedy Program: *Motown Returns to the Apollo* produced by Don Mischer; executive producer Suzanne de Passe; co-producers Suzanne Coston, Michael L. Weisbarth (NBC)

2136 Outstanding Animated Program: *Garfield in the Rough* executive producer Jay Poynor, producer/director Phil Roman, writer Jim Davis (CBS)

2137 Outstanding Writing in a Limited Series or Special: Vickie Patik for *Do You Remember Love* (CBS)

2138 Outstanding Directing in a Limited Series or Special: Lamont Johnson for *Wallenberg: A Hero's Story* (NBC)

2139 Outstanding Supporting Actor in a Limited Series or a Special: Karl Malden in *Fatal Vision* (NBC)

2140 Outstanding Supporting Actress in a Limited Series or a Special: Kim Stanley in *American Playhouse* episode "Cat on a Hot Tin Roof" (PBS)

2141 Outstanding Lead Actor in a Limited Series or a Special: Richard Crenna in *An ABC Theatre Presentation* segment "The Rape of Richard Beck" (ABC)

2142 Outstanding Lead Actress in a Limited Series or a Special: Joanne Woodward in *Do You Remember Love* (CBS)

2143 Outstanding Limited Series: *Masterpiece Theatre* series "The Jewel in the Crown" executive producer Denis Forman; producer Christopher Morahan (PBS)

2144 Outstanding Costume Design for a Series: Travilla for *Dallas* episode "Swan Song" (CBS)

2145 Outstanding Direction in a Comedy Series: Jay Sandrich for *The Cosby Show* episode "The Younger Woman" (NBC)

2146 Outstanding Drama/Comedy Special: *Do You Remember Love* executive producer Dave Bell; co-executive producer Marilyn Hall; producers Wayne Threm, James E. Thompson; co-producer Walter Halsey (CBS)

2147 Outstanding Film Editing for a Limited Series or a Special: Paul F. LaMastra, ACE for *Wallenberg: A Hero's Story* (NBC)

2148 Outstanding Film Sound Editing for a Series: supervisor Chuck Moran; editors Bruce Bell, Victor B. Lackey, Ian MacGregor-Scott, Carl Mahakian, John Oettinger, Bernie Pincus, Warren Smith, Bruce Stambler, Mike Wilhoit, Kyle Wright; music Paul Weittenberg, ADR, Jerry Sanford Cohen for the pilot of *Miami Vice* (NBC)

2149 Outstanding Graphic and Title Design: graphic designer John Tribe for *Agatha Christie's "Partners in Crime"* (PBS); title sequence creators Alex Weil,

Charles Levi for *Saturday Night Live* (NBC); title designers Rocky Morton, Annabel Jankel; executive producer Dick Ebersol for *Friday Night Videos* (NBC)

2150 Outstanding Information Special: *Cousteau: Mississippi* executive producers Jacques-Yves Cousteau, Jean-Michael Cousteau; producer Andrew Salt; host Jacques-Yves Cousteau (syndicated)

2151 Special Recognition: The National Endowment for the Arts

2152 Eighth Annual ATAS Governor's Award: Alistair Cooke

2153 Outstanding Host in a Daytime Game Show: Dick Clark in *The $25,000 Pyramid* (CBS)

2154 Outstanding Directing in a Daytime Game Show: Mark Breslow for *The Price Is Right* (CBS)

2155 Outstanding Daytime Drama Series: *The Young and the Restless* executive producers H. Wesley Kenney, William J. Bell; producer Edward Scott (CBS)

2156 Outstanding Actor in a Daytime Series: Darnell Williams in *All My Children* (ABC)

2157 Outstanding Actress in a Daytime Series: Kim Zimmer in *Guiding Light* (CBS)

2158 Outstanding Actor in a Supporting Role in a Daytime Series: Larry Gates in *Guiding Light* (CBS)

2159 Outstanding Actress in a Supporting Role in a Daytime Drama Series: Beth Maitland in *The Young and the Restless* (CBS)

2160 Outstanding Host or Hostess in a Talk or Service Series: Phil Donahue in *Donahue* (syndicated)

2161 Outstanding Writing in a Daytime Children's Special: Charles Purpura for *CBS Schoolbreak Special* episode "The Day the Senior Class Got Married" (CBS)

2162 Outstanding Directing in a Talk/ Service Show: Dick Carson for *The Merv Griffin Show* (syndicated)

2163 Outstanding Daytime Film Sound Mixing: re-recording mixers Charles "Bud" Grenzbach, Hoppy Mehterian for *Pole Position* (CBS)

2164 Outstanding Daytime Graphics and Title Design: Phil Norman for *Santa Barbara* (NBC)

2165 **Outstanding Writing in a Daytime Drama Series:** Agnes Nixon, Lorraine Broderick, Victor Miller, Art Wallace, Jack Wood, Mary K. Wells, Clarice Blackburn, Susan Kirshenbaum, Elizabeth Wallace, Elizabeth Page, Carlina Della Pietra, Wisner Washam for *All My Children* (ABC)

2166 **Outstanding Directing in Daytime Children's Programming:** Joan Darling for *ABC Afterschool Special* episode "Mom's on Strike" (ABC)

2167 **Outstanding Daytime Cinematography:** Barry Sonnenfeld for *Out of Step* (ABC)

2168 **Outstanding Daytime Drama Series Technical Team:** technical directors Robert Schulz, Harry Tatarian; electronic cameras Toby Brown, Mike Denney, Sheldon Mooney, Joe Vicens; video control David Fisher, Scha Jani; production mixers Scott Millan, Tommy Persson; post-production mixers Donald Henderson, Rafael O. Valentin; sound effects Peter Roman, Larry Maggiore; videotape editors Dan Brumett, Brian Cunneen for *The Young and the Restless* (CBS)

2169 **Outstanding Daytime Drama Design Team:** art directors Richard C. Hankins, Harry Miller, Ron Placzek; set decorators Wesley Laws, Ron Kelson, Paul Hickey; lighting directors Ralph Holmes, Jene Youtt, Lincoln John Stulik; costume designer David Dangle for *Guiding Light* (CBS)

2170 **Outstanding Daytime Hairstyling:** Deborah Holmes, Katherine Kotarakos, Mary Guerrero, Catherine Marcatto for *General Hospital* (ABC)

2171 **Outstanding Daytime Children's Series Writing:** Fred Rogers for *Mr. Rogers' Neighborhood* (PBS)

2172 **Outstanding Performer in Children's Programming:** John Carradine in *Umbrella Jack* (syndicated)

2173 **Outstanding Daytime Art Direction:** art directors Romain Johnston, Debe Hale for *Pryor's Place* (CBS)

2174 **Outstanding Daytime Film Sound Editing:** supervising music editor Richard Allen; supervising editor Bob Gillis; sound effects editors Bruce Elliot, Michael Depatie, Michael Tomack, Ron Fidele for *Jim Henson's Muppet Babies* (CBS)

2175 **Outstanding Daytime Videotape Editing:** supervising editor Ted May; editors Evamarie Keller, Vincent Sims for *Sesame Street* (PBS)

2176 **Outstanding Daytime Live and Tape Sound Mixing and Sound Effects:** pre-production mixer Joel Soifer; production mixer Mark Bovos; post-production mixer Thomas J. Huth; sound effects Doug Gray for *CBS Schoolbreak Special* episode "Contract for Life: The S.A.D.D. Story" (CBS)

2177 **Outstanding Talk or Service Series:** *Donahue* executive producers Richard Mincer, Patricia McMillen; senior producer Darlene Hayes; producers Gail Steinberg, Lorri Antosz Benson, Susan Sprecher, Marlaine Selip (syndicated)

2178 **Outstanding Daytime Children's Series:** *Sesame Street* executive producer Dulcy Singer; producer Lisa Simon (PBS)

2179 **Outstanding Daytime Lighting Direction:** Marc Palius for *Henry Hamilton, Graduate Ghost* (ABC)

2180 **Outstanding Daytime Make-Up:** Nick Schillage, Mark Landon, Ed Heim, Barry Kopper, Patti Greene for *The Young and the Restless* (CBS)

2181 **Outstanding Daytime Film Editing:** Michael Lynch for *ABC Afterschool Special* episode "Backwards: The Riddle of Dyslexia" (ABC)

2182 **Outstanding Juvenile/Young Man in a Daytime Drama Series:** Brian Bloom in *As the World Turns* (CBS)

2183 **Outstanding Ingenue/Woman in a Daytime Drama Series:** Tracy E. Bregman in *The Young and the Restless* (CBS)

2184 **Outstanding Daytime Costume Design:** Madeline Greneto for *Pryor's Place* (CBS)

2185 **Outstanding Daytime Game/Audience Participation Show:** executive producer Bob Stewart; producer Anne Marie Schmitt for *The $25,000 Pyramid* (CBS)

2186 **Outstanding Daytime Animated Program:** *Jim Henson's Muppet Babies* executive producers Lee Gunther, Jim Henson; producer Bob Richardson; directors Hank Saroyan, John Gibbs; writer Jeffrey Scott (CBS)

2187 **Outstanding Daytime Children's Special:** "All the Kids Do It" episode of *CBS Schoolbreak Special* executive producers Roger Birnbaum, Henry Winkler; producer Edna Hallinan (CBS)

2188 **Outstanding Directing in a Daytime Drama Series:** directors John Whitesell II, Bruce Barry, Matthew Diamond, Irene M. Pace; associate directors Robert D. Kochman, Joanne Sedwick for *Guiding Light* (CBS)

2189 **Outstanding Music Direction and Composition:** music director Susan Markowitz; composer Elliott Lawrence for *Edge of Night* (ABC)

2190 **Outstanding Technical Direction, Electronic Camera and Video Control:** technical director Ray Angona; electronic cameras Ted Morales, Keeth Lawrence, Martin Wagner, Jose Arvizu; video control Allen Latter for *The Price Is Right* (CBS)

2191 **Outstanding Special Class Daytime Program:** "To See a World" episode of *For Our Times* executive producer Pamela Ilott; producer Chalmers Dale (CBS)

―――――― **1 9 8 5** ――――――

2192 **Outstanding Drama Series:** *Cagney & Lacey* (CBS)

2193 **Outstanding Comedy Series:** *The Golden Girls* (NBC)

2194 **Outstanding Lead Actor in a Drama Series:** William Daniels in *St. Elsewhere* (NBC)

2195 **Outstanding Lead Actress in a Drama Series:** Sharon Gless in *Cagney & Lacey* (CBS)

2196 **Outstanding Lead Actor in a Comedy Series:** Michael J. Fox in *Family Ties* (NBC)

2197 **Outstanding Lead Actress in a Comedy Series:** Betty White in *The Golden Girls* (NBC)

2198 **Outstanding Supporting Actor in a Drama Series:** John Karlen in *Cagney & Lacey* (CBS)

2199 **Outstanding Supporting Actress in a Drama Series:** Bonnie Bartlett in *St. Elsewhere* (NBC)

2200 **Outstanding Supporting Actor in a Comedy Series:** John Larroquette in *Night Court* (NBC)

2201 **Outstanding Supporting Actress in a Comedy Series:** Rhea Perlman in *Cheers* (NBC)

2202 **Outstanding Guest Performer in a Comedy Series:** Roscoe Lee Browne in *The Cosby Show* episode "The Card Game" (NBC)

2203 **Outstanding Guest Performer in a Drama Series:** John Lithgow in *Amazing Stories* episode "The Doll" (NBC)

2204 **Outstanding Directing in a Drama Series:** Georg Stanford Brown in *Cagney & Lacey* episode "Parting Shots" (CBS)

2205 **Outstanding Directing in a Comedy Series:** Jay Sandrich for *The Cosby Show* episode "Denise's Friend" (NBC)

2206 **Outstanding Writing in a Drama Series:** Tom Fontana, John Tinker, John Masius for *St. Elsewhere* episode "Time Heals" (NBC)

2207 **Outstanding Writing in a Comedy Series:** Barry Fanaro, Mort Nathan for *The Golden Girls* episode "A Little Romance" (NBC)

2208 **Outstanding Animated Program:** *Garfield's Halloween Adventure* executive producer Jay Poynor; producer/director Phil Roman; writer Jim Davis (CBS)

2209 **Outstanding Children's Program:** *Anne of Green Gables* executive producers Wonderworks, Kevin Sullivan, Lee Polk; producers Kevin Sullivan, Ian McDougall (PBS)

2210 **Outstanding Informational Special:** *W.C. Fields Straight Up* executive producer Robert B. Weide; co-producer Ronald J. Fields (PBS)

2211 **Outstanding Sound Mixing for a Miniseries or Special:** David E. Campbell CAS, John T. Reitz CAS, Gregg C. Rudloff CAS, Keith A. Wester CAS for *An Early Frost* (NBC)

2212 **Outstanding Art Direction for a Series:** art director Jacqueline Webber; set decorator Norman Rockett for *St. Elsewhere* episodes "Time Heals, Parts I and II" (NBC)

2213 **Outstanding Costume Design for a Series:** Alfred E. Lehman for *Murder, She Wrote* episode "Widow, Weep for Me" (CBS)

2214 **Outstanding Achievement in Costuming for a Series:** costume supervisor Susan Smith-Nashold; costumes Robert M. Moore; costumers Charles Drayman, Anne Winsor, Kathy O'Rear for *St. Elsewhere* episodes "Time Heals, Parts I and II" (NBC)

2215 Outstanding Achievement in Music Sound Composition for a Series (Dramatic Underscore): Arthur B. Rubinstein for *Scarecrow and Mrs. King* episode "We're Off to See the Wizard" (CBS)

2216 Outstanding Editing for a Series (Single Camera Production): Neil Mandelberg for *Moonlighting* episode "The Dream Sequence Always Rings Twice" (ABC)

2217 Outstanding Graphics and Title Design: Betty Green for *Stingray* (NBC)

2218 Outstanding Achievement in Make-Up in a Series: Rod Wilson for *Airwolf* episode "The Horn of Plenty" (CBS)

2219 Outstanding Achievement in Hairstyling for a Series: Bernadette "Bunny" Parker for *Amazing Stories* episode "Gather Ye Acorns" (NBC)

2220 Outstanding Special Visual Effects: Phil Tippett for *Dinosaur!* (CBS) and Michael McAlister for *Ewoks: The Battle for Endor* (ABC)

2221 Outstanding Individual Achievement in Informational Programming: writer John L. Miller; director David Heeley for *The Spencer Tracy Legacy: A Tribute by Katharine Hepburn* (PBS)

2222 Outstanding Lighting Direction (Electronic) for a Series: director of photography for *Solid Gold* episode #283 (syndicated)

2223 Outstanding Cinematography for a Series: John McPherson ASC for *Amazing Stories* episode "The Mission" (NBC)

2224 Outstanding Editing for a Series (Multiple Camera Production): Henry F. Chan for *The Cosby Show* episode "Full House" (NBC)

2225 Outstanding Sound Editing for a Series: supervising sound editor Richard Anderson; sound editors Wayne Allwine, James Christopher, John Stacy, George Fredrick, Burton Weinstein; ADR editors Lettie Odney, Denise Whiting; music editor Ken Wannberg for *Amazing Stories* episode "The Mission" (NBC)

2226 Outstanding Achievement in Choreography: Walter Painter for *Great Performances* episode "Sylvia Fine Kaye's Musical Comedy Tonight III" (PBS)

2227 Outstanding Art Direction for a Variety or Music Program: production designer Roy Christopher for *The 58th Annual Academy Awards* (ABC)

2228 Outstanding Costume Design for a Variety or Music Program: Bill Hargate for *Great Performances* episode "Sylvia Fine Kaye's Musical Comedy Tonight III" (PBS)

2229 Outstanding Sound Mixing for a Drama Series: William Gazecki, Andrew MacDonald, Bill Nicholson, Blake Wilcox for *St. Elsewhere* episode "Time Heals, Part I" (NBC)

2230 Outstanding Sound Mixing for a Comedy Series or a Special: Michael Ballin, Robert Douglas, Douglas Grey, Thomas J. Huth for *Cheers* episode "Fear Is My Co-Pilot" (NBC)

2231 Outstanding Informational Series: *Great Performances* episode "Laurence Olivier — A Life" executive producers Nick Evans, Nick Elliott; producer Bob Bee (PBS) and *Planet Earth* executive producer Thomas Skinner; series producer Gregory Andorfer; coordinating producer Georgann Kane (PBS)

2232 Outstanding Achievement in Music and Lyrics: composer Larry Grossman; lyricist Buz Kohan for *My Christmas Wish, Andy Williams and the NBC Kids Search for Santa* (NBC)

2233 Outstanding Achievement in Music Direction: music director Elliott Lawrence; principal arrangers James Lawrence, Lanny Meyers, Tommy Newsom, Glen Roven, Larry Schwartz, Torrie Zito for *The 1986 Tony Awards* (CBS)

2234 Outstanding Editing for a Miniseries or Special (Multi Camera Production): Pam Marshall for *American Bandstand's 33⅓ Celebration* (ABC)

2235 Outstanding Technical Direction/ Electronic Camera/Video Control for a Miniseries or a Special: technical directors Gene Crowe, Harry Tatarian; camera personnel Toby Brown, Ed Chaney, Mike Denney, Larry Heider, Pat Kenney, Bob Keys, Dave Levisohn, Wayne Orr, Hector Ramirez, Ron Sheldon; senior video control John Polacio for *Neil Diamond—Hello Again* (CBS)

2236 Outstanding Art Direction for a Miniseries or Special: production designer Tony Walton; art director John Kasarda; set decorator Robert J. Franco for *Death of a Salesman* (CBS)

2237 Outstanding Cinematography for a Miniseries or Special: Sherwood "Woody" Omens ASC for *An Early Frost* (NBC)

2238 Outstanding Sound Mixing for a Variety or Music Special or Series: Tom Ancell and David E. Fluhr for *Mr. Previn Comes to Town* (PBS)

2239 Outstanding Classical Program in the Performing Arts: *Wolf Trap Presents the Kirov: Swan Lake* executive producer Michael B. Styer; senior producer Philip Byrd; producer John T. Potthast (PBS)

2240 Outstanding Individual Achievements in Classical Music/Dance Programming: director Franco Zeffirelli for *Great Performances* episode "Cavalleria Rusticana" (PBS)

2241 Outstanding Costume Design for a Miniseries or Special: Ella Maklakova (USSR), Syblle Ulsamer (Italy) for *Peter the Great, Part I* (NBC)

2242 Outstanding Achievement in Hairstyling for a Miniseries or a Special: K.G. Ramsey for *Second Serve* (CBS)

2243 Outstanding Achievement in Make-Up for a Miniseries or a Special: makeup creation Del Acevedo; makeup artist Paul Stanhope for *Second Serve* (CBS)

2244 Outstanding Achievement in Costuming for a Miniseries or Special: women's costume supervisor Joie Hutchinson, Vicki Sanchez; men's costume supervisor Pat McGrath for *North and South, Book I Part IV* (ABC)

2245 Outstanding Electronic Lighting Direction for a Miniseries or Special: Marilyn Lowey, John Rook, Kim Killingsworth for *Neil Diamond—Hello Again* (CBS)

2246 Outstanding Achievements in Engineering Development: Stefan Kudelski for his development of the Nagra Recorder, a development which makes it possible to record and play back stereophonic sound in synchronous double system with recorders; to CBS, Sony and Cinedco for the design and implementation of electronic editing systems for film programs

2247 Outstanding Sound Editing for a Miniseries or a Special: supervising sound editor David R. Elliott; sound editors Dino de Muro, Mark Friedgen, Mike Graham, Larry Kemp, Joe Mayer, Joseph A. Melody, Stewart Nelson, Gregory Schorer, Eric Scott, Rusty Tinsley, Scot Tinsley, Bill Williams; ADR editor Russ Tinsley; music editor Daniel A. Carlin for *Under Siege* (NBC)

2248 Outstanding Editing for a Miniseries or a Special (Single Camera Production): Jerrold L. Ludwig ACE for *An Early Frost* (NBC)

2249 Outstanding Writing in a Variety or Music Program: David Letterman, Steve O'Donnell, Sandy Frank, Joe Toplyn, Chris Elliott, Matt Wickline, Jeff Martin, Gerard Mulligan, Randy Cohen, Larry Jacobson, Kevin Curran, Fred Graver, Merrill Markoe for *Late Night with David Letterman* episode "Fourth Anniversary Special" (NBC)

2250 Outstanding Directing in a Miniseries or a Special: Joseph Sargent for *Hallmark Hall of Fame* episode "Love Is Never Silent" (NBC)

2251 Outstanding Directing in a Variety or Music Program: Waris Hussein for *Copacabana* (CBS)

2252 Outstanding Variety, Music or Comedy Program: *The Kennedy Center Honors: A Celebration of the Performing Arts* producers Nick Vanoff, George Stevens, Jr. (CBS)

2253 Outstanding Writing in a Miniseries or a Special: teleplay by Ron Cowen, Daniel Lipman; story by Sherman Yellen for *An Early Frost* (NBC)

2254 Outstanding Individual Performance in a Variety or Music Program: Whitney Houston in *The 28th Annual Grammy Awards* (CBS)

2255 Outstanding Technical Direction/Electronic Camerawork/Video Control for a Series: technical director Gerry Bucci; camera personnel Randy Baer, Dale Carlson, Steve Jones, Donna J. Quante; senior video control Victor Bagdadi for the pilot of *Golden Girls* (NBC)

2256 Outstanding Miniseries: *Peter the Great* executive producer Lawrence Schiller; producer Marvin J. Chomsky; line producer Konstantin Thoeren (NBC)

2257 Outstanding Lead Actor in a Miniseries or Special: Dustin Hoffman in *Death of a Salesman* (CBS)

2258 Outstanding Lead Actress in a Miniseries or Special: Marlo Thomas in *Nobody's Child* (CBS)

2259 Outstanding Supporting Actor in a Miniseries or Special: John Malkovich in *Death of a Salesman* (CBS)

2260 Outstanding Supporting Actress in a Miniseries or Special: Colleen Dewhurst in *Between Two Women* (ABC)

2261 Outstanding Drama/Comedy Special: *Hallmark Hall of Fame* episode "Love Is Never Silent" executive producer Marian Rees; co-executive producer Julianna Field; producer Dorothea G. Petrie (NBC)

2262 Outstanding Achievement in Music Composition for a Miniseries or Special (Dramatic Underscore): Laurence Rosenthal for *Peter the Great, Part I* (NBC)

2263 ATAS Governor's Award: Red Skelton

2264 Outstanding Daytime Animated Program: *Jim Henson's Muppet Babies* executive producers Jim Henson, Margaret Loesch, Lee Gunther; producer Bob Richardson; director John Gibbs (CBS)

2265 Outstanding Daytime Cinematography: Robert Elswit for *CBS Schoolbreak Special* "The War Between the Classes" (CBS)

2266 Outstanding Daytime Music Direction & Composition for a Drama Series: music directors Jill Diamond, Rae Kraus; composers Billy Chinnock, Patricia Stotter, James Lawrence for *Search for Tomorrow* (NBC)

2267 Outstanding Daytime Film Editing: Harvey Greenstein, Wally Katz, Douglas W. Smith for *3-2-1 Contact* (PBS)

2268 Outstanding Directing of a Daytime Game/Audience Participation Show: Dick Carson for *Wheel of Fortune* (NBC)

2269 Outstanding Daytime Film Sound Editing: supervising editor/supervising music editor David Gelfand; sound editor Laura Civiello for *ABC Afterschool Special* (ABC)

2270 Outstanding Daytime Hairstyling: Sherry Baker for *Pippi Longstocking* (ABC)

2271 Outstanding Directing of Daytime Children's Programming: Martin Sheen for *CBS Schoolbreak Special* episode "Babies Having Babies" (CBS)

2272 Outstanding Daytime Lighting Direction: Carl Gibson for *Kids Incorporated* (syndicated)

2273 Outstanding Daytime Costume Design for a Drama Series: David Dangle, Nanzi Adzima, Bud Santora for *Guiding Light* (CBS)

2274 Outstanding Writing in a Daytime Children's Special: Kathryn Montgomery, Jeffrey Auerbach for *CBS Schoolbreak Special* episode "Babies Having Babies" (CBS)

2275 Outstanding Make-Up for a Daytime Drama Series: head makeup artist Pam P.K. Cole; Diane Lewis, Donna Messina, Catherine McCann Davison, Sandi Martino, Becky Bowen for *General Hospital* (ABC)

2276 Outstanding Daytime Art Direction, Set Decoration & Scenic Design: art director Victor Di Napoli; set decorator Nat Mongioi for *Sesame Street* (PBS)

2277 Outstanding Daytime Videotape Editing for a Drama Series: Dan Brumett for *The Young and the Restless* (CBS)

2278 Outstanding Writing in a Daytime Children's Series: Norman Stiles, Sara Compton, Tom Dunsmuir, Judy Freudberg, Tony Geiss, Emily Kingsley, David Korr, Sonia Manzano, Jeff Moss, Mark Saltzman, Nancy Sans, Luis Santeiro, Cathi Rosenberg Turow for *Sesame Street* (PBS)

2279 Outstanding Daytime Live & Tape Sound Mixing and Sound Effects: production mixer Mark Bovos; post-production mixer Tom Huth; sound effects technician Mike Mitchell for *CBS Schoolbreak Special* episode "Babies Having Babies" (CBS)

2280 Outstanding Hairstyling for a Daytime Drama Series: Linda Librizzi Williams, Ralph Stanzione for *Guiding Light* (CBS)

2281 **Outstanding Lighting Direction for a Daytime Drama Series:** Frank Olson, Jene Youtt, Hal Anderson, Lincoln John Stulik for *As the World Turns* (CBS)

2282 **Outstanding Daytime Technical Direction, Electronic Camera and Video Control for a Drama Series:** technical directors Rick Labgold, Chuck Guzzi; camera personnel Gorm Erickson, Pat Kenney, Bob Welsh, Ted Morales, Toby Brown, Paul Johnson; senior video control Roberto Bosio, Janice Bendiksen for *Capitol* (CBS)

2283 **Outstanding Art Direction, Set Decoration and Scenic Design for a Daytime Drama Series:** art director Sy Tomashoff; set decorator Jay Garvin for *Capitol* (CBS)

2284 **Outstanding Special Class Daytime Programming Area:** *Chagall's Journey* executive producer Helen Marmor; producer Randolph Wands (NBC); and *Live from Lincoln Center: Chamber Music Society of Lincoln Center with Irene Worth and Horacio Gutierrez* producer John Goberman (PBS)

2285 **Outstanding Daytime Special Class Writing Area:** Catherine Faulconer for *Chagall's Journey* (NBC)

2286 **Outstanding Daytime Technical Direction, Electronic Camera & Video Control:** Dick Holden technical director/electronic camera for *This Old House* (PBS)

2287 **Outstanding Daytime Costume Design:** Bill Kellard, live actors; muppets Caroly Wilcox, Richard Termine, David Velasquez, Robert Flanagan for *Sesame Street* (PBS)

2288 **Outstanding Directing in a Daytime Talk/Service Program:** Russell F. Morash for *This Old House* (PBS)

2289 **Outstanding Daytime Videotape Editing:** Stuart Pappe for *CBS Schoolbreak Special* episode "Babies Having Babies" (CBS)

2290 **Outstanding Ingenue in a Daytime Drama Series:** Ellen Wheeler in *Another World* (NBC)

2291 **Outstanding Young Leading Man in a Daytime Drama Series:** Michael E. Knight in *All My Children* (ABC)

2292 **Outstanding Daytime Talk/Service Show Host:** Phil Donahue in *Donahue* (syndicated)

2293 **Outstanding Supporting Actor in a Daytime Drama Series:** John Wesley Shipp in *As the World Turns* (CBS)

2294 **Outstanding Daytime Graphics and Title Design:** James Castle for *New Love, American Style* (ABC)

2295 **Outstanding Daytime Film Sound Mixing:** production mixer Petur Hliddal; re-recording mixer Thomas Fleischman for *ABC Afterschool Special* episode "Can a Guy Say No" (ABC)

2296 **Outstanding Daytime Talk/Service Program:** *Donahue* executive producer Patricia McMillen; senior producer Gail Steinberg; producers Lori Antosz Benson, Janet Harrell, Marlaine Selip, Susan Sprecher (syndicated)

2297 **Outstanding Daytime Game/Audience Participation Show:** *The $25,000 Pyramid* executive producer Bob Stewart; producer Anne Marie Schmitt (CBS)

2298 **Outstanding Daytime Game Show Host:** Dick Clark for *The $25,000 Pyramid* (CBS)

2299 **Outstanding Daytime Children's Special:** "The War Between the Classes" episode of *CBS Schoolbreak Special* executive producers Frank Doelger, Mark Gordon; producer Alan C. Blomquist (CBS)

2300 **Outstanding Daytime Children's Series:** *Sesame Street* executive producer Dulcy Singer; producer Lisa Simon (PBS)

2301 **Outstanding Performer in Daytime Children's Programming:** Pearl Bailey in "Cindy Eller: A Modern Fairy Tale" episode of *ABC Afterschool Special* (ABC)

2302 **Outstanding Daytime Music Direction and Composition:** music director/composer Michael Franks for "Are You My Mother?" episode of *ABC Afterschool Special* (ABC)

2303 **Outstanding Live and Tape Sound Mixing and Sound Effects for a Daytime Drama Series:** preproduction/production mixer Scott A. Millan; production mixer Tommy Persson; post-production mixers Rafael O. Valentin, Donald D. Henderson; sound effects technicians Larry Maggiore, Peter Romano for *The Young and the Restless* (CBS)

2304 **Outstanding Daytime Drama**

Series Directing Team (Associate Directors): directors Dennis Steinmetz, Rudy Vejar, Frank Pacelli; associate directors Randy Robbins, Betty Rothenberg for *The Young and the Restless* (ABC)

2305 Outstanding Lead Actor in a Daytime Drama Series: David Canary in *All My Children* (ABC)

2306 Outstanding Lead Actress in a Daytime Drama Series: Erika Slezak in *One Life to Live* (ABC)

2307 Outstanding Daytime Drama Series: *The Young and the Restless* executive producers William J. Bell, H. Wesley Kenney; producers Edward Scott, Tom Langan (CBS)

2308 Outstanding Supporting Actress in a Daytime Drama Series: Leann Hunley in *Days of Our Lives* (NBC)

2309 Outstanding Daytime Drama Series Writing Team (Head Writers, Breakdown Writers, Associate Writers): head writers Pam Long Hammer, Jeff Ryder; breakdown writers Addie Walsh, John Kuntz, Christopher Whitesell; associate writers Megan McTavish, Stephen Demorest, Victor Gialanella, Mary Pat Gleason, Trent Jones, Pete T. Rich, N. Gail Lawrence, Nancy Curlee for *Guiding Light* (CBS)

──────── **1 9 8 6** ────────

2310 Outstanding Drama Series: *L.A. Law* (NBC)

2311 Outstanding Comedy Series: *The Golden Girls* (NBC)

2312 Outstanding Lead Actor in a Drama Series: Bruce Willis in *Moonlighting* (ABC)

2313 Outstanding Lead Actress in a Drama Series: Sharon Gless in *Cagney & Lacey* (CBS)

2314 Outstanding Lead Actor in a Comedy Series: Michael J. Fox in *Family Ties* (NBC)

2315 Outstanding Lead Actress in a Comedy Series: Rue McClanahan in *The Golden Girls* (NBC)

2316 Outstanding Supporting Actor in a Drama Series: John Hillerman in *Magnum, P.I.* (CBS)

2317 Outstanding Supporting Actress in a Drama Series: Bonnie Bartlett in *St. Elsewhere* (NBC)

2318 Outstanding Supporting Actor in a Comedy Series: John Larroquette in *Night Court* (NBC)

2319 Outstanding Supporting Actress in a Comedy Series: Jackee Harry in *227* (NBC)

2320 Outstanding Guest Performer in a Comedy Series: John Cleese in *Cheers* episode "Simon Says" (NBC)

2321 Outstanding Supporting Actress in a Miniseries or a Special: Piper Laurie in *Hallmark Hall of Fame* episode "Promise" (CBS)

2322 Outstanding Guest Performer in a Drama Series: Alfre Woodard in the pilot of *L.A. Law* (NBC)

2323 Outstanding Individual Performance in a Variety or Music Program: Robin Williams in *A Carol Burnett Special: Carol, Carl, Whoopi & Robin* (ABC)

2324 Outstanding Lead Actor in a Miniseries or a Special: James Woods in *Hallmark Hall of Fame* episode "Promise" (NBC)

2325 Outstanding Lead Actress in a Miniseries or Special: Gena Rowlands in *The Betty Ford Story* (ABC)

2326 Outstanding Supporting Actor in a Miniseries or Special: Dabney Coleman in *Sworn to Silence* (ABC)

2327 Outstanding Miniseries: *A Year in the Life* executive producers Joshua Brand, John Falsey; producer Stephen Cragg (NBC)

2328 Outstanding Informational Special: *Great Performances* episode "Dance in America: Agnes, the Indomitable DeMille" executive producer Jac Venza; producer Judy Kinberg (PBS)

2329 Outstanding Informational Series: *Smithsonian World* executive producer Adrian Malone; producer David Grubin (PBS)

2330 Outstanding Children's Program: *Jim Henson's the Story Teller: Hans My Hedgehog* executive producer Jim Henson; producer Mark Shivas (ABC)

2331 Outstanding Variety, Music or Comedy Program: *The 1987 Tony Awards* executive producer Don Mischer; producer David J. Goldberg (CBS)

2332 Outstanding Drama/Comedy Special: *Hallmark Hall of Fame* episode

"Promise" executive producers Peter K. Duchow, James Garner; producer Glenn Jordan; co-producer Richard Friedenberg (CBS)

2333 Outstanding Animated Program: *Cathy* executive producer Lee Mendelson; producer Bill Melendez; writer Cathy Guisewite (CBS)

2334 Outstanding Classical Program in the Performing Arts: *Vladimir Horowitz: The Last Romantic* executive producer Peter Gelb; producer Susan Froemke; star Vladimir Horowitz (PBS)

2335 Outstanding Directing in a Comedy Series: Terry Hughes for *The Golden Girls* episode "Isn't It Romantic" (NBC)

2336 Outstanding Directing in a Drama Series: Gregory Hoblit for the pilot of *L.A. Law* (NBC)

2337 Outstanding Directing in a Variety or Music Program: Don Mischer for *The Kennedy Center Honors: A Celebration of the Performing Arts* (CBS)

2338 Outstanding Achievement in Choreography: Dee Dee Wood, Michael Peters for *Liberty Weekend: Closing Ceremonies* (ABC)

2339 Outstanding Directing in a Miniseries or a Special: Glenn Jordan for *Hallmark Hall of Fame* episode "Promise" (CBS)

2340 Outstanding Writing in a Comedy Series: Gary David Goldberg, Alan Unger for *Family Ties* episode "A, My Name Is Alex" (NBC)

2341 Outstanding Writing in a Drama Series: Steven Bochco, Terry Louise Fisher for *L.A. Law* episode "Venus Butterfly" (NBC)

2342 Outstanding Art Direction in a Series: production designer Jeffrey L. Goldstein; set decorator Richard D. Kent for the pilot of *L.A. Law* (NBC)

2343 Outstanding Cinematography for a Series: Woody Omens ASC for the pilot of *Heart of the City* (ABC)

2344 Outstanding Cinematography for a Miniseries or Special: Philip Lathrop ASC for *Christmas Snow* (NBC)

2345 Outstanding Writing in a Miniseries or Special: teleplay by Richard Friedenberg; story by Kenneth Blackwell, Tennyson Flowers, Richard Friedenberg for *Hallmark Hall of Fame* episode "Promise" (CBS)

2346 Outstanding Writing in a Variety or Music Program: Steve O'Donnell, Sandy Frank, Joe Toplyn, Chris Elliott, Matt Wickline, Jeff Martin, Gerard Mulligan, Randy Cohen, Larry Jacobson, Kevin Curran, Fred Graver, Adam Resnick, David Letterman for *Late Night with David Letterman: Fifth Anniversary Special* (NBC)

2347 Outstanding Art Direction for a Miniseries or Special: production designer Malcolm Middleton; art director Herbert Westbrook; set decorator Harry Cordwell for *The Two Mrs. Grenvilles* (NBC)

2348 Outstanding Costume Design for a Series: Jane Robinson for *Anastasia: The Mystery of Anna* (NBC)

2349 Outstanding Achievement in Costuming for a Miniseries or Special: costume supervisor Frances Hayes for *Independence* (NBC)

2350 Outstanding Achievement in Make-Up for a Series: Michael Westmore, Mark Bussan, Charles House, Zoltan Elek, Fred Blau, Jr., for *Amazing Stories* episode "Without Diana" (NBC)

2351 Outstanding Achievement Hairstyling for a Series: Ms. Shepherd's hairstylist Katheryn Blondell; hairstylist Josee Normand for *Moonlighting* episode "Atomic Shakespeare" (ABC)

2352 Outstanding Art Direction for a Variety or Music Program: production designer Rene Lagler for *Liberty Weekend: Closing Ceremonies* (ABC)

2353 Outstanding Achievement in Music Composition for a Miniseries or Special (Dramatic Underscore): Laurence Rosenthal for *Anastasia: The Mystery of Anna* (NBC)

2354 Outstanding Editing for a Series (Single Camera Production): Roger Blondelli, Neil Mandelberg for *Moonlighting* episode "Atomic Shakespeare" (ABC)

2355 Outstanding Editing for a Miniseries or Special (Single Camera Production): Steve Cohen for *LBJ: The Early Years* (NBC)

2356 Outstanding Costume Design for a Series: Robert Turturice for *Moonlighting* episode "Atomic Shakespeare" (ABC)

2357 Outstanding Achievement in Music Composition for a Series (Dramatic Underscore): Joel Rosenbaum for *Knots Landing* episode "Cement the Relationship" (CBS)

2358 **Outstanding Achievement in Music Direction:** music director Don Pippin; principal arrangers Eric Stern, Buster Davis for *Great Performances* episode "Broadway Sings: The Music of Jule Styne" (PBS)

2359 **Outstanding Achievement in Music and Lyrics:** composer Larry Grossman; lyricist Buz Kohan for *Liberty Weekend: Opening Ceremonies* "Welcome to Liberty" (ABC)

2360 **Outstanding Achievement in Hairstyling for a Miniseries or a Special:** hairstylists Marsha Lewis, Mike Lockey; hairstylist for Ann-Margret, Sydney Guilaroff for *The Two Mrs. Grenvilles—Part 2* (NBC)

2361 **Outstanding Achievement in Make-Up for a Miniseries or a Special:** Patton makeup designed by Del Acevedo; chief makeup artists Eddie Knight, Alan Boyle for *The Last Days of Patton* (CBS)

2362 **Outstanding Achievement in Costuming for a Series:** costumer Nanrose Buchman for *All Talking, All Singing, All Dancing* (syndicated)

2363 **Outstanding Costume Design for a Variety or Music Program:** Ray Aghayan, Ret Turner for *Diana Ross—Red Hot Rhythm and Blues* (ABC)

2364 **Outstanding Editing for a Series (Multi-Camera Production):** Jerry Davis for *Night Court* episode "Her Honor—Part I" (NBC)

2365 **Outstanding Editing for a Miniseries or Special (Multi-Camera Production):** Kris Trexler for *Happy Birthday, Hollywood* (ABC)

2366 **Outstanding Sound Mixing for a Comedy Series or Special:** Michael Ballin, Bob Douglas, Doug Grey, Tom Huth for *Cheers* episode "The Proposal" (NBC)

2367 **Outstanding Sound Mixing for a Drama Series:** Gary Alexander, Joseph Kenworthy CAS, Tim Philben CAS, R. William A. Thiederman for *Max Headroom* episode "Blipverts" (ABC)

2368 **Outstanding Electronic Lighting Direction for a Series:** director of photography George Spiro Dibie for *Growing Pains* episode "My Brother, Myself" (ABC)

2369 **Outstanding Sound Editing for a Series:** supervising editors Douglas H. Grindstaff, Richard D. Corwin; editors

Clark Conrad, Brad Sherman, Richard Taylor, James Wolvington, music Richard D. Corwin ADR, Dick Bernstein for *Max Headroom* episode "Blipverts" (ABC)

2370 **Outstanding Sound Mixing for a Variety or Music Series or a Special:** Roger Cortes, Ron Estes, Carroll Pratt for *The Tonight Show Starring Johnny Carson* guests Dolly Parton, Emmylou Harris, Linda Ronstadt and George Hamilton (NBC)

2371 **Outstanding Sound Editing for a Miniseries or Special:** supervising editor Vince R. Gutierrez; editors William H. Angarola, Clark Conrad, Douglas Gray, Mace Matiosian, Anthony Mazzei, Michael Mitchell, Matthew Sawelson, Edward F. Suski, Jim Wolvington, Barbara Issak; music John Johnson ADR, Dan Carlin, Sr., for *Unnatural Causes* (NBC)

2372 **Outstanding Electronic Lighting Direction for a Miniseries or Special:** Greg Brunton for *Diana Ross—Red Hot Rhythm and Blues* (ABC)

2373 **Outstanding Technical Direction/Electronic Camera/Video Control for a Miniseries or a Special:** technical director Karl Messerschmidt; camerapersons Les Atkinson, Roy Holm, Dana Martin, J. O'Neill; senior video control Jerry Smith for *Barbara Mandrell's Christmas: A Family Reunion* (CBS)

2374 **Outstanding Sound Mixing for a Drama Miniseries or Special:** Joseph Citarella, Charles Grenzbach, David Lee, George R. West for *Unnatural Causes* (NBC)

2375 **Outstanding Technical Direction/Electronic Camerawork/Video Control for a Series:** technical director Parker Roe; camerapersons Paul Basta, Tom Dasbach, Richard Price, John Repcynski; senior video control Eric Clay for *Family Ties* episode "A, My Name Is Alex" (NBC)

2376 **Outstanding Individual Achievement—Writing for Informational Programming:** Robert McCrum, Robert MacNeil for *The Story of English, a Muse of Fire* (PBS)

2377 **Outstanding Individual Achievement—Directing Classical Music/Dance Programming:** Kirk Browning for *Great*

Performances episode "Goya with Placido Domingo" (PBS); and Albert Maysles, David Maysles for *Vladimir Horowitz: The Last Romantic* (PBS)

2378 Outstanding Individual Achievement — Performing Classical Music/ Dance Programming: Leonard Bernstein, Isaac Stern for *Carnegie Hall: The Grand Reopening* (CBS)

2379 Outstanding Graphics and Title Design: Wayne Fitzgerald, David Oliver Pfeil for *The Bronx Zoo* (NBC); and Sandy Dvore for *A Carol Burnett Special — Carol, Carl, Whoopi & Robin* (ABC)

2380 Outstanding Achievement in Engineering Development: Joseph J. Sayovitz, Jr., Jay D. Sherbon

2381 Tenth Annual ATAS Governor's Award: Grant Tinker

2382 Outstanding Daytime Drama Series: *As the World Turns* executive producer Robert Calhoun; supervising producer Ken Fritts; producers Michael Laibson, Chris Banas, Bonnie Bogard, Lisa Wilson (CBS)

2383 Outstanding Daytime Game/Audience Participation Show: *The $25,000 Pyramid* executive producer Bob Stewart; supervising producer Anne Marie Schmitt; producers David Michaels, Francine Bergman (CBS)

2384 Outstanding Daytime Children's Series: *Sesame Street* executive producer Dulcy Singer; producer Lisa Simon (PBS)

2385 Outstanding Daytime Children's Special: *ABC Afterschool Special* episode "Wanted: The Perfect Guy" executive producer Milton Justice; producer Joseph Feury (ABC)

2386 Outstanding Animated Daytime Program: *Jim Henson's Muppet Babies* executive producers Jim Henson, Lee Gunther, Margaret Loesch; producer Bob Richardson; supervising director Bob Shellhorn; writer Jeffrey Scott (CBS)

2387 Outstanding Daytime Game Show Host: Bob Barker in *The Price Is Right* (CBS)

2388 Outstanding Daytime Talk/Service Show: *The Oprah Winfrey Show* executive producer Debra DiMaio; producers Mary Kay Clinton, Christine Tardio, Dianne Hudson, Ellen Rakieten (syndicated)

2389 Outstanding Daytime Talk/Service Show Host: Oprah Winfrey in *The Oprah Winfrey Show* (syndicated)

2390 Outstanding Lead Actor in a Daytime Drama Series: Larry Bryggman in *As the World Turns* (CBS)

2391 Outstanding Lead Actress in a Daytime Drama Series: Kim Zimmer in *Guiding Light* (CBS)

2392 Outstanding Supporting Actor in a Daytime Drama Series: Gregg Marx in *As the World Turns* (CBS)

2393 Outstanding Supporting Actress in a Daytime Drama Series: Kathleen Noone in *All My Children* (ABC)

2394 Outstanding Young Leading Man in a Daytime Drama Series: Michael E. Knight in *All My Children* (ABC)

2395 Outstanding Ingenue in a Daytime Drama Series: Martha Byrne in *As the World Turns* (CBS)

2396 Outstanding Guest Performer in a Daytime Drama Series: John Wesley Shipp in *Santa Barbara* (NBC)

2397 Outstanding Performer in a Daytime Children's Program: Madeline Kahn in *ABC Afterschool Special* episode "Wanted: The Perfect Guy" (ABC)

2398 Outstanding Special Class Daytime Program Area: *ABC Notebook* episode "The Children of Ellis Island" executive producer Jane Paley (ABC); *One to Grow On* producer Charles Stepner (NBC); *Taking Children Seriously* executive producer Helen Marmor, producer Patricia Mauger (NBC)

2399 Outstanding Directing in a Daytime Game/Audience Participation Show: Mark Breslow for *The Price Is Right* (CBS)

2400 Outstanding Directing in a Daytime Talk/Service Show: Jim McPharlin for *The Oprah Winfrey Show* (syndicated)

2401 Outstanding Directing in Daytime Children's Programming: Dan F. Smith for *Square One TV* (PBS)

2402 Outstanding Daytime Drama Series Directing Team: Directors Frank Pacelli, Rudy Vejar; associate directors Betty Rothenberg, Randy Robbins for *The Young and the Restless* (CBS)

2403 Outstanding Achievement in Special Class Daytime Directing: Dick Schneider for *Macy's 60th Annual Thanksgiving Day Parade* (NBC)

2404 Outstanding Daytime Drama Series Writing Team: head writer Peggy O'Shea; associate head writers S. Michael Schnessel, Craig Carlson, Lanie Bertram, Ethel M. Brez, Mel Brez; writer Lloyd Gold for *One Life to Live* (ABC)

2405 Outstanding Daytime Children's Series Writing: Norman Stiles, Cathi Rosenberg-Turow, Jeffrey Moss, Sonia Manzano, Mark Saltzman, Belinda Ward, David Korr, Sara Compton, Tom Dunsmuir, Tony Geiss, Emily Pearl Kingsley, Judy Freudberg, Jon Stone, Nancy Sans, Luis Santeiro for *Sesame Street* (PBS)

2406 Outstanding Writing in a Daytime Children's Special: Melvin Van Peebles for *CBS Schoolbreak Special* episode "The Day They Came to Arrest the Book" (CBS)

2407 Outstanding Achievement in Daytime Special Class Writing: William Corrington, Jayne Corrington for *Superior Court* (syndicated)

2408 Outstanding Achievement in Daytime Cinematography: cinematographers Don Lenzer, Chuck Levey, Dyanna Taylor; underwater cinematographers Howard Hall, Stan Waterman, George Waterman for *3-2-1 Contact* (PBS)

2409 Outstanding Achievement in Daytime Graphics and Title Design: Prudence Fenton, Phil Trumbo for *Pee-wee's Playhouse* (CBS)

2410 Outstanding Daytime Achievement in Hairstyling: Sally Hershberger, Eric Gregg for *Pee-wee's Playhouse* (CBS)

2411 Outstanding Achievement in Hairstyling for a Daytime Drama Series: Linda Williams, Ralph Stanzione for *Guiding Light* (CBS)

2412 Outstanding Achievement in Daytime Film Editing: Harvey Greenstein, Wally Katz, Douglas W. Smith for *3-2-1 Contact* (PBS)

2413 Outstanding Achievement in Daytime Film Sound Editing: Greg Sheldon, Ira Spiegel for *ABC Afterschool Special* episode "The Gift of Amazing Grace" (ABC)

2414 Outstanding Achievement in Daytime Lighting Direction: lighting consultant John Leay; lighting designer Chenault Spence for *The Damnation of Faust* (PBS)

2415 Outstanding Achievement in Daytime Videotape Editing: Paul Dougherty, Doug Jones, Joe Castellano, Les Kaye, Howard Silver for *Pee-wee's Playhouse* (CBS)

2416 Outstanding Achievement in Lighting Direction for a Daytime Drama: John Connolly, Candice Dunn for *Ryan's Hope* (ABC)

2417 Outstanding Achievement in Daytime Art Direction/Set Decoration/Scenic Design: production designer Gary Panter; art director Sidney J. Bartholomew, Jr.; set decorator Wayne Wilkes White, Ric Heitzman for *Pee-wee's Playhouse* (CBS)

2418 Outstanding Achievement in Daytime Make-Up: Sharon Ilson Reed for *Pee-wee's Playhouse* (CBS)

2419 Outstanding Achievement in Daytime Film Sound Mixing: sound mixer Rolf Pardulal; re-recording mixer Ken Hahn for *Pee-wee's Playhouse* (CBS)

2420 Outstanding Achievement in Make-Up for a Daytime Drama Series: Joseph Cola, Sue Saccavino for *Guiding Light* (CBS)

2421 Outstanding Achievement in Art Direction/Set Decoration/Scenic Design for a Daytime Drama Series: art director William Hultstrom; set decorators Joseph Bevacqua, Andrea Joel, Eric Fischer for *The Young and the Restless* (CBS)

2422 Outstanding Achievement in Technical Direction/Electronic Camera/Video Control for a Daytime Drama Series: technical directors Ervin D. Hurd, Jr., Harry Tatarian; electronic cameras Mike Denney, Sheldon Mooney, Joseph Vicens, David Navarette; video control Dave Fisher, Scha Jani for *The Young and the Restless* (CBS)

2423 Outstanding Achievement in Daytime Live and Tape Sound Mixing and Sound Effects: production mixer Ken King; post-production mixer David E. Fluhr; for *CBS Schoolbreak Special* episode "God, the Universe and Hot Fudge Sundaes" (CBS)

2424 Outstanding Achievement in Daytime Music Direction and Composition: music director Charles Bernstein for *CBS Schoolbreak Special* episode "Little Miss Perfect" (CBS)

2425 **Outstanding Achievement in Daytime Technical Direction/Electronic Camera/Video Control:** technical director Dick Holden for *This Old House* (PBS)

2426 **Outstanding Achievement in Videotape Editing for a Daytime Drama Series:** Joseph A. Mastroberti, Steven Shatkin for *As the World Turns* (CBS)

2427 **Outstanding Achievement in Daytime Costume Design:** Jeremy Railton, Lelan Berner, Victoria deKay Bodwell for *Zoobilee Zoo* (syndicated)

2428 **Outstanding Achievement in Costume Design for a Daytime Drama Series:** Kathi Nishimoto for *The Young and the Restless* (CBS)

2429 **Outstanding Achievement in Music Direction and Composition for a Daytime Drama Series:** music director and composer Dominic Messinger for *Santa Barbara* (NBC)

2430 **Outstanding Achievement in Live and Tape Sound Mixing and Sound Effects for a Daytime Drama Series:** pre-production mixer Scott A. Millan; production mixers Scott A. Millan, Tommy Persson; post-production mixers Rafael O. Valentin, Donald D. Hendrickson; sound effects Larry Maggiore, Peter Romano for *The Young and the Restless* (CBS)

——————— **1987** ———————

2431 **Outstanding Drama Series:** *thirtysomething* executive producers Edward Zwick, Marshall Herskovitz; supervising producer Paul Haggis; producers Edward Zwick, Scott Winant; Bedford Falls Company in association with MGM/UA Television (ABC)

2432 **Outstanding Comedy Series:** *The Wonder Years* executive producers Carol Black, Neal Marlens; producer Jeff Silver; The Black Marlens Company in association with New World Television (ABC)

2433 **Outstanding Miniseries:** *The Murder of Mary Phagan* producer George Stevens, Jr.; Century Towers Productions, Inc./A George Stevens, Jr. Production in association with Orion Television (NBC)

2434 **Outstanding Variety, Music or Comedy Program:** *Irving Berlin's 100th Birthday Celebration* executive producer Don Mischer; producers Jan Cornell, David J. Goldberg; co-producer Sara Lukinson; Don Mischer Productions (CBS)

2435 **Outstanding Drama/Comedy Special:** *A.T.&T. Presents* episode "Inherit the Wind" executive producer Peter Douglas; producer Robert A. Papazian; a Vincent Pictures Production in association with David Greene/Robert Papazian/MGM/UA (NBC)

2436 **Outstanding Classical Program in the Performing Arts:** *Great Performances* episode "Nixon in China" executive producer Jac Venza; series producer David Horn, Michael Bronson; coordinating producer John Walker; a production of WNET/13 and the Houston Opera (PBS)

2437 **Outstanding Information Special:** *Dear America: Letters Home from Vietnam* producers Bill Couturie, Thomas Bird; The Couturie Company and the Vietnam Veterans Ensemble Theatre Company (HBO)

2438 **Outstanding Informational Series:** *American Masters* episode "Buster Keaton: A Hard Act to Follow" producers Kevin Brownlow, David Gill; Thames Television in association with American Masters/WNET/13 (PBS)

2439 **Outstanding Animated Program:** *A Claymation Christmas Celebration* executive producer Will Vinton; producer David Altschul, director Will Vinton; writer Ralph Liddle; Will Vinton Productions, Inc. (CBS)

2440 **Outstanding Children's Program:** *Hallmark Hall of Fame* episode "The Secret Garden" executive producer Norman Rosemont; producer Steve Lanning; Rosemont Productions, Ltd.

2441 **Outstanding Lead Actor in a Comedy Series:** Michael J. Fox in *Family Ties* (NBC)

2442 **Outstanding Lead Actor in a Drama Series:** Richard Kiley in *A Year in the Life of Me* (NBC)

2443 **Outstanding Lead Actor in a Miniseries or a Special:** Jason Robards in *A.T.&T. Presents* episode "Inherit the Wind" (NBC)

2444 Outstanding Lead Actress in a Comedy Series: Beatrice Arthur in *The Golden Girls* (NBC)

2445 Outstanding Lead Actress in a Drama Series: Tyne Daly in *Cagney & Lacey* (CBS)

2446 Outstanding Lead Actress in a Miniseries or Special: Jessica Tandy in *Hallmark Hall of Fame* episode "Foxfire" (CBS)

2447 Outstanding Supporting Actor in a Comedy Series: John Larroquette in *Night Court* (NBC)

2448 Outstanding Supporting Actor in a Drama Series: Larry Drake in *L.A. Law* (NBC)

2449 Outstanding Supporting Actor in a Miniseries or a Special: John Shea in *Baby M* (series) (ABC)

2450 Outstanding Supporting Actress in a Comedy Series: Estelle Getty in *The Golden Girls* (NBC)

2451 Outstanding Supporting Actress in a Drama Series: Patricia Wettig in *thirtysomething* (ABC)

2452 Outstanding Supporting Actress in a Miniseries or Special: Jane Seymour in *Onassis: The Richest Man in the World* (series) (ABC)

2453 Outstanding Individual Performance in a Variety or Music Program: Robin Williams in *ABC Presents a Royal Gala* (ABC)

2454 Outstanding Guest Performer in a Comedy Series: Beah Richards in *Frank's Place* episode "The Bridge" (CBS)

2455 Outstanding Guest Performer in a Drama Series: Shirley Knight in *thirtysomething* episode "The Parents Are Coming" (ABC)

2456 Outstanding Directing in a Comedy Series: Gregory Hoblit for the pilot of *Hooperman* (ABC)

2457 Outstanding Directing in a Drama Series: Mark Tinker for *St. Elsewhere* episode "Weigh In, Way Out" (NBC)

2458 Outstanding Directing in a Variety or Music Program: Patricia Birch, Humphrey Burton for *Great Performances* episode "Celebrating Gershwin" (PBS)

2459 Outstanding Directing in a Miniseries or Special: Lamont Johnson for *Gore Vidal's Lincoln* (NBC)

2460 Outstanding Achievement in Choreography: Alan Johnson for *Irving Berlin's 100th Birthday Celebration* (CBS)

2461 Outstanding Writing in a Comedy Series: Hugh Wilson for *Frank's Place* episode "The Bridge" (CBS)

2462 Outstanding Writing in a Drama Series: Paul Haggis, Marshall Herskovitz for *thirtysomething* episode "Business as Usual (a.k.a. Michael's Father's Death)" (ABC)

2463 Outstanding Writing in a Variety or Music Program: Jackie Mason for *Jackie Mason on Broadway* (HBO)

2464 Outstanding Writing in a Miniseries or a Special: William Hanley for *General Foods Golden Showcase* episode "The Attic: The Hiding of Anne Frank" (CBS)

2465 Outstanding Cinematography for a Series: Roy H. Wagner ASC for the pilot of *Beauty and the Beast* (CBS)

2466 Outstanding Cinematography for a Miniseries or a Special: Woody Omens ASC for *I Saw What You Did* (CBS)

2467 Outstanding Art Direction for a Series: art director John Mansbridge; set decorator Chuck Korian for the pilot of *Beauty and the Beast* (CBS)

2468 Outstanding Art Direction for a Miniseries or Special: production designer Jan Scott; set decorator Erica Rogalla for *Hallmark Hall of Fame* episode "Foxfire" (CBS)

2469 Outstanding Art Direction for a Variety or Music Program: production designer Charles Lisanby for *Barry Manilow: Big Fun on Swing Street* (CBS)

2470 Outstanding Achievement in Music Composition for a Series (Dramatic Underscore): Lee Holdridge for the pilot of *Beauty and the Beast* (CBS)

2471 Outstanding Achievement in Music Composition for a Miniseries or a Special (Dramatic Underscore): Laurence Rosenthal for *The Bourne Identity (Part I)* (ABC)

2472 Outstanding Achievement in Music Direction: music director Ian Frasier; principal arrangers Chris Boardman, Alexander Courage, Ian Fraser, Angela Morley for *Julie Andrews — The Sound of Christmas* (ABC)

2473 **Outstanding Achievement in Music and Lyrics:** composer Larry Grossman; lyricist Buz Kahan for *Julie Andrews — The Sound of Christmas* (ABC)

2474 **Outstanding Costume Design for a Series:** William Ware Theiss for *Star Trek: The Next Generation* episode "The Big Goodbye" (syndication)

2475 **Outstanding Costume Design for a Miniseries or a Special:** Jane Robinson for *Poor Little Rich Girl: The Barbara Hutton Story (Part II)* (NBC)

2476 **Outstanding Costume Design for a Variety or Music Program:** Pete Menefee, Ret Turner for *Las Vegas — An All-Star 75th Anniversary Special* (ABC)

2477 **Outstanding Achievement in Costuming for a Series:** women's costumer Paula Kaatz; men's costumer Darryl Levine for the pilot for *China Beach* (ABC)

2478 **Outstanding Achievement in Costuming for a Miniseries or a Special:** costume supervisor Eddie Marks; costumer Deborah Hopper for *Shakedown on the Sunset Strip* (CBS)

2479 **Outstanding Achievement in Make-Up for a Series:** Werner Keppler, Michael Westmore, Gerald Quist for *Star Trek: The Next Generation* episode "Conspiracy" (syndication)

2480 **Outstanding Achievement in Make-Up for a Miniseries or a Special:** key makeup Ronnie Specter; Ms. Fawcett's makeup Linda De Vetta, Pauline Heys for *Poor Little Rich Girl: The Barbara Hutton Story* (NBC)

2481 **Outstanding Achievement in Hairstyling for a Series:** Judy Crown, Monique de Sart for *Designing Women* episode "I'll Be Seeing You" (CBS)

2482 **Outstanding Achievement in Hairstyling for a Miniseries or a Special:** key hairstylist Claudia Thompson; Ms. Fawcett's hairstylists Aaron Quarles, Jan Archibald; key hairdresser Stephen Rose for *Poor Little Rich Girl: The Barbara Hutton Story* (NBC)

2483 **Outstanding Editing for a Series (Single Camera Production):** Elodie Keene for *L.A. Law* episode "Full Marital Jacket" (NBC)

2484 **Outstanding Editing for a Miniseries or a Special (Single Camera Production):** John A. Martinelli ACE for *The Murder of Mary Phagan (Part II)* (NBC)

2485 **Outstanding Editing for a Series (Multi-Camera Production):** Andy Ackerman for *Cheers* episode "The Big Kiss-Off" (NBC)

2486 **Outstanding Editing for a Miniseries or Special (Multi-Camera Production):** Andy Zall, Mark West, Bob Jenkis for *Julie Andrews — The Sound of Christmas* (ABC)

2487 **Outstanding Sound Editing for a Series:** supervising sound editor William Wistrom; sound editors Wilson Dyer, Mace Matiosian, James Wolvington, Keith Bilderbeck; supervising ADR editor Mace Matiosian; supervising music editor Gerry Sackman for *Star Trek: The Next Generation* episode "1100 1001" (syndication)

2488 **Outstanding Sound Editing for a Miniseries or a Special:** supervising sound editor Rich Harrison; sound editors Tom Cornwell, Peter N. Harrison; Rich Harrison, Tom McMullen, Stan Siegel; supervising ADR editor Tally Paulos, supervising music editor Allan K. Rosen for *The Murder of Mary Phagan (Part II)* (NBC)

2489 **Outstanding Sound Mixing for a Comedy Series or a Special:** Michael Ballin, M. Curtis Price, Martin P. Church, Lenore Peterson for *Frank's Place* episode "Food Fight" (CBS)

2490 **Outstanding Sound Mixing for a Variety Series or a Special:** Doug Rider, Carroll Pratt, David E. Fluhr, Doug Nelson for *Dolly Down in New Orleans* (ABC)

2491 **Outstanding Sound Mixing for a Drama Series:** Susan Chong, Thomas Huth, Tim Philben CAS, Sam Black for *Tour of Duty* episode "Under Siege" (CBS)

2492 **Outstanding Sound Mixing for a Dramatic Miniseries or Special:** Don MacDougall, Grover Helsley, Joe Citarella, Russell Williams for *Terrorist on Trial: The United States vs. Salim Ajami* (CBS)

2493 **Outstanding Technical Direction/Electronic Camerawork/Video Control for a Series:** technical director O. Tamburri; camerapersons Jack Chisholm,

Stephen A. Jones, Ritch Kenney, Ken Tamburri; senior video control Robert G. Kaufmann for *The Golden Girls* episode "Ole Friends" (NBC)

2494 Outstanding Technical Direction/Electronic Camera/Video Control for a Miniseries or a Special: technical director Mike Spencer; camerapersons David "Rocket" Barber, Bob Keys, Ron Sheldon, Gunter Degn; senior video control Mike Spencer for *Julie Andrews—The Sound of Christmas* (ABC)

2495 Outstanding Electronic Lighting Direction for a Comedy Series: Mark Buxbaum for *The Charmings* episode "The Witch Is of Van Oaks" (ABC)

2496 Outstanding Electronic Lighting Direction for a Variety/Music or Drama Series, a Miniseries or a Special: John Rook for *Julie Andrews—The Sound of Christmas* (ABC)

2497 Outstanding Daytime Drama Series: *Santa Barbara* executive producers Jill Farren Phelps, Bridget Dobson; supervising producer Steven Kent; producers Leonard Friedlander, Julie Hanan (NBC)

2498 Outstanding Daytime Game/Audience Participation Show: *The Price Is Right* executive producer Frank Wayne; producers Phillip Wayne, Roger Dobkowitz (CBS)

2499 Outstanding Daytime Children's Series: *Sesame Street* executive producer Dulcy Singer; supervising producer Lisa Simon; coordinating producer Arlene Sherman (PBS)

2500 Outstanding Daytime Children's Special: *CBS Schoolbreak Special* episode "Never Say Goodbye" executive producer Michael D. Little; producer Susan Rohrer; co-producer Craig S. Cummings (CBS)

2501 Outstanding Daytime Animated Program: *Jim Henson's Muppet Babies* executive producers Margaret Ann Loesch, Lee Gunther, Jim Henson; supervising producer Bob Richardson; producers John Ahern, Bob Shellhorn (CBS)

2502 Outstanding Daytime Talk/Service Show: *The Oprah Winfrey Show* executive producer Debra DiMaio; producers Mary Kay Clinton, Dianne Atkinson, Ellen Sue Rakieten, Christina Tardio (syndicated)

2503 Outstanding Daytime Special Class Program Area: *American Bandstand* executive producer Dick Clark; supervising producer Larry Klein; producer Barry Glazer (syndicated)

2504 Outstanding Daytime Lead Actress in a Drama Series: Helen Gallagher in *Ryan's Hope* (ABC)

2505 Outstanding Daytime Lead Actor in a Drama Series: David Canary in *All My Children* (ABC)

2506 Outstanding Daytime Supporting Actress in a Drama Series: Ellen Wheeler in *All My Children* (ABC)

2507 Outstanding Daytime Supporting Actor in a Drama Series: Justin Deas in *Santa Barbara* (NBC)

2508 Outstanding Ingenue in a Daytime Drama Series: Julianne Moore in *As the World Turns* (CBS)

2509 Outstanding Younger Leading Man in a Daytime Drama Series: Billy Warlock in *Days of Our Lives* (NBC)

2510 Outstanding Performer in Children's Daytime Programming: Philip Bosco in *ABC Afterschool Special* episode "Read Between the Lines" (ABC)

2511 Outstanding Daytime Game Show Host: Bob Barker in *The Price Is Right* (CBS)

2512 Outstanding Daytime Talk/Service Show Host: Phil Donahue in *Donahue* (syndicated)

2513 Outstanding Daytime Drama Series Directing Team: directors Rudolph L. Vejar, Frank Pacelli, Heather Hill; associate directors Randy Robbins, Betty Rothenberg for *The Young and the Restless* (CBS)

2514 Outstanding Daytime Directing of a Game/Audience Participation Show: Bruce Burmedter for *The $25,000 Pyramid* (CBS)

2515 Outstanding Daytime Directing of a Talk/Service Show: Russell Morash for *This Old House* (PBS)

2516 Outstanding Directing in Daytime Children's Programming: Jeff Brown in *CBS Schoolbreak Special* episode "What If I'm Gay?" (CBS)

2517 Outstanding Daytime Directing in a Special Class: Dick Schneider for *Macy's 61st Annual Thanksgiving Day Parade* (NBC)

2518 Outstanding Daytime Drama

Series Writing Team: Agnes Nixon, Clarice Blackburn, Lorraine Broderick, Susan Kirshenbaum, Kathleen Klein, Karen L. Lewis, Victor Miller, Megan McTavish, Elizabeth Page, Peggy Sloane, Gillian Spencer, Elizabeth Wallace, Wisner Washam, Mary K. Wells, Jack Wood for *All My Children* (ABC)

2519 Outstanding Writing in a Daytime Children's Series: head writer Norman Stiles; writers Christian Clark, Sara Compton, Judy Freudberg, Tony Geiss, Emily Kingsley, David Korr, Sonia Manzano, Jeff Moss, Cathi Rosenberg-Turow, Mark Saltzman, Nancy Sans, Luis Santeiro, Jocelyn Stevenson, Jon Stone, Belinda Ward, John Weidman for *Sesame Street* (PBS)

2520 Outstanding Writing in a Children's Daytime Special: Victoria Hochberg for *ABC Afterschool Special* episode "Just a Regular Kid: An AIDS Story" (ABC)

2521 Outstanding Achievement in Daytime Art Direction/Set Decoration/Scenic Design: production designer Gary Panzer; co-production designers Wayne White, Ric Heitzman; art director Jeremy Railton; set decorators James Higginson, Paul Reubens for *Pee-wee's Playhouse* (CBS)

2522 Outstanding Achievement in Daytime Art Direction/Set Decoration/Scenic Design for a Drama Series: art directors Sy Tomashoff, Jack Forrestel; set decorators Jay Garvin, Randy Gunderson for *The Bold and the Beautiful* (CBS)

2523 Outstanding Achievement in Daytime Technical Direction/Electronic Camera/Video Control: technical director Ray Angona; electronic cameras Jose Arvizu, Cesar Cabriera, Keeth Lawrence, Martin Wagner; video control Allen Latter for *The Price Is Right* (CBS)

2524 Outstanding Achievement in Daytime Technical Direction/Electronic Camera/Video Control for a Drama Series: technical director Chuck Guzzi; electronic cameras Ted Morales, Toby Brown, Gordon Sweeney, Mike Glenn, Pat Kenney; video control Roberto Bosio, Clive Bassett for *The Bold and the Beautiful* (CBS)

2525 Outstanding Achievement in Daytime Lighting Direction: lighting designer Chenault Spence; lighting consultant Alan Adelman for *Un Ballo in Maschera* (PBS)

2526 Outstanding Achievement in Lighting Direction for a Daytime Drama Series: Howard Sharrott for *Loving* (ABC)

2527 Outstanding Achievement in Daytime Videotape Editing: John Ward Nielsen for *Pee-wee's Playhouse* episode "Playhouse in Outer Space" (CBS)

2528 Outstanding Achievement in Daytime Videotape Editing for a Drama Series: Marc Beruti, Dan Brumett for *The Young and the Restless* (CBS)

2529 Outstanding Achievement in Daytime Live and Tape Sound Mixing and Sound Effects: production mixers Blake Norton, Tim Lester; sound effects Dick Maitland for *Sesame Street* (PBS)

2530 Outstanding Achievement in Daytime Live and Tape Sound Mixing and Sound Effects for a Drama Series: pre-production and production mixer Scott A. Millan; production mixer Tommy Persson; post-production mixers Rafael O. Valentin, Donald D. Henderson; sound effects Maurice "Smokey" Westerfeld, Peter Romano for *The Young and the Restless* (CBS)

2531 Outstanding Daytime Achievement in Costume Design: Lowell Detweiler for *Square One TV* (PBS)

2532 Outstanding Achievement in Costume Design for a Daytime Drama Series: Lee Smith for *Days of Our Lives* (NBC)

2533 Outstanding Achievement in Daytime Make-Up: Ve Neill for *Pee-wee's Playhouse* (CBS)

2534 Outstanding Achievement in Make-Up for a Daytime Drama Series: head makeup artist Carol Brown; makeup artists Keith Crary, Robert Sloan, Gail Hopkins, Lucia Blanca for *Days of Our Lives* (NBC)

2535 Outstanding Achievement in Daytime Hairstyling: wig director Bruce Geller; Mr. Pavarotti's wig Victor Callegari for *Un Ballo in Maschera* (PBS)

2536 Outstanding Achievement in Daytime Hairstyling for a Drama Series: Zora Sloan, Pauletta Lewis for *Days of Our Lives* (NBC)

2537 Outstanding Achievement in Daytime Music Direction and Composition: music directors and composers Bruce Hornsby, Peter Harris for *CBS Schoolbreak Special* episode "Soldier Boys" (CBS)

2538 Outstanding Achievement in Music Direction and Composition for a Drama Series: music director Liz Lachman; composer Dominic Messinger; principal arranger Rick Rhodes for *Santa Barbara* (NBC)

2539 Outstanding Achievement in Daytime Film Editing: John Craddock for *CBS Schoolbreak Special* episode "What If I'm Gay?" (CBS)

2540 Outstanding Achievement in Daytime Film Sound Mixing: re-recording mixer James Hodson for *Alf* (NBC)

2541 Outstanding Achievement in Daytime Film Sound Editing: supervising editor Bruce Elliot; sound effects William Koepnick; music editors Richard Gannon, Gregory K. Bowron ADR, Stuart Goetz for *Alf* (NBC)

2542 Outstanding Daytime Achievement in Cinematography: Tom Hurwitz for *ABC Afterschool Special* episode "Just a Regular Kid: An AIDS Story" (ABC)

2543 Outstanding Achievement in Daytime Graphics and Title Design: title designers Wayne Fitzgerald and David Pfeil for *The Bold and the Beautiful* (CBS)

—————— **1988** ——————

2544 Outstanding Drama Series: *L.A. Law* executive producer Steven Bochco; co-executive producer Rick Wallace; supervising producer David E. Kelley; producers Scott Goldstein, Michele Gallery; co-producers William M. Finkelstein, Judith Parker; coordinating producers Phillip M. Goldfarb, Alice West, 20th Century–Fox Film Corporation (NBC)

2545 Outstanding Comedy Series: *Cheers* executive producers James Burrows, Glen Charles, Les Charles; producers Cheri Eichen, Bill Steinkellner, Peter Casey, David Lee; co-producers Tim Berry, Phoef Sutton, a Charles/Burrows/Charles production in association with Paramount Television (NBC)

2546 Outstanding Miniseries: *War and Remembrance* executive producer Dan Curtis; producer Barbara Steele, a Dan Curtis Production in association with ABC Circle Films (ABC)

2547 Outstanding Variety, Music or Comedy Program: *The Tracey Ullman Show* executive producers James L. Brooks, Jerry Belson, Heide Perlman, Ken Estin, Sam Simon; producers Richard Sakai, Ted Bessel; co-producer Marc Flanagan; host Tracey Ullman; a Gracie Films Production in association with 20th Century–Fox Television (Fox)

2548 Outstanding Drama/Comedy Special: *A.T.&T. Presents* episode "Day One" executive producers Aaron Spelling, E. Duke Vincent; producer David W. Rintels; Aaron Spelling Productions, Inc. in association with Paragon Motion Pictures, David Rintels Productions and the World International Network (CBS)

2549 Outstanding Classical Program in the Performing Arts: *Great Performances* episode "Bernstein at 70" executive producers Harry Kraut, Klaus Hallig; producers Michael Bronson, Thomas P. Skinner; International Television Trading Corporation and WNET/New York in association with Video Music Productions, Inc. (PBS)

2550 Outstanding Information Special: *American Masters* episode "Lillian Gish: The Actor's Life for Me" executive producer Freida Lee Mock; producer Terry Sanders; co-producer William T. Cartwright; executive producer Susan Lacy, a co-production of the American Film Foundation and American Masters (PBS)

2551 Outstanding Informational Series: *Nature* executive producer David Heeley; series producer Fred Kaufman; a co-production of WNET, BBC-TV and the Australian Broadcasting Corporation (PBS)

2552 Outstanding Animated Program (for programming less than one hour): *Garfield: Babes and Bullets* producer/director Phil Roman; writer Jim Davis; co-directors John Sparey, Bob Nesler; a Film Roman Production in association with United Media/Mendelson and Paws, Inc. (CBS)

2553 **Outstanding Children's Program:** *Free to Be—A Family Affair* executive producers Marlo Thomas, Christopher Cerf (USA); producer Robert Dalrymple (USA); executive producer Leonid Zolotarevsky (USSR); producer Igor Menzelintsev (USSR); co-producer Vern T. Calhoun; Free to Be . . . Production in association with Gostelradio (Soviet TV) (ABC)

2554 **Outstanding Special Events:** *Cirque du Soleil, the Magic Circus* producer Helene Dufresne; Telemagic Productions, Inc. and Cirque du Soleil Productions, Inc. (HBO); *The 11th Annual Kennedy Center Honors: A Celebration of the Performing Arts* producers George Stevens, Jr.; Nick Vanoff; Smith-Hemion Productions and New Liberty Productions (CBS); *The 42nd Annual Tony Awards* executive producer Don Mischer; producer David J. Goldberg; co-producer Jeffrey Lane; Don Mischer Productions (CBS); *The 17th Annual Film Institute Achievement Award: A Salute to Gregory Peck*, producer George Stevens, Jr.; co-producer Jeffrey Lane; American Film Institute (NBC)

2555 **Outstanding Lead Actor in a Comedy Series:** Richard Mulligan in *Empty Nest* (NBC)

2556 **Outstanding Lead Actor in a Drama Series:** Carroll O'Connor in *In the Heat of the Night* (NBC)

2557 **Outstanding Lead Actor in a Miniseries or a Special:** James Woods in *Hallmark Hall of Fame* episode "My Name Is Bill W." (ABC)

2558 **Outstanding Lead Actress in a Comedy Series:** Candice Bergen in *Murphy Brown* (CBS)

2559 **Outstanding Lead Actress in a Drama Series:** Dana Delaney in *China Beach* (ABC)

2560 **Outstanding Lead Actress in a Miniseries or Special:** Holly Hunter in *Roe vs. Wade* (NBC)

2561 **Outstanding Supporting Actor in a Comedy Series:** Woody Harrelson in *Cheers* (NBC)

2562 **Outstanding Supporting Actor in a Drama Series:** Larry Drake in *L.A. Law* (NBC)

2563 **Outstanding Supporting Actor in a Miniseries or a Special:** Derek Jacobi in *Hallmark Hall of Fame* episode "The Tenth Man" (CBS)

2564 **Outstanding Supporting Actress in a Comedy Series:** Rhea Perlman in *Cheers* (NBC)

2565 **Outstanding Supporting Actress in a Drama Series:** Melanie Mayron in *thirtysomething* (ABC)

2566 **Outstanding Supporting Actress in a Miniseries or Special:** Colleen Dewhurst in *Those She Left Behind* (NBC)

2567 **Outstanding Individual Performance in a Variety or Music Program:** Linda Ronstadt in *Great Performances* episode "Canciones De Mi Padre" (PBS)

2568 **Outstanding Performance in Informational Programming:** Hal Holbrook in *Portrait of America* (TBS)

2569 **Outstanding Performance in Special Events:** Billy Crystal in *The 31st Annual Grammy Awards* (CBS)

2570 **Outstanding Individual Performance in Classical Music/Dance Programming:** Mikhail Baryshnikov in *Great Performances* episode "Dance in America: Baryshnikov Dances Balanchine" (PBS)

2571 **Outstanding Guest Actor in a Comedy Series:** Cleavon Little in *Dear John* episode "Stand by Your Man" (NBC)

2572 **Outstanding Guest Actress in a Comedy Series:** Colleen Dewhurst in *Murphy Brown* episode "Mama Said" (CBS)

2573 **Outstanding Guest Actor in a Drama Series:** Joe Spano in *Midnight Caller* episode "The Execution of John Saringo" (NBC)

2574 **Outstanding Guest Actress in a Drama Series:** Kay Lenz in *Midnight Caller* episode "After It Happened..." (NBC)

2575 **Outstanding Directing in a Comedy Series:** Peter Baldwin for *The Wonder Years* episode "Our Miss White," Black/Marlens Company in association with New World Television (ABC)

2576 **Outstanding Directing in a Drama Series:** Robert Altman for *Tanner '88* episode "The Boiler Room," Darkhorse Productions (HBO)

2577 **Outstanding Directing in a Variety or Music Program:** Jim Henson for *The Jim Henson Hour* episode "Dog City," Jim Henson Productions (NBC)

2578 Outstanding Directing in a Miniseries or a Special: Simon Wincer for *Lonesome Dove*, Motown Productions in association with Pangaea and Quintex Entertainment, Inc. (CBS)

2579 Outstanding Directing for Special Events: Dwight Hemion for *The 11th Annual Kennedy Center Honors: A Celebration of the Performing Arts*, Smith-Hemion Productions and the New Liberty Productions (CBS)

2580 Outstanding Casting Achievement for a Miniseries or Special: Lynn Kressel for *Lonesome Dove*, Motown Productions, Incorporated in association with Pangaea and Quintex Entertainment, Inc. (CBS)

2581 Outstanding Achievement in Choreography: Walter Painter for grand opening of Disney/MGM Studios Theme Park, a Walt Disney Production (NBC)

2582 Outstanding Writing in a Comedy Series: Diane English for the pilot of *Murphy Brown*, Shukovsky/English Productions in association with Warner Brothers Television (CBS)

2583 Outstanding Writing in a Drama Series: Joseph Dougherty for *thirtysomething* episode "First Day/Last Day," the Bedford Falls Company in association with MGM/UA Television (ABC)

2584 Outstanding Writing in a Variety or Music Program: head writer James Downey; writers John Bowman, A. Whitney Brown, Gregory Daniels, Tom Davis, Al Franken, Shannon Gaughan, Jack Handey, Phil Hartman, Lorne Michaels, Mike Myers, Conan O'Brien, Bob Odenkirk, Herb Sargent, Tom Schiller, Robert Smigel, Bonnie Turner, Terr Turner, Christine Zander; additional sketches, George Meyer for *Saturday Night Live*, a Broadway Video Incorporated Production in association with NBC Productions, Inc. (NBC)

2585 Outstanding Writing for a Miniseries or a Special: Abby Mann, Robin Vote, Ron Hutchinson for *Murderers Among Us: The Simon Weisenthal Story*, a Robert Cooper Production/Citadel Entertainment for TVS Films in association with HBO and Hungarian TV (HBO)

2586 Outstanding Writing in Infor-mation Programming: John Haminway for *The Mind: Search for the Mind*, WNET/13 in association with the BBC (PBS)

2587 Outstanding Writing for Special Events: Jeffrey Lane for *The 42nd Annual Tony Awards*, Don Mischer Productions (CBS)

2588 Outstanding Cinematography for a Series: Roy H. Wagner ASC for the pilot program of *Quantum Leap*, a Belisarius Production in association with Universal Television (NBC)

2589 Outstanding Cinematography for a Miniseries or a Special: Gayne Rescher ASC for *Shooter*, UBU Productions in association with Paramount Pictures (NBC)

2590 Outstanding Art Direction for a Series: production designer James J. Agazzi; set decorator Bill Harp; for *Moonlighting* episode "A Womb with a View" (ABC)

2591 Outstanding Art Direction for a Miniseries or a Special: production designer Jan Scott; art director Jack Taylor; set decorator Edward J. McDonald for *I'll Be Home for Christmas*, NBC Productions (NBC)

2592 Outstanding Art Direction for a Variety or Music Program: art director Bernie Yeszin; set decorator Portia Iversen for *The Tracey Ullman Show* episode "All About Tammy Lee, Maggie in Peril (Part 2)" (syndicated)

2593 Outstanding Achievement in Music Composition for a Series (Dramatic Underscore): Joel Rosenbaum for *Falcon Crest* episode "Dust to Dust," Amanda & MF Productions in association with Lorimar-Telepictures (CBS)

2594 Outstanding Achievement in Music Composition for a Miniseries or a Special (Dramatic Underscore): Basil Poledouris for *Lonesome Dove* episode "The Return (Part 4)," Motown Productions in association with Pangaea and Quintex Entertainment, Inc. (CBS)

2595 Outstanding Achievement in Music Direction: music director Ian Fraser; principal arrangers Chris Boardman, J. Hill for *Christmas in Washington*, Smith-Hemion Productions and New Liberty Productions (NBC)

2596 Outstanding Achievement in Music and Lyrics: composer Lee Holdridge, lyricist Melanie for "The First Time I Loved Forever" (song) from *Beauty and the Beast*, episode "A Distant Shore," a Witt-Thomas Production in association with Ron Koslow Films and Republic Pictures (CBS)

2597 Outstanding Costume Design for a Series: Judy Evans for *Beauty and the Beast* episode "The Outsiders," a Witt-Thomas Production in association with Ron Koslow Films and Republic Pictures (CBS)

2598 Outstanding Costume Design for a Miniseries or a Special: Van Broughton Ramsey for *Lonesome Dove* episode "On the Trail (Part 2)," Motown Productions in association with Pangaea and Quintex Entertainment, Inc. (CBS)

2599 Outstanding Costume Design for a Variety or Music Program: Daniel Orlandi for *The Magic of David Copperfield XI: The Explosive Encounter*, DCDI Productions, Inc. (CBS)

2600 Outstanding Achievement in Costuming in a Series: men's costumer Patrick R. Norris; women's costumer Julie Glick for *thirtysomething* episode "We'll Meet Again," the Bedford Falls Company in association with MGM/UA Television (ABC)

2601 Outstanding Achievement in Costuming for a Miniseries or Special: costume supervisor Paula Kaatz; L.A. women's costumer Andrea Weaver; Janet Lawler, Dallas women's costumer; men's costumer Stephen Chudez in *Pancho Barnes* for Blue Andre Productions in association with Orion Television (CBS)

2602 Outstanding Achievement in Make-Up for a Series: special makeup Thomas R. Burman; Robin Lavigne, Carol Schwartz for *The Tracey Ullman Show* episode "The Subway," Pancho Barnes, Blue Andre Productions in Association with Orion Television (Fox)

2603 Outstanding Achievement in Make-Up for a Miniseries or Special: makeup supervisor Manlio Rocchetti; makeup artists Carla Palmer, Jean Black for *Lonesome Dove (Part 4)*, Motown Productions in association with Pangaea and Quintex Entertainment Inc. (CBS)

2604 Outstanding Achievement in Hairstyling for a Series: Virginia Kearns for *Quantum Leap* episode "Double Identity," a Belisarius Production in association with Universal Television (NBC)

2605 Outstanding Achievement in Hairstyling for a Miniseries or a Special: chief hairstylist Betty Glasow; hairstylists Steve Hall, Elaine Bowerbank for *Jack the Ripper (Part I)*, Euston Films and Hill-O'Connor Entertainment in association with Lorimar (CBS)

2606 Outstanding Editing for a Series (Single-Camera Production): Steven J. Rosenblum for *thirtysomething* episode "First Day/Last Day," the Bedford Falls Company in association with MGM/UA Television (ABC)

2607 Outstanding Editing for a Miniseries or a Special (Single-Camera Production): Peter Zinner ACE, John Burnett ACE for *War and Remembrance (Part 10)*, a Dan Curtis Production in association with ABC Circle Films (ABC)

2608 Outstanding Editing for a Series (Multi-Camera Production): Tucker Wiard for the pilot of *Murphy Brown*, Shukovsky/English Production in association with Warner Brothers Television (CBS)

2609 Outstanding Editing for a Miniseries or a Special Program (Multi-Camera Production): Mark D. West for *Great Performances* episode "Dance in America: Gregory Hines Tap Dance in America," a Don Mischer Production in association with WNET/New York (PBS)

2610 Outstanding Sound Editing for a Series: supervising sound and ADR editor William Wistrom; sound editors James Wolvington, Mace Matiosian, Wilson Dyer, Guy Tsujimoto; supervising music editor Gerry Sackman for *Star Trek: The Next Generation* episode "Q Who," Paramount Pictures Corporation (syndication)

2611 Outstanding Sound Editing for a Miniseries or a Special: supervising sound editor David McMoyler; co-supervising editor Joseph Melody; sound editors Mark Steele, Rick Steele, Michael J. Wright, Gary Macheel, Stephen Grubbs, Mark Friedgen, Charles R. Beith, Scot A.

Tinsley, Karla Caldwell, George B. Bell, G. Michael Graham; ADR editor Kristi Johns; supervising music editors Tom Villano, Jamie Gelb for *Lonesome Dove* episode three, "The Plains," Motown Productions in association with Pangaea and Qintex Entertainment, Inc. (CBS)

2612 Outstanding Sound Mixing for a Comedy Series or a Special: production mixer Klaus Landsberg; re-recording mixers Craig Porter, Alan Patapoff; for *Night Court* episode "The Last Temptation of Mac," Starry Night Productions in association with Warner Brothers Television (NBC)

2613 Outstanding Sound Mixing for a Variety or Music Series or Special: SFX mixer Robert Douglass; re-recording mixer David E. Fluhr; production mixer Ed Greene; music mixer Larry Brown for *Kenny, Dolly, and Willie: Something Inside So Strong*, a Kenny Rogers–Barris Production in association with the Guber-Peters Company (NBC)

2614 Outstanding Sound Mixing for a Drama Series: dialogue re-recording mixer Chris Haire; effects re-recording mixer Doug Davey; music re-recording mixer Richard Morrison; production sound mixer Alan Bernard for *Star Trek: The Next Generation* episode "Q Who," Paramount Pictures Corporation (syndicated)

2615 Outstanding Sound Mixing for a Miniseries or a Special: sound mixer Don Johnson CAS; dialogue mixer James L. Aicholtz; music mixer Michael Herbick; sound effects mixer Kevin O'Connell for *Lonesome Dove* episode four, "The Return," Motown Productions in association with Pangaea and Qintex Entertainment, Inc. (CBS)

2616 Outstanding Sound Mixing for a Special Event: music production mixer Ed Greene; dialogue production mixer Don Worsham; production mixer audience reaction Carroll Pratt; production mixer nomination categories Paul Sandweiss for *The 31st Annual Grammy Awards*, a Pierre Cossette Production (CBS)

2617 Outstanding Technical Direction/Camera/Video for a Series: technical director Robert G. Holmes; camera operators Leigh V. Nicholson, John Repcynski, Jeffrey Wheat, Rocky Danielson; senior video control Thomas G. Tcimpidis for *Night Court* episode "Yet Another Day in the Life," Starry Night Productions in association with Warner Brothers Television (NBC)

2618 Outstanding Achievement in Special Visual Effects: supervising editors Charles Staffell, Martin Gutteridge; miniature designer Bill Cruse; directors of photography Egil Woxholt, Bill Schirmer, Godfrey Godar; miniature designers Simon Smith, Steve Anderson, Ed Williams for *War and Remembrance*, a Dan Curtis Production in association with ABC Circle Films (ABC)

2619 Outstanding Technical Direction/Camera/Video for a Miniseries or Special: technical director Ron Graft; camera operators Richard G. Price, Kenneth Patterson, Greg Harms; senior video control Mark Sanford for *American Playhouse* episode "The Meeting," a co-production of KCET/Los Angeles, Hillard Elkins Entertainment, Yagya Productions and Jeff Stetson (PBS)

2620 Outstanding Electronic Lighting Direction: Mark Levin for *Who's the Boss* episode "A Spirited Christmas," Hunter/Cohan Productions in association with Columbia Pictures Television (ABC)

2621 Governor's Award: Lucille Ball

2622 Outstanding Daytime Drama Series: *Santa Barbara* executive producer Jill Farren; senior supervising producer Steven Kent; supervising producer Charlotte Savitz; producers Julie Hanan Caruthers, Leonard Friedlander (NBC)

2623 Outstanding Daytime Game/Audience Participation Show: *The $25,000 Pyramid* executive producer Bob Stewart; supervising producer Anne Marie Schmitt; producers Francine Bergman, David Michaels (CBS)

2624 Outstanding Daytime Children's Series: *Newton's Apple* executive producer James Steinbach; supervising producers Lee Carey, Tracy Mangan; producer Lynne Reeck (PBS)

2625 Outstanding Daytime Children's Special: *ABC Afterschool Special* episode "Taking a Stand," executive producer Frank Doelger; producer Roberta Rowe (ABC)

2626 **Outstanding Daytime Animated Program:** *The New Adventures of Winnie the Pooh*, producer/director Karl Geurs; senior editor/writer Mark Zaslove; writers Bruce Talkington, Carter Crocker (ABC)

2627 **Outstanding Daytime Talk/Service Program:** *The Oprah Winfrey Show*, executive producer Debra DiMaio; supervising producer Oprah Winfrey; producers Ellen Rakieten, Dianne Hudson, Mary Kay Clinton, Angela Thame, Alice McGee (syndicated)

2628 **Outstanding Daytime Special Class Program Area:** *China: Walls and Bridges* executive producers Jimmy R. Allen, Richard T. McCartney; supervising producer and producer Robert Thornton (ABC); and *James Stewart's Wonderful Life*, executive producer Mary Frances Shea; supervising producer Phil Delbourgo; producer Dan Gurskis (Max)

2629 **Outstanding Lead Actress in a Daytime Drama Series:** Marcy Walker in *Santa Barbara* (NBC)

2630 **Outstanding Lead Actor in a Daytime Drama Series:** David Canary in *All My Children* (ABC)

2631 **Outstanding Supporting Actress in a Daytime Drama Series:** Debbi Morgan in *All My Children* (ABC)

2632 **Outstanding Supporting Actor in a Daytime Drama Series:** Justin Deas in *Santa Barbara* (NBC)

2633 **Outstanding Juvenile Male in a Daytime Drama Series:** Justin Gocke in *Santa Barbara* (NBC)

2634 **Outstanding Juvenile Female in a Daytime Drama Series:** Kimberly McCullough in *General Hospital* (ABC)

2635 **Outstanding Performer in a Daytime Children's Series:** Jim Varney in *Hey Vern, It's Ernest!* (CBS)

2636 **Outstanding Daytime Game Show Host:** Alex Trebek in *Jeopardy!* (syndicated)

2637 **Outstanding Daytime Talk/Service Show Host:** Sally Jessy Raphaël in *Sally Jessy Raphaël* (syndicated)

2638 **Outstanding Daytime Drama Series Directing Team:** directors Frank Pacelli, Heather Hill, Randy Robbins, Rudy Vejar; associate directors Betty Rothenberg, Kathryn Foster for *The Young and the Restless* (CBS)

2639 **Outstanding Directing in a Daytime Game/Audience Participation Show:** Dick Schneider for *Jeopardy!* (syndicated)

2640 **Outstanding Directing in a Daytime Talk/Service Show:** Jim McPharlin for *The Oprah Winfrey Show* (syndicated)

2641 **Outstanding Directing in a Daytime Children's Show:** Matthew Diamond for *Shining Time Station* (PBS) and Ozzie Alfonso for *3-2-1 Contact* (PBS)

2642 **Outstanding Writing Team for a Daytime Drama Series:** head writers Chuck Pratt, Jr., Anne Howard Bailey; script writers Robert Guza, Jr., Courtney Simon, Lynda Myles, Patrick Mulcahey, Gary Tomlin; breakdown/script writers Josh Griffith, Jane Atkins; breakdown writer Don Harary for *Santa Barbara* (NBC)

2643 **Outstanding Writing in a Daytime Children's Series:** head writer Norman Stiles; writers Nancy Sans, Luis Santeiro, Cathi Rosenberg-Turow, Belinda Ward, Sonia Manzano, Jeff Moss, Sara Compton, Judy Freudberg, David Korr, John Weidman, Tony Geiss, Emily Perl Kingsley, Mark Saltzman, Christian Clark, Jon Stone for *Sesame Street* (PBS)

2644 **Outstanding Daytime Art Direction/Set Decoration/Scenic Design:** production designers Anthony Sabatino, William H. Harris; art directors Phyllis Hofberg, Richard D. Bluhm for *Fun House* (syndicated)

2645 **Outstanding Daytime Art Direction/Set Decoration/Scenic Design for a Drama Series:** art directors William Hultstrom, Norman Wadell; set decorators Joseph Bevacqua, Andrea Joel, Eric Fischer for *The Young and the Restless* (CBS)

2646 **Outstanding Daytime Technical Direction/Electronic Camera/Video Control:** technical director Ray Angona; electronic camera Jose Arvizu, Cesar Cabriera, Keeth Lawrence, Martin Wagner; video control Allen Latter for *The Price Is Right* (CBS)

2647 **Outstanding Technical Direction/Electronic Camera/ Video Control for a Daytime Drama Series:** technical director Chuck Guzzi; electronic camera

Toby Brown, Ted Morales, Gordon Sweeney, Mike Glenn; video control Roberto Bosio for *The Bold and the Beautiful* (CBS)

2648 Outstanding Daytime Lighting Direction: Carl Gibson for *Kids Incorporated* (Disney)

2649 Outstanding Lighting Direction for a Daytime Drama Series: Donna Larson, Alan Blacher, Dennis M. Size for *All My Children* (ABC)

2650 Outstanding Daytime Videotape Editing: Charles Randazzo, Peter Moyer, David Pincus, Steve Purcell for *Pee-wee's Playhouse* (CBS)

2651 Outstanding Videotape Editing for a Daytime Drama Series: Dan Brumett, Marc Beruti for *The Young and the Restless* (CBS)

2652 Outstanding Daytime Live & Tape Sound Mixing and Sound Effects: production mixers Peter Miller, Rick Patterson; post-production mixers Pam Bartella, Paul D. Collins, Ferne Friedman, Ken Hahn, Grant Maxwell, John Purcell for *3-2-1 Contact* (PBS)

2653 Outstanding Achievement in Daytime Costume Design: Calista Hendrickson for *Encyclopedia* (HBO)

2654 Outstanding Achievement in Costume Design for a Daytime Drama Series: Margarita Delgado, Charles Schoonmaker for *Another World* (NBC)

2655 Outstanding Achievement in Daytime Make-Up: Paul Gebbia for *Encyclopedia* (HBO)

2656 Outstanding Live and Tape Sound Mixing and Sound Effects for a Daytime Drama Series: audio mixers Scott Millan, Tommy Persson; post-production mixers Donald Henderson, Rafael Valentin; sound effects Maurice "Smokey" Westerfeld, Peter Romano for *The Young and the Restless* (CBS)

2657 Outstanding Achievement in Make-Up for a Daytime Drama Series: Carlos Yeaggy, John Maldonado, Dawn Marando for *Santa Barbara* (NBC)

2658 Outstanding Achievement in Daytime Hairstyling: Andre Walker for *The Oprah Winfrey Show* (syndicated); and Yolanda Toussieng, Jerry Masone for *Pee-wee's Playhouse* episode "To Tell the Tooth" (CBS)

2659 Outstanding Achievement in Daytime Cinematography: Ozzie Alfonso, Larry Engel, Howard Hall, Robert Leacock, Don Lenzer, Christophe Lanzenburg, Chuck Levey, Rick Malkames, Dyanna Taylor, Jeri Sopanen for *3-2-1 Contact* (PBS)

2660 Outstanding Achievement in Daytime Graphics and Title Design: animation designer Barbara Laszewski; graphics artist Joel Anderson for *Hey Vern, It's Ernest!* (CBS)

2661 Outstanding Achievement in Hairstyling for a Daytime Drama Series: Janet Medford, Valerie Scott for *Santa Barbara* (NBC)

2662 Outstanding Achievement in Daytime Music Direction and Composition: music director/composer Joe Raposo; composers Jeff Moss, Christopher Cerf; composer/arranger Dave Conner for *Sesame Street* (PBS)

2663 Outstanding Achievement in Daytime Film Editing: Harvey Greenstein, Sam Pollard, Grace Tankersley for *3-2-1 Contact* (PBS)

2664 Outstanding Achievement in Music Direction for a Daytime Drama Series: music director/composer Jez Davidson; music director David Matthews; composers David Kurtz, Jack Allocco for *The Young and the Restless* (CBS)

2665 Outstanding Achievement in Daytime Film Sound Mixing: Jeff Haboush, Greg Russell for *Jim Henson's Muppet Babies* (CBS)

2666 Outstanding Achievement in Daytime Film Sound Editing: supervising editor Al Breittenbach; editor Ron Fedele; supervising music editor Richard Allen, sound effects editors Steve Williams, Ken Burton for *Jim Henson's Muppet Babies* (CBS); and dialogue/ADR editor Steve Michael; dialogue/music editor Peter Cole; supervising sound effects editor Steve Kirklys; sound effects/ADR editor Ken Dahlinger; sound effects editors Greg Teall, John Walker for *Pee-wee's Playhouse* episode "To Tell the Tooth" (CBS)

─────── **1 9 8 9** ───────

2667 Outstanding Drama Series: *L.A. Law* executive producer David E. Kelley; co-executive producer Rick Wallace;

supervising producer William M. Finkelstein; producers Elodie Keene, Michael M. Robin; coordinating producer Alice West; co-producer Robert M. Breech, 20th Century-Fox Film Corporation (NBC)

2668 Outstanding Comedy Series: *Murphy Brown*, executive producers Diane English, Joel Shukovsky; consulting producer Korby Siamis; producers Tom Seeley, Norm Gunzenhauser, Russ Woody, Gary Dontzig, Steven Peterman, Barnet Kellman; co-producer Deborah Smith; Shukovsky/ English Productions in association with Warner Brothers Television (CBS)

2669 Outstanding Miniseries: *Drug Wars: The Camarena Story*, executive producer Michael Mann; co-executive producer Richard Brams; supervising producers Christopher Canaan, Rose Schacht, Ann Powell; producer Branko Lustig; co-producer Mark Allan, ZZY, Incorporated (NBC)

2670 Outstanding Variety, Music or Comedy Series: *In Living Color*, executive producer Keenan Ivory Wayans; supervising producer Kevin S. Bright; producer Tamara Rawitt; co-producer Michael Petok, an Ivory Way Production in association with 20th Century-Fox Television (Fox)

2671 Outstanding Drama/Comedy Special: *Hallmark Hall of Fame* episode "Caroline?," executive producers Dan Enright, Les Alexander, Don Enright; co-executive producers Barbara Hiser, Joseph Broio; producer Dorothea G. Petrie, Barry & Enright Productions (CBS); and *A.T.&T. Presents* episode "The Incident," executive producer Robert Halmi; producers Ed Self, Bill Brademan, Qintex Productions, Inc. (CBS)

2672 Outstanding Classical Program in the Performing Arts: *The Metropolitan Opera Presents Aida*, executive producer Peter Gelb; Metropolitan Opera Association, Incorporated (CBS)

2673 Outstanding Variety, Music, or Comedy Special: *Sammy Davis Jr.'s 60th Anniversary Special*, producer George Schlatter, co-producers Jeff Margolis, Buz Kohan, Gary Necessary, Maria Schlatter; George Schlatter Productions (ABC)

2674 Outstanding Information Special: *American Masters* episode "Broadway's Dreamers: The Legacy of the Group Theatre," executive producers Jac Venza, Susan Lacy, producers Joan Kramer, David Heeley, Joanne Woodward, a production of WNET/New York (PBS); and *Great Performances* episode "Dance in America: Bob Fosse Steam Heat," executive producer Jac Venza, producer Judy Kinberg, a production of WNET/ New York (PBS)

2675 Outstanding Informational Series: *Smithsonian World*, executive producer Adrian Malone; producer Sandra W. Bradley, a co-production of WETA-TV and the Smithsonian Institution in association with Wentworth Films, Inc. (PBS)

2676 Outstanding Animated Program (for programming less than one hour): *The Simpsons*, executive producers James L. Brooks, Matt Groening, Sam Simon; producer Richard Sakai; co-producers Al Jean, Mike Reiss, Larina Jean Adamson; animation producer Margot Pipkin; supervising animation director Gabor Csupo; director David Silverman; writer John Schwartzwelder, a Gracie Films Production in association with 20th Century-Fox Television (Fox)

2677 Outstanding Children's Program: *The Magical World of Disney* episode "A Mother's Courage: The Mary Thomas Story," executive producers Ted Field, Robert W. Cort; co-executive producers Patricia Clifford, Kate Wright; producer Richard L. O'Connor, co-producer Chet Walker, Chet Walker Enterprises, Inc. and Interscope Communications, Inc. in association with Walt Disney Television (NBC)

2678 Outstanding Lead Actor in a Comedy Series: Ted Danson in *Cheers* (NBC)

2679 Outstanding Lead Actor in a Drama Series: Peter Falk in *Columbo* (ABC)

2680 Outstanding Lead Actor in a Miniseries or a Special: Hume Cronyn in *Age-Old Friends* (HBO)

2681 Outstanding Lead Actress in a Comedy Series: Candice Bergen in *Murphy Brown* (CBS)

2682 Outstanding Lead Actress in a Drama Series: Patricia Wettig in *thirtysomething* (ABC)

2683 Outstanding Lead Actress in a Miniseries or Special: Barbara Hershey in *A Killing in a Small Town* (CBS)

2684 Outstanding Supporting Actor in a Comedy Series: Alex Rocco in *The Famous Teddy Z* (CBS)

2685 Outstanding Supporting Actor in a Drama Series: Jimmy Smits in *L.A. Law* (NBC)

2686 Outstanding Supporting Actor in a Miniseries or a Special: Vincent Gardenia in *Age-Old Friends* (HBO)

2687 Outstanding Supporting Actress in a Comedy Series: Bebe Neuwirth in *Cheers* (NBC)

2688 Outstanding Supporting Actress in a Drama Series: Marg Helgenberger in *China Beach* (ABC)

2689 Outstanding Supporting Actress in a Miniseries or Special: Eva Marie Saint in *People Like Us* (NBC)

2690 Outstanding Individual Performance in a Variety or Music Program: Tracey Ullman in *The Best of the Tracey Ullman Show* (Fox)

2691 Outstanding Performance in Informational Programming: George Burns in *A Conversation With...* (Disney)

2692 Outstanding Individual Performance in Classical Music/Dance Programming: Katarina Witt, Brian Orser, Brian Boitano in *Carmen on Ice* (HBO)

2693 Outstanding Guest Actor in a Comedy Series: Jay Thomas in *Murphy Brown* episode "Heart of Gold" (CBS)

2694 Outstanding Guest Actress in a Comedy Series: Swoosie Kurtz in *Carol & Company* episode "Reunion" (NBC)

2695 Outstanding Guest Actor in a Drama Series: Patrick McGoohan in *Columbo* episode "Agenda for Murder" (ABC)

2696 Outstanding Guest Actress in a Drama Series: Viveca Lindfors in *Life Goes On* episode "Save the Last Dance for Me" (ABC)

2697 Outstanding Directing in a Comedy Series: Michael Dinner for *The Wonder Years* episode "Good-Bye," Black/Marlens Company in association with New World Television (ABC)

2698 Outstanding Directing in a Drama Series: Thomas Carter for *Equal Justice* episode "Promises to Keep," a Thomas Carter Company Production in association with Orion Television (ABC); Scott Winant for *thirtysomething* episode "The Go-Between," the Bedford Falls Company in association with MGM (ABC)

2699 Outstanding Directing in a Variety or Music Program: Dwight Hemion for *The Kennedy Center Honors: A Celebration of the Performing Arts*, Kennedy Center Television Productions (CBS)

2700 Outstanding Directing in a Miniseries or a Special: Joseph Sargent for *Hallmark Hall of Fame* episode "Caroline?," Barry & Enright Productions (CBS)

2701 Outstanding Directing for Classical Music/Dance Programming: director of concert performances Alan Skog; director Peter Rosen for *The Eighth Van Cliburn International Piano Competition: Here to Make Music*, Peter Rosen Productions, Inc. (PBS)

2702 Outstanding Directing for an Informational Program: Gene Lasko for *American Masters* episode "W. Eugene Smith: Photography Made Difficult," a co-production of Wes Foree Productions, WQED/Pittsburgh, and WNET/New York (PBS)

2703 Outstanding Achievement in Choreography: Paula Abdul, Michael Darrin, Dean Barlow for *The 17th Annual American Music Awards*, Dick Clark Productions, Inc. (ABC)

2704 Outstanding Writing in a Comedy Series: Bob Brush for *The Wonder Years* episode "Good-Bye," a Black/Marlens Company in association with New World Television (ABC)

2705 Outstanding Writing in a Drama Series: David E. Kelley for *L.A. Law* episode "Blood, Sweat & Fears," 20th Century-Fox Film Corporation (NBC)

2706 Outstanding Writing in a Variety or Music Program: Billy Crystal for *Billy Crystal: Midnight Train to Moscow*, a Robert Dalrymple/Jennilind Production (HBO); James L. Brooks, Heide Perlman, Sam Simon, Jerry Belson, Marc Flanagan, Diana Kirgo, Jay Kogen,

Wallace Wolodarsky, Ian Praiser, Marilyn Suzanne Miller, Tracey Ullman for *The Tracey Ullman Show*, a Gracie Films Production in association with 20th Century-Fox Television (Fox)

2707 Outstanding Writing for a Miniseries or a Special: Terrence McNally for *American Playhouse* episode "Andre's Mother," DBR Films Limited in association with American Playhouse (PBS)

2708 Outstanding Cinematography for a Series: Michael Watkins for *Quantum Leap* episode "Pool Hall Blues," Universal Television in association with Belisarius Productions, Inc. (NBC)

2709 Outstanding Cinematography for a Miniseries or Special: Donald M. Morgan ASC for *Murder in Mississippi,* David Wolper Productions and Elliot Friedgen & Company Inc., Productions, in association with Bernard Sofronski (NBC)

2710 Outstanding Art Direction for a Series: production designer Richard D. James; set decorator James J. Mees for *Star Trek: The Next Generation* episode "Sins of the Father," Paramount Pictures Corporation (syndicated)

2711 Outstanding Art Direction for a Miniseries or a Special: production designers Timian Alsaker, Jacques Bufnoir for *Phantom of the Opera (Part 2),* a co-production of Saban/Scherick and Hexatel in association with Starcom, TFI, Reteitalia, BetaFilm (NBC)

2712 Outstanding Art Direction for a Variety or Music Program: production designer Roy Christopher; art director Greg Richman for *The 62nd Annual Academy Awards,* ABC Television (ABC)

2713 Outstanding Achievement in Music Composition for a Series (Dramatic Underscore): Don Davis for *Beauty and the Beast* episode "A Time to Heal," a Witt-Thomas Production in association with Republic Pictures (CBS)

2714 Outstanding Achievement in Music Composition for a Miniseries or a Special (Dramatic Underscore): James Di Pasquale for *Hallmark Hall of Fame* episode "The Shell Seekers," a Marian Rees Associates, Inc., Production in association with Central Television (ABC)

2715 Outstanding Achievement in Music Direction: music director Ian Fraser; principal arrangers Chris Boardman, J. Hill, Bill Byers, Bob Florence, Angela Morley for *Great Performances* episode "Julie Andrews in Concert," WNET/13 in association with Greengage Productions, Inc. (PBS)

2716 Outstanding Achievement in Music and Lyrics: composer Larry Grossman; lyricist Buz Kohan for *From the Heart — The Very First Special Arts Festival,* a Smith-Hemion Production (NBC)

2717 Outstanding Costume Design for a Series: Patricia Norris for the pilot of *Twin Peaks,* Lynch/Frost Productions, Inc. in association with Spelling Entertainment, Inc. (ABC)

2718 Outstanding Costume Design for a Miniseries or a Special: Shelley Komarov for *The Kennedys of Massachusetts (Part 1),* an Edgar J. Scherick Associates Production in association with Orion Television (ABC)

2719 Outstanding Costume Design for a Variety or Music Program: Pat Field for *Mother Goose Rock 'n' Rhyme,* Think Entertainment (CBS)

2720 Outstanding Achievement in Costuming for a Series: Frances H. Hays for the pilot of *The Young Riders,* Ogiens/Kane Company in association with MGM/UA (ABC)

2721 Outstanding Achievement in Make-Up for a Series: makeup effects supervisor Rick Startton; head makeup artist Michele Burke; makeup artists Richard Snell, Katalin Elek, Ken Diaz for *Alien Nation* episode "Chains of Love," a Kenneth Johnson Production in association with 20th Century-Fox Film Corporation (Fox); Thomas R. Burman, Bari Dreiband-Burman, Dale Condit, Ron Walters, Greg Nelson for *The Tracey Ullman Show* episode "High School Sweethearts," a Gracie Films Production in association with 20th Century-Fox Television (Fox)

2722 Outstanding Achievement in Makeup for a Miniseries or Special: Ken Chase for *Billy Crystal: Midnight Train to Moscow,* a Robert Dalrymple/Jennilind Production (HBO)

2723 Outstanding Achievement in

Hairstyling for a Series: Linle White, Peggy Shannon for *The Tracey Ullman Show* episode "My Date with Il Duce, the Thrill Is Gone, the Wrong Message," a Gracie Films Production in association with 20th Century–Fox Television (Fox)

2724 Outstanding Achievement in Hairstyling for a Miniseries or a Special: Ms. Peter's hairstylist Janice Alexander; hairstylist Dorothy Andre for *Fall from Grace*, NBC Productions (NBC); Cedric Chami for *Phantom of the Opera (Part 1)*, a co-production of Saban/Scherick and Hexatel in association with Starcom, TFI, Reteitalia, BetaFilm (NBC)

2725 Outstanding Editing for a Series (Single Camera Production): Duwayne Dunham for the pilot of *Twin Peaks*, Lynch/Frost Productions, Inc. in association with Spelling Entertainment, Inc. (ABC)

2726 Outstanding Editing for a Miniseries or a Special (Single Camera Production): Paul LaMastra ACE for *Hallmark Hall of Fame* episode "Caroline?," Barry & Enright Productions (CBS)

2727 Outstanding Editing for a Series (Multi-Camera Production): Douglas Hines ASC, M. Pam Blumenthal for *The Tracey Ullman Show* episode "...And God Created, Tillman, Rare Talent," a Gracie Films Production in association with 20th Century–Fox Television (Fox)

2728 Outstanding Editing for a Miniseries or a Special (Multi-Camera Production): M. Pam Blumenthal, Douglas Hines, Brian K. Roberts for *The Best of the Tracey Ullman Show*, a Gracie Films Production in association with 20th Century–Fox Television (Fox)

2729 Outstanding Sound Editing for a Series: supervising sound editor William Wistrom; sound editors James Wolvington, Mace Matiosian, Wilson Dyer, Rick Freeman; supervising music editor Gerry Sackman for *Star Trek: The Next Generation* episode "Yesterday's Enterprise," Paramount Pictures Corporation (syndication)

2730 Outstanding Sound Editing for a Miniseries or a Special: supervising sound editor Vince Gutierrez; sound editors Randal S. Thomas, Ken Gladden, Mace Matiosian, Joseph A. Johnston, T.W.

Davis, Douglas Gray, John Orr, Gary Gelfand, Andre Caporaso, Russell Brower, David Scharf; supervising ADR editor Philip Jamtaas; supervising music editor John Caper, Jr. for *Challenger*, the Indie/Prod Company in association with King Phoenix Entertainment (ABC); supervising sound editors Burton Weinstein, Michael Gutierrez; sound editors Randal S. Thomas, Joseph A. Johnston, Ken Gladden, George R. Groves, Philip Jamtaas, Sam Black, Andre Caporaso, Clark Conrad, Gary Gelfand, John Orr, David Scharf, Terence Thomas, T.W. Davis; supervising music editor Abby Treloggen for *Family of Spies (Part 1)*, King Phoenix Entertainment, Inc. (CBS)

2731 Outstanding Sound Mixing for a Comedy Series or a Special: production mixer Robert Crosby, Jr. CAS; re-recording mixers Thomas J. Huth CAS, Sam Black, Bobby Douglass; for *Cheers* episode "The Stork Brings a Crane," Charles/Burrows/Charles Productions in association with Paramount (NBC)

2732 Outstanding Sound Mixing for a Variety or Music Series or Special: production mixers Gordon Klimuck, Barton Michael Chiate for *The Arsenio Hall Show* episode #292, Arsenio Hall Communications, Ltd. in association with Paramount Domestic Television (syndicated)

2733 Outstanding Sound Mixing for a Drama Miniseries or a Special: production mixer Fred Schultz; re-recording mixers William McCaughey, Richard D. Rogers, Grover Helmsley for *Cross of Fire (Part 1)*, Leonard Hill Films (NBC)

2734 Outstanding Technical Direction/Camera/Video for a Series: technical director Terry Rohnke; camera operators Steve Jambeck, Joe De Bonis, Jan Kasoff, John Pinto, Robert Reese; senior video control Bruce Shapiro for *Saturday Night Live* episode "Host: Christopher Walken," a Broadway Video, Inc. Production in association with NBC Productions (NBC)

2735 Outstanding Technical Direction/Camera/Video for a Miniseries or a Special: technical director and senior video control Keith Winikoff; camera operators Gary Childs, Dave Banks, Sam Drummy, Hank Geving, Dean Hall, Dave Levisohn, Bill Philbin, Hector Ramirez, for *The Magic of David Copperfield XII: The Niagara Falls Challenge*, DCDI Productions, Inc. (CBS)

2736 Outstanding Achievement in Special Visual Effects: special visual effects supervisor Craig Barron; effects art direction supervisor Michael Pangrazio; motion control camera Charlie Mullen; matte artist Bill Mather for *By Dawn's Early Light*, a Jack Sholder Film in association with Panavision International and HBO Pictures (HBO); visual effects supervisor William Mesa; visual effects art director Tony Tremblay; matte supervisor Tim Donahue; technical director John Coats; miniatures supervisor David B. Sharp for *Miracle Landing*, a CBS Entertainment Production (CBS); conceived and directed by Zbig Rybczynski; visual effects editor John O'Connor; ultimatte operator Ryszard Welnowski; motion control operator Paul Bachman for *Great Performances* episode "The Orchestra," ZBIG Vision, Ltd. (PBS)

2737 Outstanding Electronic Lighting Design for a Comedy Series: George Spiro Dibie for *Highway to Heaven* episode "Just the Ten of Us," a GSM Production in association with Warner Brothers Television (ABC)

2738 Outstanding Electronic Lighting Direction for a Drama Series, Variety Series, Miniseries or a Special: Olin Younger for *The 17th Annual American Music Awards*, Dick Clark Productions, Incorporated (ABC); John Rook for *Time Warner Presents "The Earth Day Special,"* People of the Earth Foundation, Richard Baskin, Inc., Beacon Pictures and Sum Entertainment Group, Inc. in association with Warner Brothers Television (ABC)

2739 Outstanding Achievement in Engineering Development: Emmy Award to Comark Communications, Inc. and Varian/Elmac (and its creative team members Merald Shrader, Don Priest, and Nat Osteroff) for the Klystrode UHF Power Amplifier Tube and Transmitter; Zaxcom Video, Inc. (and Glenn Sanders) for the TBC Control System; Engineering Plaque to Alan Gordon Enterprises (and Grant Loucks and Geoff Williamson) for

the Image 300 35mm High Speed Camera; Samuelson Alga Cinema (and its creative team members Jean Marie Lavalou, Alain Masseron, David Samuelson and Herve Theys) for the Louma Camera

2740 Governor's Award: Leonard Goldenson

2741 Outstanding Daytime Drama Series: *Santa Barbara* senior executive producer John Conboy; executive producer Jill Farren Phelps; senior supervising producer Steve Kent; supervising producer Charlotte Savitz; producer Julie Hanan Caruthers (NBC)

2742 Outstanding Daytime Game/Audience Participation Show: *Jeopardy!*, executive producer Merv Griffin, producer George Vosburgh (syndicated)

2743 Outstanding Daytime Children's Series: *Reading Rainbow* executive producers Twila Liggett, Tony Buttino; supervising producer/producer Cecily Truett; producers Orly Berger, Jill Gluckson, Ronnie Krauss; contributing producer LeVar Burton (PBS)

2744 Outstanding Daytime Children's Special: *CBS Schoolbreak Special* episode "A Matter of Conscience," executive producer Eve Silverman; producer Susan Aronson (CBS)

2745 Outstanding Daytime Animated Program: *The New Adventures of Winnie the Pooh*, producers/directors Ken Kessel, Karl Geurs; producer Ed Ghertner; director Terence Harrison; story editors Bruce Talkington, Mark Zaslove; writers Steven Sustarsic, Carter Crocker (ABC); *Beetlejuice* executive producers David Geffen, Tim Burton; supervising producer Lenora Hume; coordinating producer Steven Hodgins; producers Hicjael Hirsh, Patrick Loubert, Clive A. Smith; story editors Patsy Cameron, Ted Anasti (ABC)

2746 Outstanding Daytime Talk/Service Program: *Sally Jessy Raphaël*, executive producer Burt Dubrow; senior producer Kari Sagan; producers Linda Fennell, Alex Williamson, Donna Benner Ingber, Mary Duffy (syndicated)

2747 Outstanding Daytime Directing for a Children's Series: *Square One TV/Mathnet*, series director Mike Gargiulo; series director (*Mathnet*) Charles S. Dubin (PBS)

2748 **Outstanding Lead Actress in a Daytime Drama Series:** Kim Zimmer in *Guiding Light* (CBS)

2749 **Outstanding Lead Actor in a Daytime Drama Series:** A Martinez in *Santa Barbara* (NBC)

2750 **Outstanding Supporting Actress in a Daytime Drama Series:** Julia Barr in *All My Children* (ABC)

2751 **Outstanding Supporting Actor in a Daytime Drama Series:** Henry Darrow in *Santa Barbara* (NBC)

2752 **Outstanding Juvenile Male in a Daytime Drama Series:** Andrew Kavovit in *As the World Turns* (CBS)

2753 **Outstanding Juvenile Female in a Daytime Drama Series:** Cady McClain in *All My Children* (ABC)

2754 **Outstanding Performer in a Daytime Children's Series:** Kevin Clash in *Sesame Street* (PBS)

2755 **Outstanding Daytime Game Show Host:** Alex Trebek in *Jeopardy!* (syndicated)

2756 **Outstanding Daytime Talk/Service Show Host:** Joan Rivers in *The Joan Rivers Show* (syndicated)

2757 **Outstanding Performer in a Daytime Children's Special:** Greg Spottiswood in *Looking for Miracles* (Disney)

2758 **Daytime Drama Series Directing Team:** directors Michael Gliona, Rick Bennewitz, Robert Schiller; associate directors Pamela Fryman, Jeanine Guarneri-Frons for *Santa Barbara* (NBC)

2759 **Outstanding Directing in a Daytime Game/Audience Participation Show:** Joseph Behar for *Fun House* (syndicated)

2760 **Outstanding Directing in a Daytime Talk/Service Show:** Russell Morash for *This Old House* (PBS)

2761 **Outstanding Directing in a Special Class Area:** Victoria Hochberg for *Wonderworks* episode "Sweet 15" (PBS)

2762 **Outstanding Writing Team for a Daytime Drama Series:** head writer Pamela K. Long; associate head writers Nancy Curlee, Trent Jones; story consultant Jeff Ryder; script editor Stephen Demorest; breakdown writers Garrett Foster, Peter Brash, Nancy Williams; breakdown/script writers Patty Gideon Sloan, Richard Culliton; script writers N. Gail Lawrence, Pete T. Rich, Melissa Salmons for *Guiding Light* (CBS)

2763 **Outstanding Writing in a Daytime Children's Series:** head writer Norman Stiles; series writers Nancy Sans, Luis Santeiro, Cathi Rosenberg-Turow, Belinda Ward, Sonia Manzano, Jeff Moss, Sara Compton, Judy Freudberg, David Korr, John Weidman, Tony Geiss, Emily Perl Kingsley, Mark Saltzman, Josh Selig, Jon Stone for *Sesame Street* (PBS)

2764 **Writing in a Daytime Children's Special:** Paul Cooper for *CBS Schoolbreak Special* episode "A Matter of Conscience" (CBS)

2765 **Outstanding Achievement in Daytime Art Direction/Set Decoration/Scenic Design:** art director Victor Di Napoli; scenic designer Mike Pantuso for *Sesame Street* (PBS)

2766 **Outstanding Achievement in Daytime Art Direction/Set Decoration/Scenic Design for a Drama Series:** art director Lawrence King; scenic designer Elmon Webb; set decorators Holmes Easley, David Harnish, Paul W. Hickey for *As the World Turns* (CBS)

2767 **Outstanding Achievement in Daytime Technical Direction/Electronic Camera/Video Control for a Daytime Drama Series:** technical directors Janice Bendiksen, Ervin D. Hurd, Jr.; electronic camera Joel Binger, Joseph Vicens, Dave Navarette; video control Roberto Bosio, Scha Jani for *The Young and the Restless* (CBS)

2768 **Outstanding Achievement in Daytime Live and Tape Sound Mixing and Sound Effects:** production sound mixer Galen Handy; re-recording mixer David E. Fluhr for *ABC Afterschool Special* episode "Torn Between Two Fathers" (ABC)

2769 **Outstanding Achievement in Daytime Live and Tape Sound Mixing and Sound Effects for a Drama Series:** audio mixers Pat Lucatorio, Tommy Persson; music mixer Don Henderson; postproduction mixers Rafael Valentin, Harold Linstrot; sound effects Maurice "Smokey" Westerfeld, Peter Romano for *The Young and the Restless* (CBS)

2770 **Outstanding Achievement in Daytime Make-Up:** David Abbott, Gil Mosko for *The Munsters Today* (syndicated)

2771 Outstanding Achievement in Make-Up for a Daytime Drama Series: Mark Landon, Steve Artmont, Ed Heim, for *The Young and the Restless* (CBS)

2772 Outstanding Achievement in Daytime Graphics and Title Design: Penelope Gottlieb for *Generations* (NBC)

2773 Outstanding Achievement in Daytime Writing — Special Class Area: Glenn Kirschbaum for *Remembering World War II* episode "Hitler: Man & Myth" (syndicated); Robert Kirk for *Remembering World War II* episode "Pearl Harbor" (syndicated)

2774 Outstanding Achievement in Daytime Costume Design: costume designer — live actors Bill Kellard; costume designers — muppets Caroly Wilcox, Kermit Love, Connie Peterson, Paul Hartis, Barry Link, Peter MacKennan, Stephen Rotondaro, Mark Zeszotek (PBS)

2775 Outstanding Achievement in Costume Design for a Daytime Drama Series: Carol Luiken, Charles Clute for *All My Children* (ABC); Margarita Delgado, Charles Schoonmaker for *Another World* (NBC)

2776 Outstanding Achievement in Daytime Videotape Editing: supervising editor Robert J. Emerick; editor Evamarie Keller for *Sesame Street* (PBS)

2777 Outstanding Achievement in Videotape Editing for a Daytime Drama Series: Dan Brumett, Marc Beruti for *The Young and the Restless* (CBS)

2778 Outstanding Achievement in Daytime Film Editing: Stan Salfas for *ABC Afterschool Special* episode "All That Glitters" (ABC)

2779 Outstanding Achievement in Daytime Music Direction and Composition: composers Christopher Cerf, Jeff Moss, Tony Geiss, Sarah Durkee; composers/arrangers Stephen Lawrence, Cheryl Hardwick, Paul Jacobs, David Conner for *Sesame Street* (PBS)

2780 Outstanding Achievement in Music Direction and Composition for a Daytime Drama Series: music director/composer Marty Davich; music supervisor Amy Burkhard; composer Ken Corday for *Days of Our Lives* (NBC)

2781 Outstanding Achievement in Daytime Hairstyling: Andre Walker for *The Oprah Winfrey Show* (syndicated)

2782 Outstanding Achievement in Hairstyling for a Daytime Drama Series: head hairstylist Angel De Angelis; hairstylists John Quaglia, Annette Bianco, Joyce Sica for *Another World* (NBC)

2783 Outstanding Achievement in Daytime Film Sound Mixing: production mixer Kim Ornitz, re-recording mixers Douglas Gray, T.W. Davis; sound effects Brian Risner for *CBS Schoolbreak Special* episode "The Girl with the Crazy Brother" (CBS)

2784 Outstanding Achievement in Daytime Lighting Direction: Jim Tetlow, Bill Berner for *Sesame Street* (PBS)

2785 Outstanding Achievement in Daytime Film Sound Editing: supervising editor Charles King; sound editors Rick Hinson, Richard Harrison for *Ducktales* (syndication)

2786 Outstanding Achievement in Lighting Direction for a Daytime Drama Series: Brian McRae, Ted C. Polmarski for *Santa Barbara* (NBC)

2787 Outstanding Achievement in Daytime Cinematography: James Carter for *ABC Afterschool Special* episode "Torn Between Two Fathers" (ABC)

2788 Lifetime Achievement Award for Daytime Television: Mark Goodson

—————— **1990** ——————

2789 Outstanding Drama Series: *L.A. Law*; executive producers David E. Kelley, Rick Wallace; supervising producer Patricia Green; producers Elodie Keene, James C. Hart, Alan Brennert, Robert Breech, John Hill; coordinating producer Alice West; 20th Century–Fox Film Corporation (NBC)

2790 Outstanding Comedy Series: *Cheers*; executive producers James Burrows, Glen Charles, Les Charles, Cheri Eichen, Bill Steinkellner, Phoef Sutton; producer Tim Berry; co-producers Andy Ackerman, Brian Pollack, Mert Rich, Dan O'Shannon, Tom Anderson, Larry Balmagia; Charles/Burrows/Charles Productions in association with Paramount (NBC)

2791 Outstanding Drama/Comedy Special and Miniseries: *A General Motors Mark of Excellence Presentation* episode "Separate but Equal"; executive producers George Stevens, Jr., Stan Marguilies; a New Liberty Production in association with Republic Pictures Television (ABC)

2792 Outstanding Variety, Music or Comedy Program: *The 63rd Annual Academy Awards*; producer Gilbert Cates; ABC Television (ABC)

2793 Outstanding Classical Program in the Performing Arts: *Tchaikovsky 150th Birthday Gala from Leningrad*; executive producer Peter Gelb; producer Helmut Rost; coordinating producers Anne Cauvin, Laura Mitgang; a co-production of Cami Video, ZDF, TLE and Antenna 2, BBC, MBS, NOS, ORF, PBS, RA13 & Bertlesman Music (PBS)

2794 Outstanding Informational Special: *American Masters* episode "Edward R. Murrow: This Reporter"; executive producer Susan Lacy; producer Susan Steinberg; co-producers Elizabeth Kreutz, Harlene Freezer; Thirteen/WNET in association with CBS Enterprises (PBS)

2795 Outstanding Informational Series: *A General Motors Mark of Excellence Presentation* episode "The Civil War"; producers Ken Burns, Rick Burns; co-producers Steven Ives, Julie Dunfey, Mike Hill; coordinating producer Catherine Eisele; Florentine Films in association with WETA (PBS)

2796 Outstanding Animated Program (for programming of one hour or less): *The Simpsons*; executive producers James L. Brooks, Matt Groening, Sam Simon; supervising producers Al Jean, Mike Reiss; producers Jay Kogen, Wallace Wolodarsky, Richard Sakai, Larina Jean Adamson; co-producer George Meyer; executive animation producer Gabor Csupo; animation producer Sherry Gunther; writer Steve Repoon; director Rich Moore; a Gracie Films Production in association with 20th Century-Fox Television (Fox)

2797 Outstanding Children's Program: *You Can't Grow Home Again: A 3-2-1 Contact Extra*; executive producer Anne MacLeod; producer Tom Cammisa; a Children's Television Workshop Production (PBS)

2798 Outstanding Lead Actor in a Comedy Series: Burt Reynolds in *Evening Shade*; a production of CBS Entertainment in association with Mozark Productions and MTM (CBS)

2799 Outstanding Lead Actor in a Drama Series: James Earl Jones in *Gabriel's Fire*; Crystal Beach Entertainment and Coleman Luck Productions in association with Lorimar Television (ABC)

2800 Outstanding Lead Actor in a Miniseries or Special: John Gielgud in *Masterpiece Theatre* episode "Summer's Lease"; a BBC Television Production in association with WGBH Boston, Australian Broadcasting Corporation and Television New Zealand (PBS)

2801 Outstanding Lead Actress in a Comedy Series: Kirstie Alley in *Cheers*; Charles/Burrows/Charles Productions in association with Paramount (NBC)

2802 Outstanding Lead Actress in a Drama Series: Patricia Wettig in *thirtysomething*; the Bedford Falls Company in association with MGM (ABC)

2803 Outstanding Lead Actress in a Miniseries or Special: Lynn Whitfield in *The Josephine Baker Story*; HBO Pictures in association with RHI Entertainment, Inc. and Anglia Television, Ltd. (HBO)

2804 Outstanding Supporting Actor in a Comedy Series: Jonathan Winters in *Davis Rules*; a Carsey-Werner Production (ABC)

2805 Outstanding Supporting Actor in a Drama Series: Timothy Busfield in *thirtysomething*; the Bedford Falls Company in association with MGM (ABC)

2806 Outstanding Supporting Actor in a Miniseries or Special: James Earl Jones in *Heat Wave*; the Avnet/Kerner Company and Propaganda Films in association with TNT (TNT)

2807 Outstanding Supporting Actress in a Comedy Series: Bebe Neuwirth in *Cheers*; Charles/Burrows/Charles Productions in association with Paramount (NBC)

2808 Outstanding Supporting Actress in a Drama Series: Madge Sinclair in *Gabriel's Fire*; Crystal Beach Entertainment and Coleman Luck Productions in association with Lorimar Television (ABC)

2809 Outstanding Supporting Actress in a Miniseries or Special: Ruby Dee in *Hallmark Hall of Fame* episode "Decoration Day"; Marian Rees Associates, Inc. (NBC)

2810 Outstanding Individual Performance in a Variety or Music Program: Billy Crystal as host of *The 63rd Annual Academy Awards*; ABC Television (ABC)

2811 Outstanding Performance in Classical Music/Dance Programming: Kurt Moll in *The Metropolitan Opera Presents* episode "The Ring of Nibelung"; Metropolitan Opera Association, Inc. (PBS); Yo-Yo Ma in *Tchaikovsky 150th Birthday Gala from Leningrad*; a co-production of Cami Video, ZDF, YLE and Antenna 2, BBC, MBS, NOS, ORF, PBS, RA13 and Bertlesman Music (PBS)

2812 Outstanding Guest Actor in a Comedy Series: Jay Thomas in *Murphy Brown* episode "Gold Rush"; Shukovsky/English Productions in association with Warner Brothers Television (CBS)

2813 Outstanding Guest Actress in a Comedy Series: Colleen Dewhurst in *Murphy Brown* episode "Bob and Murphy and Ted and Avery"; Shukovsky/English Productions in association with Warner Brothers Television (CBS)

2814 Outstanding Guest Actor in a Drama Series: David Opatoshu in *Gabriel's Fire* episode "A Prayer for the Goldsteins"; Crystal Beach Entertainment and Coleman Luck Productions in association with Lorimar Television (ABC)

2815 Outstanding Guest Actress in a Drama Series: Peggy McCay in *The Trials of Rosie O'Neill* episode "State of Mind"; MTM Distribution and the Rosenzweig Company (CBS)

2816 Outstanding Directing in a Comedy Series: James Burrows for *Cheers* episode "Woody Interruptus"; Charles/Burrows/Charles Productions in association with Paramount (NBC)

2817 Outstanding Directing in a Drama Series: Thomas Carter for *Equal Justice* episode "In Confidence"; the Thomas Carter Company in association with Orion Television (ABC)

2818 Outstanding Directing in a Variety or Music Program: Hal Gurnee for *Late Night with David Letterman*, show #1425; NBC Productions in association with Carson Productions and Worldwide Pants, Inc. (NBC)

2819 Outstanding Directing in a Miniseries or a Special: Brian Gibson for *The Josephine Baker Story*; HBO Pictures in association with RHI Entertainment, Inc. and Anglia Television Ltd. (HBO)

2820 Outstanding Directing in Informational Programming: directors Peter Gelb, Susan Froemke, Albert Maysles, Bob Eisenhardt for *Soldiers of Music: Rostropovich Returns to Russia*; a co-production of Channel 4, NOS, ORF, PBS, Sony Classical and ZDF (PBS)

2821 Outstanding Achievement in Casting for a Miniseries or Special: Alixe Gordin CSA for *A General Motors Mark of Excellence Presentation* episode "Separate but Equal"; a New Liberty Production in association with Republic Pictures Television (ABC)

2822 Outstanding Achievement in Choreography: Debbie Allen for *Motown 30: What's Goin' On!* dance number "African American Odyssey"; Don Mischer Productions (CBS)

2823 Outstanding Writing in a Comedy Series: Gary Dontzig, Steven Peterman for *Murphy Brown* episode "Jingle Hell, Jingle Hell, Jingle All the Way"; Shukovsky/English Productions in association with Warner Brothers Television (CBS)

2824 Outstanding Writing in a Drama Series: David E. Kelley for *L.A. Law* episode "On the Toad Again"; 20th Century–Fox Film Corporation (NBC)

2825 Outstanding Writing in a Variety or Music Program: writers Hal Kanter, Buz Kohan; special material Billy Crystal, David Steinberg, Bruce Vilanch, Robert Wuhl for *The 63rd Annual Academy Awards*; ABC Television (ABC)

2826 Outstanding Writing in a Miniseries or a Special: Andrew Davies for *Masterpiece Theatre* episode "House of Cards"; BBC Television (PBS)

2827 Outstanding Writing in Informational Programming: Geoffrey C. Ward, Rick Burns, Ken Burns for *A General Motors Mark of Excellence Presentation* episode "The Civil War"; Florentine Films in association with WETA (PBS); Todd McCarthy for *American Masters* episode "Preston Sturges: The Rise and Fall of an American Dreamer"; a Barking Dog Production in association with WNET/New York (PBS)

2828 Outstanding Cinematography for a Series: Michael Watkins ASC for *Quantum Leap* episode "The Leap Home (Vietnam) — April 7, 1970 Part 2"; Universal Television in association with Belisarius Productions, Inc. (NBC)

2829 Outstanding Cinematography for a Miniseries or Special: Gayne Rescher ASC for *Jackie Collins' Lucky Chances Part 1*; NBC Productions (NBC)

2830 Outstanding Art Direction for a Series: production designer John C. Mula; art director Kevin Pfeiffer; set decorator Brian Savegar for *Dinosaurs* episode "The Mating Dance"; Michael Jacobs Productions (ABC)

2831 Outstanding Art Direction for a Miniseries or Special: production designer Jozsef Romvari; art director Dean Tschetter for *The Josephine Baker Story*; HBO Pictures in association with RHI Entertainment, Inc. and Anglia Television, Ltd. (HBO)

2832 Outstanding Art Direction for a Variety or Music Program: production designers John Shaffner, Joe Stewart for *The Magic of David Copperfield XIII: Mystery on the Orient Express*; DCDI Productions (CBS)

2833 Outstanding Achievement in Music Composition for a Series (Dramatic Underscore): John Debney for *The Young Riders* episode "Kansas"; Ogiens/Kane Company in association with MGM/UA (ABC)

2834 Outstanding Achievement in Music Composition for a Miniseries or Special (Dramatic Underscore): Richard Bellis for *Stephen King's "It," Part 1*; Green/Epstein Productions in association with Lorimar (ABC)

2835 Outstanding Achievement in Music Direction: music director Ian Fraser; principal arrangers Bill Byers, Chris Boardman, J. Hill for *The Walt Disney Company Presents "The American Teacher Awards"*; Smith-Hemion Productions (Disney)

2836 Outstanding Achievement in Music and Lyrics: composer and lyricist Randy Newman for the pilot of *Cop Rock*; Steven Bochco Productions in association with 20th Century–Fox Television (ABC)

2837 Outstanding Costume Design for a Series: Bill Hargate for *Murphy Brown* episode "Eldin Imitates Life"; Shukovsky/English Productions in association with Warner Brothers Television (CBS)

2838 Outstanding Costume Design for a Miniseries or Special: Maria Hruby, Gyorgyi Vidak for *The Josephine Baker Story*; HBO Pictures in association with RHI Entertainment, Inc. and Anglia Television Ltd. (HBO)

2839 Outstanding Costume Design for a Variety or Music Program: costume designer Ret Turner; costume designer for Carol Burnett, Bob Mackie for *Carol & Company* episode "The Little Extra Something"; Kalola Productions, Inc. and Wind Dancer Productions, Inc. in association with Touchstone Television (NBC)

2840 Outstanding Achievement in Costuming for a Series: costume supervisor Patrick R. Norris; women's costume supervisor Linda Serijan-Fasmer for *thirtysomething* episode "A Wedding"; the Bedford Falls Company in association with MGM (ABC)

2841 Outstanding Achievement in Costuming for a Miniseries or Special: military costume supervisor Michael T. Boyd; American Indian costume supervisor Cathy A. Smith; civilian costume supervisor Bud Clark for *Son of the Morning Star, Part 2*; a co-production of the Mount Company and the Preston Stephen Fischer Co. in association with Republic Television (ABC)

2842 Outstanding Achievement in Make-Up for a Series: Gerald Quist, Michael Mills, Jeremy Swan, Douglas D. Kelly for *Quantum Leap* episode "The Leap Home — November 25, 1969, Part 1"; Universal Television in association with Belisarius Productions, Inc. (NBC)

2843 Outstanding Achievement in Make-Up for a Miniseries or Special: makeup supervisors Joe McKinney, Hank Edds; key makeup Paul Sanchez; American Indian makeup T.C. Williams for *Son of the Morning Star, Part 2*; a co-production of the Mount Company and the Preston Stephen Fischer Co. in association with Republic Television (ABC)

2844 **Outstanding Achievement in Hairstyling for a Series:** Dee Dee Petty, Jan Van Uchelen, Susan Boyd for *Dark Shadows* episode #8; Dan Curtis Television Productions, Inc. in association with MGM (NBC)

2845 **Outstanding Achievement in Hairstyling for a Miniseries or Special:** Miss Whitfield's hairstylist Aldo Signoretti; hairstylists Ferdinando Merolla, Katalin Kajtar for *The Josephine Baker Story*; HBO Pictures in association with RHI Entertainment, Inc. and Anglia Television Ltd. (HBO)

2846 **Outstanding Editing for a Series (Single Camera Production):** Joe Ann Fogle for the pilot of *Cop Rock*; Steven Bochco Productions in association with 20th Century–Fox Television (ABC)

2847 **Outstanding Editing for a Miniseries or Special (Single Camera Production):** John Wright for *Hallmark Hall of Fame* episode "Sara, Plain and Tall"; a Self Productions, Inc. and Trillium Productions, Inc. Production (CBS)

2848 **Outstanding Editing for a Series (Multi-Camera Production):** Tucker Wiard for *Murphy Brown* episode "On Another Plane"; Shukovsky/English Productions in association with Warner Brothers Television (CBS)

2849 **Outstanding Editing for a Series (Multi-Camera Production):** David Gumpel, Girish Bhargava for *The Muppets Celebrate Jim Henson*; Jim Henson Productions, Don Mischer Productions and Walt Disney Television (CBS)

2850 **Outstanding Sound Editing for a Series:** supervising editor and supervising ADR editor William Wistrom; sound editors James Wolvington, Mace Matiosian, Wilson Dyer, Masanobu "Tomi" Tomita, Dan Yale; supervising music editor Gerry Sackman for *Star Trek: The Next Generation* episode "The Best of Both Worlds, Part 2"; Paramount Pictures (syndicated)

2851 **Outstanding Sound Editing for a Miniseries or Special:** supervising editors G. Michael Graham, Joseph A. Melody; sound editors Rick Steele, Mark Steele, Gary Macheel, Charles Beith, Jr., Mark Friedgen, Dan Luna, Michael J. Wright, Bob Costanza, Chris Assels, David

McMoyler, Bill Bell, Scot Tinsley, Philip Jamtaas, Andre Caporaso, Stephen Grubbs; supervising ADR editor Kristi Johns; supervising music editor John Caper for *Son of the Morning Star, Part 2*; a co-production of the Mount Company and the Preston Stephen Fischer Company in association with Republic Television (ABC)

2852 **Outstanding Sound Mixing for a Comedy Series or a Special:** production mixer Joe Kenworthy CAS; re-recording mixers Dean Okrand, William Thiederman, Michael Getlin for *Doogie Howser, M.D.* episode "Doogenstein"; Steven Bochco Productions in association with 20th Century–Fox Television (ABC)

2853 **Outstanding Sound Mixing for a Drama Series:** production mixer Alan Bernard CAS; re-recording mixers Doug Davey CAS, Chris Haire CAS, Richard Morrison CAS for *Star Trek: The Next Generation* episode "The Best of Both Worlds, Part 2"; Paramount Pictures Television (syndicated)

2854 **Outstanding Sound Mixing for a Variety or Music Series or Special:** Ed Greene, Terry Kulchar for *Carnegie Hall: Live at 100*; Don Mischer Productions, Carnegie Hall and 13/WNET (PBS)

2855 **Outstanding Sound Mixing for a Drama Miniseries or a Special:** production mixer Nelson Stoll; re-recording mixers Thomas J. Huth CAS, Sam Black, Anthony Costantini for *Son of the Morning Star, Part 2*; a co-production of the Mount Company and the Preston Stephen Fischer Co. in association with Republic Television (ABC)

2856 **Outstanding Technical Direction/Camera/Video for a Series:** technical director Terry Rohnke; camera operators Steve Jambeck, Joe De Bonis, Jan Kasoff, John Pinto, Robert Reese; senior video control Bruce Shapiro for *Saturday Night Live* episode "Host: Christopher Walken," a Broadway Video, Inc. Production in association with NBC Productions (NBC)

2857 **Outstanding Technical Direction/Camera/Video for a Series:** technical director Jerry Weiss; electronic camera operators Marty Brown, Dave Owen, Marvin Shearer, Mark Warshaw; senior video control Rich Rose for

Married People episode "Dance Ten, Friends Zero"; Sternin/Fraser Ink, Inc. in association with Columbia Pictures Television (ABC)

2858 Outstanding Technical Direction/Camera Work/Video for a Miniseries or Special: technical director and senior video control Keith Winikoff; electronic camera operators Sam Drummy, Dave Levisohn, Bill Philbin, Hector Ramirez for *The Magic of David Copperfield XIII: Mystery on the Orient Express*; DCDI Productions (CBS)

2859 Outstanding Achievement in Graphic Design and Title Sequences: designer/director Steve Martino; designer director "Chinese Lion" sequence Jeff Doud; creative director John Townley; designer Thomas Barham for *ABC World of Discovery*; ABC/Kane Productions International, Inc. (ABC)

2860 Outstanding Electronic Lighting Direction for a Drama Series, Variety Series, Miniseries or a Special: William Klages for *The 33rd Annual Emmy Awards*; Pierre Cossette Productions (CBS); Bob Dickinson for *The Magic of David Copperfield XIII: Mystery on the Orient Express*; DCDI Productions (CBS)

2861 Outstanding Individual Achievement in Animation: Teresa Drilling, Jeff Mulcaster for *Will Vinton's Claymation Comedy of Horrors*; Will Vinton Productions (CBS)

2862 Outstanding Electronic Lighting Direction for a Comedy Series: George Spiro Dibie for *Growing Pains* episodes "Happy Halloween Parts 1 and 2"; a GSM Production in association with Warner Brothers Television (ABC)

2863 Outstanding Achievement in Engineering Development: Emmy Awards to Vari-Lite, Inc. (and its creative team members Jim Bornhorst, John Covington, Brooks Taylor and Tom Walsh) for the VARI-LITE Series 200 Lighting System; Camera Platforms International, Inc. (and Keith Gillum) for the Shotmaker Elite Camera Car Crane; Graham-Patten Systems, Inc. (and Michael D. Patten) for the D/ESAM Digital Mixer; engineering plaques to Denecks, Inc. (and Mike Denecks) for the Dcode TS-1 Time Code Slate; Camera Platforms International, Inc. (and Dr. Paul Kiankhooy) for the Lightmaker AC/DC HMI Ballast; Op Tex UK (and George Hill) and Litton Electronic Devices (and Charles E. Scholz) for the Mini Image Intensifier for ENG cameras; Grass Valley Group, Inc. (and its creative team members John Abt, Richard S. Bannister, Ron Barnett, Jim Blecksmith, Steven P. DeLaney, Richard Frasier, Thomas A. Grancey, Sandra Hershberger, Richard A. Jackson, William C. Lange, Roshan Mazhar, Neil Olmstead, John M. Pichitino, Peter D. Symes, Kevin Windrem, Andy Witek and Dallas Wivholm) for the Kadenza Digital Picture Processor

2864 ATAS Governor's Award: *Masterpiece Theatre*

2865 Syd Cassyd Founders Award: Syd Cassyd

2866 Outstanding Daytime Drama Series: *As the World Turns*; executive producer Laurence Caso; supervising producer Kenneth L. Fitts; producers Christine S. Banas, David Domedian; coordinating producer Lisa Anne Wilson (CBS)

2867 Outstanding Daytime Game/Audience Participation Show: *Jeopardy!*, executive producer Merv Griffin, producer George Vosburgh (syndicated)

2868 Outstanding Daytime Children's Series: *Sesame Street*; executive producer Dulcy Singer; producer Lisa Simon; coordinating producer Arlene Sherman (PBS)

2869 Outstanding Daytime Children's Special: *Lost in the Barrens*; executive producers Michael MacMillan, Michael Scott; producers Seaton McLean, Derek Mazur, Joan Scott (Disney)

2870 Outstanding Daytime Animated Program: *Tiny Toon Adventures*; executive producer Steven Spielberg; producer Tom Ruegger; directors Ken Boyer, Art Leonardi, Art Vitello; story editor Paul Dini; writer Sherri Stoner (syndicated)

2871 Outstanding Daytime Talk/Service Program: *The Oprah Winfrey Show*; executive producer Debra DiMaio; senior producer Ray Nunn; supervising producer Oprah Winfrey; producers David Boul, Mary Kay Clinton, Rudy Guido, Dianne

Hudson, Alice McGee, Sally Lou Oaks, Ellen Rakieten (syndicated)

2872 Outstanding Special Class Daytime Program: *Live from Lincoln Center* episode "Yo-Yo Ma in Concert"; executive producer John Goberman; coordinating producer Marc Bauman; host Hugh Downs (PBS)

2873 Outstanding Lead Actress in a Daytime Drama Series: Finola Hughes in *General Hospital* (ABC)

2874 Outstanding Lead Actor in a Daytime Drama Series: Peter Bergman in *The Young and the Restless* (CBS)

2875 Outstanding Supporting Actress in a Daytime Drama Series: Jess Walton in *The Young and the Restless* (CBS)

2876 Outstanding Supporting Actor in a Daytime Drama Series: Bernie Barrow in *Loving* (ABC)

2877 Outstanding Younger Actor in a Daytime Drama Series: Rick Hearst in *Guiding Light* (CBS)

2878 Outstanding Younger Actress in a Daytime Drama Series: Charlotte Ross in *Days of Our Lives* (NBC)

2879 Outstanding Performer in a Daytime Children's Series: Tim Curry in *Fox's Peter Pan and the Pirates* (Fox)

2880 Outstanding Daytime Game Show Host: Bob Barker in *The Price Is Right* (CBS)

2881 Outstanding Daytime Talk/Service Show Host: Oprah Winfrey in *The Oprah Winfrey Show* (syndicated)

2882 Outstanding Performer in a Daytime Children's Special: Joanne Vannicola in *CBS Schoolbreak Special* episode "Maggie's Secret" (CBS)

2883 Daytime Drama Series Directing Team: directors Michael Giliona, Rick Bennewitz, Robert Schiller, Peter Brinckerhoff; associate directors Pamela Fryman, Jeanine Guarneri-Frons, Robin Raphaelian for *Santa Barbara* (NBC)

2884 Outstanding Directing in a Daytime Game/Audience Participation Show: Dick Schneider for *Jeopardy!* (syndicated)

2885 Outstanding Directing in a Daytime Talk/Service Show: Peter Kimball for *The Oprah Winfrey Show* (syndicated)

2886 Outstanding Directing in a Special Class Area: Kristoffer Siegel-Tabori for *ABC Afterschool Special* episode "The Perfect Date" (ABC)

2887 Outstanding Directing in a Daytime Children's Series: series directors Brian Henson, Michael J. Kerrigan for *Jim Henson's Mother Goose Stories* (Disney)

2888 Outstanding Writing Team for a Daytime Drama Series: head writer Chuck Pratt, Jr.; co-head writers Sheri Anderson, Sam Ratcliffe, Marilyn Thoma; associate head writers John Griffith, Robert Guza; breakdown writer Linda Hamner; script writers Lynda Myles, Frank Salisbury; script writer/editor Richard Culliton for *Santa Barbara* (NBC)

2889 Outstanding Writing in a Daytime Children's Series: head writer Norman Stiles; series writers Nancy Sans, Luis Santeiro, Cathi Rosenberg-Turow, Belinda Ward, Sonia Manzano, Jeff Moss, Sara Compton, Judy Freudberg, David Korr, John Weidman, Tony Geiss, Emily Kingsley, Mark Saltzman, Josh Selig, Lou Berger, Jon Stone for *Sesame Street* (PBS)

2890 Writing in a Daytime Children's Special: teleplay and story Courtney Flavin; story Tracey Thompson, Beth Thompson for *ABC Afterschool Special* episode "A Question About Sex" (ABC)

2891 Outstanding Achievement in Daytime Special Class Writing: Harry Eisenberg, Steven Dorfman, Kathy Easterling, Frederik Pohl IV, Steve Tamerius, Debbie Griffin, Michele Johnson, Carol Campbell for *Jeopardy!* (syndicated)

2892 Outstanding Achievement in Daytime Art Direction/Set Decoration/Scenic Design: production designer Gary Panter; co-production designers Ric Heitzman, Wayne White; art director Jimmy Cuomo, set decorators Debbie Madalena, Paul Reubens for *Pee-wee's Playhouse* (CBS)

2893 Outstanding Achievement in Daytime Technical Direction/Electronic Camera/Video Control: technical directors Ray Angona; electronic camera Jose Arvizu, Cesar Cabriera, Wayne Getchell, Keeth Lawrence, Martin Wagner; video control Allen Latter for *The Price Is Right* (CBS)

2894 Outstanding Achievement in Daytime Cinematography: Hanania Baer for *CBS Schoolbreak Special* episode "But He Loves Me" (CBS)

2895 Outstanding Achievement in Daytime Music Direction and Composition: William Ross for "Fields of Honey" on *Tiny Toon Adventures* (syndicated)

2896 Outstanding Original Daytime Song: composer and lyricist A.J. Gundell for "Love Like This" on *Guiding Light* (CBS); composer and lyricist Bruce Broughton; lyricists Wayne Kaatz, Tom Ruegger for the main title theme for *Tiny Toon Adventures* (syndicated)

2897 Outstanding Achievement in Daytime Graphics and Title Design: title designer Paul Reubens; co-designers Prudence Fenton, Dome Huebler for *Pee-wee's Playhouse* (CBS)

2898 Outstanding Achievement in Daytime Make-Up: David Abbott, Gil Mosko, Carlos Yeaggy for *The Munsters Today* (syndicated)

2899 Outstanding Achievement in Daytime Hairstyling: Jody Ann Lawrence for *The Munsters Today* (syndicated)

2900 Outstanding Achievement in Daytime Videotape Editing: James C. Wright for *Reading Rainbow* (PBS)

2901 Outstanding Achievement in Daytime Live and Tape Sound Mixing and Sound Effects: re-recording mixer David E. Fluhr; production mixer Mark Bovos for *ABC Afterschool Special* episode "A Question About Sex" (ABC)

2902 Outstanding Achievement in Daytime Film Editing: Barbara Pokras for *ABC Afterschool Special* episode "The Perfect Date" (ABC)

2903 Outstanding Achievement in Daytime Film Sound Editing: dialogue/ADR editor Peter Cole; dialogue editor Chris Trent; supervising music editor Glenn Jordan; supervising sound effects editor Steve Kirklys; sound effects editors Ken Dahlinger, John Walker for *Pee-wee's Playhouse* (CBS)

2904 Outstanding Achievement in Daytime Film Sound Mixing: production sound mixer Bo Harwood; re-recording mixers Peter Cole, Chris Trent, Troy Smith for *Pee-wee's Playhouse* (CBS)

2905 Outstanding Achievement in Daytime Lighting Direction: Bill Berner for *Sesame Street* (PBS)

2906 Outstanding Achievement in Daytime Costume Design: Jacqueline Mills, Jill Thraves for *Jim Henson's Mother Goose Stories* (Disney)

2907 Outstanding Achievement in Art Direction/Set Decoration/Scenic Design for a Daytime Drama Series: production designer Sy Tomashoff; art director Jack Forrestel; set decorators Jay Garvin, Randy Gunderson for *The Bold and the Beautiful* (CBS)

2908 Outstanding Achievement in Technical Direction/Electronic Camera/Video Control for a Daytime Drama Series: technical directors Janice L. Bendiksen, Ervin D. Hurd, Jr.; electronic camera Sheldon L. Mooney, Joseph M. Vicens, David Navarette, Joel D. Binger; senior video control Roberto A. Bosio, Scha Jani for *The Young and the Restless* (CBS)

2909 Outstanding Achievement in Music Direction and Composition for a Daytime Drama Series: music director/supervisor Barbara Miller-Gidaly; music director A.J. Gundell; composers Rob Mounsey, John Henry, Richard Hazard, Barry de Vorzon, Theodore Irwin; composer/arranger James Elliot Lawrence for *Guiding Light* (CBS)

2910 Outstanding Achievement in Make-Up for a Daytime Drama Series: head makeup artist Carol Brown; makeup artists Keith Crary, Robert Sloan, Gail Hopkins, Lucia Bianca for *Days of Our Lives* (NBC)

2911 Outstanding Achievement in Hairstyling for a Daytime Drama Series: Janet Medford, Valerie Scott for *Santa Barbara* (NBC)

2912 Outstanding Achievement in Videotape Editing for a Daytime Drama Series: Dan Brumett, Marc Beruti, Steve Pierron for *The Young and the Restless* (CBS)

2913 Outstanding Achievement in Lighting Direction for a Daytime Drama Series: Brian McRae, Ted C. Polmarski for *Santa Barbara* (NBC)

2914 Outstanding Achievement in Live and Sound Mixing for a Daytime Drama Series: mixers Otto Svoboda,

Tommy Persson; music mixer/sound effects Donald D. Henderson; post-production mixers Harold "Lanky" Linstrot, Bob Marencovich; sound effects Jack Ten Hoor, Maurice "Smokey" Westerfeld for *The Young and the Restless* (CBS)

2915 Outstanding Achievement in Costume Design for a Daytime Drama Series: Sandra Bojin-Sedlik for *The Bold and the Beautiful* (CBS)

———————— **1 9 9 1** ————————

2916 Outstanding Drama Series: *Northern Exposure*; executive producers Joshua Brand, John Falsey; co-executive producer Andrew Schneider; supervising producers Diane Frolov; Jeff Melvoin, Cheryl Bloch, Robin Green; producers Matthew Nodella, Rob Thompson; the Finnegan Pinchuk Company/Austin Street Productions in association with Universal (CBS)

2917 Outstanding Comedy Series: *Murphy Brown*; executive producers Diane English, Joel Shukovsky; supervising producers Steven Peterman, Gary Dontzig; co-supervising producer Tom Palmer; consulting producer Korby Siamis; producer Deborah Smith; co-producer Peter Tolan; Shukovsky/English Productions in association with Warner Brothers Television (CBS)

2918 Outstanding Miniseries: *A Woman Named Jackie*; executive producer Lester Persky; producer Lorin Bennett; co-producer Tomlinson Dean; Lester Persky Productions, Inc. and World International Network, Inc. (NBC)

2919 Outstanding Variety, Music or Comedy Series Program: *The Tonight Show Starring Johnny Carson*; executive producers Fred De Cordova, Peter Lassally; producer Jeff Sontag; co-producer Jim McCawley; host Johnny Carson; Carson Tonight (NBC)

2920 Outstanding Variety, Music or Comedy Special Program: *Cirque du Soleil II: A New Experience*; producer Helene Dufresne; an HBO Production (HBO)

2921 Outstanding Classical Program in the Performing Arts: *Perlman in Russia*;

producer Robert Dalrymple; performer Itzhak Perlman; Dalrymple Productions in association with Steinhardt Baer Pictures Company (PBS)

2922 Outstanding Informational Special: *Abortion: Desperate Choices*; executive producer Susan Froemke; a production of Maysles Films, Inc. (HBO)

2923 Outstanding Informational Series: *MGM: When the Lion Roars*; producer Joni Levin; Point Black Productions in association with Turner Network Television (TNT)

2924 Outstanding Animated Program (for programming of one hour or less): *A Claymation Easter*; executive producer Will Vinton; producer Paul Diener; director/writer Mark Gustafson; writers Barry Breuce, Ryan Holznagel; Will Vinton Productions (CBS)

2925 Outstanding Children's Program: *Mark Twain and Me*; executive producers Geoffrey Cowan; Julian Fowles; Walt Disney Company Productions (Disney)

2926 Outstanding Made for Television Movie: *Hallmark Hall of Fame* episode "Miss Rose White"; executive producer Marian Rees; co-executive producers Andrea Baynes, Francine LeFrak; producer Anne Hopkins; a Marian Rees Associates Production in association with Lorimar Television (NBC)

2927 Outstanding Lead Actor in a Comedy Series: Craig T. Nelson in *Coach*; Bungalow 78 Productions in association with Universal Television (ABC)

2928 Outstanding Lead Actor in a Drama Series: Christopher Lloyd in *Avonlea*; a Sullivan Films Production (Disney)

2929 Outstanding Lead Actor in a Miniseries or Special: Beau Bridges in *Without Warning: The James Brady Story*; the Next Picture Company (HBO)

2930 Outstanding Lead Actress in a Comedy Series: Candice Bergen in *Murphy Brown*: Shukovsky/English Productions in association with Warner Brothers Television (CBS)

2931 Outstanding Lead Actress in a Drama Series: Dana Delaney in *China Beach*; Sacret, Inc., in association with Warner Brothers Television (ABC)

2932 Outstanding Lead Actress in a Miniseries or Special: Gena Rowlands in *Face of a Stranger*; Viacom Productions (CBS)

2933 Outstanding Supporting Actor in a Comedy Series: Michael Jeter in *Evening Shade*; CBS Entertainment Productions in association with Mozark Productions and MTM (CBS)

2934 Outstanding Supporting Actor in a Drama Series: Richard Dysart in *L.A. Law*; 20th Century–Fox Film Corporation (NBC)

2935 Outstanding Supporting Actor in a Miniseries or Special: Hume Cronyn in *Neil Simon's "Broadway Bound"*; AKA Productions and ABC Productions (ABC)

2936 Outstanding Supporting Actress in a Comedy Series: Laurie Metcalf in *Roseanne*; a Carsey-Werner Production (ABC)

2937 Outstanding Supporting Actress in a Drama Series: Valerie Mahaffey in *Northern Exposure*; Finnegan Pinchuk Company, Falahey/Austin Street Productions in association with Universal (CBS)

2938 Outstanding Supporting Actress in a Miniseries or Special: Amanda Plummer in *Hallmark Hall of Fame* episode "Miss Rose White"; a Marian Rees Associates Production in association with Lorimar Television (NBC)

2939 Outstanding Individual Performance in a Variety or Music Program: Bette Midler in *The Tonight Show Starring Johnny Carson*; Carson Tonight (NBC)

2940 Outstanding Voice-Over Performance: Nancy Cartwright, Jackie Mason, Julie Kavner, Yeardley Smith, Marcia Wallace, Dan Castellaneta in *The Simpsons*; a Gracie Films Production in association with 20th Century–Fox Television (Fox)

2941 Outstanding Individual Achievement in Classical Music/Dance Programming Performance: Placido Domingo, Kathleen Battle in *The Metropolitan Opera Silver Anniversary Gala*; a Cablevision/NBC/Polygram PPV Production in association with the Metropolitan Opera co-production with Max Japan (PBS)

2942 Outstanding Individual Achievement in Directing a Comedy Series: Barnet Kellman for *Murphy Brown* episode "Birth 101"; Shukovsky/English Productions in association with Warner Brothers Television (CBS)

2943 Outstanding Individual Achievement in Directing in a Drama Series: Eric Laneuville for *I'll Fly Away* episode "All God's Children"; Falahey/Austin Street Productions in association with Lorimar Television (CBS)

2944 Outstanding Individual Achievement in Directing a Variety or Music Program: Patricia Birch for *Great Performances* episode "Unforgettable, with Love: Natalie Cole Sings the Songs of Nat King Cole"; a production of 13/WNET in association with Knight Productions, Inc. (PBS)

2945 Outstanding Individual Achievement in Directing a Miniseries or a Special: Daniel Petrie for *Mark Twain and Me*; a Walt Disney Company Production (Disney)

2946 Outstanding Individual Achievement in Directing Informational Programming: directors George Hickenlooper, Eleanor Coppola for *Hearts of Darkness: A Filmmaker's Apocalypse*; a ZM Production in association with Zoetrope Studios (Showtime)

2947 Outstanding Individual Achievement in Directing Classical Music/Dance Programming: Brian Large for *The Metropolitan Opera Silver Anniversary Gala*; a Cablevision/NBC/Polygram PPV Production in association with the Metropolitan Opera in co-production with Max Japan (PBS)

2948 Outstanding Individual Achievement in Animation: Ron Ashlee Prat for *A Claymation Easter*; Will Vinton Productions (CBS)

2949 Outstanding Individual Achievement in Art Direction for a Series: production designer Woody Crocker; art director Ken Berg; set decorator Gene Serdena for *Northern Exposure* episode "Cecily"; the Finnegan Pinchuk Company, Falahey/Austin Street Productions in association with Universal (CBS)

2950 Outstanding Individual Achievement in Art Direction for a Miniseries or Special: production designer Gavin

Bocquet; art directors Keith Pain, Lucy Richardson; set decorator Maggie Gray for the pilot of *Young Indiana Jones*; Lucasfilm Ltd. Television Production in association with Paramount Television (ABC)

2951 Outstanding Individual Achievement in Art Direction for a Variety or Music Program: production designers Joe Stewart, John Shaffner for *The Magic of David Copperfield XIV: Flying—Live the Dream*; DCDI Productions, Inc. (CBS)

2952 Outstanding Individual Achievement in Casting: Joyce Gallie for *One Against the Wind*; a Karen Mack Production in association with Republic Pictures (CBS)

2953 Outstanding Individual Achievement in Choreography: Paul Taylor for *Great Performances* episode "Paul Taylor's 'Speaking in Tongues'—Dance in America"; Thirteen/WNET in association with Amaya Distribution (PBS)

2954 Outstanding Individual Achievement in Cinematography for a Series: Frank Prinzi for *Northern Exposure* episode "Cecily"; the Finnegan Pinchuk Company, Falahey/Austin Street Productions in association with Universal (CBS)

2955 Outstanding Individual Achievement in Cinematography for a Miniseries or Special: Bradford May for *Lady Against the Odds*; Robert Greenwald Productions and MGM/UA (NBC)

2956 Outstanding Individual Achievement in Cinematography in Informational Programming: field cinematographers Michael Boland, Vic Sarin for *Millennium: Tribal Wisdom and the Modern World* (PBS)

2957 Outstanding Individual Achievement in Costuming for a Series: costume supervisors Chic Gennarelli, Lyn Paolo for *Homefront* episode "At Your Age"; Roundelay Productions, Latham/Lechowick Productions in association with Lorimar Television (ABC)

2958 Outstanding Individual Achievement in Costuming for a Miniseries or Special: costume supervisor Darryl Levine; key costumers Molly Harris Campbell, Bridget Ostersehlte for *The Babe Ruth Story*; a Lyttle Production Company and Warner Brothers Television (NBC)

2959 Outstanding Individual Achievement in Music Costume Design for a Series: Robert Blackman for *Star Trek: The Next Generation* episode "Cost of Living"; Paramount Pictures (syndication)

2960 Outstanding Individual Achievement in Costume Design for a Miniseries or Special: Charlotte Holdich for the pilot of *Young Indiana Jones*; Lucasfilm Ltd. Television Production in association with Paramount Television (ABC)

2961 Outstanding Individual Achievement in Costume Design for a Variety or Music Program: Raymond Aghayan for *The 64th Annual Academy Awards*; ABC Television (ABC)

2962 Outstanding Individual Achievement in Editing for a Series (Single Camera Production): Thomas R. Moore for *Northern Exposure* episode "Cecily"; the Finnegan Pinchuk Company, Falahey/Austin Street Productions in association with Universal (CBS)

2963 Outstanding Individual Achievement in Editing for a Miniseries or Special: Edgar Burcksen for the pilot of *Young Indiana Jones*; Lucasfilm Ltd. Television Production in association with Paramount Television (ABC)

2964 Outstanding Individual Achievement in Editing for a Series (Multi-Camera Production): Janet Ashikaga for *Seinfeld* episode "The Subway"; a Shapiro/West Production in association with Castle Rock Entertainment (NBC)

2965 Outstanding Individual Achievement in Editing for a Miniseries or Special (Multi-Camera Production): Ray Miller, Jeff U'Ren for *The Magic of David Copperfield XIV: Flying—Live the Dream*; DCDI Productions, Inc. (CBS)

2966 Outstanding Individual Achievement in Editing for an Informational Program: Michael Greer, Jay Miracle for *Hearts of Darkness: A Filmmaker's Apocalypse* (Showtime)

2967 Outstanding Individual Achievement in Graphic Design and Title Sequences: designer/animator Ken Pearce; designer Mark Malmberg for *MTV Liquid TV*; and MTV: Music Television Production (MTV)

2968 Outstanding Individual Achievement in Hairstyling for a Series: hairstylists Generio Gugliemotto, Barbara Ronci for

Homefront episode "Man This Joint Is Jumping"; Roundelay Productions, Latham/Lechowick Productions in association with Lorimar Television (ABC)

2969 Outstanding Individual Achievement in Hairstyling for a Series or Special: Terry Baliel for *Hallmark Hall of Fame* episode "Miss Rose White"; a Marian Rees Associates Production in association with Lorimar Television (NBC)

2970 Outstanding Individual Achievement in Electronic Lighting for a Comedy Series: Donald A. Morgan for *Home Improvement* episode "Luck Be a Taylor Tonight"; Wind Dancer Productions, Inc. in association with Walt Disney/Touchstone Television (ABC)

2971 Outstanding Individual Achievement in Electronic Lighting for a Drama Series, Variety Series, Miniseries or Special: Robert A. Dickinson for *The Magic of David Copperfield XIV: Flying—Live the Dream*; DCDI Productions, Inc. (CBS)

2972 Outstanding Individual Achievement in Make-Up for a Series: makeup supervisor and designer Michael Westmore; makeup artists Gerald Quist, Ron Walters, June Haymore, Robert Scribner, Kenneth Diaz, Karen J. Westerfield, Richard Snell, Tania McComas for *Star Trek: The Next Generation* episode "Cost of Living"; Paramount Pictures (syndicated)

2973 Outstanding Individual Achievement in Make-Up for a Series or Special: makeup for Jason Robards, Kevin Haney; makeup Donald Mowat for *Mark Twain and Me*; Walt Disney Company Productions (Disney)

2974 Outstanding Individual Achievement in Music Composition for a Series (Dramatic Underscore): Bruce H. Babcock for *Matlock* episode "The Strangler"; Dean Hargrave Productions, the Fred Silverman Company and Viacom (NBC)

2975 Outstanding Individual Achievement in Music Composition for a Miniseries or Special (Dramatic Underscore): Bruce Broughton for *Hallmark Hall of Fame* episode "O Pioneers"; Craig Anderson Productions (CBS)

2976 Outstanding Individual Achievement in Music Direction: music director Bill Conti; arrangers Jack Eskew, Julie Giroux, Ashley Irwin, Hummie Mann for *The 64th Annual Academy Awards*; ABC Television (ABC)

2977 Outstanding Individual Achievement in Music and Lyrics: composer Curt Sobel; lyricist Dennis Spiegel for *Cast a Deadly Spell* "Why Do I Lie" (song); a Pacific Western Production (HBO)

2978 Outstanding Individual Achievement in Sound Editing for a Series: sound supervisor David Hankins; supervising sound editor Frank Andrew; sound editors Peter Bergren, David A. Cohen, Rich Thomas, Barbara Issak; ADR editors Jim Hebenstreit, Albert Lord; music editor Barbara Schechter for *Law and Order* episode "Heaven"; Wolf Films in association with Universal Television (NBC)

2979 Outstanding Individual Achievement in Sound Editing for a Miniseries or Special: supervising sound editor Stephen Grubbs; sound editors Randal S. Thomas, Clark Conrad, Gary Gelfand, Terence Thomas MPSE, Joseph A. Johnston, David Scharf, Craig Otte; ADR editors Andre Caporaso, Philip Jamtaas; music editor Stan Jones for *Crash Landing: The Rescue of Flight 232*; a Dorothea G. Petrie Production, Helios Production, Bob Banner Associates and the Gary L. Pudney Company in association with World International Network (WIN)

2980 Outstanding Individual Achievement in Sound Mixing for a Comedy Series or Special: production mixer Joe Kenworthy CAS; re-recording mixers R. William A. Thiederman, Dean Okrand, Michael Getlin for *Doogie Howser, M.D.* episode "Lonesome Doog"; Steven Bochco Productions and 20th Century-Fox (ABC)

2981 Outstanding Individual Achievement in Sound Mixing for a Variety or Music Series or a Special: production sound mixer Bill Schnee; re-recording mixers John Bickelhaupt, Fred Tator for *Great Performances* episode "Unforgettable, with Love: Natalie Cole Sings the Songs of Nat King Cole"; a production of WNET/13 in association with Knight Production, Inc. (PBS)

2982 **Outstanding Technical Direction/Camera/Video for a Series:** technical director Kenneth Tamburri; camera operators Rich Kenney, Stephen A. Jones, Dave Heckman, Chester Jackson, Non Keys SOC; video control Randy Johnson, Richard Steiner, John O'Brien for *The Golden Girls* episode "One Flew Out of the Cuckoo's Nest, Parts 1 and 2"; a Witt/Thomas/Harris Production in association with Touchstone Pictures and Television (NBC)

2983 **Outstanding Individual Achievement in Sound Mixing for a Drama Series:** production sound mixer David Stephenson; re-recording mixer Gary Summers for *The Young Indiana Jones Chronicles* episode "Verdun 1916"; Lucasfilm Ltd. Television Production in association with Paramount Television (ABC)

2984 **Outstanding Sound Mixing for a Drama Miniseries or Special:** re-recording mixers Thomas J. Huth CAS, Anthony Costantini CAS, Sam Black CAS and production mixer Trevor Black for *Hallmark Hall of Fame* episode "One Against the Wind"; a Karen Mack Production in association with Republic Pictures (CBS)

2985 **Outstanding Individual Achievement in Special Visual Effects:** animation producer Brad Lewis; director of opening and miniature effects Dale Fay; produced open and miniature effects Paul Boyington; animation director Henry Anderson for *The Last Halloween* (CBS); visual effects supervisor; visual effects coordinator Gary Hutzel; visual effects compositor Patrick Clancey; visual effects associate David Takemura; motion control operator Adrian Hurley; animation supervisor Adam Howard; visual effects editor Don Lee; motion control technician Dennis Hoerter for *Star Trek: The Next Generation* episode "Conundrum"; Paramount Pictures (syndicated); visual effects supervisor Dan Curry; visual effects coordinator Ronald B. Moore; visual effects associate David Takemura; motion control photography Erik Nash; visual effects editors Don Lee, Peter Sternlicht; visual effects animator Adam Howard; matte artists Syd Dutton, Robert Stromberg for *Star Trek: The*

Next Generation episode "A Matter of Time" (syndicated)

2986 **Outstanding Individual Achievement in Writing in a Comedy Series:** Elaine Pope, Larry Charles for *Seinfeld* episode "The Fix Up"; a Shapiro/West Production in association with Castle Rock Entertainment (NBC)

2987 **Outstanding Individual Achievement in Writing in a Drama Series:** Andrew Schneider, Diane Frolov for *Northern Exposure* episode "Seoul Mates"; the Finnegan/Pinchuk Company, Falahey/Austin Street Productions in association with Universal (CBS)

2988 **Outstanding Individual Achievement in Writing in a Variety or Music Program:** writers Hal Kanter, Buz Kohan; writer special material Billy Crystal, Marc Shaiman, David Steinberg, Robert Wuhl, Bruce Vilanch for *The 64th Annual Academy Awards*; ABC Television (ABC)

2989 **Outstanding Individual Achievement in Writing in a Miniseries or Special:** John Falsey, Joshua Brand for the pilot of *I'll Fly Away*; Falahey/Austin Street Productions in association with Lorimar Television (NBC)

2990 **Outstanding Individual Achievement in Technical Direction/Camera/ Video for a Miniseries or Special:** technical director John B. Field; camera operator Sam Drummy, John Feher, Tom Geren, Jim Goldsmith, Manny Gutierrez, Charlie Huntley, Dave Levisohn, Mike Lieberman, Bob Mikkelson, Jake Ostroff, Hector Ramirez, Manny Rodriguez, George Schaafsma, Ron Sheldon, Bill Sullivan, Ron Washburn; video control Mark Sanford, Keith Winikoff for *Paul Simon Concert in Central Park*; an Eighty-Twenty Production in association with Broadway Video and Ian E. Hoblyn Productions (HBO)

2991 **Outstanding Individual Achievement in Writing in Informational Programming:** Fax Bahr, George Hickenlooper for *Hearts of Darkness: A Filmmaker's Apocalypse*; a ZM Production in association with Zoetrope Studios (HBO)

2992 **Outstanding Achievement in Engineering Development:** Emmy Award: Charlie Douglass for the invention and development of the post-production sweetener; engineering plaques to Accom, Inc. (Luigi Gallo, Sohei Takemoto, Doug George) for the Accom D-Bridge 122 Video Encoder; Filmlook, Inc. (Robert A. Faber) for the Filmlook process for film simulation; the Charles F. Jenkins Engineering Award: to Kerns H. Powers for his ongoing contributions of ideas, inventions and research projects directed toward theoretical and applied improvements in communications systems.

2993 Outstanding Daytime Drama Series: *All My Children*; executive producer Felicia Minei Behr; supervising producers Terry Cacavio, Thomas de Villiers; coordinating producer Nancy Horwich (ABC)

2994 Outstanding Daytime Game/Audience Participation Show: *Jeopardy!*, executive producer Merv Griffin, producer George Vosburgh (syndicated)

2995 Outstanding Daytime Children's Series: *Sesame Street*; executive producer Dulcy Singer; producer Lisa Simon; coordinating producer Arlene Sherman (PBS)

2996 Outstanding Daytime Children's Special: *Vincent and Me*; producer Rock Demers; line producer Daniel Louis; co-producer Claude Nedjar (Disney)

2997 Outstanding Daytime Animated Program: *Rugrats*; executive producers Vanessa Coffey, Gabor Csupo, Arlene Klasky; creative producer Paul Germain; supervising producers Mary Harrington, Sherry Gunther; producer David Blum; co-producer Bee Beckman; directors Norton Virgien, Howard Baker, Dan Thompson (Nickelodeon)

2998 Outstanding Daytime Talk/Service Program: *The Oprah Winfrey Show*; executive producer Debra DiMaio; supervising producer Oprah Winfrey; producers David Boul, Mary Kay Clinton, Dianne Hudson, Rudy Guido, Alice McGee, Ellen Rakieten (syndicated)

2999 Outstanding Special Class Daytime Program: *Spaceship Earth: Our Global Environment*; executive producer Kirk Bergstrom; producer Kit Thomas, host Khrystyne Haje (Disney)

3000 Outstanding Lead Actress in a Daytime Drama Series: Erika Slezak in *One Life to Live* (ABC)

3001 Outstanding Lead Actor in a Daytime Drama Series: Peter Bergman in *The Young and the Restless* (CBS)

3002 Outstanding Supporting Actress in a Daytime Drama Series: Maeve Kinkead in *Guiding Light* (CBS)

3003 Outstanding Supporting Actor in a Daytime Drama Series: Thom Christopher in *One Life to Live* (ABC)

3004 Outstanding Younger Actor in a Daytime Drama Series: Kristoff St. John in *The Young and the Restless* (CBS)

3005 Outstanding Younger Actress in a Daytime Drama Series: Tricia Cast in *The Young and the Restless* (CBS)

3006 Outstanding Performer in a Daytime Children's Series: Shari Lewis in *Lamb Chop's Play-Along* (PBS)

3007 Outstanding Daytime Game Show Host: Bob Barker in *The Price Is Right* (CBS)

3008 Outstanding Daytime Talk/Service Show Host: Oprah Winfrey in *The Oprah Winfrey Show* (syndicated)

3009 Outstanding Performer in a Daytime Children's Special: Josh Hamilton in *CBS Schoolbreak Special* episode "Abby, My Love" (CBS)

3010 Daytime Drama Series Directing Team: directors Michael Eilbaum, Bob Schwarz, Casey Childs, Susan Strickler; associate directors Carol Sedwick, Mary Madeiras, Janet Andrews for *Another World* (NBC)

3011 Outstanding Directing in a Daytime Game/Audience Participation Show: Dick Schneider for *Jeopardy!* (syndicated)

3012 Outstanding Directing in a Daytime Talk/Service Show: Russell Morash for *This Old House* (PBS)

3013 Outstanding Directing in a Daytime Children's Series: Larry Lancit, Ed Wiseman, Mark Mannussi for *Reading Rainbow* (PBS)

3014 Outstanding Directing in a Daytime Children's Special: David Cobham for *Woof!* (Disney)

3015 Outstanding Directing in Daytime Special Class: Dick Schneider for *Macy's 65th Annual Thanksgiving Day Parade* (NBC)

3016 Writing Team for a Daytime Drama Series: head writer William J. Bell; co-head writer Kay Alden; writers

Jerry Birn, John F. Smith, Eric Freiwald, Rex M. Best, Janice Ferri, Frederick Johnson, Jim Houghton for *The Young and the Restless* (CBS)

3017 Outstanding Writing in a Daytime Children's Series: head writer Norman Stiles; series writers Nancy Sans, Luis Santeiro, Cathi Rosenberg-Turow, Belinda Ward, Sonia Manzano, Jeff Moss, Sara Compton, Judy Freudberg, David Korr, John Weidman, Tony Geiss, Emily Perl Kingsley, Mark Saltzman, Josh Selig, Lou Berger, Jon Stone, Molly Boylan for *Sesame Street* (PBS)

3018 Writing in a Daytime Children's Special: Paul W. Cooper for *CBS Schoolbreak Special* episode "Abby, My Love" (CBS)

3019 Outstanding Achievement in Writing a Daytime Animated Program: writers Nicholas Hollander, Tom Ruegger; story editors Paul Dini; Sherri Stoner for *Tiny Toon Adventures* (syndicated)

3020 Outstanding Achievement in Special Class Daytime Writing: Kerry Millerick, Julie Engleman, Neal Rogin for *Spaceship Earth: Our Global Environment* (Disney)

3021 Outstanding Achievement in Daytime Art Direction/Set Decoration/Scenic Design: James Fenhagen for *Where in the World Is Carmen Sandiego?* (PBS)

3022 Outstanding Achievement in Daytime Technical Direction/Electronic Camera/Video Control: electronic camera Dick Holden; video control Bill Fairweather for *This Old House* (PBS)

3023 Outstanding Achievement in Daytime Cinematography: Eli Adler, Lex Fletcher for *Scenic Wonders of America* (Disney)

3024 Outstanding Achievement in Daytime Music Direction and Composition: Mark Watters for *Tiny Toon Adventures* "The Love Disconnection" (syndicated)

3025 Outstanding Original Daytime Song: composer and lyricist A.J. Gundell for "I Knew That I'd Fall" on *Guiding Light* (CBS)

3026 Outstanding Achievement in Daytime Graphics and Title Design: Wayne Fitzgerald for *Guiding Light* (CBS)

3027 Outstanding Achievement in Daytime Make-Up: Mark Sanchez for *The Joan Rivers Show* (syndicated)

3028 Outstanding Achievement in Daytime Hairstyling: hair designer Richard Sabre; hairstylist Tish Simpson for *Adventures in Wonderland* (Disney)

3029 Outstanding Achievement in Daytime Live and Tape Sound Mixing and Sound Effects: mixers Blake Norton, Tim Lester; sound effects Dick Maitland for *Sesame Street* (PBS)

3030 Outstanding Achievement in Daytime Multiple Camera Film Editing: supervising editor Robert J. Emerick; editor Evamarie Keller for *Sesame Street* (PBS)

3031 Outstanding Achievement in Daytime Single Camera Editing: editor for *Mathnet* John Tierney for *Square One TV* (PBS)

3032 Outstanding Achievement in Daytime Film Sound Editing: supervising sound editors William Koepnick MPSE, Russell Brower; sound editors James C. Hodson CAS, Aaron King, Matt Thorne, Mark Keatts for *Back to the Future* (CBS)

3033 Outstanding Achievement in Daytime Film Sound Mixing: re-recording mixers James C. Hodson CAS, William Koepnick MPSE; production mixer Harry Andronis for *Back to the Future* (CBS)

3034 Outstanding Achievement in Daytime Lighting Direction: Carl Gibson for *Kids Incorporated* (Disney)

3035 Outstanding Achievement in Daytime Costume Design: Jacqueline Saint Anne for *Riders in the Sky* (CBS)

3036 Outstanding Achievement in Art Direction/Set Decoration/Scenic Design for a Daytime Drama Series: production designer Sy Tomashoff; art director Jack Forrestel; set decorator Jay Garvin for *The Bold and the Beautiful* (CBS)

3037 Outstanding Achievement in Technical Direction/Electronic Camera/Video Control for a Daytime Drama Series: technical director Charles Guzzi; electronic camera Gordon T. Sweeney, Ted L. Morales, David G. Navarette, Jim

Velarde; senior video control Roberto A. Bosio, Scha Jani for *The Bold and the Beautiful* (CBS)

3038 Outstanding Achievement in Music Direction and Composition for a Daytime Drama Series: music director/supervisor Barbara Miller-Gidaly; music director A.J. Gundell; composers John Henry, Richard Hazard, Barry de Vorzon, Theodore Irwin, Michael Licari, Wes Boatman for *Guiding Light* (CBS)

3039 Outstanding Achievement in Make-Up for a Daytime Drama Series: head makeup artist Carol Brown; makeup artists Keith Crary, Robert Sloan, Gail Hopkins, Lucia Bianca for *Days of Our Lives* (NBC)

3040 Outstanding Achievement in Hairstyling for a Daytime Drama Series: head hairstylist Angel De Angelis; hairstylists Annette Bianco, John Quaglia, Joyce Sica for *Another World* (NBC)

3041 Outstanding Achievement in Editing for a Daytime Drama Series: Dan Brumett, Marc Beruti, Steve Pierron for *The Young and the Restless* (CBS)

3042 Outstanding Achievement in Lighting Direction for a Daytime Drama Series: Lauri Moorman, Tim Sheldon for *The Bold and the Beautiful* (CBS)

3043 Outstanding Achievement in Live and Sound Mixing for a Daytime Drama Series: audio mixers Otto Svoboda, Tommy Persson; music mixer Don Henderson; Maurice "Smokey" Westerfeld; post-production mixers Harold "Lanky" Linstrot, Bob Marencovich; sound effects technicians Jack Ten Hoor, David Golba for *The Young and the Restless* (CBS)

3044 Outstanding Achievement in Costume Design for a Daytime Drama Series: Sandra Bojin-Sedlik for *The Bold and the Beautiful* (CBS)

———————— 1992 ————————

3045 Outstanding Drama Series: *Picket Fences*, executive producer David E. Kelley; co–executive producer Michael Pressman; senior producer Alice West; producers Robert Breech, Mark B. Perry; co-producer Jonathan Pontell,

David E. Kelley Productions, Inc. in association with 20th Century–Fox (CBS)

3046 Outstanding Comedy Series: *Seinfeld*; executive producers Larry David, Andrew Scheinman, George Shapiro, Howard West; supervising producers Larry Charles, Tom Cherones; producer Jerry Seinfeld; line producer Joan Van Horn; coordinating producer Tim Kaiser; a West/Shapiro Production in association with Castle Rock Entertainment (NBC)

3047 Outstanding Miniseries: "Prime Suspect 2" on *Mystery*; executive producer Sally Head; producer Paul Marcus; Granada Television in association with WGBH/Boston (PBS)

3048 Outstanding Made for Television Movie: *Barbarians at the Gate*; executive producers Thomas M. Hammel, Glenn Jordan; producer Ray Stark; co-producer Marykay Powell; HBO Pictures in association with Columbia Pictures and Rastar Productions (HBO) and *Stalin*; producer Mark Carliner; line producer Don West; co-producer Ilene Kahn; a Mark Carliner Production in association with HBO and Hungarian Television-Channel 1 (HBO)

3049 Outstanding Variety, Music or Comedy Series: *Saturday Night Live*; executive producer Lorne Michaels; a Broadway Video Inc. Production in association with NBC Productions (NBC)

3050 Outstanding Classical Program in the Performing Arts: *Tosca in the Settings and at the Times of Tosca*; executive producer Rada Rassimov; producer Andrea Andermann; conductor Zubin Mehta; Rada Film-Rai Uno in association with Cami Video and WNET/13 (PBS)

3051 Outstanding Informational Special: *Lucy and Desi: A Home Movie*; executive producers Lucie Arnaz, Laurence Luckinbill; producer Don Buford; an Arluck Entertainment Production (NBC)

3052 Outstanding Informational Series: *Healing and the Mind with Bill Moyers*; executive producer/producer David Grubin; producer Alice Markowitz; editorial producer/host Bill

Moyers; editorial producer Judith Moyers; a production of David Grubin Productions, Inc. and Public Television, Inc. (PBS)

3053 Outstanding Animated Program (for programming of one hour or less): *Batman: The Series*; executive producers Jean H. MacCurdy, Tom Ruegger; producers Alan Burnett, Eric Radomski, Bruce W. Timm; writer Randy Rogel; director Dick Sebast; Warner Brothers Television (Fox)

3054 Outstanding Children's Program: *Avonlea*; executive producers Kevin Sullivan, Trudy Grant; line producer Brian Leslie Parker; a Sullivan Entertainment, Inc. Production, Rose Cottage Productions, Inc., in association with the Canadian Broadcasting Corporation, the Disney Channel and the participation of Telefilm Canada (DIS) and *Beethoven Lives Upstairs*; executive producer Terence E. Robinson; producers David Denine, Richard Mozer; Eros Financial Investments, Inc. in association with Classical Productions for Children, Inc. (HBO)

3055 Outstanding Variety, Music or Comedy Special: *Bob Hope: The First 90 Years*; executive producer Linda Hope; supervising producer Nancy Malone; producer Don Mischer; a Hope Enterprises, Inc. Television Production (NBC)

3056 Outstanding Lead Actor in a Comedy Series: Ted Danson in *Cheers*; Charles/Burrows/Charles Production in association with Paramount Pictures (NBC)

3057 Outstanding Lead Actor in a Drama Series: Tom Skerritt in *Picket Fences*; David E. Kelley Productions, Inc. in association with 20th Century–Fox (CBS)

3058 Outstanding Lead Actor in a Miniseries or Special: Robert Morse in "Tru" episode of *American Playhouse*; a production of KCET/Los Angeles (PBS)

3059 Outstanding Lead Actress in a Comedy Series: Roseanne Arnold in *Roseanne*; a Carsey-Werner Production (ABC)

3060 Outstanding Lead Actress in a Drama Series: Kathy Baker in *Picket Fences*; David E. Kelley Productions, Inc. in association with 20th Century–Fox (CBS)

3061 Outstanding Lead Actress in a Miniseries or Special: Holly Hunter in *The Positively True Adventures of the Alleged Texas Cheerleader-Murdering Mom*; a Frederick S. Pierce Company & Sudden Entertainment Production and HBO (HBO)

3062 Outstanding Supporting Actor in a Comedy Series: Michael Richards in *Seinfeld*; a West/Shapiro Production in association with Castle Rock Entertainment (NBC)

3063 Outstanding Supporting Actor in a Drama Series: Chad Lowe in *Life Goes On*; a Toots Production in association with Warner Brothers Television (ABC)

3064 Outstanding Supporting Actor in a Miniseries or Special: Beau Bridges in *The Positively True Adventures of the Alleged Texas Cheerleader-Murdering Mom*; a Frederick S. Pierce Company & Sudden Entertainment Production and HBO (HBO)

3065 Outstanding Supporting Actress in a Comedy Series: Laurie Metcalf in *Roseanne*; a Carsey-Werner Production (ABC)

3066 Outstanding Supporting Actress in a Drama Series: Mary Alice in *I'll Fly Away*; Brand/Falsey Production in association with Lorimar Television (NBC)

3067 Outstanding Supporting Actress in a Miniseries or Special: Mary Tyler Moore in *Stolen Babies*; a production of ABC Video Enterprises in association with Sander/Moss Productions, Inc. (LIF)

3068 Outstanding Individual Performance in a Variety or Music Program: Dana Carvey in "*Saturday Night Live*'s Presidential Bash" episode of *Saturday Night Live*; a Broadway Video, Inc. Production in association with NBC Productions (NBC)

3069 Outstanding Guest Actor in a Comedy Series: David Clennon in "For Peter's Sake" episode of *Dream On*; Malkis Productions, Inc. in association with MCA Television Entertainment (HBO)

3070 Outstanding Guest Actor in a Drama Series: Laurence Fishburne in "The Box" episode of *Tribeca*; San Vincente Productions in association with Tri-Star Television (Fox)

3071 **Outstanding Guest Actress in a Comedy Series:** Tracey Ullman in "The Prima Dava" episode of *Love and War*; Love and War Productions in association with Shukovsky/English Entertainment (CBS)

3072 **Outstanding Guest Actress in a Drama Series:** Elaine Stritch in "Point of View" episode of *Law and Order*; Wolf Films in association with Universal Television (NBC)

3073 **Outstanding Individual Achievement in Art Direction for a Series:** production designer Dean E. Mitzner; set decorator Tom Pedigo for "The Traveling Lemo All-Stars" episode of *Homefront*; a Roundelay Production, a Latham/Lechowick Production in association with Lorimar Television (ABC)

3074 **Outstanding Individual Achievement in Art Direction for a Miniseries or a Special:** production designer Keith Wilson; art director Alistair Kay; set decorators Vladimir Bashkin, Peter Drozd, Eugene Kamaev, Vladimir Rybin, Yuri Shuyer, Valery Tsvetkov, Alexander Kazmischev for *Stalin*; a Mark Carliner Production in association with HBO and Hungarian Television-Channel 1 (HBO)

3075 **Outstanding Individual Achievement in Art Direction for a Variety or Music Program:** production designers John Shaffner, Joe Stewart for *The Magic of David Copperfield XV: Fires of Passion*; DCDI Productions (CBS)

3076 **Outstanding Individual Achievement in Choreography:** Michael Peters for *The Jacksons: An American Dream*; KJ Films, Inc. in association with the Stan Marguiles Company/de Passe Entertainment, Motown Record Company, L.P., Polygram, Filmed Entertainment (ABC)

3077 **Outstanding Individual Achievement in Cinematography for a Series:** Constantine Makris for "Conspiracy" episode of *Law and Order*; Wolf Films in association with Universal Television (NBC)

3078 **Outstanding Individual Achievement in Cinematography for a Miniseries or a Special:** Vilmos Zsigmond, ASC for *Stalin*; a Mark Carliner Production in association with HBO and Hungarian Television-Channel 1 (HBO)

3079 **Outstanding Individual Achievement in Costuming for a Series:** costumer supervisors M.J. Chic Gennarelli, Lyn Paolo for "Like Being There When You're Not" episode of *Homefront*; a Roundelay Production, a Latham/Lechowick Production in association with Lorimar Television (ABC)

3080 **Outstanding Individual Achievement in Costume Design for a Series:** Peggy Farrell for "Young Indiana Jones and the Scandal of 1920" episode of *The Young Indiana Jones Chronicles*; Lucasfilms, Ltd. in association with Paramount Pictures Television (ABC)

3081 **Outstanding Individual Achievement in Costume Design for a Miniseries or a Special:** Shelley Komarov for "Part One" of *Sinatra*; a TS Production in association with Warner Brothers Television (CBS)

3082 **Outstanding Individual Achievement in Costume Design for a Variety or Music Program:** costume designer Emi Wada; mask and body sculpture designer Julie Taymor for *Oedipus Rex*; Cami Video and NHK in association with Channel 4, Czech TV, DR, NOS, ORF, Phillips Classics, S4C, WNET/13 and ZDF (PBS)

3083 **Outstanding Individual Achievement in Directing in a Comedy Series:** Betty Thomas for "For Peter's Sake" episode of *Dream On*; Melkis Productions, Inc. in association with MCA Television Entertainment (NBC)

3084 **Outstanding Individual Achievement in Directing in a Drama Series:** Barry Levinson for "Gone for Goode" episode of *Homicide—Life on the Street*; Reeves Entertainment in association with Baltimore Pictures (NBC)

3085 **Outstanding Individual Achievement in Directing in a Variety or Music Program:** Jeff Margolic for *The 65th Annual Academy Awards*; ABC Television Production (ABC)

3086 **Outstanding Individual Achievement in Directing for a Miniseries or Special:** James Sandwith for *Sinatra*; a TS Production in association with Warner Brothers Television (CBS)

3087 **Outstanding Individual Achievement in Editing for a Series—Single Camera Production:** Jon Koslowsky,

ACE for "Lee Harvey Oswald" episode of *Quantum Leap*; Belisarius Productions in association with Universal Television (NBC)
3088 Outstanding Individual Achievement in Editing for a Miniseries or Special – Single Camera Production: Peter Zinner, ACE for *Citizen Cohn*; a Spring Creek Production in association with Breakheart Films (HBO)
3089 Outstanding Individual Achievement in Editing for a Series – Multi-Camera Production: Robert Bramwell for "One for the Road" episode of *Cheers*; Charles/Burrows/Charles Productions in association with Paramount Pictures (NBC)
3090 Outstanding Individual Achievement in Editing for a Miniseries or a Special – Multi-Camera Production: editors Jeff U'Ren, Ray Miller, Larry Lyman for *The Magic of David Copperfield XV: Fires of Passion*; DCDI Productions (CBS)
3091 Outstanding Individual Achievement in Hairstyling for a Series: hair designer Joy Zapata; hairstylists Candy Neal, Patty Miller, Laura Connelly, Richard Sabre, Julia Walker, Josee Normand for "Time's Arrow, Part 2" episode of *Star Trek: The Next Generation*; a Paramount Pictures Production (syndicated)
3092 Outstanding Individual Achievement in Hairstyling for a Miniseries or a Special: Linda De Andrea for "Part Two" of *Alex Haley's Queen;* Wolper Organization in association with Bernard Sofronski and Warner Brothers (CBS)
3093 Outstanding Individual Achievement in Electronic Lighting Direction for a Comedy Series: Donald A. Morgan for "Bye Bye Birdie" episode of *Home Improvement*; Wind Dancer Productions, Inc. in association with Touchstone Television (ABC)
3094 Outstanding Individual Achievement in Electronic Lighting Direction for a Drama Series, Variety Series, Miniseries or Special: John Rook for *The 52nd Presidential Inaugural Gala*; Smith-Hemion Productions (CBS)
3095 Outstanding Individual Achievement in Make-Up for a Series: makeup designer and supervisor Michael G.

Westmore; makeup artists Jill Rockow, Karen J. Westerfield, Gil Mosko, Dean Jones, Michael Key, Craig Reardon, Vincent Niebla for "Captive Pursuit" segment of *Star Trek: Deep Space Nine* (syndicated)
3096 Outstanding Individual Achievement in Make-Up for a Miniseries or a Special: key makeup Lynne Eagan; special makeup Mathew Mungle, John E. Jackson; James Woods' makeup Deborah La Mia Denaver for *Citizen Cohn*; a Spring Creek Production in association with Breakheart Films (HBO)
3097 Outstanding Individual Achievement in Music Composition for a Series (Dramatic Underscore): Joel McNeely for "Young Indiana Jones and the Scandal of 1920" episode of *The Young Indiana Jones Chronicles*; Lucasfilm, Ltd. in association with Paramount Pictures Television (ABC)
3098 Outstanding Individual Achievement in Music Composition for a Miniseries or a Special (Dramatic Underscore): Patrick Williams for "Part One" of *Danielle Steel's Jewels*; List/Estrin Productions and RCS Video in association with NBC Productions (NBC)
3099 Outstanding Individual Achievement in Music Direction: Ian Fraser for *The 52nd Presidential Inaugural Gala*; Smith-Hemion Productions (CBS)
3100 Outstanding Individual Achievement in Music and Lyrics: composer John Kander; lyricist Fred Ebb for the song "Sorry I Asked" from *Liza Minnelli Live from Radio City Music Hall*; a Live Live Ltd. production in association with Sony Music Video Enterprises (PBS)
3101 Outstanding Individual Achievement in Main Title Theme Music: Dennis McCarthy for the series *Star Trek: Deep Space Nine*; a Paramount Pictures Production (syndicated)
3102 Outstanding Individual Achievement in Sound Editing for a Series: supervising sound editor Tom Bellfort; sound editors Larry Oatfield, Chris Scarabosio, Michael Silvers; music editors David Slusser, Tom Villano, Jamie Gelb-Forester for "Somme, 1916" episode of *The Young Indiana Jones Chronicles*;

Lucasfilm, Ltd. in association with Paramount Pictures Television (ABC)

3103 Outstanding Individual Achievement in Sound Editing for a Miniseries or Special: supervising sound editor Charles R. Beith, Jr.; sound editors Phil Hess, Bill Bell, David Eichhorn, Tim Terusa, Rusty Tinsley, Scott Eilers, Mark Steele, Rick Steele, Mike Graham, Mark Friedgen, Gary Shinkle, Gary Macheel, Mike Dickeson, Dan Luna; supervising ADR editor Kristi Johns; ADR editors J. Michael Hooser, Bob Costanza; music editors Roy Prendergast, Jerry Rothchild for "Part 1" of *The Fire Next Time*; RHI Entertainment, Inc. in association with the Koch Group (CBS)

3104 Outstanding Individual Achievement in Sound Mixing for a Comedy Series or a Special: production mixer Joe Kenworthy, CAS; re-recording mixers Michael Getlin; Dean Okrand, Liam A. Thiederman for "Doogie Gotta Gun" episode of *Doogie Howser, M.D.*; Steven Bochco Productions and 20th Century-Fox (ABC)

3105 Outstanding Individual Achievement in Sound Mixing for a Variety or Music Series or Special: pre-production mixer/re-recording mixer Gregg Rabin; production mixer Randy Ezratty; re-recording mixer John Alberts for *Harry Connick, Jr.: The New York Big Band Concert*; Scorched Earth Productions in association with HC Productions, Inc. (DIS)

3106 Outstanding Individual Achievement in Sound Mixing for a Drama Series: production mixer Alan Bernard; re-recording mixers Doug Davey, Richard Morrison, Christopher Haire for "A Fistful of Datas" episode of *Star Trek: The Next Generation* (syndicated)

3107 Outstanding Sound Mixing for a Drama Miniseries or a Special: production mixer Drew Kunin; re-recording mixers Grover Helsley, Robert W. Glass, Jr., Richard D. Rogers, Michael Jiron, Scott Millan, Tim Philben, CAS for *Stalin*, a Mark Carliner Production in association with HBO and Hungarian Television-Channel 1 (HBO)

3108 Outstanding Technical Direction/Camera/Video for a Series: technical director Allan Wells; cameras John Gillis, Larry Heider, Robert L. Highton, Dave Hilmer, Michael Malone, Bruce Oldham, Kenneth A. Patterson, David A. Plakos; video control Steven C. Berry, Rick Edwards for the 1,000th show episode of *The Arsenio Hall Show*; Arsenio Hall Communications and Paramount Pictures (syndicated)

3109 Outstanding Individual Achievement in Technical Direction/Camera/ Video for a Miniseries or Special: technical director/video control Keith Winikoff, Mark Sanford; cameras Tom Banzoi, David Eastwood, Skip Eppley, Neal Gallagher, Hank Geving, Scott McClain, Ken Patterson, Hector Ramirez, Gordy Sager for *The Magic of David Copperfield XV: Fires of Passion*; DCDI Productions (CBS)

3110 Outstanding Individual Achievement in Writing for a Comedy Series: Larry David for "The Contest" episode of *Seinfeld*; a West/Shapiro Production in association with Castle Rock Entertainment (NBC)

3111 Outstanding Individual Achievement in Writing in a Drama Series: Tom Fontana for "Three Men and Adena" episode of *Homicide — Life on the Street*; Reeves Entertainment in association with Baltimore Pictures (NBC)

3112 Outstanding Individual Achievement in Writing in a Variety or Music Program: writers Judd Apatow, Robert Cohen, Brent Forrester, Jeff Kahn, Bruce Kirschbaum, Bob Odenkirk, Sultan Pepper, Ben Stiller, Sino Stamatopoulos for *The Ben Stiller Show*; an HBO Independent Production (Fox)

3113 Outstanding Individual Achievement in Writing in a Miniseries or a Special: Jane Anderson for *The Positively True Adventures of the Alleged Texas Cheerleader-Murdering Mom*; a Frederick S. Pierce Company and Sudden Entertainment Production and HBO (HBO)

3114 Outstanding Individual Achievement — Informational Programming: cinematographers Lionel Friedberg, Sid Perou; for "Mysteries Underground" episode of *National Geographic*; National Geographic Television (PBS) and director Lee Stanley for *Gridiron Gang*;

Stanhaven Productions, Inc. (syndicated) and editor Gary Weimberg for *Earth and the American Dream*; an HBO Presentation (HBO) and host Audrey Hepburn for "Flower Gardens" episode of *Gardens of the World*; Perennial Productions, Inc. in association with KCET/Los Angeles (PBS)

3115 Outstanding Individual Achievement — Classical Music/Dance Programming: directors Guiseppe Patroni Griffi, Brian Large; Catherine Malfitano for portraying Floria Tosca in *Tosca in the Settings and at the Times of Tosca*; Rada Film-Rai Uno in association with Cami Video and WNET/13 (PBS)

3116 Outstanding Engineering Development Award: Avid Technology, Incorporated (William J. Warner, Eric C. Peters, Jeffrey J. Bedell, Joseph H. Rice, Stephen J. Reber, Thomas A. Ohanian); and Newtek, Incorporated (Tim Jenison, Robert P. Seidel, Les Aseere); CBS, Incorporated (Robert P. Seidel); Les Aseere

3117 Charles Jenkins Engineering Award: Richard S. O'Brien

3118 Outstanding Daytime Children's Series: executive producers Twila C. Liggett, Tony Buttino; supervising producers Cecily Truett, Larry Lancit, Orly Berger; contributing producer LeVar Burton; producers Ronnie Krauss, Jill Gluckson, Kathy Kinsner for *Reading Rainbow* (PBS)

3119 Outstanding Daytime Children's Special: executive producer Debra DiMaio; supervising producer Oprah Winfrey; coordinating producer Tod Solomon Lending; senior producer Ray Nunn; producers John Watkin, Eamon Harrington for "Shades of a Single Protein" episode of *ABC Afterschool Special* (ABC)

3120 Outstanding Daytime Animated Children's Program: executive producer Steven Spielberg; senior producer Tom Ruegger; producer Sherri Stoner; directors Rich Arons, Byron Vaughns, Ken Boyer, Alfred Gimeno, David West for *Tiny Toon Adventures* (Fox)

3121 Outstanding Daytime Game/Audience Participation Show: executive producer Merv Griffin; producer George Vosburgh for *Jeopardy!* (syndicated)

3122 Outstanding Daytime Talk/Service Show: executive producer Jack Reilly; senior producer Steve Lewis; producers Frederica Gaffney, Kevin Magee, Roni Selig, Bob Reichblum, Roberta Dougherty; coordinating producer Randall Barone for *Good Morning America* (ABC)

3123 Outstanding Daytime Drama Series: executive producers William J. Bell, Sr., Edward J. Scott; producer David Shaughnessy; coordinating producer Nancy Bradley Wiard for *The Young and the Restless* (CBS)

3124 Outstanding Lead Actor in a Daytime Drama Series: David Canary in *All My Children* (ABC)

3125 Outstanding Lead Actress in a Daytime Drama Series: Linda Dano in *Another World* (NBC)

3126 Outstanding Supporting Actor in a Daytime Drama Series: Gerald Anthony in *General Hospital* (ABC)

3127 Outstanding Supporting Actress in a Daytime Drama Series: Ellen Parker in *Guiding Light* (CBS)

3128 Outstanding Younger Actor in a Daytime Drama Series: Monti Sharp in *Guiding Light* (CBS)

3129 Outstanding Younger Actress in a Daytime Drama Series: Heather Tom in *The Young and the Restless* (CBS)

3130 Outstanding Daytime Talk/Service Show Host: Oprah Winfrey in *The Oprah Winfrey Show* (syndicated)

3131 Outstanding Daytime Game Show Host: Pat Sajak in *Wheel of Fortune* (syndicated)

3132 Outstanding Daytime Drama Series Directing Team: directors Paul Lammers, Maria Wagner, Dan Hamilton, Charles C. Dyer, Larry Carpenter; associate directors Joel Arnowitz, Michael Kerner for *As the World Turns* (CBS)

3133 Outstanding Daytime Drama Series Writing Team: head writers Nancy Curlee, Stephen Demorest, Lorraine Broderick, James E. Reilly; associate head writer Nancy Williams Watt; writers Michael Conforti, Bill Elverman, Barbara Esensten, James Harmon Brown, Trent Jones, N. Gail Lawrence, Pete T. Rich, Sally Mandel, Patrick Mulcahey, Roger Newman, Dorothy Purser, Peggy Schibi, Courtney Simon, Wisner Washam for *Guiding Light* (CBS)

George Foster Peabody Awards

The National Association of Broadcasters (NAB) decided to establish an award honoring outstanding achievements in broadcasting. It was to be similar to the Pulitzer Prizes administered by the Journalism School at Columbia University. The Journalism School at the University of Georgia was chosen.

The award was named in honor of a native Georgian who was a benefactor of the University, George Foster Peabody. His image is on the medal presented to the winner. The first Peabody Awards were for radio only and they were presented during a banquet held at the Commodore Hotel in New York City. The awards were for radio programs broadcast in 1940.

This first ceremony was broadcast nationwide by the CBS radio network. Television awards were added to radio program awards in 1948. The awards continue to expand to keep up with technology. Cable television was honored for the first time in 1981.

Unlike most other awards, the total number has been kept low. Although over 30,000 nominations have been made, only 1,000 awards have been made. This makes the Peabody one of the rarest and most sought after awards.

For the years 1964, 1972 and 1974 through 1992 awards were not made for specific categories. Only recipients were named.

───────── **1 9 4 0** ─────────

3134 Network Public Service: CBS
3135 Public Service by a Large Station: WLW Radio in Cincinnati, Ohio
3136 Public Service by a Medium-Sized Station: WGAR Radio in Cleveland, Ohio
3137 Public Service by a Small Station: KRFU in Columbia, Missouri
3138 News Reporting: Elmer Davis

───────── **1 9 4 1** ─────────

3139 News Reporting: Cecil Brown, CBS
3140 Drama Entertainment: Sandra Michael and John Gibbs for *Against the Storm* and Norman Corwin for *The Bill of Rights*
3140a Music Entertainment: Alfred Wallenstein, Mutual Network
3141 Educational Program: *Chicago Roundtable of the Air*, NBC
3142 Public Service: The International Shortwave Broadcasters

───────── **1 9 4 2** ─────────

3143 News Reporting: Charles Collingwood, CBS
3144 Drama Entertainment: *The Man Behind the Gun*, CBS
3145 Music Entertainment: *The Standard Symphony*, NBC Pacific Coast Network
3146 Educational Program: *Afield with Ranger Mac*, WHA Radio, Madison, Wisconsin
3147 Public Service by a Local Station: *Our Hidden Enemy—Venereal Disease*, KOAC Radio, Corvallis, Oregon
3148 Public Service by a Regional Station: *The Home Front*, WCHS Radio, Charleston, West Virginia

───────── **1 9 4 3** ─────────

3149 News Reporting: Edward R. Murrow
3150 Drama Entertainment: *Lux Radio Theater*, CBS and *An Open Letter to the American People*, CBS
3151 Music Entertainment: *Music and the Spoken Word*, KSL Radio, Salt Lake City, Utah
3152 Educational Program: *American*

Town Meeting, the Blue Network (ABC)
3153 Public Service by a Regional Station: *These Are Americans*, KNX Radio, Los Angeles, California
3154 Community Service by a Local Station: *Calling Longshoremen*, KYA Radio, San Francisco, California
3155 Children's Program: *Let's Pretend*, CBS
3156 Special Citation: Bob Hope

───────── **1 9 4 4** ─────────

3157 News Reporting: WLW, Cincinnati, Ohio
3158 Commentary: Raymond Gram Swing, Blue Network (ABC)
3159 Drama Entertainment: *Cavalcade of America*, NBC
3160 Special Award for Comedy: Fred Allen
3161 Entertainment in Music: *Telephone Hour*, NBC
3162 Educational Program: *Human Adventure*, Mutual Network
3163 Program for Youth: *Philharmonic Young Artist Series*, KFI Radio, Los Angeles, California
3164 Public Service by a Regional Station: *Worcester and the World*, WTAG Radio, Worcester, Massachusetts
3165 Public Service by a Local Station: *Cross-Rhoads*, WIBX Radio, Ithaca, New York and WNYC Radio and Mayor Fiorello LaGuardia, New York, New York
3166 Regional Awards: *Song of the Columbia*, KOIN Radio, Portland, Oregon; *Syracuse on Trial*, WFBL Radio, Syracuse, New York; *Southwest Forum*, KVOO Radio, Tulsa, Oklahoma; and *St. Louis Speaks*, KMOX Radio, St. Louis, Missouri
3167 Special Award for Adaptation of Radio to the Requirements of the Armed Forces and the Home Front: Colonel Edward M. Kirby, War Department, Radio Branch

───────── **1 9 4 5** ─────────

3168 News Reporting: CBS and Paul White
3169 Drama Entertainment: Edgar Bergen, NBC, and Arch Obler, Mutual Network
3170 Music Entertainment: *The NBC Symphony of the Air* and Howard

Hanson, Eastman School of Music and WHAM Radio, Rochester, New York
3171 **Educational Program:** George V. Denney, Jr.
3172 **Children's Program:** *We March with Faith*, KUWH Radio, Omaha, Nebraska
3173 **Regional Public Service:** *Arnold Hartley* and *Wake Up Kentucky*, WHAS Radio, Louisville, Kentucky; and *Mr. Columbo Discovers America*, WOV Radio, New York, New York
3174 **Local Public Service:** *Save a Life*, KOMA Radio, Oklahoma City, Oklahoma
3175 **News Reporting, Special Citation:** KRNT Radio, Des Moines, Iowa
3176 **Special Citation, Regional Public Service:** *Toward a Better World*, KFWB Radio, Hollywood, California

———————— **1 9 4 6** ————————

3177 **News Reporting and Interpretation:** William L. Shirer, CBS
3178 **Special News Citation:** *Meet the Press*, Mutual Network
3179 **Drama Entertainment:** *The Columbia Workshop*
3180 **Special Drama Citations:** Henry Morgan, CBS and *Suspense*, CBS
3181 **Music Entertainment:** *Orchestras of the Nation*, NBC
3182 **Special Citation for Music Entertainment:** *Invitation to Music*, CBS
3183 **Educational Program:** WMCA Radio, New York, New York
3184 **Special Education Citation:** *Hiroshima* by Robert Saudek, ABC
3185 **Special Children's Program Citation:** *Books Bring Adventure* by the Junior League of America
3186 **Special Award for Contribution to Radio Through Writing:** John Crosby of *The New York Herald Tribune*
3187 **Public Service by Regional Station:** *Operation Big Muddy*, WOW Radio, Omaha, Nebraska
3188 **Special Citation for Regional Public Service:** *The Harbor We Seek*, WSB Radio, Atlanta, Georgia
3189 **Public Service by Local Station:** *Our Town*,WELL Radio, Battle Creek, Michigan
3190 **Special Citation for Local Public**

Service: *The Radio Edition of the Weekly Press*, WCHU Radio, Ithaca, New York

———————— **1 9 4 7** ————————

3191 **News Reporting and Interpretation:** *CBS Views the Press* and Elmer Davis, ABC
3192 **Drama Entertainment:** *Theater Guild on the Air*, ABC
3193 **Special Drama Citation:** *Studio One*, CBS
3194 **Music Entertainment:** *The Boston Symphony Orchestra*, ABC
3195 **Educational Program:** CBS Documentary Unit Series, CBS
3196 **Children's Program:** *The Children's Hour*, WQQW, Washington, DC
3197 **Special Citation:** *United Nations Today*, United Nations Network
3198 **Public Service by a Regional Station:** *Report Uncensored*, WBBM Radio, Chicago, Illinois
3199 **Special Citation for Regional Public Service:** *As the Twig Is Bent*, WCCO Radio, Minneapolis, Minnesota
3200 **Public Service by a Local Station:** *Disaster Broadcast from Cotton Valley*, KXAR Radio, Hope, Arkansas

———————— **1 9 4 8** ————————

3201 **News Reporting and Interpretation:** Edward R. Murrow, CBS
3202 **Drama Entertainment:** *The NBC University Theater*, NBC and *The Groucho Marx Show*, ABC
3203 **Education Program:** *Communism – US Brand*, ABC
3204 **Special Education Citation:** Rocky Mountain Education Council and Lowell Institute of Broadcasting
3205 **Children's Program:** *Howdy Doody*, NBC
3206 **Overall Contributions of Broadcasting Good Music, Music Entertainment:** NBC
3207 **Special Citation:** *Little Songs About U.N.*, WNEW, New York, New York
3208 **Contribution to Television Art:** *Actor's Studio*, ABC
3209 **Overall Contributions (especially for Larry LeSeur's Broadcasts) Promotion of International Understanding:** CBS

3210 **Public Service by Regional Public Station:** *Forests Aflame*, KNBC Radio, San Francisco, California
3211 **Public Service by Local Station:** *You and Youth*, WDAR Radio, Atlanta, Georgia

———————— **1 9 4 9** ————————

RADIO:
3212 **News Reporting and Interpretation:** Eric Sevareid, CBS
3213 **Special News Citations:** Erwin Canham, *The Monitor Views of the News*, ABC; and WMAZ Radio, CBS, Macon, Georgia
3214 **Drama Entertainment:** Jack Benny, CBS
3215 **Special Citation:** *The Greatest Story Ever Told*, ABC
3216 **Music Entertainment:** WQXR, New York, New York
3217 **Children's Program:** *Mind Your Manners* WTIC, NBC, Hartford, Connecticut
3218 **Educational Program:** *Author Meets the Critics*, ABC
3219 **Contribution to International Understanding:** *United Nations Project*, NBC
3220 **Public Service by a Regional Station:** WWJ Radio, NBC, Detroit, Michigan
3221 **Public Service by a Local Station:** KXLJ Radio, NBC, Helena, Montana

TELEVISION:
3222 **Entertainment:** *The Ed Wynn Show*, CBS
3223 **Education:** *Crusade in Europe*, ABC
3224 **Children's Program:** *Kukla, Fran and Ollie*, NBC
3225 **News Reporting and Interpretation:** *United Nations in Action*, CBS
3226 **Special Citation:** Harold W. Ross, *The New Yorker*
3227 **Special Citation:** H. T. Webster, cartoon
3228 **Special Citation:** *Unseen Audience*, United Nations and American broadcasters generally

———————— **1 9 5 0** ————————

RADIO:
3229 **News Reporting and Interpretation:** Elmer Davis, ABC

3230 **Special News Citation:** *Hear It Now*, CBS
3231 **Drama Entertainment:** *Halls of Ivy*, NBC
3232 **Music Entertainment:** *Metropolitan Opera*, ABC
3233 **Special Music Citation:** Ira Hirschman, WABF-FM, New York, New York
3234 **Education:** *The Quick and the Dead*, NBC
3235 **Contribution to International Understanding:** Radio Free Europe
3236 **Special Citations for Contributing to International Understanding:** WNYC, New York, New York; and *Pursuit of Peace*, Mutual and United Nations Radio
3237 **Public Service by a Regional Station:** *The Quiet Answer*, WBBM, CBS, Chicago, Illinois
3238 **Public Service by a Local Station:** WEPL-FM, Louisville Free Public Library, Louisville, Kentucky

TELEVISION:
3239 **Entertainment:** Jimmy Durante, NBC
3240 **Education:** *The Johns Hopkins Science Review*, WAAM-TV, Dumont Network, Baltimore, Maryland
3241 **Children's Programs:** *Zoo Parade*, NBC and *Saturday at the Zoo*, ABC
3242 **Special Citation:** ABC, specifically to President Robert E. Kitner and his associates, and to Robert Saudek and Joseph McDonald
3243 **Special Citation:** *Providence Journal* specifically to Editor Sellvon Brown and Reporter Ben Bagdikian

———————— **1 9 5 1** ————————

3244 **Radio Educational Program:** *The Nation's Nightmare*, CBS
3245 **Radio Youth Program:** *The New York Times Youth Forums*, WQXR, New York, New York
3246 **Non-Musical Radio Entertainment:** *Bob and Ray*, NBC
3247 **Radio's Contribution to International Understanding:** *Letter from America*, Alistair Cooke, British Broadcasting Corporation

3248 Television Educational Program: *What in the World*, WCAU, CBS, Philadelphia, Pennsylvania

3249 Television Musical Entertainment: *Amahl and the Night Visitors*, NBC

3250 Television Non-Musical Entertainment: *Celanese Theatre*, ABC

3251 Television News and Interpretation: Edward R. Murrow, *See It Now*, CBS

3252 Local Public Service by Radio: *Careers Unlimited*, KPOJ, Mutual Network, Portland, Oregon

3253 Regional Public Service by Radio and Television: WSB, NBC, Atlanta, Georgia

——————— 1952 ———————

3254 Radio News: Martin Agronsky, ABC

3255 Radio Music: *The New York Philharmonic Symphony Orchestra*, CBS and *The Standard Symphony*, NBC

3256 Television Education: *The Johns Hopkins Science Review*, WAAM-TV, Dumont Network, Baltimore, Maryland

3257 Television News: *Meet the Press*, NBC

3258 Television Entertainment: *Mister Peepers*, NBC and *Your Hit Parade*, NBC

3259 Youth and Children's Program: *Ding Dong School* NBC

3260 Television Special Award: *Victory at Sea*, NBC

3261 Regional Public Service Including Promotion of International Understanding: WISC Radio, NBC, Columbia, South Carolina

3262 Local Public Service Radio: WEWS-TV, ABC and CBS, Cleveland, Ohio

——————— 1953 ———————

3263 Radio News: Chet Huntley, KABC, ABC, Los Angeles, California

3264 Television News: Gerald W. Johnson, WAAM-TV, Baltimore, Maryland

3265 Television Music: *NBC Television Opera Theater*, NBC

3266 Television Entertainment: *Tele-*

vision Playhouse, NBC and *Imogene Coca*, NBC

3267 Television Education: *Cavalcade of Books*, KNXT, CBS, Los Angeles, California; and *Camera Three*, WCBS-TV, CBS, New York

3268 Television Youth and Children's Program: *Mr. Wizard*, NBC

3269 Promotion of International Understanding Through Television: Coverage of the Coronation, British Broadcasting Company

3270 Public Service by Local Radio-TV Station: WSB-AM-FM-TV, NBC, Atlanta, Georgia

3271 Public Service by a Local Station: WBAW, Barnwell, South Carolina

3272 Special Award: Edward R. Murrow

——————— 1954 ———————

3273 Radio-Television News: John Daly, ABC

3274 Television Entertainment: George Gobel, NBC

3275 Television Education: *Adventure*, CBS

3276 Television Special Awards: *Omnibus*, CBS and *The Search*, CBS

3277 Youth and Children's Programs: *Disneyland*, ABC

3278 Television National Public Service: *Industry on Parade*, National Association of Manufacturers

3279 Television Regional Public Service: *Hurricane Carol*, WJAR-TV, Providence, Rhode Island

3280 Radio Entertainment: *Conversation*, NBC

3281 Public Education: *Man's Right to Knowledge*, CBS

3282 Radio Contribution to International Understanding: *Pauline Frederick at the U.N.*, NBC

3283 Radio Local Public Service: *The Navajo Hour*, KGAK, Gallup, New Mexico

3284 Radio Music Special Citation: Boris Goldovsky, Metropolitan Opera, NBC

——————— 1955 ———————

3285 Television News: Douglas Edwards, CBS

3286 **Television Entertainment:** Perry Como, NBC and Jackie Gleason, CBS
3287 **Television Dramatic Entertainment:** *Producer's Showcase*, NBC
3288 **Television Youth and Children's Program:** *Lassie*, CBS
3289 **Television Education:** Frank Baxter, KNXT, CBS
3290 **Special Television Education Citation:** *Omnibus* and *Adams Family Series*, CBS
3291 **Radio-Television Music:** *Voice of Firestone*, ABC
3292 **Radio-Television Public Service for Pioneering Programming Concepts:** Sylvester L. Weaver, Jr., NBC
3293 **Radio-Television Promotion of International Understanding:** Quincy Howe, ABC
3294 **Special Citation for Promotion of International Understanding:** *Assignment: India*, NBC
3295 **Radio Education:** *Biographies in Sound*, NBC
3296 **Local Radio Public Service:** KIRO, Seattle, Washington
3297 **Special Citation for Radio Public Service:** KFYO, CBS, Lubbock, Texas
3298 **Special Citations for Local Radio Public Service:** WMT, CBS, Cedar Rapids, Iowa; and KQED, San Francisco, California

──────── **1 9 5 6** ────────

3299 **Television News:** John Charles Daly and associates, ABC convention coverage
3300 **Television Entertainment:** *The Ed Sullivan Show*, CBS
3301 **Television Education:** *You Are There*, CBS
3302 **Television Children's and/or Youth Program:** *Youth Wants to Know*, NBC
3303 **Television Public Service:** *World in Crisis*, CBS
3304 **Television Promotion of International Understanding:** *The Secret Life of Danny Kaye*, UNICEF
3305 **Television Writing:** Rod Serling
3306 **Radio News:** *Edward P. Morgan and the News*, ABC
3307 **Radio Entertainment:** *Bob and Ray*, Mutual and NBC

3308 **Radio Education:** *Books in Profile*, WNYC, New York, New York
3309 **Radio Youth and/or Children's Program:** *Little Orchestra Society Concerts*, WNYC, New York, New York
3310 **Radio/Television Local-Regional Public Service:** *Regimented Raindrops*, WOW, Omaha, Nebraska
3311 **Special Award for Promotion of International Understanding:** United Nations Radio and Television
3312 **Special Award for Contributions to Radio and Television Through Writing:** Jack Gould, *The New York Times*

──────── **1 9 5 7** ────────

3313 **Television News:** John Charles Daly and associates, *Prolog '58*
3314 **Depth and Range of Radio and Television News:** CBS News, CBS
3315 **Local Radio Television News:** Louis M. Lyons, WGBH, Boston, Massachusetts
3316 **Musical Entertainment:** *The Dinah Shore Chevy Show*, NBC
3317 **Non-Musical Entertainment:** *Hallmark Hall of Fame*, NBC
3318 **Television Education:** *The Heritage Series*, WQED, Pittsburgh, Pennsylvania
3319 **Local Radio Education:** *You Are the Jury*, WKAR, East Lansing, Michigan
3320 **Television Youth and Children's Program:** *Captain Kangaroo*, CBS
3321 **Local Television Youth and Children's Program:** *Wunda, Wunda*, KING-TV, ABC, Seattle, Washington
3322 **Television Contribution to International Understanding:** Bob Hope, NBC
3323 **Special Radio-Television Awards:** Education programs fed to educational stations and *Know Your Schools*, NBC stations and Westinghouse Broadcasting Company Boston Conference
3324 **Local Television Public Service:** *Panorama*, KLZ-TV, CBS, Denver, Colorado
3325 **Television Public Service:** *The Last Word*, CBS
3326 **Local Radio Public Service:** KPFA-FM, Berkeley, California

——————— **1 9 5 8** ———————

3327 **Television News:** *NBC News— The Huntley-Brinkley Report*, NBC

3328 **Television Dramatic Entertainment:** *Playhouse 90*, CBS

3329 **Television Musical Entertainment:** *Lincoln Presents Leonard Bernstein and the New York Philharmonic*, CBS

3330 **Television Entertainment with Humor:** *The Steve Allen Show*, NBC

3331 **Television Education:** *Continental Classroom*, NBC

3332 **Television Program for Youth:** *College News Conference*, ABC

3333 **Television Program for Children:** *The Blue Fairy*, WGN-TV, Chicago, Illinois

3334 **Television Contribution to International Understanding:** *M. D. International*, NBC

3335 **Television Writing:** James Costigan for "Little Moon of Alban," *Hallmark Hall of Fame*, NBC

3336 **Television Special Awards:** *An Evening with Fred Astaire*, NBC; and Orson Welles, *Fountain of Youth*, *Colgate Theatre*, NBC

3337 **Radio News:** WNEW, New York, New York

3338 **Radio Education:** *Standard School Broadcast*, Standard Oil Company of California

3339 **Radio Contribution to International Understanding:** *Easy as ABC*, ABC-UNESCO

3340 **Television Public Service:** CBS-TV

3341 **Radio Public Service:** *The Hidden Revolution*, CBS

——————— **1 9 5 9** ———————

3342 **Television News:** *Khrushchev Abroad*, ABC

3343 **Television Musical Entertainment:** *The Bell Telephone Hour*, NBC and *Great Music from Chicago*, WGN-TV, Chicago, Illinois

3344 **Television Non-Musical Entertainment:** *Play of the Week*, WNTA-TV, Newark, New Jersey and David Susskind, *The Moon and Sixpence*, NBC

3345 **Television Education:** *The Pop-*

ulation Explosion, CBS; and *Decisions*, WGBH, Boston, Massachusetts and the World Affairs Council

3346 **Television Contribution to International Understanding:** *The Ed Sullivan Show*, CBS and *Small World*, CBS

3347 **Radio News:** *World News Tonight*, CBS

3348 **Television Special Awards:** Frank Stanton, CBS and *The Lost Class of '59*, CBS

3349 **Local Television Public Service:** WDSU-TV, New Orleans, Louisiana

3350 **Radio Public Service:** *Family Living '59*, NBC

3351 **Local Radio Public Service:** WCCO, Minneapolis, Minnesota

——————— **1 9 6 0** ———————

3352 **Television News:** *The Texaco Huntley-Brinkley Report*, NBC

3353 **Television Entertainment:** *The Fabulous Fifties*, CBS

3354 **Television Education:** *NBC White Paper* Series, NBC

3355 **Television Youth Program:** *G.E. College Bowl*, CBS

3356 **Television Contribution to International Understanding:** CBS Olympic Coverage

3357 **Radio Entertainment:** *Musical Spectaculars*, WQXR, New York, New York

3358 **Radio Children's Program:** Irene Wicker, WNYC, New York, New York

3359 **Locally Produced Radio-Television:** WOOD and WOOD-TV, Grand Rapids, Michigan; KPFK, Los Angeles, California; WCKT, Miami, Florida; and WCCO-TV, Minneapolis, Minnesota

3360 **Radio-Television Public Service, Various Programs on Different Networks and Local Stations:** Broadcasting and Film Commission, National Council of Churches of Christ in the U.S.A.

3361 **Special Award:** Frank Stanton, CBS

3362 **Radio Public Service:** Texaco-Metropolitan Opera Network

3363 **Television Public Service:** *CBS Reports,* CBS

---------------- 1 9 6 1 ----------------

3364 **Television News:** *David Brinkley's Journal*, NBC

3365 **Television Entertainment:** *The Bob Newhart Show*, NBC

3366 **Television Education:** *An Age of Kings*, BBC and *Vincent Van Gogh: A Self Portrait*, NBC

3367 **Television Youth and Children's Program:** *Expedition!*, ABC

3368 **Television Contribution to International Understanding:** Walter Lippman, CBS

3369 **Radio Entertainment:** *Fine Arts Entertainment*, WFMT, Chicago, Illinois

3370 **Radio Education:** *The Reader's Almanac* and *Teen Age Book Talk*, WNYC, New York, New York

3371 **Special Awards:** Fred Friendly, CBS, Capital Cities Broadcasting Corporation, *Verdict for Tomorrow: The Eichmann Trial on Television* and Newton N. Minow, chairman of the Federal Communications Commission

3372 **Radio Contribution to International Understanding:** WRUL, Worldwide Broadcasting, New York, New York for coverage of the U.N. General Assembly proceedings in English and Spanish

3373 **Television Public Service:** *Let Freedom Ring*, KSL-TV, CBS, Salt Lake City, Utah

---------------- 1 9 6 2 ----------------

3374 **Television News:** Walter Cronkite, CBS

3375 **Television Entertainment:** *Dupont Show of the Week*, NBC and Carol Burnett, CBS

3376 **Television Education:** *Biography!*, Official Films, Incorporated

3377 **Television Youth and Children's Programming:** *Exploring*, NBC and Walt Disney, NBC

3378 **Television Contribution to International Understanding:** *Adlai Stevenson Reports*, ABC

3379 **Radio News:** WQXR, New York, New York

3380 **Radio Entertainment:** *Adventures in Good Music*, WJR, Detroit, Michigan and *The Eternal Light*, NBC

3381 **Radio Education:** *Science Editor*, KNX, CBS, Los Angeles, California

3382 **Radio Youth and Children's Program:** *Carnival of Books*, WMAQ, NBC, Chicago, Illinois

3383 **Special Award:** William R. McAndrew and NBC News and National Association of Broadcasters for study of television's effects on the young viewer

3384 **Locally Produced Television:** *Elliot Norton Reviews*, WGBH-TV, Boston, Massachusetts; *Books of Our Time*, WNDT (now WNET/13), New York, New York; and *San Francisco Pageant*, KPIX-TV

3385 **Television Public Service:** *A Tour of the White House with Mrs. John F. Kennedy*, CBS

---------------- 1 9 6 3 ----------------

3386 **Television News Commentary:** Eric Sevareid

3387 **Television Entertainment:** *The Danny Kaye Show*, CBS and *Mr. Novak*, NBC

3388 **Television Education:** *American Revolution '63*, NBC and *The Saga of Western Man*, ABC

3389 **Television Youth Program:** *The Dorothy Gordon Forum*, WNBC-TV and Radio, New York, New York

3390 **Television Children's Program:** *Treetop House*, WGN-TV, Chicago, Illinois

3391 **Television Contribution to International Understanding:** *Town Meeting of the World*, CBS and Frank Stanton

3392 **Radio News:** *Sunday Night Monitor*, NBC

3393 **Radio Education:** WLW Radio, Cincinnati, Ohio

3394 **Radio Contribution to International Understanding:** *Voice of America* and Edward R. Murrow

3395 **Special Award:** Broadcast Industry of the U. S. for coverage of the assassination of President Kennedy and related events

3396 **Television Public Service:** *CBS Reports: Storm Over the Supreme Court*

3397 **Radio Public Service:** KSTP Radio, Minneapolis, Minnesota

---------------- 1 9 6 4 ----------------

3398 *CBS Reports*

3399 *Profiles in Courage*, NBC

3400 William H. (Bill) Lawrence, ABC

3401 Joyce Hall, *Hallmark Hall of Fame*
3402 Julia Child, *The French Chef*, WGBH-TV, Boston, Massachusetts and NET
3403 INTERTEL: International Television Federation
3404 *Off the Cuff*, WBKB, ABC, Chicago, Illinois
3405 Riverside Radio, WRVR-FM, New York, New York
3406 *The Louvre*, NBC
3407 Burr Tillstrom
3408 The networks and the broadcasting industry for confronting the American public with the realities of racial discontent

———————— 1 9 6 5 ————————

3409 **Television News:** Frank McGee, NBC and Morley Safer, CBS and KTLA, Los Angeles, California
3410 **Television Entertainment:** *The Julie Andrews Show*, NBC; *My Name Is Barbra*, CBS; and *Frank Sinatra — A Man and His Music*, NBC
3411 **Television Education:** National Educational Television
3412 **Television Youth and Children's Programming:** *A Charlie Brown Christmas*, CBS
3413 **Television Contribution to International Understanding:** Xerox Corporation
3414 **Television Innovation:** *The National Driver's Test*, CBS
3415 **Television's Most Inventive Art Documentary:** *The Mystery of Stonehenge*, CBS
3416 **Television Special Award:** *A Visit to Washington with Mrs. Lyndon B. Johnson — On Behalf of a More Beautiful America*, ABC
3417 **Television Public Service:** *CBS Reports: KKK — The Invisible Empire*, CBS
3418 **Radio Entertainment:** *Music 'til Dawn*, CBS
3419 **Radio Public Service:** WCCO Radio, Minneapolis, Minnesota

———————— 1 9 6 6 ————————

3420 **Television News:** Harry Reasoner, CBS

3421 **Television Entertainment:** *A Christmas Memory: ABC Stage 67*, ABC
3422 **Television Education:** *National Geographic Special*, CBS and *American White Paper: Organized Crime in the United States*, NBC
3423 **Television Youth and Children's Program:** *The World of Stuart Little*, NBC
3424 **Television Promotion of International Understanding:** *ABC's Wide World of Sports*, ABC and *Siberia: A Day in Irkutsk*, NBC
3425 **Television Special Awards:** *Bell Telephone Hour*, NBC; Tom John, CBS; National Educational Television; and *CBS Reports: The Poisoned Air*, CBS
3426 **Local Television News-Entertainment:** *Kup's Show*, WBKB-TV, Chicago, Illinois
3427 **Local Television Music:** *Artists' Showcase*, WGN-TV, Chicago, Illinois and *A Polish Millennium Concert*, WTMJ-TV, Milwaukee, Wisconsin
3428 **Television-Radio Public Service:** *The Dorothy Gordon Youth Forum: Youth and Narcotics — Who Has the Answer?*, WNBC-TV and WNBC Radio, New York, New York
3429 **Local Television Public Service:** *Assignment Four*, KRON-TV, San Francisco, California
3430 **Radio News:** Edwin Newman, NBC
3431 **Local Radio Public Service:** Elmo Ellis, WSB, Atlanta, Georgia
3432 **Local Radio Education:** *Community Opinion*, WLIB, New York, New York

———————— 1 9 6 7 ————————

3433 **Radio News:** Elie Abel, *The World and Washington*, NBC
3434 **Radio Education:** *The Eternal Light*, NBC
3435 **Radio-Television News Analysis and Commentary:** Eric Sevareid, CBS
3436 **Television Entertainment:** *CBS Playhouse* and NBC Television *An Evening at Tanglewood*
3437 **Television Youth or Children's Program:** *The Children's Film Festival*, CBS and *Mr. Knozit*, WIS-TV

3438 **Television Promotion of International Understanding:** *Africa*, ABC
3439 **Television Special Award:** *The Ed Sullivan Show*, CBS
3440 **Special Broadcasting Education Award:** James H. Killiam, Jr., Chairman, Massachusetts Institute of Technology
3441 **Radio-Television Special Awards:** *Meet the Press*, NBC and Bob Hope
3442 **Television Public Service:** *The Opportunity Line*, WBBM-TV, Chicago, Illinois

——————— **1 9 6 8** ———————

3443 **Television News:** Charles Kuralt, *On the Road*, CBS
3444 **Television Entertainment:** *Playhouse*, NET
3445 **Television Education:** Robert Cromie, *Book Beat*, WTTW, Chicago, Illinois and ABC for its creative 1968 documentaries, ABC
3446 **Television Youth or Children's Program:** *Mister Rogers' Neighborhood*, NET
3447 **Television Promotion of International Understanding:** *The 1968 Olympic Games*, ABC
3448 **Television Special Award:** *CBS Reports: Hunger in America*, CBS
3449 **Radio News:** *Second Sunday*, NBC
3450 **Radio Education:** Leonard Reiffel, *The World Tomorrow*, WEEI, CBS, Boston, Massachusetts
3451 **Radio Entertainment:** *Steinway Hall*, WQXR, New York, New York
3452 **Television Public Service:** *One Nation Indivisible*, Westinghouse Broadcasting
3453 **Radio Public Service:** *Kaleidoscope*, WJR, CBS, Detroit, Michigan

——————— **1 9 6 9** ———————

3454 **Television News:** *Newsroom*, KQED, San Francisco, California and Frank Reynolds, ABC, New York, New York
3455 **Television Education:** *The Advocates*, WGBH-TV, Boston, Massachusetts and KCET, Los Angeles, California, and *Who Killed Lake Erie?*, NBC

3456 **Television Entertainment:** *Experiment in Television*, NBC and Curt Gowdy
3457 **Television Youth or Children's Program:** *Sesame Street*, Children's Television Workshop, New York, New York
3458 **Television Promotion of International Understanding:** *The Japanese*, CBS
3459 **Television Special Award:** Chet Huntley
3460 **Special Individual Award:** Bing Crosby
3461 **Special Television Writing Award:** *J. T.*, CBS
3462 **Radio News:** *When Will It End?*, WRNG, Atlanta, Georgia
3463 **Radio Education:** *On Trial: The Man in the Middle*, NBC, New York, New York
3464 **Radio Promotion of International Understanding:** *Voice of America*, Washington, DC
3465 **Network Television Public Service:** Tom Pettit, investigative reporting for NBC
3466 **Local Television Public Service:** *The Negro in Indianapolis*, WFBM-TV, Indianapolis, Indiana
3467 **Radio Public Service:** *Higher Horizons*, WLIB, New York, New York

——————— **1 9 7 0** ———————

3468 **Television News:** *60 Minutes*, CBS and *Politithon '70*, WPBT, Miami, Florida
3469 **Television Entertainment:** *Flip Wilson Show*, NBC; *Evening at the Pops* and *The Andersonville Trial*, PBS; and KCET, Los Angeles, California
3470 **Television Education:** *Eye of the Storm*, ABC
3471 **Television Youth and Children's Program:** The Doctor Seuss Programs, CBS and *Hot Dog*, NBC
3472 **Television Promotion of International Understanding:** *Civilization*, BBC and *This New Frontier*, WWL-TV, New Orleans, Louisiana
3473 **Television Special Award:** *The Selling of the Pentagon*, CBS
3474 **Radio News:** Douglas Kiker, *Jordan Reports*, NBC

3475 **Radio Education:** *Danger Within: A Study of Disunity in America*, NBC

3476 **Radio Promotion of International Understanding:** *Voice of America* and Gary Moore

3477 **Radio Youth or Children's Program:** *Listening/4*, WFBE-FM, Flint, Michigan

3478 **Radio Public Service:** *Medical Viewpoint* and *Pearl Harbor: Lest We Forget*, WAHT, Lebanon, Pennsylvania

3479 **Television Public Service:** *Peace— On Our Time* and *The Death of Reuben Salazar*, KMEX-TV, Los Angeles, California; and *Migrant: An NBC White Paper*, NBC

———————— **1971** ————————

3480 **Broadcast News:** John Rich, NBC Radio and Television

3481 **Television Entertainment:** NBC Dramatic Programming, *The American Revolution: 1770–1783, a Conversation with Lord North*, CBS and *Brian's Song*, ABC

3482 **Television Youth or Children's Program:** *Make a Wish*, ABC News

3483 **Television Education:** *The Turned-on Crisis*, WQED, Pittsburgh, Pennsylvania

3484 **Special Television Education:** Mississippi Authority for Educational Television

3485 **Television Promotion of International Understanding:** *United Nations Day Concert with Pablo Casals*, United Nations Television, New York, New York

3486 **Television Public Service:** *This Child Is Rated X: An NBC News White Paper on Juvenile Justice*, NBC

3487 **Special Television Award:** George Heinemann, NBC

3488 **Special Award:** Frank Stanton

3489 **Radio Education:** *Wisconsin on the Move*, WHA, Madison, Wisconsin

3490 **Radio Promotion of International Understanding:** *Voice of America*, Washington, DC

3491 **Radio Youth or Children's Program:** *Junior Town Meeting of the Air*, WWVA, Wheeling, West Virginia

3492 **Radio Public Service:** *Second Sunday*, NBC

3493 **Radio Special Awards:** *The Heart of the Matter*, WCCO, Minneapolis, Minnesota and Arthur Godfrey

———————— **1972** ————————

3494 Bill Monroe for news reporting, *Today*, NBC

3495 *The Waltons*, CBS

3496 Three programs on twentieth century American music, NBC

3497 Overall classroom programming, WHRO-TV, Norfolk, Virginia

3498 *The Search for the Nile*, BBC and NBC

3499 *ABC Afternoon Specials*, ABC

3500 *The Restless Earth*, WNET, New York, New York and BBC

3501 *Captain Kangaroo*, CBS

3502 *China '72: A Hole in the Bamboo Curtain*, WWL-TV, New Orleans, Louisiana

3503 *Pensions: The Broken Promise*, NBC

3504 *Willowbrook: The Last Disgrace*, WABC, New York, New York

3505 *XX Olympiad*

3506 Alistair Cooke

3507 *NBC Monitor*, NBC Radio Network

3508 *Conversations with Will Shakespeare and Certain of His Friends*, KOAC, Corvallis, Oregon

3509 *The Noise Show*, Washington, DC Schools Radio Project

3510 *Open Door*, KGW, Portland, Oregon

3511 Broadcasting Foundation of America, New York, New York

3512 *Voice of America*

3513 *Breakdown*, Group W, Westinghouse Broadcasting Corporation, New York, New York

3514 *No Fault Insurance—Right Road or Wrong?* and *Second Sunday*, NBC and NBC owned stations

3515 *All Things Considered*, National Public Radio, Washington, DC

———————— **1973** ————————

3516 **Television News:** *Close-up*, ABC News

3517 **Special News Award:** Peter Lisagor, *Chicago Daily News*

3518 **Television Entertainment:** *Myshkin*, WTIU, Bloomington, Indiana; *Pueblo*, ABC; *The Red Pony*, ABC; "The Catholics" on *CBS Playhouse 90*, CBS
3519 **Television Education:** *The First and Essential Freedom*, ABC; *Learning Can Be Fun* and *Dusty's Treehouse*, KNXT, Los Angeles, California
3520 **Television Youth and Children's Program:** *The Borrowers*, NBC and *Street of the Flower Boxes*, NBC
3521 **Television Promotion of International Understanding:** *Overture to Friendship: The Philadelphia Orchestra in China*, WCAU, Philadelphia, Pennsylvania
3522 **Television Special Award:** *The Energy Crisis . . . An American White Paper*, NBC
3523 **Special Sports Award:** Joe Garagiola on *The Baseball World of Joe Garagiola*, NBC
3524 **Radio News:** Lowell Thomas
3525 **Radio Entertainment:** *Lyric Opera Live Broadcasts* and *Music in Chicago*, WFMT, Chicago, Illinois; and *Project Experiment*, NBC Radio Live Concerts
3526 **Radio Education:** *Second Sunday*, NBC Radio and *The American Past: Introduction*, KANU-FM, Lawrence, Kansas
3527 **Radio Promotion of International Understanding:** *From 18th Street: Destination Peking*, WIND, Chicago, Illinois
3528 **Television Public Service:** "Home Rule Campaign," WRC, NBC
3529 **Television Personal Public Service Award:** Pamela Ilott for *Lamp Unto My Feet* and *Look Up and Live*, CBS News
3530 **Radio Public Service:** *Marijuana and the Law*, KNOW, Austin, Texas

──────── **1 9 7 4** ────────

3531 WCKT-TV, Miami, Florida, investigative reporting
3532 *The Execution of Private Slovak*, *The Law* and *IBM Presents Clarence Darrow*, NBC Television Network
3533 *Benjamin Franklin*, CBS Television Network
3534 *Theater in America*, WNET and the Public Broadcasting Service

3535 *Nova*, WGBH-TV, Boston, Massachusetts
3536 *Free to Be—You and Me*, ABC Television Network
3537 *Go!*, NBC Television Network
3538 *How Come?*, KING-TV, Seattle, Washington
3539 *From Belfast with Love*, WCCO-TV, Minneapolis, Minnesota
3540 *Sadat: Action Biography*, ABC Television Network
3541 *Tornado! 4:40 P.M.*, *Xenia, Ohio*, NBC Television Network
3542 NPACT, National Public Affairs Center for Television, Washington, DC
3543 *The Right Man*, KPRC, Houston, Texas
3544 Carl Stern, NBC News
3545 Fred Graham, CBS News
3546 Marilyn Baker, formerly of KPRC, Houston, Texas
3547 Julian Goodman, chairman NBC
3548 *Hit and Run Players*, KTW Radio, Seattle, Washington
3549 *The CBS Radio Mystery Theatre*, CBS Radio Network
3550 *The Second Sunday*, NBC Radio Network
3551 *Through the Looking Glass*, KFAC Radio, Los Angeles, California
3552 *Conversations from Wingspread*, The Johnson Foundation, Racine, Wisconsin
3553 WSB-Radio, Atlanta, Georgia for public and community service
3554 *Battles Just Begun*, WMAL Radio, Washington, DC
3555 *Pledge a Job*, WNBC Radio, New York, New York

──────── **1 9 7 5** ────────

3556 Charles Kuralt for *On the Road to '76*, CBS News
3557 *The Dale Car: A Dream or a Nightmare?*, KABC-TV, Los Angeles, California
3558 *M*A*S*H*, CBS-TV
3559 *ABC Theatre: Love Among the Ruins*, KABC-TV, Los Angeles, California
3560 *Weekend*, NBC-TV
3561 WCVB-TV Boston, Massachusetts
3562 *Call It Macaroni*, Group W, Westinghouse Broadcasting Corporation, New York, New York

3563 *The ABC Afternoon Specials*, ABC

3564 *Snipets*, Kaiser Broadcasting, San Francisco

3565 *Big Blue Marble*, Alphaventure, New York, New York

3566 *Mr. Rooney Goes to Washington*, CBS News

3567 *A Sunday Journal*, WWL-TV, New Orleans, Louisiana

3568 *The American Assassins*, CBS News

3569 *Las Rosas Blancas*, WAPA-TV, San Juan, Puerto Rico

3570 James Killian, Boston

3571 *Harambee: For My People* and *Everywoman: The Hidden World*, WTOP, Washington, DC

3572 Jim Laurie, NBC News

3573 *Sleeping Watchdogs*, KMOX Radio, St. Louis, Missouri

3574 *The Collector's Shelf* and *200 Years of Music in America*, WGMS, Bethesda, Maryland, and WGMS-FM, Bethesda, Maryland

3575 Standard School of Broadcast, San Francisco, California

3576 *Music in Chicago '75*, WFMT, Chicago, Illinois

3577 *Land of Poetry*, WSOU-FM, South Orange, New Jersey

3578 "The Battle of Lexington," *Voice of America*

3579 *A Life to Share*, WCBS Radio, New York, New York

3580 KDKB, Mesa, Arizona for community service

3581 *Suffer the Little Children* and *Legend of the Bermuda Triangle*, WMAL Radio, Washington, DC

3582 Paul Porter, special posthumous award as former member of Peabody Awards National Advisory Board

——————— **1976** ———————

3583 *Power Politics in Mississippi*, WLBT-TV, Jackson, Mississippi

3584 *Primary Colors, an Artist on the Campaign Trail*, Franklin McMahon, WBBM-TV, Chicago, Illinois

3585 Charles Barthold, WHO-TV, Des Moines, Iowa for filming tornadoes

3586 *The CBS Morning News*, Hughes Rudd and Bruce Morton

3587 *Weekend's* "Sawyer Brothers" segment, Sy Perlman, NBC

3588 *Visions*, KCET/28, Los Angeles, California

3589 *Sybil*, NBC-TV

3590 *Eleanor and Franklin*, ABC

3591 *Animals*, ABC

3592 *The 1976 Winter Olympic Games* and *The 1976 Summer Olympic Games*, ABC Sports

3593 *Judge Horton and the Scottsboro Boys*, Tomorrow Entertainment, Inc., New York, New York

3594 *In Performance at Wolftrap*, WETA-TV, Arlington, Virginia

3595 *Perry Como's Christmas in Austria*, NBC-TV

3596 *In the News*, CBS News

3597 *A Thirst in the Garden*, KERA-TV, Dallas, Texas

3598 *'76 Presidential Debates*, Jim Karyn and the League of Women Voters

3599 *The Adams Chronicles*, WNET/13 New York, New York

3600 *In Celebration of US*, CBS News

3601 *Suddenly an Eagle*, ABC News

3602 *A Conversation with Jimmy Carter*, WETA-TV, Arlington, Virginia, and WNET/13 New York, New York

3603 *60 Minutes*, CBS News

3604 *American Popular Song with Alec Wilder and Friends*, South Carolina Educational Radio Network, Columbia, South Carolina

3605 *Flashback 1976*, WGIR-AM-FM, Manchester, New Hampshire

3606 *The Garden Plot: Food as a Weapon*, Associated Press Radio, Washington, DC

——————— **1977** ———————

3607 ABC Television and David Wolper for *Roots*

3608 ABC Television and Lorimar Productions for *Green Eyes,* an ABC Theatre Production

3609 Steve Allen, KCET-TV, Los Angeles, California, Personal Award for *Meeting of the Minds*

3610 Paul Hume, WGMS Radio, Rockville, Maryland, Personal Award for *A Variable Feast*

3611 KABC-TV, Los Angeles, California for *Police Accountability*

3612 KCMO-TV (now KCTV), Kansas City, Missouri for *Where Have All the Flood Cars Gone?*
3613 KPFA-FM, Berkeley, California for *Science Story*
3614 KSJN Radio, St. Paul, Minnesota for *The Prairie Was Quiet*
3615 Norman Lear, personal award for *All in the Family*
3616 London Weekend Television for *Upstairs, Downstairs*
3617 Lorimar Productions and ABC Television for *Green Eyes*, an *ABC Theatre* Production
3618 Metropolitan Opera Association, New York, New York for *Live from the Met*
3619 MTM Enterprises for *The Mary Tyler Moore Show*
3620 Multimedia Program Productions, Cincinnati, Ohio for *Joshua's Confusion*
3621 National Public Radio for *Crossroads: Sea Island Sketches*
3622 NBC Television for *Tut: The Boy King*
3623 NBC Television, Arthur Rankin and Jules Bass for *The Hobbit*
3624 WBTV, Charlotte, North Carolina for *The Rowe String Quartet Plays on Your Imagination*
3625 WCBS-TV, New York, New York for *Camera Three*
3626 WETA-TV, Arlington, Virginia and WNET/13, New York, New York for *MacNeil/Lehrer Report*
3627 WHA Radio, Madison, Wisconsin for *Earplay*
3628 WHLN Radio, Harlan, Kentucky for coverage of the April flood
3629 WNBC-TV, New York, New York for *F.I.N.D. Investigative Reports*
3630 WNBC-TV, New York, New York for *Buyline: Betty Furness*
3631 WNET/13, New York, New York for *A Good Dissonance Like a Man*
3632 WNET/13, New York, New York for *Police Tapes*
3633 WNET/13, New York, New York for *The Lifer's Group, I Am My Brother's Keeper*
3634 WXYZ Radio (now WXYT Radio), Detroit, Michigan for *Winter's Fear: The Children, the Killer, the Search*

——————— **1 9 7 8** ———————

3635 ABC Television and Four D Productions/Trisene Corporation for *Barney Miller*
3636 Baptist Radio and TV Commission, Ft. Worth, Texas for *A River to the Sea*
3637 CBS News for *The Battle for South Africa*
3638 CBS News for *30 Minutes*
3639 CBS Radio News for *CBS World News Roundup*
3640 CBS Television and MTM Enterprises for *Lou Grant*
3641 CBS Television and Tomorrow Entertainment/Medcom Company for *The Body Human: The Vital Connection*
3642 Henson Associates, New York, New York, for *The Muppet Show*
3642a CBS Television, personal award for Bob Keeshan (*Captain Kangaroo*)
3643 KGO-TV, San Francisco, California for *Old Age: Do Not Go Gentle*
3644 KHET-TV, Honolulu, Hawaii for *Damien*
3645 KQED-TV, San Francisco for *Over Easy*
3646 Charles Kuralt, CBS News, personal award for *On the Road*
3647 National Public Radio for *Dialogues on a Tightrope: An Italian Mosaic*
3648 NBC Radio and the Jewish Theological Seminary for *The Eternal Light*
3649 NBC Radio network for *Second Tuesday*
3650 NBC Television and Survival Anglia Ltd./World Wildlife Fund for *Mysterious Castles of Clay*
3651 NBC Television and Titus Productions for *Holocaust*
3652 Newsweek Broadcasting, New York, New York for *Cartoon-a-Torial*
3653 Personal award to Richard S. Salant, New York, New York
3654 The National Radio Theatre of Chicago for *Chicago Radio Theatre*
3655 WABE-FM, Atlanta, Georgia for *The Eyewitness Who Wasn't*
3656 WAVE-TV, Louisville, Kentucky for *Whose Child Is This?*
3656a WDVM-TV (now WUSA), Washington, DC for *Your Health and Your Wallet*
3657 WDVM-TV (now WUSA), Washington, DC for *Race War in Rhodesia*

3657a WENH-TV, Durham, New Hampshire for *Arts in New Hampshire*

3658 WMUK Radio, Kalamazoo, Michigan for live radio drama

3658a WOCB Radio, West Yarmouth, Massachusetts for *The Last Voyage of Cap'n Bill*

3659 WQED-TV, Pittsburgh, Pennsylvania for *A Connecticut Yankee in King Arthur's Court*

———————— **1979** ————————

3660 ABC Television for *Valentine*

3661 ABC Television for *Friendly Fire*

3662 ABC Television for "A Special Gift" on *ABC Afterschool Special*

3663 Canadian Broadcasting Corporation for *The Longest Journey*

3664 CBS Entertainment for *Dummy*

3665 CBS News for *CBS News Sunday Morning*

3666 CBS News for *The Boston Goes to China*

3667 Children's Radio Theatre, Washington, DC for *Henny Penny Playwrighting Contest*

3668 Sylvia Fine Kaye, Beverly Hills, California, Personal Award for *Musical Comedy Tonight*

3669 KNXT-TV (now KCBS-TV), Los Angeles, California for *Down at the Dunbar*

3670 KOOL-TV (now KSTP-TV), Phoenix, Arizona for *The Long Eyes of Kitt Peak*

3671 KRON-TV, San Francisco, California for *Politics of Poison*

3672 KSJN and Minnesota Public Radio, St. Paul, Minnesota for *The Way to 8-A*

3673 KTVI-TV, St. Louis, Missouri for *The Adventures of Whistling Sam*

3674 Roger Mudd, CBS News, Personal Award for *Teddy*

3675 NBC Television for *When Hell Was in Session*

3676 NBC Television and the BBC for *Treasures of the British Crown*

3677 Robert Trout, ABC News, Personal Award

3678 WCBS Radio, New York, New York for *Follow That Cab: The Great Taxi Rip-off*

3679 WGBH Radio, Boston, Massachusetts for *Currier Bell, Esquire*

3680 WGBH-TV, Boston, Massachusetts for *World*

3681 WMAQ-TV, Chicago, Illinois for *Strip and Search*

———————— **1980** ————————

3682 ABC Television for *IBM Presents Baryshnikov on Broadway*

3683 ABC Television for *Amber Waves*

3684 BBC Television for *All Creatures Great and Small*

3685 Canadian Broadcasting Corporation for *The Wonderful World of Science*

3686 Canadian Broadcasting Corporation for *Peniel*

3687 CBS Entertainment for *Gideon's Trumpet*

3688 CBS Entertainment for *Playing for Time*

3689 CBS News for *Universe*

3690 Personal Award for Walter Cronkite, CBS News

3691 Personal Award for Phil Donahue

3692 Elaine Green, WCPO-TV, Cincinnati, Ohio, Personal Award for *The Hoskins Interview*

3693 KCET-TV, Adrian Malone and Dr. Carl Sagan, Los Angeles, California for *Cosmos*

3694 KQED-TV, San Francisco, California for *Broken Arrow: Can a Nuclear Accident Happen Here?*

3695 KTEH-TV, Carol Mon Pere and Sandra Nichols, San Jose, California for *The Battle of Wetlands*

3696 KUED-TV, Salt Lake City, Utah and WNET/13, New York, New York for *The MX Debate*

3697 Maryland Instructional Television, Owings Mills, Maryland for *Terra: Our World*

3698 Minnesota Public Radio, St. Paul, Minnesota for *A Prairie Home Companion*

3699 National Geographic Society and WQED-TV, Pittsburgh, Pennsylvania for *The National Geographic Specials*

3700 National Public Radio for *Jazz Alive!*

3701 NBC Radio for *The Hallelujah Caucus*

3702 NBC Television and Paramount Television for *Shogun*

3703 Personal Award to Mary Nissenson, WTVJ-TV, Miami, Florida for *Poland: A Changing Nation*

3704 Personal Award to Carroll O'Connor for "Edith's Death" on *All in the Family*

3705 Public Broadcasting Service and Robert Geller for *The American Short Story*

3706 San Francisco Opera for *the San Francisco Opera Broadcasts*

3707 Personal Award to Sol Taishoff, Washington, DC

3708 Personal Award to Studs Terkel, WFMT Radio, Chicago, Illinois

3709 WNCN Radio, New York, New York for overall performance as exemplified by *Conversations with Horowitz*

──────── **1 9 8 1** ────────

3710 ABC News, *Viewpoint*, *Nightline* and *America Held Hostage: The Secret Negotiations*

3711 ABC Television and T.A.T. Communications for *The Wave*

3712 Canadian Broadcasting Corporation for *Carl Sandburg at Connemara*

3713 CBS Television and Alan Landesburg Productions for *Bill*

3714 Eighth Decade Consortium (KOMO-TV Seattle, Washington; KSTP-TV Minneapolis/St. Paul, Minnesota; WCVB-TV, Boston, Massachusetts; WJLA-TV, Washington, DC; WRAL-TV, Raleigh, North Carolina) for *Fed Up with Fear*

3715 Home Box Office, New York, New York and *Ms.* magazine (first cable award) for *She's Nobody's Baby: A History of American Women in the 20th Century*

3716 KATU-TV, Portland, Oregon for a series of significant television documentaries

3717 Danny Kaye, New York, New York for *An Evening with Danny Kaye and the New York Philharmonic; Zubin Mehta, Music Director* and *Skokie*

3718 KJRH-TV, Tulsa, Oklahoma for *Project China*

3719 KTEH-TV, San Jose, California for *The Day After Trinity: J. Robert Oppenheimer and the Atomic Bomb*

3720 Personal Award to Bill Leonard, CBS Television

3721 National Radio Theatre, Chicago, Illinois for *The Odyssey of Homer*

3722 NBC Television and MTM Enterprises for *Hill Street Blues*

3723 Nebraska Educational Television Network and the Great Amwell Company for *The Private History of a Campaign That Failed*

3724 Société Radio-Canada, Montreal, Canada for *Klimbo: Le Lion et la Souris (The Lion and the Mouse)*

3725 Timothy and Susan Todd, Middlebury, Vermont for *The Todds' Teddy Bears Picnic*

3726 WDVM-TV, John Goldsmith, Washington, DC for *Now That We've Got Your Interest*

3727 WGBH-TV, Boston, Massachusetts and Granada TV London for *The Red Army*

3728 WJR Radio, Detroit, Michigan for *Newsfile: A Bankrupt Court*

3729 WLS-TV, Chicago, Illinois for *Eyewitness News*

3730 WNET/13, New York, New York and the Public Broadcasting Service for *Dance in America: Nureyev and the Joffrey Ballet/In Tribute to Nijinsky*

3731 WQDR-FM, Raleigh, North Carolina for *Our Forgotten Warriors: Vietnam Veterans Face the Challenge of the 80's*

3732 WSMV-TV, Nashville, Tennessee for a series of significant television documentaries

──────── **1 9 8 2** ────────

3733 ABC News for *Vietnam Requiem*

3734 BBC Television, Paramount Television and Operation Prime Time for *Smiley's People*

3735 Canadian Broadcasting Corporation for *Morningside/1905*

3736 CBS Entertainment and Cinetex International for *The Wall*

3737 CBS News for *Juilliard and Beyond: A Life in Music*

3738 Personal Award to Alistair Cooke

3739 Daniel Wilson Productions and Taurus Films for *Blood and Honor, Youth Under Hitler*
3740 KGMB-TV, Honolulu, Hawaii and Lee Productions, Inc. for *Beyond the Great Wall: Journey to the End of China*
3741 KOCO-TV, Oklahoma City, Oklahoma for *Oklahoma Shame*
3742 KQED-TV, San Francisco, California for *Current Affairs: The Case of Dashiell Hammett*
3743 KYW-TV, Philadelphia, Pennsylvania for *Sweet Nothing*
3744 Metropolitan Opera Association, Texaco, Inc. and the Texaco Foundation for their commitment to both radio and television presentation of great opera
3745 Mutual Broadcasting System for *The Larry King Show*
3746 National Public Radio for *The Sunday Show*
3747 National Public Radio for *Taylor Made Piano: A Jazz History*
3748 NBC News for *The Man Who Shot the Pope: A Study in Terrorism*
3749 NBC Radio News for *Bank on the Brink*
3750 NBC Television and Highgate Pictures for *The Electric Grandmother*
3751 NBC Television, Margie-Lee Enterprises, the Blue Marble Company in association with ITC Productions, Inc. for *Skeezer*
3752 Radio Foundation, New York, New York for *The Bob and Ray Public Radio Show*
3753 Television Corporation of America, Washington, DC for *The 784 Days That Changed America—From Watergate to Resignation*
3754 WAGA-TV, Atlanta, Georgia for *Paradise Saved*
3755 Warner Amex Satellite Entertainment Company, New York, New York for *Nickelodeon*
3756 WBBM-TV, Chicago, Illinois, for *Killing Crime: A Police Cop-Out*
3757 WCVB-TV, Boston, Massachusetts for *Ground Zero: Victory Road*
3758 WMAL Radio, Washington, DC for *They Served with Honor*
3759 WQED-TV, Pittsburgh, Pennsylvania for *Firebird*

3760 WTSP-TV, St. Petersburg, Florida for *Prisoners of the Harvest*
3761 WWL-TV, New Orleans, Louisiana for *Search for Alexander*

1983

3762 ABC Television and Dick Clark Productions for *The Woman Who Willed a Miracle*
3763 Cable News Network (CNN), Atlanta, Georgia for significant news and information programming
3764 CBS Entertainment and Mendelson-Melendez Productions for *What Have We Learned, Charlie Brown?*
3765 CBS Entertainment and Smith-Hemion Productions for *Romeo and Juliet on Ice*
3766 CBS News for *The Plane That Fell from the Sky*
3767 CBS News for *60 Minutes: Lenell Geter's in Jail*
3768 KCTS-TV, Seattle, Washington for *Diagnosis: AIDS*
3769 KMOX Radio, St. Louis, Missouri for *Times Beach: Born 1925, Died 1983*
3770 KRON-TV, San Francisco, California for *Climate of Death*
3771 Thomas Looker, Montague, Maine for *New England Almanac: Portraits in Sound of New England Life and Landscape*
3772 Personal Award to Don McGannon (Group W, Westinghouse Broadcasting Corporation)
3773 NBC Television and Chrysalis-Yellen Productions for *Prisoner Without a Name, Cell Without a Number*
3774 NBC Television and Edgar J. Scherick Associates for *He Makes Me Feel Like Dancin'*
3775 NBC Television and Motown Productions for *Motown 25: Yesterday, Today, Forever*
3776 South Carolina Educational Radio Network, Columbia, South Carolina for *Marian McPartland's Piano Jazz*
3777 Sunbow Productions, New York, New York for *The Great Space Coaster*
3778 The Grand Ole Opry, Nashville, Tennessee for *The Grand Ole Opry*
3779 WBBM-TV, Chicago, Illinois for *Studebaker: Less Than They Promised*

3780 WBRZ-TV, Baton Rouge, Louisiana for *Give Me That Bigtime Religion*

3781 WCCO Radio, Minneapolis, Minnesota for *Debbie Pielow: Waiting for a Heart That Never Came*

3782 WCCO-TV, Minneapolis, Minnesota for *I-Team: Ambulance*

3783 WGBH-TV, Boston, Massachusetts for *Nova: The Miracle of Life*

3784 WGBH-TV, Boston, Massachusetts, Central Independent Television, London and Antenna 2, Paris for *Vietnam: A Television History*

3785 WMAL Radio, Washington, DC for *The Jeffersonian World of Dumas Malone*

3786 WNBC-TV, New York, New York for *Asylum in the Streets*

3787 WRAL Radio, Raleigh, North Carolina for *Victims*

3788 WTBS-TV, Atlanta, Georgia for *Portrait of America*

3789 WTTW-TV, Chicago, Illinois for *The Merry Widow*

3790 WTTW-TV, Chicago, Illinois and the BBC, London for *The Making of a Continent*

1984

3791 ABC News for *To Save Our Schools, to Save Our Children*

3792 ABC News and Ted Koppel for *Nightline*

3793 ABC Television for *Heartsounds*

3794 Personal Award to Roone Arledge, ABC Television

3795 Brigham Young University, Provo, Utah for *Bradbury 13*

3796 CBS Entertainment and The David Gerber Company for *George Washington*

3797 Central Independent Television, London for *Seeds of Despair*

3798 Corporation for Entertainment and Learning, Inc./Bill Moyers, Washington, DC for *A Walk Through the 20th Century with Bill Moyers*

3799 Frontline, Boston, Massachusetts for *Frontline*

3800 Grenada Television of England, London for *The Jewel in the Crown*

3801 KDFW-TV, Dallas, Texas for *A Call for Help*

3802 KFGO Radio, Fargo, North Dakota for *24 Hour Blizzard Coverage*

3803 KGW-TV, Portland, Oregon for *Rajneesh Update*

3804 KNX NewsRadio, Los Angeles, California for *The Immigration Problem*

3805 MacNeil/Lehrer NewsHour for *Essays by Roger Rosenblatt*

3806 NBC Television and MTM Enterprises for *St. Elsewhere*

3807 Protestant Radio and Television Center, Atlanta, Georgia for *The Protestant Hour*

3808 Showtime for *Faerie Tale Theatre*

3809 Turner Broadcasting System, Atlanta, Georgia for *Cousteau/Amazon*

3810 WAFX Radio, Ft. Wayne, Indiana for *D-Day: 40 Years Later*

3811 WCAX-TV, Burlington, Vermont for *Patterns of Practice*

3812 WCCO-TV, Minneapolis, Minnesota for *The Hollow Victory: Vietnam Under Communism*

3813 WCVB-TV, Boston, Massachusetts for *Sommerville High*

3814 WDVM-TV (now WUSA-TV), Washington, DC for *Investigation of Dr. Milan Vuitch*

3815 WFMT Radio and Raymond Nordstrand, Chicago, Illinois for fine arts programming

3816 WMAQ-TV, Chicago, Illinois for *Political Parasites*

3817 WNET/13, New York, New York for *Heritage: Civilization and the Jews*

3818 WNET/13, New York, New York for *The Brain*

3819 WNYC Radio, New York, New York for *Small Things Considered*

1985

3820 Personal Award to Johnny Carson, NBC Television

3821 CBS Entertainment and Dave Bell Productions for *Do You Remember Love*

3822 CBS News for *The Numbers Man — Bach at Three Hundred*

3823 CBS News for *Whose America Is It?*

3824 Central Independent Television, London and WETA-TV, Arlington, Virginia for *The Skin Horse*

3825 Columbia University Graduate School of Journalism, New York, New York for *Seminars on Media and Society*

3826 Personal Award to Lawrence Fraiberg, Westinghouse Broadcasting Corporation, Group W

3827 Frontline, Boston, Massachusetts for *Crisis in Central America*

3828 Personal Award to Bob Geldof and Live Aid

3829 Home Box Office and Spinning Reels for *Braingames*

3830 KDKA-TV, Pittsburgh, Pennsylvania for *Second Chance*

3831 KDTV-TV, San Francisco, California for coverage of the Mexican earthquake

3832 KGO-TV, San Francisco, California for *The American West: Steinbeck Country*

3833 Lincoln Center for the Performing Arts, New York, New York for *Live from Lincoln Center*

3834 MacNeil/Lehrer NewsHour, New York, New York for *Apartheid's People*

3835 NBC News for *Vietnam Ten Years After*

3836 NBC Television for *An Early Frost*

3837 TV Ontario, Ontario, Canada for *The Final Chapter?*

3838 Marjorie Van Halteren for *Breakdown and Back*

3839 WBBM-TV, Chicago, Illinois for *Armed and Dangerous*

3840 WBUR-FM, Boston, Massachusetts for *Liberation Remembered*

3841 WBZ-TV, Boston, Massachusetts for *Tender Places*

3842 WCCO-TV, Minneapolis, Minnesota for *I-Team: Home Health Care*

3843 WGBH Radio, Boston, Massachusetts for overall programming and its Leadership in State-of-the-Art Broadcasting

3844 WHAS Radio, Louisville, Kentucky for *Down and Outside: On the Streets of Louisville*

3845 WNET/13, New York, New York and the Harvey Milk Film Project, Inc. for *The Times of Harvey Milk*

3846 WSMV-TV, Nashville, Tennessee for *A Higher Standard*

————— **1 9 8 6** —————

3847 ABC News for *This Week with David Brinkley*

3848 ABC Television Entertainment and Churchill Films for *The Mouse and the Motorcycle*

3849 BBC, London and MacNeil/Lehrer Productions, New York, New York for *The Story of English*

3850 Personal Award to Mrs. Dorothy Bullitt (King Broadcasting), Seattle, Washington

3851 Canadian Broadcasting Corporation for *Paris: From Oscar Wilde to Jim Morrison*

3852 CBS Entertainment and Garner-Duchow Productions for *Promise*

3853 CBS News for *Newsmark: Where in the World Are We?*

3854 CBS News for *Sunday Morning: Vladimir Horowitz*

3855 CBS News for *CBS Reports: The Vanishing Family — Crisis in Black America*

3856 Connecticut Public Radio for *One-on-One*

3857 Fine Arts Society of Indianapolis, Indiana for their overall programming

3858 Personal Award to Jim Henson and the Muppets

3859 John F. Kennedy Center for the Performing Arts, Washington, DC for *The 1986 Kennedy Center Honors: A Celebration of the Performing Arts*

3860 KPIX-TV, San Francisco, California for *AIDS Lifeline*

3861 MacNeil/Lehrer Productions, New York, New York and the BBC, London for *The Story of English*

3862 NBC Radio News for coverage of the attack on Tripoli, Libya

3863 NBC Television for *The Cosby Show*

3864 Thames Television International, London and D.L. Taffner, Ltd., New York, New York for *Unknown Chaplin*

3865 WCCO-TV and WCCO Radio, Minneapolis, Minnesota for *Project Lifesaver*

3866 WCVB-TV, Boston, Massachusetts for *A World of Difference*

3867 WFAA-TV, Dallas, Texas for *S.M.U. Investigation*

3868 WGBH-TV, Boston, Massachusetts and Thames TV, London for *Paradise Postponed*
3869 WHAS Radio, Louisville, Kentucky for *A Disaster Called Schizophrenia*
3870 WQED-TV, Pittsburgh, Pennsylvania for *Anne of Green Gables*
3871 WQED-TV, Pittsburgh, Pennsylvania and the National Geographic Society, Washington, DC for the *National Geographic Specials*
3872 WSB-TV, Atlanta, Georgia for *The Boy King*
3873 WTMJ-TV, Milwaukee, Wisconsin for *Who's Behind the Wheel?*

──────── **1 9 8 7** ────────

3874 ABC News for *Earnest Will: Americans in the Gulf*
3875 Blackside, Incorporated, Boston, Massachusetts for *Eyes on the Prize: America's Civil Rights Years*
3876 Personal Awards for Kevin Brownlow and David Gill, London
3877 Cable News Network, Atlanta, Georgia for coverage of the stock market crash
3878 CBS Television and *Hallmark Hall of Fame* for *Foxfire* and *Pack of Lies*
3879 CKVU-TV, Vancouver, British Columbia, Canada for *AIDS and You*
3880 Personal Award to Karl Haas, Cleveland, Ohio
3881 Home Box Office for *Mandela*
3882 Home Box Office for *America Undercover: Drunk and Deadly*
3883 KNBC-TV, Los Angeles, California for *Some Place Like Home*
3884 KPAL Radio, Little Rock, Arkansas, K-pal Radio for overall programming for children
3885 KQED-TV (in association with El Teatro Campesino), San Francisco, California for *Corridos! Tales of Passion and Revolution*
3886 Long Bow Group, Incorporated, New York, New York for *Small Happiness: Women of a Chinese Village*
3887 MacNeil/Lehrer NewsHour, New York, New York for *Japan Series*
3888 Mutual Broadcasting System, Arlington, Virginia for *Charities That Give and Take*

3889 National Public Radio, Washington, DC for "Ryan Martin" as presented on *Weekend Edition*
3890 NBC Television for *L.A. Law*
3891 NBC Television and Louis Rudolph Films for *LBJ: The Early Years*
3892 Paramount Pictures Corporation, Los Angeles, California for *Star Trek: The Next Generation*, "The Big Goodbye"
3893 Center for New American Media, New York, New York for *American Tongues*
3894 WCPO-TV, Cincinnati, Ohio for *Drake Hospital Investigation*
3895 WCVB-TV, Boston, Massachusetts for *Inside Bridgewater*
3896 WGBH-TV, Boston, Massachusetts and KCET-TV Los Angeles, California for *Nova: Spy Machines*
3897 WNET/13, New York, New York for *Nature: A Season in the Sun*
3898 WNET/13, New York, New York for *Shoah*
3899 WRC-TV, Washington, DC for *Deadly Mistakes*
3900 WSM Radio, Nashville, Tennessee for *Of Violence and Victims*
3901 WSMV-TV, Nashville, Tennessee for *For the Family* project
3902 WXXI-TV, Rochester, New York for *Safe Haven*

──────── **1 9 8 8** ────────

3903 ABC Television and The Bedford Falls Company in association with MGM/UA Television for *thirtysomething*
3904 Personal Award for Ambassador Walter Annenberg, Sunnyvale, California
3905 BBC, London and WNET/13, New York, New York for *The Singing Detective*
3905a BBC Radio (World Service for Africa), London for *Nothing Political/ Mandela at 70*
3906 CBS Entertainment and Telecom Entertainment in association with Yorkshire Television for *The Attic: The Hiding of Anne Frank*
3907 CBS News for "Mr. Snow Goes to Washington," part of *60 Minutes*
3908 CBS News for "Abortion Battle" and "On Runaway Street," part of *48 Hours*

3909 Children's Television Workshop, New York, New York for *3-2-1 Contact Extra: I Have AIDS, a Teenager's Story*

3910 Christian Science Monitor Reports, New York, New York for *Islam in Turmoil*

3911 Frontline, Boston, Massachusetts and Time, Incorporated, New York, New York for *Frontline: The Choice*

3912 Personal Award for Don Hewitt, CBS Television

3913 Home Box Office for *Dear America: Letters Home from Vietnam*

3914 Home Box Office and Pro Image Productions, Sydney, Australia for *Suzy's Story*

3915 KCBS-TV, Los Angeles, California for *MCA and the Mob*

3916 KMOX Radio, St. Louis, Missouri for *Hate Crimes: America's Cancer*

3917 KTAR Radio, Phoenix, Arizona for *The Impeachment of Evan Mecham*

3918 MacNeil/Lehrer Productions, New York, New York for the *MacNeil/Lehrer NewsHour* Election '88 Coverage

3919 Personal Award to Jim McKay, ABC Sports

3920 National Public Radio, Washington, DC for *Cowboys on Everest*

3921 NBC Television for *The Murder of Mary Phagan*

3922 Public Affairs Television, New York, New York for *Bill Moyers' World of Ideas*

3923 South Carolina ETV Network, Columbia, South Carolina and the Mosaic Group, Incorporated, New York, New York for *Children's Express Newsmagazine: Campaign '88*

3924 Turner Network Television, Atlanta, Georgia for *The Making of a Legend: Gone with the Wind*

3925 WBRZ-TV, Baton Rouge, Louisiana for *The Best Insurance Commissioner Money Can Buy*

3926 WBUR-FM, Boston, Massachusetts for *Speaking for Everyman: Ian McKellen Celebrates Shakespeare's Birthday*

3927 WHAS Radio News, Louisville, Kentucky for *A Matter of Time: The Crisis in Kentucky Corrections*

3928 WJLA-TV, Washington, DC for the Radon Watch Campaign

3929 WPLG-TV, Miami, Florida for *Caution: Precious Cargo*

3930 WTTW-TV, Chicago, Illinois and Chloe Productions, Incorporated for *...and the Pursuit of Happiness*

——————— **1 9 8 9** ———————

3931 ABC Television and Black/Marlens Company in association with New World Television for *The Wonder Years*

3932 ABC Television, Lou Rudolph Films, Motown Productions, Allarcom Limited and Fries Entertainment for *Small Sacrifices*

3933 ABC Television and Sacret, Incorporated in association with Warner Brothers Television for *China Beach: Vets*

3934 Beyond International Group, Sydney, Australia for *The Great Wall of Iron*

3935 Personal Award to David Brinkley, ABC Television

3936 Canadian Broadcasting Corporation, Toronto, Ontario, Canada for *Lost Innocence: The Children of World War II*

3937 CBS Radio News for *China in Crisis*

3938 CBS Television, Motown-Pangaea Productions in association with Qintex Entertainment for *Lonesome Dove*

3939 Central Independent Television, London, England for *Cambodia Year Ten*

3940 Cable News Network (CNN), Atlanta, Georgia for CNN's coverage of China

3941 Children's Television Workshop, New York, New York for *Sesame Street*

3942 Film News Now and WTVS, Detroit, Michigan in association with P.O.V., New York, New York for *Who Killed Vincent Chin?*

3943 Home Box Office (HBO), New York, New York for *Common Threads: Stories from the Quilt*

3944 KCBS-AM, San Francisco, California for *Earthquake '89*

3945 KCNC-TV, Denver, Colorado for *Yellowstone: Four Seasons After Fire*

3946 KGO-TV, San Francisco, California for *'89 San Francisco Earthquake*

3947 KING-TV, Seattle, Washington for *Project Home Team*
3948 KRON-TV, San Francisco, California for *I Want to Go Home*
3949 Music Television (MTV), New York, New York for *Decade*
3950 NBC News for *NBC News Special: To Be an American*
3951 National Public Radio (NPR), Washington, DC for *Scott Simon's Radio Essays*
3952 Public Affairs Television and Alvin H. Perlmutter, Incorporated, New York, New York for *The Public Mind*
3953 D. Roberts, independent producer, American Public Radio's "Soundprint" series *Mel: A Daughter's Song*
3954 Personal Award to J. Leonard Reinsch
3955 Texaco and the Metropolitan Opera for *Metropolitan Opera Saturday Afternoon Broadcasts*
3956 WCSC-TV, Charleston, South Carolina for *Hurricane Hugo Aftermath*
3957 WLOX-TV, Biloxi, Mississippi for *Did They Die in Vain?*

———————— **1 9 9 0** ————————

3958 ABC News and Koppel Communications, New York, New York for *The Koppel Report: Death of a Dictator*
3959 ABC News/TIME, New York, New York for *Peter Jennings Reporting: Guns*
3960 *American Playhouse* series, New York, New York
3961 Personal Award to Red Barber
3962 Blackside, Incorporated, Boston, Massachusetts for *Eyes on the Prize II: America at the Racial Crossroads (1965–1985)*
3963 Cable News Network, Atlanta, Georgia for its coverage of the Persian Gulf War
3964 CBS Music Video Enterprises and American Masters in association with Perry Films for *John Hammond: From Bessie Smith to Bruce Springsteen*
3965 Connecticut Public Radio, New Haven, Connecticut for *The Shubert Theatre: 75 Years of Memories*

3966 FASE Productions (Foundation for Advancement in Science and Education), Los Angeles, California for *Futures*
3967 Personal Award to Paul Fine and Holly Fine
3968 Florentine Films and WETA-TV, Arlington, Virginia for *The Civil War*
3969 Personal Award to the John D. and Catherine T. MacArthur Foundation, Chicago, Illinois
3970 KCTS-TV, Seattle, Washington and MacNeil/Lehrer NewsHour, New York, New York for *Backhauling*
3971 KPTV News, Portland, Oregon for *Mt. St. Helens: A Decade Later*
3972 Lynch/Frost Productions in association with Propaganda Films and Worldvision Enterprises, Incorporated for the premiere episode of *Twin Peaks*
3973 Worth McDougal on occasion of his retirement for over two decades in service to the Peabody Awards as director
3974 Mouchette Films/P.O.V. for *P.O.V.: Days of Waiting*
3975 Murray Street Enterprises in association with KQED-FM and distributed by NPR, New York, New York for *Heat with John Hockenberry*
3976 National Public Radio, Washington, DC for *Manicu's Story: The War in Mozambique*
3977 NBC Television, New York, New York for *Saturday Night Live*
3978 The Southern Center for International Studies, Atlanta, Georgia
3979 Think Entertainment as presented on the Disney Channel for *Mother Goose Rock 'n' Rhyme*
3980 Vermont Folklife Festival, Middlebury, Vermont for *Journey's End: The Memories and Traditions of Daisy Turner and Family*
3981 Personal Award to Frederick Wiseman
3982 WKYC-TV, Cleveland, Ohio for *Dick Faegler Commentaries*
3983 WXPN-FM, Philadelphia, Pennsylvania for *Kid's Corner*
3984 Young Visions, Incorporated, Los Angeles, California and The Rotary Club of Los Altos, California for *Rotary and AIDS: The Los Altos Story*

——————— **1991** ———————

3985 ABC News, New York, New York and NHK, Japan for *Pearl Harbor: Two Hours That Changed the World*

3986 Armed Forces Radio and Television Service (AFRTS), Mission, Texas on the occasion of its 50th anniversary

3987 Brand/Falsey Productions, Los Angeles, California for *I'll Fly Away*, NBC, and *Northern Exposure*, CBS

3988 Cable News Network, Atlanta, Georgia for its coverage of the Soviet coup

3989 Caedmon Audio (a division of HarperAudio, HarperCollins), New York, New York for a distinguished and unmatched record of preserving our rich oral tradition in poetry, drama and spoken word performance

3990 CBS News, New York, New York for *60 Minutes: Friendly Fire*

3991 CBS Sports, New York, New York for *The Masters*

3992 CBS, New York, New York and Shukovsky/English Productions in association with Warner Brothers, Burbank, California for *Murphy Brown*

3993 Central Independent Television, Nottingham, England presented on WETA-TV, Arlington, Virginia public broadcasting system version of *Soviets: Red Hot*

3994 Personal Award to Peggy Charren

3995 The Discovery Channel, Bethesda, Maryland for *People of the Forest: The Chimps of Gombe*

3996 Home Box Office, New York, New York for *America Undercover: Heil Hitler! Confessions of a Hitler Youth*

3997 Home Box Office, New York, New York and Black Canyon Productions for *When It Was a Game*

3998 KARK-TV, Little Rock, Arkansas and the Arkansas Department of Health for *Arkansas' Timebomb: Teen Pregnancy*

3999 KCRW, Santa Monica, California for *Joe Frank: Work in Progress*

4000 KSTP-TV, St. Paul, Minnesota for *Who's Watching the Store?*

4001 KTLA-TV, Los Angeles, California for *Rodney King: Videotaped Beating*

4002 Lucky Duck Production for MTV Network, New York, New York for *Nickelodeon Special Edition: It's Only Television*

4003 National Public Radio, New York, New York for "The Case Against Women: Sexism in the Courts" on *NPR's Horizons*

4004 National Public Radio, Washington, DC for coverage of the Clarence Thomas Confirmation

4005 NBC News, New York, New York for *Brian Ross Reports on B.C.C.I.*

4006 NBC Productions, Incorporated, New York, New York, Carson Productions, Burbank, California and Worldwide Pants, New York, New York for *Late Night with David Letterman*

4007 WNET/13, New York, New York for *Dance in America: Everybody Dance Now!*

4008 Turner Multimedia, Atlanta, Georgia for *Coup d'État: The Week That Changed the World*

4009 WNCN-FM, New York, New York for *New York City Musicbox*

4010 WRAL-TV, Raleigh, North Carolina for WRAL environmental reporting

4011 Zouk Productions, Philadelphia, Pennsylvania for *The Miles Davis Radio Project*

——————— **1992** ———————

4012 ABC-TV and the Carsey-Werner Company for *Roseanne*

4013 An institutional award to the BBC Radio, London, England

4014 Cable News Network, Atlanta, Georgia for *Larry King Live Election Coverage 1992*

4015 CBS-TV and Grenada Television, London, England for *Age Seven in America*

4016 CBS-TV and Finnegan Pinchuk Company in association with Brand/Falsey Productions for *Northern Exposure: "Cecily"*

4017 Canamedia Productions, Limited and TV Ontario, Toronto, Canada for *Threads of Hope*

4018 Capital Cities/ABC, Incorporated for *ABC News Nightline Special: 72 Hours to Victory*

4019 Capital Cities/ABC, Incorporated for *ABC News Nightline Special: Moment of Crisis, Anatomy of a Riot*

4020 Channel One/Whittle Communications, Los Angeles, California for *AIDS*

4021 Institutional award to C-SPAN, Washington, DC

4022 GPN/Nebraska ETV Network, Lincoln, Nebraska for *Reading Rainbow: The Wall*

4023 Home Box Office and Spring Creek Productions in association with Breakheart Films for *Citizen Cohn*

4024 HKO Media Incorporated and WKBD-TV, Detroit, Michigan for *Close to Home: The Tammy Boccomino Story*

4025 The Institute of American Indian Arts, Santa Fe, New Mexico and KNME-TV, Albuquerque, New Mexico for *Surviving Columbus*

4026 David Isay, independent producer for *American Folklife Radio Project*

4027 KFFA Radio, Helena, Arkansas for *King Biscuit Time*

4028 KIRO-TV, Seattle, Washington for *When the Salmon Runs Dry*

4029 KJLH Radio, Los Angeles, California for coverage of the Los Angeles Riots

4030 KTTV-TV, Los Angeles, California for gavel to gavel coverage of the Rodney King Trial

4031 Maysles Films, Incorporated, New York, New York and Home Box Office for *Abortion: Desperate Choices*

4032 MTV Music Television for *Choose or Lose*

4033 National Broadcasting Company for *The More You Know*

4034 NBC-TV and Castle Rock Entertainment for *Seinfeld*

4035 National Public Radio for *Prisoners in Bosnia*, Sylvia Poggioli, correspondent

4036 Propaganda Films and Fox Broadcasting Company for *Rock the Vote*

4037 Personal award to Fred Rogers

4038 Personal award to Daniel Schorr

4039 Signifyin' Works, Berkeley, California and the Public Broadcasting Service for *Color Adjustment*

4040 WBUR Radio, Boston, Massachusetts and National Public Radio for *Car Talk*

4041 WCVB-TV, Boston, Massachusetts for *The Incredible Voyage of Bill Pinkney*

4042 WGBH-TV, Boston, Massachusetts for *The Health Quarterly: The AIDS Report Series*

4043 WGBH-TV, Boston, Massachusetts, the British Broadcasting Corporation, London, England and NDR, Hamburg, Germany for *The Machine That Changed the World*

4044 WQED-TV, Pittsburgh, Pennsylvania and WGBH-TV, Boston, Massachusetts for *Where in the World Is Carmen Sandiego?*

4045 WTVJ-TV, Miami, Florida for *Hurricane Andrew: As It Happened*

Golden Globe Awards

The Golden Globe Awards were first presented in 1944. With the increasing popularity of broadcasting, television was added at the 13th annual ceremonies in 1956. *Dinah Shore, Lucy & Desi, The American Comedy* and *Davy Crockett* were winners of the first Golden Globe Awards for television. These four programs were winners for the best television shows of 1956.

Like most other awards, they have increased in number. For six years only the best shows were honored regardless of the type of program (news, drama, comedy, etc.). Then in 1962 the best male and female stars on television were named. The Golden Globe Awards for television were limited to these three categories until the 27th annual awards presented in 1970.

The awards were doubled by expanding the categories to include drama and musical comedy winners in each of the three categories. The next year awards were added for supporting actor and actress.

Members of the Hollywood Foreign Press Association vote on the winners for both television and motion pictures listed earlier in this book. The Hollywood Foreign Press Association is made up of representatives of the press from other countries who are located in Hollywood.

Foreign Press Organizations represented include the *London Daily Mail*, the *London Times*, the *London Standard* and the *Sunday Mirror* from England, *L'Espress* from Italy, *Women's World* from Israel, *Bazaar* from Germany, the *Australian Women's Weekly*, and many others.

——————— **1 9 5 6** ———————

4046 Best Television Shows: *The American Comedy, Davy Crockett, Dinah Shore* and *Luci & Desi*

——————— **1 9 5 7** ———————

4047 Best Television Shows: *Cheyenne, Mickey Mouse Club, Playhouse 90, Matinee Theater* and *This Is Your Life*

——————— **1 9 5 8** ———————

4048 Best Television Shows: *Eddie Fisher, Alfred Hitchcock, Jack Benny* and *Mike Wallace*

——————— **1 9 5 9** ———————

4049 Best Television Shows: *Paul Coates, Ann Sothern, Loretta Young, Red Skelton, Ed Sullivan* and William Orr (producer)

——————— **1 9 6 0** ———————

4050 Best Television Shows: *David Susskind, Chuck Connors, Pat Boone, 77 Sunset Strip, Dinah Shore, Ed Sullivan* and *Edward R. Murrow*

——————— **1 9 6 1** ———————

4051 Best Television Shows: *Hanna Barbera Presents, Perry Mason, Bell Telephone Hour, Hong Kong* and *Walter Cronkite*

——————— **1 9 6 2** ———————

4052 Best Television Shows: *What's My Line?* and *My Three Sons*
4053 Best Television Star—Female: Pauline Fredericks
4054 Best Television Star—Male: Bob Newhart and John Daly

——————— **1 9 6 3** ———————

4055 Best Television Shows: *The Dick Powell Show, The Defenders, Mr. Ed* and *Telstar*
4056 Best Television Star—Female: Donna Reed

4057 Best Television Star—Male: Richard Chamberlain and Rod Serling

——————— **1 9 6 4** ———————

4058 Best Television Shows: *The Richard Boone Show, The Danny Kaye Show* and *The Dick Van Dyke Show*
4059 Best Television Star—Female: Inger Stevens
4060 Best Television Star—Male: Mickey Rooney

——————— **1 9 6 5** ———————

4061 Best Television Shows: *The Rogues* and *Burke's Law*
4062 Best Television Star—Female: Mary Tyler Moore
4063 Best Television Star—Male: Gene Barry

——————— **1 9 6 6** ———————

4064 Best Television Show: *The Man from U.N.C.L.E.*
4065 Best Television Star—Female: Anne Francis in *Honey West*
4066 Best Television Star—Male: David Janssen in *The Fugitive*

——————— **1 9 6 7** ———————

4067 Best Television Show: *I Spy*
4068 Best Television Star—Female: Marlo Thomas in *That Girl*
4069 Best Television Star—Male: Dean Martin in *The Dean Martin Show*

——————— **1 9 6 8** ———————

4070 Best Television Show: *Mission: Impossible*
4071 Best Television Star—Female: Carol Burnett in *The Carol Burnett Show*
4072 Best Television Star—Male: Martin Landau in *Mission: Impossible*

——————— **1 9 6 9** ———————

4073 Best Television Show: *Laugh-In*
4074 Best Television Star—Female: Diahann Carroll in *Julia*
4075 Best Television Star—Male: Carl Betz in *Judd for the Defense*

─────────── **1 9 7 0** ───────────

4076 Best Television Show — Drama: *Marcus Welby, M.D.*

4077 Best Television Show — Musical/ Comedy: *The Governor and J.J.*

4078 Best Television Actress — Drama: Linda Crystal in *High Chaparral*

4079 Best Television Actor — Drama: Mike Connors in *Mannix*

4080 Best Television Actress — Musical/ Comedy: Carol Burnett and Julie Sommers

4081 Best Television Actor — Musical/ Comedy: Dan Dailey in *The Governor and J.J.*

─────────── **1 9 7 1** ───────────

4082 Best Television Show — Drama: *Medical Center*

4083 Best Television Show — Musical/ Comedy: *The Carol Burnett Show*

4084 Best Television Actress — Drama: Peggy Lipton in *Mod Squad*

4085 Best Television Actor — Drama: Peter Graves in *Mission: Impossible*

4086 Best Television Actress — Musical/ Comedy: Mary Tyler Moore

4087 Best Television Actor — Musical/ Comedy: Flip Wilson

4088 Best Television Supporting Actress: Gail Fisher in *Mannix*

4089 Best Television Supporting Actor: James Brolin in *Marcus Welby, M.D.*

─────────── **1 9 7 2** ───────────

4090 Best Television Show — Drama: *Mannix*

4091 Best Television Show — Musical/ Comedy: *All in the Family*

4092 Best Television Actress — Drama: Patricia Neal in *The Homecoming*

4093 Best Television Actor — Drama: Robert Young in *Marcus Welby, M.D.*

4094 Best Made for Television Movie: *The Snow Goose*

4095 Television Actress — Musical/ Comedy: Carol Burnett in *The Carol Burnett Show*

4096 Best Television Actor — Musical/ Comedy: Carroll O'Connor in *All in the Family*

4097 Best Television Supporting Actress: Sue Ane Langdon in *Arnie*

4098 Best Television Supporting Actor: Edward Asner in *The Mary Tyler Moore Show*

─────────── **1 9 7 3** ───────────

4099 Best Television Show — Drama: *Columbo*

4100 Best Television Show — Musical/ Comedy: *All in the Family*

4101 Best Movie Made for Television: *That Certain Summer*

4102 Best Television Special: *Life of Leonardo daVinci*

4103 Best Television Actress — Drama: Gail Fisher in *Mannix*

4104 Best Television Actor — Drama: Peter Falk in *Columbo*

4105 Best Television Actress — Musical/Comedy: Jean Stapleton in *All in the Family*

4106 Best Television Actor — Musical/ Comedy: Redd Foxx in *Sanford & Son*

4107 Best Television Supporting Actress: Ruth Buzzi in *Laugh-In*

4108 Best Television Supporting Actor: James Brolin in *Marcus Welby, M.D.*

─────────── **1 9 7 4** ───────────

4109 Best Television Show — Drama: *The Waltons*

4110 Best Television Show — Musical/ Comedy: *All in the Family*

4111 Best Television Actress — Drama: Lee Remick in *The Blue Knight*

4112 Best Television Actor — Drama: James Stewart in *Hawkins*

4113 Best Television Actress — Musical/Comedy: Jean Stapleton in *All in the Family* and Cher Bono in *Sonny and Cher*

4114 Best Television Actor — Musical/ Comedy: Jack Klugman in *The Odd Couple*

4115 Best Television Supporting Actress: Ellen Corby in *The Waltons*

4116 Best Television Supporting Actor: McLean Stevenson in *M*A*S*H*

─────────── **1 9 7 5** ───────────

4117 Best Television Show — Drama: *Upstairs — Downstairs*

4118 **Best Television Show — Comedy/ Musical:** *Rhoda*

4119 **Best Television Actress — Drama:** Angie Dickinson in *Police Woman*

4120 **Best Television Actor — Drama:** Telly Savalas in *Kojak*

4121 **Best Television Actress — Comedy Musical:** Valerie Harper in *Rhoda*

4122 **Best Television Actor — Comedy/Musical:** Alan Alda in *M*A*S*H*

4123 **Best Television Supporting Actress:** Betty Garrett in *All in the Family*

4124 **Best Television Supporting Actor:** Harvey Korman in *The Carol Burnett Show*

──────── **1976** ────────

4125 **Best Television Series — Drama:** *Kojak*

4126 **Best Television Series — Musical/ Comedy:** *Barney Miller*

4127 **Best Television Actress — Drama:** Lee Remick in *Jennie*

4128 **Best Television Actor — Drama:** Robert Blake in *Baretta* and Telly Savalas in *Kojak*

4129 **Best Television Actress — Musical/Comedy:** Cloris Leachman in *Phyllis*

4130 **Best Television Actor — Musical/ Comedy:** Alan Alda in *M*A*S*H*

4131 **Best Television Supporting Actress:** Hermione Baddeley in *Maude*

4132 **Best Television Supporting Actor:** Edward Asner in *The Mary Tyler Moore Show* and Tim Conway in *The Carol Burnett Show*

4133 **Best Motion Picture Made for Television:** *Babe*

──────── **1977** ────────

4134 **Best Television Series — Drama:** *Rich Man, Poor Man (Book I)*

4135 **Best Television Series — Musical/ Comedy:** *Barney Miller*

4136 **Best Motion Picture Made for Television:** *Eleanor and Franklin*

4137 **Best Television Actor — Drama:** Richard Jordan in *Captains and the Kings*

4138 **Best Television Actress — Drama:** Susan Blakely in *Rich Man, Poor Man (Book I)*

4139 **Best Television Actor — Musical/ Comedy:** Henry Winkler in *Happy Days*

4140 **Best Television Actress — Musical/Comedy:** Carol Burnett in *The Carol Burnett Show*

4141 **Best Supporting Actor in a Television Series:** Ed Asner in *Rich Man, Poor Man (Book I)*

4142 **Best Supporting Actress in a Television Series:** Josette Banzet in *Rich Man, Poor Man (Book I)*

──────── **1978** ────────

4143 **Best Television Series — Drama:** *Roots*

4144 **Best Television Series — Musical/ Comedy:** *All in the Family*

4145 **Best Motion Picture Made for Television:** *Raid on Entebbe*

4146 **Best Television Actor — Drama:** Ed Asner in *Lou Grant*

4147 **Best Television Actress — Drama:** Lesley Ann Warren in *79 Park Avenue*

4148 **Best Television Actor — Musical/ Comedy:** Henry Winkler in *Happy Days*

4149 **Best Television Actress — Musical/Comedy:** Carol Burnett in *The Carol Burnett Show*

──────── **1979** ────────

4150 **Best Television Series — Drama:** *60 Minutes*

4151 **Best Television Series — Musical/ Comedy:** *Taxi*

4152 **Best Motion Picture Made for Television:** *A Family Upside Down*

4153 **Best Television Actor — Drama:** Michael Moriarty in *Holocaust*

4154 **Best Television Actress — Drama:** Rosemary Harris in *Holocaust*

4155 **Best Television Actor — Musical/ Comedy:** Robin Williams in *Mork and Mindy*

4156 **Best Television Actress — Musical/Comedy:** Linda Lavin in *Alice*

4157 **Best Television Actor in a Supporting Role:** Norman Fell in *Three's Company*

4158 **Best Television Actress in a Supporting Role:** Polly Holiday in *Alice*

──────── **1980** ────────

4159 **Best Television Series — Drama:** *Lou Grant*

4160 Best Television Series — Musical/Comedy: *Alice* and *Taxi*

4161 Best Motion Picture Made for Television: *All Quiet on the Western Front*

4162 Best Television Actor — Drama (Series): Ed Asner in *Lou Grant*

4163 Best Television Actress — Drama (Series): Natalie Wood in *From Here to Eternity*

4164 Best Television Actor — Musical/Comedy: Alan Alda in *M*A*S*H*

4165 Best Television Actress — Musical/Comedy: Linda Lavin in *Alice*

4166 Best Television Actor in a Supporting Role: Danny De Vito in *Taxi* and Vic Tayback in *Alice*

4167 Best Television Actress in a Supporting Role: Polly Holiday in *Alice*

————— **1 9 8 1** —————

4168 Best Television Series — Drama: *Shogun*

4169 Best Television Series — Musical/Comedy: *Taxi*

4170 Best Motion Picture Made for Television: *The Shadow Box*

4171 Best Television Actor — Drama (Series): Richard Chamberlain in *Shogun*

4172 Best Television Actress — Drama (Series): Yoko Shimada in *Shogun*

4173 Best Television Actor — Musical/Comedy: Alan Alda in *M*A*S*H*

4174 Best Television Actress — Musical/Comedy: Katherine Helmond in *Soap*

4175 Best Television Actor in a Supporting Role: Pat Harrington, Jr., in *One Day at a Time* and Vic Tayback in *Alice*

4176 Best Television Actress in a Supporting Role: Valerie Bertinelli in *One Day at a Time* and Diane Ladd in *Alice*

————— **1 9 8 2** —————

4177 Best Television Series — Drama: *Hill Street Blues*

4178 Best Television Series — Musical/Comedy: *M*A*S*H*

4179 Best Miniseries or Motion Picture Made for Television: *Bill* and *East of Eden*

4180 Best Television Special — Musical/Variety: *The Kennedy Center Honors: A Celebration of the Performing Arts*

4181 Best Television Actor in a Series — Drama: Barbara Bel Geddes in *Dallas* and Linda Evans in *Dynasty*

4182 Best Television Actor in a Series — Comedy or Musical: Alan Alda in *M*A*S*H*

4183 Best Television Actress in a Series — Comedy or Musical: Eileen Brennan in *Private Benjamin*

4184 Best Supporting Actor in a Television Series: John Hillerman in *Magnum, P.I.*

4185 Best Supporting Actress in a Television Series: Valerie Bertinelli in *One Day at a Time*

4186 Best Actor in a Miniseries or Motion Picture: Mickey Rooney in *Bill*

4187 Best Actress in a Miniseries or Motion Picture: Jane Seymour in *East of Eden*

————— **1 9 8 3** —————

4188 Best Television Series — Drama: *Hill Street Blues*

4189 Best Television Series — Comedy/Musical: *Fame*

4190 Best Television Actress and Actor — Series (Drama): Joan Collins in *Dynasty* and John Forsythe in *Dynasty*

4191 Best Television Actress and Actor — Series (Musical/Comedy): Debbie Allen in *Fame* and Alan Alda in *M*A*S*H*

4192 Best Supporting Actress and Actor in a Television Series: Shelley Long in *Cheers* and Lionel Stander in *Hart to Hart*

4193 Best Miniseries or Motion Picture Made for Television: *Brideshead Revisited*

4194 Best Actress and Actor in a Miniseries or Motion Picture Made for Television: Ingrid Bergman in *A Woman Named Golda* and Anthony Andrews in *Brideshead Revisited*

————— **1 9 8 4** —————

4195 Best Television Series — Drama: *Dynasty*

4196 Best Television Series — Comedy/Musical: *Fame*

4197 Best Miniseries or Motion Picture Made for Television: *The Thorn Birds*

4198 Best Performance by an Actress in a Television Series – Drama: Jane Wyman in *Falcon Crest*

4199 Best Performance by an Actor in a Television Series – Drama: John Forsythe in *Dynasty*

4200 Best Performance by an Actress in a Television Series – Musical/Comedy: Joanna Cassidy in *Buffalo Bill*

4201 Best Performance by an Actor in a Television Series – Musical/Comedy: John Ritter in *Three's Company*

4202 Best Performance by an Actress in a Miniseries or Motion Picture Made for Television: Ann-Margret in *Who Will Love My Children?*

4203 Best Performance by an Actor in a Miniseries or Motion Picture Made for Television: Richard Chamberlain in *The Thorn Birds*

4204 Best Performance by an Actress in a Supporting Role in a Series, Miniseries or Motion Picture Made for Television: Barbara Stanwyck in *The Thorn Birds*

4205 Best Performance by an Actor in a Supporting Role in a Series, Miniseries or Motion Picture Made for Television: Richard Kiley in *The Thorn Birds*

——————— **1985** ———————

4206 Best Television Series – Drama: *Murder, She Wrote*

4207 Best Television Series – Comedy/Musical: *The Bill Cosby Show*

4208 Best Miniseries or Motion Picture Made for Television: *Something About Amelia*

4209 Best Performance by an Actress in a Television Series – Drama: Angela Lansbury in *Murder, She Wrote*

4210 Best Performance by an Actor in a Television Series – Drama: Tom Selleck in *Magnum, P.I.*

4211 Best Performance by an Actress in a Television Series – Musical/Comedy: Shelley Long in *Cheers*

4212 Best Performance by an Actor in a Television Series – Musical/Comedy: Bill Cosby in *The Bill Cosby Show*

4213 Best Performance by an Actress in a Miniseries or Motion Picture Made for Television: Ann-Margret in *Streetcar Named Desire*

4214 Best Performance by an Actor in a Miniseries or Motion Picture Made for Television: Ted Danson in *Something About Amelia*

4215 Best Performance by an Actress in a Supporting Role in a Series, Miniseries or Motion Picture Made for Television: Faye Dunaway in *Ellis Island*

4216 Best Performance by an Actor in a Supporting Role in a Series, Miniseries or Motion Picture Made for Television: Paul LeMat in *The Burning Bed*

——————— **1986** ———————

4217 Best Television Series – Drama: *Murder, She Wrote*

4218 Best Television Series – Comedy/Musical: *The Golden Girls*

4219 Best Miniseries or Motion Picture Made for Television: *The Jewel in the Crown*

4220 Best Performance by an Actress in a Television Series – Drama: Sharon Gless in *Cagney & Lacey*

4220a Best Performance by an Actor in a Television Series – Drama: Don Johnson in *Miami Vice*

4221 Best Performance by an Actress in a Television Series – Musical/Comedy: Estelle Getty in *The Golden Girls* and Cybill Shepherd in *Moonlighting*

4221a Best Performance by an Actor in a Television Series – Musical/Comedy: Bill Cosby in *The Bill Cosby Show*

4222 Best Performance by an Actress in a Miniseries or Motion Picture Made for Television: Liza Minnelli in *A Time to Live*

4222a Best Performance by an Actor in a Miniseries or Motion Picture Made for Television: Dustin Hoffman in *Death of a Salesman*

4223 Best Performance by an Actress in a Supporting Role in a Series, Miniseries or Motion Picture Made for Television: Sylvia Sidney in *An Early Frost*

4223a Best Performance by an Actor in a Supporting Role in a Series, Miniseries or Motion Picture Made for Television: Edward James Olmos in *Miami Vice*

——————— **1 9 8 7** ———————

4224 Best Television Series – Drama:
L.A. Law

4224a Best Television Series – Comedy/Musical: *The Golden Girls*

4225 Best Miniseries or Motion Picture Made for Television: *Promise*

4225a Best Performance by an Actress in a Television Series – Drama: Angela Lansbury in *Murder, She Wrote*

4226 Best Performance by an Actor in a Television Series – Drama: Edward Woodward in *The Equalizer*

4226a Best Performance by an Actress in a Television Series – Musical/Comedy: Cybill Shepherd in *Moonlighting*

4227 Best Performance by an Actor in a Television Series – Musical/Comedy: Bruce Willis in *Moonlighting*

4227a Best Performance by an Actress in a Miniseries or Motion Picture Made for Television: Loretta Young in *Christmas Eve*

4228 Best Performance by an Actor in a Miniseries or Motion Picture Made for Television: James Woods in *Promise*

4228a Best Performance by an Actress in a Supporting Role in a Series, Miniseries or Motion Picture Made for Television: Olivia De Havilland in *Anastasia, The Mystery of Anna*

4229 Best Performance by an Actor in a Supporting Role in a Series, Miniseries or Motion Picture Made for Television: Jan Niklas in *Anastasia: The Mystery of Anna*

——————— **1 9 8 8** ———————

4229a Best Television Series – Drama:
L.A. Law

4230 Best Television Series – Comedy/Musical: *The Golden Girls*

4231 Best Miniseries or Motion Picture Made for Television: *Escape from Sobibor* and *Poor Little Rich Girl: The Barbara Hutton Story*

4232 Best Performance by an Actress in a Television Series – Drama: Susan Dey in *L.A. Law*

4233 Best Performance by an Actor in a Television Series – Drama: Richard Kiley in *A Year in the Life*

4234 Best Performance by an Actress in a Television Series – Musical/Comedy: Tracey Ullman in *The Tracey Ullman Show*

4235 Best Performance by an Actor in a Television Series – Musical/Comedy: Dabney Coleman in *The "Slap" Maxwell Story*

4236 Best Performance by an Actress in a Miniseries or Motion Picture Made for Television: Gena Rowlands in *The Betty Ford Story*

4237 Best Performance by an Actor in a Miniseries or Motion Picture Made for Television: Randy Quaid in *LBJ: The Early Years*

4238 Best Performance by an Actress in a Supporting Role in a Series, Miniseries or Motion Picture Made for Television: Claudette Colbert in *The Two Mrs. Grenvilles*

4239 Best Performance by an Actor in a Supporting Role in a Series, Miniseries or Motion Picture Made for Television: Rutger Hauer in *Escape from Sobibor*

——————— **1 9 8 9** ———————

4240 Best Television Series – Drama:
thirtysomething

4241 Best Television Series – Comedy/Musical: *The Wonder Years*

4242 Best Miniseries or Motion Picture Made for Television: *War and Remembrance*

4243 Best Performance by an Actress in a Television Series – Drama: Jill Eikenberry in *L.A. Law*

4244 Best Performance by an Actor in a Television Series – Drama: Ron Perlman in *Beauty and the Beast*

4245 Best Performance by an Actress in a Television Series – Musical/Comedy: Candice Bergen in *Murphy Brown*

4246 Best Performance by an Actor in a Television Series – Musical/Comedy: Michael J. Fox in *Family Ties*, Judd Hirsch in *Dear John* and Richard Mulligan in *Empty Nest*

4247 Best Performance by an Actress in a Miniseries or Motion Picture Made for Television: Ann Jillian in *The Ann Jillian Story*

**4248 Best Performance by an Actor in a Miniseries or Motion Picture Made for

Television: Michael Caine in *Jack the Ripper* and Stacy Keach in *Hemingway*

4249 Best Performance by an Actress in a Supporting Role in a Series, Miniseries or Motion Picture Made for Television: Katherine Helmond in *Who's the Boss?*

4250 Best Performance by an Actor in a Supporting Role in a Series, Miniseries or Motion Picture Made for Television: Barry Bostwick in *War and Remembrance* and John Gielgud in *War and Remembrance*

──────── **1 9 9 0** ────────

4251 Best Television Series – Drama: *China Beach*

4252 Best Television Series – Comedy/Musical: *Murphy Brown*

4253 Best Miniseries or Motion Picture Made for Television: *Lonesome Dove*

4254 Best Performance by an Actress in a Television Series – Drama: Angela Lansbury in *Murder, She Wrote*

4255 Best Performance by an Actor in a Television Series – Drama: Ken Wahl in *Wiseguy*

4256 Best Performance by an Actress in a Television Series – Musical/Comedy: Jamie Lee Curtis in *Anything but Love*

4257 Best Performance by an Actor in a Television Series – Musical/Comedy: Ted Danson in *Cheers*

4258 Best Performance by an Actress in a Miniseries or Motion Picture Made for Television: Christine Lahti in *No Place Like Home*

4259 Best Performance by an Actor in a Miniseries or Motion Picture Made for Television: Robert Duvall in *Lonesome Dove*

4260 Best Performance by an Actress in a Supporting Role in a Series, Miniseries or Motion Picture Made for Television: Amy Madigan in *Roe vs. Wade*

4261 Best Performance by an Actor in a Supporting Role in a Series, Miniseries or Motion Picture Made for Television: Dean Stockwell in *Quantum Leap*

──────── **1 9 9 1** ────────

4262 Best Television Series – Drama: *Twin Peaks*

4263 Best Television Series – Comedy/Musical: *Cheers*

4264 Best Miniseries or Motion Picture Made for Television: *Decoration Day*

4265 Best Performance by an Actress in a Television Series – Drama: Sharon Gless in *The Trials of Rosie O'Neill* and Patricia Wettig in *thirtysomething*

4266 Best Performance by an Actor in a Television Series – Drama: Kyle McLachlan in *Twin Peaks*

4267 Best Performance by an Actress in a Television Series – Musical/Comedy: Kirstie Alley in *Cheers*

4268 Best Performance by an Actor in a Television Series – Musical/Comedy: Ted Danson in *Cheers*

4269 Best Performance by an Actress in a Miniseries or Motion Picture Made for Television: Barbara Hershey in *A Killing in a Small Town*

4270 Best Performance by an Actor in a Miniseries or Motion Picture Made for Television: James Garner in *Decoration Day*

4271 Best Performance by an Actress in a Supporting Role in a Series, Miniseries or Motion Picture Made for Television: Piper Laurie in *Twin Peaks*

4272 Best Performance by an Actor in a Supporting Role in a Series, Miniseries or Motion Picture Made for Television: Charles Durning in *The Kennedys of Massachusetts*

──────── **1 9 9 2** ────────

4273 Best Television Series – Drama: *Northern Exposure*

4274 Best Television Series – Comedy/Musical: *Brooklyn Bridge*

4275 Best Performance by an Actress in a Television Series – Drama: Angela Lansbury in *Murder, She Wrote*

4276 Best Performance by an Actor in a Television Series – Drama: Scott Bakula in *Quantum Leap*

4277 Best Performance by an Actress in a Television Series – Musical/Comedy: Candice Bergen in *Murphy Brown*

4278 Best Performance by an Actor in a Television Series – Musical/Comedy: Burt Reynolds in *Evening Shade*

4279 Best Miniseries or Motion Picture Made for Television: *One Against the Wind*

4280 Best Performance by an Actress in a Miniseries or Motion Picture Made for Television: Judy Davis in *One Against the Wind*

4281 Best Performance by an Actor in a Miniseries or Motion Picture Made for Television: Beau Bridges in *Without Warning: The James Brady Story*

4282 Best Performance by an Actress in a Supporting Role in a Series, Miniseries or Motion Picture Made for Television: Amanda Donohoe in *L.A. Law*

4283 Best Performance by an Actor in a Supporting Role in a Series, Miniseries or Motion Picture Made for Television: Louis Gossett, Jr., in *The Josephine Baker Story*

————— **1993** —————

4284 Best Performance by an Actor in a Musical or Comedy Television Series: John Goodman in *Roseanne*

4285 Best Performance by an Actress in a Musical or Comedy Television Series: Roseanne Arnold in *Roseanne*

4286 Best Musical or Comedy Television Series: *Roseanne*, the Carsey-Werner Company

4287 Best Performance by an Actress in a Supporting Role in a Series, Miniseries or Motion Picture Made for Television: Joan Plowright in *Stalin*

4288 Best Performance by an Actor in a Supporting Role in a Series, Miniseries or Motion Picture Made for Television: Maximillian Schell in *Stalin*

4289 Best Miniseries or Motion Picture Made for Television: *Sinatra Parts I & II*, Warner Brothers Television

4290 Best Performance by an Actress in a Miniseries or a Motion Picture Made for Television: Laura Dern in *Afterburn*

4291 Best Performance by an Actor in a Miniseries or a Motion Picture Made for Television: Robert Duvall in *Stalin*

4292 Best Performance by an Actress in a Drama Television Series: Regina Taylor in *I'll Fly Away*

4293 Best Performance by an Actor in a Drama Television Series: Sam Waterston in *I'll Fly Away*

4294 Best Drama Television Series: *Northern Exposure*, Finnegan Pinchuk Company Productions/Brand Falsey Productions/MCA TV

Part Two

MUSIC

Grammy Awards

The Grammy Award is presented by the National Academy of Recording Arts & Sciences (NARAS) annually for excellence in the recording industry.

The award statuette is a composite of early recording machines. Since those early machines were called gramophones, the award is called a "Grammy." Both the award and its name are registered trademarks of the National Academy of Recording Arts & Sciences.

In 1957, the Hollywood Beautification Committee was faced with a problem. They needed names to put in the stars in the sidewalk on Hollywood's "Walk of Fame." So the committee asked a group of recording executives to name the best recording artists who would then have their names put into the stars in the sidewalk.

Those same recording executives realized that recognition was needed which was based on excellence rather than merely popular recognition. The National Academy of Recording Arts & Sciences was formed and the Grammy Awards developed out of that meeting.

The first awards, for achievements in 1958, were handed out on May 4, 1959. Today, winners in categories unfamiliar or less popular than the major awards are announced early in the evening before the national telecast begins. Entertainment by some of the nominated artists accompanies the televised envelope opening during the ceremonies.

Members of the National Academy of Recording Arts & Sciences are classified as either active or associate. Active members are involved in the creative aspects of recording and only active members are allowed to vote for the Grammy.

As musical tastes change, new categories are added and old ones dropped. Folk Recordings were added at the 1962 ceremonies only to be replaced by Ethnic or Traditional Recordings in 1970. Latin recordings were added in 1976. At the 1982 ceremonies, the Video of the Year first appeared, now there are two music video categories.

──────── **1 9 5 9** ────────

4295 Record of the Year: "Nel Blu Dipinto di Blu" *(Volare)*, by Domenico Modugno on Decca

4296 Album of the Year: *The Music from Peter Gunn*, by Henry Mancini on RCA

4297 Song of the Year (Award to the Songwriter): Domenico Modugno for "Nel Blu Dipinto di Blu" *(Volare)* on Decca

4298 Best Male Vocal Performance: Perry Como for "Catch a Falling Star" on RCA-Victor

4299 Best Female Vocal Performance: Ella Fitzgerald for *Ella Fitzgerald Sings the Irving Berlin Songbook* on Verve

4300 Best Individual Jazz Performance: Ella Fitzgerald for *Ella Fitzgerald Sings the Duke Ellington Song Book* on Verve

4301 Best Country & Western Performance: Kingston Trio for "Tom Dooley" on Capitol

4302 Best Rhythm & Blues Performance: The Champs for "Tequila" on Challenge

4303 Best Recording for Children: David Seville for "The Chipmunk Song" on Liberty

4304 Best Comedy Performance: David Seville for "The Chipmunk Song" on Liberty

4305 Best Performance by an Orchestra: Billy May for *Billy May's Big Fat Brass* on Capitol

4306 Best Arrangement: Henry Mancini for *The Music from Peter Gunn* on RCA

4307 Best Jazz Performance by a Group: Count Basie for *Basie* on Roulette

4308 Best Performance by a Dance Band: Count Basie for *Basie* on Roulette

4309 Best Original Cast Album, Broadway or TV: Meredith Willson for *The Music Man* on Capitol

4310 Best Performance by a Vocal Group or Chorus: Louis Prima and Keely Smith for "That Old Black Magic" on Capitol

4311 Best Performance, Documentary or Spoken Word: Stan Freberg for *The Best of the Stan Freberg Show* on Capitol

4312 Best Composition Over 5 Minutes First Recorded and Released During the Year: Nelson Riddle for *Cross Country Suite* on Dot

4313 Best Soundtrack Album, Dramatic Picture Score or Original Cast: Andre Previn for *Gigi* on MGM

4314 Best Instrumental Classical Performance (with Concerto Scale Accompaniment): Van Cliburn, pianist, and Kiril Kondrashin and His Symphony Orchestra, for *Tchaikovsky: Concerto No. 1 in B-Flat Minor, Op. 23* on RCA

4315 Best Instrumental Classical Performance (Other Than Concerto Scale): Andres Segovia for *Segovia Golden Jubilee* on Decca

4316 Best Orchestral Classical Performance: Felix Slatkin and the Hollywood Bowl Symphony Orchestra for *Gaieté Parisienne* on Capitol

4317 Best Classical Performance, Vocal Soloist (with or without Orchestra): Renata Tebaldi for *Operatic Recital* on London

4318 Best Classical Performance, Operatic or Choral: Roger Wagner Chorale for *Virtuoso* on Capitol

4319 Best Classical Performance, Chamber Music (Including Chamber Orchestra): Hollywood String Quartet for *Beethoven Quartet 130* on Decca

4320 Best Engineered Record, Non-Classical: Ted Keep for "The Chipmunk Song" on Liberty

4321 Best Engineered Record, Classical: Sherwood Hall III for "Duets with a Spanish Guitar" on Capitol

4322 Best Album Cover: art director: Frank Sinatra for *Only the Lonely* on Capitol

──────── **1 9 6 0** ────────

4323 Record of the Year: "Mack the Knife" by Bobby Darin on Atco

4324 Album of the Year: *Come Dance with Me* by Frank Sinatra on Capitol

4325 Song of the Year (Award to the Songwriter): Jimmy Driftwood for "The Battle of New Orleans" on Columbia

4326 Best Male Vocal Performance: Frank Sinatra for "Come Dance with Me" on Capitol

4327 Best Female Vocal Performance: Ella Fitzgerald for "But Not for Me" on Verve

4328 **Best Jazz Soloist:** Ella Fitzgerald for "Ella Swings Lightly" on Verve

4329 **Best Jazz Group:** Jonah Jones for "I Dig Chicks" on Capitol

4330 **Best Country & Western:** Johnny Horton for "The Battle of New Orleans"

4331 **Best Rhythm & Blues:** Dinah Washington for "What a Diff'rence a Day Makes" on Mercury

4332 **Best Album for Children:** *Peter and the Wolf* narrated by Peter Ustinov, Philharmonic Orchestra conducted by Herbert von Karajan on Angel

4333 **Best Comedy, Spoken Word:** Shelly Berman for *Inside Shelly Berman* on Verve

4334 **Best Comedy, Musical:** Homer & Jethro for *The Battle of Kookamonga* on RCA

4335 **Best Dance Band Performance:** Duke Ellington for *Anatomy of a Murder* on Columbia

4336 **Best Orchestra:** Andre Previn conducting the David Rose Orchestra for *Like Young* on MGM

4337 **Best Folk:** The Kingston Trio for "The Kingston Trio at Large" on Capitol

4338 **Best Documentary or Spoken Word (Other Than Comedy):** *A Lincoln Portrait* by Carl Sandburg on Columbia

4339 **Best Original Cast Soundtrack Album:** *Porgy and Bess* by the motion picture cast on Columbia

4340 **Best Broadway Show Albums:** *Gypsy* by Ethel Merman on Columbia, and *Redhead* by Gwen Verdon on RCA

4341 **Best Soundtrack Album, Original Cast, Motion Picture or Television:** *Anatomy of a Murder* (Motion Picture) by Duke Ellington on Columbia

4342 **Best Over 5 Minute Musical Composition First Recorded and Released This Year:** *Anatomy of a Murder* composed by Duke Ellington on Columbia

4343 **Best Choral Performance:** The Mormon Tabernacle Choir conducted by Richard Condie for "Battle Hymn of the Republic" on Columbia

4344 **Best Classical Orchestra:** Boston Symphony conducted by Charles Munch for *Debussy: Images for Orchestra* on RCA

4345 **Best Classical Instrumental Soloist (Other Than Full Orchestral Accompaniment):** Artur Rubinstein, Pianist for *Beethoven: Sonata No. 21, in C, Op. 53, No. 3* on RCA

4346 **Best Classical Concerto or Instrumental Soloist (Full Orchestra):** Van Cliburn, pianist accompanying the Symphony of the Air conducted by Kiril Kondrashin for *Rachmaninoff Piano Concerto No. 3* on RCA

4347 **Best Classical Chamber Music (Including Chamber Orchestra):** Artur Rubinstein, pianist for *Beethoven Sonata No. 21, in C, Op. 53, Sonata No. 18, in E-Flat, Op. 31, No. 3* on RCA

4348 **Best Classical Vocal Soloist (with or without orchestra):** Jussi Bjoerling for *Bjoerling in Opera* on London

4349 **Best Classical Opera Cast or Choral:** Vienna Philharmonic Orchestra conducted by Erich Leinsdorf for *Mozart: The Marriage of Figaro* on RCA

4350 **Best Engineered Record (Classical):** Lewis W. Layton for "Victory at Sea, Vol. 1" by Robert Russell Bennett on RCA

4351 **Best Engineered Record (Novelty):** Ted Keep for "Alvin's Harmonica" on Liberty

4352 **Best Engineered Record (Other Than Classical or Novelty):** Robert Simpson for "Belafonte at Carnegie Hall" on RCA

4353 **Best Arrangement:** Billy May for "Come Dance with Me" on Capitol

4354 **Best Album Cover:** Robert Jones for *Shostakovich Symphony No. 5* on RCA

4355 **Best Performance by a "Top-40" Artist:** Nat "King" Cole for "Midnight Flyer" on Capitol

4356 **Special National Trustees' Award for Artists and Repertoire Contribution:** Bobby Darin for "Mack the Knife" produced by Ahmet Ertegun on Atco; Frank Sinatra for "Come Dance with Me" produced by Dave Cavanaugh on Capitol

4357 **Best New Artist of 1959:** Bobby Darin on Atco

———— **1 9 6 1** ————

4358 **Record of the Year:** "Theme from *A Summer Place*" by Percy Faith on Columbia

4359 **Album of the Year:** *Button Down Mind* by Bob Newhart on Warner Brothers

4360 **Song of the Year (Award to the Songwriter):** Ernest Gold for "Theme from Exodus" on RCA

4361 **Best Male Vocal Single Record Performance:** Ray Charles for "Georgia on My Mind" on RCA

4362 **Best Male Vocal Album Performance:** Ray Charles for *Genius of Ray Charles* on RCA

4363 **Best Female Vocal Single Record Performance:** Ella Fitzgerald for "Mack the Knife" on Verve

4364 **Best Female Vocal Album Performance:** Ella Fitzgerald for *Mack the Knife — Ella in Berlin* on Verve

4365 **Best Jazz Solo or Small Group:** Andre Previn for *West Side Story* on Contemporary

4366 **Best Jazz Large Group:** Henry Mancini for *Blues and the Beat* on RCA

4367 **Best Jazz Composition of More Than 5 Minutes:** Miles Davis and Gil Evans for *Sketches of Spain* on Columbia

4368 **Best Pop Single Artist:** Ray Charles for "Georgia on My Mind" on ABC

4369 **Best Country & Western:** Marty Robbins for "El Paso" on Columbia

4370 **Best Rhythm & Blues:** Ray Charles for "Let the Good Times Roll" on Atlantic

4371 **Best Album for Children:** *Let's All Sing with the Chipmunks* by David Seville on Liberty

4372 **Best Comedy, Spoken Word:** Bob Newhart for *Button Down Mind Strikes Back* on Warner Brothers

4373 **Best Comedy, Musical:** Jo Stafford and Paul Weston for *Jonathan and Darlene Edwards in Paris* on Columbia

4374 **Best Dance Band Performance:** Count Basie for *Dance with Basie* on Roulette

4375 **Best Orchestra:** Henry Mancini for *Mr. Lucky* on RCA

4376 **Best Arrangement:** Henry Mancini for *Mr. Lucky* on RCA

4377 **Best Folk:** Harry Belafonte for *Swing Dat Hammer* on RCA

4378 **Best Spoken Word (Other Than Comedy):** Robert Bialek for *FDR Speaks* on Washington

4379 **Best Original Cast Soundtrack Music Score from Motion Picture or Television:** Ernest Gold for *Exodus* on RCA

4380 **Best Show Album (Original Cast):** Mary Martin in *The Sound of Music* by Richard Rodgers and Oscar Hammerstein II on Columbia

4381 **Best Soundtrack Original Cast:** Frank Sinatra in *Can Can* by Cole Porter on Capitol

4382 **Best Vocal Group:** Steve Lawrence & Eydie Gorme for "We Got Us" on ABC

4383 **Best Chorus:** Norman Luboff Choir for *Songs of the Cowboy* on Columbia

4384 **Best Classical Orchestra:** Chicago Symphony conducted by Fritz Reiner for *Bartok: Music for Strings, Percussion and Celeste* on RCA

4385 **Best Classical Concerto or Instrumental Soloist:** Sviatoslav Richter, pianist for *Brahms: Piano Concerto No. 2 in B-Flat* on RCA

4386 **Best Classical Chamber Music:** Laurindo Almeida for *Conversations wtih the Guitar* on Capitol

4387 **Best Classical Vocal Soloist:** Leontyne Price for *A Program of Song* on RCA

4388 **Best Classical Opera:** Erich Leinsdorf conducting the Rome Opera House Orchestra and Chorus in *Puccini: Turandot* on RCA

4389 **Best Contemporary Classical Composition:** Aaron Copland for *Orchestral Suite from Tender Land Suite* on RCA

4390 **Best Classical Choral (Including Oratorio):** Sir Thomas Beecham conducting the Royal Philharmonic Orchestra and Chorus in *Handel: The Messiah* on RCA

4391 **Best Classical Instrumentalist Soloist or Duo:** Laurindo Almeida for *The Spanish Guitars of Laurindo Almeida* on Capitol

4392 **Best Engineered Record (Classical):** Hugh Davies for *The Spanish Guitars of Laurindo Almeida* on Capitol

4393 **Best Engineered Record (Novelty):** John Kraus for *The Old Payola Roll Blues* by Stan Freberg on Capitol

4394 **Best Engineering (Pop):** Luis P. Valentin for *Ella Fitzgerald Sings the George and Ira Gershwin Songbook* on Verve

4395 **Best Album Cover (Award to Art Director):** Marvin Schwartz for *Latin Ala Lee* on Capitol

4396 **Best New Artist of 1960:** Bob Newhart on Warner Brothers

4397 **Special National Trustees' Awards for Artists and Repertoire Contribution:** Ernest Altschuler producer for *Theme from a Summer Place* on Columbia; George Avakian producer for *Button Down Mind* on Warner Brothers

———————— **1962** ————————

4398 **Record of the Year:** "Moon River" by Henry Mancini on RCA

4399 **Album of the Year:** *Judy at Carnegie Hall* by Judy Garland on Capitol

4400 **Song of the Year (Award to the Songwriter):** Henry Mancini and Johnny Mercer for "Moon River" on RCA

4401 **Classical Album of the Year:** Igor Stravinsky conducting the Columbia Symphony Orchestra in *Stravinsky Conducts, 1960: Le Sacre du Printemps; Petrouchka* on Columbia

4402 **Best Male Solo Vocal:** Jack Jones for "Lollipops and Roses" on Kapp

4403 **Best Female Solo Vocal:** Judy Garland for *Judy at Carnegie Hall* on Capitol

4404 **Best Jazz Solo or Small Group:** Andre Previn for *Andre Previn Plays Harold Arlen* on Contemporary

4405 **Best Jazz Large Group:** Stan Kenton for *West Side Story* on Capitol

4406 **Best Original Jazz Composition:** Galt MacDermot for *African Waltz* on Roulette

4407 **Best Instrumental Theme:** Galt MacDermot for *African Waltz* on Roulette

4408 **Best Country & Western:** Jimmy Dean for "Big Bad John" on Columbia

4409 **Best Rhythm & Blues:** Ray Charles for "Hit the Road Jack" on Am-Par

4410 **Best Album for Children:** Leonard Bernstein conducting the New York Philharmonic Orchestra in *Prokofiev: Peter and the Wolf* on Columbia

4411 **Best Comedy:** *An Evening with Mike Nichols and Elaine May* on Mercury

4412 **Best Orchestra for Dancing:** Si Zetner for *Up a Lazy River* on Liberty

4413 **Best Orchestra Not for Dancing:** Henry Mancini for *Breakfast at Tiffany's* on RCA

4414 **Best Spoken Word:** Leonard Bernstein conducting the New York Philharmonic for *Humor in Music* on Columbia

4415 **Best Rock & Roll:** Chubby Checker for "Let's Twist Again" on Parkway

4416 **Best Folk:** Belafonte Folk Singers for *Belafonte Folk Singers at Home and Abroad* on RCA

4417 **Best Gospel or Other Religious:** Mahalia Jackson for "Everytime I Feel the Spirit" on Columbia

4418 **Best Original Cast Show Album:** Frank Loesser for *How to Succeed in Business Without Really Trying* on RCA

4419 **Best Soundtrack Score:** Henry Mancini for *Breakfast at Tiffany's* on RCA

4420 **Best Soundtrack Original Cast:** Johnny Green, Saul Chaplin, Sid Ramin and Irwin Kostal for *West Side Story* on Columbia

4421 **Best Arrangement:** Henry Mancini for "Moon River" on RCA

4422 **Best Vocal Group:** Lambert, Hendricks and Ross for *High Flying* on Columbia

4423 **Best Chorus:** Johnny Mann Singers with the Si Zetner Orchestra for *Great Band with Great Voices* on Liberty

4424 **Best Classical Orchestra:** Boston Symphony Orchestra conducted by Charles Munch for *Ravel: Daphnis et Chloe* on RCA

4425 **Best Classical Chamber Music:** Jascha Heifetz, Gregor Piatigorsky, and William Primrose for *Beethoven: Serenade, Op. 8 Kodaly Duo for Violin and Cello, Op. 7* on RCA

4426 **Best Classical Vocal Soloist:** Joan Sutherland for *The Art of the Prima Donna* with Molinari-Pradelli conducting the Royal House Orchestra on London

4427 **Best Opera:** Gabriele Santini conducting the Rome Opera Chorus and Orchestra in *Puccini: Madame Butterfly* on Capitol

4428 **Best Classical Instrumental Soloist with Orchestra:** Isaac Stern, violinist for *Bartok: Concerto No. 1 for Violin and Orchestra* with Eugene Ormandy conducting the Philharmonia Orchestra on Columbia

4429 **Best Classical Choral:** Robert Shaw Chorale for "Bach: B-Minor Mass" on RCA

4430 **Best Classical Instrumentalist Soloist or Duo Without Orchestra:** Laurindo Almeida for *Reverie for Spanish Guitars* on Capitol

4431 **Best Contemporary Classical Compositions:** Laurindo Almeida for *Discantus* on Capitol, and Igor Stravinsky for *Movements for Piano and Orchestra* on Columbia

4432 **Best Engineered Record (Classical):** Lewis W. Layton for "Ravel: Daphnis et Chloe" with Charles Munch conducting the Boston Symphony Orchestra on RCA

4433 **Best Engineered Record (Novelty):** John Kraus for "Stan Freberg Presents the United States of America" on Capitol

4434 **Best Engineering (Pop):** Robert Arnold for *Judy at Carnegie Hall* on Capitol

4435 **Best Album Cover (Award to Art Director):** Jim Silke for *Judy at Carnegie Hall* on Capitol

4436 **Best Album Cover (Classical):** Marvin Schwartz for *Puccini: Madame Butterfly* on Angel

4437 **Best New Artist of 1961:** Peter Nero on RCA

———— **1 9 6 3** ————

4438 **Record of the Year:** "I Left My Heart in San Francisco" by Tony Bennett on Columbia

4439 **Album of the Year:** *The First Family* by Vaughn Meader on Cadence

4440 **Song of the Year (Award to the Songwriter):** Leslie Bricusse and Anthony Newley for "What Kind of Fool Am I?" on London

4441 **Classical Album of the Year:** *Columbia Records Presents Vladimir Horowitz* on Columbia

4442 **Best Male Solo Vocal:** Tony Bennett for "I Left My Heart in San Francisco" on Columbia

4443 **Best Female Solo Vocal:** Ella Fitzgerald for "Ella Swings Brightly with Nelson Riddle" on Verve

4444 **Best Jazz Solo or Small Group:** Stan Getz for *Desafinado* on Verve

4445 **Best Jazz Large Group:** Stan Kenton for *Adventures in Jazz* on Capitol

4446 **Best Original Jazz Composition:** Vince Guaraldi for "Cast Your Fate to the Winds" on Fantasy

4447 **Best Instrumental Theme:** Bobby Scott and Ric Marlow for "A Taste of Honey" on Reprise

4448 **Best Country & Western:** Burl Ives for "Funny Way of Laughin'" on Decca

4449 **Best Rhythm & Blues:** Ray Charles for "I Can't Stop Loving You" on ABC

4450 **Best Album for Children:** Leonard Bernstein conducting the New York Philharmonic Orchestra in *Saint-Saëns: Carnival of the Animals/Britten: Young Person's Guide to the Orchestra* on Columbia

4451 **Best Comedy:** Vaughn Meader for *The First Family* on Cadence

4452 **Best Orchestra for Dancing:** Joe Harnell for *Fly Me to the Moon Bossa Nova* on Kapp

4453 **Best Orchestra or Instrumentalist with Orchestra Not for Jazz or Dancing:** *The Colorful Peter Nero* on RCA

4454 **Best Spoken Word:** *The Story-Teller: A Session with Charles Laughton* on Capitol

4455 **Best Rock & Roll:** Bent Fabric for "Alley Cat" on Atco

4456 **Best Folk:** Peter, Paul & Mary for "If I Had a Hammer" on Warner Brothers

4457 **Best Gospel or Other Religious:** Mahalia Jackson for *Great Songs of Love and Faith* on Columbia

4458 **Best Original Cast Show Album:** Richard Rodgers for *No Strings* on Capitol

4459 **Best Instrumental Arrangement:** Henry Mancini for "Baby Elephant Walk" on RCA

4460 **Best Background Arrangement:** Marty Manning for "I Left My Heart in San Francisco" on Columbia

4461 **Best Vocal Group:** Peter, Paul & Mary for "If I Had a Hammer" on Warner Brothers

4462 Best Chorus: The New Christy Minstrels for *Presenting the New Christy Minstrels* on Columbia

4463 Best Classical Orchestra: The Columbia Symphony Orchestra conducted by Igor Stravinsky for *Stravinsky: The Firebird Ballet* on Columbia

4464 Best Classical Chamber Music: Jascha Heifetz, Gregor Piatigorsky, and William Primrose for *The Heifetz/Piatigorsky Concerts with Primrose, Pennario and Guests* on RCA

4465 Best Classical Vocal Soloist: Eileen Farrell for *Wagner: Götterdämmerung-Brunhilde's Immolation Scene/Wesendonck Songs* with Leonard Bernstein conducting the N.Y. Philharmonic on Columbia

4466 Best Opera: Georg Solti conducting the Rome Opera House Chorus and Orchestra in *Verdi: Aida* on RCA

4467 Best Classical Instrumental Soloist with Orchestra: Isaac Stern, violinist for *Stravinsky: Concerto in D for Violin* with Igor Stravinsky conducting the Columbia Symphony Orchestra on Columbia

4468 Best Classical Choral: Philharmonic Choir with choral director Wilhelm Pitz for *Bach: St. Matthew Passion* with Otto Klemperer conducting the Philharmonia Orchestra on Angel

4469 Best Classical Instrumentalist Soloist or Duo Without Orchestra: *Columbia Records Presents Vladimir Horowitz* on Columbia

4470 Best Contemporary Classical Compositions: Igor Stravinsky for *The Flood* on Columbia

4471 Best Engineered Record (Classical): Lewis W. Layton for "Strauss: Also Sprach Zarathustra Op. 30" with Fritz Reiner conducting the Chicago Symphony Orchestra on RCA

4472 Best Engineered Record (Novelty): Robert Fine for "The Civil War, Volume 1" on Mercury

4473 Best Engineering (Other Than Novelty or Classical): Al Schmitt for "Hatari!" on RCA

4474 Best Album Cover (Award to Art Director): Robert Jones for *Lena ... Lovely and Alive* on RCA

4475 Best Album Cover (Classical): Marvin Schwartz for *The Intimate Bach* on Capitol

4476 Best New Artist of 1962: Robert Goulet on Columbia

───────── **1 9 6 4** ─────────

4477 Record of the Year: "The Days of Wine and Roses" by Henry Mancini on RCA

4478 Album of the Year: *The Barbra Streisand Album* on Columbia

4479 Song of the Year (Award to the Songwriter): Henry Mancini and Johnny Mercer for "The Days of Wine and Roses" on RCA

4480 Classical Album of the Year: *Britten: War Requiem* by Benjamin Britten conducting the London Symphony Orchestra and Chorus on London

4481 Best Male Solo Vocal: Jack Jones for "Wives and Lovers" on Kapp

4482 Best Female Solo Vocal: Barbra Streisand for "The Barbra Streisand Album" on Columbia

4483 Best Jazz Solo or Small Group: Bill Evans for *Conversations with Myself* on Verve

4484 Best Jazz Large Group: *Encore Woody Herman, 1963* on Philips

4485 Best Original Jazz Composition: Steve Allen and Ray Brown for "Gravy Waltz"

4486 Best Instrumental Theme: Norman Newell, Nino Oliviero, and Riz Ortolani for "More" (The Theme from *Mondo Cane*) on United Artists

4487 Best Country & Western: Bobby Bare for "Detroit City" on RCA

4488 Best Rhythm & Blues: Ray Charles for "Busted" on ABC-Paramount

4489 Best Album for Children: Leonard Bernstein conducting the New York Philharmonic Orchestra in *Bernstein Conducts for Young People* on Columbia

4490 Best Comedy: Allan Sherman for *Hello Mudduh, Hello Faddah* on Warner Brothers

4491 Best Orchestra for Dancing: Count Basie for *This Time by Basie! Hits of the 50's and 60's* on Reprise

4492 Best Orchestra or Instrumentalist with Orchestra Not for Jazz or Dancing: Al Hirt for *Java* on RCA

4493 Best Spoken Word: *Who's Afraid of Virginia Woolf?* by Edward Albee on Warner Brothers

4494 **Best ·Rock & Roll:** Nino Tempo and April Stevens for "Deep Purple" on Atco

4495 **Best Folk:** Peter, Paul & Mary for "Blowin' in the Wind" on Warner Brothers

4496 **Best Gospel or Other Religious:** Soeur Sourire, the Singing Nun for *Dominique* on Philips

4497 **Best Original Cast Show Album:** Jerry Bock and Sheldon Harnick for *She Loves Me* on MGM

4498 **Best Original Score:** John Addison for *Tom Jones* on United Artists

4499 **Best Instrumental Arrangement:** Quincy Jones for "I Can't Stop Loving You" on Reprise

4500 **Best Background Arrangement:** Henry Mancini for "The Days of Wine and Roses" on RCA

4501 **Best Vocal Group:** Peter, Paul & Mary for "Blowin' in the Wind" on Warner Brothers

4502 **Best Chorus:** The Swingle Singers for *Bach's Greatest Hits* on Philips

4503 **Best Classical Orchestra:** The Boston Symphony conducted by Erich Leinsdorf for *Bartok: Concerto for Orchestra* on RCA

4504 **Best Classical Chamber Music:** Julian Bream Consort for *Evening of Elizabethan Music* on RCA

4505 **Best Classical Vocal Soloist:** Leontyne Price for *Great Scenes from Gershwin's Porgy and Bess* on RCA

4506 **Best Opera:** Erich Leinsdorf conducting the RCA Italiana Opera orchestra and chorus in *Puccini: Madame Butterfly* on RCA

4507 **Best Classical Instrumental Soloist with Orchestra:** Artur Rubinstein, pianist for *Tchaikovsky: Concerto No. 1 in B-Flat Minor for Piano and Orchestra* with Erich Leinsdorf conducting the Boston Symphony Orchestra on RCA

4508 **Best Classical Instrumental Soloist Without Orchestra:** Vladimir Horowitz for *The Sound of Horowitz* on Columbia

4509 **Best Classical Choral:** David Willcocks director of the Bach Choir, Edward Chapman director of the Highgate School Choir for *Britten: War Requiem* with Benjamin Britten conducting the London Symphony Orchestra and Chorus on London

4510 **Best Contemporary Classical Compositions:** Benjamin Britten for *War Requiem* on London

4511 **Best Engineered Record (Classical):** Lewis Layton for *Puccini: Madame Butterfly* on RCA

4512 **Best Engineered Record (Non-classical):** James Malloy for "Charade" on RCA

4513 **Best Engineering (Novelty):** Robert Fine for *Civil War, Vol. 2* on Mercury

4514 **Best Album Cover:** John Berg for *The Barbra Streisand Album* on Columbia

4515 **Best Album Notes (Award to Annotator):** Stanley Dance and Leonard Feather for *The Ellington Era* on Columbia

4516 **Best Album Cover (Classical):** Robert Jones for *Puccini: Madame Butterfly* on RCA

4517 **Most Promising New Classical Recording Artist:** Andre Watts on Columbia

4518 **Best New Artist of 1963:** Swingle Singers on Philips

———————— **1 9 6 5** ————————

4519 **Record of the Year:** "The Girl from Impanema" by Stan Getz and Astrud Gilberto on Verve

4520 **Album of the Year:** *Getz/Gilberto* by Stan Getz and Joao Gilberto

4521 **Song of the Year (Award to the Songwriter):** Jerry Herman for "Hello, Dolly!" on Kapp

4522 **Classical Album of the Year:** *Bernstein: Symphony No. 3* by Leonard Bernstein conducting the New York Philharmonic on Columbia

4523 **Best Male Solo Vocal:** Louis Armstrong for "Hello, Dolly!" on Kapp

4524 **Best Female Solo Vocal:** Barbra Streisand for "People" on Columbia

4525 **Best Jazz Solo or Small Group:** Stan Getz for *Getz/Gilberto* on Verve

4526 **Best Jazz Large Group:** Laurindo Almeida for *Guitar from Impanema* on Capitol

4527 **Best Original Jazz Composition:** Lalo Schifrin for "The Cat" on Verve

4528 **Best Instrumental (Non-jazz):** Henry Mancini for "The Pink Panther Theme" on RCA

4529 Best Country & Western Single: Roger Miller for "Dang Me" on Smash

4530 Best Country & Western Album: Roger Miller for "Dang Me"/*Chug-a-Lug* on Smash

4531 Best Country & Western Female Vocal: Dottie West for "Here Comes My Baby" on RCA

4532 Best Country & Western Male Vocal: Roger Miller for "Dang Me" on Smash

4533 Best Country & Western Song: Roger Miller for "Dang Me" on Smash

4534 Best Rhythm & Blues: Nancy Wilson for "How Glad I Am" on Capitol

4535 Best Album for Children: Julie Andrews and Dick Van Dyke for *Mary Poppins* on Buena Vista

4536 Best Comedy: Bill Cosby for *I Started Out as a Child* on Warner Brothers

4537 Best Spoken Word: *BBC Tribute to John Kennedy* by the cast of "That Was the Week That Was" on Decca

4538 Best Rock & Roll: Petula Clark for "Downtown" on Warner Brothers

4539 Best Folk: Gayle Garnett for "We'll Sing in the Sunshine" on RCA

4540 Best Gospel or Other Religious: Tennessee Ernie Ford for *Great Gospel Songs* on Capitol

4541 Best Original Score: Richard M. Sherman and Robert B. Sherman for *Mary Poppins* on Buena Vista

4542 Best Score from an Original Show Album: Jule Styne and Bob Merrill for *Funny Girl* on Capitol

4543 Best Instrumental Arrangement: Henry Mancini for *Pink Panther* on RCA

4544 Best Accompaniment Arrangement: Peter Matz for "People" on Columbia

4545 Best Vocal Group: The Beatles for "A Hard Day's Night" on Capitol

4546 Best Chorus: The Swingle Singers for *The Swingle Singers Going Baroque* on Philips

4547 Best Classical Orchestra: The Boston Symphony conducted by Erich Leinsdorf for *Mahler: Symphony No. 5 in C-Sharp Minor; Berg: "Wozzeck" Excerpts* on RCA

4548 Best Classical Chamber Music: Jascha Heifetz, Gregor Piatigorsky and Jacob Lateiner for *Beethoven: Trio No. 1 in E-Flat Op. 1, No. 1* on RCA

4549 Best Classical Vocal Chamber Music: Noah Greenberg conducting the New York Pro Musica for *It Was a Lover and His Lass (Morley, Byrd and Others)* on Decca

4550 Best Performance Instrumental Soloist with Orchestra: Isaac Stern, violinist for *Prokofiev: Concerto No. 1 in D Major for Violin* on Columbia

4551 Best Performance Instrumental Soloist Without Orchestra: *Vladimir Horowitz Plays Beethoven, Debussy, Chopin* (Beethoven: "Sonata No. 8 'Pathetique,'" Debussy: "Preludes," Chopin: "Etudes and Scherzos 1 Through 4") on Columbia

4552 Best Opera: Herbert von Karajan conducting the Vienna Philharmonic Orchestra and Chorus for *Bizet: Carmen* on RCA

4553 Best Vocal Soloist: Leontyne Price for *Berlioz: Nuits d'Été (Song Cycle)/Falla: El Amor Brujo* with Fritz Reiner conducting the Chicago Symphony Orchestra on RCA

4554 Best Classical Choral: Robert Shaw Chorale for *Britten: A Ceremony of Carols* on RCA

4555 Best Classical Composition: Samuel Barber for "Piano Concerto" on Columbia

4556 Best Engineered Classical Record: Douglas Larter for "Britten: Young Person's Guide to the Orchestra" on Angel

4557 Best Engineered Record: Phil Ramone for "Getz/Gilberto" on Verve

4558 Best Engineered Novelty Record: Dave Hassinger for "The Chipmunks Sing the Beatles" on Liberty

4559 Best Album Cover (Award to the Art Director): Robert Cato and Don Bronstein for *People* on Columbia

4560 Best Album Notes (Award to Annotator): Stanton Catlin and Carleton Beals for *Mexico (Legacy Collection)* on Columbia

4561 Best Album Cover (Classical): Robert Jones and Jan Balet for *Saint-Saëns: Carnival of the Animals/Britten: Young Person's Guide to the Orchestra* on RCA

4562 Best Instrumental Performance (Non-Jazz): Henry Mancini for *Pink Panther* on RCA

4563 **Best New Artist:** The Beatles on Capitol

4564 **Best New Country & Western Artist:** Roger Miller on Smash

4565 **Most Promising New Recording Artist:** Marilyn Horne on London

————— **1 9 6 6** —————

4566 **Record of the Year:** "A Taste of Honey" by Herb Alpert and the Tijuana Brass on A&M

4567 **Album of the Year:** *September of My Years* by Frank Sinatra on Reprise

4568 **Song of the Year (Award to the Songwriter):** Paul Francis Webster and Johnny Mandel for "The Shadow of Your Smile" on Mercury

4569 **Classical Album of the Year:** *Horowitz at Carnegie Hall (An Historic Return)* by Vladimir Horowitz on Columbia

4570 **Best Male Solo Vocal:** Frank Sinatra for "It Was a Very Good Year"

4571 **Best Female Solo Vocal:** Barbra Streisand for "My Name Is Barbra" on Columbia

4572 **Best Jazz Solo or Small Group:** Ramsey Lewis Trio for *The "In" Crowd* on Cadet

4573 **Best Jazz Large Group:** Duke Ellington Orchestra for *Ellington '66* on Reprise

4574 **Best Original Jazz Composition:** Lalo Schifrin for "Jazz Suite on the Mass Texts" on RCA

4575 **Best Instrumental (Non-Jazz):** Herb Alpert and the Tijuana Brass for "A Taste of Honey" on A&M

4576 **Best Country & Western Single:** Roger Miller for "King of the Road" on Smash

4577 **Best Country & Western Album:** Roger Miller for *The Return of Roger Miller* on Smash

4578 **Best Country & Western Female Vocal:** Jody Miller for "Queen of the House" on Capitol

4579 **Best Country & Western Male Vocal:** Roger Miller for "King of the Road" on Smash

4580 **Best Country & Western Song:** Roger Miller for "King of the Road" on Smash

4581 **Best Rhythm & Blues:** James Brown for "Papa's Got a Brand New Bag" on King

4582 **Best Album for Children:** Marvin Miller for *Dr. Seuss Presents* "Fox in Socks — Green Eggs and Ham" on RCA/Camden

4583 **Best Comedy:** Bill Cosby for *Why Is There Air?* on Warner Brothers

4584 **Best Spoken Word:** *John F. Kennedy — As We Remember Him* producer Goddard Lieberson on Columbia

4585 **Best Folk:** Harry Belafonte and Miriam Makeba for *An Evening with Belafonte/Makeba* on RCA

4586 **Best Gospel or Other Religious:** George Beverly Shea and the Anita Kerr Singers for *Southland Favorites* on RCA

4587 **Best Original Score:** Johnny Mandel for *The Sandpiper* on Mercury

4588 **Best Score from an Original Show Album:** Alan Lerner and Burton Lane for *On a Clear Day* on RCA

4589 **Best Instrumental Arrangement:** Herb Alpert and the Tijuana Brass for "A Taste of Honey" on A&M

4590 **Best Background Arrangement:** Gordon Jenkins for "It Was a Very Good Year" on Reprise

4591 **Best Vocal Group:** Anita Kerr Singers for *We Dig Mancini* on RCA

4592 **Best Chorus:** The Swingle Singers for *Anyone for Mozart?* on Philips

4593 **Best Contemporary Single:** Roger Miller for "King of the Road" on Smash

4594 **Best Single Contemporary Male Vocal:** Roger Miller for "King of the Road" on Smash

4595 **Best Single Contemporary Female Vocal:** Petula Clark for "I Know a Place" on Warner Brothers

4596 **Best Contemporary Group:** The Statler Brothers for *Flowers on the Wall* on Columbia

4597 **Best Classical Orchestra:** American Symphony Orchestra conducted by Leopold Stokowski for *Ives: Symphony No. 4* on Columbia

4598 **Best Classical Chamber Music:** Juilliard String Quartet for *Bartok: The Six String Quartets* on Columbia

4599 **Best Performance Instrumental Soloist with Orchestra:** Artur Rubinstein, pianist for *Beethoven: Concerto No. 4 in G Major for Piano and Orchestra* with

Erich Leinsdorf conducting the Boston Symphony Orchestra on RCA

4600 Best Performance Instrumental Soloist Without Orchestra: Vladimir Horowitz for *Horowitz at Carnegie Hall—An Historic Return* on Columbia

4601 Best Opera: Karl Bohm conducting the Orchestra of the German Opera, Berlin for *Berg: Wozzeck* on DG

4602 Best Vocal Soloist: Leontyne Price for "Strauss: Salome" (Dance of the Seven Veils, Interlude, Final Scene), "The Egyptian Helen" (Awakening Scene) on RCA

4603 Best Classical Choral: Robert Shaw Chorale for *Stravinsky: Symphony of Psalms/Poulenc: Gloria* with the RCA Victor Symphony on RCA

4604 Best Contemporary Classical Composition: Charles Ives for *Symphony Number 4* on Columbia

4605 Best Engineered Record (Classical): Fred Plaut for "Horowitz at Carnegie Hall—An Historic Return" on Columbia

4606 Best Engineered Record: Larry Levine for "A Taste of Honey" on A&M

4607 Best Album Cover Photography: Bob Jones and Ken Whitmore for *Jazz Suite on the Mass Texts* on RCA

4608 Best Album Notes (Award to Annotator): Stan Cornyn for *September of My Years* on Reprise

4609 Best Album Cover (Classical): George Estes and James Alexander for *Bartok: Concerto No. 2 for Violin/ Stravinsky: Concerto for Violin* on RCA

4610 Most Promising New Recording Artist: Peter Serkin on RCA

4611 Best New Country and Western Artist: The Statler Brothers on Columbia

4612 Best New Artist: Tom Jones on Parrot

1967

4613 Record of the Year: "Strangers in the Night" by Frank Sinatra on Reprise

4614 Album of the Year: *Sinatra a Man and His Music* by Frank Sinatra on Reprise

4615 Song of the Year (Award to the Songwriter): John Lennon and Paul McCartney for "Michelle" on Capitol

4616 Classical Album of the Year: *Ives: Symphony Number 1 in D Minor* Morton Gould conducting the Chicago Symphony Orchestra on RCA

4617 Best Male Solo Vocal: Frank Sinatra for "Strangers in the Night" on Reprise

4618 Best Female Solo Vocal: Eydie Gorme for "If He Walked Into My Life" on Columbia

4619 Best Instrumental Jazz Group: Wes Montgomery for *Goin' Out of My Head* on Verve

4620 Best Original Jazz Composition: Duke Ellington for "In the Beginning God" on RCA

4621 Best Instrumental (Non-Jazz): Herb Alpert and the Tijuana Brass for "What Now My Love" on A&M

4622 Best Country & Western: David Houston for "Almost Persuaded" on Epic

4623 Best Country & Western Song: Billy Sherrill and Glenn Sutton for "Almost Persuaded" on Epic

4624 Best Country & Western Female Vocal: Jeannie Seely for "Don't Touch Me" on Monument

4625 Best Country & Western Male Vocal: David Houston for "Almost Persuaded" on Epic

4626 Best Rhythm & Blues: Ray Charles for "Crying Time" on ABC-Paramount

4627 Best Rhythm & Blues Solo Vocal: Ray Charles for "Crying Time" on ABC-Paramount

4628 Best Rhythm & Blues Group: Ramsey Lewis for "Hold It Right There" on Cadet

4629 Best Album for Children: Marvin Miller for *Dr. Seuss Presents* "If I Ran the Zoo" and "Sleep Book" on RCA-Camden

4630 Best Comedy: Bill Cosby for *Wonderfulness* on Warner Brothers

4631 Best Spoken Word: *Edward R. Murrow—A Reporter Remembers, Vol. 1: The War Years* on Columbia

4632 Best Folk: Cortelia Clark for "Blues in the Street" on RCA

4633 Best Sacred: Porter Wagoner and the Blackwood Brothers for *Grand Old Gospel* on RCA

4634 Best Original Score: Maurice Jarre for *Dr. Zhivago* on MGM

4635 **Best Score from an Original Cast Show Album:** Jerry Herman for *Mame* on Columbia

4636 **Best Instrumental Theme:** Neal Hefti for "Batman" on RCA

4637 **Best Instrumental Arrangement:** Herb Alpert for "What Now My Love" on A&M

4638 **Best Accompaniment Arrangement:** Ernie Freeman for "Strangers in the Night" on Reprise

4639 **Best Vocal Group:** Anita Kerr Singers for "A Man and a Woman" on Warner Brothers

4640 **Best Chorus:** Ray Coniff Singers for "Somewhere My Love" ("Lara's Theme" from *Dr. Zhivago*) on Columbia

4641 **Best Contemporary Rock & Roll:** New Vaudeville Band for *Winchester Cathedral* on Fontana

4642 **Best Contemporary Solo Vocal:** Paul McCartney for "Eleanor Rigby" on Capitol

4643 **Best Contemporary Group:** The Mamas and the Papas for "Monday, Monday" on Dunhill

4644 **Best Classical Orchestra:** The Boston Symphony Orchestra conducted by Erich Leinsdorf for *Mahler: Symphony No. 6 in A Minor* on RCA

4645 **Best Classical Chamber Music:** *Boston Symphony Chamber Players* on RCA

4646 **Best Performance Instrumental Soloist:** Julian Bream for "Baroque Guitar" on RCA

4647 **Best Classical Chorales:** Robert Shaw Chorale and Orchestra for *Handel: Messiah* on RCA, and Gregg Smith Singers and Ithaca College Concert Choir with the Texas Boys Choir for *Ives: Music for Chorus (Gen. Wm. Booth Enters Into Heaven, Serenity, the Circus Band, etc.)* on Columbia

4648 **Best Opera:** Georg Solti conducting the Vienna Philharmonic for *Wagner: Die Walküre* on London

4649 **Best Vocal Soloist:** Leontyne Price for "Prima Donna" on RCA

4650 **Best Album Cover (Award to Art Director):** Klaus Voormann for *Revolver* on Capitol

4651 **Best Album Cover Photography:** Robert Jones and Les Leverette for *Confessions of a Broken Man* on RCA

4652 **Best Album Notes (Award to Annotator):** Stan Cornyn for *Sinatra at the Sands* on Reprise

4653 **Best Engineered Classical:** Anthony Salvatore for *Wagner: Lohengrin* on RCA

4654 **Best Engineered Non-Classical:** Eddie Brackett and Lee Herschberg for *Strangers in the Night* on Reprise

1968

4655 **Record of the Year:** "Up, Up and Away" by the 5th Dimension on Soul City

4656 **Album of the Year:** *Sgt. Pepper's Lonely Hearts Club Band* by the Beatles on Capitol

4657 **Song of the Year (Award to the Songwriter):** Jim Webb for "Up, Up and Away" on Soul City

4658 **Classical Albums of the Year:** *Mahler: Symphony Number 8 in E-Flat Major (Symphony of a Thousand)* by Leonard Bernstein conducting the London Symphony Orchestra on Columbia, and *Berg: Wozzeck* by Pierre Boulez conducting the Paris National Opera on Columbia

4659 **Best Male Solo Vocal:** Glen Campbell for "By the Time I Get to Phoenix" on Capitol

4660 **Best Female Solo Vocal:** Bobbie Gentry for "Ode to Billie Joe" on Capitol

4661 **Best Instrumental Jazz Small Group:** Cannonball Adderley Quintet for *Mercy, Mercy, Mercy* on Capitol

4662 **Best Instrumental Jazz Large Group:** Duke Ellington for *Far East Suite* on RCA

4663 **Best Country & Western:** Glen Campbell for "Gentle on My Mind" on Capitol

4664 **Best Country & Western Song:** John Hartford for "Gentle on My Mind" on Capitol

4665 **Best Country & Western Female Vocal:** Tammy Wynette for "I Don't Wanna Play House" on Epic

4666 **Best Country & Western Male Vocal:** Glen Campbell for "Gentle on My Mind" on Capitol

4667 **Best Country and Western Duet, Trio or Group:** Johnny Cash and June Carter for "Jackson" on Columbia

4668 **Best Rhythm & Blues:** Aretha Franklin for "Respect" on Atlantic

4669 **Best Rhythm & Blues Female Solo Vocal:** Aretha Franklin for "Respect" on Atlantic

4670 **Best Rhythm & Blues Male Solo Vocal:** Lou Rawls for "Dead End Street" on Capitol

4671 **Best Rhythm & Blues Group:** Sam & Dave for "Soul Man" on Stax

4672 **Best Album for Children:** Boris Karloff for *Dr. Seuss: How the Grinch Stole Christmas* on MGM

4673 **Best Comedy:** Bill Cosby for *Revenge* on Warner Brothers/7 Arts

4674 **Best Spoken Word:** *Gallant Men* by Senator Everett M. Dirksen on Capitol

4675 **Best Folk:** John Hartford for "Gentle on My Mind" on RCA

4676 **Best Sacred:** Elvis Presley for "How Great Thou Art" on RCA

4677 **Best Gospel:** Porter Wagoner and the Blackwood Brothers for *More Grand Old Gospel* on RCA

4678 **Best Original Score:** Lalo Schifrin for *Mission: Impossible* on Dot

4679 **Best Score from an Original Cast Show Album:** Fred Ebb and John Kander for *Cabaret* on Columbia

4680 **Best Instrumental Theme:** Lalo Schifrin for *Mission: Impossible* on Dot

4681 **Best Instrumental Arrangement:** Burt Bacharach for "Alfie" on A&M

4682 **Best Instrumental:** *Chet Atkins Picks the Best* on RCA

4683 **Best Accompaniment Arrangement:** Jimmie Haskell for "Ode to Billie Joe" on Capitol

4684 **Best Vocal Group:** The 5th Dimension for "Up, Up and Away" on Soul City

4685 **Best Chorus:** Johnny Mann Singers for "Up, Up and Away" on Liberty

4686 **Best Contemporary Single:** The 5th Dimension for "Up, Up and Away" on Soul City

4687 **Best Contemporary Male Vocal:** Glen Campbell for "By the Time I Get to Phoenix" on Capitol

4688 **Best Contemporary Female Vocal:** Bobbie Gentry for "Ode to Billie Joe" on Capitol

4689 **Best Contemporary Group:** The 5th Dimension for "Up, Up and Away" on Soul City

4690 **Best Contemporary Album:** *Sgt. Pepper's Lonely Hearts Club Band* by the Beatles on Capitol

4691 **Best Classical Orchestra:** The Columbia Symphony Orchestra conducted by Igor Stravinsky for *Stravinsky: Firebird and Petrouchka Suites* on Columbia

4692 **Best Classical Chamber Music:** Ravi Shankar and Yehudi Menuhin for *West Meets East* on Angel

4693 **Best Performance Instrumental Soloist:** Vladimir Horowitz for *Horowitz in Concert* on Columbia

4694 **Best Classical Chorales:** Temple University Chorus conducted by Robert Page for *Orff: Catulli Carmina* with Eugene Ormandy conducting the Philadelphia Orchestra on Columbia, and Leonard Bernstein conducting the London Symphony Orchestra for *Mahler: Symphony No. 8 in E-Flat Major* on Columbia

4695 **Best Opera:** Pierre Boulez conducting the Paris National Opera for *Berg: Wozzeck* on Columbia

4696 **Best Vocal Soloist:** Leontyne Price for "Prima Donna, Volume 2" with Molinari-Pradelli conducting the RCA Italian Opera Orchestra on RCA

4697 **Best Album Cover (Award to Art Director):** Peter Blake and Jann Haworth for *Sgt. Pepper's Lonely Hearts Club Band* on Capitol

4698 **Best Album Cover Photography:** John Berg, Bob Cato and Roland Scherman for *Bob Dylan's Greatest Hits* on Columbia

4699 **Best Album Notes (Award to Annotator):** John D. Loudermilk for *Suburban Attitudes in Country Verse* on RCA

4700 **Best Engineered Classical:** Edward T. Graham for "The Glorious Sound of Brass" on Capitol

4701 **Best Engineered Non-Classical:** Geoff Emerick for "Sgt. Pepper's Lonely Hearts Club Band" on Capitol

4702 **Best New Artist:** Bobbie Gentry on Capitol

——————— **1969** ———————

4703 **Record of the Year:** "Mrs. Robinson" by Simon and Garfunkel on Columbia

4704 **Album of the Year:** *By the Time I Get to Phoenix* by Glen Campbell on Capitol

4705 **Song of the Year (Award to the Songwriter):** Bobby Russell for "Little Green Apples" on Columbia

4706 **Best Contemporary/Pop Male Solo Vocal:** Jose Feliciano for "Light My Fire" on RCA

4707 **Best Contemporary/Pop Female Solo Vocal:** Dionne Warwick for "Do You Know the Way to San Jose?" on Scepter

4708 **Best Contemporary/Pop Vocal Duo or Group:** Simon and Garfunkel for "Mrs. Robinson" on Columbia

4709 **Best Contemporary/Pop Chorus:** Alan Copeland Singers for *Mission: Impossible/Norwegian Wood* on ABC

4710 **Best Instrumental Arrangement:** Mike Post for "Classical Gas" on Warner Brothers

4711 **Best Contemporary/Pop Instrumental:** Mason Williams for "Classical Gas" on Warner Brothers/7 Arts

4712 **Best Accompaniment Arrangement:** Jim Webb for "MacArthur Park" on Dunhill

4713 **Best Instrumental Jazz Small Group:** Bill Evans Trio for *Bill Evans at the Montreux Jazz Festival* on Verve

4714 **Best Instrumental Jazz Large Group:** Duke Ellington for *And His Mother Called Him Bill* on RCA

4715 **Best Country & Western Song:** Bobby Russell for "Little Green Apples" on Smash

4716 **Best Country & Western Female Vocal:** Jeannie C. Riley for "Harper Valley P.T.A." on Plantation

4717 **Best Country & Western Male Vocal:** Johnny Cash for "Folsom Prison Blues" on Columbia

4718 **Best Country & Western Duet, Trio or Group:** Flatt and Scruggs for "Foggy Mountain Breakdown" on Columbia

4719 **Best Rhythm & Blues Song:** Otis Redding and Steve Cropper for "(Sittin' on) the Dock of the Bay" on Volt

4720 **Best Rhythm & Blues Female Solo Vocal:** Aretha Franklin for "Chain of Fools" on Atlantic

4721 **Best Rhythm & Blues Male Solo Vocal:** Otis Redding for "(Sittin' on) the Dock of the Bay" on Volt

4722 **Best Rhythm & Blues Group:** The Temptations for "Cloud Nine" on Soul/Gordy

4723 **Best Comedy:** Bill Cosby for *To Russell, My Brother, Whom I Slept With* on Warner Brothers/7 Arts

4724 **Best Spoken Word:** *Lonesome Cities* by Rod McKuen on Warner Brothers/7 Arts

4725 **Best Folk:** Judy Collins for "Both Sides Now" on Elektra

4726 **Best Sacred:** Jake Hess for "Beautiful Isle of Somewhere" on RCA

4727 **Best Gospel:** The Happy Goodman Family for *The Happy Gospel of the Happy Goodmans* on Word

4728 **Best Soul Gospel:** Dottie Rambo for "The Soul of Me" on Heartwarming

4729 **Best Original Score:** Paul Simon with additional music by Dave Grusin for *The Graduate* on Columbia

4730 **Best Score from an Original Cast Show Album:** Gerome Ragni, James Rado and Galt MacDermot for *Hair* on RCA

4731 **Best Instrumental Theme:** Mason Williams for "Classical Gas" on Warner Brothers/7 Arts

4732 **Best Classical Orchestra:** New Philharmonia Orchestra conducted by Pierre Boulez for *Boulez Conducts Debussy* on Columbia

4733 **Best Classical Chamber Music:** E. Power Biggs with the Edward Tarr Ensemble and Gabrieli Consort conducted by Vittorio Negri for *Gabrieli: Canzoni for Brass, Winds, Strings and Organ* on Columbia

4734 **Best Performance Instrumental Soloist:** Vladimir Horowitz for "Horowitz on Television" on Columbia

4735 **Best Classical Chorale:** The Gregg Smith Singers, Texas Boys Choir, George Bragg director, Vittorio Negri conductor for *The Glory of Gabrieli* with E. Power Biggs and the Edward Tarr Ensemble on Columbia

4736 **Best Opera:** Erich Leinsdorf conducting the New Philharmonic Orchestra and the Ambrosian Opera Chorus for *Mozart: Cosi Fan Tutte* on RCA

4737 **Best Vocal Soloist:** Montserrat Caballe for "Rossini Rarities." Cillario conducting the RCA Italiana Opera Orchestra and Chorus on RCA

4738 **Best Engineered Classical:** Gordon Parry for "Mahler: Symphony No. 9 in D Major" on London

4739 **Best Engineered Non-Classical:** Joe Polito and Hugh Davies for "Wichita Lineman" on Capitol

4740 **Best Album Cover (Award to Art Director):** John Berg and Richard Mantel for *Underground* on Columbia

4741 **Best Album Notes:** Johnny Cash for *Johnny Cash at Folsom Prison* on Columbia

4742 **Best New Artist of 1968:** Jose Feliciano

———— **1 9 7 0** ————

4743 **Record of the Year:** "Aquarius/Let the Sunshine In" by the 5th Dimension on Soul City

4744 **Album of the Year:** *Blood, Sweat and Tears* by Blood, Sweat and Tears on Columbia

4745 **Song of the Year (Award to the Songwriter):** Joe South for "Games People Play"

4746 **Best Contemporary/Pop Male Solo Vocal:** Harry Nilsson for *Everybody's Talkin'* on United Artists

4747 **Best Contemporary/Pop Female Solo Vocal:** Peggy Lee for *Is That All There Is?* on Capitol

4748 **Best Contemporary/Pop Vocal Duo or Group:** The 5th Dimension for "Aquarius/Let the Sunshine In" on Soul City

4749 **Best Contemporary/Pop Chorus:** Percy Faith Orchestra and Chorus for "Love Theme from *Romeo and Juliet*" on RCA

4750 **Best Instrumental Arrangement:** Henry Mancini for "Love Theme from *Romeo and Juliet*" on RCA

4751 **Best Contemporary/Pop Instrumental:** Blood, Sweat and Tears for "Variations on a Theme by Eric Satie" on Columbia

4752 **Best Contemporary Song:** Joe South for "Games People Play"

4753 **Best Accompaniment Arrangement:** Fred Lipsius for "Spinning Wheel" on Columbia

4754 **Best Instrumental Jazz Small Group:** Wes Montgomery for *Willow Weep for Me* on Verve

4755 **Best Instrumental Jazz Large Group:** Quincy Jones for *Walking in Space* on A&M

4756 **Best Country & Western Song:** Shel Silverstein for "A Boy Named Sue"

4757 **Best Country & Western Female Vocal:** Tammy Wynette for "Stand by Your Man" on Epic

4758 **Best Country & Western Male Vocal:** Johnny Cash for "A Boy Named Sue" on Columbia

4759 **Best Country & Western Duet, Trio or Group:** Waylon Jennings and the Kimberleys for "MacArthur Park" on RCA

4760 **Best Country & Western Instrumental:** *Danny Davis and the Nashville Brass Play More Nashville Sounds* on RCA

4761 **Best Rhythm & Blues Song:** Richard Spencer for "Color Him Father"

4762 **Best Rhythm & Blues Female Solo Vocal:** Aretha Franklin for "Share Your Love with Me" on Atlantic

4763 **Best Rhythm & Blues Male Solo Vocal:** Joe Simon for "The Chokin' Kind" on Sound Stage 7

4764 **Best Rhythm & Blues Vocal or Duo Blues Group:** The Isley Brothers for "It's Your Thing" on T-neck

4765 **Best Rhythm & Blues Instrumental:** King Curtis for "Games People Play" on Atco

4766 **Best Comedy:** Bill Cosby for *Bill Cosby* on Uni

4767 **Best Spoken Word:** *We Love You, Call Collect* by Art Linkletter and Diane on Word/Cap

4768 **Best Folk:** Joni Mitchell for "Clouds" on Warner Brothers

4769 **Best Sacred:** Jake Hess for "Ain't That Beautiful Singing?" on RCA

4770 **Best Gospel:** Porter Wagoner and the Blackwood Brothers for "In Gospel Country" on RCA

4771 **Best Soul Gospel:** The Edwin Hawkins Singers for "Oh Happy Day" on Buddah

4772 **Best Original Score:** Burt Bacharach for *Butch Cassidy and the Sundance Kid* on A&M

4773 **Best Score from an Original Cast Show Album:** Burt Bacharach and Hal David for *Promises, Promises* on Liberty/United Artists

4774 **Best Instrumental Theme:** John Barry for *Midnight Cowboy*

4775 **Best Children:** Peter, Paul & Mary for "Peter, Paul & Mommy" on Warner Brothers

4776 **Classical Album of the Year:** Walter Carlos for *Switched-on Bach* on Columbia

4777 **Best Classical Orchestra:** The Cleveland Orchestra conducted by Pierre Boulez for *Boulez Conducts Debussy, Vol. 2 "Images Pour Orchestre"* on Columbia

4778 **Best Classical Chamber Music:** The Philadelphia, Cleveland and Chicago Brass Ensembles for *Gabrieli: Antiphonal Music of Gabrieli (Canzoni for Brass Choirs)* on Columbia

4779 **Best Performance Instrumental Soloist:** Walter Carlos for *Switched-on Bach* on Columbia

4780 **Best Classical Chorales:** The Swingle Singers for *Berio: Sinfonia* the New York Philharmonic conducted by Luciano Berio on Columbia

4781 **Best Opera:** Herbert von Karajan conducting the Berlin Philharmonic for *Wagner: Siegfried* on DG

4782 **Best Vocal Soloist:** Leontyne Price for "Barber: Two Scenes from *Antony and Cleopatra*"/"Knoxville: Summer of 1915" the New Philharmonia Orchestra conducted by Thomas Schippers on RCA

4783 **Best Engineered Classical:** Walter Carlos for *Switched-on Bach*

4784 **Best Engineered Non-Classical:** Geoff Emerick and Phillip McDonald for *Abbey Road* on Apple

4785 **Best Album Cover/Album Package:** Evelyn J. Kelbish and David Stahlberg for *America the Beautiful*

4786 **Best Album Notes:** Johnny Cash for *Nashville Skyline* on Columbia

4787 **Best New Artist of 1969:** Crosby, Stills & Nash

————— **1971** —————

4788 **Record of the Year:** "Bridge Over Troubled Water" by Simon and Garfunkel on Columbia

4789 **Album of the Year:** *Bridge Over Troubled Water* by Simon and Garfunkel on Columbia

4790 **Song of the Year (Award to the Songwriter):** Paul Simon for "Bridge Over Troubled Water" on Columbia

4791 **Best Contemporary/Pop Male Solo Vocal:** Ray Stevens for "Everything Is Beautiful" on Barnaby

4792 **Best Contemporary/Pop Female Solo Vocal:** Dionne Warwick for "I'll Never Fall in Love Again" on Scepter

4793 **Best Contemporary/Pop Vocal Duo or Group:** The Carpenters for "Close to You" on A&M

4794 **Best Instrumental Arrangement:** Henry Mancini for "Theme from *Z*" on RCA

4795 **Best Contemporary/Pop Instrumental:** Henry Mancini for *Theme from Z and Other Films* on RCA

4796 **Best Contemporary Song:** Paul Simon for "Bridge Over Troubled Water" on Columbia

4797 **Best Accompaniment Arrangement:** Paul Simon, Arthur Garfunkel, Jimmie Haskell, Ernie Freeman and Larry Knechtel for "Bridge Over Troubled Water" on Columbia

4798 **Best Instrumental Jazz Small Group:** Bill Evans for *Alone* on MGM

4799 **Best Instrumental Jazz Large Group:** Miles Davis for *Bitches Brew* on Columbia

4800 **Best Country & Western Song:** Marty Robbins for "My Woman, My Woman, My Wife" on Columbia

4801 **Best Country & Western Female Vocal:** Lynn Anderson for "Rose Garden" on Columbia

4802 **Best Country & Western Male Vocal:** Ray Price for "For the Good Times" on Columbia

4803 **Best Country & Western Duet, Trio or Group:** Johnny Cash and June Carter for "If I Were a Carpenter" on Columbia

4804 **Best Country & Western Instrumental:** Chet Atkins and Jerry Reed for "Me & Jerry" on RCA

4805 **Best Rhythm & Blues Song:** Ronald Dunbar and General Johnson for "Patches" on Atlantic

4806 **Best Rhythm & Blues Female Solo Vocal:** Aretha Franklin for "Don't Play That Song" on Atlantic

4807 **Best Rhythm & Blues Male Solo Vocal:** B.B. King for "The Thrill Is Gone" on ABC

4808 **Best Rhythm & Blues Vocal or Duo Blues Group:** The Delfonics for "Didn't I (Blow Your Mind This Time)" on Philly Groove

4809 **Best Comedy:** Flip Wilson for *The Devil Made Me Buy This Dress* on Little David

4810 **Best Spoken Word:** *Why I Oppose the War in Vietnam* by Dr. Martin Luther King, Jr., on Black Forum

4811 **Best Sacred:** Jake Hess for "Everything Is Beautiful" on RCA

4812 **Best Gospel:** The Oak Ridge Boys for "Talk About the Good Times" on Heartwarming

4813 **Best Soul Gospel:** The Edwin Hawkins Singers for "Every Man Wants to Be Free" on Buddah

4814 **Best Ethnic or Traditional:** T-bone Walker for "Good Feelin'" on Polydor

4815 **Best Original Score:** John Lennon, Paul McCartney, Ringo Starr and George Harrison for "Let It Be" on Apple

4816 **Best Score from an Original Cast Show Album:** Stephen Sondheim for *Company* on Columbia

4817 **Best Instrumental Composition:** Alfred Newman for "Airport Love Theme" on Decca

4818 **Best Children:** Joan Cooney producer of *Sesame Street* on Columbia

4819 **Classical Album of the Year:** Colin Davis conducting the Royal Opera House Orchestra and Chorus for *Berlioz: Les Troyens* on Philips

4820 **Best Classical Orchestra:** The Cleveland Orchestra conducted by Pierre Boulez for *Stravinsky: Le Sacre du Printemps* on Columbia

4821 **Best Classical Chamber Music:** Eugene Istomin, Isaac Stern and Leonard Rose for *Beethoven: The Complete Piano Trios* on Columbia

4822 **Best Performance Instrumental Soloists:** David Oistrakh and Mstislav Rostropovich for *Brahms: Double Concerto (Concerto in A Minor for Violin and Cello)* on Angel

4823 **Best Classical Chorale:** The Gregg Smith Singers and the Columbia Chamber Ensemble for *Ives: New Music of Charles Ives* on Columbia

4824 **Best Opera:** Colin Davis conducting the Royal Opera House Chorus and Orchestra for *Berlioz: Les Troyens* on Philips

4825 **Best Vocal Soloist:** Dietrick Fischer-Dieskau for *Schubert: Lieder* on DG

4826 **Best Engineered Classical:** Fred Plaut, Ray Moore and Arthur Kennedy for "Stravinsky: Le Sacre du Printemps" with Pierre Boulez conducting the Cleveland Orchestra on Columbia

4827 **Best Engineered Non-Classical:** Roy Halee for "Bridge Over Troubled Water" on Columbia

4828 **Best Album Cover/Album Package:** Robert Lockart and Ivan Nagy for *Indianola Mississippi Seeds* on ABC

4829 **Best Album Notes:** Chris Albertson for *The World's Greatest Blues Singer* on Columbia

4830 **Best New Artist of the Year:** The Carpenters on A&M

──────── **1972** ────────

4831 **Record of the Year:** "It's Too Late" by Carole King on Ode

4832 **Album of the Year:** *Tapestry* by Carole King on Ode

4833 **Song of the Year (Award to the Songwriter):** Carole King for "You've Got a Friend" on Ode

4834 **Best Contemporary/Pop Male Solo Vocal:** James Taylor for "You've Got a Friend" on Warner Brothers

4835 **Best Contemporary/Pop Female Solo Vocal:** Carole King for "Tapestry" on Ode

4836 **Best Contemporary/Pop Vocal Duo or Group:** The Carpenters for *The Carpenters* on A&M

4837 **Best Instrumental Arrangement:** Isaac Hayes and Johnny Allen for "Theme from *Shaft*" on Enterprise

4838 **Best Contemporary/Pop Instrumental:** Quincy Jones for "Smackwater Jack" on A&M

4839 **Best Accompaniment Arrangement:** Paul McCartney for "Uncle Albert/Admiral Halsey" on Apple

4840 **Best Instrumental Jazz Small Group:** Bill Evans Trio for *The Bill Evans Album* on Columbia

4841 **Best Instrumental Jazz Large Group:** Duke Ellington for *New Orleans Suite* on Atlantic

4842 **Best Jazz Soloist:** Bill Evans for *The Bill Evans Album* on Columbia

4843 **Best Country & Western Song:** Kris Kristofferson for "Help Me Make It Through the Night" on Mega

4844 **Best Country & Western Female Vocal:** Sammi Smith for "Help Me Make It Through the Night" on Mega

4845 **Best Country & Western Male Vocal:** Jerry Reed for "When You're Hot, You're Hot" on RCA

4846 **Best Country & Western Duet, Trio or Group:** Conway Twitty & Loretta Lynn for "After the Fire Is Gone" on Decca

4847 **Best Country & Western Instrumental:** Chet Atkins for "Snowbird" on RCA

4848 **Best Rhythm & Blues Song:** Bill Withers for "Ain't No Sunshine" on Sussex

4849 **Best Rhythm & Blues Female Solo Vocal:** Aretha Franklin for "Bridge Over Troubled Water" on Atlantic

4850 **Best Rhythm & Blues Male Solo Vocal:** Lou Rawls for "A Natural Man" on MGM

4851 **Best Rhythm & Blues Vocal or Duo Blues Group:** Ike and Tina Turner for "Proud Mary" on United Artists

4852 **Best Comedy:** Lily Tomlin for *This Is a Recording* on Polydor

4853 **Best Spoken Word:** *Desiderata* by Les Crane on Warner Brothers

4854 **Best Sacred:** Charley Pride for "Did You Think to Pray?" on RCA

4855 **Best Gospel:** Charley Pride for "Let Me Live" on RCA

4856 **Best Soul Gospel:** Shirley Caesar for "Put Your Hand in the Hand of the Man from Galilee" on Hob

4857 **Best Ethnic:** Muddy Waters for *They Call Me Muddy Waters* on Chess

4858 **Best Original Motion Picture Score:** Isaac Hayes for *Shaft* on Enterprise

4859 **Best Score from an Original Cast Show Album:** Stephen Schwartz for *Godspell* on Bell Records

4860 **Best Instrumental Composition:** Michel Legrand for "Theme from *Summer of '42*" on Warner Brothers

4861 **Best Children:** Bill Cosby for *Bill Cosby Talks to Kids About Drugs* on Uni

4862 **Classical Album of the Year:** Vladimir Horowitz, pianist for *Horowitz Plays Rachmaninoff* on Columbia

4863 **Best Classical Orchestra:** Carlo Maria Giulini conducting the Chicago Symphony Orchestra for *Mahler: Symphony No. 1 in D Major* on Angel

4864 **Best Classical Chamber Music:** Juilliard Quartet for *Debussy: Quartet in G Minor/Ravel: Quartet in F Major* on Columbia

4865 **Best Performance Instrumental Soloists (with Orchestra):** Julian Bream for *Villa-Lobos: Concerto for Guitar* Andre Previn conducting the London Symphony on RCA

4866 **Best Performance Instrumental Soloists (Without Orchestra):** Vladimir Horowitz for *Horowitz Plays Rachmaninoff* on Columbia

4867 **Best Opera:** Erich Leinsdorf conducting the London Symphony Orchestra for *Verdi: Aida* on RCA

4868 **Best Vocal Soloist:** Leontyne Price for "Leontyne Price Sings Robert Schumann" on RCA

4869 **Best Classical Chorale:** Russell Burgess conducting the Wadsworth School Boys Choir, and Arthur Oldham conducting the London Symphony Chorus for *Berlioz: Requiem* with Colin Davis conducting the London Symphony Orchestra on Philips

4870 **Best Engineered Classical:** Vittorio Negri for "Berlioz: Requiem" on Philips

4871 **Best Engineered Non-Classical:** David Purple, Ron Capone and Henry Bush for "Theme from *Shaft*" on Enterprise

4872 **Best Album Cover (Award to Art Director):** Dean O. Torrence and Gene Brownell for *Pollution* on Prophesy

4873 **Best Album Notes (Award to Annotator):** Sam Samudio for *Sam, Hard and Heavy* on Atlantic

4874 **Best New Artist of the Year:** Carly Simon on Elektra

———— **1973** ————

4875 **Record of the Year:** "The First Time Ever I Saw Your Face" by Roberta Flack on Atlantic

4876 **Album of the Year:** *The Concert for Bangla Desh* by George Harrison, Ravi Shankar, Bob Dylan, Leon Russell, Eric Clapton, Ringo Starr, Billy Preston and Klaus Voormann on Apple

4877 Song of the Year (Award to the Songwriter): Ewan MacColl for "The First Time Ever I Saw Your Face"

4878 Best Contemporary/Pop Male Solo Vocal: Harry Nilsson for "Without You" on RCA

4879 Best Contemporary/Pop Female Solo Vocal: Helen Reddy for "I Am Woman" on Capitol

4880 Best Contemporary/Pop Vocal Duo or Group: Roberta Flack and Donny Hathaway for "Where Is the Love?" on Atlantic

4881 Best Instrumental Arrangement: Don Ellis for "Theme from *The French Connection*" on Columbia

4882 Best Contemporary/Pop Instrumental: Isaac Hayes for "Black Moses" for Enterprise

4883 Best Pop Instrumental Performer: Billy Preston for "Out-a-Space" on A&M

4884 Best Accompaniment Arrangement: Michel Legrand for "What Are You Doing the Rest of Your Life?" on Mainstream

4885 Best Instrumental Jazz Small Group: Freddy Hubbard for *First Flight* on CTI

4886 Best Instrumental Jazz Large Group: Duke Ellington for *Toga Brava Suite* on United Artists

4887 Best Jazz Soloist: Gary Burton for "Alone at Last" on Atlantic

4888 Best Country & Western Song: Ben Peters for "Kiss an Angel Good Mornin'"

4889 Best Country & Western Female Vocal: Donna Fargo for "The Happiest Girl in the Whole USA" on Dot

4890 Best Country & Western Male Vocal: Charley Pride for *Charley Pride Sings Heart Songs* on RCA

4891 Best Country & Western Duet, Trio or Group: The Statler Brothers for *Class of '57* on Mercury

4892 Best Country & Western Instrumental: Charlie McCoy for *Charlie McCoy/The Real McCoy* on Monument

4893 Best Rhythm & Blues Song: Barrett Strong and Norman Whitfield for "Papa Was a Rolling Stone"

4894 Best Rhythm & Blues Female Solo Vocal: Aretha Franklin for "Young, Gifted & Black" on Atlantic

4895 Best Rhythm & Blues Male Solo Vocal: Billy Paul for "Me & Mrs. Jones" on Philadelphia International

4896 Best Rhythm & Blues Vocal or Duo Blues Group: The Temptations for "Papa Was a Rolling Stone" on Gordy/Motown

4897 Best Rhythm and Blues Instrumental: Paul Riser conducting the Temptations for "Papa Was a Rolling Stone" on Gordy/Motown

4898 Best Comedy: George Carlin for *FM & AM* on Little David

4899 Best Spoken Word: *Lenny* produced by Bruce Botnik on Blue Thumb

4900 Best Inspirational: Elvis Presley for "He Touched Me" on RCA

4901 Best Gospel: The Blackwood Brothers for "Love" on RCA

4902 Best Soul Gospel: Aretha Franklin for "Amazing Grace" on Atlantic

4903 Best Ethnic or Traditional: Muddy Waters for *The London Muddy Waters Sessions* on Chess

4904 Best Original Motion Picture Score: Nino Rota for "The Godfather" on Paramount

4905 Best Score from an Original Cast Show Album: Micki Grant for "Don't Bother Me, I Can't Cope" on Polydor

4906 Best Instrumental Composition: Michel Legrand for *Brian's Song*

4907 Best Children: Producer and music director Joe Raposo for *The Electric Company* project directors Christopher Cerf, Bill Cosby, Rita Moreno and Lee Chamberlain on Warner Brothers

4908 Classical Album of the Year: Georg Solti conducting the Chicago Symphony Orchestra for *Mahler: Symphony No. 8* with the Vienna State Opera Chorus and Vienna Singverein Chorus and Soloists on London

4909 Best Classical Orchestra: Georg Solti conducting the Chicago Symphony Orchestra for *Mahler, Symphony No. 7* on London

4910 Best Classical Chamber Music: Julian Bream and John Williams for *Julian & John* on RCA

4911 Best Performance Instrumental Soloists (with Orchestra): Artur Rubinstein for *Brahms: Concerto No. 2* on RCA

4912 **Best Performance Instrumental Soloist (Without Orchestra):** Vladimir Horowitz for *Horowitz Plays Chopin* on Columbia

4913 **Best Opera:** Erik Smith for *Berlioz: Benvenuto Cellini* with Colin Davis conducting the BBC Symphony and the Chorus of the Covent Garden on Philips

4914 **Best Vocal Soloist:** Dietrick Fischer-Dieskau for "Brahms: Die Schone Magelone" on Angel

4915 **Best Classical Choral:** Georg Solti conductor for *Mahler: Symphony No. 8* on London

4916 **Best Engineered Classical:** Gordon Parry and Kenneth Wilkinson for "Mahler: Symphony No. 8" on London

4917 **Best Engineered Non-Classical:** Armin Steiner for "Moods" on Uni

4918 **Best Album Cover (Award to Art Director):** Acy Lehman and Harvey Dinnerstein for *The Siegel Schwall Band* on Wooden Nickel

4919 **Best Album Notes (Award to Annotator):** Tom T. Hall for *Tom T. Hall's Greatest Hits* on Mercury

4920 **Best Album Notes/Classical (Award to Annotator):** James Lyons for *Vaughan Williams: Symphony No. 2* on RCA

4921 **Best New Artist of the Year:** America on Warner Brothers

——————— **1974** ———————

4922 **Record of the Year:** "Killing Me Softly with His Song" by Roberta Flack on Atlantic

4923 **Album of the Year:** *Innervisions* by Stevie Wonder on Tamla/Motown

4924 **Song of the Year (Award to the Songwriter):** Norman Gimbel and Charles Fox for "Killing Me Softly with His Song"

4925 **Best Contemporary/Pop Male Solo Vocal:** Stevie Wonder for "You Are the Sunshine of My Life" on Tamla/Motown

4926 **Best Contemporary/Pop Female Solo Vocal:** Roberta Flack for "Killing Me Softly with His Song" on Atlantic

4927 **Best Contemporary/Pop Vocal Duo or Group:** Gladys Knight and the Pips for "Neither One of Us (Wants to Be the First to Say Goodbye)" on Soul/Motown

4928 **Best Instrumental Arrangement:** Quincy Jones for "Summer in the City" on A&M

4929 **Best Contemporary/Pop Instrumental:** Eumir Deodato for "Also Sprach Zarathustra" (Used in the movie *2001: A Space Odyssey*) on CTI

4930 **Best Instrumental Composition:** Gato Barbieri for "Last Tango in Paris"

4931 **Best Accompaniment Arrangement:** George Martin for "Live and Let Die" on Apple

4932 **Best Instrumental Jazz Small Group:** Supersax for *Supersax Plays Bird* on Capitol

4933 **Best Instrumental Jazz Large Group:** Woody Herman for *Giant Steps* on Fantasy

4934 **Best Jazz Soloist:** Art Tatum for *God Is in the House* on Onyx

4935 **Best Country & Western Song:** Kenny O'Dell for "Behind Closed Doors"

4936 **Best Country & Western Female Vocal:** Olivia Newton-John for "Let Me Be There" on MCA

4937 **Best Country & Western Male Vocal:** Charlie Rich for "Behind Closed Doors" on Epic/Columbia

4938 **Best Country & Western Duo or Group:** Kris Kristofferson and Rita Coolidge for "From the Bottle to the Bottom" on A&M

4939 **Best Country & Western Instrumental:** Eric Weissberg and Steve Mandell for "Dueling Banjos" on Warner Brothers

4940 **Best Rhythm & Blues Song:** Stevie Wonder for "Superstition"

4941 **Best Rhythm & Blues Female Solo Vocal:** Aretha Franklin for "Master of Eyes" on Atlantic

4942 **Best Rhythm & Blues Male Solo Vocal:** Stevie Wonder for "Superstition" on Tamla/Motown

4943 **Best Rhythm & Blues Vocal or Duo Blues Group:** Gladys Knight and the Pips for "Midnight Train to Georgia" on Buddah

4944 **Best Rhythm & Blues Instrumental:** Ramsey Lewis for "Hang On Sloopy" on Columbia

4945 **Best Comedy:** Cheech and Chong for *Los Cochinos* on Ode

4946 **Best Spoken Word:** *Jonathan Livingston Seagull* by Richard Harris on ABC/Dunhill

4947 **Best Inspirational:** The Bill Gaither Trio for "Let's Just Praise the Lord" on Impact

4948 **Best Gospel:** The Blackwood Brothers for "Release Me (from My Sin)" on Skylite

4949 **Best Soul Gospel:** The Dixie Hummingbirds for "Loves Me Like a Rock" on ABC

4950 **Best Ethnic or Traditional:** Doc Watson for *Then and Now* on United Artists

4951 **Best Original Motion Picture Score:** Neil Diamond for *Jonathan Livingston Seagull* on Columbia

4952 **Best Score from an Original Cast Show Album:** Stephen Sondheim for *A Little Night Music* on Columbia

4953 **Best Children:** Joe Raposo producer for *Sesame Street Live* on Columbia

4954 **Classical Album of the Year:** Pierre Boulez conducting the New York Philharmonic Orchestra for *Bartok: Concerto for Orchestra* on Columbia

4955 **Best Classical Orchestra:** The New York Philharmonic Orchestra conducted by Pierre Boulez for *Bartok: Concerto for Orchestra* on Columbia

4956 **Best Classical Chamber Music:** Gunther Schuller and the New England Conservatory Ragtime Ensemble for *Joplin: The Red Back Book* on Angel

4957 **Best Performance Instrumental Soloists (with Orchestra):** Vladimir Ashkenazy for *Beethoven: Concerto (5) for Piano and Orchestra* with Georg Solti conducting the Chicago Symphony Orchestra on London

4958 **Best Performance Instrumental Soloists (Without Orchestra):** Vladimir Horowitz, pianist for *Horowitz Plays Scriabin* on Columbia

4959 **Best Opera:** Leonard Bernstein conducting the Metropolitan Opera Chorus for *Bizet: Carmen* on DG

4960 **Best Vocal Soloist:** Leontyne Price for *Puccini: Heroines (La Bohème, La Rondine, Tosca* and *Manon Lescaut)* on RCA

4961 **Best Classical Chorale:** Andre Previn conducting the London Symphony Orchestra for *Walton: Belshazzar's Feast*

with the London Symphony Orchestra Chorus conducted by Arthur Oldham on Angel

4962 **Best Engineered Classical:** Edward T. Graham and Raymond Moore for "Bartok: Concerto for Orchestra" on Columbia

4963 **Best Engineered Non-Classical:** Robert Margouleff and Malcolm Cecil for "Innervisions" on Tamla/Motown

4964 **Best Album Cover (Award to Art Director):** Wilkes and Braun, Inc. for *Tommy* on Ode

4965 **Best Album Notes (Award to Annotator):** Dan Morgenstern for *God Is in the House* on Onyx

4966 **Best Album Notes/Classical (Award to Annotator):** Glenn Gould for *Hindemith: Sonatas for Piano (Complete)* on Columbia

4967 **Best New Artist of the Year:** Bette Midler on Atlantic

──────── **1975** ────────

4968 **Record of the Year:** "I Honestly Love You" by Olivia Newton-John on MCA

4969 **Album of the Year:** *Fulfillingness' First Finale* by Stevie Wonder on Tamla/Motown

4970 **Song of the Year (Award to the Songwriter):** Marilyn Bergman, Alan Bergman and Marvin Hamlisch for "The Way We Were"

4971 **Best Contemporary/Pop Male Solo Vocal:** "Fulfillingness' First Finale" by Stevie Wonder on Tamla/Motown

4972 **Best Contemporary/Pop Finale Solo Vocal:** Olivia Newton-John for "I Honestly Love You" on MCA

4973 **Best Contemporary/Pop Vocal Duo or Group:** Paul McCartney and Wings for "Band on the Run" on Apple/Capitol

4974 **Best Instrumental Arrangement:** Pat Williams for "Threshold" on Capitol

4975 **Best Contemporary/Pop Instrumental:** "The Entertainer" by Marvin Hamlisch on MCA

4976 **Best Instrumental Composition:** Mike Oldfield for "Tubular Bells (Theme from *The Exorcist*)"

4977 **Best Accompaniment Arrangement:** Joni Mitchell and Tom Scott for "Down to You" on Asylum

4978 Best Instrumental Jazz Small Group: Oscar Peterson, Joe Pass and Niels Pedersen for "The Trio" on Pablo

4979 Best Instrumental Jazz Large Group: Woody Herman for *Thundering Herd* on Fantasy

4980 Best Jazz Soloist: Charlie Parker for *First Recordings* on Onyx

4981 Best Country & Western Song: Norris Wilson and Billy Sherrill for "A Very Special Love Song"

4982 Best Country & Western Female Vocal: Anne Murray for "A Love Song" on Capitol

4983 Best Country & Western Male Vocal: Ronnie Milsap for "Please Don't Tell Me How the Story Ends" on RCA

4984 Best Country & Western Duo or Group: The Pointer Sisters for "Fairytale" on Blue Thumb

4985 Best Country & Western Instrumental: Chet Atkins and Merle Travis for *The Atkins-Travis Travelling Show* on ABC

4986 Best Rhythm & Blues Song: Stevie Wonder for "Living for the City"

4987 Best Rhythm & Blues Female Solo Vocal: Aretha Franklin for "Ain't Nothing Like the Real Thing" on Atlantic

4988 Best Rhythm & Blues Male Solo Vocal: Stevie Wonder for "Boogie On Reggae Woman" on Tamla/Motown

4989 Best Rhythm & Blues Vocal or Duo Blues Group: Rufus for "Tell Me Something Good" on ABC

4990 Best Rhythm & Blues Instrumental: MFSB for *TSOP (The Sound of Philadelphia)* on Philadelphia International/Epic

4991 Best Comedy: Richard Pryor for *That Nigger's Crazy* on Partee/Stax

4992 Best Spoken Word: *Good Evening* by Peter Cook and Dudley Moore on Island

4993 Best Inspirational: Elvis Presley for "How Great Thou Art" on RCA

4994 Best Gospel: The Oak Ridge Boys for "The Baptism of Jesse Taylor" on Columbia

4995 Best Soul Gospel: James Cleveland and the Southern California Community Choir for "In the Ghetto" on Savoy

4996 Best Ethnic or Traditional: Doc Watson and Merle Watson for *Two Days in November* on United Artists

4997 Best Original Motion Picture Score: Marvin Hamlisch, Marilyn Bergman and Alan Bergman for *The Way We Were* on Columbia

4998 Best Score from an Original Cast Show Album: Judd Woldin and Robert Brittan for *Raisin* on Columbia

4999 Best Children: Sebastian Cabot, Sterling Holloway and Paul Winchell for *Winnie the Pooh & Tigger Too* on Disneyland

5000 Classical Album of the Year: Georg Solti conducting the Chicago Symphony Orchestra for *Berlioz: Symphonie Fantastique* on London

5001 Best Classical Orchestra: The Chicago Symphony conducted by Georg Solti for *Berlioz: Symphonie Fantastique* on London

5002 Best Classical Chamber Music: Artur Rubinstein, Henryk Szeryng and Pierre Fournier for *Brahms and Schumann Trios* on RCA

5003 Best Performance Instrumental Soloists (with Orchestra): David Oistrakh for *Shostakovich: Violin Concerto No. 1* on Angel

5004 Best Performance Instrumental Soloists (Without Orchestra): Alicia de Larrocha for *Albéniz: Iberia* on London

5005 Best Opera: Georg Solti conducting for *Puccini: La Bohème* on RCA

5006 Best Vocal Soloist: Leontyne Price for "Leontyne Price Sings Richard Strauss" on RCA

5007 Best Classical Choral: Colin Davis conducting for *Berlioz: The Damnation of Faust* on Philips

5008 Best Engineered Classical: Kenneth Wilkinson for "Berlioz: Symphonie Fantastique" on London

5009 Best Engineered Non-Classical: Geoff Emerick for "Band on the Run" on Apple/Capitol

5010 Best Album Cover (Award to Art Director): Christopher Whorf and Ed Thrasher for *Come and Gone* on Warner Brothers

5011 Best Album Notes (Award to Annotator): Charles R. Townsend for *For the Last Time* on United Artists and Dan Morgenstern for *The Hawk Flies* on Milestone

5012 Best Album Notes/Classical (Award to Annotator): Rory Guy for *The*

Classic Erich Wolfgang Korngold on Angel

5013 **Producer of the Year:** Thom Bell

5014 **Best New Artist of the Year:** Marvin Hamlisch on MCA

———————— **1 9 7 6** ————————

5015 **Record of the Year:** "Love Will Keep Us Together" by the Captain and Tennille on A&M

5016 **Album of the Year:** *Still Crazy After All These Years* by Paul Simon on Columbia

5017 **Song of the Year (Award to the Songwriter):** Stephen Sondheim for "Send In the Clowns"

5018 **Best Contemporary/Pop Male Solo Vocal:** Paul Simon for "Still Crazy After All These Years" on Columbia

5019 **Best Contemporary/Pop Female Solo Vocal:** "At Seventeen" by Janis Ian on Columbia

5020 **Best Contemporary/Pop Vocal Duo or Group:** The Eagles for "Lyin' Eyes" on Asylum

5021 **Best Instrumental Arrangement:** Mike Post and Pete Carpenter for *The Rockford Files* on MGM

5022 **Best Contemporary/Pop Instrumental:** "The Hustle" by Van McCoy and the Soul City Symphony on AVCO

5023 **Best Instrumental Composition:** Michel Legrand for "Images"

5024 **Best Accompaniment Arrangement:** Ray Stevens for "Misty" on Barnaby

5025 **Best Instrumental Jazz Small Group:** Chick Corea and Return to Forever for *No Mystery* on Polydor

5026 **Best Instrumental Jazz Large Group:** Phil Woods with Michel Legrand and His Orchestra for *Images* on Gryphon/RCA

5027 **Best Jazz Soloist:** Dizzy Gillespie for *Oscar Peterson and Dizzy Gillespie* on Pablo

5028 **Best Country & Western Song:** Chips Moman and Larry Butler for "(Hey Won't You Play) Another Somebody Done Somebody Wrong Song"

5029 **Best Country & Western Female Vocal:** Linda Ronstadt for "I Can't Help It (If I'm Still in Love with You)" on Capitol

5030 **Best Country & Western Male Vocal:** Willie Nelson for "Blue Eyes Crying in the Rain" on Columbia

5031 **Best Country & Western Duo or Group:** Kris Kristofferson and Rita Coolidge for "Lover Please" on Monument

5032 **Best Country & Western Instrumental:** Chet Atkins for "The Entertainer" on RCA

5033 **Best Rhythm & Blues Song:** Harry Wayne Casey, Richard Finch, Willie Clarke and Betty Wright for "Where Is the Love?"

5034 **Best Rhythm & Blues Female Solo Vocal:** Natalie Cole for "This Will Be" on Capitol

5035 **Best Rhythm & Blues Male Solo Vocal:** Ray Charles for "Living for the City" on Crossover

5036 **Best Rhythm & Blues Vocal or Duo Blues Group:** Earth, Wind & Fire for "Shining Star" on Columbia

5037 **Best Rhythm & Blues Instrumental:** Silver Convention for "Fly, Robin Fly" on Midland/RCA

5038 **Best Comedy:** Richard Pryor for *Is It Something I Said?* on Reprise

5039 **Best Spoken Word:** *Give 'Em Hell, Harry* by James Whitmore on United Artists

5040 **Best Inspirational:** The Bill Gaither Trio for *Jesus, We Just Want to Thank You* on Impact

5041 **Best Gospel:** The Imperials for "No Shortage" on Impact

5042 **Best Soul Gospel:** Andrae Crouch and the Disciples for "Take Me Back" on Light

5043 **Best Ethnic or Traditional:** Muddy Waters for *The Muddy Waters Woodstock Album* on Chess

5044 **Best Original Motion Picture Score:** John Williams for *Jaws* on MCA

5045 **Best Original Cast:** Jerry Wexler and Charlie Smalls for *The Wiz* on Atlantic

5046 **Best Latin:** Eddie Palmieri for *Sun of Latin Music* on Coco

5047 **Best Children:** Richard Burton for *The Little Prince* on PIP

5048 **Classical Album of the Year:** Georg Solti conducting the Chicago Symphony Orchestra for *Beethoven: Symphonies (9) Complete* on London

5049 **Best Classical Orchestra:** Pierre Boulez conducting the New York Philharmonic Orchestra for *Ravel: Daphnis et Chloe (Complete Ballet)* on Columbia

5050 **Best Classical Chamber Music:** Artur Rubinstein, Henryk Szeryng and Pierre Fournier for *Schubert: Trios No. 1 in B-Flat Major Op. 99 and 2 in E-Flat Major Op. 100 (The Piano Trios)* on RCA

5051 **Best Performance Instrumental Soloists (with Orchestra):** Alicia de Larrocha for *Ravel: Concerto for Left Hand and Concerto for Piano in G Major/ Faure: Fantasie for Piano and Orchestra* with De Burgos & Foster conducting the London Philharmonic Orchestra on London

5052 **Best Performance Instrumental Soloists (Without Orchestra):** Nathan Milstein for *Bach: Sonatas and Partitas for Violin Unaccompanied* on DG

5053 **Best Opera:** Colin Davis conducting the Royal Opera House, Covent Garden for *Mozart: Cosi Fan Tutte* on Philips

5054 **Best Vocal Soloist:** Janet Baker for *Mahler: Kindertotenlieder* with Leonard Bernstein conducting the Israel Philharmonic Orchestra on Columbia

5055 **Best Classical Choral:** Robert Page directing the Cleveland Orchestra Chorus and Boys Choir for *Orff: Carmina Burana* with Michael Tilson Thomas conducting the Cleveland Orchestra on Columbia

5056 **Best Engineered (Classical):** Bud Graham, Ray Moore and Milton Cherin for "Ravel: Daphnis et Chloe" on Columbia

5057 **Best Engineered (Non-Classical):** Brooks Arthur, Larry Alexander and Russ Payne for "Between the Lines" on Columbia

5058 **Best Album Cover (Award to Art Director):** Jim Ladwig for *Honey* on Mercury

5059 **Best Album Notes (Award to Annotator):** Pete Hamill for *Blood on the Tracks* on Columbia

5060 **Best Album Notes/Classical (Award to the Annotator):** Gunther Schuller for *Footlifters* on Columbia

5061 **Best Producer of the Year:** Arif Mardin

5062 **Best New Artist of the Year:** Natalie Cole on Capitol

——————— **1 9 7 7** ———————

5063 **Record of the Year:** "This Masquerade" by George Benson on Warner Brothers

5064 **Album of the Year:** *Songs in the Key of Life* by Stevie Wonder on Tamla/ Motown

5065 **Song of the Year (Award to the Songwriter):** Bruce Johnston for "I Write the Songs"

5066 **Best Contemporary/Pop Male Solo Vocal:** Stevie Wonder for "Songs in the Key of Life" on Tamla/Motown

5067 **Best Contemporary/Pop Female Solo Vocal:** Linda Ronstadt for "Hasten Down the Wind" on Asylum

5068 **Best Contemporary/Pop Vocal Duo or Group:** Chicago for "If You Leave Me Now" on Columbia

5069 **Best Instrumental Arrangement:** Chick Corea for "Leprechaun's Dream" on Polydor

5070 **Best Contemporary/Pop Instrumental:** "Breezin'" by George Benson on Warner Brothers

5071 **Best Arrangement for Voices (Duo, Group or Chorus):** Starland Vocal Band for "Afternoon Delight" on Windsong/RCA

5072 **Best Instrumental Composition:** Chuck Mangione for "Bellavia"

5073 **Best Accompaniment Arrangement:** Jimmie Haskell and James William Guerico for "If You Leave Me Now" on Columbia

5074 **Best Instrumental Jazz Small Group:** Chick Corea for *The Leprechaun* on Polydor

5075 **Best Instrumental Jazz Large Group:** Duke Ellington for *The Ellington Suites* on Pablo

5076 **Best Jazz Soloist:** Count Basie for *Basie and Zoot* on Pablo

5077 **Best Jazz Vocal:** Ella Fitzgerald for *Fitzgerald & Pass . . . Again* on Pablo

5078 **Best Country & Western Song:** Larry Gatlin for "Broken Lady"

5079 **Best Country & Western Female Vocal:** Emmylou Harris for "Elite Hotel" on Reprise/Warner Brothers

5080 **Best Country & Western Male Vocal:** Ronnie Milsap for "(I'm a) Stand by My Woman Man" on RCA

5081 **Best Country & Western Duo or Group:** The Amazing Rhythm Aces for "The End Is Not in Sight (The Cowboy Tune)" on ABC

5082 **Best Country & Western Instrumental:** Chet Atkins and Les Paul for "Chester and Lester" on RCA

5083 **Best Rhythm & Blues Song:** Boz Scaggs and David Paich for "Lowdown"

5084 **Best Rhythm & Blues Female Solo Vocal:** Natalie Cole for "Sophisticated Lady (She's a Different Lady)" on Capitol

5085 **Best Rhythm & Blues Male Solo Vocal:** Stevie Wonder for "I Wish" on Tamla/Motown

5086 **Best Rhythm & Blues Vocal or Duo Blues Group:** Marilyn McCoo and Billy Davis, Jr., for "You Don't Have to Be a Star (To Be in My Show)" on ABC

5087 **Best Rhythm & Blues Instrumental:** George Benson for "Theme from *Good King Bad*" on CIT

5088 **Best Comedy:** Richard Pryor for *Bicentennial Nigger* on Warner Brothers

5089 **Best Spoken Word:** *Great American Documents* by Orson Welles, Henry Fonda, Helen Hayes and James Earl Jones on CBS

5090 **Best Inspirational:** Gary S. Paxton for *The Astonishing, Outrageous, Amazing, Incredible, Unbelievable, Different World of Gary S. Paxton* on Newpax

5091 **Best Gospel:** The Oak Ridge Boys for "Where the Soul Never Dies" on Columbia

5092 **Best Soul Gospel:** Mahalia Jackson for "How I Got Over" on Columbia

5093 **Best Ethnic or Traditional:** John Hartford for *Mark Twang* on Flying Fish

5094 **Best Original Motion Picture Score:** Norman Whitfield for *Car Wash* on MCA

5095 **Best Original Cast Show Album:** Hugo and Luigi, producers for *Bubbling Brown Sugar* on H&L

5096 **Best Latin:** Eddie Palmieri for *Unfinished Masterpiece* on Coco

5097 **Best Children:** Hermione Gingold for *Prokofiev: Peter and the Wolf/ Saint-Saëns: Carnival of the Animals* on DG

5098 **Classical Album of the Year:** Artur Rubinstein and Daniel Barenboim

conducting the London Philharmonic Orchestra for *Beethoven: The Five Concertos* on RCA

5099 **Best Classical Orchestra:** Georg Solti conducting the Chicago Symphony Orchestra for *Strauss: Also Sprach Zarathustra* on London

5100 **Best Classical Chamber Music:** David Munrow conducting the Early Music Consort of London for *The Art of Courtly Love* on Seraphim

5101 **Best Performance Instrumental Soloists (with Orchestra):** Artur Rubinstein for *Beethoven: The Five Concertos* with Daniel Barenboim conducting the London Philharmonic on RCA

5102 **Best Performance Instrumental Soloists (Without Orchestra):** Vladimir Horowitz for *Horowitz Concerts 1975/76* on RCA

5103 **Best Opera:** Lorin Maazel conducting the Cleveland Orchestra and Chorus for *Gershwin: Porgy and Bess* on London

5104 **Best Vocal Soloist:** Beverly Sills for *Herbert: The Music of Victor Herbert* on Angel

5105 **Best Classical Choral:** Arthur Oldham, chorus master of the London Symphony Chorus for *Rachmaninoff: The Bells* with Andre Previn conducting the London Symphony Orchestra on Angel

5106 **Best Engineered (Classical):** Edward Graham, Ray Moore and Milton Cherin for "Gershwin: Rhapsody in Blue" on Columbia

5107 **Best Engineered (Non-Classical):** Al Schmitt for "Breezin'" on Warner Brothers

5108 **Best Album Cover (Award to Art Director):** John Berg for *Chicago X* on Columbia

5109 **Best Album Notes (Award to Annotator):** Dan Morgenstern for *The Changing Face of Harlem, the Savoy Sessions* on Savoy

5110 **Producer of the Year:** Stevie Wonder

5111 **Best New Artist of the Year:** Starland Vocal Band on Windsong/RCA

——————— **1 9 7 8** ———————

5112 **Record of the Year:** "Hotel California" by the Eagles on Asylum

5113 **Album of the Year:** *Rumours* by Fleetwood Mac on Warner Brothers

5114 **Songs of the Year (Award to the Songwriter):** Barbra Streisand and Paul Williams for "Evergreen," and Joe Brooks for "You Light Up My Life"

5115 **Best Contemporary/Pop Male Solo Vocal:** James Taylor for "Handy Man" on Columbia

5116 **Best Contemporary/Pop Female Solo Vocal:** Barbra Streisand for "Love Theme from *A Star Is Born* (Evergreen)" on Columbia

5117 **Best Contemporary/Pop Vocal Duo or Group:** Bee Gees for "How Deep Is Your Love?" on RSO

5118 **Best Instrumental Arrangement:** Harry Betts, Perry Botkin, Jr., and Barry de Vorzon for "Nadia's Theme" *(The Young and the Restless)* on Arista

5119 **Best Contemporary/Pop Instrumental:** *Star Wars* by John Williams conducting the London Symphony Orchestra on 20th Century

5120 **Best Arrangement for Voices:** Eagles for "New Kid in Town" on Asylum

5121 **Best Instrumental Composition:** John Williams for "Main Title Theme from *Star Wars*"

5122 **Best Accompaniment Arrangement:** Ian Freebairn-Smith for "Love Theme from *A Star Is Born* (Evergreen)" on Columbia

5123 **Best Instrumental Jazz Small Group:** Phil Woods for *The Phil Woods Six, Live from Showboat* on RCA

5124 **Best Instrumental Jazz Large Group:** Count Basie and His Orchestra for *Prime Time* on Pablo

5125 **Best Jazz Vocal:** Al Jarreau for "Look to the Rainbow" on Warner Brothers

5126 **Best Jazz Instrumentalist:** Oscar Peterson for *The Giants* on Pablo

5127 **Best Country & Western Song:** Richard Leigh for "Don't It Make My Brown Eyes Blue?"

5128 **Best Country & Western Female Vocal:** Crystal Gayle for "Don't It Make My Brown Eyes Blue?" on United Artists

5129 **Best Country & Western Male Vocal:** Kenny Rogers for "Lucille" on United Artists

5130 **Best Country & Western Duo or Group:** The Kendalls for "Heaven's Just a Sin Away" on Ovation

5131 **Best Country & Western Instrumental:** Hargus "Pig" Robbins for *Hargus "Pig" Robbins* on Elektra

5132 **Best Rhythm & Blues Song:** Leo Sayer and Vini Poncia for "You Make Me Feel Like Dancing"

5133 **Best Rhythm & Blues Female Solo Vocal:** Thelma Houston for "Don't Leave Me This Way" on Motown

5134 **Best Rhythm & Blues Male Solo Vocal:** Lou Rawls for "Unmistakably Lou" on PIR/Epic

5135 **Best Rhythm & Blues Vocal or Duo Blues Group:** The Emotions for "Best of My Love" on Columbia

5136 **Best Rhythm & Blues Instrumental:** The Brothers Johnson for *Q* on A&M

5137 **Best Comedy:** Steve Martin for *Let's Get Small* on Warner Brothers

5138 **Best Spoken Word:** *The Belle of Amherst* by Julie Harris on Credo

5139 **Best Inspirational:** B.J. Thomas for "Home Where I Belong" on Myrrh/Word

5140 **Best Traditional Gospel:** The Oak Ridge Boys for "Just a Little Talk with Jesus" on Rockland Road

5141 **Best Contemporary Gospel:** The Imperials for "Sail On" on Dayspring/Word

5142 **Best Contemporary Soul Gospel:** Edwin Hawkins and the Edwin Hawkins Singers for "Wonderful" on Birthright

5143 **Best Traditional Soul Gospel:** James Cleveland for *James Cleveland Live at Carnegie Hall* on Savoy

5144 **Best Ethnic or Traditional:** Muddy Waters for *Hard Again* on Blue Sky/CBS

5145 **Best Original Motion Picture Score:** John Williams for *Star Wars* on 20th Century

5146 **Best Original Cast Show Album:** Charles Strouse and Martin Charnin for *Annie* on Columbia

5147 **Best Latin:** Mongo Santamaria for *Dawn* on Vaya

5148 **Best Children:** Christopher Cerf and Jim Timmens for *Aren't You Glad You're You?* on Sesame Street

5149 **Classical Album of the Year:** *Concert of the Century* with Leonard Bernstein, Vladimir Horowitz, Isaac Stern, Mstislav Rostropovich, Dietrick Fischer-Dieskau, Yehudi Menuhin and Lyndon Woodside on Columbia

5150 **Best Classical Orchestra:** Carlo Maria Giulini conducting the Chicago Symphony Orchestra for *Mahler: Symphony No. 9* on DG

5151 **Best Classical Chamber Music:** Juilliard Quartet for *Schönberg: Quartets for Strings* on Columbia

5152 **Best Performance Instrumental Soloists (with Orchestra):** Itzhak Perlman and the London Philharmonic Orchestra for *Vivaldi: The Four Seasons* on Angel

5153 **Best Performance Instrumental Soloists (Without Orchestra):** Artur Rubinstein for *Beethoven: Sonata for Piano No. 18/Schumann: Fantasiestucke* on RCA

5154 **Best Opera:** John de Main conducting the Sherwin M. Goldman/Houston Grand Orchestra for *Gershwin: Porgy and Bess* on RCA

5155 **Best Vocal Soloist:** Janet Baker for *Bach: Arias* on Angel

5156 **Best Classical Choral:** Margaret Hillis choral director of the Chicago Symphony Chorus for *Verdi: Requiem* with Georg Solti conducting the Chicago Symphony Orchestra on RCA

5157 **Best Engineered (Classical):** Kenneth Wilkinson for *Ravel: Bolero* on London

5158 **Best Engineered (Non-Classical):** Roger Nichols, Elliot Scheiner, Bill Schnee and Al Schmitt for *AJA* on ABC

5159 **Best Album Cover (Award to Art Director):** Kosh for *Simple Dreams* on Asylum

5160 **Best Album Notes (Award to Annotator):** George T. Simon for *Bing Crosby: A Legendary Performer* on RCA

5161 **Producer of the Year:** Peter Asher

5162 **Best New Artist of the Year:** Debby Boone on Warner Brothers/Curb

——————— **1 9 7 9** ———————

5163 **Record of the Year:** "Just the Way You Are" by Billy Joel on Columbia

5164 **Album of the Year:** *Saturday Night Fever* by the Bee Gees, David Shire, Yvonne Elliman, Tavares, Kool and the Gang, K.C. and the Sunshine Band, MFSB, the Trammps, Walter Murphy and Ralph MacDonald on RSO

5165 **Song of the Year (Award to the Songwriter):** Billy Joel for "Just the Way You Are"

5166 **Best Contemporary/Pop Male Solo Vocal:** Barry Manilow for "Copacabana (At the Copa)" on Arista

5167 **Best Contemporary/Pop Female Solo Vocal:** Anne Murray for "You Need Me" on Capitol

5168 **Best Contemporary/Pop Vocal Duo or Group:** Bee Gees for "Saturday Night Fever" on RSO

5169 **Best Instrumental Arrangement:** Quincy Jones and Robert Freedman for "The Main Title (Overture Part One)" from *The Wiz Original Soundtrack*" on MCA

5170 **Best Contemporary/Pop Instrumental:** Chuck Mangione Group for "Children of Sanchez" on A&M

5171 **Best Arrangement for Voices (Duo, Group or Chorus):** The Bee Gees for "Stayin' Alive" on RSO

5172 **Best Instrumental Composition:** John Williams for "Close Encounters of the Third Kind"

5173 **Best Accompaniment Arrangement:** Maurice White for "Got to Get You Into My Life" on RSO

5174 **Best Instrumental Jazz Small Group:** Chick Corea for *Friends* on Polydor

5175 **Best Instrumental Jazz Large Group:** Thad Jones and Mel Lewis for *Live in Munich* on Horizon/A&M

5176 **Best Jazz Vocal:** Al Jarreau for "All Fly Home" on Warner Brothers

5177 **Best Jazz Instrumentalist:** Oscar Peterson for *Montreux '77 — Oscar Peterson Jam* on Pablo

5178 **Best Country & Western Song:** Don Schlitz for "The Gambler"

5179 **Best Country & Western Female Vocal:** Dolly Parton for "Here You Come Again" on RCA

5180 **Best Country & Western Male Vocal:** Willie Nelson for "Georgia on My Mind" on Columbia

5181 **Best Country & Western Duo or Group:** Waylon Jennings and Willie Nelson for "Mamas Don't Let Your Babies Grow Up to Be Cowboys" on RCA

5182 **Best Country & Western Instrumental:** Asleep at the Wheel for "One O'Clock Jump" on Capitol

5183 **Best Rhythm & Blues Song:** Paul Jabara for "Last Dance"
5184 **Best Rhythm & Blues Female Solo Vocal:** Donna Summer for "Last Dance" on Casablanca
5185 **Best Rhythm & Blues Male Solo Vocal:** George Benson for "On Broadway" on Warner Brothers
5186 **Best Rhythm & Blues Vocal or Duo Blues Group:** Earth, Wind & Fire for "All 'n All" on Columbia
5187 **Best Rhythm & Blues Instrumental:** Earth, Wind & Fire for "Runnin'" on Columbia
5188 **Best Comedy:** Steve Martin for *A Wild and Crazy Guy* on Warner Brothers
5189 **Best Spoken Word:** *Citizen Kane Soundtrack* by Orson Welles on Mark 56
5190 **Best Inspirational:** B.J. Thomas for "Happy Man" on Myrrh
5191 **Best Traditional Gospel:** The Happy Goodman Family for "Refreshing" on Canaan
5192 **Best Contemporary Gospel:** Larry Hart for "What a Friend" on Genesis
5193 **Best Contemporary Soul Gospel:** Andrae Crouch and the Disciples for *Live in London* on Light
5194 **Best Traditional Soul Gospel:** Mighty Clouds of Joy for *Live and Direct* on ABC
5195 **Best Ethnic or Traditional:** Muddy Waters for *I'm Ready* on Blue Sky
5196 **Best Original Motion Picture Score:** John Williams for *Close Encounters of the Third Kind* on Arista
5197 **Best Original Cast Show Album:** Thomas Z. Shepard for *Ain't Misbehavin'* on RCA Victor Red Seal Records
5198 **Best Latin:** Tito Puente for *Homenaje a Beny More* on Tico
5199 **Best Children:** Jim Henson for *The Muppet Show* on Arista
5200 **Classical Album of the Year:** *Brahms: Concerto for Violin in D Major* Itzhak Perlman with Carlo Maria Giulini conducting the Chicago Symphony Orchestra on Angel
5201 **Best Classical Orchestra:** Herbert von Karajan conducting the Berlin Philharmonic Orchestra for *Beethoven: Symphonies (9)* on DG

5202 **Best Classical Chamber Music:** Itzhak Perlman and Vladimir Ashkenazy for *Beethoven: Sonatas for Violin and Piano* on London
5203 **Best Performance Instrumental Soloists (with Orchestra):** Vladimir Horowitz for *Rachmaninoff: Concerto No. 3 in D Minor for Piano* with Eugene Ormandy conducting the Philadelphia Orchestra on RCA
5204 **Best Performance Instrumental Soloists (Without Orchestra):** Vladimir Horowitz for *The Horowitz Concerts 1977/78* on RCA
5205 **Best Opera:** Julius Rudel conducting the New York City Opera Orchestra and Chorus for *Lehar: The Merry Widow* on Angel
5206 **Best Vocal Soloist:** Luciano Pavarotti for *Luciano Pavarotti: Hits from Lincoln Center* on London
5207 **Best Classical Choral:** Margaret Hillis choral director of the Chicago Symphony Chorus for *Beethoven: Missa Solemnis* with Georg Solti conducting the Chicago Symphony Orchestra on London
5208 **Best Engineered (Classical):** Bud Graham, Arthur Kennedy and Ray Moore for *Varese: Ameriques/Arcana/Ionisation (Boulez Conducts Varese)* on Columbia
5209 **Best Engineered (Non-Classical):** Roger Nichols and Al Schmitt for "FM (No Static at All)" on MCA
5210 **Best Album Cover (Award to Art Director):** Johnny Lee and Tony Lane for *Boys in the Trees* on Elektra
5211 **Best Album Notes (Award to Annotator):** Michael Brooks for *A Bing Crosby Collection, Vols. I and II*
5212 **Producer of the Year:** Bee Gees, Albhy Galuten and Karl Richardson
5213 **Best New Artist of the Year:** A Taste of Honey on Capitol

———————— **1 9 8 0** ————————

5214 **Record of the Year:** "What a Fool Believes" by the Doobie Brothers on Warner Brothers
5215 **Album of the Year:** *52nd Street* by Billy Joel on Columbia
5216 **Song of the Year (Award to the Songwriter):** Kenny Loggins and Michael McDonald for "What a Fool Believes"

5217 **Best Contemporary/Pop Male Solo Vocal:** Billy Joel for "52nd Street" on Columbia

5218 **Best Contemporary/Pop Female Solo Vocal:** Dionne Warwick for "I'll Never Love This Way Again" on Arista

5219 **Best Contemporary/Pop Vocal Duo or Group:** The Doobie Brothers for "Minute by Minute" on Warner Brothers

5220 **Best Instrumental Arrangement:** Claus Ogerman for "Soulful Strut" on Warner Brothers

5221 **Best Contemporary/Pop Instrumental:** Herb Alpert for "Rise" on A&M

5222 **Best Rock Performance for Voices (Duo, Group or Chorus):** The Eagles for "Heartbreak Tonight" on Asylum

5223 **Best Rock Instrumental Performance:** Wings for "Rockstra Theme" on Columbia

5224 **Best Female Rock Performance:** Donna Summer for "Hot Stuff" on Casablanca

5225 **Best Male Rock Performance:** Bob Dylan for "Gotta Serve Somebody" on Columbia

5226 **Best Instrumental Composition:** John Williams for "Main Title Theme from *Superman*"

5227 **Best Accompaniment Arrangement:** Michael McDonald for "What a Fool Believes" on Warner Brothers

5228 **Best Instrumental Jazz Small Group:** Gary Burton and Chick Corea for *Duet* on ECM/Warner Brothers

5229 **Best Instrumental Jazz Large Group:** Duke Ellington for *At Fargo, 1940 Live* on Book-of-the-Month Records

5230 **Best Jazz Vocal:** Ella Fitzgerald for "Fine and Mellow" on Pablo

5231 **Best Jazz Instrumentalist:** Oscar Peterson for "Jousts" on Pablo

5232 **Best Jazz Fusion Performance:** Weather Report for *8:30* on ARC/CBS

5233 **Best Country & Western Song:** Debbie Hupp and Bob Morrison for "You Decorated My Life"

5234 **Best Country & Western Female Vocal:** Emmylou Harris for "Blue Kentucky Girl" on Warner Brothers

5235 **Best Country & Western Male Vocal:** Kenny Rogers for "The Gambler" on United Artists

5236 **Best Country & Western Duo or Group:** The Charlie Daniels Band for "The Devil Went Down to Georgia" on Epic

5237 **Best Country & Western Instrumental:** Doc and Merle Watson for *Big Sandy/Leather Britches* on United Artists

5238 **Best Rhythm & Blues Song:** David Foster, Jay Graydon and Bill Champlin for "After the Love Has Gone"

5239 **Best Rhythm & Blues Female Solo Vocal:** Dionne Warwick for "Deja Vu" on Arista

5240 **Best Rhythm & Blues Male Solo Vocal:** Michael Jackson for "Don't Stop Till You Get Enough" on Epic

5241 **Best Rhythm & Blues Vocal, Duo or Blues Group:** Earth, Wind & Fire for "After the Love Has Gone" on ARC/CBS

5242 **Best Rhythm & Blues Instrumental:** Earth, Wind & Fire for "Boogie Wonderland" on ARC/CBS

5243 **Best Disco Recording:** Gloria Gaynor for "I Will Survive" on Polydor

5244 **Best Comedy:** Robin Williams for *Reality . . . What a Concept* on Casablanca

5245 **Best Spoken Word:** *Ages of Man (Readings from Shakespeare)* by John Gielgud on Caedmon

5246 **Best Inspirational:** B.J. Thomas for "You Gave Me Love (When Nobody Gave Me a Prayer)" on Myrrh

5247 **Best Traditional Gospel:** The Blackwood Brothers for "Lift Up the Name of Jesus" on Skylite

5248 **Best Contemporary Gospel:** The Imperials for "Heed the Call" on Dayspring

5249 **Best Contemporary Soul Gospel:** Andrae Crouch for "I'll Be Thinking of You" on Light

5250 **Best Traditional Soul Gospel:** Mighty Clouds of Joy for "Changing Times" on Epic

5251 **Best Ethnic or Traditional:** Muddy Waters for *Muddy "Mississippi" Waters Live* on Blue Sky/CBS

5252 **Best Original Motion Picture Score:** John Williams for *Superman* on Warner Brothers

5253 **Best Original Cast Show Album:** Stephen Sondheim for *Sweeney Todd* on RCA

5254 **Best Latin:** Irakere for *Irakere* on Columbia

5255 **Best Children:** Jim Henson for *The Muppet Movie* on Atlantic

5256 **Classical Album of the Year:** *Brahms: Symphonies Complete* by the Chicago Symphony Orchestra conducted by Sir Georg Solti on London

5257 **Best Classical Orchestra:** The Chicago Symphony Orchestra conducted by Sir Georg Solti for *Brahms: Symphonies Complete* on London

5258 **Best Classical Chamber Music:** Dennis Russell Davies conducting the St. Paul Chamber Orchestra for *Copland: Appalachian Spring* on Sound 80

5259 **Best Performance Instrumental Soloists (with Orchestra):** Maurizio Pollini for *Bartok: Concertos for Piano Nos. 1 and 2* on DG

5260 **Best Performance Instrumental Soloists (Without Orchestra):** Vladimir Horowitz for *The Horowitz Concerts 1978/79* on RCA

5261 **Best Classical Vocal Soloist:** Luciano Pavarotti for *O Sole Mio* on London

5262 **Best Opera:** Colin Davis conducting the Orchestra and Chorus of the Royal Opera House for *Britten: Peter Grimes* on Philips

5263 **Best Classical Choral:** Margaret Hillis choral director of the Chicago Symphony Chorus for *Brahms: A German Requiem* with Sir Georg Solti conducting the Chicago Symphony Orchestra on London

5264 **Best Engineered (Classical):** Anthony Salvatore for *Sondheim: Sweeney Todd* on RCA

5265 **Best Engineered (Non-Classical):** Peter Henderson for *Breakfast in America* on A&M

5266 **Best Album Cover (Award to Art Director):** Mike Doud and Mick Haggerty for *Breakfast in America* on A&M

5267 **Best Album Notes (Award to Annotator):** Bob Porter and James Patrick for *Charlie Parker: The Complete Savoy Sessions* on Savoy

5268 **Best Historical Reissue:** Michael Brooks and Jerry Korn for *Billie Holiday (Giants of Jazz)* on Time Life

5269 **Non-Classical Producer of the Year:** Larry Butler

5270 **Classical Producer of the Year:** James Mallinson

5271 **Best New Artist of the Year:** Rickie Lee Jones on Warner Brothers

———————— **1981** ————————

5272 **Record of the Year:** "Sailing" by Christopher Cross on Warner Brothers

5273 **Album of the Year:** *Christopher Cross* by Christopher Cross on Warner Brothers

5274 **Song of the Year (Award to the Songwriter):** Christopher Cross for "Sailing"

5275 **Best Contemporary/Pop Male Solo Vocal:** Kenny Loggins for "This Is It" on Columbia

5276 **Best Contemporary/Pop Female Solo Vocal:** Bette Midler for "The Rose" on Atlantic

5277 **Best Contemporary/Pop Vocal Duo or Group:** Barbra Streisand and Barry Gibb for "Guilty" on Columbia

5278 **Best Instrumental Arrangement:** Quincy Jones and Jerry Hey for "Dinorah, Dinorah" on Warner Brothers

5279 **Best Contemporary/Pop Instrumental:** Bob James and Earl Klugh for "One on One" on Columbia

5280 **Best Arrangement for Voices (Duo, Group or Chorus):** Janis Siegel for *Birdland* on Atlantic

5281 **Best Rock Instrumental Performance:** The Police for "Regatta de Blanc" on A&M

5282 **Best Female Rock Performance:** Pat Benatar for "Crimes of Passion" on Chrysalis

5283 **Best Male Rock Performance:** Billy Joel for "Glass Houses" on Columbia

5284 **Best Rock Performance by a Duo or Group with Vocal:** Bob Seger and the Silver Bullet Band for "Against the Wind" on Capitol

5285 **Best Instrumental Composition:** John Williams for *The Empire Strikes Back*

5286 **Best Accompanying Arrangement:** Michael Omartian and Christopher Cross for "Sailing" on Warner Brothers

5287 **Best Instrumental Jazz Small Group:** Bill Evans for *We Shall Meet Again* on Warner Brothers

5288 **Best Instrumental Jazz Large Group:** Count Basie and His Orchestra for *On the Road* on Pablo

5289 **Best Female Jazz Vocal:** Ella Fitzgerald for *A Perfect Match/Ella and Basie* on Pablo

5290 **Best Male Jazz Vocal:** George Benson for "Moody's Mood" on Q West/Warner Brothers

5291 **Best Jazz Instrumentalist:** Bill Evans for "I Will Say Goodbye" on Warner Brothers

5292 **Best Jazz Fusion Performance:** Manhattan Transfer for "Birdland" on Atlantic

5293 **Best Country & Western Song:** "On the Road Again" by Willie Nelson

5294 **Best Country & Western Female Vocal:** "Could I Have This Dance" by Anne Murray on Capitol

5295 **Best Country & Western Male Vocal:** "He Stopped Loving Her Today" by George Jones on Epic

5296 **Best Country & Western Duo or Group:** Roy Orbison and Emmylou Harris for "That Lovin' You Feelin' Again" on Warner Brothers

5297 **Best Country & Western Instrumental:** Gilley's "Urban Cowboy" Band for *Orange Blossom Special/Hoedown* on Full Moon/Asylum

5298 **Best Rhythm & Blues Song:** Reggie Lucas and James Mtume for "Never Knew Love Like This Before"

5299 **Best Rhythm & Blues Female Solo Vocal:** Stephanie Mills for "Never Knew Love Like This Before" on 20th Century

5300 **Best Rhythm & Blues Male Solo Vocal:** George Benson for "Give Me the Night" on Q West/Warner Brothers

5301 **Best Rhythm & Blues Vocal or Duo Blues Group:** The Manhattans for "Shining Star" on Columbia

5302 **Best Rhythm & Blues Instrumental:** George Benson for "Off Broadway" on Q West/Warner Brothers

5303 **Best Comedy:** Rodney Dangerfield for *No Respect* on Casablanca

5304 **Best Spoken Word:** *Gertrude Stein, Gertrude Stein, Gertrude Stein* by Pat Carroll on Caedmon

5305 **Best Inspirational:** Debby Boone for "With My Song I Will Praise Him" on Lamb & Lion

5306 **Best Traditional Gospel:** The Blackwood Brothers for "We Come to Worship" on Voice Box

5307 **Best Contemporary Gospel:** Reba Rambo, Dony McGuire, B.J. Thomas, Andrae Crouch, the Archers, Cynthia Clawson, Walter and Tramaine Hawkins for *The Lord's Prayer* on Light

5308 **Best Contemporary Soul Gospel:** Shirley Caesar for "Rejoice" on Myrrh

5309 **Best Traditional Soul Gospel:** James Cleveland and the Charles Ford Singers for "Lord, Let Me Be an Instrument" on Savoy

5310 **Best Ethnic or Traditional:** Dr. Isiah Ross, Big Joe Williams, Maxwell Street Jimmy, Son House, Rev. Robert Wilkins, Little Brother Montgomery and Sunnyland Slim for *Rare Blues* on Takoma

5311 **Best Original Motion Picture Score:** John Williams for *The Empire Strikes Back* on RSO

5312 **Best Original Cast Show Album:** Andrew Lloyd Webber and Tim Rice for *Evita — Premier American Recording* on MCA

5313 **Best Latin:** Cal Tjader for *La Onda Va Bien* on Concord Jazz

5314 **Best Children:** The Doobie Brothers, James Taylor, Carly Simon, Bette Midler, the Muppets, Al Jarreau, Linda Ronstadt, Wendy Waldman, Libby Titus & Dr. John, Livingston Taylor, George Benson & Pauline Wilson, Lucy Simon, Kate Taylor and the Simon/Taylor Family for *In Harmony/ A Sesame Street Record* on Sesame Street/Warner Brothers

5315 **Classical Album of the Year:** *Berg: Lulu (Complete Version)* with Pierre Boulez conducting the Orchestre de l'Opera de Paris on DG

5316 **Best Classical Orchestra:** The Chicago Symphony Orchestra conducted by Sir Georg Solti for *Bruckner: Symphony No. 6 in A Major* on London

5317 **Best Classical Chamber Music:** Itzhak Perlman and Pinchas Zukerman for *Music for Two Violins (Moszkowski: Suite for Two Violins/Shostakovich: Duets/Prokofiev: Sonata for Two Violins)* on Angel

5318 **Best Performance Instrumental Soloists (with Orchestra):** Itzhak Perlman for *Berg: Concerto for Violin and Orchestra/Stravinsky: Concerto in D Major* *for Violin and Orchestra* with Seiji Ozawa conducting the Boston Symphony Orchestra on DG and Itzhak Perlman and Mstislav Rostropovich for *Brahms: Concerto in A Minor for Violin and Cello (Double Concerto)* with Haitink conducting the Concert-Gebouw Orchestra on Angel

5319 Best Performance Instrumental Soloists (Without Orchestra): Itzhak Perlman for *The Spanish Album* on Angel

5320 Best Classical Vocal Soloist: Leontyne Price for *Prima Donna, Volume 5 Great Soprano Arias from Handel to Britten* with Henry Lewis conducting the Philharmonia Orchestra on RCA

5321 Best Opera: Pierre Boulez conducting the Orchestre de l'Opera de Paris for *Berg: Lulu (Complete Version)* on DG

5322 Best Classical Choral: Norbert Balatsch chorus master of the Philharmonia Orchestra and Chorus for *Mozart: Requiem* with Carlo Maria Giulini conducting on Angel

5323 Best Engineered (Classical): Karl-August Naegler for *Berg: Lulu (Complete Version)* on DG

5324 Best Engineered (Non-Classical): James Guthrie for *The Wall* on Columbia

5325 Best Album Cover (Award to Art Director): Roy Kohara for *Against the Wind* on Capitol

5326 Best Album Note (Award to Annotator): David McClintock for *Trilogy: Past, Present and Future* on Reprise/ Warner Brothers

5327 Best Historical Reissue: Keith Hardwick for *Segovia — The EMI Recordings 1927-39* on Angel

5328 Non-Classical Producer of the Year: Phil Ramone

5329 Classical Producer of the Year: Robert Woods

5330 Best New Artist of the Year: Christopher Cross on Warner Brothers

----------- **1982** -----------

5331 Record of the Year: "Bette Davis Eyes" by Kim Carnes on EMI/America

5332 Album of the Year: *Double Fantasy* by John Lennon and Yoko Ono on Geffen/Warner Brothers

5333 Song of the Year (Award to the Songwriter): Donna Weiss and Jackie DeShannon for "Bette Davis Eyes"

5334 Best Contemporary/Pop Male Solo Vocal: Al Jarreau for *Breakin' Away* on Warner Brothers

5335 Best Contemporary/Pop Female Solo Vocal: Lena Horne for *Lena Horne: The Lady and Her Music Live on Broadway* on Q West/Warner Brothers

5336 Best Contemporary/Pop Vocal Duo or Group with Vocal: The Manhattan Transfer for "Boy from New York City" on Atlantic

5337 Best Instrumental Arrangement: Quincy Jones and Johnny Mandel for "Velas" on A&M

5338 Best Contemporary/Pop Instrumental: Mike Post featuring Larry Carlton for "Theme from *Hill Street Blues*" on Elektra/Asylum

5339 Best Arrangement for Voices (Duo, Group or Chorus): Quincy Jones and Jerry Hey for *Al No Corrida* on A&M

5340 Best Rock Instrumental Performance: The Police for "Behind My Camel" on A&M

5341 Best Female Rock Performance: Pat Benatar for "Fire and Ice" on Chrysalis

5342 Best Male Rock Performance: Rick Springfield for "Jessie's Girl" on RCA

5343 Best Rock Performance by a Duo or Group with Vocal: The Police for "Don't Stand So Close to Me" on A&M

5344 Best Instrumental Arrangement Accompanying Vocals: Mike Post for the "Theme from *Hill Street Blues*"

5345 Best Vocal Arrangement for Two or More Voices: Gene Puerling for "A Nightingale Sang in Berkeley Square" on Atlantic

5346 Best Instrumental Jazz Small Group: Chick Corea and Gary Burton for *Chick Corea and Gary Burton in Concert, Zurich, October 28, 1979* on ECM

5347 Best Instrumental Jazz Large Group: Gerry Mulligan and His Orchestra for *Walk on the Water* on DRG

5348 Best Female Jazz Vocal: Ella Fitzgerald for "Digital III at Montreux" on Pablo Live

5349 Best Male Jazz Vocal: Al Jarreau for "Blue Rondo a la Turk" on Warner Brothers

5350 **Best Jazz Instrumentalist:** John Coltrane for "Bye Bye Blackbird" on Pablo

5351 **Best Duo or Group Jazz Vocal Performance:** The Manhattan Transfer

5352 **Best Jazz Fusion Performance:** Grover Washington, Jr., for "Winelight" on Elektra/Asylum

5353 **Best Country & Western Song:** "9 to 5" by Dolly Parton

5354 **Best Country & Western Female Vocal:** "9 to 5" by Dolly Parton

5355 **Best Country & Western Male Vocal:** Ronnie Milsap for "(There's) No Gettin' Over Me" on RCA

5356 **Best Country & Western Duet, Trio or Group:** The Oak Ridge Boys for "Elvira" on MCA

5357 **Best Country & Western Instrumental:** Chet Atkins for "Country— After All These Years" on RCA

5358 **Best Rhythm & Blues Song:** Bill Withers, William Salter and Ralph MacDonald for "Just the Two of Us"

5359 **Best Rhythm & Blues Female Solo Vocal:** Aretha Franklin for "Hold On I'm Comin'" on Arista

5360 **Best Rhythm & Blues Male Solo Vocal:** James Ingram for "One Hundred Ways" on A&M

5361 **Best Rhythm & Blues Vocal or Duo Blues Group:** Quincy Jones for *The Dude* on A&M

5362 **Best Rhythm & Blues Instrumental:** David Sanborn for "All I Need Is You" on Warner Brothers

5363 **Best Comedy:** Richard Pryor for *Rev. Du Rite* on Laff

5364 **Best Spoken Word:** *Donovan's Brain* by Orson Welles on Radiola

5365 **Best Inspirational:** B.J. Thomas for "Amazing Grace" on Myrrh/Word

5366 **Best Traditional Gospel:** J.D. Sumner, Hovie Lister, James Blackwood, Rosie Rozell and Jake Hess for *The Masters V* on Skylite

5367 **Best Contemporary Gospel:** The Imperials for "Priority" on Dayspring/ Word

5368 **Best Contemporary Soul Gospel:** Andrae Crouch for "Don't Give Up" on Warner Brothers

5369 **Best Traditional Soul Gospel:** Al Green for "The Lord Will Make a Way" on Hi-Myrrh/Word

5370 **Best Ethnic or Traditional:** B.B. King for *There Must Be a Better World Somewhere* on MCA

5371 **Best Original Motion Picture Score:** John Williams for *Raiders of the Lost Ark*

5372 **Best Original Cast Show Album:** Quincy Jones for *Lena Horne: The Lady and Her Music Live on Broadway*

5373 **Best Latin:** Clare Fischer for *Guajira Pa' la Jeva* on Pause

5374 **Best Children:** The Muppets, Glen Campbell, Crystal Gayle, Loretta Lynn, Tanya Tucker and Jim Henson for *Sesame Street* on Sesame Street

5375 **Classical Album of the Year:** *Mahler: Symphony No. 2 in C Minor* with Sir Georg Solti conducting the Chicago Symphony Orchestra on London

5376 **Best Classical Orchestra:** The Chicago Symphony Orchestra conducted by Sir Georg Solti for *Mahler: Symphony No. 2 in C Minor* on London

5377 **Best Classical Chamber Music:** Itzhak Perlman, Lynn Harrell and Vladimir Ashkenazy for *Tchaikovsky: Piano Trio in A Minor* on Angel

5378 **Best Performance Instrumental Soloists (with Orchestra):** Itzhak Perlman, Isaac Stern and Pinchas Zukerman for *Isaac Stern 60th Anniversary Celebration* with Zubin Mehta conducting the New York Philharmonic Orchestra on CBS

5379 **Best Performance Instrumental Soloists (Without Orchestra):** Vladimir Horowitz for *The Horowitz Concerts 1979–1980* on RCA

5380 **Best Opera:** Sir Charles Mackerras conducting the Vienna Philharmonic Orchestra for *Janacek: From the House of the Dead* on London

5381 **Best Vocal Soloist:** Joan Sutherland, Marilyn Horne and Luciano Pavarotti for *Live from Lincoln Center— Sutherland—Horne—Pavarotti* on London

5382 **Best Classical Choral:** Neville Marriner conducting the Chorus of the Academy of St. Martin-in-the-Fields for *Haydn: The Creation* on Philips

5383 **Best Engineered (Classical):** Bud Graham, Ray Moore and Andrew Kazdan for *Isaac Stern 60th Anniversary Celebration* on CBS

5384 **Best Engineered (Non-Classical):** Bill Schnee and Jerry Garszva for *Gaucho* on MCA

5385 **Best Album Cover (Award to Art Director):** Peter Corriston for *Tatoo You* on Rolling Stones/Atlantic

5386 **Best Album Notes (Award to Annotator):** Dan Morgenstern for *Errol Garner: Master of the Keyboard* on Book-of-the-Month Records

5387 **Best Historical Album:** George Spitzer and Michael Brooks for *Hoagy Carmichael from "Star Dust" to "Ole Buttermilk Sky"* on Book-of-the-Month Records

5388 **Non-Classical Producer of the Year:** Quincy Jones

5389 **Classical Producer of the Year:** James Mallinson

5390 **Best New Artist of the Year:** Sheena Easton on EMI/America

5391 **Best Video of the Year:** Michael Nesmith for *Michael Nesmith in Elephant Parts* on Pacific Arts Video

———— **1 9 8 3** ————

5392 **Record of the Year:** "Rosanna" by Toto on Columbia

5393 **Album of the Year:** *Toto IV* by Toto on Columbia

5394 **Song of the Year (Award to the Songwriter):** Johnny Christopher, Mark James and Wayne Carson for "Always on My Mind"

5395 **Best Contemporary/Pop Male Solo Vocal:** Lionel Richie for "Truly" on Motown

5396 **Best Contemporary/Pop Female Solo Vocal:** Melissa Manchester for "You Should Hear How She Talks About You" on Arista

5397 **Best Contemporary/Pop Vocal Duo or Group with Vocal:** Joe Cocker and Jennifer Warnes for "Up Where We Belong"

5398 **Best Instrumental Arrangement:** John Williams for "Flying" (The Theme from *E.T., the Extra-Terrestrial*) on MCA

5399 **Best Contemporary/Pop Instrumental:** Ernie Watts for the dance version of the "Theme from *Chariots of Fire*" on Qwest/Warner Brothers

5400 **Best Arrangement for Voices (Duo, Group or Chorus):** David Paich for *Rosanna* on Columbia

5401 **Best Rock Instrumental Performance:** A Flock of Seagulls for "D.N.A." on Jive/Arista

5402 **Best Female Rock Performance:** Pat Benatar for "Shadows of the Night" on Chrysalis

5403 **Best Male Rock Performance:** John Cougar for "Hurts So Good" on Riva/Polygram

5404 **Best Rock Performance by a Duo or Group with Vocal:** Survivor for "Eye of the Tiger" on Scotti Brothers/CBS

5405 **Best Instrumental Arrangement Accompanying Vocals:** Jerry Hey, David Paich and Jeff Porcaro for "Rosanna" on Columbia

5406 **Best Instrumental Composition:** John Williams for "Flying (The Theme from *E.T., the Extra-Terrestrial*)

5407 **Best Instrumental Jazz Small Group:** The Phil Woods Quartet for *"More" Live* on Adelphi

5408 **Best Instrumental Jazz Large Group:** Count Basie and His Orchestra for *Warm Breeze* on Pablo Today

5409 **Best Female Jazz Vocal:** Sarah Vaughan for *Gershwin Live!* on CBS

5410 **Best Male Jazz Vocal:** Mel Tormé for *An Evening with George Shearing and Mel Tormé* on Concord Jazz

5411 **Best Jazz Instrumentalist:** Miles Davis for "We Want Miles" on Columbia

5412 **Best Duo or Group Jazz Vocal Performance:** The Manhattan Transfer for "Route 66" on Atlantic

5413 **Best Jazz Fusion Performance:** Pat Metheny Group for *Offramp* on ECM/Warner Brothers

5414 **Best Country & Western Song:** "Always on My Mind" by Wayne Carson, Johnny Christopher and Mark James

5415 **Best Country & Western Female Vocal:** "Break It Gently" by Juice Newton on Capitol

5416 **Best Country & Western Male Vocal:** Willie Nelson for "Always on My Mind" on Columbia

5417 **Best Country & Western Duet, Trio or Group:** Alabama for "Mountain Music" on RCA

5418 **Best Country & Western Instrumental:** Roy Clark for "Alabama Jubilee" on Churchill

5419 Best Rhythm & Blues Song: Jay Graydon, Steve Lukather and Bill Champlin for "Turn Your Love Around"

5420 Best Rhythm & Blues Female Solo Vocal: Jennifer Holliday for "And I Am Telling You I'm Not Going" on Geffen/Warner Brothers

5421 Best Rhythm & Blues Male Solo Vocal: Marvin Gaye for "Sexual Healing" on Columbia

5422 Best Rhythm & Blues Performance by a Vocal or Duo Blues Group: Dazz Band for "Let It Whip" on Motown, and Earth, Wind & Fire for "Wanna Be With You" on ARC/CBS

5423 Best Rhythm & Blues Instrumental: Marvin Gaye for "Sexual Healing" on Columbia

5424 Best Traditional Blues: Clarence Gatemouth Brown for *Alright Again* on Rounder

5425 Best Comedy: Richard Pryor for *Live on Sunset Strip* on Warner Brothers

5426 Best Spoken Word, Documentary or Drama Recording: *Raiders of the Lost Ark: The Movie on Record* by Tom Voegeli on Columbia

5427 Best Inspirational: Barbara Mandrell for "He Set My Life to Music" on Songbird/MCA

5428 Best Traditional Gospel: The Blackwood Brothers for "I'm Following You" on Voice Box

5429 Best Contemporary Gospel: Amy Grant for "Age to Age" on Myrrh/Word

5430 Best Contemporary Soul Gospel: Al Green for "Higher Plane" on Myrrh/Word

5431 Best Traditional Soul Gospel: Al Green for "Precious Lord" by Myrrh/Word

5432 Best Ethnic or Traditional Folk: Queen Ida for *Queen Ida and the Ben Temps Zydeco Band on Tour* on GNP/Crescendo

5433 Best Original Motion Picture Score: John Williams for *E.T., the Extra-Terrestrial*

5434 Best Original Cast Show Album: Tom Eyen and Henry Krieger for *Dreamgirls* on Geffen/Warner Brothers

5435 Best Latin: Machito for *Machito and His Salsa Big Band '82* on Timeless

5436 Best Children: Billy Joel, Bruce Springsteen, James Taylor, Kenny Loggins, Carly and Lucy Simon, Teddy Pendergrass, Crystal Gayle, Lou Rawls, Deniece Williams, Janis Ian and Dr. John for *In Harmony* on CBS

5437 Classical Album of the Year: *Bach: The Goldberg Variations* by Glenn Gould on CBS

5438 Best Classical Orchestra: The Chicago Symphony Orchestra conducted by James Levine for *Mahler: Symphony No. 7 in E Minor* on RCA

5439 Best Classical Chamber Music: Richard Stoltzman and Richard Goode for *Brahms: The Sonatas for Clarinet and Piano Op. 120* on RCA

5440 Best Performance Instrumental Soloists (with Orchestra): Itzhak Perlman for *Elgar: Concerto for Violin in B Minor* with Daniel Barenboim conducting the Chicago Symphony Orchestra on DG

5441 Best Performance Instrumental Soloists (Without Orchestra): Glenn Gould for *Bach: The Goldberg Variations* on CBS

5442 Best Classical Vocal Soloist: Leontyne Price for *Leontyne Price Sings Verdi* with Zubin Mehta conducting the Israel Philharmonic Orchestra on London

5443 Best Opera: Pierre Boulez conducting the Bayreuth Festival Orchestra for *Wagner: Der Ring Des Nibelungen* on Philips

5444 Best Classical Choral: Margaret Hillis chorus director for the Chicago Symphony Chorus for *Berlioz: The Damnation of Faust* with Sir Georg Solti conducting the Chicago Symphony Orchestra on London

5445 Best Engineered (Classical): Paul Goodman for *Mahler: Symphony No. 7 in E Minor* on RCA

5446 Best Engineered (Non-Classical): Al Schmitt, Tom Knox, Greg Ladanyi and David Leonard for *Toto IV* on Columbia

5447 Best Album Cover (Award to Art Director): Kosh and Ron Larson for *Get Closer* on Elektra/Asylum

5448 Best Album Notes (Award to Annotator): John Chilton and Richard Sudhalter for *Bunny Berrigan (Giants of Jazz)* on Time Life

5449 **Best Historical Album:** Alan Dell, Ethel Gabriel and Don Wardell on *The Tommy Dorsey/Frank Sinatra Sessions Vols. 1, 2, & 3*

5450 **Non-Classical Producer of the Year:** Toto

5451 **Classical Producer of the Year:** Robert Woods

5452 **Best New Artist of the Year:** Men at Work on Columbia

5453 **Best Video of the Year:** Olivia Newton-John for *Olivia Physical* on MCA Video

——————— **1 9 8 4** ———————

5454 **Record of the Year:** "Beat It" by Michael Jackson on Epic/CBS

5455 **Album of the Year:** *Thriller* by Michael Jackson on Epic/CBS

5456 **Song of the Year (Award to the Songwriter):** Sting for "Every Breath You Take"

5457 **Best Contemporary/Pop Male Solo Vocal:** Michael Jackson for "Thriller" on Epic/CBS

5458 **Best Contemporary/Pop Female Solo Vocal:** Irene Cara for "Flashdance ... What a Feeling" on Casablanca/Polygram

5459 **Best Contemporary/Pop Vocal Duo or Group with Vocal:** The Police for "Every Breath You Take" on A&M

5460 **Best Instrumental Arrangement:** Dave Grusin for "Summer Sketches '82" on GRP

5461 **Best Contemporary/Pop Instrumental:** George Benson for "Being with You" on Warner Brothers

5462 **Best Instrumental Arrangement Accompanying Voices:** Nelson Riddle for "What's New" on Asylum/EA

5463 **Best Rock Instrumental Performance:** Sting for "Brimstone & Treacle" on A&M

5464 **Best Female Rock Performance:** Pat Benatar for "Love Is a Battlefield" on Chrysalis

5465 **Best Male Rock Performance:** Michael Jackson for "Beat It" on Epic/CBS

5466 **Best Rock Performance by a Duo or Group with Vocal:** The Police for "Synchronicity" on A&M

5467 **Best Vocal Arrangement for Two or More Voices:** Arif Mardin and Chaka Khan for "Be Bop Medley" on Warner Brothers

5468 **Best Instrumental Composition:** Giorgio Moroder for "Love Theme from *Flashdance*"

5469 **Best Instrumental Jazz Small Group:** The Phil Woods Quartet for *At the Vanguard* on Antilles/Island

5470 **Best Instrumental Jazz Large Group:** Rob McConnell and the Boss Brass for *All in Good Time* on Dark Orchid

5471 **Best Female Jazz Vocal:** Ella Fitzgerald for "The Best Is Yet to Come" on Pablo Today

5472 **Best Male Jazz Vocal:** Mel Tormé for "Top Drawer" on Concord Jazz

5473 **Best Jazz Instrumentalist:** Wynton Marsalis for *Think of One* on Columbia

5474 **Best Duo or Group Jazz Vocal Performance:** The Manhattan Transfer for "Why Not?" on Atlantic

5475 **Best Jazz Fusion Performance:** Pat Metheny Group for *Travels* on ECM/Warner Brothers

5476 **Best Country & Western Song:** "Stranger in My House" by Mike Reid

5477 **Best Country & Western Female Vocal:** "A Little Good News" by Anne Murray on Capitol

5478 **Best Country & Western Male Vocal:** Lee Greenwood for "I.O.U." on MCA

5479 **Best Country & Western Duet, Trio or Group:** Alabama for *Alabama* on RCA

5480 **Best Country & Western Instrumental:** The New South (Ricky Skaggs, Tony Rice, Jerry Douglas, J.D. Crowe and Todd Philips) for "Fireball" on Sugar Hill

5481 **Best Rhythm & Blues Song:** Michael Jackson for "Billie Jean"

5482 **Best Rhythm & Blues Female Solo Vocal:** Chaka Khan for "Chaka Khan" on Warner Brothers

5483 **Best Rhythm & Blues Male Solo Vocal:** Michael Jackson for "Billie Jean" on Epic/CBS

5484 **Best Rhythm & Blues Performance by a Vocal or Duo Blues Group:** Rufus and Chaka Khan for "Ain't Nobody" on Warner Brothers

5485 Best Rhythm & Blues Instrumental: Herbie Hancock for *Rockit* on Columbia

5486 Best Traditional Blues: B.B. King for *Blues and Jazz* on MCA

5487 Best Comedy: Eddie Murphy for *Eddie Murphy: Comedian* on the Entertainment Company/Columbia

5488 Best Spoken Word or Non-Musical Recording: *Copland: Lincoln Portrait* by William Warfield on Mercury/Philips

5489 Best Inspirational: Donna Summer for *He's a Rebel* on Mercury/Polygram

5490 Best Female Gospel: Amy Grant for *Ageless Medley* on Myrrh/Word

5491 Best Male Gospel: Russ Taff for *Walls of Glass* on Myrrh/Word

5492 Best Gospel Performance by a Duo or Group: Sandi Patti and Larnelle Harris for *More Than Wonderful* on Impact/Benson

5493 Best Female Soul Gospel: Sandra Crouch for *We Sing Praises* on Light/Lexicon

5494 Best Male Soul Gospel: Al Green for *I'll Rise Again* on Myrrh/Word

5495 Best Soul Gospel by a Duo or Group: Bobby Jones and New Life with Barbara Mandrell for *I'm So Glad I'm Standing Here Today* on Myrrh/Word

5496 Best Original Motion Picture Score: Giorgio Moroder, Keith Forsey, Irene Cara, Shandi Sinnamon, Ronald Magness, Douglas Cotler, Richard Gilbert, Michael Boddicker, Jerry Hey, Phil Ramone, Michael Sembello, Kim Carnes, Duane Hitchings, Craig Krampf and Dennis Matosky for *Flashdance* on Casablanca/Polygram

5497 Best Original Cast Show Album: Andrew Lloyd Webber for *Cats* on Geffen/Warner Brothers

5498 Best Latin: Jose Feliciano for *Me Enamore* on Profono/TPI

5499 Best Tropical Latin: Tito Puente and His Latin Ensemble for *On Broadway* on Concord Picante

5500 Best Mexican/American: Los Lobos for *Anselma* on Slash/Warner Brothers

5501 Best Ethnic or Traditional Folk: Clifton Chenier and His Red Hot Louisiana Band for *I'm Here* on Alligator

5502 Best Children: Quincy Jones for *E.T., the Extra-Terrestrial* with Michael Jackson, Narration and Vocals on MCA

5503 Classical Album of the Year: *Mahler: Symphony No. 9 in D Major* with Sir Georg Solti conducting the Chicago Symphony Orchestra on London

5504 Best Classical Orchestra: The Chicago Symphony Orchestra conducted by Sir Georg Solti for *Mahler: Symphony No. 9 in D Major* on London

5505 Best Classical Chamber Music: Mstislav Rostropovich and Rudolf Serkin for *Brahms: Sonata for Cello and Piano in E Minor, Op. 38 & Sonata in F Major, Op. 99* on DG

5506 Best Performance Instrumental Soloists (with Orchestra): Wynton Marsalis for *Haydn: Concerto for Trumpet and Orchestra in E-Flat Major; Mozart: Concerto for Trumpet and Orchestra in D Major; Hummel: Concerto for Trumpet and Orchestra in E-Flat Major* on CBS

5507 Best Performance Instrumental Soloists (Without Orchestra): Glenn Gould for *Beethoven: Sonata for Piano No. 12 in A-Flat Major, Op. 26 and No. 13 in E-Flat Major, Op. 27, No. 1* on CBS

5508 Best Classical Vocal Soloist: Leontyne Price and Marilyn Horne for *Leontyne Price and Marilyn Horne in Concert at the Met* on RCA

5509 Best Opera Recordings: Sir Georg Solti conducting for *Mozart: Le nozze di Figaro* on London and James Levine conducting for *Verdi: La Traviata* on Elektra

5510 Best Classical Choral: Margaret Hillis chorus director for the Chicago Symphony Chorus for *Haydn: The Creation* with Sir Georg Solti conducting the Chicago Symphony Orchestra on London

5511 Best Engineered (Classical): James Lock for *Mahler: Symphony No. 9 in D Minor* on London

5512 Best Engineered (Non-Classical): Bruce Swedien for *Thriller* on Epic/CBS

5513 Best Album Cover (Award to Art Director): Robert Rauschenberg for *Speaking in Tongues* on Sire/Warner Brothers

5514 Best Album Notes (Award to Annotator): Orrin Keepnews for *The "Interplay" Sessions* on Milestone

5515 **Best Historical Album:** Stanley Walker and Allan Steckler for *The Greatest Recordings of Arturo Toscanini Symphonies Vol. 1* on Franklin Mint

5516 **Non-Classical Producers of the Year:** Quincy Jones and Michael Jackson

5517 **Classical Producers of the Year:** Marc J. Aubort and Joanna Nickrenz

5518 **Best New Artist of the Year:** Culture Club on Epic/CBS

5519 **Best Short Form Video of the Year:** Duran Duran for *Girls on Film/Hungry Like a Wolf* on Picture Music International/Thorne

5520 **Best Video Album:** Duran Duran for *Duran Duran* on Picture Music International/Thorne EMI/Pioneer Artists

—————— **1 9 8 5** ——————

5521 **Record of the Year:** "What's Love Got to Do with It" by Tina Turner, produced by Terry Britten on Capitol Records

5522 **Album of the Year:** *Can't Slow Down* by Lionel Richie, album producers Lionel Richie and James Anthony Carmichael on Motown Records

5523 **Song of the Year:** "What's Love Got to Do with It" by Tina Turner, songwriters Graham Lyle and Terry Britten

5524 **Best New Artist:** Cyndi Lauper on Portrait/CBS Records

5525 **Best Female Pop Vocal Performance:** "What's Love Got to Do with It" by Tina Turner on Capitol Records

5526 **Best Male Pop Vocal Performance:** "Against All Odds (Take a Look at Me Now)" by Phil Collins on Atlantic Records

5527 **Best Duo or Group with Vocal Pop Performance:** "Jump (for My Love)" by the Pointer Sisters on Planet/RCA Records

5528 **Best Pop Instrumental Performance:** "Ghostbusters" (Instrumental Version) (track from movie *Ghostbusters*) by Ray Parker, Jr., on Arista Records

5529 **Best Female Rock Vocal Performance:** "Better Be Good to Me" by Tina Turner on Capitol Records

5530 **Best Male Rock Vocal Performance:** "Dancing in the Dark" by Bruce Springsteen on Columbia Records

5531 **Best Duo or Group Vocal Rock Performance:** *Purple Rain Music from the Motion Picture* by Prince and the Revolution on Warner Brothers Records

5532 **Best Rock Instrumental Performance:** "Cinema" (track from *90125*) by Yes on Atco/Atlantic Records

5533 **Best Female Rhythm & Blues Vocal Performance:** "I Feel for You" by Chaka Khan on Warner Brothers Records

5534 **Best Male Rhythm & Blues Vocal Performance:** "Caribbean Queen (No More Love on the Run)" by Billy Ocean on Jive/Arista Records

5535 **Best Duo or Group with Vocal Rhythm & Blues Performance:** "Yah Mo B There" by James Ingram and Michael McDonald on Qwest/Warner Brothers Records

5536 **Best Rhythm & Blues Instrumental Performance:** *Sound-System* by Herbie Hancock on Columbia Records

5537 **Best New Rhythm & Blues Song:** "I Feel for You" performed and written by Prince

5538 **Best Vocal or Instrumental Jazz Fusion Performance:** *First Circle* by the Pat Metheny Group on ECM/Warner Brothers Records

5539 **Best Female Country Vocal Performance:** "In My Dreams" by Emmylou Harris on Warner Brothers Records

5540 **Best Male Country Vocal Performance:** "That's the Way Love Goes" by Merle Haggard on Epic/CBS Records

5541 **Best Duo or Group with Vocal Group Performance:** "Mama, He's Crazy" by the Judds on RCA Records

5542 **Best Country Instrumental Performance:** "Wheel Hoss" (track from *Country Boy*) by Ricky Skaggs on Columbia Records

5543 **Best Country Song:** "City of New Orleans" by Steve Goodman

5544 **Best Female Gospel Performance:** "Angels" (track from *Straight Ahead*) by Amy Grant on Myrrh/Word Records

5545 **Best Male Gospel Performance:** *Michael W. Smith* by Michael W. Smith on Reunion/Word Records

5546 **Best Duo or Group Gospel Performance:** "Keep the Flame Burning" (track from *Debby Boone Surrender*) by Debby Boone and Phil Driscoll on Lamb & Lion/Sparrow Records

5547 **Best Female Soul Gospel Performance:** *Sailin'* by Shirley Caesar on Myrrh/Word Records

5548 **Best Male Soul Gospel Performance:** "Always Remember" (track from *No Time to Lose*) by Andrae Crouch on Light/Lexicon Records

5549 **Best Duo or Group Soul Gospel Performance:** "Sailin' on the Sea of Your Love" (track from *Sailin'*) by Shirley Caesar and Al Green on Myrrh/Word Records

5550 **Best Inspirational Performance:** "Forgive Me" (track from *Cats Without Claws*) by Donna Summer on Geffen/Warner Brothers Records

5551 **Best Latin Pop Performance:** *Always in My Heart (Siempre en mi Corazon)* by Placido Domingo on CBS Masterworks Records

5552 **Best Tropical Latin Performance:** *Palo Pa Rumba* by Eddie Palmieri on Musica Latina International Records

5553 **Best Mexican/American Performance:** "Me Gustas Tal Como Eres" by Sheena Easton and Luis Miguel on Top Hits Records

5554 **Best Traditional Blues Recording:** *Blues Explosion* by John Hammond, Stevie Ray Vaughan & Double Trouble, Sugar Blue, Koko Taylor & the Blues Machine, Luther "Guitar Junior" Johnson, J.B. Hutto & the Night Hawks on Atlantic Records

5555 **Best Ethnic or Traditional Folk Recording:** *Elizabeth Cotton Live!* by Elizabeth Cotton on Arhoolie Records

5556 **Best Reggae Recording:** *Anthem* by Black Uhuru on Island Records

5557 **Best Recording for Children:** *Where the Sidewalk Ends* by Shel Silverstein, album producer Ron Haffkine on Columbia Records

5558 **Best Comedy Recording:** "Eat It" (track from *Weird Al Yankovic in 3-D*) by "Weird Al" Yankovic on Rock 'n' Roll Records

5559 **Best Spoken Word or Non-Musical Recording:** *The Words of Gandhi* by Ben Kingsley on Caedmon Records

5560 **Best Instrumental Composition:** "The Natural" (track from *The Natural*) composed by Randy Newman on Warner Brothers Records, and "Olympic Fanfare and Theme" (track from *The Official Music of the XXIIIrd Olympiad in Los Angeles*) composed by John Williams on Columbia Records

5561 **Best Album of Original Score Written for a Motion Picture or a Television Special:** *Purple Rain* songwriters Prince, John L. Nelson, Lisa & Wendy on Warner Brothers Records

5562 **Best Cast Show Album:** *Sunday in the Park with George* composer and lyricist Stephen Sondheim, album producer Thomas Z. Shepard on RCA Records

5563 **Best Video, Short Form:** *David Bowie* (Beta) by David Bowie on Sony/Picture Makers Video

5564 **Best Video Album:** *Making of Michael Jackson's Thriller* (VHS) by Michael Jackson on Vestron Music Video

5565 **Best Jazz Vocal Performance:** *Nothin' but the Blues* by Joe Williams on Delos Records

5566 **Best Jazz Instrumental Performance by a Soloist:** *Hot House Flowers* by Wynton Marsalis on Columbia Records

5567 **Best Jazz Instrumental Performance by a Group:** "New York Scene" by Art Blakely on Concord Jazz Records

5568 **Best Jazz Instrumental Performance by a Big Band:** *88 Basie Street* by Count Basie and His Orchestra on Pablo Records

5569 **Best Arrangement on an Instrumental:** "Grace" (gymnastics theme) (track from *Official Music of the XXIIIrd Olympiad in Los Angeles*) by Quincy Jones, arranged by Quincy Jones and Jeremy Lubbock on Columbia Records

5570 **Best Instrumental Arrangement Accompanying Vocals:** "Hard Habit to Break" by Chicago, arranged by David Foster and Jeremy Lubbock on Full Moon/Warner Brothers Records

5571 **Best Vocal Arrangement for Two or More Voices:** "Automatic" (track from *Breakout*) arranged and performed by the Pointer Sisters on Planet/RCA Records

5572 **Best Album Package:** *She's So Unusual* by Cyndi Lauper, art director Janet Perr on Portrait/CBS Records

5573 **Best Album Notes:** *Big Band Jazz* by Paul Whiteman, Fletcher Henderson,

Chick Webb, Tommy Dorsey, Count Basie, Benny Goodman and others, album note writers Gunther Schuller and Martin Williams on Smithsonian Records

5574 Best Historical Album: *Big Band Jazz* by Paul Whiteman, Fletcher Henderson, Chick Webb, Tommy Dorsey, Count Basie, Benny Goodman and others, album producer J.R. Taylor on Smithsonian Records

5575 Best Engineered Non-Classical Record: *17* by Chicago, engineered by Humberto Gatica on Full Moon/Warner Brothers Records

5576 Non-Classical Producer of the Year: David Foster, Lionel Richie and James Anthony Carmichael

5577 Best Classical Album: *Amadeus* (original soundtrack) by Neville Marriner conducting the Academy of St. Martin-in-the-Fields/Ambrosian Opera Chorus, Choristers of Westminster Abbey/ Soloists, album producer John Strauss on Fantasy Records

5578 Best Classical Orchestral Performance: *Prokofiev: Symphony No. 5 in B Flat, Op. 100* by Leonard Slatkin conducting the St. Louis Symphony Orchestra, album producer Jay David Saks on RCA Records

5579 Best Opera Recording: *Bizet: Carmen* (original soundtrack) by Loren Mazel conducting the Orchestre National de France/Choeurs et Maitrise de Radio France/Principal soloists: Julia Migenes Johnson, Faith Esham, Placido Domingo, Ruggero Raimondi, album producer Michel Glotz on Erato Records

5580 Best Non-Opera Choral Performance: *Brahms: A German Requiem* by James Levine conducting the Chicago Symphony Orchestra with Margaret Hillis choral director of the Chicago Symphony Chorus on RCA Records

5581 Best Classical Performance by an Instrumental Soloist or Soloists with Orchestra: *Wynton Marsalis — Edita Gruberova — Handel, Purcell, Torelli, Fasch, Molter* by Wynton Marsalis with Raymond Leppard conducting the English Chamber Orchestra on CBS Masterworks Records

5582 Best Classical Performance by an Instrumental Soloist or Soloists Without Orchestra: *Bach: The Unaccompanied Cello Suites* by Yo-Yo Ma on CBS Masterworks Records

5583 Best Chamber Music Performance: *Beethoven: The Late String Quartets* by the Juilliard String Quartet on CBS Masterworks Records

5584 Best Classical Vocal Soloist Performance: *Ravel: Songs of Maurice Ravel* by Jessye Norman, Jose Van Dam, Heather Harper with Pierre Boulez conducting the Members of Ensemble Intercontemporian & BBC Symphony Orchestra on CBS Masterworks Records

5585 Best New Classical Composition: *Antony and Cleopatra* composed by Samuel Barber on New World Records

5586 Best Engineered Classical Recording: *Prokofiev: Symphony Number 5 in B Flat, Opus 100* by Leonard Slatkin conducting the St. Louis Symphony Orchestra, engineered by Paul Goodman on RCA Records

5587 Classical Producer of the Year: Steven Epstein

———— **1986** ————

5588 Record of the Year: "We Are the World" by USA for Africa, produced by Quincy Jones for Columbia/CBS Records

5589 Album of the Year: *No Jacket Required* by Phil Collins, album producers Phil Collins and Hugh Padgham on Atlantic Records

5590 Song of the Year: "We Are the World" songwriters Michael Jackson and Lionel Richie

5591 Best New Artist: Sade on Portrait/CBS Records

5592 Best Female Pop Vocal Performance: "Saving All My Love for You" by Whitney Houston on Arista Records

5593 Best Male Pop Vocal Performance: *No Jacket Required* by Phil Collins on Atlantic Records

5594 Best Duo or Group with Vocal Pop Performance: "We Are the World" by USA for Africa, album producer Quincy Jones for Columbia/CBS Records

5595 Best Pop Instrumental Performance: "Miami Vice Theme" by Jan Hammer on RCA Records

5596 Best Female Rock Vocal Performance: "One of the Living" by Tina Turner on Capitol Records

5597 Best Male Rock Vocal Performance: "The Boys of Summer" by Don Henley on Geffen Records

5598 Best Duo or Group Vocal Rock Performance: "Money for Nothing" by Dire Straits on Warner Brothers Records

5599 Best Rock Instrumental Performance: "Escape" (track from *Flash*) by Jeff Beck on Epic/CBS Records

5600 Best Female Rhythm & Blues Vocal Performance: "Freeway of Love" by Aretha Franklin on Arista Records

5601 Best Male Rhythm & Blues Vocal Performance: "In Square Circle" by Stevie Wonder on Tamla/Motown Records

5602 Best Duo or Group with Vocal Rhythm & Blues Performance: "Nightshift" by the Commodores on Gordy/Motown Records

5603 Best Rhythm & Blues Instrumental Performance: *Musician* by Ernie Watts on Q West Records

5604 Best New Rhythm & Blues Song: "Freeway of Love" songwriters Narada Michael Walden and Jeffrey Cohen

5605 Best Vocal or Instrumental Jazz Fusion Performance: *Straight to the Heart* by David Sanborn on Warner Brothers Records

5606 Best Female Jazz Vocal Performance: *Cleo at Carnegie* (The 10th Anniversary Concert) by Cleo Laine on DRG Records

5607 Best Male Jazz Vocal Performance: "Another Night in Tunisia" (track from *Vocalese*) by Jon Hendricks and Bobby McFerrin on Atlantic Records

5608 Best Duo or Group Jazz Vocal Group Performance: *Vocalese* by the Manhattan Transfer on Atlantic Records

5609 Best Soloist Jazz Instrumental Performance: *Black Codes from the Underground* by Wynton Marsalis on Columbia/CBS Records

5610 Best Group Jazz Instrumental Performance: *Black Codes from the Underground* by Wynton Marsalis on Columbia/CBS Records

5611 Best Big Band Jazz Instrumental Performance: *The Cotton Club/Original Motion Picture Soundtrack* by John Barry and Bob Wilber on Geffen Records

5612 Best Female Country Vocal Performance: "I Don't Know Why You Want Me" by Rosanne Cash on CBS Records

5613 Best Male Country Vocal Performance: "Lost in the Fifties Tonight (In the Still of the Night)" by Ronnie Milsap on RCA Records

5614 Best Duo or Group with Vocal Country Performance: *Why Not Me* by the Judds on RCA Records

5615 Best Country Instrumental Performance: "Cosmic Square Dance" (track from *Stay Tuned*) by Chet Atkins and Mark Knopfler on Columbia/CBS Records

5616 Best Country Song: "Highwayman" by Jimmy L. Webb

5617 Best Female Gospel Performance: *Unguarded* by Amy Grant on Myrrh/Word Records

5618 Best Male Gospel Performance: "How Excellent Is Thy Name" (track from *I've Just Seen Jesus*) by Larnelle Harris on Benson Records

5619 Best Duo or Group Gospel Performance: "I've Just Seen Jesus" (track from *I've Just Seen Jesus*) by Larnelle Harris and Sandi Patti on Impact/Benson Records

5620 Best Female Soul Gospel Performance: "Martin" by Shirley Caesar on Rejoice/Word Records

5621 Best Male Soul Gospel Performance: "Bring Back the Days of Yea and Nay" (track from *Tomorrow*) by Marvin Winans on Light Records

5622 Best Duo or Group Gospel Performance: *Tomorrow* by the Winans on Light Records

5623 Best Inspirational Performance: "Come Sunday" (track from *Say You Love Me*) by Jennifer Holliday on Geffen Records

5624 Best Latin Performance: *Es Facil Amar* by Lani Hall on A&M Records

5625 Best Tropical Latin Performance: *Mambo Diablo* by Tito Puente and His Latin Ensemble on Concord Jazz Records and *Solito* by Eddie Palmieri on Musica Latina International Records

5626 Best Mexican/American Performance: *Simplemente Mujer* by Vikki Carr on Discos International/CBS Records

5627 **Best Traditional Blues Recording:** "My Guitar Sings the Blues" (track from *Six Silver Strings*) by B.B. King on MCA Records

5628 **Best Ethnic or Traditional Folk Recording:** "My Toot Toot" by Rockin' Sidney on Maison De Soul Records

5629 **Best Polka Recording:** *70 Years of Hits* by Frankie Yankovic on Cleveland International/CBS Records

5630 **Best Reggae Recording:** *Cliff Hanger* by Jimmy Cliff on Columbia/CBS Records

5631 **Best Recording for Children:** *Follow That Bird* (original motion picture soundtrack) by Jim Henson's Muppets and the Sesame Street Cast, album producer Steve Buckingham on RCA Records

5632 **Best Comedy Recording:** *Whoopi Goldberg* (original Broadway show recording) by Whoopi Goldberg on Geffen Records

5633 **Best Spoken Word or Non-Musical Recording:** *Ma Rainey's Black Bottom* (original Broadway cast), album producer Mike Berniker on Manhattan Records

5634 **Best Music Video, Short Form:** *We Are the World—The Video Event* (VHS) (Beta) by USA for Africa, video directed by Tom Trbovich, record produced by Quincy Jones on RCA/Columbia Pictures Home Video

5635 **Best Music Video, Long Form:** *Huey Lewis and the News: The Heart of Rock 'n' Roll* (VHS) (Beta) by Huey Lewis and the News, video directed by Bruce Gowers on Warner Home Video

5636 **Best Instrumental Composition:** "Miami Vice Theme" composed by Jan Hammer on MCA Records

5637 **Best Album of Original Score Written for a Motion Picture or Television Special:** *Beverly Hills Cop* composers and songwriters Sharon Robinson, Jon Gilutin, Bunny Hull, Hawk, Howard Hewett, Micki Free, Sue Sheridan, Howie Rice, Keith Forsey, Harold Faltermeyer, Alee Willis, Dan Sembello, Marc Benno and Richard Theisen on MCA Records

5638 **Best Cast Show Album:** *West Side Story* album produced by John McClure on DG Records

5639 **Best Arrangement on an Instrumental:** "Early A.M. Attitude" (track from *Harlequin*) arranged and performed by Lee Ritenour and Dave Grusin on GRP Records

5640 **Best Instrumental Arrangement Accompanying Vocals:** "Lush Life" (track from *Lush Life*) by Linda Ronstadt, arranged by Nelson Riddle on Asylum Records

5641 **Best Vocal Arrangement for Two or More Voices:** "Another Night in Tunisia" by the Manhattan Transfer, arranged by Cheryl Bentyne and Bobby McFerrin on Atlantic Records

5642 **Best Album Package:** *Lush Life* by Linda Ronstadt, art directors Kosh and Ron Larson on Asylum Records

5643 **Best Album Notes:** *Sam Cooke Live at the Harlem Square Club, 1963* by Sam Cooke, annotator Peter Guralnick on RCA Records

5644 **Best Historical Album:** *RCA/MET—100 Singers—100 Years* from Melba, Schumann-Heink, Caruso through Price, Verrett, Domingo and 94 others, produced by John Pfeiffer on RCA Victor Red Seal Records

5645 **Best Engineered Non-Classical Recording:** *Brothers in Arms* by Dire Straits, engineered by Neil Dorfsman on Warner Brothers Records

5646 **Non-Classical Producer of the Year:** Phil Collins and Hugh Padgham

5647 **Best Classical Album:** *Berlioz: Requiem* by Robert Shaw conducting the Atlanta Symphony Orchestra and Chorus, album produced by Robert E. Woods on Telarc Records

5648 **Best Classical Orchestral Recording:** *Faure: Pelleas et Mallisande* by Robert Shaw conducting the Atlanta Symphony Orchestra, album produced by Robert E. Woods on Telarc Records

5649 **Best Opera Recording:** *Schönberg: Moses und Aron* by Sir Georg Solti conducting the Chicago Symphony Orchestra and Chorus, principal soloists Franz Mazur and Philip Langridge, album produced by James Mallinson on London Records

5650 **Best Non-Opera Choral Performance:** *Berlioz: Requiem* by Robert Shaw conducting the Atlanta Symphony Orchestra and Chorus on Telarc Records

5651 **Best Classical Performance by an Instrumental Soloist or Soloists with Orchestra:** *Elgar: Cello Concerto Opus 85/Walton Concerto for Cello and Orchestra* by Yo-Yo Ma with Andre Previn conducting the London Symphony Orchestra on CBS Masterworks Records

5652 **Best Classical Performance by an Instrumental Soloist or Soloists Without Orchestra:** *Ravel: Gaspard de la Nuit, Pavane pour une Infante Defunte, Valses Nobles et Sentimentales* by Vladimir Ashkenazy on London Records

5653 **Best Chamber Music Performance:** *Brahms: Cello and Piano Sonatas in E Minor & F Major* by Emanuel Ax and Yo-Yo Ma on RCA Records

5654 **Best Classical Vocal Soloist Performance:** *Berlioz: Requiem* by John Aler with Robert Shaw conducting the Atlanta Symphony Orchestra and Chorus on Telarc Records

5655 **Best New Classical Artist:** Chicago Pro Musica on Reference Records

5656 **Best Contemporary Composition:** *Andrew Lloyd Webber: Requiem* composed by Andrew Lloyd Webber on Angel Records

5657 **Best Engineered Classical Recording:** *Berlioz: Requiem* by Robert Shaw conducting the Atlanta Symphony Orchestra and Chorus, engineered by Jack Renner on Telarc Records

5658 **Classical Producer of the Year:** Robert Woods

――――――― **1987** ―――――――

5659 **Record of the Year:** "Higher Love" by Steve Winwood, produced by Russ Titelman and Steve Winwood on Island Records

5660 **Album of the Year:** *Graceland* album produced and performed by Paul Simon on Warner Brothers Records

5661 **Song of the Year:** "That's What Friends Are For" by Dionne Warwick, Elton John, Gladys Knight, Stevie Wonder, songwriters Burt Bacharach and Carol Bayer Sager

5662 **Best New Artist:** Bruce Hornsby and the Range on RCA Records

5663 **Best Female Pop Vocal Performance:** *The Broadway Album* by Barbra Streisand on Columbia/CBS Records

5664 **Best Male Pop Vocal Performance:** "Higher Love" by Steve Winwood on Island Records

5665 **Best Duo or Group with Vocal Pop Performance:** "That's What Friends Are For" by Dionne Warwick, Elton John, Gladys Knight, Stevie Wonder on Columbia/CBS Records

5666 **Best Pop Instrumental Performance by an Orchestra, Group or Soloist:** "Top Gun Anthem" (track from *Top Gun*) (original motion picture soundtrack) by Harold Faltermeyer and Steve Stevens on Columbia/CBS Records

5667 **Best New Age Recording:** *Down to the Moon* by Andreas Vollenweider on FM/CBS Records

5668 **Best Female Rock Vocal Performance:** "Back Where You Started" (track from *Break Every Rule*) by Tina Turner on Capitol Records

5669 **Best Male Rock Vocal Performance:** "Addicted to Love" by Robert Palmer on Island Records

5670 **Best Duo or Group Vocal Rock Performance:** "Missionary Man" by the Eurythmics on Island Records

5671 **Best Rock Instrumental Performance by Orchestra, Group or Soloist:** "Peter Gunn" (track from *In Visible Silence*) by the Art of Noise featuring Duane Eddy on China/Chrysalis Records

5672 **Best Female Rhythm & Blues Vocal Performance:** *Rapture* by Anita Baker on Elektra Records

5673 **Best Male Rhythm & Blues Vocal Performance:** "Living in America" by James Brown on Scotti Brothers/CBS Records

5674 **Best Duo or Group with Vocal Rhythm & Blues Performance:** "Kiss" by Prince and the Revolution on Paisley Park Records

5675 **Best Rhythm & Blues Instrumental Performance (Orchestra, Group or Soloist):** "And You Know That" (track from *Shades*) by the Yellowjackets on MCA Records

5676 **Best New Rhythm & Blues Song:** "Sweet Love" songwriters Anita Baker, Louis A. Johnson and Gary Bias on Elektra Records

5677 **Best Vocal or Instrumental Jazz Fusion Performance:** *Double Vision* by Bob James and David Sanborn on Warner Brothers Records

5678 **Best Female Jazz Vocal Performance:** *Timeless* by Diane Schuur on GRP Records

5679 **Best Male Jazz Vocal Performance:** "Round Midnight" (track from soundtrack for *Round Midnight*) by Bobby McFerrin on Columbia/CBS Records

5680 **Best Duo or Group Jazz Vocal Group Performance:** *Free Fall* by 2 + 2 (Clare Fischer and His Latin Jazz Sextet) on Discovery Records

5681 **Best Soloist Jazz Instrumental Performance:** *Tutu* by Miles Davis on Warner Brothers Records

5682 **Best Group Jazz Instrumental Performance:** *J Mood* by Wynton Marsalis on Columbia/CBS Records

5683 **Best Big Band Jazz Instrumental Performance:** *The Tonight Show Band with Doc Severinson* by the Tonight Show Band with Doc Severinson on Amherst Records

5684 **Best Female Country Vocal Performance:** "Whoever's in New England" by Reba McEntire on MCA Records

5685 **Best Male Country Vocal Performance:** *Lost in the Fifties Tonight* by Ronnie Milsap on RCA Records

5686 **Best Duo or Group with Vocal Country Performance:** "Grandpa (Tell Me 'Bout the Good Old Days)" by the Judds on RCA Records

5687 **Best Country Instrumental Performance:** "Raisin' the Dickens" (track from *Love's Gonna Get Ya*) by Ricky Skaggs on Epic/CBS Records

5688 **Best Country Song:** "Grandpa (Tell Me 'Bout the Good Old Days)" songwriter Jamie O'Hara on RCA records

5689 **Best Female Gospel Performance:** "Morning Like This" by Sandi Patti on Word Records

5690 **Best Male Gospel Performance:** "Triumph" by Philip Bailey on Myrrh/Word Records

5691 **Best Duo or Group, Choir or Chorus Gospel Performance:** "They Say" (track from *So Glad I Know*) by Sandi Patti and Deniece Williams on Sparrow Records

5692 **Best Female Soul Gospel Performance:** "I Surrender All" (track from *So Glad I Know*) by Deniece Williams on Sparrow Records

5693 **Best Male Soul Gospel Performance:** "Going Away" by Al Green on A&M Records

5694 **Best Duo or Group, Choir or Chorus Gospel Performance:** *Let My People Go* by the Winans on Q West Records

5695 **Best Latin Pop Performance:** "Leolai" (track from *Te Amare*) by Jose Feliciano on RCA Records

5696 **Best Tropical Latin Performance:** *Escenas* by Ruben Blades on Elektra Records

5697 **Best Mexican/American Performance:** *Ay Te Dejo en San Antonio* by Flaco Jiminez on Arhoolie Records

5698 **Best Traditional Blues Recording:** *Showdown!* by Albert Collins, Robert Cray and Johnny Copeland on Alligator Records

5699 **Best Traditional Folk Recording:** *Riding the Midnight Train* by Doc Watson on Sugar Hill Records

5700 **Best Contemporary Folk Recording:** *Tribute to Steve Goodman* by Arlo Guthrie, John Hartford, Richie Havens, Bonnie Koloc, Nitty Gritty Dirt Band, John Prine, and others, album produced by Hank Neuberger, Al Bunetta and Dan Einstein on Red Pajamas Records

5701 **Best Polka Recording:** *Another Polka Celebration* by Eddie Blazonczyk's Versatones on Bel Aire Records and *I Remember Warsaw* by Jimmy Sturr and His Orchestra on Starr Records

5702 **Best Reggae Recording:** *Babylon the Bandit* by Steel Pulse on Elektra Records

5703 **Best Recording for Children:** *The Alphabet* (cassette recording) by the Sesame Street Muppets, Muppets creator Jim Henson, album produced by Kathryn King and Geri Van Rees on Golden Books

5704 **Best Comedy Recording:** *Those of You with or Without Children, You'll Understand* by Bill Cosby on Geffen Records

5705 **Best Spoken Word or Non-Musical Recording:** *Interviews from the Class of '55 Recording Sessions* by Carl Perkins, Jerry Lee Lewis, Roy Orbison, Johnny Cash, Sam Phillips, Rick Nelson and Chips Moman on America Record Corporation

5706 **Best Musical Cast Show Album:** *Follies in Concert* album produced by Thomas Z. Shepard on RCA Records

5707 **Best Instrumental Compositions:** "Out of Africa" (music from the motion picture soundtrack) composed by John Barry

5708 **Best Music Video, Short Form (VHS):** *Dire Straits Brothers in Arms* by Dire Straits on Warner Reprise Video

5709 **Best Music Video, Long Form (VHS) (Beta) (Disc):** *Bring On the Night* by Sting, video produced by Michael Apted on Karl Lorimar Home Video

5710 **Best Arrangement on an Instrumental:** "Suite Memories" (track from *Someplace Else*) by Bill Watrous with Patrick Williams and His Orchestra, album arranged by Patrick Williams on Soundwings Records

5711 **Best Arrangement on an Instrumental Accompanying Vocals:** "Somewhere" (track from *The Broadway Album*) by Barbra Streisand, arranged by David Foster on Columbia/CBS Records

5712 **Best Album Package:** *Tutu* by Miles Davis, art director Eiko Ishioka on Warner Brothers Records

5713 **Best Album Notes:** *The Voice: The Columbia Years 1943-1952* by Frank Sinatra, album notators Gary Giddens, Wilfred Sheed, Jonathan Schwartz, Murray Kempton, Andrew Sarris, Stephen Holden and Frank Conroy on Columbia/CBS Records

5714 **Best Historical Album:** *Atlantic Rhythm and Blues 1947-1974 Volumes 1 Through 7* by Brook Benton, Ray Charles, the Coasters, the Drifters, Roberta Flack, Aretha Franklin, Otis Redding and many others, albums produced by Bob Porter and Aziz Goksel on Atlantic Records

5715 **Best Engineered Non-Classical Recording:** *Back in the High Life* by Steve Winwood, engineered by Tom Lord Alge and Jason Corsaro on Island Records

5716 **Non-Classical Producer of the Year:** Jimmy Jam and Terry Lewis

5717 **Best Classical Album:** *Horowitz: The Studio Recordings, New York 1985* by Vladimir Horowitz, album produced by Thomas Frost on Deutsche Grammophon Records

5718 **Best Classical Orchestral Recording:** *Liszt: A Faust Symphony* by Sir Georg Solti conducting the Chicago Symphony Orchestra, album produced by Michael Haas on London Records

5719 **Best Opera Recording:** *Bernstein: Candide* by John Mauceri conducting the New York City Opera Chorus and Orchestra, principal soloists Erie Mills, David Eisler, John Langston, Joyce Castle, Scott Reeve, Jack Harrold, James Billings and Maris Clement, album produced by Elizabeth Ostrow on New World Records

5720 **Best Non-Opera Choral Performance:** *Orff: Carmina Burana* by James Levine conducting the Chicago Symphony Orchestra and Chorus with Margaret Hillis, choral director on Deutsche Grammophon Records

5721 **Best Classical Performance by an Instrumental Soloist:** *Horowitz: The Studio Recordings, New York 1985* by Vladimir Horowitz on Deutsche Grammophon Records

5722 **Best Instrumental or Vocal Chamber Music Performance:** *Beethoven: Cello and Piano Sonata Number 4 in C Major and Variations* by Yo-Yo Ma and Emanuel Ax on CBS Masterworks Records

5723 **Best Classical Performance by Vocalist:** *Mozart: Kathleen Battle Sings Mozart* by Kathleen Battle on Angel Records

5724 **Best Contemporary Composition:** *Lutoslawski: Symphony Number 3* composed by Witold Lutoslawski on CBS Masterworks Records

5725 **Best Engineered Classical Recording:** *Horowitz: The Studio Recordings, New York 1985* by Vladimir Horowitz, engineered by Paul Goodman on Deutsche Grammophon Records

5726 **Classical Producer of the Year:** Thomas Frost

——————— **1988** ———————

5727 **Record of the Year:** "Graceland" produced and performed by Paul Simon on Warner Brothers Records

5728 **Album of the Year:** *Joshua Tree* by U2, album producers Daniel Lanois and Brian Eno on Island Records

5729 Song of the Year: "Somewhere Out There" by Linda Ronstadt and James Ingram, songwriters James Horner, Barry Mann, Cynthia Weil on MCA Records

5730 Best New Artist: Jody Watley on MCA Records

5731 Best Female Pop Vocal Performance: "I Wanna Dance with Somebody (Who Loves Me)" by Whitney Houston on Arista Records

5732 Best Male Pop Vocal Performance: *Bring On the Night* by Sting on A&M Records

5733 Best Duo or Group with Vocal Pop Performance: "(I've Had) the Time of My Life" (track from *Dirty Dancing* original soundtrack) by Bill Medley and Jennifer Warnes on BMG Music/RCA Records

5734 Best Pop Instrumental Performance by an Orchestra, Group or Soloist: "Minute by Minute" by Larry Carlton on MCA Records

5735 Best New Age Performance: *Yusef Lateef's Little Symphony* by Yusef Lateef on Atlantic Records

5736 Best Solo Rock Vocal Performance: *Tunnel of Love* by Bruce Springsteen on Columbia/CBS Records

5737 Best Duo or Group Rock Vocal Performance: *Joshua Tree* by U2 on Island Records

5738 Best Rock Instrumental Performance by Orchestra, Group or Soloist: *Jazz from Hell* by Frank Zappa on Barking Pumpkin/Rykodisc Records

5739 Best Female Rhythm & Blues Vocal Performance: "Aretha" by Aretha Franklin on Arista Records

5740 Best Male Rhythm & Blues Vocal Performance: "Just to See Her" by Smokey Robinson on Motown Records

5741 Best Duo or Group with Vocal Rhythm & Blues Performance: "I Knew You Were Waiting (for Me)" (track from *Aretha*) by Aretha Franklin and George Michael on Arista Records

5742 Best Rhythm & Blues Instrumental Performance: "Chicago Song" by David Sanborn on Warner Brothers Records

5743 Best Rhythm & Blues Song: "Lean on Me" by Club Nouveau, written by Bill Withers on King Jay/Warner Brothers Records

5744 Best Vocal or Instrumental Jazz Fusion Performance: *Still Life (Talking)* by the Pat Metheny Group on Geffen Records

5745 Best Female Jazz Vocal Performance: *Diane Schuur and the Count Basie Orchestra* by Diane Schuur on GRP Records

5746 Best Male Jazz Vocal Performance: "What Is This Thing Called Love" (track from *The Other Side of Round Midnight—Dexter Gordon*) by Bobby McFerrin on Blue Note Records

5747 Best Soloist Jazz Instrumental Performance: *The Other Side of Round Midnight* by Dexter Gordon on Blue Note Records

5748 Best Group Jazz Instrumental Performance: *Marsalis Standard Time—Volume 1* by Wynton Marsalis on Columbia/CBS Records

5749 Best Big Band Jazz Instrumental Performance: *Digital Duke* by the Duke Ellington Orchestra conducted by Mercer Ellington on GRP Records

5750 Best Female Country Vocal Performance: "80's Ladies" (track from *80's Ladies*) by K.T. Oslin on BMG Music/RCA Records

5751 Best Male Country Vocal Performance: *Always & Forever* by Randy Travis on Warner Brothers Records

5752 Best Country Performance by a Duo or Group with a Vocal: *Trio* by Dolly Parton, Emmylou Harris and Linda Ronstadt on Warner Brothers Records

5753 Best Country Vocal Duet Performance: "Make No Mistake, She's Mine" by Kenny Rogers and Ronnie Milsap on BMG Music/RCA Records

5754 Best Country Instrumental Performance by an Orchestra, Group or Soloist: "String of Pars" (track from *Asleep at the Wheel*) by Asleep at the Wheel on Epic Records

5755 Best Country Song: "Forever and Ever, Amen" by Randy Travis, songwriters Paul Overstreet and Don Schlitz on Warner Brothers Records

5756 Best Female Gospel Performance: "I Believe in You" (track from *Water Under the Bridge*) by Deniece Williams on Columbia/CBS Records

5757 Best Male Gospel Performance: "The Father Hath Provided" by Larnelle Harris on Benson Records

5758 Best Duo or Group, Choir or Chorus Gospel Performance: *Crack the Sky* by Mylon LeFevre and Broken Heart on Myrrh/Word Records

5759 Best Female Soul Gospel Performance: "For Always" (track from *Bebe and CeCe Winans*) by CeCe Winans on Sparrow Records

5760 Best Male Soul Gospel Performance: "Everything's Gonna Be Alright" (track from *Soul Survivor*) by Al Green on A&M Records

5761 Best Duo or Group Gospel Performance: "Ain't No Need to Worry" by the Winans and Anita Baker on Q West Records

5762 Best Latin Pop Performance: *Un Hombre Solo* by Julio Iglesias on Discos International/CBS Records

5763 Best Tropical Latin Performance: *La Verdad—The Truth* by Eddie Palmieri on Fania/Musica Latina International Records

5764 Best Mexican/American Performance: *Gracias! America Sin Fronteras* by Los Tigres Del Norte on Profuno International Records

5765 Best Traditional Blues Recording: *Houseparty New Orleans Style* by Professor Longhair on Rounder Records

5766 Best Contemporary Blues Recording: *Strong Persuader* by the Robert Cray Band on Mercury/Hightone Records

5767 Best Traditional Folk Recording: *Shaka Zulu* by Ladysmith Black Mambazo on Warner Brothers Records

5768 Best Contemporary Folk Recording: *Unfinished Business* by Steve Goodman on Red Pajamas Records

5769 Best Polka Recording: *A Polka Just for Me* by Jimmy Sturr and His Orchestra on Starr Records

5770 Best Reggae Recording: *No Nuclear War* by Peter Tosh on EMI/America Records

5771 Best Recording for Children: *The Elephant's Child* narration by Jack Nicholson, music by Bobby McFerrin, album produced by Bobby McFerrin, Tom Bradshaw, Mark Sottnick on Windham Hill Records

5772 Best Comedy Recording: *A Night at the Met* by Robin Williams on Columbia/CBS Records

5773 Best Spoken Word or Non-Musical Recording: *Lake Wobegon Days* (cassette) by Garrison Keillor on PHC

5774 Best Musical Cast Show Album: *Les Misérables* (original Broadway cast recording) lyricist Herbert Kretzmer, composer Claude-Michel Schönberg, album producers Alain Boublil and Claude-Michel Schonberg on Geffen Records

5775 Best Instrumental Composition: "Call Sheet Blues" (track from *The Other Side of Round Midnight—Dexter Gordon*) composed and performed by Wayne Shorter, Herbie Hancock, Ron Carter and Billy Higgins on Blue Note Records

5776 Best Album of Original Instrumental Background Score Written for a Motion Picture or Television: *The Untouchables* (original motion picture soundtrack) composed and performed by Ennio Morricone on A&M Records

5777 Best Song Specifically Written for a Motion Picture or Television: "Somewhere Out There" by Linda Ronstadt and James Ingram, songwriters James Horner, Barry Mann, Cynthia Weil on MCA Records

5778 Best Performance Music Video: *The Prince's Trust All-Star Rocket Concert* (VHS) by Elton John, Tina Turner, Sting and others, video producer Anthony Eaton on MGM Home Video

5779 Best Concept Music Video: *Land of Confusion* (VHS) by Genesis, Video directors John Lloyd and Jim Yurich, video producer John Blair for Atlantic Video

5780 Best Instrumental Arrangement: "Take the 'A' Train" (track from *The Tonight Show Band with Doc Severinson, Volume II*) by the Tonight Show Band with Doc Severinson, instrumental arranger Bill Holman on Amherst Records

5781 Best Instrumental Arrangement Accompanying Vocals: "Deedle's Blues" (track from *Diane Schuur and the Count Basie Orchestra*) by Diane Schuur and the Count Basie Orchestra, instrumental arranger Frank Foster on GRP Records

5782 Best Album Package: *King's Record Shop* by Rosanne Cash, art director Bill Johnson on Columbia/CBS Records

5783 **Best Album Notes:** *Thelonius Monk – The Complete Riverside Recordings* by Thelonius Monk, album notes writer Orrin Keepnews on Riverside Records

5784 **Best Historical Album:** *Thelonius Monk – The Complete Riverside Recordings* by Thelonius Monk, album producer Orrin Keepnews on Riverside Records

5785 **Best Engineered Non-Classical Recording:** *Bad* by Michael Jackson, engineers Bruce Swedien and Humberto Gatica on Epic Records

5786 **Non-Classical Producer of the Year:** Narada Michael Walden

5787 **Best Classical Album:** *Horowitz in Moscow* by Vladimir Horowitz, album producer Thomas Frost on Deutsche Grammophon Records

5788 **Best Classical Orchestral Recording:** *Beethoven: Symphony Number 9 in D Minor (Choral)* by Sir Georg Solti conducting the Chicago Symphony Orchestra, album producer Michael Haas on London Records

5789 **Best Opera Recording:** *(R.) Strauss: Ariadne auf Naxos* by James Levine conducting the Vienna Philharmonic Orchestra with principal soloists Anna Tomowa-Sintow, Kathleen Battle, Agnes Baltsa, Gary Lakes, Hermann Prey, album producer Cord Garben on Deutsche Grammophon Records

5790 **Best Non-Opera Choral Performance:** *Hindemith: When Lilacs Last in the Dooryard Bloom'd (A Requiem for Those We Love)* by Robert Shaw conducting the Atlanta Symphony Orchestra and Chorus on Telarc Records

5791 **Best Classical Performance by an Instrumental Soloist or Soloists with Orchestra:** *Mozart: Violin Concertos Numbers 2 and 4 in D* by Itzhak Perlman with James Levine conducting the Vienna Philharmonic Orchestra on Deutsche Grammophon Records

5792 **Best Classical Performance by an Instrumental Soloist or Soloists Without Orchestra:** *Horowitz in Moscow* by Vladimir Horowitz on Deutsche Grammophon Records

5793 **Best Instrumental or Vocal Chamber Music Performance:** *Beethoven: The Complete Piano Trios* by Itzhak Perlman, Lynn Harrell and Vladimir Ashkenazy on Angel Records

5794 **Best Classical Vocal Soloist Performance:** *Kathleen Battle – Salzburg Recital* by Kathleen Battle, accompanied by James Levine on Deutsche Grammophon Records

5795 **Best Contemporary Composition:** *Penderecki: Cello Concerto Number 2* composed by Krzystof Penderecki on Erato-Editions Records

5796 **Best Engineered Classical Recording:** *Faure: Requiem, Opus 48/Durufle-Requiem, Opus 9* by Robert Shaw conducting the Atlanta Symphony Orchestra and Chorus, engineered by Jack Renner on Telarc Records

5797 **Classical Producer of the Year:** Robert Woods

—————— **1 9 8 9** ——————

5798 **Record of the Year:** "Don't Worry, Be Happy" by Bobby McFerrin, produced by Linda Goldstein on EMI/USA Records

5799 **Album of the Year:** *Faith* performed and produced by George Michael on Columbia/CBS Records

5800 **Song of the Year:** "Don't Worry, Be Happy" performed and written by Bobby McFerrin on EMI/USA Records

5801 **Best New Artist:** Tracy Chapman on Elektra Records

5802 **Best Female Pop Vocal Performance:** "Fast Car" by Tracy Chapman on Elektra Records

5803 **Best Male Pop Vocal Performance:** "Don't Worry, Be Happy" by Bobby McFerrin on EMI/USA Records

5804 **Best Duo or Group with Vocal Pop Performance:** *Brazil* by the Manhattan Transfer on Atlantic Records

5805 **Best Pop Instrumental Performance by an Orchestra, Group or Soloist:** *Close-up* by David Sanborn on Reprise Records

5806 **Best Female Rock Vocal Performance:** *Tina Live in Europe* by Tina Turner on Capitol Records

5807 **Best Male Rock Vocal Performance:** "Simply Irresistible" by Robert Palmer on EMI/Manhattan Records

5808 **Best Duo or Group Rock Vocal Performance:** "Desire" by U2 on Island Records

5809 **Best Rock Instrumental Performance by Orchestra, Group or Soloist:** *Blues for Salvador* by Carlos Santana on Columbia/CBS Records

5810 **Best Hard Rock/Metal Performance by a Duo or Group with Vocal:** *Chest of a Knave* by Jethro Tull on Chrysalis Records

5811 **Best Female Rhythm & Blues Vocal Performance:** "Giving You the Best That I Got" by Anita Baker on Elektra Records

5812 **Best Male Rhythm & Blues Vocal Performance:** *Introducing the Hardline According to Terence Trent D'Arby* by Terence Trent D'Arby on Columbia/CBS Records

5813 **Best Rhythm & Blues Performance by a Duo or Group with Vocal:** "Love Overboard" by Gladys Knight and the Pips on MCA Records

5814 **Best Rhythm & Blues Instrumental Orchestral Performance with Group or Soloists:** "Light Years" (track from *GRP Super Live in Concert, Volumes 1 & 2*) by Chick Corea on GRP Records

5815 **Best Rhythm & Blues Song:** "Giving You the Best That I Got" by Anita Baker, songwriters Anita Baker, Skip Scarborough and Randy Holland on Elektra Records

5816 **Best Rap Performance:** "Parents Just Don't Understand" (track from *He's Just the D.J. I'm the Rapper*) by D.J. Jazzy Jeff and the Fresh Prince

5817 **Best New Age Performance:** *Folksongs for a Nuclear Age* by Shadowfax on Capitol Records

5818 **Best Jazz Fusion Performance:** *Politics* by the Yellowjackets on MCA Records

5819 **Best Female Jazz Vocal Performance:** *Look What I Got* by Betty Carter on Verve Records

5820 **Best Male Jazz Vocal Performance:** "Brothers" (track from Rob Wasserman's *Duets*) by Bobby McFerrin on MCA Records

5821 **Best Duo or Group Jazz Vocal Performance:** "Spread Love" by Take 6 on Reprise Records

5822 **Best Jazz Instrumental Performance by a Soloist on a Jazz Recording:** *Don't Try This at Home* by Michael Brecker on MCA Impulse Records

5823 **Best Group Jazz Instrumental Performance:** *Blues for Coltrane, a Tribute to John Coltrane* by McCoy Turner, Pharoah Sanders, David Murray, Cecil McBee and Roy Haynes on MCA Impulse Records

5824 **Best Big Band Jazz Instrumental Performance:** *Bud & Bird* by Gil Evans and the Monday Night Orchestra on Intersound Records

5825 **Best Female Country Vocal Performance:** "Hold Me" (track from *This Woman*) by K.T. Oslin on RCA Records

5826 **Best Male Country Vocal Performance:** *Old 8 x 10* by Randy Travis on Warner Brothers Records

5827 **Best Duo or Group Vocal Country Performance:** "Give a Little Love" (track from *Greatest Hits*) by the Judds on RCA Records

5828 **Best Country Vocal Collaboration:** "Crying" by Roy Orbison and k.d. lang on Virgin Records

5829 **Best Country Instrumental Performance by an Orchestra, Group or Soloist:** "Sugarfoot Rag" (track from *Western Standard Time*) by Asleep at the Wheel on Epic Records

5830 **Best Vocal or Instrumental Bluegrass Recording:** *Southern Flavor* by Bill Monroe on MCA Records

5831 **Best Country Song:** "Hold Me" written and performed by K.T. Oslin

5832 **Best Female Gospel Performance:** "Lead Me On" by Amy Grant on A&M Records

5833 **Best Male Gospel Performance:** *Christmas* by Larnelle Harris on Benson Records

5834 **Best Gospel Performance by a Duo, Group, Choir or Chorus:** *The Winans Live at Carnegie Hall* by the Winans on Q West Records

5835 **Best Female Soul Gospel Performance:** "One Lord, One Faith, One Baptism" by Aretha Franklin on Arista Records

5836 **Best Male Soul Gospel Performance:** "Abundant Life" (track from *Ron Winans Family & Friends Choir*) by BeBe Winans on Selah Records

5837 **Best Soul Gospel Performance**

by a Duo or Group, Choir or Chorus: *Take Six* by Take 6 on Reprise Records

5838 **Best Latin Pop Performance:** *Roberto Carlos* by Roberto Carlos on Discos International/CBS Records

5839 **Best Tropical Latin Performance:** *Antecedent* by Ruben Blades on Elektra Records

5840 **Best Mexican/American Performance:** *Canciones De Mi Padre* by Linda Ronstadt on Elektra Records

5841 **Best Traditional Blues Recording:** *Hidden Charms* by Willie Dixon on Bug/Capitol Records

5842 **Best Contemporary Blues Recording:** "Don't Be Afraid of the Dark" by the Robert Cray Band on Mercury Records

5843 **Best Traditional Folk Recording:** *Folkways: A Vision Shared—A Tribute to Woody Guthrie and Leadbelly* produced by Don DeVito, Joe McEwen, Harold Leventhal and Ralph Rinzler on Columbia/CBS Records

5844 **Best Contemporary Folk Recording:** *Tracy Chapman* by Tracy Chapman on Elektra Records

5845 **Best Polka Recording:** *Born to Polka* by Jimmy Sturr and His Orchestra on Starr Records

5846 **Best Reggae Recording:** *Conscious Party* by Ziggy Marley and the Melody Makers on Virgin Records

5847 **Best Recording for Children:** *Pecos Bill* narrated by Robin Williams, music by Ry Cooder, produced by Mark Sottnick and Ry Cooder on Windham Hill Records

5848 **Best Comedy Recording:** *Good Morning, Vietnam* by Robin Williams on A&M Records

5849 **Best Spoken Word or Non-Musical Recording:** "Speech by Reverend Jesse Jackson—July 27" (track from Aretha Franklin's *One Lord, One Faith, One Baptism*) by the Reverend Jesse Jackson on Arista Records

5850 **Best Musical Cast Show Album:** *Into the Woods* composer and lyricist Stephen Sondheim, produced by Jay David Saks on RCA Records

5851 **Best Instrumental Composition:** "The Theme from *L.A. Law*" (track from *Music from L.A. Law and Otherwise*) composed by Mike Post on Polydor Records

5852 **Best Album of Original Instrumental Background Score Written for a Motion Picture or Television:** *The Last Emperor* composed by Ryuichi Sakamoto, David Byrne and Cong Su on Virgin Records

5853 **Best Song Written Specifically for a Motion Picture or Television:** "Two Hearts" (track from *Buster*) performed by Phil Collins, songwriters Phil Collins and Lamont Dozier on Atlantic Records

5854 **Best Performance Music Video:** *Where the Streets Have No Name* by U2, video director Meiert Avis, video producers Michael Hamlyn and Ben Dossett on Island Video

5855 **Best Concept Music Video:** *Fat* by "Weird Al" Yankovic, video director Jay Levey, video producer Susan Zwertman on Rock 'n' Roll/Epic Records

5856 **Best Arrangement of an Instrumental:** "Memos from Paradise" (track from *Memos from Paradise*) by Eddie Daniels, arranged by Roger Kellaway on GRP Records

5857 **Best Instrumental Arrangement Accompanying Vocals:** "No One Is Alone" (track from *Cleo Sings Sondheim*) by Cleo Laine, arranged by Jonathan Tunick on RCA Records

5858 **Best Album Package:** *Tired of Runnin'* by the O'Kanes, art director Bill Johnson

5859 **Best Album Notes:** *Crossroads* by Eric Clapton, annotator Anthony DeCurtis on Polydor Records

5860 **Best Historical Album:** *Crossroads* by Eric Clapton, album producer Bill Levinson on Polydor Records

5861 **Best Engineered Non-Classical Recording:** *Roll with It* by Steve Winwood, album engineered by Tom Lord Alge on Virgin Records

5862 **Non-Classical Producer of the Year:** Neil Dorfsman

5863 **Best Classical Album:** *Verdi: Requiem and Operatic Choruses* by Robert Shaw conducting the Atlanta Symphony Orchestra and Chorus, album produced by Robert Woods on Telarc Records

5864 **Best Orchestral Recording:** *Rorem: String Symphony; Sunday Morning; Eagles* by Robert Shaw conducting the Atlanta Symphony Orchestra for "String Symphony" and Louis Lane conducting the Atlanta Symphony Orchestra for "Sunday Morning" and "Eagles," album produced by Robert Woods for New World Records

5865 Best Opera Recording: *Wagner: Lohengrin* by Sir Georg Solti conducting the Vienna State Opera Choir and the Vienna Philharmonic, principal soloists Placido Domingo, Jessye Norman, Eva Randova, Siegmund Nimsgern, Hans Sotin and Dietrick Fischer-Dieskau, produced by Christopher Raeburn on London Records

5866 Best Non-Opera Choral Performance: *Verdi: Requiem & Operatic Choruses* by Robert Shaw conducting the Atlanta Symphony Chorus and Orchestra on Telarc Records

5867 Best Classical Performance by an Instrumental Soloist with Orchestra: *Mozart: Piano Concerto Number 23 in A* by Vladimir Horowitz with Giulini conducting the LaScala Opera Orchestra on Deutsche Grammophon Records

5868 Best Classical Performance by an Instrumental Soloist Without Orchestra: *Albeniz: Iberia; Navarra; Suite Espagnola* by Alicia de Larrocha on London Records

5869 Best Instrumental or Vocal Chamber Music Performance: *Bartok: Sonata for Two Pianos and Percussion/Brahms: Variations on a Theme by Joseph Haydn for Two Pianos* by Murray Perahia and Sir Georg Solti pianists with David Corkhill and Evelyn Glennie, percussionists on CBS Masterworks Records

5870 Best Classical Vocal Soloist Performance: *Luciano Pavarotti in Concert* by Luciano Pavarotti on CBS Masterworks Records

5871 Best Contemporary Composition: *Adams: Nixon in China* composed by John Adams on Elektra/Nonesuch Records

5872 Best Engineered Classical Recording: *Verdi: Requiem and Operatic Choruses* by Robert Shaw conducting the Atlanta Symphony Orchestra and Chorus, engineered by Jack Renner on Telarc Records

5873 Classical Producer of the Year: Robert Woods

———————— **1 9 9 0** ————————

5874 Record of the Year: "Wind Beneath My Wings" by Bette Midler, produced by Arif Mardin on Atlantic Records

5875 Album of the Year: *Nick of Time* by Bonnie Raitt, produced by Don Was on Capitol Records

5876 Song of the Year: "Wind Beneath My Wings" by Bette Midler, songwriters Larry Henley and Jeff Silbar on Atlantic Records

5877 Best Female Pop Vocal Performance: "Nick of Time" (track from *Nick of Time*) by Bonnie Raitt on Capitol Records

5878 Best Male Pop Vocal Performance: "How Am I Supposed to Live Without You" by Michael Bolton on Columbia/CBS Records

5879 Best Duo or Group with Vocal Pop Performance: "Don't Know Much" by Linda Ronstadt and Aaron Neville on Elektra Records

5880 Best Pop Instrumental Performance: "Healing Chant" (track from *Yellow Moon*) by the Neville Brothers on A&M Records

5881 Best Female Rock Vocal Performance: *Nick of Time* by Bonnie Raitt on Capitol Records

5882 Best Male Rock Vocal Performance: *The End of Innocence* by Don Henley on Geffen Records

5883 Best Duo or Group Rock Vocal Performance: *Travelling Wilburys Volume One* by the Travelling Wilburys on Wilbury/Warner Brothers Records

5884 Best Rock Instrumental Performance: *Jeff Beck's Guitar Shop with Terry Bozzio and Tony Hymas* by Jeff Beck, Terry Bozzio and Tony Hymas on Epic Records

5885 Best Hard Rock Performance: "Cult of Personality" by Living Colour on Epic Records

5886 Best Metal Performance: "One" by Metallica on Elektra Records

5887 Best Female Rhythm & Blues Vocal Performance: "Giving You the Best That I Got" by Anita Baker on Elektra Records

5888 Best Male Rhythm & Blues Vocal Performance: "Every Little Step" by Bobby Brown on MCA Records

5889 Best Rhythm & Blues Performance by a Duo or Group with Vocal: "Back to Life" by Soul II Soul featuring Caron Wheeler on Virgin Records

5890 Best Rhythm & Blues Instrumental

Performance: "African Dance" (track from *Keep On Movin'*) by Soul II Soul on Virgin Records

5891 Best Rhythm & Blues Song: *If You Don't Know Me by Now* by Simply Red, songwriters Kenny Gamble and Leon Huff on Elektra Records

5892 Best Rap Performance: "Bust a Move" by Young MC on Delicious Vinyl Records

5893 Best New Age Performance: *Passion—Music from the Last Temptation of Christ* by Peter Gabriel on Geffen Records

5894 Best Jazz Fusion Performance: *Letter from Home* by the Pat Metheny Group on Geffen Records

5895 Best Female Jazz Vocal Performance: *Blues on Broadway* by Ruth Brown on Fantasy Records

5896 Best Male Jazz Vocal Performance: *When Harry Met Sally* by Harry Connick, Jr., on Columbia/CBS Records

5897 Best Duo or Group Jazz Vocal Performance: "Makin' Whoopie" by Dr. John and Rickie Lee Jones on Warner Brothers Records

5898 Best Jazz Instrumental Performance by a Soloist on a Jazz Recording: *Aura* by Miles Davis on Columbia/CBS Records

5899 Best Group Jazz Instrumental Performance: *Chick Corea Akoustic Band* by the Chick Corea Akoustic Band on GRP Records

5900 Best Big Band Jazz Instrumental Performance: *Aura* by Miles Davis on Columbia/CBS Records

5901 Best Female Country Vocal Performance: *Absolute Torch and Twang* by k.d. lang on Sire Records

5902 Best Male Country Vocal Performance: *Lyle Lovett and His Large Band* by Lyle Lovett on MCA Records

5903 Best Duo or Group Vocal Country Performance: *Will the Circle Be Unbroken Volume Two* by the Nitty Gritty Dirt Band on Universal Records

5904 Best Country Vocal Collaboration: "There's a Tear in My Beer" by Hank Williams, Jr., and Hank Williams, Sr., on Curb Records

5905 Best Country Instrumental Performance: "Amazing Grace" (track from *Will the Circle Be Unbroken Volume Two*) by Randy Scruggs on Universal Records

5906 Best Vocal or Instrumental Bluegrass Recording: "The Valley Road" (track from *Will the Circle Be Unbroken Volume Two*) Bruce Hornsby and the Nitty Gritty Dirt Band on Universal Records

5907 Best Country Song: "After All This Time" written and performed by Rodney Crowell on Columbia Records

5908 Best Female Gospel Vocal Performance: "Don't Cry" (track from *Heaven*) by CeCe Winans on Capitol Records

5909 Best Male Gospel Vocal Performance: "Meantime" (track from *Heaven*) by BeBe Winans on Capitol Records

5910 Best Gospel Performance by a Duo, Group, Choir or Chorus: "The Savior Is Waiting" (track from *Our Hymns/ Various Artists*) by Take 6 on Word Records

5911 Best Female or Male Soul Gospel Performance: "As Long as We're Together" by Al Green on A&M Records

5912 Best Soul Gospel Vocal Performance by a Group, Duo, Choir or Chorus: "Let Brotherly Love Continue" (track from *Brotherly Love*) by Daniel Winans and Chorus on Rejoice Records

5913 Best Latin Pop Performance: "Cielito Lindo" by Jose Feliciano on EMI Records

5914 Best Tropical Latin Performance: *Ritmo en el Corazon* by Celia Cruz and Ray Baretto on Fania Records

5915 Best Mexican/American Performance: *La Pistola el Corazon* by Los Lobos on Warner Brothers/Slash Records

5916 Best Traditional Blues Recording: "I'm in the Mood" (track from *The Healer*) by John Lee Hooker and Bonnie Raitt on Chameleon Music Group Records

5917 Best Contemporary Blues Recording: *In Step* by Stevie Ray Vaughan & Double Trouble on Epic Records

5918 Best Traditional Folk Recording: *Le Mystere des voix Bulgares, Volume II* by the Bulgarian State Female Vocal Choir, produced by Marcel Cellier on Elektra/ Nonesuch Records

5919 Best Contemporary Folk Recording: *Indigo Girls* by the Indigo Girls on Epic Records

5920 Best Polka Recording: *All in My Love for You* by Jimmy Sturr and His Orchestra on Starr Records

5921 **Best Reggae Recording:** *One Bright Day* by Ziggy Marley and the Melody Makers on Virgin Records

5922 **Best Recording for Children:** *The Rock-a-Bye Collection* Tanya Goodman, produced by David Lehman and J. Aaron Brown on Jaba Records

5923 **Best Comedy Recording:** *P.D.Q. Bach: 1712 Overture & Other Musical Assaults* by Professor Peter Schickele on Telarc Records

5924 **Best Spoken Word or Non-Musical Recording:** *It's Always Something* by Gilda Radner on Simon & Schuster Audio

5925 **Best Musical Cast Show Album:** *Jerome Robbins' Broadway* by Jason Alexander, Debbie Shapiro, Robert La Fasse, produced by Jay David Saks on RCA-Victor Records

5926 **Best Instrumental Composition:** "The Batman Theme" by the Sinfonia of London Orchestra, composed by Danny Elfman on Warner Brothers Records

5927 **Best Album of Original Instrumental Background Score Written for a Motion Picture or Television:** *The Fabulous Baker Boys* composed and conducted by Dave Grusin on GRP Records

5928 **Best Song Written Specifically for a Motion Picture or Television:** "Let the River Run" (from *Working Girl*) composed and performed by Carly Simon on Arista Records

5929 **Best Music Video—Short Form:** *Leave Me Alone* (VHS) by Michael Jackson, video director Jim Blashfield, video producers Frank DiLeo, Michael Jackson, Jim Blashfield, Jerry Kramer, Paul Diener on Epic Records

5930 **Best Music Video—Long Form:** *Rhythm Nation 1814* (VHS) by Janet Jackson, video directors Dominic Sena, Jonathan Dayton, Valerie Faris, video producers Aris McGarry, Jonathan Dayton and Valerie Faris on A&M Records

5931 **Best Arrangement of an Instrumental:** "Suite from *The Milagro Beanfield War*" (track from *Migration*) arranged and performed by Dave Grusin on GRP Records

5932 **Best Instrumental Arrangement Accompanying Vocals:** "My Funny Valentine" (track from *The Fabulous Baker Boys Motion Picture Soundtrack*) by Michelle Pfeiffer, arranged by Dave Grusin on GRP Records

5933 **Best Album Package:** *Sound + Vision* by David Bowie, art director Roger Gorman on Rykodisc, Incorporated Records

5934 **Best Album Notes:** *Bird: The Complete Charlie Parker on Verve* by Charlie Parker, annotator Phil Schaap on Verve Records

5935 **Best Historical Album:** *Chuck Berry—The Chess Box* by Chuck Berry, producer Andy McKaie on Chess/MCA Records

5936 **Best Engineered Non-Classical Recording:** *Cry Like a Rainstorm—Howl Like the Wind* by Linda Ronstadt, engineer George Massenburg on Elektra Records

5937 **Non-Classical Producer of the Year:** Peter Asher

5938 **Best Classical Album:** *Bartok: 6 String Quartets* by the Emerson String Quartet, produced by Wolf Erichson on Deutsche Grammophon Records

5939 **Best Orchestral Performance:** *Mahler: Symphony Number 3 in D Minor* by Leonard Bernstein conducting the New York Philharmonic Orchestra on Deutsche Grammophon Records

5940 **Best Opera Recording:** *Wagner: Die Walküre* by James Levine conducting the Metropolitan Opera Orchestra, principal soloists Lakes, Moll, Morris, Norman, Behrens, Ludwig, produced by Cord Garben on Deutsche Grammophon Records

5941 **Best Non-Opera Choral Performance:** *Britten: War Requiem* by Robert Shaw conducting the Atlanta Symphony Orchestra & Chorus & Atlanta Boys Choir on Telarc Records

5942 **Best Classical Performance by an Instrumental Soloist with Orchestra:** *Barber: Cello Concerto, Opus 22/Britten: Symphony for Cello & Orchestra, Opus 68* by cellist Yo-Yo Ma with David Zinman conducting the Baltimore Symphony Orchestra on CBS Masterworks Records

5943 **Best Classical Performance by an Instrumental Soloist Without Orchestra:** *Bach: English Suites, BMW 806-11* by pianist Andras Schiff on London Records

5944 **Best Chamber Music Performance:** *Bartok: 6 String Quartets* by the Emerson String Quartet on Deutsche Grammophon Records

5945 **Best Classical Vocal Soloist Performance:** *Knoxville—Summer 1915 (Music of Barber, Menotti, Harbison, Stravinsky)* by Dawn Upshaw soprano with David Zinman conducting the Orchestra of St. Luke's on Elektra/ Nonesuch Records

5946 **Best Contemporary Composition:** *Reich: Different Trains* by the Kronos Quartet, composed by Steve Reich on Elektra/Nonesuch Records

5947 **Best Engineered Classical Recording:** *Britten: War Requiem* by Robert Shaw conducting the Atlanta Symphony Orchestra & Chorus & Atlanta Boys Choir & Solos, engineered by Jack Renner on Telarc Records

5948 **Classical Producer of the Year:** Robert Woods

———— **1 9 9 1** ————

5949 **Record of the Year:** "Another Day in Paradise" by Phil Collins, produced by Phil Collins and Hugh Padgham on Atlantic Records

5950 **Album of the Year:** *Back on the Block* produced and performed by Quincy Jones on Q West/Warner Brothers Records

5951 **Song of the Year:** "From a Distance" by Bette Midler, songwriter Julie Gold on Atlantic Records

5952 **Best New Artist:** Mariah Carey on Columbia/CBS Records

5953 **Best Female Pop Vocal Performance:** "Vision of Love" by Mariah Carey on Columbia/CBS Records

5954 **Best Male Pop Vocal Performance:** "Oh, Pretty Woman" (track from *A Black and White Night Live*) by Roy Orbison on Virgin Records

5955 **Best Duo or Group with Vocal Pop Performance:** "All My Life" by Linda Ronstadt and Aaron Neville on Elektra Entertainment Records

5956 **Best Pop Instrumental Performance:** "Twin Peaks Theme" (track from *Twin Peaks Soundtrack*) by Angelo Badalamenti on Warner Brothers Records

5957 **Best Female Rock Vocal Performance:** "Black Velvet" by Alannah Myles on Atlantic Records

5958 **Best Male Rock Vocal Performance:** "Bad Love" by Eric Clapton on Reprise/Duck Records

5959 **Best Duo or Group Rock Vocal Performance:** "Janie's Got a Gun" by Aerosmith on Geffen Records

5960 **Best Rock Instrumental Performance:** "D/FW" (track from *Family Style*) by the Vaughan Brothers on Epic Associated Records

5961 **Best Hard Rock Performance:** *Time's Up* by Living Colour on Epic Records

5962 **Best Metal Performance:** "Stone Cold Crazy" (track from *Rubaiyat/ Various Artists*) by Metallica on Elektra Entertainment Records

5963 **Alternative Music Performance:** *I Do Not Want What I Haven't Got* by Sinéad O'Connor on Ensign/Chrysalis Records

5964 **Best Female Rhythm & Blues Vocal Performance:** *Compositions* by Anita Baker on Elektra Entertainment Records

5965 **Best Male Rhythm & Blues Vocal Performance:** "Here and Now" by Luther Vandross on Epic Records

5966 **Best Rhythm & Blues Performance by a Duo or Group with Vocal:** "I'll Be Good to You" by Ray Charles and Chaka Khan on Q West/Warner Brothers Records

5967 **Best Rhythm & Blues Song:** "U Can't Touch This" by M.C. Hammer, songwriters Rick James, Alonzo Miller, M.C. Hammer on Capitol Records

5968 **Best Rap Performance:** "U Can't Touch This" by M.C. Hammer on Capitol Records

5969 **Best Duo or Group Rap Performance:** "Back on the Block" (track from *Quincy Jones/Back on the Block*) by Ice-T, Melle Mel, Big Daddy Kane, Kool Moe Dee, Quincy D. III and Quincy Jones on Q West/Warner Brothers Records

5970 **Best New Age Performance:** *Mark Isham* by Mark Isham on Virgin Records

5971 **Best Jazz Fusion Performance:** "Birdland" (track from *Back on the Block*) by Quincy Jones on Q West/ Warner Brothers Records

5972 **Best Female Jazz Vocal Performance:** *All That Jazz* by Ella Fitzgerald on Pablo Records

5973 **Best Male Jazz Vocal Performance:** *We Are in Love* by Harry Connick, Jr., on Columbia/CBS Records

5974 **Best Jazz Instrumental Performance by a Soloist:** *The Legendary Oscar Peterson Trio Live at the Blue Note* by Oscar Peterson on Telarc Records

5975 **Best Group Jazz Instrumental Performance:** *The Legendary Oscar Peterson Trio Live at the Blue Note* by Oscar Peterson on Telarc Records

5976 **Best Big Band Jazz Instrumental Performance:** "Basie's Bag" (track from *Big Boss Band*) by George Benson featuring the Count Basie Orchestra conducted by Frank Foster on Warner Brothers Records

5977 **Best Female Country Vocal Performance:** "Where've You Been" by Kathy Mattea on Mercury Records

5978 **Best Male Country Vocal Performance:** "When I Call Your Name" by Vince Gill on MCA Records

5979 **Best Duo or Group Vocal Country Performance:** *Pickin' on Nashville* by the Kentucky HeadHunters on Mercury Records

5980 **Best Country Vocal Collaboration:** "Poor Boy Blues" by Chet Atkins and Mark Knopfler on Columbia/CBS Records

5981 **Best Country Instrumental Performance:** "So Soft, Your Goodbye" (track from *Neck and Neck*) by Chet Atkins and Mark Knopfler on Columbia/CBS Records

5982 **Best Bluegrass Recording:** *I've Got That Old Feeling* by Alison Krauss on Rounder Records

5983 **Best Country Song:** "Where've You Been" by Kathy Mattea, songwriters Jon Vezner and Don Henry on Mercury Records

5984 **Best Rock/Contemporary Gospel Album:** *Beyond Belief* by Petra on Dayspring/Word Records

5985 **Best Pop Gospel Album:** *Another Time ... Another Place* by Sandi Patti on A&M/Word Records

5986 **Best Southern Gospel Album:** *The Great Exchange* by Bruce Carroll on Word Records

5987 **Best Traditional Soul Gospel Album:** *Tramaine Hawkins Live* by Tramaine Hawkins on Sparrow Corporation Records

5988 **Best Contemporary Soul Gospel Album:** *So Much 2 Say* by Take 6 on Reprise/Warner/Alliance Records

5989 **Best Choir or Chorus Gospel Album:** *Having Church* by Reverend James Cleveland on Savoy Records

5990 **Best Latin Pop Performance:** "Por Que Te Tengo Qeu Olvidar?" (track from *Nina*) by Jose Feliciano on Capitol/EMI Latin Records

5991 **Best Tropical Latin Performance:** "Lambada Timbales" (track from *Goza Mi Timbal*) by Tito Puente on Concord Picante Records

5992 **Best Mexican/American Performance:** "Soy de San Luis" (track from *Texas Tornadoes*) by the Texas Tornadoes on Reprise Records

5993 **Best Traditional Blues Recording:** *Live at San Quentin* by B.B. King on MCA Records

5994 **Best Contemporary Blues Recording:** *Family Style* by the Vaughan Brothers on Epic Associated Records

5995 **Best Traditional Folk Recording:** *On Praying Ground* by Doc Watson on Sugar Hill Records

5996 **Best Contemporary Folk Recording:** *Steady On* by Shawn Colvin on Columbia/CBS Records

5997 **Best Polka Recording:** *When It's Polka Time at Your House* by Jimmy Sturr and His Orchestra on Starr Records

5998 **Best Reggae Recording:** *Time Will Tell — A Tribute to Bob Marley* by Bunny Wailer on Sunachie Records

5999 **Best Recording for Children:** *The Little Mermaid — Original Motion Picture Soundtrack* composed by Howard Ashman and Alan Menken on Disneyland Records

6000 **Best Comedy Recording:** *P.D.Q. Bach: Oedipus Tex & Other Choral Calamities* by Professor Peter Schickele on Telarc Records

6001 **Best Spoken Word or Non-Musical Recording:** *Gracie: A Love Story* by George Burns on Simon & Schuster Audio

6002 **Best Musical Cast Show Album:** *Les Misérables, the Complete Symphonic Recording* produced by David Caddick on Relativity Records

6003 **Best Instrumental Composition:** "Change of Heart" (track from *Question and Answer*) composed by Pat Metheny on Geffen Records

6004 Best Instrumental Composition Written for a Motion Picture or Television: *Glory* composed by James Horner on Virgin Records

6005 Best Song Written Specifically for a Motion Picture or Television: "Under the Sea" (track from *The Little Mermaid Original Soundtrack*) composed by Alan Menken and Howard Ashman on Walt Disney Records

6006 Best Music Video—Short Form: *Opposites Attract* by Paula Abdul, video directors Michael Patterson & Candice Reckinger, video producer Sharon Oreck on Virgin Records

6007 Best Music Video—Long Form: *Please Hammer Don't Hurt 'Em The Movie* by M.C. Hammer, video director Rupert Wainwright, video producer John Oetjen on Capitol Home Video

6008 Best Arrangement of an Instrumental: "Birdland" (track from *Back on the Block*) by Quincy Jones & various artists, arranged by Quincy Jones, Ian Prince, Rod Temperton, Jerry Hey on Q West/Warner Brothers Records

6009 Best Instrumental Arrangement Accompanying Vocals: "The Places You Find Love" (track from *Back on the Block*) by Siedah Garrett & Chaka Khan on Quincy Jones Album, arrangers Jerry Hey, Glen Ballard, Clif Magness & Quincy Jones on Q West/Warner Brothers Records

6010 Best Album Package: *Days of Open Hand* (special edition Hologram Digipack) by Suzanne Vega, art directors Len Peltier, Jeffrey Gold, Suzanne Vega on A&M Records

6011 Best Album Notes: *Brownie: The Complete Emarcy Recordings of Clifford Brown* by Clifford Brown, annotator Dan Morgenstern on Emarcy Records

6012 Best Historical Album: *Robert Johnson—The Complete Recordings* by Robert Johnson, produced by Lawrence Cohn, Stephen Lavere on Columbia/CBS Records

6013 Best Engineered Non-Classical Recording: *Back on the Block* by Quincy Jones, engineer Bruce Swedien on Q West/Warner Brothers Records

6014 Non-Classical Producer of the Year: Quincy Jones

6015 Best Classical Album: *Ives: Symphony Number 2 (and Three Short Works)* by Leonard Bernstein conducting the New York Philharmonic, producer Hans Weber on Deutsche Grammophon Records

6016 Best Orchestral Performance: *Shostakovich: Symphonies Number 1 and 7* by Leonard Bernstein conducting the Chicago Symphony Orchestra on Deutsche Grammophon Records

6017 Best Opera Recording: *Wagner: Das Rheingold* by James Levine conducting the Metropolitan Opera Orchestra, principal soloists Morris, Ludwig, Jerusalem, Wlaschiha, Moll, Zednik, Rootering, produced by Cord Garben on Deutsche Grammophon Records

6018 Best Non-Opera Choral Performance: *Walton: Belshazzar's Feast/Bernstein: Chichester Psalms; Missa Brevis* by Robert Shaw conducting the Atlanta Symphony Orchestra and Chorus on Telarc Records

6019 Best Classical Performance by an Instrumental Soloist with Orchestra: *Shostakovich: Violin Concerto Number 1/Glazunov: Violin Concerto* by Itzhak Perlman violinist with Zubin Mehta conducting the Israel Philharmonic Orchestra on Angel Records

6020 Best Classical Performance by an Instrumental Soloist Without Orchestra: *The Last Recording (Chopin, Haydn, Liszt, Wagner)* by Vladimir Horowitz on Sony Classical Records

6021 Best Chamber Music or Other Small Ensemble Performance: *Brahms: The Three Violin Sonatas* by violinist Itzhak Perlman, pianist Daniel Barenboim on Sony Classical Records

6022 Best Classical Vocal Performance: *Carreras, Domingo, Pavarotti in Concert* by tenors Jose Carreras, Placido Domingo and Luciano Pavarotti, Zubin Mehta conducting the Orchestra del Maggio Musicale Fiorentino & Orchestra del teatro dell' Opera di Roma on London Records

6023 Best Contemporary Composition: *Bernstein: Arias & Barcarolles* by Sharp, Kaye, Barrett & Blier), composed by Leonard Bernstein on Koch International Records

6024 Best Engineered Classical Recording: *Rachmaninoff: Vespers* by Robert

Shaw conducting the Robert Shaw Festival Singers, engineered by Jack Renner on Telarc Records

6025 Classical Producer of the Year: Adam Stern

———— **1 9 9 2** ————

6026 Record of the Year: *Unforgettable* by Natalie Cole and Nat "King" Cole, produced by David Foster on Elektra Entertainment Records

6027 Album of the Year: *Unforgettable* by Natalie Cole and Nat "King" Cole, album produced by Natalie Cole, Andre Fischer, David Foster and Tommy Lipuma on Elektra Records

6028 Song of the Year: "Unforgettable" by Natalie Cole with Nat "King" Cole, songwriter Irving Gordon on Elektra Entertainment Records

6029 Best New Artist: Mark Cohn on Atlantic Records

6030 Best Female Pop Vocal Performance: "Something to Talk About" by Bonnie Raitt on Capitol Records

6031 Best Male Pop Vocal Performance: "When a Man Loves a Woman" by Michael Bolton on Columbia Records

6032 Best Duo or Group with Vocal Pop Performance: "Losing My Religion" by R.E.M. on Warner Brothers Records

6033 Best Traditional Pop Performance: "Unforgettable" by Natalie Cole and Nat "King" Cole on Elektra Entertainment Records

6034 Best Pop Instrumental Performance: *Robin Hood: Prince of Thieves* by Michael Kamen conducting the Greater Los Angeles Orchestra on Morgan Creek Records

6035 Best Solo Rock Vocal Performance: *Luck of the Draw* by Bonnie Raitt on Capitol Records

6036 Best Duo or Group Rock Vocal Performance: "Good Man, Good Woman" (track from *Luck of the Draw*) by Bonnie Raitt on Capitol Records

6037 Best Hard Rock Performance with Vocal: *For Unlawful Carnal Knowledge* by Van Halen on Warner Brothers Records

6038 Best Metal Performance with Vocal: *Metallica* by Metallica on Elektra Records

6039 Best Rock Instrumental Performance: "Cliffs of Dover" by Eric Johnson on Capitol Records

6040 Best Rock Song: "Soul Cages" written and performed by Sting on A&M Records

6041 Best Alternative Music Album: *Out of Time* by R.E.M. on Warner Brothers Records

6042 Best Female Rhythm & Blues Vocal Performance: *Burnin'* by Patti LaBelle on Warner Brothers Records and "How Can I Ease the Pain" by Lisa Fischer on Elektra Records

6043 Best Male Rhythm & Blues Vocal Performance: *Power of Love* by Luther Vandross on Epic Records

6044 Best Rhythm & Blues Performance by a Duo or Group with Vocal: *Cooley High Harmony* by Boyz II Men on Motown Records

6045 Best Rhythm & Blues Song: "Power of Love/Love Power" by Luther Vandross, songwriters Luther Vandross, Marcus Miller, Teddy Van on Epic Records

6046 Best Rap Solo Performance: "Mama Said Knock You Out" by L.L. Cool J. on Def Jam/Columbia Records

6047 Best Duo or Group Rap Performance: "Summertime" by D.J. Jazzy Jeff and the Fresh Prince on Jive Records

6048 Best New Age Album: *Fresh Aire 7* by the Mannheim Steamroller on American Grammophon Records

6049 Best Contemporary Jazz Performance: "Sassy" (track from *The Offbeat of Avenues*) by the Manhattan Transfer on Columbia Records

6050 Best Jazz Vocal Performance: *He Is Christmas* by Take 6 on Reprise Records

6051 Best Solo Jazz Instrumental: "I Remember You" (track from *Serenity*) by Stan Getz on Emarcy Records

6052 Best Jazz Group Instrumental Performance: *Saturday Night at the Blue Note* by the Oscar Peterson Trio on Telarc Records

6053 Best Large Jazz Ensemble Performance: *Live at the Royal Festival Hall* by Dizzy Gillespie and the United Nations Orchestra on Enja Records

6054 **Best Female Country Vocal Performance:** "Down at the Twist and Shout" by Mary Chapin-Carpenter on Columbia Records

6055 **Best Male Country Vocal Performance:** *Ropin' the Wind* by Garth Brooks on Capitol Records

6056 **Best Duo or Group Vocal Country Performance:** "Love Can Build a Bridge" by the Judds on Curb/RCA Records

6057 **Best Country Vocal Collaboration:** "Restless" (track from the *Mark O'Connor & the New Nashville Cats*) by Steve Wariner, Ricky Skaggs & Vince Gill on Warner Brothers Records

6058 **Best Country Instrumental Performance:** *The New Nashville Cats* by Mark O'Connor on Warner Brothers Records

6059 **Best Bluegrass Album:** *Spring Training* by Carl Jackson and John Starling (& the Nash Ramblers) on Sugar Hill Records

6060 **Best Country Song:** "Love Can Build a Bridge" by the Judds, songwriters John Jarvis, Naomi Judd and Paul Overstreet on Curb/RCA Records

6061 **Best Rock/Contemporary Gospel Album:** *Under Their Influence* by Russ Taff on Myrrh Records

6062 **Best Pop Gospel Album:** *For the Sake of the Call* by Steven Curtis Chapman on Sparrow Records

6063 **Best Southern Gospel Album:** *Homecoming* by the Gaither Vocal Band on Star Song Records

6064 **Best Traditional Soul Gospel Album:** *Pray for Me* by Mighty Clouds of Joy on Word Records

6065 **Best Contemporary Soul Gospel Album:** *Different Lifestyles* by BeBe and CeCe Winans on Capitol/Sparrow Records

6066 **Best Choir or Chorus Gospel Album:** *The Evolution of Gospel* by the Sounds of Blackness, choir director Gary Hines on Perspective/A&M Records

6067 **Best Latin Pop Album:** *Cosas del Amor* by Vikki Carr on Sony Discos International Records

6068 **Best Tropical Latin Album:** *Bachata Rosa* by Juan Luis Guerra on Karen Records

6069 **Best Mexican/American Album:** *16 de Septembre* by Little Joe on Sony Discos International Records

6070 **Best Traditional Blues Album:** *Live at the Apollo* by B.B. King on GRP Records

6071 **Best Contemporary Blues Album:** *Damn Right, I've Got the Blues* by Buddy Guy on Silvertone Records

6072 **Best Traditional Folk Album:** *The Civil War (Geoffrey Ward with Ric Burns and Ken Burns)* (original soundtrack) by various artists, producers Ken Burns and John Colby on Elektra/Nonesuch Records

6073 **Best Contemporary Folk Album:** *The Missing Years* by John Prine on Oh Boy Records

6074 **Best Polka Album:** *Live! At Gilley's* by Jimmy Sturr and His Orchestra on Starr Records

6075 **Best Reggae Album:** *As Raw as Ever* by Shabba Ranks on Epic Records

6076 **Best World Music Album:** *Planet Drum* by Mickey Hart on Rykodisc, Incorporated Records

6077 **Best Album for Children:** *A Cappella Kids* by the Maranatha! Kids, produced by Clifford "Barney" Robertson on Marantha Records

6078 **Best Comedy Album:** *P.D.Q. Bach: WTWP Classical Talkity-Talk Radio* by Professor Peter Schickele on Telarc Records

6079 **Best Spoken Word or Non-Musical Album:** *The Civil War (Geoffrey Ward with Ric Burns and Ken Burns)* by Ken Burns on Sound Editions Records

6080 **Best Musical Cast Show Album:** *The Will Rogers Follies* (original Broadway cast show album) by Keith Carradine & cast, produced by Cy Coleman and Mike Berniker, lyricists Betty Comden and Adolph Green, new score composer Cy Coleman on Columbia Records

6081 **Best Instrumental Composition:** "Basque" (track from *The Wind Beneath My Wings*) by Elton John, composed by John Barry on Epic Records

6082 **Best Instrumental Composition Written for a Motion Picture or for Television:** *Dances with Wolves* composed and performed by John Barry on Epic Records

6083 **Best Song Written Specifically for a Motion Picture or Television:** "(Everything I Do) I Do It for You" (track from

Robin Hood: Prince of Thieves) by Bryan Adams, Robert John "Mutt" Lange and Michael Kamen, songwriter Bryan Adams on A&M/ Morgan Creek Records

6084 Best Music Video—Short Form: *Losing My Religion* by R.E.M. video director Tarsem, video producer Dave Ramser on Warner Brothers Records

6085 Best Music Video—Long Form: *Madonna: Blonde Ambition World Tour Live* by Madonna, video directors Dave Mallet and Mark "Aldo" Miceli, video producer Tony Eaton on Pioneer LDCA, Incorporated

6086 Best Arrangement of an Instrumental: "Medley: Bess You Is My Woman/I Love You Porgy" (track from *The Gershwin Connection*) arranged and performed by Dave Grusin on GRP Records

6087 Best Instrumental Arrangement Accompanying Vocals: "Unforgettable" by Natalie Cole, arranged by Johnny Mandel on Elektra Records

6088 Best Album Package: *Billie Holiday: The Complete Decca Recordings* by Billie Holiday, art director Vartan on GRP Records

6089 Best Album Notes: *Star Time* by James Brown, annotators James Brown, Cliff White, Harry Weinger, Nelson George, Alan M. Leeds on Polydor Records

6090 Best Historical Album: *Billie Holiday: The Complete Decca Recordings* by Billie Holiday, producers Steven Lasker and Andy McKaie on GRP Records

6091 Best Engineered Non-Classical Recording: *Unforgettable* by Natalie Cole, engineers Al Schmitt, Woody Woodruff, Armin Steiner, David Reitzas on Elektra Records

6092 Non-Classical Producer of the Year: David Foster

6093 Best Classical Album: *Bernstein: Candide* by Leonard Bernstein conducting the London Symphony Orchestra, principal soloists Hadley, Anderson, Ludwig, Green, Gedda, Jones, Ollmann, producer Hans Weber on Deutsche Grammophon Records

6094 Best Orchestral Performance: *Corigliano: Symphony Number 1* by Daniel Barenboim conducting the Chi-

cago Symphony Orchestra on Erato/ Elektra International Classics Records

6095 Best Opera Recording: *Wagner: Götterdämmerung* by James Levine conducting the Metropolitan Opera Orchestra and Chorus, principal soloists Behrens, Studer, Schwarz, Goldberg, Weikl, Wlaschiha, Salminen, produced by Cord Garben on Deutsche Grammophon Records

6096 Best Performance of a Choral Work: *Bach: Mass in B Minor* by Sir Georg Solti conducting the Chicago Symphony Orchestra and Chorus, choral director Margaret Hillis on London Records

6097 Best Classical Performance by an Instrumental Soloist with Orchestra: *Barber: Piano Concerto* pianist John Browning with Leonard Slatkin conducting the St. Louis Symphony Orchestra on RCA Victor Red Seal Records

6098 Best Classical Performance by an Instrumental Soloist Without Orchestra: *Granados: Goyescas; Allegro de Concierto; Danza Lenta* by pianist Alicia de Larrocha on RCA Victor Red Seal Records

6099 Best Chamber Music Performance: *Brahms: Piano Quartets* by violinists Isaac Stern and Jamime Laredo, cellist Yo-Yo Ma, pianist Emanuel Ax on Sony Classical Records

6100 Best Classical Vocal Performance: *The Girl with Orange Lips (DeFalla, Ravel, Kim, Stravinsky, Delage)* by Dawn Upshaw with ensemble accompaniment on Elektra/Nonesuch Records

6101 Best Contemporary Composition: *Corigliano: Symphony Number 1* composed by John Corigliano, with Daniel Barenboim conducting the Chicago Symphony Orchestra on Erato/Elektra International Classics Records

6102 Best Engineered Classical Recording: *Bernstein: Candide* by Leonard Bernstein conducting the London Symphony Orchestra and Soloists, engineered by Gregor Zielinsky on Deutsche Grammophon Records

6103 Classical Producer of the Year: James Mallinson

──────── **1 9 9 3** ────────

6104 Record of the Year: "Tears in Heaven" by Eric Clapton, produced by Russ Titelman on Reprise Records

6105 Album of the Year: *Unplugged* by Eric Clapton, produced by Russ Titelman on Reprise Records

6106 Song of the Year: "Tears in Heaven" by Eric Clapton and Will Jennings, songwriter Eric Clapton on Reprise Records

6107 Best New Artist: Arrested Development on Chrysalis Records

6108 Best Female Pop Vocal Performance: "Constant Craving" by k.d. lang on Warner Brothers/Sire Records

6109 Best Male Pop Vocal Performance: "Tears in Heaven" by Eric Clapton on Reprise Records

6110 Best Duo or Group with Vocal Pop Performance: "Beauty and the Beast" by Celine Dion and Peabo Bryson on Epic/Walt Disney Records

6111 Best Traditional Pop Vocal Performance: *Perfectly Frank* by Tony Bennett on Columbia Records

6112 Best Pop Instrumental Performance: "Beauty and the Beast" (track from *Symphonic Hollywood*) by Richard Kaufman conducting the Nuremberg Symphony Orchestra on Varese Sarabande Records

6113 Best Female Vocal Rock Performance: "Ain't It Heavy" (track from *Never Enough*) by Melissa Etheridge on Island Records

6114 Best Male Vocal Rock Performance: *Unplugged* by Eric Clapton on Reprise Records

6115 Best Duo or Group Rock Vocal Performance: *Achtung Baby* by U2 on Island Records

6116 Best Hard Rock Performance with Vocal: "Give It Away" by the Red Hot Chili Peppers on Warner Brothers Records

6117 Best Metal Performance with Vocal: "Wish" (track from *Broken*) by the Nine Inch Nails on Interscope/Halo Five Records

6118 Best Rock Instrumental Performance: "Little Wing" (track from *The Sky Is Crying*) by Stevie Ray Vaughan & Double Trouble on Epic Records

6119 Best Rock Song: "Layla" by Eric Clapton, songwriters Eric Clapton and Jim Gordon on Reprise Records

6120 Best Alternative Music Album: *Bone Machine* by Tom Waits on Island Records

6121 Best Female Rhythm & Blues Vocal Performance: *The Woman I Am* by Chaka Khan on Warner Brothers Records

6122 Best Male Rhythm & Blues Vocal Performance: *Heaven and Earth* by Al Jarreau on Reprise Records

6123 Best Rhythm & Blues Performance by a Duo or Group with Vocal: "End of the Road" by Boyz II Men on Motown Records

6124 Best Rhythm & Blues Instrumental Performance: *Doo-Bop* by Miles Davis on Warner Brothers Records

6125 Best Rhythm & Blues Song: "End of the Road" by Boyz II Men, songwriters L.A. Reid, Babyface & Daryl Simmons on Motown Records

6126 Best Rap Solo Performance: "Baby Got Back" (track from *Mack Daddy*) by Sir Mix-A-Lot on Def American/Rhyme Cartel Records

6127 Best Duo or Group Rap Performance: "Tennessee" by Arrested Development on Chrysalis Records

6128 Best New Age Album: *Shepherd Moons* by Enya on Reprise Records

6129 Best Contemporary Jazz Instrumental Performance: *Secret Story* by Pat Metheny on Geffen Records

6130 Best Jazz Vocal Performance: "'Round Midnight" (track from play *Round Midnight* by Bobby McFerrin and Chick Corea) performed by Bobby McFerrin on Blue Note Records

6131 Best Solo Jazz Instrumental: "Lush Life" (track from *Lush Life – The Music of Billy Strayhorn*) by Joe Henderson on Verve Records

6132 Best Jazz Group or Individual Instrumental Performance: *I Heard You Twice the First Time* by Branford Marsalis on Columbia Records

6133 Best Large Jazz Ensemble Performance: *The Turning Point* by the McCoy Turner Big Band on Verve Records

6134 Best Female Country Vocal Performance: "I Feel Lucky" by Mary Chapin-Carpenter on Columbia Records

6135 Best Male Country Vocal Performance: *I Still Believe in You* by Vince Gill on MCA Records

6136 Best Duo or Group Vocal Country Performance: *Emmylou Harris and the Nash Ramblers at the Ryman* by Emmylou Harris and the Nash Ramblers on Reprise Records

6137 Best Country Vocal Collaboration: "The Whiskey Ain't Workin'" by Travis Tritt and Marty Stuart on Warner Brothers Records

6138 Best Country Instrumental Performance: *Sneakin' Around* by Chet Atkins and Jerry Reed on Columbia Records

6139 Best Bluegrass Album: *Every Time You Say Goodbye* by Alison Krauss & Union Station on Rounder Records

6140 Best Country Song: "I Still Believe in You" by Vince Gill and John Barlow Jarvis, songwriter Vince Gill on MCA Records

6141 Best Rock/Contemporary Gospel Album: *Unseen Power* by Petra on Dayspring Records

6142 Best Pop Gospel Album: *The Great Adventure* by Steven Curtis Chapman on Sparrow Records

6143 Best Southern Gospel Album: *Sometimes Miracles Hide* by Bruce Carroll on Word Records

6144 Best Traditional Soul Gospel Album: *He's Working It Out for You* by Shirley Caesar on Word Records

6145 Best Contemporary Soul Gospel Album: *Handel's Messiah—A Soulful Celebration* by various artists, produced by Mervyn Warren on Reprise Records

6146 Best Choir or Chorus Gospel Album: *Edwin Hawkins Music & Arts Seminar Mass Choir—Recorded Live in Los Angeles* by Edwin Hawkins, choir director of the Music & Arts Seminar Mass Choir on Fixit Records

6147 Best Latin Pop Album: *Otro Dia Mas Sin Verte* by Jon Secada on Capitol/EMI Latin Records

6148 Best Tropical Latin Album: *Frenesi* by Linda Ronstadt on Elektra Entertainment Records

6149 Best Mexican/American Album: *Más Canciones* by Linda Ronstadt on Elektra Records

6150 Best Traditional Blues Album: *Goin' Back to New Orleans* by Dr. John on Warner Brothers Records

6151 Best Contemporary Blues Album: *The Sky Is Crying* by Stevie Ray Vaughan & Double Trouble on Epic Records

6152 Best Traditional Folk Album: *An Irish Evening Live at the Grand Opera House, Belfast with Roger Daltrey and Nanci Griffith* by the Chieftains on RCA Victor Records

6153 Best Contemporary Folk Album: *Another Country* by the Chieftains on RCA Victor Records

6154 Best Polka Album: *35th Anniversary* by Walter Ostanek on World Renowned Sound Records

6155 Best Reggae Album: *X-Tra Naked* by Shabba Ranks on Epic Records

6156 Best World Music Album: *Brasileiro* by Sergio Mendes on Elektra Entertainment Records

6157 Best Album for Children: *Beauty and the Beast—Original Motion Picture Soundtrack* by various artists, songwriters Alan Menken and Howard Ashman on Walt Disney Records

6158 Best Comedy Album: *P.D.Q. Bach: Music for an Awful Lot of Winds & Percussion* by Professor Peter Schickele on Telarc Records

6159 Best Spoken Word or Non-Musical Album: *What You Can Do to Avoid AIDS* by Earvin "Magic" Johnson & Robert O'Keefe on Random House AudioBooks

6160 Best Musical Cast Show Album: *Guys & Dolls—The New Broadway Cast Recording* by the New Broadway cast, composer and lyricist Frank Loesser, producer Jay David Saks on Mercury Records

6161 Best Instrumental Composition: "Harlem Renaissance Suite" (track from *Harlem Renaissance*) composed and performed by Benny Carter on Musicmasters Records

6162 Best Instrumental Composition Written for a Motion Picture or for Television: *Beauty and the Beast* (instrumental portion of the album) composed by Alan Menken on Walt Disney Records

6163 **Best Song Written Specifically for a Motion Picture or Television:** "Beauty and the Beast" (track from *Beauty and the Beast*) by Celine Dion and Peabo Bryson, songwriters Alan Menken and Howard Ashman on Epic/Walt Disney Records

6164 **Best Music Video—Short Form:** *Digging in the Dirt* by Peter Gabriel, video director and line producer John Downer on Geffen Records

6165 **Best Music Video—Long Form:** *Diva* by Annie Lennox, video director Sophie Muller, video line producer Rob Small on 6 West Home Video

6166 **Best Arrangement of an Instrumental:** "Strike Up the Band" (track from *Brassy & Sassy*) by Rob McConnell and the Boss Brass, arranged by Rob McConnell on Concord Jazz Records

6167 **Best Instrumental Arrangement Accompanying Vocals:** "Here's to Life" (track from *Here's to Life*) by Shirley Horn, arranged by Johnny Mandel on Verve Records

6168 **Best Album Package:** *Spellbound—Compact* (Special Package) by Paula Abdul, art director Melanie Nissen on Capitol/Virgin Records

6169 **Best Album Notes:** *Queen of Soul—The Atlantic Recordings* by Aretha Franklin, annotators Dave Marsh, Jerry Wexler, David Ritz, Thulani Davis, Ahmet Ertegun, Tom Dowd, Arif Mardin on Rhino Records

6170 **Best Historical Album:** *The Complete Capitol Recordings of the Nat King Cole Trio* by the Nat King Cole Trio, produced by Michael Cuscuna on Mosaic Records

6171 **Best Engineered Non-Classical Recording:** *Dangerous* by Michael Jackson, engineered by Bruce Swedien and Ted Riley on Epic Records

6172 **Non-Classical Producer of the Year:** Daniel Lanois & Brian Eno, and L.A. Reid & Babyface

6173 **Best Classical Album:** *Mahler: Symphony Number 9* by Leonard Bernstein conducting the Berlin Philharmonic Orchestra, producer Horst Dittberner on Deutsche Grammophon Records

6174 **Best Orchestral Performance:** *Mahler: Symphony Number 9* by Leonard Bernstein conducting the Berlin Philharmonic Orchestra on Deutsche Grammophon Records

6175 **Best Opera Recording:** *Richard Strauss: Die Frau Ohne Schatten* by Sir Georg Solti conducting the Vienna Philharmonic Orchestra, principal soloists Domingo, Varady, Van Dam, Behrens, Runkel, Jo; producers Christopher Raeburn, Morton Winding, Stephen Trainor on London Records

6176 **Best Performance of a Choral Work:** *Orff: Carmina Burana* by Herbert Blomstedt conducting the San Francisco Girls/Boys Chorus, the San Francisco Symphony and Chorus on London Records

6177 **Best Classical Performance by an Instrumental Soloist with Orchestra:** *Prokofiev: Sinfonia Concertante/Tchaikovsky: Variations on a Rococo Theme* by cellist Yo-Yo Ma with Loren Mazel conducting the Pittsburgh Symphony Orchestra on Sony Classical Records

6178 **Best Classical Performance by an Instrumental Soloist Without Orchestra:** *Horowitz: Discovered Treasures (Chopin, Clementi, Liszt, Scarlatti, Scriabin)* by pianist Vladimir Horowitz on Sony Classical Records

6179 **Best Chamber Music Performance:** *Brahms: Sonatas for Cello and Piano* by cellist Yo-Yo Ma, pianist Emanuel Ax on Sony Classical Records

6180 **Best Classical Vocal Performance:** *Kathleen Battle at Carnegie Hall (Handel, Mozart, Liszt, Strauss, Carpentier, etc.)* by soprano Kathleen Battle accompanied by Margo Garrett on Deutsche Grammophon Records

6181 **Best Contemporary Composition:** *Barber: The Lovers* composed by Samuel Barber with Andrew Schenck conducting the Chicago Symphony Orchestra on Koch International Records

6182 **Best Engineered Classical Recording:** *Richard Strauss: Die Frau Ohne Schatten* by Sir Georg Solti conducting the Vienna Philharmonic Orchestra, principal soloists Domingo, Varady, Van Dam, Behrens; engineered by James Lock, John Pellowe, Jonathan Stokes, Philip Siney on London Records

6183 **Classical Producer of the Year:** Michael Fine

CMA Awards

The Country Music Association was formed in Nashville in 1958, but the CMA Awards did not come into existence until the Country Music Association was nine years old.

During the 1967 anniversary banquet, country performers and songwriters were presented with the first CMA statuettes. The next year, the award presentation was held October 19, 1968, separate from the annual banquet, at the Grand Ole Opry House. The presentation was videotaped for later broadcast on the "Kraft Music Hall."

Dale Evans and Roy Rogers hosted the first televised presentation. Today various country artists host and present the CMA awards. Originally there were ten awards presented. Like many national award ceremonies some classifications of awards have remained. Others have been dropped and replaced by still other awards.

In 1970, Porter Wagoner and Dolly Parton were named the first winners of the Vocal Duo of the Year. Also in 1970, Roy Clark was awarded the last Comedian of the Year Award.

In 1981, the Horizon Award was introduced. The Horizon Award is for career development by an individual or an act that has never won the CMA Award. The first recipient was Terri Gibbs.

The Song of the Year Award is determined by the national chart listing of the song in music trade magazines in combination with total membership votes. All other awards are determined by the combined votes of all members of the Country Music Association.

──────── **1 9 6 7** ────────

6184 Entertainer of the Year: Eddy Arnold

6185 Song of the Year: "There Goes My Everything" by Dallas Frazier

6186 Female Vocalist of the Year: Loretta Lynn

6187 Male Vocalist of the Year: Jack Greene

6188 Album of the Year: *There Goes My Everything* by Jack Greene on Decca Records

6189 Single of the Year: "There Goes My Everything" by Jack Greene on Decca Records

6190 Vocal Group of the Year: The Stoneman Family

6191 Instrumentalist of the Year: Chet Atkins

6192 Comedian of the Year: Don Bowman

6193 Instrumental Group of the Year: The Buckaroos

──────── **1 9 6 8** ────────

6194 Entertainer of the Year: Glen Campbell

6195 Song of the Year: "Honey" by Bobby Russell

6196 Female Vocalist of the Year: Tammy Wynette

6197 Male Vocalist of the Year: Glen Campbell

6198 Album of the Year: *Johnny Cash at Folsom Prison* by Johnny Cash on Columbia Records

6199 Single of the Year: "Harper Valley P.T.A." by Jeannie C. Riley on Plantation Records

6200 Vocal Group of the Year: Porter Wagoner and Dolly Parton

6201 Instrumentalist of the Year: Chet Atkins

6202 Comedian of the Year: Ben Colder

6203 Instrumental Group of the Year: The Buckaroos

──────── **1 9 6 9** ────────

6204 Entertainer of the Year: Johnny Cash

6205 Song of the Year: "Carroll County Accident" by Bob Ferguson

6206 Female Vocalist of the Year: Tammy Wynette

6207 Male Vocalist of the Year: Johnny Cash

6208 Album of the Year: *Johnny Cash at San Quentin Prison* by Johnny Cash on Columbia Records

6209 Single of the Year: "A Boy Named Sue" by Johnny Cash on Columbia Records

6210 Vocal Group of the Year: Johnny Cash and June Carter

6211 Instrumentalist of the Year: Chet Atkins

6212 Comedian of the Year: Archie Campbell

6213 Instrumental Group of the Year: Danny Davis & the Nashville Brass

──────── **1 9 7 0** ────────

6214 Entertainer of the Year: Merle Haggard

6215 Song of the Year: "Sunday Morning Coming Down" by Kris Kristofferson

6216 Female Vocalist of the Year: Tammy Wynette

6217 Male Vocalist of the Year: Merle Haggard

6218 Album of the Year: *Okie from Muskogee* by Merle Haggard on Capitol Records

6219 Single of the Year: "Okie from Muskogee" by Merle Haggard on Capitol Records

6220 Vocal Group of the Year: The Glaser Brothers

6221 Instrumentalist of the Year: Jerry Reed

6222 Comedian of the Year: Roy Clark

6223 Instrumental Group of the Year: Danny Davis & the Nashville Brass

6224 Vocal Duo of the Year: Porter Wagoner and Dolly Parton

──────── **1 9 7 1** ────────

6225 Entertainer of the Year: Charley Pride

6226 Song of the Year: "Easy Loving" by Freddie Hart

6227 Female Vocalist of the Year: Lynn Anderson

6228 **Male Vocalist of the Year:** Charley Pride
6229 **Album of the Year:** *I Won't Mention It Again* by Ray Price on Columbia Records
6230 **Single of the Year:** "Help Me Make It Through the Night" by Sammi Smith on Mega Records
6231 **Vocal Group of the Year:** The Osborne Brothers
6232 **Instrumentalist of the Year:** Jerry Reed
6233 **Vocal Duo of the Year:** Porter Wagoner and Dolly Parton
6234 **Instrumental Group of the Year:** Danny Davis & the Nashville Brass

———— **1 9 7 2** ————

6235 **Entertainer of the Year:** Loretta Lynn
6236 **Song of the Year:** "Easy Loving" by Freddie Hart
6237 **Female Vocalist of the Year:** Loretta Lynn
6238 **Male Vocalist of the Year:** Charley Pride
6239 **Album of the Year:** *Let Me Tell You About a Song* by Merle Haggard on Capitol Records
6240 **Single of the Year:** "The Happiest Girl in the Whole U.S.A." by Donna Fargo on Dot Records
6241 **Vocal Group of the Year:** The Statler Brothers
6242 **Instrumentalist of the Year:** Charlie McCoy
6243 **Vocal Duo of the Year:** Conway Twitty and Loretta Lynn
6244 **Instrumental Group of the Year:** Danny Davis & the Nashville Brass

———— **1 9 7 3** ————

6245 **Entertainer of the Year:** Roy Clark
6246 **Song of the Year:** "Behind Closed Doors" by Kenny O'Dell
6247 **Female Vocalist of the Year:** Loretta Lynn
6248 **Male Vocalist of the Year:** Charlie Rich
6249 **Album of the Year:** *Behind Closed Doors* by Charlie Rich on Epic Records

6250 **Single of the Year:** "Behind Closed Doors" by Charlie Rich on Epic Records
6251 **Vocal Group of the Year:** The Statler Brothers
6252 **Instrumentalist of the Year:** Charlie McCoy
6253 **Vocal Duo of the Year:** Conway Twitty and Loretta Lynn
6254 **Instrumental Group of the Year:** Danny Davis & the Nashville Brass

———— **1 9 7 4** ————

6255 **Entertainer of the Year:** Charlie Rich
6256 **Song of the Year:** "Country Bumpkin" by Don Wayne
6257 **Female Vocalist of the Year:** Olivia Newton-John
6258 **Male Vocalist of the Year:** Ronnie Milsap
6259 **Album of the Year:** *A Very Special Love Song* by Charlie Rich on Epic Records
6260 **Single of the Year:** "Country Bumpkin" by Cal Smith on MCA Records
6261 **Vocal Group of the Year:** The Statler Brothers
6262 **Instrumentalist of the Year:** Don Rich
6263 **Vocal Duo of the Year:** Conway Twitty and Loretta Lynn
6264 **Instrumental Group of the Year:** Danny Davis & the Nashville Brass

———— **1 9 7 5** ————

6265 **Entertainer of the Year:** John Denver
6266 **Song of the Year:** "Back Home Again" by John Denver
6267 **Female Vocalist of the Year:** Dolly Parton
6268 **Male Vocalist of the Year:** Waylon Jennings
6269 **Album of the Year:** *A Legend in My Own Time* by Ronnie Milsap on RCA Records
6270 **Single of the Year:** "Before the Next Teardrop Falls" by Freddy Fender on ABC-Dot Records
6271 **Vocal Group of the Year:** The Statler Brothers

6272 **Instrumentalist of the Year:** Johnny Gimble
6273 **Vocal Duo of the Year:** Conway Twitty and Loretta Lynn
6274 **Instrumental Group of the Year:** Roy Clark and Buck Trent

──────── **1 9 7 6** ────────

6275 **Entertainer of the Year:** Mel Tillis
6276 **Song of the Year:** "Rhinestone Cowboy" by Larry Weiss
6277 **Female Vocalist of the Year:** Dolly Parton
6278 **Male Vocalist of the Year:** Ronnie Milsap
6279 **Album of the Year:** *Wanted— The Outlaws* by Waylon Jennings, Willie Nelson, Tompall Glaser and Jessi Colter on RCA Records
6280 **Single of the Year:** "Good Hearted Woman" by Waylon Jennings and Willie Nelson on RCA Records
6281 **Vocal Group of the Year:** The Statler Brothers
6282 **Instrumentalist of the Year:** Hargus "Pig" Robbins
6283 **Vocal Duo of the Year:** Waylon Jennings and Willie Nelson
6284 **Instrumental Group of the Year:** Roy Clark and Buck Trent

──────── **1 9 7 7** ────────

6285 **Entertainer of the Year:** Ronnie Milsap
6286 **Song of the Year:** "Lucille" by Roger Bowling and Hal Bynum
6287 **Female Vocalist of the Year:** Crystal Gayle
6288 **Male Vocalist of the Year:** Ronnie Milsap
6289 **Album of the Year:** *Ronnie Milsap Live* by Ronnie Milsap on RCA Records
6290 **Single of the Year:** "Lucille" by Kenny Rogers on United Artists Records
6291 **Vocal Group of the Year:** The Statler Brothers
6292 **Instrumentalist of the Year:** Roy Clark
6293 **Vocal Duo of the Year:** Jim Ed Brown and Helen Cornelius
6294 **Instrumental Group of the Year:** The Original Texas Playboys

──────── **1 9 7 8** ────────

6295 **Entertainer of the Year:** Dolly Parton
6296 **Song of the Year:** "Don't It Make My Brown Eyes Blue" by Richard Leigh
6297 **Female Vocalist of the Year:** Crystal Gayle
6298 **Male Vocalist of the Year:** Don Williams
6299 **Album of the Year:** *It Was Almost Like a Song* by Ronnie Milsap on RCA Records
6300 **Single of the Year:** "Heaven's Just a Sin Away" by the Kendalls on Ovation Records
6301 **Vocal Group of the Year:** The Oak Ridge Boys
6302 **Instrumentalist of the Year:** Roy Clark
6303 **Vocal Duo of the Year:** Kenny Rogers and Dottie West
6304 **Instrumental Group of the Year:** The Oak Ridge Boys Band

──────── **1 9 7 9** ────────

6305 **Entertainer of the Year:** Willie Nelson
6306 **Song of the Year:** "The Gambler" by Don Schlitz
6307 **Female Vocalist of the Year:** Barbara Mandrell
6308 **Male Vocalist of the Year:** Kenny Rogers
6309 **Album of the Year:** *The Gambler* by Kenny Rogers on United Artists Records
6310 **Single of the Year:** "The Devil Went Down to Georgia" by the Charlie Daniels Band on Epic Records
6311 **Vocal Group of the Year:** The Statler Brothers
6312 **Instrumentalist of the Year:** Charlie Daniels
6313 **Vocal Duo of the Year:** Kenny Rogers and Dottie West
6314 **Instrumental Group of the Year:** The Charlie Daniels Band

──────── **1 9 8 0** ────────

6315 **Entertainer of the Year:** Barbara Mandrell
6316 **Song of the Year:** "He Stopped

Loving Her Today" by Bobby Braddock and Curly Putnam

6317 **Female Vocalist of the Year:** Emmylou Harris

6318 **Male Vocalist of the Year:** George Jones

6319 **Album of the Year:** *Coal Miner's Daughter* original motion picture soundtrack on MCA Records

6320 **Single of the Year:** "He Stopped Loving Her Today" by George Jones on Epic Records

6321 **Vocal Group of the Year:** The Statler Brothers

6322 **Instrumentalist of the Year:** Roy Clark

6323 **Vocal Duo of the Year:** Moe Bandy and Joe Stampley

6324 **Instrumental Group of the Year:** The Charlie Daniels Band

———— **1 9 8 1** ————

6325 **Entertainer of the Year:** Barbara Mandrell

6326 **Song of the Year:** "He Stopped Loving Her Today" by Bobby Braddock and Curly Putnam

6327 **Female Vocalist of the Year:** Barbara Mandrell

6328 **Male Vocalist of the Year:** George Jones

6329 **Album of the Year:** *I Believe in You* by Don Williams on MCA Records

6330 **Single of the Year:** "Elvira" by the Oak Ridge Boys on MCA Records

6331 **Vocal Group of the Year:** Alabama

6332 **Instrumentalist of the Year:** Chet Atkins

6333 **Horizon Award:** Terri Gibbs

6334 **Instrumental Group of the Year:** Alabama

6335 **Vocal Duo of the Year:** David Frizzell and Shelly West

———— **1 9 8 2** ————

6336 **Entertainer of the Year:** Alabama

6337 **Song of the Year:** "Always on My Mind" by Johnny Christopher, Wayne Carson and Mark James

6338 **Female Vocalist of the Year:** Janie Fricke

6339 **Male Vocalist of the Year:** Ricky Skaggs

6340 **Album of the Year:** *Always on My Mind* by Willie Nelson on Columbia Records

6341 **Single of the Year:** "Always on My Mind" by Willie Nelson on Columbia Records

6342 **Vocal Group of the Year:** Alabama

6343 **Instrumentalist of the Year:** Chet Atkins

6344 **Horizon Award:** Ricky Skaggs

6345 **Instrumental Group of the Year:** Alabama

6346 **Vocal Duo of the Year:** David Frizzell and Shelly West

———— **1 9 8 3** ————

6347 **Entertainer of the Year:** Alabama

6348 **Song of the Year:** "Always on My Mind" by Johnny Christopher, Wayne Carson and Mark James

6349 **Female Vocalist of the Year:** Janie Fricke

6350 **Male Vocalist of the Year:** Lee Greenwood

6351 **Album of the Year:** *The Closer You Get* by Alabama on RCA Records

6352 **Single of the Year:** "Swingin'" by John Anderson on Warner Brothers Records

6353 **Vocal Group of the Year:** Alabama

6354 **Instrumentalist of the Year:** Chet Atkins

6355 **Horizon Award:** John Anderson

6356 **Instrumental Group of the Year:** The Ricky Skaggs Band

6357 **Vocal Duo of the Year:** Merle Haggard and Willie Nelson

———— **1 9 8 4** ————

6358 **Entertainer of the Year:** Alabama

6359 **Song of the Year:** "Wind Beneath My Wings" by Larry Henley and Jeff Silbar

6360 **Female Vocalist of the Year:** Reba McEntire

6361 **Male Vocalist of the Year:** Lee Greenwood

6362 **Album of the Year:** *A Little Good News* by Anne Murray on Capitol Records

6363 **Single of the Year:** "A Little Good News" by Anne Murray on Capitol Records

6364 **Vocal Group of the Year:** The Statler Brothers

6365 **Instrumentalist of the Year:** Chet Atkins

6366 **Horizon Award:** The Judds

6367 **Instrumental Group of the Year:** The Ricky Skaggs Band

6368 **Vocal Duo of the Year:** Willie Nelson and Julio Iglesias

─────── **1 9 8 5** ───────

6369 **Entertainer of the Year:** Ricky Skaggs

6370 **Song of the Year:** "God Bless the USA" by Lee Greenwood

6371 **Female Vocalist of the Year:** Reba McEntire

6372 **Male Vocalist of the Year:** George Strait

6373 **Album of the Year:** *Does Fort Worth Ever Cross Your Mind?* by George Strait on MCA Records

6374 **Single of the Year:** "Why Not Me" by the Judds on RCA Records

6375 **Vocal Group of the Year:** The Judds

6376 **Instrumentalist of the Year:** Chet Atkins

6377 **Horizon Award:** Sawyer Brown

6378 **Music Video of the Year:** *All My Rowdy Friends Are Comin' Over Tonight* by Hank Williams, Jr., on Warner Brothers Records

6379 **Instrumental Group of the Year:** The Ricky Skaggs Band

6380 **Vocal Duo of the Year:** Anne Murray and Dave Loggins

─────── **1 9 8 6** ───────

6381 **Entertainer of the Year:** Reba McEntire

6382 **Song of the Year:** "On the Other Hand" by Paul Overstreet and Don Schlitz

6383 **Female Vocalist of the Year:** Reba McEntire

6384 **Male Vocalist of the Year:** George Strait

6385 **Album of the Year:** *Lost in the Fifties Tonight* by Ronnie Milsap on RCA Records

6386 **Single of the Year:** "Bop" by Dan Seals on EMI/America Records

6387 **Vocal Group of the Year:** The Judds

6388 **Instrumentalist of the Year:** Johnny Gimble

6389 **Horizon Award:** Randy Travis

6390 **Music Video of the Year:** *Who's Gonna Fill Their Shoes* by George Jones on Epic Records

6391 **Instrumental Group of the Year:** The Oak Ridge Boys Band

6392 **Vocal Duo of the Year:** Dan Seals and Marie Osmond

─────── **1 9 8 7** ───────

6393 **Entertainer of the Year:** Hank Williams, Jr.

6394 **Song of the Year:** "Forever and Ever, Amen" by Paul Overstreet and Don Schlitz

6395 **Female Vocalist of the Year:** Reba McEntire

6396 **Male Vocalist of the Year:** Randy Travis

6397 **Album of the Year:** *Always & Forever* by Randy Travis on Warner Brothers Records

6398 **Single of the Year:** "Forever and Ever, Amen" by Randy Travis on Warner Brothers Records

6399 **Vocal Group of the Year:** The Judds

6400 **Instrumentalist of the Year:** Johnny Gimble

6401 **Horizon Award:** Holly Dunn

6402 **Music Video of the Year:** *My Name Is Bocephus* by Hank Williams, Jr., on Warner Brothers Records

6403 **Vocal Duo of the Year:** Ricky Skaggs and Sharon White

─────── **1 9 8 8** ───────

6404 **Entertainer of the Year:** Hank Williams, Jr.

6405 **Song of the Year:** "80's Ladies" by K. T. Oslin

6406 **Female Vocalist of the Year:** K. T. Oslin

6407 **Male Vocalist of the Year:** Randy Travis

6408 **Album of the Year:** *Born to Boogie* by Hank Williams, Jr., on Warner Brothers Records

6409 **Single of the Year:** "Eighteen Wheels and a Dozen Roses" by Kathy Mattea on Polygram Records

6410 **Vocal Group of the Year:** Highway 101

6411 **Musician of the Year:** Chet Atkins

6412 **Vocal Event of the Year:** *Trio* Dolly Parton/Emmylou Harris/Linda Ronstadt

6413 **Horizon Award:** Ricky Van Shelton

6414 **Vocal Duo of the Year:** The Judds

———————— **1 9 8 9** ————————

6415 **Entertainer of the Year:** George Strait

6416 **Song of the Year:** "Chiseled in Stone" by Max D. Barnes and Vern Gosdin

6417 **Female Vocalist of the Year:** Kathy Mattea

6418 **Male Vocalist of the Year:** Ricky Van Shelton

6419 **Album of the Year:** *Will the Circle Be Unbroken, Vol. II* by the Nitty Gritty Dirt Band on Universal Records

6420 **Single of the Year:** "I'm No Stranger to the Rain" by Keith Whiteley on RCA Records

6421 **Vocal Group of the Year:** Highway 101

6422 **Musician of the Year:** Johnny Gimble

6423 **Vocal Event of the Year:** Hank Williams, Jr./Hank Williams, Sr.

6424 **Horizon Award:** Clint Black

6425 **Music Video of the Year:** *There's a Tear in My Beer* by Hank Williams, Jr., and Hank Williams, Sr., directed by Ethan Russell on Warner Brothers Records

6426 **Vocal Duo of the Year:** The Judds

———————— **1 9 9 0** ————————

6427 **Entertainer of the Year:** George Strait

6428 **Song of the Year:** "Where You've Been" by Jon Vezner

6429 **Female Vocalist of the Year:** Kathy Mattea

6430 **Male Vocalist of the Year:** Clint Black

6431 **Album of the Year:** *Pickin' on Nashville* by the Kentucky HeadHunters on Mercury Records

6432 **Single of the Year:** "When I Call Your Name" by Vince Gill on MCA Records

6433 **Vocal Group of the Year:** The Kentucky HeadHunters

6434 **Musician of the Year:** Johnny Gimble

6435 **Vocal Event of the Year:** Lorrie Morgan/Keith Whiteley

6436 **Horizon Award:** Garth Brooks

6437 **Music Video of the Year:** *The Dance* by Garth Brooks, directed by John Lloyd Miller on Capitol Nashville Records

6438 **Vocal Duo of the Year:** The Judds

———————— **1 9 9 1** ————————

6439 **Entertainer of the Year:** Garth Brooks

6440 **Song of the Year:** "When I Call Your Name" by Vince Gill and Tommy DuBois

6441 **Female Vocalist of the Year:** Tanya Tucker

6442 **Male Vocalist of the Year:** Vince Gill

6443 **Album of the Year:** *No Fences* by Garth Brooks on Capitol Nashville Records

6444 **Single of the Year:** "Friends in Low Places" by Garth Brooks on Capitol Nashville Records

6445 **Vocal Group of the Year:** The Kentucky HeadHunters

6446 **Musician of the Year:** Mark O'Connor

6447 **Vocal Event of the Year:** Mark O'Connor & the New Nashville Cats (featuring Vince Gill, Ricky Skaggs and Steve Wariner)

6448 **Horizon Award:** Travis Tritt

6449 **Music Video of the Year:** *The Thunder Rolls* by Garth Brooks, directed by Bud Schaetzle on Capitol Nashville Records

6450 **Vocal Duo of the Year:** The Judds

———————— **1 9 9 2** ————————

6451 **Entertainer of the Year:** Garth Brooks

6452 **Song of the Year:** "Look at Us" by Vince Gill and Max D. Barnes

6453 **Female Vocalist of the Year:** Mary Chapin-Carpenter

6454 **Male Vocalist of the Year:** Vince Gill

6455 **Album of the Year:** *Ropin' the Wind* by Garth Brooks on Liberty Records

6456 **Single of the Year:** "Achy Breaky Heart" by Billy Ray Cyrus on Mercury Records

6457 **Vocal Group of the Year:** Diamond Rio

6458 **Musician of the Year:** Mark O'Connor

6459 **Vocal Event of the Year:** Marty Stuart/Travis Tritt

6460 **Horizon Award:** Suzy Bogguss

6461 **Music Video of the Year:** *Midnight in Montgomery* by Alan Jackson, directed by Jim Shea on Arista Records

6462 **Vocal Duo of the Year:** Brooks & Dunn

———————— **1 9 9 3** ————————

6463 **Entertainer of the Year:** Vince Gill

6464 **Song of the Year:** "I Still Believe in You" by Vince Gill and John Barlow Larvis

6465 **Female Vocalist of the Year:** Mary Chapin-Carpenter

6466 **Male Vocalist of the Year:** Vince Gill

6467 **Album of the Year:** *I Still Believe in You* by Vince Gill on MCA Records

6468 **Single of the Year:** "Chattahoochee" by Alan Jackson on Arista Records

6469 **Vocal Group of the Year:** Diamond Rio

6470 **Musician of the Year:** Mark O'Connor

6471 **Vocal Event of the Year:** George Jones with Vince Gill, Mark Chestnutt, Garth Brooks, Travis Tritt, Joe Diffie, Alan Jackson, Pam Tillis, T. Graham Brown, Patty Loveless, Clint Black—*I Don't Need Your Rockin' Chair*

6472 **Horizon Award:** Mark Chestnutt

6473 **Music Video of the Year:** *Chattahoochee* by Alan Jackson, directed by Martin Kahan on Arista Records

6474 **Vocal Duo of the Year:** Brooks & Dunn

Pulitzer Prize for Music

When Joseph Pulitzer died his will established awards for journalism, drama, poetry, history and biography. Although the first Pulitzer prizes were awarded in 1917, the music award did not begin until 1943. He had left instructions to establish a scholarship for a music student. But in 1943 the Pulitzer Board decided to change the scholarship to a Pulitzer Prize Award.

The original stated intent was to honor American composers. But in the early years the awards were presented to American composers whose compositions imitated European musical structure.

Those early decisions were more a reflection of the taste of the people making up the Pulitzer Prize Board than the wishes of Joseph Pulitzer. His intent was to honor American composers. Selections were made according to the tastes of the Pulitzer Board rather than for original contributions to music. Symphonic works were honored, jazz was not.

As was frequently the case, the shortcoming of these awards prompted other organizations to create awards more reflective of Pulitzer's original intent: to honor American composers and not be limited by the tastes of the Pulitzer Board.

--------------- **1 9 4 3** ---------------

6475 William Schuman for his *Secular Cantata No. 2, a Free Song*, performed by the Boston Symphony Orchestra and published by G. Schirmer, Incorporated, New York.

--------------- **1 9 4 4** ---------------

6476 Howard Hanson for his *Symphony Number 4, Opus 34*, performed by the Boston Symphony Orchestra on December 3, 1943.

--------------- **1 9 4 5** ---------------

6477 Aaron Copland for his *Appalachian Spring*, a ballet written for and presented by Martha Graham and group, commissioned by Mrs. E. S. Coolidge, first presented at the Library of Congress, Washington, D.C., October 1944.

--------------- **1 9 4 6** ---------------

6478 Leo Sowerby for *The Canticle of the Sun*, commissioned by the Alice M. Ditson Fund, first performed by the Schola Cantorum in New York, April 1945.

--------------- **1 9 4 7** ---------------

6479 Charles Ives for his *Symphony No. 3*, first performed by Lou Harrison and Chamber Orchestra in New York, April 1946.

--------------- **1 9 4 8** ---------------

6480 Walter Piston for his *Symphony No. 3*, first performed by the Boston Symphony Orchestra in Boston, January 1948.

--------------- **1 9 4 9** ---------------

6481 Virgil Thomson for his music for the film *Louisiana Story*, released in 1948 by Robert Flaherty Productions.

--------------- **1 9 5 0** ---------------

6482 Gian-Carlo Menotti for his music in *The Consul*, produced at the Barrymore Theater, New York.

--------------- **1 9 5 1** ---------------

6483 Douglas S. Moore for his music in *Giants in the Earth*, produced by the Columbia Opera Workshop, March 28, 1951.

--------------- **1 9 5 2** ---------------

6484 Gail Kubik for his *Symphony Concertante*, performed at Town Hall, January 7, 1952.

--------------- **1 9 5 3** ---------------

No Award.

--------------- **1 9 5 4** ---------------

6485 Quincy Porter for *Concerto for Two Pianos and Orchestra*, first performed by the Louisville Symphony Orchestra, March 17, 1954. This was one of the works commissioned under a grant of the Rockefeller Foundation for new American compositions for orchestra, or soloists and orchestra.

--------------- **1 9 5 5** ---------------

6486 Gian-Carlo Menotti for *The Saint of Bleecker Street*, an opera first performed at the Broadway Theater, New York, December 27, 1954.

--------------- **1 9 5 6** ---------------

6487 Ernst Toch for *Symphony No. 3*, first performed by the Pittsburgh Symphony Orchestra, December 2, 1955.

--------------- **1 9 5 7** ---------------

6488 Norman Dello Joio for his *Meditations on Ecclesiastes*, first performed at the Juilliard School of Music on April 20, 1956.

──────── **1 9 5 8** ────────

6489 Samuel Barber for *Vanessa*, an opera in four acts, libretto by Gian-Carlo Menotti. First presented January 15, 1958, at the Metropolitan Opera House.

──────── **1 9 5 9** ────────

6490 John LaMontaine for his *Concerto for Piano and Orchestra*, first performed in Washington, D.C., by the National Symphony Orchestra on November 25, 1958.

──────── **1 9 6 0** ────────

6491 Elliott Carter for *Second String Quartet*, first performed at the Juilliard School of Music, March 25, 1960.

──────── **1 9 6 1** ────────

6492 Walter Piston for his *Symphony No. 7*, first performed by the Philadelphia Orchestra on February 10, 1961, and commissioned by the Philadelphia Orchestra Association.

──────── **1 9 6 2** ────────

6493 Robert Ward for *The Crucible*, an opera in three acts, libretto by Berrard Stambler, based on the play by Arthur Miller. First performed at New York City Center, on October 26, 1961, by the New York City Opera Company.

──────── **1 9 6 3** ────────

6494 Samuel Barber for *Piano Concerto No. 1*, which had its world premiere with the Boston Symphony Orchestra at Philharmonic Hall on September 24, 1962.

──────── **1 9 6 4** ────────

No Award.

──────── **1 9 6 5** ────────

No Award.

──────── **1 9 6 6** ────────

6495 Leslie Bassett for his *Variations for Orchestra*. It was first performed in the United States by Eugene Ormandy and the Philadelphia Orchestra at the Academy of Music in Philadelphia on October 22, 1965.

──────── **1 9 6 7** ────────

6496 Leon Kirchner for his *Quartet No. 3*, first performed by the Beaux Arts Quartet in Town Hall January 27, 1967.

──────── **1 9 6 8** ────────

6497 George Crumb for his orchestral suite, *Echoes of Time and the River*, first performed on May 26, 1967, by the Chicago Symphony Orchestra at Mandel Hall, University of Chicago, having been commissioned by the University in connection with the celebration of its 75th anniversary.

──────── **1 9 6 9** ────────

6498 Karel Husa for his *String Quartet No 3*, first performed at the Goodman Theatre, Chicago, on October 14, 1968, by the Fine Arts Quartet.

──────── **1 9 7 0** ────────

6499 Charles Wuorinen for *Time's Ecomium*, premiered in its entirety at the Berkshire Music Festival on August 16, 1969.

──────── **1 9 7 1** ────────

6500 Mario Davidovsky for *Synchronisms No. 6 for Piano and Electronic Sound (1970)*. Premiered August 19, 1970, at the Berkshire Music Festival.

──────── **1 9 7 2** ────────

6501 Jacob Druckman for *Windows*. Premiered by the Chicago Symphony Orchestra on March 16, 1972, at Orchestra Hall, Chicago.

─────── **1 9 7 3** ───────

6502 Elliott Carter for *String Quartet No. 3*. Premiered by the Juilliard String Quartet at Tully Hall, Lincoln Center, New York City, January 23, 1973.

─────── **1 9 7 4** ───────

6503 Donald Martino for his chamber music piece *Notturno*, commissioned by the Walter W. Naumburg Foundation and first performed May 15, 1973, at Alice Tully Hall, New York City, by Speculum Musicae.

6504 Special citation to Roger Sessions for his life's work as a distinguished American composer.

─────── **1 9 7 5** ───────

6505 Dominick Argento for *From the Diary of Virginia Woolf*, for medium voice and piano, commissioned by the Shubert Club of St. Paul, and premiered January 5, 1975.

─────── **1 9 7 6** ───────

6506 Ned Rorem for *Air Music*, first performed by the Cincinnati Symphony Orchestra December 5, 1975. It was subtitled "Ten Etudes for Orchestra."

6507 Special award bestowed posthumously on Scott Joplin, in this bicentennial year, for his contribution to American music.

─────── **1 9 7 7** ───────

6508 Richard Wernick for *Visions of Terror and Wonder* for mezzo-soprano and orchestra, premiered at the Aspen Music Festival, July 19, 1976. It was commissioned by the festival's Conference on Contemporary Music, with assistance from the National Endowment for the Arts.

─────── **1 9 7 8** ───────

6509 Michael Colgrass for *Déjà Vu for Percussion Quartet and Orchestra*, commissioned by the New York Philhar-

monic and premiered by that orchestra on October 20, 1977.

─────── **1 9 7 9** ───────

6510 Joseph Schwantner for *Aftertones of Infinity*, first performed by the American Composers Orchestra on January 29, 1979, in Alice Tully Hall, New York City.

─────── **1 9 8 0** ───────

6511 David Del Tredici for *In Memory of a Summer Day*, a work for soprano solo and orchestra, commissioned by the St. Louis Symphony for its 100th anniversary and premiered by that orchestra February 23, 1980.

─────── **1 9 8 1** ───────

No Award.

─────── **1 9 8 2** ───────

6512 Roger Sessions for *Concerto for Orchestra*, first performed by the Boston Symphony Orchestra on October 23, 1981, Seiji Ozawa conductor.

6513 Special citation to Milton Babbitt for his life's work as distinguished and seminal American composer.

─────── **1 9 8 3** ───────

6514 Ellen Taaffe Zwilch for *Symphony No. 1* (three movements for orchestra), commissioned by the American Composers Orchestra and premiered by that orchestra May 5, 1982 in Alice Tully Hall, New York City.

─────── **1 9 8 4** ───────

6515 Bernard Rands for *"Canti del Sole" for Tenor and Orchestra*, premiered by the New York Philharmonic Orchestra June 8, 1983.

─────── **1 9 8 5** ───────

6516 Stephen Albert for *Symphony River Run*, premiered by the National Symphony Orchestra January 17, 1985.

6517 Special citation to William Schuman for more than a half century of contribution to American music as composer and educational leader.

——————— **1 9 8 6** ———————

6518 George Perle for *Wind Quintet IV*, premiered October 2, 1985, at Merkin Concert Hall in New York City.

——————— **1 9 8 7** ———————

6519 John Harbison for *The Flight Into Egypt*, premiered by the Cantata Singers and Ensemble on November 21, 1986, at the New England Conservatory in Boston.

——————— **1 9 8 8** ———————

6520 William Bolcom for *12 New Etudes for Piano*, first complete performance by Marc-Andre Hamelin, pianist on March 30, 1987, at Temple University, Philadelphia, Pennsylvania.

——————— **1 9 8 9** ———————

6521 Roger Reynolds for *Whispers out of Time* premiered December 11, 1988, at Buckley Recital Hall, Amherst College, Massachusetts.

——————— **1 9 9 0** ———————

6522 Mel Powell for *"Duplicates": A Concerto for Two Pianos and Orchestra*, premiered by the Los Angeles Philharmonic January 26, 1990.

——————— **1 9 9 1** ———————

6523 Shulamit Ran for *Symphony*, commissioned by the Philadelphia Orchestra and premiered by that orchestra October 19, 1990.

——————— **1 9 9 2** ———————

6524 Wayne Peterson for *The Face of the Night, the Heart of the Dark*.

——————— **1 9 9 3** ———————

6525 Christopher Rouse for *Trombone Concerto*.

Part Three

CINEMA

Academy Awards — Oscars

The Academy of Motion Picture Arts and Sciences (AMPAS) was founded in 1927. Part of the stated purpose was to encourage the growth and recognition of motion pictures through the presentation of awards for distinctive achievements. The first award ceremony took place just one week after the formation of AMPAS. This first ceremony took place at a banquet held at the Hollywood Roosevelt Hotel.

After 1943, increasing popularity and commercial success of the award presentation caused an end to presentations at banquet ceremonies. The award presentation has been an event in its own right ever since.

The statuette was sculpted in 1928 and was originally cast in bronze standing on Belgian black marble. The 13 1/2 inch tall sculpture is now made of a tin, copper and antimony alloy called "Britannia" and the statuette stands on a metal base. During World War II (from 1942 to 1945) the Academy Award was made of plaster. When materials became available again, the metal statuettes reappeared.

Legend says that the award was nameless until 1931 when the original librarian for AMPAS, Margaret Herrick, saw the statuette for the first time and commented, "It looks just like my uncle Oscar." The Academy Award has been referred to as the "Oscar" ever since.

At the first award ceremonies, 15 statuettes were awarded. The next year only seven were given. Since that time, the number of awards has steadily increased. An example of awards given in the first ceremony but no longer needed is the one for title writing. Since sound came to films and title writing was not needed any more, the award for title writing was never given again.

Early films were made in black and white. When the use of color became more frequent, cinematography, costume design, art direction and set decoration awards were doubled with awards given for both black and white and color films. This practice of dual awards ended in 1957.

Assistant Director awards were given between 1932 and 1937. An award for Dance Director only lasted three years. The greatest growth was in scientific or technical awards, begun at the 1930 ceremonies.

The Academy members allowed to vote for the award recipients are limited to those in the same classification: actors for actors, directors for directors, editors for editors, etc. Thus the Academy Awards show respect for the winner among his or her peers in the business.

──────── **1 9 2 8** ────────

6526 **Best Picture:** *Wings*
6527 **Best Actor:** Emil Jannings in *The Way of All Flesh* and *The Last Command*
6528 **Best Actress:** Janet Gaynor in *Seventh Heaven, Street Angel* and *Sunrise*
6529 **Best Director (Comedy Picture):** Lewis Milestone for *Two Arabian Nights*
6530 **Best Director (Dramatic Picture):** Frank Borzage for *Seventh Heaven*
6531 **Best Art Direction:** William Menzies for *The Dove* and *The Tempest*
6532 **Best Cinematography:** Charles Rosher and Karl Struss for *Sunrise*
6533 **Best Writing/Original Story:** Ben Hecht for *Underworld*
6534 **Best Writing/Adaptation:** Benjamin Glazer for *Seventh Heaven*
6535 **Best Writing/Title Writing:** Joseph Farnham
6536 **Best Engineering Effects:** Roy Pomeroy for *Wings*
6537 **Most Unique and Artistic Picture:** *Sunrise*
6538 **Special Award:** To Warner Brothers for producing *The Jazz Singer*, the pioneer talking picture, which has revolutionized the industry. To Charles Chaplin for his versatility and genius in writing, acting, directing and producing *The Circus.*

──────── **1 9 2 9** ────────

6539 **Best Picture:** *The Broadway Melody*
6540 **Best Actor:** Warner Baxter in *In Old Arizona*
6541 **Best Actress:** Mary Pickford in *Coquette*
6542 **Best Director:** Frank Lloyd for *The Divine Lady*
6543 **Best Art Direction:** Cedric Gibbons for *The Bridge of San Luis Rey*
6544 **Best Cinematography:** Clyde De Vinna for *White Shadows in the South Seas*
6545 **Best Writing:** Hans Kraly for *The Patriot*

──────── **1 9 3 0** ────────

6546 **Best Picture:** *All Quiet on the Western Front*

6547 **Best Actor:** George Arliss in *Disraeli*
6548 **Best Actress:** Norma Shearer in *The Divorcee*
6549 **Best Director:** Lewis Milestone for *All Quiet on the Western Front*
6550 **Best Art Direction:** Herman Rosse for *King of Jazz*
6551 **Best Cinematography:** Joseph T. Rucker and Willard Van Der Veer for *With Byrd at the South Pole*
6552 **Best Writing:** Frances Marion for *The Big House*

──────── **1 9 3 1** ────────

6553 **Best Picture:** *Cimarron*
6554 **Best Actor:** Lionel Barrymore in *A Free Soul*
6555 **Best Actress:** Marie Dressler in *Min and Bill*
6556 **Best Director:** Norman Taurog for *Skippy*
6557 **Best Art Direction:** Max Ree for *Cimarron*
6558 **Best Cinematography:** Floyd Crosby for *Tabu*
6559 **Best Writing/Original Story:** John Monk Saunders for *The Dawn Patrol*
6560 **Best Writing/Adaptation:** Howard Estabrook for *Cimarron*
6561 **Best Sound Recording:** Paramount Studio Sound Department
6562 **Scientific or Technical/Class I (Academy Statuette with Engraved Plaque and Individual Certificates of First Award):** To Electrical Research Products, Inc., RCA-Photophone Pictures, Inc., and RKO Radio Pictures, Inc. for noise reduction recording equipment. To DuPont Film Manufacturing Corp. and Eastman Kodak Co. for supersensitive panchromatic film.
6563 **Scientific or Technical/Class II (Certificate of Honorable Mention):** To Fox Film Corp. for effective use of synchro-projection composite photography.
6564 **Scientific or Technical/Class III (Honorable Mention in Report of Board of Judges):** To Electrical Research Products, Inc., for moving coil microphone transmission. To RKO Radio Pictures, Inc., for reflex-type microphone concentrators. To RCA-Photophone Pictures, Inc., for ribbon microphone transmitters.

——————— **1 9 3 2** ———————

6565 Best Picture: *Grand Hotel*
6566 Best Actor (tie): Fredric March in *Dr. Jekyll and Mr. Hyde* and Wallace Beery in *The Champ*
6567 Best Actress: Helen Hayes in *The Sin of Madelon Claudet*
6568 Best Director: Frank Borzage for *Bad Girl*
6569 Best Art Direction: Gordon Wiles for *Transatlantic*
6570 Best Cinematography: Lee Garmes for *Shanghai Express*
6571 Best Writing/Original Story: Frances Marion for *The Champ*
6572 Best Writing/Adaptation: Edwin Burke for *Bad Girl*
6573 Best Sound Recording: Paramount Studio Sound Department
6574 Best Short Subject/Cartoon: *Flowers and Trees*
6575 Best Short Subject/Comedy: *The Music Box*
6576 Best Short Subject/Novelty: *Wrestling Swordfish*
6577 Scientific or Technical/Class II (Certificate of Honorable Mention): To Technicolor Motion Picture Corp. for color cartoon process.
6578 Scientific or Technical/Class III (Honorable Mention in Report of Board of Judges): To Eastman Kodak Co. for type II-B Sensitometer
6579 Special Honorary Award: Walt Disney for creating Mickey Mouse.

——————— **1 9 3 3** ———————

6580 Best Picture: *Cavalcade*
6581 Best Actor: Charles Laughton in *The Private Life of Henry VIII*
6582 Best Actress: Katharine Hepburn in *Morning Glory*
6583 Best Director: Frank Lloyd for *Cavalcade*
6584 Best Art Direction: William S. Darling for *Cavalcade*
6585 Best Cinematography: Charles Bryant Lang, Jr. for *A Farewell to Arms*
6586 Best Writing/Original Story: Robert Lord for *One Way Passage*
6587 Best Writing/Adaptation: Sarah Y. Mason and Victor Heerman for *Little Women*

6588 Best Assistant Director: William Tummel — 20th Century-Fox, Charles Dorian — Metro-Goldwyn-Mayer, Charles Barton — Paramount, Dowey Starkey — RKO Radio Pictures, Fred Fox — United Artists, Scott Beal — Universal and Gordon Hollingshead — Warner Brothers
6589 Best Sound Recording: Paramount Studio Sound Department (Franklin Hansen, sound director) for *A Farewell to Arms*
6590 Best Short Subject/Cartoon: *The Three Little Pigs*
6591 Best Short Subject/Comedy: *So This Is Harris*
6592 Best Short Subject/Novelty: *Krakatoa*
6593 Scientific or Technical/Class I (Certificate of Honorable Mention): To Electrical Research Products, Inc., for their high-fidelity recording and reproducing system. To RCA-Victor Co. for their high-fidelity recording and reproducing system.
6594 Scientific or Technical/Class III (Honorable Mention in Report of Board of Judges): To Fox Film Corp., Fred Jackman and Warner Brothers Pictures, Inc., and Sydney Sanders of RKO Studios, Inc., for their development and effective use of the translucent cellulose screen in composite photography.

——————— **1 9 3 4** ———————

6595 Best Picture: *It Happened One Night*
6596 Best Actor: Clark Gable in *It Happened One Night*
6597 Best Actress: Claudette Colbert in *It Happened One Night*
6598 Best Director: Frank Capra for *It Happened One Night*
6599 Best Art Direction: Cedric Gibbons and Frederic Hope for *The Merry Widow*
6600 Best Cinematography: Victor Milner for *Cleopatra*
6601 Best Writing/Original Story: Arthur Caesar for *Manhattan Melodrama*
6602 Best Writing/Adaptation: Robert Riskin for *It Happened One Night*
6603 Best Assistant Director: John Waters for *Viva Villa!*
6604 Best Music/Score: Columbia

Studio Music Department (Louis Silvers, department head; thematic music by Victor Schertzinger and Gus Kahn) for *One Night of Love*

6605 **Best Music/Best Song:** "The Continental" from *The Gay Divorcee*, music by Con Conrad, lyrics by Herb Magidson

6606 **Best Sound Recording:** Columbia Studio Sound Department (John Livadary, sound director) for *One Night of Love*

6607 **Film Editing:** Conrad Nervig for *Eskimo*

6608 **Best Short Subject/Cartoon:** *The Tortoise and the Hare*

6609 **Best Short Subject/Comedy:** *La Cucaracha*

6610 **Best Short Subject/Novelty:** *City of Wax*

6611 **Scientific or Technical/Class I (Certificate of Honorable Mention):** To Electrical Research Products, Inc., for their development of the vertical-cut disc method of sound recording for motion pictures (hill and dale recording).

6612 **Scientific or Technical/Class III (Honorable Mention in Report of Board of Judges):** To Columbia Pictures Corp. for the application of the vertical-cut disc method (hill and dale recording) to actual studio production, with their recording of the sound on the picture *One Night of Love*. To Bell & Howell Co. for their development of the Bell and Howell fully automatic sound and picture printer.

6613 **Special Award (Miniature Statuette):** To Shirley Temple in recognition of her outstanding contribution to screen entertainment during 1934.

───────── **1935** ─────────

6614 **Best Picture:** *Mutiny on the Bounty*

6615 **Best Actor:** Victor McLaglen in *The Informer*

6616 **Best Actress:** Bette Davis in *Dangerous*

6617 **Best Director:** John Ford for *The Informer*

6618 **Best Art Direction:** Richard Day for *The Dark Angel*

6619 **Best Cinematography:** Hal Mohr for *A Midsummer Night's Dream*

6620 **Best Writing/Original Story:** Ben Hecht and Charles MacArthur for *The Scoundrel*

6621 **Best Writing/Best Written Screenplay:** Dudley Nichols for *The Informer*

6622 **Best Assistant Director:** Clem Beauchamp and Paul Wing for *Lives of a Bengal Lancer*

6623 **Best Music/Score:** RKO Studio Music Department (Max Steiner, department head and composer of winning score) for *The Informer*

6624 **Best Music/Best Song:** "Lullaby of Broadway" from *Gold Diggers of 1935*, music by Harry Warren, lyrics by Al Dubin

6625 **Best Dance Direction:** Dave Gould for "I've Got a Feeling You're Fooling" from *Broadway Melody of 1936* and "Straw Hat" from *Folies-Bergere*

6626 **Best Sound Recording:** Metro-Goldwyn-Mayer Sound Department (Douglas Shearer, sound director) for *Naughty Marietta*

6627 **Best Film Editing:** Ralph Dawson for *A Midsummer Night's Dream*

6628 **Best Short Subject/Cartoon:** *Three Orphan Kittens*

6629 **Best Short Subject/Comedy:** *How to Sleep*

6630 **Best Short Subject/Novelty:** *Wings Over Mt. Everest*

6631 **Scientific or Technical/Class I (Certificate of Honorable Mention):** To AGFA Ansco Corp. for their development of AGFA Infra-red film. To Eastman Kodak Co. for their development of the Eastman Pola-Screen.

6632 **Scientific or Technical/Class III (Honorable Mention in Report of the Board of Judges):** To Metro-Goldwyn-Mayer Studio for the development of anti-directional negative and positive development by means of jet turbulation and the application of the method to all negative and print processing of the entire product of a major producing company. To William A. Mueller of Warner Brothers–First National Studio Sound Department for his method of dubbing, in which the level of dialog automatically controls level of accompanying music and sound effects. To Mole-Richardson Co. for their development of "Solar-Spot" spot lamps. To Douglas Shearer and

Metro-Goldwyn-Mayer Studio Sound Department for their automatic control system for cameras and sound recording machines and auxiliary stage equipment. To Electrical Research Products, Inc., for their study and development of equipment to analyze and measure flutter resulting from the travel of film through the mechanisms used in the recording and reproduction of sound. To Paramount Productions, Inc., for their design and construction of the Paramount transparency air turbine developing machine. To Nathan Levinson, Director of Sound Recording for Warner Brothers–First National Studio for method of intercutting variable area and variable density soundtracks to secure an increase in the effective volume recorded for motion pictures.

6633 Special Award: David Wark Griffith for distinguished creative achievements as director and producer and lasting contributions to the progress of the motion picture arts.

———————— **1 9 3 6** ————————

6634 Best Picture: *The Great Ziegfeld*

6635 Best Actor: Paul Muni in *The Story of Louis Pasteur*

6636 Best Actress: Luise Rainer in *The Great Ziegfeld*

6637 Best Director: Frank Capra for *Mr. Deeds Goes to Town*

6638 Best Supporting Actor: Walter Brennan in *Come and Get It*

6639 Best Supporting Actress: Gale Sondergaard in *Anthony Adverse*

6640 Best Art Direction: Richard Day for *Dodsworth*

6641 Best Cinematography: Tony Gaudio for *Anthony Adverse*

6642 Best Writing/Original Story: Pierre Collings and Sheridan Gibney for *The Story of Louis Pasteur*

6643 Best Writing/Best Written Screenplay: Pierre Collings and Sheridan Gibney for *The Story of Louis Pasteur*

6644 Best Assistant Director: Jack Sullivan for *The Charge of the Light Brigade*

6645 Best Music/Score: Warner Brothers Studio Music Department (Leo Forbstein, department head; Erich Wolfgang Korngold, composer) for *Anthony Adverse*

6646 Best Music/Best Song: Jerome Kern, music and Dorothy Fields, lyrics for "The Way You Look Tonight" from *Swingtime*

6647 Best Dance Direction: Seymour Felix for "A Pretty Girl Is Like a Melody" from *The Great Ziegfeld*

6648 Best Sound Recording or Sound: Metro-Goldwyn-Mayer Sound Department (Douglas Shearer, sound director) for *San Francisco*

6649 Best Film Editing: Ralph Dawson for *Anthony Adverse*

6650 Best Short Subject/Cartoon: *Country Cousin*

6651 Best Short Subject/One Reel: *Bored of Education*

6652 Best Short Subject/Two Reel: *The Public Pays*

6653 Best Short Subject/Color: *Give Me Liberty*

6654 Scientific or Technical/Class I (Academy Statuette and Individual Certificate of First Award): To Douglas Shearer and the Metro-Goldwyn-Mayer Studio Sound Department for the development of a practical two-way horn system and a biased Class A push-pull recording system.

6655 Scientific or Technical/Class I (Certificate of Honorable Mention): To E. C. Wente and the Bell Telephone Laboratories for multi-cellular high-frequency horn and receiver. To RCA Manufacturing Co., Inc., for their rotary stabilizer sound head.

6656 Scientific or Technical/Class III (Honorable Mention in Report of Board of Judges): To RCA Manufacturing Co., Inc., for their development of a method of recording and printing sound records utilizing a restricted spectrum (known as ultra-violet light recording). To Electrical Research Products, Inc., for the ERPI "Type Q" portable recording channel. To RCA Manufacturing Co., Inc., for furnishing a practical design and specifications for a non-slip printer. To United Artists Studio Corp. for the development of a practical, efficient and quiet wind machine.

6657 Special Award: *March of Time* for its significance to motion pictures and for having revolutionized one of the most important branches of the industry—the newsreel. To W. Howard Greene and Harold Rosson for the color cinematography of *The Garden of Allah.*

─────────── **1 9 3 7** ───────────

6658 **Best Picture:** *The Life of Emile Zola*
6659 **Best Actor:** Spencer Tracy in *Captains Courageous*
6660 **Best Actress:** Luise Rainer in *The Good Earth*
6661 **Best Director:** Leo McCarey for *The Awful Truth*
6662 **Best Supporting Actor:** Joseph Schildkraut in *The Life of Emile Zola*
6663 **Best Supporting Actress:** Alice Brady in *In Old Chicago*
6664 **Best Art Direction:** Stephen Goosson for *Lost Horizon*
6665 **Best Cinematography:** Karl Freund for *The Good Earth*
6666 **Best Writing/Original Story:** Robert Carson and William A. Wellman for *A Star Is Born*
6667 **Best Writing/Best Written Screenplay:** Norman Reilly Raine, Heinz Herald and Geza Herczeg for *The Life of Emile Zola*
6668 **Best Assistant Director:** Robert Webb for *In Old Chicago*
6669 **Best Music/Score:** Universal Studio Music Department (Charles Previn, department head) for *One Hundred Men and a Girl*
6670 **Best Music/Song:** Harry Owens for "Sweet Leilani" from *Waikiki Wedding*
6671 **Best Dance Direction:** Hermes Pan for "Fun House" from *A Damsel in Distress*
6672 **Best Sound Recording:** Samuel Goldwyn Studio Sound Department (Thomas T. Moulton, sound director) for *The Hurricane*
6673 **Best Film Editing:** Gene Milford and Gene Havlick for *Lost Horizon*
6674 **Best Short Subject/Cartoon:** *The Old Mill*
6675 **Best Short Subject/Color:** *Penny Wisdom*
6676 **Best Short Subject/One Reel:** *Private Life of the Gannets*
6677 **Best Short Subject/Two Reel:** *Torture Money*

6678 **Scientific or Technical/Class I (Academy Statuette and Individual Certificate of First Award):** To AGFA Ansco Corp. for AGFA Supreme and AGFA Ultra Speed pan motion picture negatives.
6679 **Scientific or Technical/Class II (Certificate of Honorable Mention):** To Walt Disney Productions, Ltd. for design and application of Multi-Plane camera. To Eastman Kodak Co. for two fine-grain duplicating film stocks. To Farciot Edouart and Paramount Pictures, Inc., for the development of the dual screen transparency camera set-up. To Douglas Shearer and Metro-Goldwyn-Mayer Studio Sound Department for a method of varying scanning width of variable density sound tracks (squeeze tracks) to obtain increased amount of noise reduction.
6680 **Scientific or Technical/Class III (Honorable Mention in Report of Board of Judges):** To John Arnold and Metro-Goldwyn-Mayer Studio Camera Department for their improvement of the semi-automatic focus device and its application to all cameras used by the Metro-Goldwyn-Mayer studio. To John Livadary, Director of Sound Recording for Columbia Pictures Corp. for the application of the bi-planar light valve to motion picture sound recording. To Thomas T. Moulton and the United Artists Studio Sound Department for the application to motion picture sound recording of volume indicators which have peak reading response and linear decibel scales. To RCA Manufacturing Co., Inc., for the introduction of the modulated high frequency method of determining optimum photographic processing conditions for variable sound tracks. To Joseph E. Robbins and Paramount Pictures, Inc., for an exceptional application of acoustic principles to the sound-proofing of gasoline generators and water pumps. To Douglas Shearer and Metro-Goldwyn-Mayer Studio Sound Department for the design of the film drive mechanism incorporated in the ERPI 1010 Reproducer.
6681 **Irving G. Thalberg Memorial Award:** Darryl F. Zanuck
6682 **Special Award:** To Mack Sennett for his lasting contribution to the comedy

technique of the screen, the basic principles of which are as important today as when they were first put into practice, the Academy presents a Special Award to that master of fun, discoverer of stars, sympathetic, kindly, understanding comedy genius. To Edgar Bergen for his outstanding comedy creation, Charlie McCarthy. To the Museum of Modern Art Film Library for its significant work in collecting films dating from 1895 to the present and for the first time making available to the public the means of studying the historical and asthetic development of the motion picture as one of the major arts. To W. Howard Greene for color photography of *A Star Is Born.*

———— **1938** ————

6683 **Best Picture:** *You Can't Take It with You*

6684 **Best Actor:** Spencer Tracy in *Boys Town*

6685 **Best Actress:** Bette Davis in *Jezebel*

6686 **Best Director:** Frank Capra for *You Can't Take It with You*

6687 **Best Supporting Actor:** Walter Brennan in *Kentucky*

6688 **Best Supporting Actress:** Fay Bainter in *Jezebel*

6689 **Best Art Direction:** Carl Weyl for *The Adventures of Robin Hood*

6690 **Best Cinematography:** Joseph Ruttenberg for *The Great Waltz*

6691 **Best Writing/Original Story:** Dory Schary and Eleanore Griffin for *Boys Town*

6692 **Best Writing/Screenplay:** George Bernard Shaw for *Pygmalion*, adapted by W. P. Lipscomb, Cecil Lewis and Ian Dalrymple

6693 **Best Music/Score:** Alfred Newman for *Alexander's Ragtime Band*

6694 **Best Music/Original Score:** Erich Wolfgang Korngold for *The Adventures of Robin Hood*

6695 **Best Music/Song:** Ralph Rainger, music and Leo Robin, lyrics for "Thanks for the Memory" from *The Big Broadcast of 1938*

6696 **Best Sound Recording:** Samuel Goldwyn Studio Sound Department (Thomas T. Moulton, Sound Director) for *The Cowboy and the Lady*

6697 **Best Film Editing:** Ralph Dawson for *The Adventures of Robin Hood*

6698 **Best Short Subject/Cartoon:** *Ferdinand the Bull*

6699 **Best Short Subject/One Reel:** *That Mothers Might Live*

6700 **Best Short Subject/Two Reel:** *Declaration of Independence*

6701 **Scientific or Technical/Class III (Certificate of Honorable Mention):** To John Aalberg and the RKO Studio Sound Department for application of compression to variable area recording in motion picture production. To Byron Haskin and the Special Effects Department of Warner Brothers Studio for pioneering the development and for the first practical application to motion picture production of the triple-head background projector.

6702 **Irving G. Thalberg Memorial Award:** Hal B. Wallis

6703 **Special Award:** To Deanna Durbin and Mickey Rooney for their significant contribution to bringing to the screen the spirit and personification of youth, and as juvenile players setting a high standard of ability and achievement. To Harry M. Warner in recognition of patriotic service in the production of historical short subjects presenting significant episodes in the early struggle of the American people for liberty. To Walt Disney for *Snow White and the Seven Dwarfs* recognized as a significant screen innovation which has charmed millions and pioneered a great new entertainment field for the motion picture cartoon. To Oliver Marsh and Allen Davey for the color cinematography of *Sweethearts*. To J. Arthur Ball for his outstanding contributions to the advancement of color in motion picture photography. To Gordon Jennings, assisted by Jan Domela, Dev Jennings, Irmin Roberts and Art Smith for the special effects. To Farciot Edouart assisted by Loyal Griggs for the transparencies. To Loren Ryder assisted by Harry Mills, Louis Mesenkop and Walter Oberst for the sound effects. All for outstanding achievement in creating Special Effects for the Paramount production *Spawn of the North.*

———— **1 9 3 9** ————

6704 Best Picture: *Gone with the Wind*

6705 Best Actor: Robert Donat in *Goodbye, Mr. Chips*

6706 Best Actress: Vivien Leigh in *Gone with the Wind*

6707 Best Director: Victor Fleming for *Gone with the Wind*

6708 Best Supporting Actor: Thomas Mitchell in *Stagecoach*

6709 Best Supporting Actress: Hattie McDaniel in *Gone with the Wind*

6710 Best Art Direction: Lyle Wheeler for *Gone with the Wind*

6711 Best Cinematography/Color: Ernest Haller and Ray Rennahan for *Gone with the Wind*

6712 Best Cinematography/Black & White: Gregg Toland for *Wuthering Heights*

6713 Best Writing/Original Story: Lewis R. Foster for *Mr. Smith Goes to Washington*

6714 Best Writing/Screenplay: Sidney Howard for *Gone with the Wind*

6715 Best Music/Score: Richard Hageman, W. Franke Harling, John Leipold, Louis Gruenberg and Leo Shuken for *Stagecoach*

6716 Best Music/Original Score: Herbert Stothart for *The Wizard of Oz*

6717 Best Music/Song: Harold Arlen music and E. Y. Harburg, lyrics for "Over the Rainbow" from *The Wizard of Oz*

6718 Best Sound Recording: Universal Studio Sound Department (Bernard B. Brown, Sound Director) for *When Tomorrow Comes*

6719 Best Film Editing: Hal C. Kern and James E. Newcom for *Gone with the Wind*

6720 Best Short Subject/Cartoon: *The Ugly Duckling*

6721 Best Short Subject/One Reel: *Busy Little Bears*

6722 Best Short Subject/Two Reel: *Sons of Liberty*

6723 Scientific or Technical/Class III (Certificate of Honorable Mention): To George Anderson of Warner Brothers Studio for an improved positive head for sun arcs. To John Arnold of Metro-Goldwyn-Mayer Studio for the M-G-M mobile camera crane. To Thomas T. Moulton, Fred Albin and the Sound Department of Samuel Goldwyn Studio for the origination and application of Delta db test to sound recording in motion pictures. To Farciot Edouart, Joseph E. Robbins, William Rudolph and Paramount Pictures, Inc., for the design and construction of a quiet portable treadmill. To Emery Huse and Ralph B. Atkinson of Eastman Kodak Co. for their specifications for chemical analysis of photographic developers and fixing baths. To Harold Nye of Warner Brothers Studio for a miniature incandescent spot lamp. To A. J. Tondreau of Warner Brothers Studio for the design and manufacture of an improved sound track printer. Multiple Award for important contributions in cooperative development of new improved process Projection Equipment: To F. R. Abbott, Haller Belt, Alan Cook and Bausch & Lomb Optical Company for faster projection lens. To Mitchell Camera Co. for new type process projection head. To Mole-Richardson Co. for new type automatically controlled projection arc lamp. To Charles Handley, David Joy and National Carbon Co. for improved and more stable high-intensity carbons. To Winton Hoch and Technicolor Motion Picture Corp. for auxiliary optical system. To Don Musgrave and Selznick International Pictures, Inc., for pioneering in the use of coordinated equipment in the production of *Gone with the Wind*.

6724 Irving G. Thalberg Memorial Award: David O. Selznick

6725 Special Award: To Douglas Fairbanks (Commemorative Award) recognizing his unique and outstanding contribution as first president of the Academy to the international development of the motion picture. To the Motion Picture Relief Fund acknowledging the outstanding services to the industry during the past year of the Motion Picture Relief Fund and its progressive leadership. Presented to Jean Hersholt, President; Ralph Morgan, Chairman of the Executive Committee; Ralph Block, First Vice-President; and Conrad Nagel. To the Technicolor Motion Picture Corp. for its contributions in successfully bringing three-color feature production to the screen. To Judy Garland for her outstanding performance as a screen juvenile during the past year. To William Cameron Menzies for outstanding achievement in the use of color for the enhancement of dramatic mood in the production *Gone with the Wind.*

─────── **1940** ───────

6726 **Best Picture:** *Rebecca*

6727 **Best Actor:** James Stewart in *The Philadelphia Story*

6728 **Best Actress:** Ginger Rogers in *Kitty Foyle*

6729 **Best Director:** John Ford for *The Grapes of Wrath*

6730 **Best Supporting Actor:** Walter Brennan in *The Westerner*

6731 **Best Supporting Actress:** Jane Darwell in *The Grapes of Wrath*

6732 **Best Art Direction/Color:** Vincent Korda for *The Thief of Bagdad*

6733 **Best Art Direction/Black & White:** Cedric Gibbons and Paul Groesse for *Pride and Prejudice*

6734 **Best Cinematography/Color:** George Perrinal for *The Thief of Bagdad*

6735 **Best Cinematography/Black & White:** George Barnes for *Rebecca*

6736 **Best Writing/Original Story:** Benjamin Glazer and John S. Toddy for *Arise, My Love*

6737 **Best Writing/Screenplay:** Donald Ogden Stewart for *The Philadelphia Story*

6738 **Best Writing/Original Screenplay:** Preston Sturges for *The Great McGinty*

6739 **Best Music/Score:** Alfred Newman for *Tin Pan Alley*

6740 **Best Music/Original Score:** Leigh Harline, Paul J. Smith and Ned Washington for *Pinocchio*

6741 **Best Music/Song:** Leigh Harline, music and Ned Washington, lyrics for "When You Wish Upon a Star" from *Pinocchio*

6742 **Best Sound Recording:** Metro-Goldwyn-Mayer Studio Sound Department (Douglas Shearer, Sound Director) for *Strike Up the Band*

6743 **Best Special Effects:** Lawrence Butler (Photographic) and Jack Whitney (Sound) for *The Thief of Bagdad*

6744 **Best Film Editing:** Anne Bauchens for *North West Mounted Police*

6745 **Best Short Subject/Cartoon:** *Milky Way*

6746 **Best Short Subject/One Reel:** *Quicker'n a Wink*

6747 **Best Short Subject/Two Reel:** *Teddy, the Tough Rider*

6748 **Scientific or Technical/Class I (Academy Statuette):** To 20th Century–Fox Film Corp. for the design and construction of the 20th Century Silenced Camera, developed by Daniel Clark, Grover Laube, Charles Miller and Robert W. Stevens.

6749 **Scientific or Technical/Class III (Certificate of Honorable Mention):** To Warner Brothers Studio Art Department and Anton Grot for the design and perfection of the Warner Brothers water ripple and wave illusion machine.

6750 **Special Award:** To Bob Hope in recognition of his unselfish services to the motion picture industry. To Colonel Nathan Levinson for his outstanding service to the industry and the Army during the past nine years, which has made possible the present efficient mobilization of the motion picture industry facilities for the production of Army Training Films.

─────── **1941** ───────

6751 **Best Picture:** *How Green Was My Valley*

6752 **Best Actor:** Gary Cooper in *Sergeant York*

6753 **Best Actress:** Joan Fontaine in *Suspicion*

6754 **Best Director:** John Ford for *How Green Was My Valley*

6755 **Best Supporting Actor:** Donald Crisp in *How Green Was My Valley*

6756 **Best Supporting Actress:** Mary Astor in *The Great Lie*

6757 **Best Art Direction/Color:** Cedric Gibbons and Urie McCleary, interior decoration by Thomas Little for *Blossoms in the Dust*

6758 **Best Art Direction/Black & White:** Richard Day and Nathan Juran, interior decoration by Thomas Little for *How Green Was My Valley*

6759 Best Cinematography/Color: Ernest Palmer and Ray Rennahan for *Blood and Sand*

6760 Best Cinematography/Black & White: Arthur Miller for *How Green Was My Valley*

6761 Best Writing/Original Story: Harry Segall for *Here Comes Mr. Jordan*

6762 Best Writing/Screenplay: Sidney Buchman and Seton I. Miller for *Here Comes Mr. Jordan*

6763 Best Writing/Original Screenplay: Herman J. Mankiewicz and Orson Welles for *Citizen Kane*

6764 Best Music/Score of a Musical Picture: Frank Churchill and Oliver Wallace for *Dumbo*

6765 Best Music/Score of a Dramatic or Comedy Picture: Bernard Herrmann for *All That Money Can Buy*

6766 Best Music/Song: Jerome Kern, music and Oscar Hammerstein II, lyrics for "The Last Time I Saw Paris" from *Lady Be Good*

6767 Best Sound Recording: Alexander Korda, United Artists; General Services Sound Department (Jack Whitney, Sound Director) for *That Hamilton Woman*

6768 Best Special Effects: Farciot Edouart and Gordon Jennings (Photographic) and Louis Mesenkop (Sound) for *I Wanted Wings*

6769 Best Film Editing: William Holmes for *Sergeant York*

6770 Best Short Subject/Cartoon: *Lend a Paw*

6771 Best Short Subject/One Reel: *Of Pups and Puzzles*

6772 Best Short Subject/Two Reel: *Main Street on the March*

6773 Scientific or Technical/Class II (Academy Plaque): To Electrical Research Products Division of Western Electric Co. for the development of the precision integrating sphere densitometer. To RCA Manufacturing Co. for the design and development of the MI-3043 Uni-directional microphone.

6774 Scientific or Technical/Class III (Certificate of Honorable Mention): To Ray Wilkinson and the Paramount Studio Laboratory for pioneering in the use of and the first application to release printing of fine-grain positive stock. To Charles Lootens and the Republic Studio Sound Department for pioneering the use of and for the first practical application to motion picture production of Class B push-pull variable-area recording. To Wilbur Silvertooth and the Paramount Studio Engineering Department for the design and computation of a relay condenser system applicable to transparency process projection, delivering more usable light. To Paramount Pictures, Inc., and 20th Century–Fox Film Corp. for the development and first practical application to motion picture production of an automatic scene slating device. To Douglas Shearer and Metro-Goldwyn-Mayer Studio Sound Department and to Loren Ryder and the Paramount Studio Sound Department for pioneering the development of fine grain emulsions for variable-density original sound recording in studio production.

6775 Irving G. Thalberg Memorial Award: Walter E. Disney

6776 Special Award: Citation for distinctive achievement in short documentary subject to Canadian National Film Board for *Churchill's Island*. To Rey Scott for his extraordinary achievement in producing *Kukan* a film record of China's struggle, including its photography with a 16mm camera under the most difficult and dangerous conditions. To the British Ministry of Information for its vivid and dramatic presentation of the heroism of the R. A. F. in the documentary film *Target for Tonight*. To Walt Disney, William Garrity, John N. A. Hawkins and the RCA Manufacturing Co. for their outstanding contribution to the advancement of the use of sound in motion pictures through the production of *Fantasia*. To Leopold Stokowski and his associates for their unique achievement in the creation of a new form of visualized music in Walt Disney's production of *Fantasia*, thereby widening the scope of the motion picture as entertainment and as an art form.

—————— **1942** ——————

6777 Best Picture: *Mrs. Miniver*

6778 Best Actor: James Cagney in *Yankee Doodle Dandy*

6779 Best Actress: Greer Garson in *Mrs. Miniver*

6780 Best Director: William Wyler for *Mrs. Miniver*

6781 Best Supporting Actor: Van Heflin in *Johnny Eager*

6782 Best Supporting Actress: Teresa Wright in *Mrs. Miniver*

6783 Best Art Direction/Color: Richard Day and Joseph Wright, interior decoration by Thomas Little for *My Gal Sal*

6784 Best Art Direction/Black & White: Richard Day and Joseph Wright, interior decoration by Thomas Little for *This Above All*

6785 Best Cinematography/Color: Leon Shamroy for *The Black Swan*

6786 Best Cinematography/Black & White: Joseph Ruttenberg for *Mrs. Miniver*

6787 Best Writing/Original Story: Emeric Pressburger for *The Invaders*

6788 Best Writing/Screenplay: Arthur Wimperis, George Froeschell, James Hilton and Claudine West for *Mrs. Miniver*

6789 Best Writing/Original Screenplay: Ring Lardner, Jr., and Michael Kanin for *Woman of the Year*

6790 Best Music/Score of a Musical Picture: Ray Heindorf and Hans Roemheld for *Yankee Doodle Dandy*

6791 Best Music/Score of a Dramatic or Comedy Picture: Max Steiner for *Now, Voyager*

6792 Best Music/Song: "White Christmas" from *Holiday Inn*, music and lyrics by Irving Berlin

6793 Best Sound Recording: Warner Brothers Studio Sound Department (Nathan Levinson, Sound Director) for *Yankee Doodle Dandy*

6794 Best Special Effects: Gordon Jennings, Farciot Edouart and William L. Pereira (Photographic) and Louis Mesenkop (Sound) for *Reap the Wild Wind*

6795 Film Editing: Daniel Mandell for *The Pride of the Yankees*

6796 Best Short Subject/Cartoon: *Der Fuehrer's Face*

6797 Best Short Subject/One Reel: *Speaking of Animals and Their Families*

6798 Best Short Subject/Two Reel: *Beyond the Line of Duty*

6799 Best Documentary/Feature: *Battle of Midway, Kokoda Front Line, Moscow Strikes Back* and *Prelude to War*

6800 Scientific or Technical/Class II (Academy Plaque): To Carroll Clark, F. Thomas Thompson and the RKO Studio Art and Miniature departments for the design and construction of a moving cloud and horizon machine. To Daniel B. Clark and the 20th Century–Fox Film Corp. for the development of a lens calibration system and the application of this system to exposure control in cinematography.

6801 Scientific or Technical/Class III (Certificate of Honorable Mention): To Robert Henderson and the Paramount Studio Engineering and Transparency departments for the design and construction of adjustable light bridges and frames for transparency process photography. To Daniel J. Bloomberg and the Republic Studio Sound Department for the design and application to motion picture production of a device for marking action negative for preselection purposes.

6802 Irving G. Thalberg Memorial Award: Sidney Franklin

6803 Special Award: Charles Boyer for his progressive cultural achievement in establishing the French Research Foundation in Los Angeles as a source of reference for the Hollywood Motion Picture Industry. To Noel Coward for his outstanding production achievement, *In Which We Serve*. To the Metro-Goldwyn-Mayer Studio for its achievement in representing the American Way of Life in the production of the "Andy Hardy" series of films.

——————— **1943** ———————

6804 Best Picture: *Casablanca*

6805 Best Actor: Paul Lukas in *Watch on the Rhine*

6806 Best Actress: Jennifer Jones in *The Song of Bernadette*

6807 Best Director: Michael Curtiz for *Casablanca*

6808 Best Supporting Actor: Charles Coburn in *The More the Merrier*

6809 Best Supporting Actress: Katina Paxinou in *For Whom the Bell Tolls*

6810 Best Art Direction/Color: Alexander Golitzen and John B. Goodman, Interior Decoration by Russell A. Gausman and Ira S. Webb for for *The Phantom of the Opera*

6811 Best Art Direction/Black & White: James Basevi and William Darling, Interior Decoration by Thomas Little for *The Song of Bernadette*

6812 Best Cinematography/Color: Hal Mohr and W. Howard Greene for *The Phantom of the Opera*

6813 Best Cinematography/Black & White: Arthur Miller for *The Song of Bernadette*

6814 Best Writing/Original Story: William Saroyan for *The Human Comedy*

6815 Best Writing/Screenplay: Julius J. Epstein, Philip G. Epstein and Howard Koch for *Casablanca*

6816 Best Writing/Original Screenplay: Norman Krasna for *Princess O'Rourke*

6817 Best Music/Score of a Musical Picture: Ray Heindorf for *This Is the Army*

6818 Best Music/Score of a Dramatic or Comedy Picture: Alfred Newman for *The Song of Bernadette*

6819 Best Music/Song: Harry Warren, music and Mack Gordon, lyrics for "You'll Never Know" from *Hello, Frisco, Hello*

6820 Best Sound Recording: RKO Radio Studio Sound Department (Stephen Dunn, Sound Director) for *This Land Is Mine*

6821 Best Special Effects: Fred Sersen (Photographic) and Roger Heman (Sound) for *Crash Dive*

6822 Best Film Editing: George Amy for *Air Force*

6823 Best Short Subject/Cartoon: *Yankee Doodle Mouse*

6824 Best Short Subject/One Reel: *Amphibious Fighters*

6825 Best Short Subject/Two Reel: *Heavenly Music*

6826 Best Documentary/Feature: *Desert Victory*

6827 Best Documentary/Short Subject: *December 7th*

6828 Scientific or Technical/Class II (Academy Plaque): To Farciot Edouart, Earle Morgan, Barton Thompson and the Paramount Studio and Engineering and Transparency departments for the development and practical application to motion picture production of a method of duplicating and enlarging natural color photographs, transferring the image emulsions to glass plates and projecting these slides by especially designed stereopticon equipment. To the Photo Products Department of E. I. duPont de Nemours and Co., Inc., for the development of fine-grain motion picture films.

6829 Scientific or Technical/Class III (Certificate of Honorable Mention): To Daniel J. Bloomberg and the Republic Studio Sound Department for the design and development of an inexpensive method of converting Moviolas to Class B push-pull reproduction. To Charles Galloway Clarke and the 20th Century–Fox Studio Camera Department for the development and practical application of a device for composing artificial clouds into motion picture scenes during production photography. To Farciot Edouart and the Paramount Studio Transparency Department for an automatic electric transparency cueing timer. To Willard H. Turner and the RKO Studio Sound Department for the design and construction of the phono-cue starter.

6830 Irving G. Thalberg Memorial Award: Hal B. Wallis

6831 Special Award: To George Pal for the development of novel methods and techniques in the production of the short subjects known as Puppetoons.

———— **1944** ————

6832 Best Picture: *Going My Way*

6833 Best Actor: Bing Crosby in *Going My Way*

6834 Best Actress: Ingrid Bergman in *Gaslight*

6835 Best Director: Leo McCarey for *Going My Way*

6836 Best Supporting Actor: Barry Fitzgerald in *Going My Way*

6837 **Best Supporting Actress:** Ethel Barrymore in *None But the Lonely Heart*

6838 **Best Art Direction/Color:** Wiard Ihnen, Interior Decoration by Thomas Little for *Wilson*

6839 **Best Art Direction/Black & White:** Cedric Gibbons and William Ferrari, Interior Decoration by Edwin B. Willis and Paul Huldschinsky for *Gaslight*

6840 **Best Cinematography/Color:** Leon Shamroy for *Wilson*

6841 **Best Cinematography/Black & White:** Joseph LaShelle for *Laura*

6842 **Best Writing/Original Story:** Leo McCarey for *Going My Way*

6843 **Best Writing/Screenplay:** Frank Butler and Frank Cavett for *Going My Way*

6844 **Best Writing/Original Screenplay:** Lamar Trotti for *Wilson*

6845 **Best Music/Score of a Musical Picture:** Morris Stoloff and Carmen Dragon for *Cover Girl*

6846 **Best Music/Score of a Dramatic or Comedy Picture:** Max Steiner for *Since You Went Away*

6847 **Best Music/Song:** James Van Heusen, music and Mack Gordon, lyrics for "Swinging on a Star" from *Going My Way*

6848 **Best Sound Recording:** 20th Century–Fox Studio Sound Department (E. H. Hansen, Sound Director) for *Wilson*

6849 **Best Special Effects:** A. Arnold Gillespie, Donald Jahraus and Warren Newcombe (Photographic) and Douglas Shearer (Sound) for *Thirty Seconds Over Tokyo*

6850 **Best Film Editing:** Barbara McLean for *Wilson*

6851 **Best Short Subject/Cartoon:** *Mouse Trouble*

6852 **Best Short Subject/One Reel:** *Who's Who in Animal Land*

6853 **Best Short Subject/Two Reel:** *I Won't Play*

6854 **Best Documentary/Feature:** *The Fighting Lady*

6855 **Best Documentary/Short Subject:** *With the Marines at Tarawa*

6856 **Scientific or Technical/Class II (Academy Plaque):** To Stephen Dunn and the RKO Radio Studio Sound Department and Radio Corporation of America for the design and development of the electronic compressor-limiter.

6857 **Scientific or Technical/Class III (Certificate of Honorable Mention):** To Linwood Dunn, Cecil Love and Acme Tool and Manufacturing Co. for the design and construction of the Acme-Dunn Optical Printer. To Grover Laube and the 20th Century–Fox Studio Camera Department for the development of a continuous-loop projection device. To Western Electric Co. for the design and construction of the 1126A Limiting Amplifier for variable density sound recording. To Russell Brown, Ray Hinsdale and Joseph E. Robbins for the development and production use of the Paramount floating hydraulic boat rocker. To Gordon Jennings for the design and construction of the Paramount nodal point tripod. To Radio Corporation of America and RKO Radio Studio Sound Department for the design and construction of the RKO reverberation chamber. To Daniel J. Bloomberg and the Republic Studio Sound Department for the design and development of multi-interlock selector switch. To Bernard B. Brown and John P. Livadary for the design and engineering of a separate soloist and chorus recording room. To Paul Zeff, S. J. Twining and George Seid of the Columbia Studio Laboratory for the formula and application to production of a simplified variable area sound negative developer. To Paul Lerpae the design and construction of the Paramount travelling matte projection and photographing device.

6858 **Irving G. Thalberg Memorial Award:** Darryl F. Zanuck

6859 **Special Award:** To Margaret O'Brien as outstanding child actress of 1944. To Bob Hope for his many services to the Academy, a Life Membership in the Academy of Motion Picture Arts and Sciences.

——————— **1945** ———————

6860 **Best Picture:** *The Lost Weekend*

6861 **Best Actor:** Ray Milland in *The Lost Weekend*

6862 **Best Actress:** Joan Crawford in *Mildred Pierce*

6863 **Best Director:** Billy Wilder for *The Lost Weekend*

6864 **Best Supporting Actor:** James Dunn in *A Tree Grows in Brooklyn*

6865 **Best Supporting Actress:** Anne Revere in *National Velvet*

6866 **Best Art Direction/Color:** Hans Dreier and Ernst Fegte, Interior Decoration by Sam Comer for *Frenchman's Creek*

6867 **Best Art Direction/Black & White:** Wiard Ihnen, Interior Decoration by A. Roland Fields for *Blood on the Sun*

6868 **Best Cinematography/Color:** Leon Shamroy for *Leave Her to Heaven*

6869 **Best Cinematography/Black & White:** Harry Stradling for *The Picture of Dorian Gray*

6870 **Best Writing/Original Story:** Charles G. Booth for *The House on 92nd Street*

6871 **Best Writing/Screenplay:** Charles Brackett and Billy Wilder for *The Lost Weekend*

6872 **Best Writing/Original Screenplay:** Richard Schweizer for *Marie-Louise*

6873 **Best Music/Score of a Musical Picture:** Georgie Stoll for *Anchors Aweigh*

6874 **Best Music/Score of a Dramatic or Comedy Picture:** Miklos Rozsa for *Spellbound*

6875 **Best Music/Song:** Richard Rodgers, music and Oscar Hammerstein II, lyrics for "It Might as Well Be Spring" from *State Fair*

6876 **Best Sound Recording or Sound:** RKO Radio Studio Sound Department (Stephen Dunn, Sound Director) for *The Bells of St. Mary's*

6877 **Best Special Effects:** John Fulton (Photographic) and Arthur W. Johns (Sound) for *Wonder Man*

6878 **Best Film Editing:** Robert J. Kern for *National Velvet*

6879 **Best Short Subject/Cartoon:** *Quiet, Please*

6880 **Best Short Subject/One Reel:** *Stairway to Light*

6881 **Best Short Subject/Two Reel:** *Star in the Night*

6882 **Best Documentary/Feature:** *The True Glory*

6883 **Best Documentary/Short Subject:** *Hitler Lives?*

6884 **Scientific or Technical/Class III (Certificate of Honorable Mention):** To Loren L. Ryder, Charles R. Daily and the Paramount Studio Sound Department for the design and construction and use of the first dial controlled, step-by-step sound channel line-up and test circuit. To Michael S. Leshing, Benjamin C. Robinson, Arthur B. Chatelain and Robert C. Stevens of 20th Century-Fox Studio and John G. Capstaff of Eastman Kodak Co. for the 20th Century-Fox film processing machine.

6885 **Special Award:** To Walter Wanger for his six years service as president of the Academy. To Peggy Ann Garner as the outstanding child actress of 1945. To Frank Ross and Mervyn LeRoy (producers), Mervyn LeRoy (director), Albert Maltz (screenplay), Earl Robinson and Lewis Allen (title song – "The House I Live In") and Frank Sinatra (star) for *The House I Live In*, a short subject promoting tolerance. To Republic Studios, Daniel J. Bloomberg and the Republic Studio Sound Department for the building of an outstanding musical scoring auditorium which provides optimum recording conditions and combines all elements of acoustic and engineering design.

─────── **1 9 4 6** ───────

6886 **Best Picture:** *The Best Years of Our Lives*

6887 **Best Actor:** Fredric March in *The Best Years of Our Lives*

6888 **Best Actress:** Olivia de Havilland in *To Each His Own*

6889 **Best Director:** William Wyler for *The Best Years of Our Lives*

6890 **Best Supporting Actor:** Harold Russell in *The Best Years of Our Lives*

6891 **Best Supporting Actress:** Anne Baxter in *The Razor's Edge*

6892 **Best Art Direction/Color:** Cedric Gibbons and Paul Groesse, Interior Decoration by Edwin B. Willis for *The Yearling*

6893 **Best Art Direction/Black & White:** Lyle Wheeler and William Darling, Interior Decoration by Thomas Little for *Anna and the King of Siam*

6894 **Best Cinematography/Color:**

Charles Rosher, Leonard Smith and Arthur Arling for *The Yearling*

6895 Best Cinematography/Black & White: Arthur Miller for *Anna and the King of Siam*

6896 Best Writing/Original Story: Clemence Dane for *Vacation from Marriage*

6897 Best Writing/Screenplay: Robert E. Sherwood for *The Best Years of Our Lives*

6898 Best Writing/Original Screenplay: Muriel Box and Sidney Box for *The Seventh Veil*

6899 Best Music/Score of a Musical Picture: Morris Stoloff for *The Jolson Story*

6900 Best Music/Score of a Dramatic or Comedy Picture: Hugo Friedhofer for *The Best Years of Our Lives*

6901 Best Music/Song: Harry Warren, music and Johnny Mercer, lyrics for "On the Atchison, Topeka and Santa Fe" from *The Harvey Girls*

6902 Best Sound Recording: Columbia Studio Sound Department (John Livadary, Sound Director) for *The Jolson Story*

6903 Best Special Effects: Thomas Howard (Photographic) for *Blithe Spirit*

6904 Best Film Editing: Daniel Mandell for *The Best Years of Our Lives*

6905 Best Short Subject/Cartoon: *The Cat Concerto*

6906 Best Short Subject/One Reel: *Facing Your Danger*

6907 Best Short Subject/Two Reel: *A Boy and His Dog*

6908 Best Documentary/Short Subject: *Seeds of Destiny*

6909 Scientific or Technical/Class III (Certificate of Honorable Mention): To Harlan L. Baumbach and the Paramount West Coast Laboratory for an improved method for the quantitative determination of hydroquinone and metal in photographic development baths. To Herbert E. Britt for the development and application of formulas and equipment for producing cloud and smoke effects. To Burton F. Miller and the Warner Brothers Studio Sound and Electrical departments for the design and construction of motion picture arc lighting generator filter. To Carl Faulkner of the 20th Century–Fox Studio Sound Department for reversed bias method, including a double bias method for light valve and galvonometer density recording. To Mole-Richardson Co. for Type 450 super high intensity carbon arc lamp. To Arthur F. Blinn, Robert O. Cook, C. O. Slyfield and the Walt Disney Studio Sound Department for the design and development of an audio finder and track viewer for checking and locating noise in soundtracks. To Burton F. Miller and the Warner Brothers Studio Sound Department for the design and application of an equalizer to eliminate relative spectral energy distortion in electronic compressors. To Marty Martin and Hal Adkins of the RKO Radio Studio Miniature Department for the design and construction of equipment providing visual bullet effects. To Harold Nye and the Warner Brothers Studio Electrical Department for the development of the electronically controlled fire and gaslight effect.

6910 Irving G. Thalberg Memorial Award: Samuel Goldwyn

6911 Special Award: To Laurence Olivier for his outstanding achievement as actor, producer, and director in bringing *Henry V* to the screen. To Harold Russell for bringing hope and courage to his fellow veterans through his appearance in *The Best Years of Our Lives*. To Ernst Lubitsch for his distinguished contributions to the art of the motion picture. To Claude Jarman, Jr., as the outstanding child actor of 1946.

———————— **1 9 4 7** ————————

6912 Best Picture: *Gentleman's Agreement*

6913 Best Actor: Ronald Coleman in *A Double Life*

6914 Best Actress: Loretta Young in *The Farmer's Daughter*

6915 Best Director: Elia Kazan for *Gentleman's Agreement*

6916 Best Supporting Actor: Edmund Gwenn in *Miracle on 34th Street*

6917 Best Supporting Actress: Celeste Holm in *Gentleman's Agreement*

6918 Best Art Direction/Color:

Alfred Junge, Set Decoration by Alfred Junge for *Black Narcissus*

6919 Best Art Direction/Black & White: John Bryan, Set Decoration by Wilfred Shingleton for *Great Expectations*

6920 Best Cinematography/Color: Jack Cardiff for *Black Narcissus*

6921 Best Cinematography/Black & White: Guy Green for *Great Expectations*

6922 Best Writing/Original Story: Valentine Davies for *Miracle on 34th Street*

6923 Best Writing/Screenplay: George Seaton for *Miracle on 34th Street*

6924 Best Writing/Original Screenplay: Sidney Sheldon for *The Bachelor and the Bobbysoxer*

6925 Best Music/Score of a Musical Picture: Alfred Newman for *Mother Wore Tights*

6926 Best Music/Score of a Dramatic or Comedy Picture: Miklos Rozsa for *A Double Life*

6927 Best Music/Song: Allie Wrubel, music and Ray Gilbert, lyrics for "Zip-A-Dee-Do-Dah" from *Song of the South*

6928 Best Sound Recording or Sound: Samuel Goldwyn Studio Sound Department (Gordon Sawyer, Sound Director) for *The Bishop's Wife*

6929 Best Special Effects: A. Arnold Gillespie and Warren Newcombe (Visual) and Douglas Shearer and Michael Steinore (Audible) for *Green Dolphin Street*

6930 Best Film Editing: Francis Lyon and Robert Parish for *Body and Soul*

6931 Best Short Subject/Cartoon: *Tweetie Pie*

6932 Best Short Subject/One Reel: *Goodbye, Miss Turlock*

6933 Best Short Subject/Two Reel: *Climbing the Matterhorn*

6934 Best Documentary/Feature: *Design for Death*

6935 Best Documentary/Short Subject: *First Steps*

6936 Scientific or Technical/Class II (Academy Plaque): To C. C. Davis and Electical Research Products Division of Western Electric Company for the development and application of an improved film drive filter mechanism. To C. R. Daily and the Paramount Studio Film Laboratory, Still and Engineering departments for the development and first practical application to motion picture and still photography of a method of increasing film speed as first suggested to the industry by the E. I. duPont de Nemours & Co.

6937 Scientific or Technical/Class III (Certificate of Honorable Mention): To Nathan Levinson and the Warner Brothers Studio Sound Department for the design and construction of a constant-speed sound editing machine. To Farciot Edouart, C. R. Daily, Hal Corl, H. G. Cartwright and the Paramount Studio Transparency and Engineering departments for the first application of special anti-solarizing glass to high intensity background and spot arc projectors. To Fred Ponedel of Warner Brothers Studio for pioneering the fabrication and practical application to motion picture color photography of large translucent photographic backgrounds. To Kurt Singer and the RCA-Victor Division of Radio Corporation of America for the design and development of a continuously variable band elimination filter. To James Gibbons of Warner Brothers Studio for the development and production of large dyed plastic filters for motion picture photography.

6938 Special Award: To *Bill and Coo* for a novel and entertaining use of the medium of motion pictures. To *Shoe-Shine*, an Italian production of superlative quality made under adverse circumstances. To Colonel William N. Selig, Albert E. Smith, George K. Spoor and Thomas Armat, motion picture pioneers, for their contributions to the development of the film industry. To James Baskett for his characterization of "Uncle Remus" in *Song of the South*.

———————— **1948** ————————

6939 Best Picture: *Hamlet*

6940 Best Actor: Laurence Olivier in *Hamlet*

6941 Best Actress: Jane Wyman in *Johnny Belinda*

6942 Best Director: John Huston for *Treasure of the Sierra Madre*

6943 **Best Supporting Actor:** Walter Huston in *Treasure of the Sierra Madre*

6944 **Best Supporting Actress:** Claire Trevor in *Key Largo*

6945 **Best Art Direction/Color:** Hein Heckroth, Set Decoration by Arthur Lawson for *The Red Shoes*

6946 **Best Art Direction/Black & White:** Roger K. Furse, Set Decoration by Carmen Dillon for *Hamlet*

6947 **Best Cinematography/Color:** Joseph Valentine, William V. Skall and Winton Hoch for *Joan of Arc*

6948 **Best Cinematography/Black & White:** William Daniels for *The Naked City*

6949 **Best Writing/Motion Picture Story:** Richard Schweizer and David Wechsler for *The Search*

6950 **Best Writing/Screenplay:** John Huston for *Treasure of Sierra Madre*

6951 **Best Costume Design/Black & White:** Roger K. Furse for *Hamlet*

6952 **Best Costume Design/Color:** Dorothy Jeakins and Karinska for *Joan of Arc*

6953 **Best Music/Score of a Musical Picture:** Johnny Green and Roger Edens for *Easter Parade*

6954 **Best Music/Score of a Dramatic or Comedy Picture:** Brian Easdale for *The Red Shoes*

6955 **Best Music/Song:** Jay Livingston and Ray Evans, music and lyrics for "Buttons and Bows" from *The Paleface*

6956 **Best Sound Recording or Sound:** 20th Century–Fox Studio Sound Department (Thomas T. Moulton, Sound Director) for *The Snake Pit*

6957 **Best Special Effects:** Paul Eagler, J. McMillan Johnson, Russell Shearman and Clarence Slifer (Visual) and Charles Freeman and James G. Stewart (Audible) for *Portrait of Jennie*

6958 **Best Film Editing:** Paul Weatherwax for *The Naked City*

6959 **Best Short Subject/Cartoon:** *The Little Orphans*

6960 **Best Short Subject/One Reel:** *Symphony of a City*

6961 **Best Short Subject/Two Reel:** *Seal Island*

6962 **Best Documentary/Feature:** *The Secret Land*

6963 **Best Documentary/Short Subject:** *Toward Independence*

6964 **Best Foreign Language Film:** *Monsieur Vincent*—France

6965 **Scientific or Technical/Class II (Academy Plaque):** To Victor Caccialanza, Maurice Ayers and the Paramount Studio Set Construction Department for the development and application of "Paralite," new lightweight plaster process for set construction. To Nick Kalten, Louis J. Witti and the 20th Century–Fox Studio Mechanical Effects Department for a process of preserving and flameproofing foliage.

6966 **Scientific or Technical/Class III (Certificate of Honorable Mention):** To Marty Martin, Jack Lannon, Russell Shearman and the RKO Radio Studio Special Effects Department for the development of a new method of simulating falling snow on motion picture sets. To A. J. Moran and the Warner Brothers Studio Electrical Department for a method of remote control for shutters on motion picture arc lighting equipment.

6967 **Irving G. Thalberg Memorial Award:** Jerry Wald

6968 **Honorary Foreign Language Film Award:** *Monsieur Vincent* from France

6969 **Special Award:** To Ivan Jandl for the outstanding juvenile performance of 1948 in *The Search*. To Sid Grauman, master showman, who raised the standing of exhibition of motion pictures. To Adolph Zukor for his services to the industry over a period of fifty years. To Walter Wanger for distinguished service to the industry in adding to its moral stature in the world community through production of the picture *Joan of Arc*.

—————— **1 9 4 9** ——————

6970 **Best Picture:** *All the King's Men*

6971 **Best Actor:** Broderick Crawford in *All the King's Men*

6972 **Best Actress:** Olivia de Havilland in *The Heiress*

6973 **Best Director:** Joseph L. Mankiewicz for *A Letter to Three Wives*

6974 **Best Supporting Actor:** Dean Jagger in *Twelve O'Clock High*

6975 **Best Supporting Actress:** Mercedes McCambridge in *All the King's Men*

6976 **Best Art Direction/Color:** Cedric Gibbons and Paul Groesse, Set Decoration by Edwin B. Willis and Jack D. Moore for *Little Women*

6977 **Best Art Direction/Black & White:** Harry Horner and John Meehan, Set Decoration by Emile Kuri for *The Heiress*

6978 **Best Cinematography/Color:** Winton Hoch for *She Wore a Yellow Ribbon*

6979 **Best Cinematography/Black & White:** Paul C. Vogel for *Battleground*

6980 **Best Writing/Motion Picture Story:** Douglas Marrow for *The Stratton Story*

6981 **Best Writing/Screenplay:** Joseph L. Mankiewicz for *A Letter to Three Wives*

6982 **Best Writing/Story and Screenplay:** Robert Pirosh for *Battleground*

6983 **Best Costume Design/Black & White:** Edith Head and Gile Steele for *The Heiress*

6984 **Best Costume Design/Color:** Leah Rhodes, Travilla and Marjorie Best for *Adventures of Don Juan*

6985 **Best Music/Score of a Musical Picture:** Roger Edens and Lennie Hayton for *On the Town*

6986 **Best Music/Score of a Dramatic or Comedy Picture:** Aaron Copland for *The Heiress*

6987 **Best Music/Song:** Frank Loesser, music and lyrics for "Baby, It's Cold Outside" from *Neptune's Daughter*

6988 **Best Sound Recording:** 20th Century-Fox Studio Sound Department (Thomas T. Moulton, Sound Director) for *Twelve O'Clock High*

6989 **Best Special Effects:** ARKO Productions for *Mighty Joe Young*

6990 **Best Film Editing:** Harry Gerstad for *Champion*

6991 **Best Short Subject/Cartoon:** *For Scent-imental Reasons*

6992 **Best Short Subject/One Reel:** *Aquatic House-Party*

6993 **Best Short Subject/Two Reel:** *Van Gogh*

6994 **Best Documentary/Feature:** *Daybreak in Udi*

6995 **Best Documentary/Short Subject:** *A Chance to Live* and *So Much for So Little*

6996 **Best Foreign Language Film:** *The Bicycle Thief*—Italy

6997 **Scientific or Technical/Class I (Academy Statuette):** To Eastman Kodak Co. for the development and introduction of an improved safety base motion picture film.

6998 **Scientific or Technical/Class III (Certificate of Honorable Mention):** To Loren L. Ryder, Bruce H. Denney, Robert Carr and the Paramount Studio Sound Department for the development and application of the supersonic playback and public address system. To M. B. Paul for the first successful large-area seamless translucent backgrounds. To Herbert Britt for the development and application of formulas and equipment producing artificial snow and ice for dressing motion picture sets. To Andre Coutant and Jacques Mathot for the design of the Eclair camerette. To Charles R. Daily, Steve Csillag and the Paramount Studio Engineering, Editorial and Music departments for a new precision method of computing variable tempo-click tracks. To International Projector Corp. for a simplified and self-adjusting take-up device for projection machines. To Alexander Velcoff for the application to production of the infra-red photographic evaluator.

6999 **Special Award:** To Bobby Driscoll as the outstanding juvenile actor of 1949. To Fred Astaire for his unique artistry and his contributions to the technique of musical pictures. To Cecil B. DeMille, distinguished motion picture pioneer, for 37 years of brilliant showmanship. To Jean Hersholt for distinguished service to the motion picture industry.

——————— **1 9 5 0** ———————

7000 **Best Picture:** *All About Eve*

7001 **Best Actor:** Jose Ferrer in *Cyrano de Bergerac*

7002 **Best Actress:** Judy Holliday in *Born Yesterday*

7003 **Best Director:** Joseph L. Mankiewicz for *All About Eve*

7004 **Best Supporting Actor:** George Sanders in *All About Eve*

7005 **Best Supporting Actress:** Josephine Hull in *Harvey*

7006 **Best Art Direction/Color:** Hans Dreier and Walter Tyler, Set Decoration by Sam Comer and Ray Moyer for *Samson and Delilah*

7007 **Best Art Direction/Black & White:** Hans Dreier and John Meehan, Set Decoration by Sam Comer and Ray Moyer for *Sunset Boulevard*

7008 **Best Cinematography/Color:** Robert Surtees for *King Solomon's Mines*

7009 **Best Cinematography/Black & White:** Robert Krasker for *The Third Man*

7010 **Best Writing/Motion Picture Story:** Edna Anhalt and Edward Anhalt for *Panic in the Streets*

7011 **Best Writing/Story and Screenplay:** Charles Brackett, Billy Wilder and D. M. Marshman, Jr., for *Sunset Boulevard*

7012 **Best Writing/Screenplay:** Joseph L. Mankiewicz for *All About Eve*

7013 **Best Costume Design/Black & White:** Edith Head and Charles Le Maire for *All About Eve*

7014 **Best Costume Design/Color:** Edith Head, Dorothy Jeakins, Elois Jenssen, Gile Steele and Gwen Wakeling for *Samson and Delilah*

7015 **Best Music/Score of a Musical Picture:** Adolph Deutsch and Roger Edens for *Annie Get Your Gun*

7016 **Best Music/Score of a Dramatic or Comedy Picture:** Franz Waxman for *Sunset Boulevard*

7017 **Best Music/Song:** Ray Evans and Jay Livingston, music and lyrics for "Mona Lisa" from *Captain Carey, USA*

7018 **Best Sound Recording or Sound:** 20th Century-Fox Studio Sound Department (Thomas T. Moulton, Sound Director) for *All About Eve*

7019 **Best Special Effects:** George Pal (Producer) for *Destination Moon*

7020 **Best Film Editing:** Ralph E. Winters and Conrad A. Nervig for *King Solomon's Mines*

7021 **Best Short Subject/Cartoon:** *Gerald McBoing-Boing*

7022 **Best Short Subject/One Reel:** *Grandad of Races*

7023 **Best Short Subject/Two Reel:** *In Beaver Valley*

7024 **Best Documentary/Feature:** *The Titan: The Story of Michelangelo*

7025 **Best Documentary/Short Subject:** *Why Korea?*

7026 **Best Foreign Language Film:** *The Walls of Malapaga* — France-Italy

7027 **Scientific or Technical/Class II (Academy Plaque):** To James B. Gordon and the 20th Century-Fox Studio Camera Department for the design and development of a multiple-image film viewer. To John Paul Livadary, Floyd Campbell, Lloyd Russell and the Columbia Studio Sound Department for the development of a multi-track magnetic re-recording system. To Loren L. Ryder and the Paramount Studio Sound Department for the first studio-wide application of magnetic sound recording to motion picture production.

7028 **Irving G. Thalberg Memorial Award:** Darryl F. Zanuck

7029 **Honorary Awards:** To George Murphy for his services in interpreting the film industry to the country at large. To Louis B. Mayer for distinguished service to the motion picture industry.

———————— **1951** ————————

7030 **Best Picture:** *An American in Paris*

7031 **Best Actor:** Humphrey Bogart in *The African Queen*

7032 **Best Actress:** Vivien Leigh in *A Streetcar Named Desire*

7033 **Best Director:** George Stevens for *A Place in the Sun*

7034 **Best Supporting Actor:** Karl Malden in *A Streetcar Named Desire*

7035 **Best Supporting Actress:** Kim Hunter in *A Streetcar Named Desire*

7036 **Best Art Direction/Color:** Cedric Gibbons and Preston Ames, Set Decoration by Edwin B. Willis and Keogh Gleason for *An American in Paris*

7037 **Best Art Direction/Black & White:** Richard Day, Set Decoration by George James Hopkins for *A Streetcar Named Desire*

7038 **Best Cinematography/Color:** Alfred Gilks and John Alton for *An American in Paris*

7039 Best Cinematography/Black & White: William C. Mellor for *A Place in the Sun*

7040 Best Writing/Motion Picture Story: Paul Dehn and James Bernard for *Seven Days to Noon*

7041 Best Writing/Story and Screenplay: Alan Jay Lerner for *An American in Paris*

7042 Best Writing/Screenplay: Michael Wilson and Harry Brown for *A Place in the Sun*

7043 Costume Design/Black & White: Edith Head for *A Place in the Sun*

7044 Best Costume Design/Color: Orry-Kelly, Walter Plunkett and Irene Sharaff for *An American in Paris*

7045 Best Music/Score of a Musical Picture: Johnny Green and Saul Chaplin for *An American in Paris*

7046 Best Music/Score of a Dramatic or Comedy Picture: Franz Waxman for *A Place in the Sun*

7047 Best Music/Song: Hoagy Carmichael, music and Johnny Mercer, lyrics for "In the Cool, Cool, Cool of the Evening" from *Here Comes the Groom*

7048 Best Sound Recording: Metro-Goldwyn-Mayer Studio Sound Department (Douglas Shearer, Sound Director) for *The Great Caruso*

7049 Best Film Editing: William Hornbeck for *A Place in the Sun*

7050 Best Short Subject/Cartoon: *Two Mouseketeers*

7051 Best Short Subject/One Reel: *World of Kids*

7052 Best Short Subject/Two Reel: *Nature's Half Acre*

7053 Best Documentary/Feature: *Kon-Tiki*

7054 Best Documentary/Short Subject: *Benji*

7055 Best Special Effects: *When Worlds Collide*

7056 Best Foreign Language Film: *Rashomon* — Japan

7057 Scientific or Technical/Class II (Academy Plaque): To Gordon Jennings, S. L. Stancliffe and the Paramount Studio Special Photographic and Engineering departments for the design, construction and application of a servo-operated recording and repeating device. To Olin L. Dupy of Metro-Goldwyn-Mayer Studio for the design, construction and application of a motion picture reproducing system. To Victor Division of the Radio Corporation of America for pioneering direct positive recording with anticipatory noise reduction.

7058 Scientific or Technical/Class III (Certificate of Honorable Mention): To Richard M. Haff, Frank P. Herrnfeld, Garland C. Misener and the Ansco Film Division of General Aniline and Film Corp. for the development of the Ansco color scene tester. To Fred Ponedel, Ralph Ayers and George Brown of Warner Brothers Studio for an air-driven water motor to provide flow, wake and white water for marine sequences in motion pictures. To Glen Robinson and the Metro-Goldwyn-Mayer Studio Construction Department for the development of a new music wire and cable cutter. To Jack Gaylord and the Metro-Goldwyn-Mayer Studio Construction Department for the development of balsa falling snow. To Carlos Rivas of Metro-Goldwyn-Mayer Studio for the development of an automated magnetic film splicer.

7059 Irving G. Thalberg Memorial Award: Arthur Freed

7060 Honorary Award: To Gene Kelly in appreciation of his versatility as an actor, singer, director, dancer and specifically for his brilliant achievement in the art of choreography on film.

———————— **1 9 5 2** ————————

7061 Best Picture: *The Greatest Show on Earth*

7062 Best Actor: Gary Cooper in *High Noon*

7063 Best Actress: Shirley Booth in *Come Back, Little Sheba*

7064 Best Director: John Ford for *The Quiet Man*

7065 Best Supporting Actor: Anthony Quinn in *Viva Zapata!*

7066 Best Supporting Actress: Gloria Grahame in *The Bad and the Beautiful*

7067 Best Art Direction/Color: Paul Sheriff, Set Decoration by Marcel Vertes for *Moulin Rouge*

7068 Best Art Direction/Black & White: Cedric Gibbons and Edward Carfagno, Set Decoration by Edwin B. Willis and Keogh Gleason for *The Bad and the Beautiful*

7069 Best Cinematography/Color: Winton C. Hoch and Archie Stout for *The Quiet Man*

7070 Best Cinematography/Black & White: Robert Surtees for *The Bad and the Beautiful*

7071 Best Writing/Motion Picture Story: Frederic M. Frank, Theodore St. John and Frank Cavett for *The Greatest Show on Earth*

7072 Best Writing/Story and Screenplay: T. E. B. Clarke for *The Lavender Hill Mob*

7073 Best Writing/Screenplay: Charles Schnee for *The Bad and the Beautiful*

7074 Best Costume Design/Black & White: Helen Rose for *The Bad and the Beautiful*

7075 Best Costume Design/Color: Marcel Vertes for *Moulin Rouge*

7076 Best Music/Score of a Musical Picture: Alfred Newman for *With a Song in My Heart*

7077 Best Music/Score of a Dramatic or Comedy Picture: Dimitri Tiomkin for *High Noon*

7078 Best Music/Song: Dimitri Tiomkin, music and Ned Washington, lyrics for "High Noon (Do Not Forsake Me, Oh My Darlin')" from *High Noon*

7079 Best Sound Recording: London Films Studio Sound Department (British) for *Breaking the Sound Barrier*

7080 Best Film Editing: Elmo Williams and Harry Gerstad for *Hign Noon*

7081 Best Short Subject/Cartoon: *Johann Mouse*

7082 Best Short Subject/One Reel: *Light in the Window*

7083 Best Short Subject/Two Reel: *Water Birds*

7084 Best Documentary/Feature: *The Sea Around Us*

7085 Best Documentary/Short Subject: *Neighbours*

7086 Best Foreign Language Film: *Forbidden Games*—France

7087 Best Special Effects: *Plymouth Adventure*

7088 Scientific or Technical/Class I (Academy Statuette): To Eastman Kodak Co. for the introduction of Eastman color negative and Eastman color print films. To Ansco Film Division of the General Aniline and Film Corp. for the introduction of Ansco color negative and Ansco color print film.

7089 Scientific or Technical/Class II (Academy Plaque): To Technicolor Motion Picture Corp. for an improved method of color motion picture photography under incandescent light.

7090 Scientific or Technical/Class III (Certificate of Honorable Mention): To the Projection, Still Photographic and Development Engineering departments of Metro-Goldwyn-Mayer Studio for an improved method of projecting photographic backgrounds. To John G. Frayne and R. R. Scoville and Westrex Corp. for a method of measuring distortion in sound reproduction. To Photo Research Corp. for creating the Spectra color temperature meter. To Gustav Jirouch for the design of the Robot automatic film splicer. To Carlos Rivas of Metro-Goldwyn-Mayer Studio for the development of a sound reproducer for magnetic film.

7091 Irving G. Thalberg Memorial Award: Cecil B. DeMille

7092 Honorary Award: To George Alfred Mitchell for the design and development of the camera which bears his name and for his continued and dominant presence in the field of cinematography. To Joseph M. Schenck for long and distinguished service to the motion picture industry. To Merian C. Cooper for his many innovations and contributions to the art of motion pictures. To Harold Lloyd, master comedian and good citizen. To Bob Hope for his contribution to the laughter of the world, his service to the industry and his devotion to the American premise.

—————— **1953** ——————

7093 Best Picture: *From Here to Eternity*

7094 Best Actor: William Holden in *Stalag 17*

7095 Best Actress: Audrey Hepburn in *Roman Holiday*

7096 Best Director: Fred Zinnemann for *From Here to Eternity*

7097 Best Supporting Actor: Frank Sinatra in *From Here to Eternity*

7098 **Best Supporting Actress:** Donna Reed in *From Here to Eternity*

7099 **Best Art Direction/Color:** Lyle Wheeler and George W. Davis, Set Decoration by Walter M. Scott and Paul S. Fox for *The Robe*

7100 **Best Art Direction/Black & White:** Cedric Gibbons and Edward Carfagno, Set Decoration by Edwin B. Willis and Hugh Hunt for *Julius Caesar*

7101 **Best Cinematography/Color:** Loyal Griggs for *Shane*

7102 **Best Cinematography/Black & White:** Burnett Guffey for *From Here to Eternity*

7103 **Best Writing/Motion Picture Story:** Ian McLellan Hunter for *Roman Holiday*

7104 **Best Writing/Story and Screenplay:** Charles Brackett, Walter Reisch and Richard Breen for *Titanic*

7105 **Best Writing/Screenplay:** Daniel Taradash for *From Here to Eternity*

7106 **Best Costume Design/Black & White:** Edith Head for *Roman Holiday*

7107 **Best Costume Design/Color:** Charles Le Maire and Emile Santiago for *The Robe*

7108 **Best Music/Score of a Musical Picture:** Alfred Newman for *Call Me Madam*

7109 **Best Music/Score of a Dramatic or Comedy Picture:** Bronislau Kaper for *Lili*

7110 **Best Music/Song:** Sammy Fain, music and Paul Francis Webster, lyrics for "Secret Love" from *Calamity Jane*

7111 **Best Sound Recording:** Columbia Studio Sound Department (John P. Livadary, Sound Director) for *From Here to Eternity*

7112 **Best Film Editing:** William Lyon for *From Here to Eternity*

7113 **Best Short Subject/Cartoon:** *Toot, Whistle, Plunk and Boom*

7114 **Best Short Subject/One Reel:** *The Merry Wives of Windsor Overture*

7115 **Best Short Subject/Two Reel:** *Bear Country*

7116 **Best Documentary/Feature:** *The Living Desert*

7117 **Best Documentary/Short Subject:** *The Alaskan Eskimo*

7118 **Best Special Effects:** *War of the Worlds*

7119 **Scientific or Technical/Class I (Academy Statuette):** To Professor Henri Chretien and Earl Sponable, Sol Halprin, Lorin Grignon, Herbert Bragg and Carl Faulkner of 20th Century-Fox Studios for creating, developing and engineering the equipment, process and techniques of known as CinemaScope. To Fred Waller for designing and developing the multiple photographic and projection systems which culminated in Cinerama.

7120 **Scientific or Technical/Class II (Academy Plaque):** To Reeves Soundcraft Corp. for their development of a process of applying stripes of magnetic oxide to motion picture film for sound recording and reproduction.

7121 **Scientific or Technical/Class III (Certificate of Honorable Mention):** To Westrex Corp. for the design and construction of a new film editing machine.

7122 **Irving G. Thalberg Memorial Award:** George Stevens

7123 **Honorary Award:** To Pete Smith for his witty and pungent observations on the American scene in his series "Pete Smith Specialties." To the 20th Century-Fox Film Corp. in recognition of their imagination, showmanship and foresight in introducing the revolutionary process known as CinemaScope. To Joseph I. Breen for his conscientious, open-minded and dignified management of the Motion Picture Production Code. To Bell & Howell Co. for their pioneering and basic achievements in the advancement of the motion picture industry.

1954

7124 **Best Picture:** *On the Waterfront*

7125 **Best Actor:** Marlon Brando in *On the Waterfront*

7126 **Best Actress:** Grace Kelly in *The Country Girl*

7127 **Best Director:** Elia Kazan for *On the Waterfront*

7128 **Best Supporting Actor:** Edmond O'Brien in *The Barefoot Contessa*

7129 **Best Supporting Actress:** Eva Marie Saint in *On the Waterfront*

7130 **Best Art Direction/Color:** John Meehan, Set Decoration by Emile Kuri for *20,000 Leagues Under the Sea*

7131 **Best Art Direction/Black &**

White: Richard Day for *On the Waterfront*

7132 **Best Cinematography/Color:** Milton Krasner for *Three Coins in the Fountain*

7133 **Best Cinematography/Black & White:** Boris Kaufman for *On the Waterfront*

7134 **Best Writing/Motion Picture Story:** Philip Yordan for *Broken Lance*

7135 **Best Writing/Story and Screenplay:** Budd Schulberg for *On the Waterfront*

7136 **Best Writing/Screenplay:** George Seaton for *The Country Girl*

7137 **Best Costume Design/Black & White:** Edith Head for *Sabrina*

7138 **Best Costume Design/Color:** Sanzo Wada for *Gate of Hell*

7139 **Best Music/Score of a Musical Picture:** Adolph Deutsch and Saul Chaplin for *Seven Brides for Seven Brothers*

7140 **Best Music/Score of a Dramatic or Comedy Picture:** Dimitri Tiomkin for *The High and the Mighty*

7141 **Best Music/Song:** Jule Styne, music and Sammy Kahn, lyrics for "Three Coins in the Fountain" from *Three Coins in the Fountain*

7142 **Best Sound Recording:** Universal-International Studio Sound Department (Leslie I. Carey, Sound Director) for *The Glenn Miller Story*

7143 **Best Special Effects:** Walt Disney Studios for *20,000 Leagues Under the Sea*

7144 **Best Film Editing:** Gene Milford for *On the Waterfront*

7145 **Best Short Subject/Cartoon:** *When Magoo Flew*

7146 **Best Short Subject/One Reel:** *This Mechanical Age*

7147 **Best Short Subject/Two Reel:** *A Time Out of War*

7148 **Best Documentary/Feature:** *The Vanishing Prairie*

7149 **Best Documentary/Short Subject:** *Thursday's Children*

7150 **Best Foreign Language Film:** *Gate of Hell* — Japan

7151 **Scientific or Technical/Class I (Academy Statuette):** To Paramount Pictures, Inc., Loren L. Ryder, John Bishop and all the members of the technical and engineering staff for developing a method of producing and exhibiting motion pictures known as VistaVision.

7152 **Scientific or Technical/Class III (Certificate of Honorable Mention):** To David S. Horsley and the Universal-International Studio Special Photographic Department for a portable remote control device for process projectors. To Karl Freund and Frank Crandell of Photographic Research Corp. for the design and development of a direct reading brightness meter. To Wesley C. Miller, J. W. Stafford, K. M. Frierson and the Metro-Goldwyn-Mayer Studio Sound Department for an electronic sound printing comparison device. To John P. Livadary, Lloyd Russell and the Columbia Studio Sound Department for an improved limiting amplifier as applied to sound level comparison devices. To Roland Miller and Max Goeppinger of Magnascope Corp. for the design and development of a cathode ray magnetic sound track viewer. To Carlos Rivas, G. M. Sprague and the Metro-Goldwyn-Mayer Studio Sound Department for the design of a magnetic sound editing machine. To Fred Wilson of Samuel Goldwyn Studio Sound Department for the design of a variable multiple-band equalizer. To P. C. Young of the Metro-Goldwyn-Mayer Studio Projection Department for the practical application of a variable focal length attachment to motion picture projection lenses. To Fred Knoth and Orien Ernest of the Universal-International Studio Technical Department for the development of a hand portable, electric, dry oil-fog machine.

7153 **Honorary Award:** To Bausch & Lomb Optical Co. for their contributions to the advancement of the motion picture industry. To Kemp R. Niver for the development of the Renovare Process which has made possible the restoration of the Library of Congress Paper Film Collection. To Greta Garbo for her unforgettable screen performances. To Danny Kaye for his unique talents, service to the Academy, the motion picture industry and the American people. To Jon Whitely for his outstanding juvenile performance in *The Little Kidnappers*. To Vincent Winter for his outstanding juvenile performance in *The Little Kid-nappers.*

─────── 1 9 5 5 ───────

7154 **Best Picture:** *Marty*
7155 **Best Actor:** Ernest Borgnine in *Marty*
7156 **Best Actress:** Anna Magnani in *The Rose Tattoo*
7157 **Best Director:** Delbert Mann for *Marty*
7158 **Best Supporting Actor:** Jack Lemmon in *Mister Roberts*
7159 **Best Supporting Actress:** Jo Van Fleet in *East of Eden*
7160 **Best Art Direction/Color:** William Flannery and Jo Mielziner, Set Decoration by Robert Priestley for *Picnic*
7161 **Best Art Direction/Black & White:** Hal Pereira and Tambi Larsen, Set Decoration by Sam Comer and Arthur Krams for *The Rose Tattoo*
7162 **Best Cinematography/Color:** Robert Burks for *To Catch a Thief*
7163 **Best Cinematography/Black & White:** James Wong Howe for *The Rose Tattoo*
7164 **Best Writing/Motion Picture Story:** Daniel Fuchs for *Love Me or Leave Me*
7165 **Best Writing/Story and Screenplay:** William Ludwig and Sonya Levien for *Interrupted Melody*
7166 **Best Writing/Screenplay:** Paddy Chayefsky for *Marty*
7167 **Best Costume Design/Black & White:** Helen Rose for *I'll Cry Tomorrow*
7168 **Best Costume Design/Color:** Charles Le Maire for *Love Is a Many-Splendored Thing*
7169 **Best Music/Score of a Musical Picture:** Robert Russell Bennett, Jay Blackton and Adolph Deutsch for *Oklahoma!*
7170 **Best Music/Score of a Dramatic or Comedy Picture:** Alfred Newman for *Love Is a Many-Splendored Thing*
7171 **Best Music/Song:** Sammy Fain, music and Paul Francis Webster, lyrics for "Love Is a Many-Splendored Thing" from *Love Is a Many-Splendored Thing*
7172 **Best Sound Recording:** Todd-AO

Sound Department (Fred Hynes, Sound Director) for *Oklahoma!*
7173 **Best Special Effects:** Paramount Studio for *The Bridges at Toko-Ri*
7174 **Best Film Editing:** Charles Nelson and William A. Lyon for *Picnic*
7175 **Best Short Subject/Cartoon:** *Speedy Gonzales*
7176 **Best Short Subject/One Reel:** *Survival City*
7177 **Best Short Subject/Two Reel:** *The Face of Lincoln*
7178 **Best Documentary/Feature:** *Helen Keller in Her Story*
7179 **Best Documentary/Short Subject:** *Men Against the Arctic*
7180 **Best Foreign Language Film:** *Samurai* — Japan
7181 **Scientific or Technical/Class I (Academy Statuette):** To National Carbon Co. for the development and production of a high efficiency yellow flame carbon for motion picture color photography.
7182 **Scientific or Technical/Class II (Academy Plaque):** To Eastman Kodak Co. for Eastman Tri-X panchromatic negative film. To Farciot Edouart, Hal Corl and the Paramount Studio Transparency Department for the engineering and development of a double-frame, triple-head background projector.
7183 **Scientific or Technical/Class III (Certificate of Honorable Mention):** To 20th Century–Fox Studio and Bausch & Lomb Co. for the new combination lenses for CinemaScope photography. To Walter Jolley, Maurice Larson and R. H. Spies of 20th Century–Fox Studio for a spraying process which creates simulated metallic surfaces. To Steve Krilanovich for an improved camera dolly incorporating multi-directional steering. To Dave Anderson of 20th Century–Fox Studio for an improved spotlight capable of maintaining a fixed circle of light at constant intensity over varied distances. To Loren L. Ryder, Charles West, Henry Fracker and Paramount Studio for a projection film index to establish proper framing for various aspect ratios. To Farciot Edouart, Hal Corl and the Paramount Studio Transparency Department for an improved dual stereopticon background projector.

───────── **1 9 5 6** ─────────

7184 **Best Picture:** *Around the World in 80 Days*

7185 **Best Actor:** Yul Brynner in *The King and I*

7186 **Best Actress:** Ingrid Bergman in *Anastasia*

7187 **Best Director:** George Stevens for *Giant*

7188 **Best Supporting Actor:** Anthony Quinn in *Lust for Life*

7189 **Best Supporting Actress:** Dorothy Malone in *Written on the Wind*

7190 **Best Art Direction/Color:** Lyle R. Wheeler and John de Cuir, Set Decoration by Walter M. Scott and Paul Fox for *The King and I*

7191 **Best Art Direction/Black & White:** Cedric Gibbons and Malcolm F. Brown, Set Decoration by Edwin B. Willis and Keogh Gleason for *Somebody Up There Likes Me*

7192 **Best Cinematography/Color:** Lionel Lindon for *Around the World in 80 Days*

7193 **Best Cinematography/Black & White:** Joseph Ruttenberg for *Somebody Up There Likes Me*

7194 **Best Writing/Motion Picture Story:** Dalton Trumbo (aka "Robert Rich") for *The Brave One*

7195 **Best Writing/Screenplay-Adapted:** James Poe, John Farrow and S. J. Perlman for *Around the World in 80 Days*

7196 **Best Writing/Screenplay-Original:** Albert Lamorisse for *The Red Balloon*

7197 **Best Costume Design/Black & White:** Jean Louis for *The Solid Gold Cadillac*

7198 **Best Costume Design/Color:** Irene Sharaff for *The King and I*

7199 **Best Music/Score of a Musical Picture:** Alfred Newman and Ken Darby for *The King and I*

7200 **Best Music/Score of a Dramatic or Comedy Picture:** Victor Young for *Around the World in 80 Days*

7201 **Best Music/Song:** Ray Evans and Jay Livingston, music and lyrics for "Whatever Will Be, Will Be (Que Sera, Sera)" from *The Man Who Knew Too Much*

7202 **Best Sound Recording:** 20th Century-Fox Studio Sound Department (Carl Faulkner, Sound Director) for *The King and I*

7203 **Best Special Effects:** John Fulton for *The Ten Commandments*

7204 **Best Film Editing:** Gene Ruggiero and Paul Weatherwax for *Around the World in 80 Days*

7205 **Best Foreign Language Film:** *La Strada* — Italy

7206 **Best Short Subject/Cartoon:** *Mister Magoo's Puddle Jumper*

7207 **Best Short Subject/One Reel:** *Crashing the Water Barrier*

7208 **Best Short Subject/Two Reel:** *The Bespoke Overcoat*

7209 **Best Documentary/Feature:** *The Silent World*

7210 **Best Documentary/Short Subject:** *The True Story of the Civil War*

7211 **Scientific or Technical/Class III (Certificate of Honorable Mention):** To Richard H. Ranger of Rangertone, Inc. for the development of a synchronous recording and reproducing system for quarter-inch magnetic tape. To Ted Hirsch, Carl Hauge and Edward Reichard of Consolidated Film Laboratories for an automatic scene counter for laboratory projection rooms. To the Technical Departments of Paramount Pictures Corp. for the engineering and development of the Paramount lightweight, horizontal-movement Vista-Vision camera. To Roy C. Stewart and Sons of Stewart-Trans Lux Corp., Dr. C. R. Daily and the Transparency Department of Paramount Pictures Corp. for the engineering and development of the HiTrans and Para-HiTrans rear projection screens. To the Construction Department of Metro-Goldwyn-Mayer Studio for new hand-portable fog machine. To Daniel J. Bloomberg, John Pond, William Wade and the Enginering and Camera departments of Republic Studio for the Naturama adaptation to the Mitchell camera.

7212 **Jean Hersholt Humanitarian Award:** Y. Frank Freeman

7213 **Irving G. Thalberg Memorial Award:** Buddy Adler

7214 **Honorary Awards:** Eddie Cantor for distinguished service to the film industry.

1957

7215 **Best Picture:** *The Bridge on the River Kwai*
7216 **Best Actor:** Alec Guinness in *The Bridge on the River Kwai*
7217 **Best Actress:** Joanne Woodward in *The Three Faces of Eve*
7218 **Best Director:** David Lean for *The Bridge on the River Kwai*
7219 **Best Supporting Actor:** Red Buttons in *Sayonara*
7220 **Best Supporting Actress:** Miyoshi Umeki in *Sayonara*
7221 **Best Art Direction:** Ted Haworth, Set Decoration by Robert Priestley for *Sayonara*
7222 **Best Cinematography:** Jack Hildyard for *The Bridge on the River Kwai*
7223 **Best Writing/Story and Screenplay Written Directly for the Screen:** George Wells for *Designing Woman*
7224 **Best Writing/Screenplay Based on Material from Another Medium:** Michael Wilson, Carl Foreman and Pierre Boulle for *The Bridge on the River Kwai*
7225 **Best Costume Design:** Orry-Kelly for *Les Girls*
7226 **Best Music/Scoring:** Malcolm Arnold for *The Bridge on the River Kwai*
7227 **Best Music/Song:** James Van Heusen, music and Sammy Kahn, lyrics for "All the Way" from *The Joker Is Wild*
7228 **Best Sound Recording:** Warner Brothers Studio Sound Department (George R. Groves, Sound Director) for *Sayonara*
7229 **Best Special Effects:** Walter Rossi (Audible) for *The Enemy Below*
7230 **Best Film Editing:** Peter Taylor for *The Bridge on the River Kwai*
7231 **Best Foreign Language Film:** *The Nights of Cabiria* — Italy
7232 **Best Short Subject/Cartoon:** *Birds Anonymous*
7233 **Best Short Subject/Live Action:** *The Wetback Hound*
7234 **Best Documentary/Feature:** *Albert Schweitzer*
7235 **Scientific or Technical/Class I (Academy Statuette):** To the Todd-AO Corp. and Westrex Corp. for developing method of producing and exhibiting wide-film motion pictures known as the Todd-AO System. To the Motion Picture Research Council for the design and development of a high-efficiency projection screen for drive-in theaters.
7236 **Scientific or Technical/Class II (Academy Plaque):** To the Société d'Optique et de Mécanique de Haute Précision for the development of a high-speed vari-focal photographic lens. To Harlan L. Baumbach, Lorand Wargo, Howard M. Little and the Unicorn Engineering Corp. for the development of an automatic printer light selector.
7237 **Scientific or Technical/Class III (Certificate of Honorable Mention):** To Charles E. Sutter, William B. Smith, Paramount Pictures Corp. and General Cable Corp. for the engineering and application to studio use of aluminum lightweight electrical cable and connectors.
7238 **Jean Hersholt Humanitarian Award:** Samuel Goldwyn
7239 **Honorary Award:** To Charles Brackett for outstanding service to the Academy. To B. B. Kahane for distinguished service to the motion picture industry. To Gilbert M. ("Broncho Billy") Anderson, motion picture pioneer, for his contributions to the development of motion pictures as entertainment. To the Society of Motion Picture and Television Engineers for their contributions to the advancement of the motion picture industry.

1958

7240 **Best Picture:** *Gigi*
7241 **Best Actor:** David Niven in *Separate Tables*
7242 **Best Actress:** Susan Hayward in *I Want to Live!*
7243 **Best Director:** Vincente Minnelli for *Gigi*
7244 **Best Supporting Actor:** Burl Ives in *The Big Country*
7245 **Best Supporting Actress:** Wendy Hiller in *Separate Tables*
7246 **Best Art Direction:** William A. Horning and Preston Ames, Set Decoration by Henry Grace and Keogh Gleason for *Gigi*
7247 **Best Cinematography/Color:** Joseph Ruttenberg for *Gigi*
7248 **Best Cinematography/Black & White:** Sam Leavitt for *The Defiant Ones*

7249 **Best Writing/Story and Screenplay Written Directly for the Screen:** Nathan E. Douglas and Harold Jacob Smith for *The Defiant Ones*

7250 **Best Writing/Screenplay Based on Material from Another Medium:** Alan Jay Lerner for *Gigi*

7251 **Best Costume Design:** Cecil Beaton for *Gigi*

7252 **Best Music/Score of a Musical Picture:** Andre Previn for *Gigi*

7253 **Best Music/Score of a Dramatic or Comedy Picture:** Dimitri Tiomkin for *The Old Man and the Sea*

7254 **Best Music/Song:** Frederick Loewe, music and Alan Jay Lerner, lyrics for "Gigi" from *Gigi*

7255 **Best Sound Recording:** Todd-AO Sound Department (Fred Hynes, Sound Director) for *South Pacific*

7256 **Best Special Effects:** Tom Howard (Visual) for *tom thumb*

7257 **Best Film Editing:** Adrienne Fazan for *Gigi*

7258 **Best Foreign Language Film:** *My Uncle*—France

7259 **Best Short Subject/Cartoon:** *Knightly Knight Bugs*

7260 **Best Short Subject/Live Action:** *Grand Canyon*

7261 **Best Documentary/Feature:** *White Wilderness*

7262 **Best Documentary/Short Subject:** *Ama Girls*

7263 **Scientific or Technical/Class II (Academy Plaque):** To Don W. Prideaux, LeRoy G. Leighton and the Lamp Division of General Electric Co. for the development and production of an improved 10 kilowatt lamp for motion picture set lighting. To Panavision, Inc. for the design and development of the Auto Panatar anamorphic photographic lens for 35mm CinemaScope photography.

7264 **Scientific or Technical/Class III (Certificate of Honorable Mention):** To Willy Borberg of the General Precision Laboratory, Inc. for the development of a high-speed intermittent movement for 35mm theater projection equipment. To Fred Ponedel, George Brown and Conrad Boye of the Warner Brothers Special Effects Department for the design and fabrication of a new rapid-fire marble gun.

7265 **Irving G. Thalberg Memorial Award:** Jack L. Warner

7266 **Honorary Award:** To Maurice Chevalier for his contributions to the world of entertainment for more than half a century.

─────── **1959** ───────

7267 **Best Picture:** *Ben-Hur*

7268 **Best Actor:** Charlton Heston in *Ben-Hur*

7269 **Best Actress:** Simone Signoret in *Room at the Top*

7270 **Best Director:** William Wyler for *Ben-Hur*

7271 **Best Supporting Actor:** Hugh Griffith in *Ben-Hur*

7272 **Best Supporting Actress:** Shelley Winters in *The Diary of Anne Frank*

7273 **Best Art Direction/Color:** William A. Horning and Edward Carfagno, Set Design by Hugh Hunt for *Ben-Hur*

7274 **Best Art Direction/Black & White:** Lyle R. Wheeler and George W. Davis, Set Decoration by Walter M. Scott and Stuart A. Reiss for *The Diary of Anne Frank*

7275 **Best Cinematography/Color:** Robert L. Surtees for *Ben-Hur*

7276 **Best Cinematography/Black & White:** William C. Mellor for *The Diary of Anne Frank*

7277 **Best Writing/Story and Screenplay Written Directly for the Screen:** Russell Rouse and Clarence Greene (story), Stanley Shapiro and Maurice Richlin (screenplay) for *Pillow Talk*

7278 **Best Writing/Screenplay Based on Material from Another Medium:** Neil Paterson for *Room at the Top*

7279 **Best Costume Design/Black & White:** Orry-Kelly for *Some Like It Hot*

7280 **Best Costume Design/Color:** Elizabeth Haffenden for *Ben-Hur*

7281 **Best Music/Score of a Musical Picture:** Andre Previn and Ken Darby for *Porgy and Bess*

7282 **Best Music/Score of a Dramatic or Comedy Picture:** Miklos Rozsa for *Ben-Hur*

7283 **Best Music/Song:** James Van Heusen, music and Sammy Kahn, lyrics for "High Hopes" from *A Hole in the Head*

7284 **Best Sound Recording:** Metro-Goldwyn-Mayer Sound Department (Franklin E. Milton, Sound Director) for *Ben-Hur*

7285 **Best Special Effects:** A. Arnold Gillespie and Robert MacDonald (Visual) and Milo Lory (Audible) for *Ben-Hur*

7286 **Best Film Editing:** Ralph E. Winters and John D. Dunning for *Ben-Hur*

7287 **Foreign Language Film:** *Black Orpheus* — France

7288 **Best Short Subject/Cartoon:** *Moonbird*

7289 **Best Short Subject/Live Action:** *The Golden Fish*

7290 **Best Documentary/Feature:** *Serengeti Shall Not Die*

7291 **Best Documentary/Short Subject:** *Glass*

7292 **Scientific or Technical/Class II (Academy Plaque):** To Douglas G. Shearer of Metro-Goldwyn-Mayer, Inc. and Robert E. Gottschalk and John R. Moore of Panavision, Inc. for the development of a system of producing and exhibiting wide-film motion pictures known as Camera 65. To Wadsworth E. Pohl, William Evans, Werner Hopf, S. E. Howse, Thomas P. Dixon, Stanford Research Institute and Technicolor Motion Picture Corp. for the design and development of Technicolor electronic printing timer. To Wadsworth E. Pohl, Jack Alford, Henry Imus, Joseph Schmit, Paul Fassnacht, Al Lofquist and Technicolor Motion Picture Corp. for the development and practical application of equipment for wet printing. To Dr. Howard S. Coleman, Dr. A. Francis Turner, Harold H. Schroeder, James R. Benford and Harold E. Rosenberger of the Bausch and Lomb Optical Co. for the design and development of the Bacold projection mirror. To Robert P. Gutterman of General Kinetics Inc. and Lipsner Smith Corp. for the design and development of the CF-2 Ultra-Sonic Film Cleaner.

7293 **Scientific or Technical/Class III (Certificate of Honorable Mention):** To Ub Iwerks of Walt Disney Productions, Ltd., for the design of an improved optical printer for special effects and matte shots. To E. L. Stones, Glen Robinson, Winfield Hubbard and Luthur Newman

of Metro-Goldwyn-Mayer Construction Department for the design of a multiple cable remote-controlled winch.

7294 **Jean Hersholt Humanitarian Award:** Bob Hope

7295 **Honorary Award:** To Lee de Forest for his pioneering inventions which brought sound to the motion picture. To Buster Keaton for his unique talents which brought immortal comedies to the screen.

——————— **1 9 6 0** ———————

7296 **Best Picture:** *The Apartment*

7297 **Best Actor:** Burt Lancaster in *Elmer Gantry*

7298 **Best Actress:** Elizabeth Taylor in *Butterfield 8*

7299 **Best Director:** Billy Wilder for *The Apartment*

7300 **Best Supporting Actor:** Peter Ustinov in *Spartacus*

7301 **Best Supporting Actress:** Shirley Jones in *Elmer Gantry*

7302 **Best Art Direction/Color:** Alexander Golitzen and Eric Orbom, Set Decoration by Russell A. Gausman for *Spartacus*

7303 **Best Art Direction/Black & White:** Alexander Trauner, Set Decoration by Edward G. Boyle for *The Apartment*

7304 **Best Cinematography/Color:** Russell Metty for *Spartacus*

7305 **Best Cinematography/Black & White:** Freddie Francis for *Sons and Lovers*

7306 **Best Writing/Story and Screenplay Written Directly for the Screen:** Billy Wilder and I. A. L. Diamond for *The Apartment*

7307 **Best Writing/Screenplay Based on Material from Another Medium:** Richard Brooks for *Elmer Gantry*

7308 **Best Costume Design/Black & White:** Edith Head and Howard Stevenson for *The Facts of Life*

7309 **Best Costume Design/Color:** Valles and Bill Thomas for *Spartacus*

7310 **Best Music/Score of a Musical Picture:** Morris Stoloff and Harry Sukman for *Song Without End (The Story of Franz Liszt)*

7311 **Best Music/Score of a Dramatic or Comedy Picture:** Ernest Gold for *Exodus*

7312 **Best Music/Song:** Manos Hadjidakis for "Never on Sunday" from *Never on Sunday*

7313 **Best Sound Recording:** Samuel Goldwyn Studio Sound Department (Gordon E. Sawyer, Sound Director) and Todd-AO Sound Department (Fred Hynes, Sound Director) for *The Alamo*

7314 **Best Special Effects:** Gene Warren and Tim Baar (Visual) for *The Time Machine*

7315 **Best Film Editing:** Daniel Mandell for *The Apartment*

7316 **Best Foreign Language Film:** *The Virgin Spring* — Sweden

7317 **Best Short Subject/Cartoon:** *Munro*

7318 **Best Short Subject/Live Action:** *Day of the Painter*

7319 **Best Documentary/Feature:** *The Horse with the Flying Tail*

7320 **Best Documentary/Short Subject:** *Guiseppina*

7321 **Scientific or Technical/Class II (Academy Plaque):** To Ampex Professional Products Co. for the production of a well-engineered, multi-purpose sound system combining high standards of quality with convenience of control, dependable operation and simplified emergency provisions.

7322 **Scientific or Technical/Class III (Certificate of Honorable Mention):** To Arthur Holcomb, Petro Vlahos and Columbia Studio Camera Department for a camera flicker-indicating device. To Anthony Paglia and the 20th Century-Fox Studio Mechanical Effects Department for the design and construction of a miniature flak gun and ammunition. To Carl Hauge, Robert Grubel and Edward Reichard of Consolidated Film Laboratories for the development of an automatic developer replenisher system.

7323 **Jean Hersholt Humanitarian Award:** Sol Lesser

7324 **Honorary Award:** To Gary Cooper for his many memorable screen performances and the international recognition he, as an individual, has gained for the motion picture industry. To Stan Laurel for his creative pioneering in the field of cinema comedy. To Hayley Mills for outstanding juvenile performance in 1960 in *Polyanna*.

———— **1 9 6 1** ————

7325 **Best Picture:** *West Side Story*

7326 **Best Actor:** Maximillian Schell in *Judgment at Nuremberg*

7327 **Best Actress:** Sophia Loren in *Two Women*

7328 **Best Director:** Robert Wise and Jerome Robbins for *West Side Story*

7329 **Best Supporting Actor:** George Chakiris in *West Side Story*

7330 **Best Supporting Actress:** Rita Moreno in *West Side Story*

7331 **Best Art Direction/Color:** Boris Levin, Set Decoration by Victor A. Gangelin for *West Side Story*

7332 **Best Art Direction/Black & White:** Harry Horner, Set Decoration by Gene Callahan for *The Hustler*

7333 **Best Cinematography/Color:** Daniel L. Fapp for *West Side Story*

7334 **Best Cinematography/Black & White:** Eugen Shuftan for *The Hustler*

7335 **Best Writing — Story and Screenplay Written Directly for the Screen:** William Inge for *Splendor in the Grass*

7336 **Best Writing — Screenplay Based on Material from Another Medium:** Abby Mann for *Judgment at Nuremberg*

7337 **Best Costume Design/Black & White:** Piero Gherardi for *La Dolce Vita*

7338 **Best Costume Design/Color:** Irene Sharaff for *West Side Story*

7339 **Best Music/Score of a Musical Picture:** Saul Chaplin, Johnny Green, Sid Ramin and Irwin Kostal for *West Side Story*

7340 **Best Music/Score of a Dramatic or Comedy Picture:** Henry Mancini for *Breakfast at Tiffany's*

7341 **Best Music/Song:** Henry Mancini, music and Johnny Mercer, lyrics for "Moon River" from *Breakfast at Tiffany's*

7342 **Best Sound Recording:** Todd-AO Sound Department (Fred Hynes, Sound Director) and Samuel Goldwyn Studio Sound Department (Gordon E. Sawyer, Sound Director) for *West Side Story*

7343 **Best Special Effects:** Bill Warrington (Visual) and Vivian C. Greenham (Audible) for *The Guns of Navarone*

7344 **Best Film Editing:** Thomas Stanford for *West Side Story*

7345 Best Foreign Language Film: *Through a Glass Darkly* — Sweden
7346 Best Short Subject/Cartoon: *Ersatz*
7347 Best Short Subject/Live Action: *Seawards the Great Ships*
7348 Best Feature Documentary: *Le Ciel et la Boue (Sky Above and Mud Beneath)*
7349 Best Documentary/Short Subject: *Project Hope*
7350 Scientific or Technical/Class II (Academy Plaque): To Sylvania Electric Products, Inc., for the development of a hand-held, high-power photographic lighting unit known as the Sun Gun Professional. To James Dale, S. Wilson, H. E. Rice, John Rude, Laurie Atkin, Wadsworth E. Pohl, H. Peasgood and Technicolor Corp. for a process of automatic selective printing. To the 20th Century-Fox Research Department under E. I. Sponable and Herbert E. Bragg, and DeLuxe Laboratories, Inc., with the assistance of F. D. Leslie, R. D. Whitmore, A. A. Alden, Endel Pool and James B. Gordon for a system of decompressing and recomposing Cinema-Scope pictures for conventional aspect ratios.
7351 Scientific or Technical/Class III (Certificate of Honorable Mention): To Electric Eye Equipment Division of Hurletron, Inc., for an automatic light changing system for motion picture printers. To Wadsworth E. Pohl and Technicolor Corp. for an integrated sound and picture transfer process.
7352 Jean Hersholt Humanitarian Award: George Seaton
7353 Irving G. Thalberg Memorial Award: Stanley Kramer
7354 Honorary Award: To William L. Hendricks for his outstanding patriotic service in the conception, writing and production of the Marine Corps film *A Force in Readiness*, which has brought honor to the Academy and the motion picture industry. To Jerome Robbins for his brilliant achievements in the art of choreography on film. To Fred L. Metzler for his dedication and outstanding service to the Academy of Motion Picture Arts and Sciences.

———— **1962** ————

7355 Best Picture: *Lawrence of Arabia*
7356 Best Actor: Gregory Peck in *To Kill a Mockingbird*
7357 Best Actress: Anne Bancroft in *The Miracle Worker*
7358 Best Director: David Lean for *Lawrence of Arabia*
7359 Best Supporting Actor: Ed Begley in *Sweet Bird of Youth*
7360 Best Supporting Actress: Patty Duke in *The Miracle Worker*
7361 Best Art Direction/Color: John Box and John Stoll, Set Decoration by Dario Simoni for *Lawrence of Arabia*
7362 Best Art Direction/Black & White: Alexander Golitzen and Henry Bumstead, Set Decoration by Oliver Emert for *To Kill a Mockingbird*
7363 Best Cinematography/Color: Fred A. Young for *Lawrence of Arabia*
7364 Best Cinematography/Black & White: Jean Bourgoin and Walter Wottitz for *The Longest Day*
7365 Best Writing — Story and Screenplay Written Directly for the Screen: Ennio de Concini, Alfredo Gianetti and Pietro Germi for *Divorce — Italian Style*
7366 Best Writing — Screenplay Based on Material from Another Medium: Horton Foote for *To Kill a Mockingbird*
7367 Best Costume Design/Black & White: Norma Koch for *Whatever Happened to Baby Jane?*
7368 Best Costume Design/Color: Mary Wills for *The Wonderful World of the Brothers Grimm*
7369 Best Music/Score Substantially Original: Maurice Jarre for *Lawrence of Arabia*
7370 Best Music/Adaptation or Treatment: Ray Heindorf for *The Music Man*
7371 Best Music/Song: Henry Mancini, music and Johnny Mercer, lyrics for "Days of Wine and Roses" from *Days of Wine and Roses*
7372 Best Sound Recording: Shepperton Studio Sound Department (John Cox, Sound Director) for *Lawrence of Arabia*
7373 Best Special Effects: Robert MacDonald (Visual) and Jacques Maumont (Audible) for *The Longest Day*
7374 Best Film Editing: Anne Coates for *Lawrence of Arabia*

7375 **Best Foreign Language Film:** *Sundays and Cybele*—France

7376 **Best Short Subject/Cartoon:** *The Hole*

7377 **Best Short Subject/Live Action:** *Heureux Anniversaire*

7378 **Best Documentary/Feature:** *Black Fox*

7379 **Best Documentary/Short Subject:** *Dylan Thomas*

7380 **Scientific or Technical/Class II (Academy Plaque):** to Ralph Chapman for the design and development of an advanced motion picture camera crane. To Albert S. Pratt, James L. Wassell and Hans C. Wohlrab of the Professional Division of Bell and Howell Company for the design and development of a new and improved automatic motion picture additive color printer. To North American Phillips Co., Inc. for the design and engineering of the Norelco Universal 35/70mm motion picture projector. To Charles E. Sutter, William Bryson Smith and Louis C. Kennell of Paramount Pictures Corp. for the engineering and application to motion picture production of a new system of electric power distribution.

7381 **Scientific or Technical/Class III (Certificate of Honorable Mention):** To Electro-Voice, Inc. for a highly directional dynamic line microphone. To Louis G. MacKenzie for a selective sound effects repeater.

7382 **Jean Hersholt Humanitarian Award:** Steve Broidy

——————— **1 9 6 3** ———————

7383 **Best Picture:** *Tom Jones*

7384 **Best Actor:** Sidney Poitier in *Lilies of the Field*

7385 **Best Actress:** Patricia Neal in *Hud*

7386 **Best Director:** Tony Richardson for *Tom Jones*

7387 **Best Supporting Actor:** Melvyn Douglas in *Hud*

7388 **Best Supporting Actress:** Margaret Rutherford in *The V.I.P.s*

7389 **Best Art Direction/Color:** John de Cuir, Jack Martin Smith, Hilyard Brown, Herman Blumenthal, Elven Webb, Maurice Pelling and Boris Juraga,

Set Decoration by Walter M. Scott, Paul S. Fox and Ray Moyer for *Cleopatra*

7390 **Best Art Direction/Black & White:** Gene Callahan for *America, America*

7391 **Best Cinematography/Color:** Leon Shamroy for *Cleopatra*

7392 **Best Cinematography/Black & White:** James Wong Howe for *Hud*

7393 **Best Writing—Story and Screenplay Written Directly for the Screen:** James R. Webb for *How the West Was Won*

7394 **Best Writing—Screenplay Based on Material from Another Medium:** John Osborn for *Tom Jones*

7395 **Best Costume Design/Black & White:** Piero Gherardi for *Federico Felini's 8½*

7396 **Best Costume Design/Color:** Irene Sharaff, Vittorio Nino Novarese and Renie for *Cleopatra*

7397 **Best Music/Score Substantially Original:** John Addison for *Tom Jones*

7398 **Best Music/Scoring Adaptation or Treatment:** Andre Previn for *Irma la Douce*

7399 **Best Music/Best Song:** James Van Heusen, music and Sammy Kahn, lyrics for "Call Me Irresponsible" from *Papa's Delicate Condition*

7400 **Best Sound Recording:** Metro-Goldwyn-Mayer Studio Sound Department (Franklin E. Milton, Sound Director) for *How the West Was Won*

7401 **Best Sound Effects:** Walter G. Elliott for *It's a Mad, Mad, Mad, Mad World*

7402 **Best Special Effects:** Emil Kosa, Jr. for *Cleopatra*

7403 **Best Film Editing:** Harold F. Kress for *How the West Was Won*

7404 **Best Foreign Language Film:** *Federico Fellini's 8½*—Italy

7405 **Best Documentary/Feature:** *Robert Frost: A Lover's Quarrel with the World*

7406 **Best Documentary/Short Subject:** *Chagall*

7407 **Best Short Subject/Cartoon:** *The Critic*

7408 **Best Short Subject/Live Action:** *An Occurrence at Owl Creek Bridge*

7409 **Scientific or Technical/Class III (Certificate of Honorable Mention):** To

Douglas G. Shearer and A. Arnold Gillespie of Metro-Goldwyn-Mayer Studios for the engineering of an improved Background Process Projection System.

7410 Irving G. Thalberg Memorial Award: Sam Spiegel

———————— **1 9 6 4** ————————

7411 Best Picture: *My Fair Lady*

7412 Best Actor: Rex Harrison in *My Fair Lady*

7413 Best Actress: Julie Andrews in *Mary Poppins*

7414 Best Director: George Cukor for *My Fair Lady*

7415 Best Supporting Actor: Peter Ustinov in *Topkapi*

7416 Best Supporting Actress: Lila Kedrova in *Zorba the Greek*

7417 Best Art Direction/Color: Gene Allen and Cecil Beaton, Set Decoration by George James Hopkins for *My Fair Lady*

7418 Best Art Direction/Black & White: Vassilis Fotopoulos for *Zorba the Greek*

7419 Best Cinematography/Color: Harry Stradling for *My Fair Lady*

7420 Best Cinematography/Black & White: Walter Lassally for *Zorba the Greek*

7421 Best Writing—Story and Screenplay Written Directly for the Screen: S. H. Barnett (Story) and Peter Stone and Frank Tarloff (screenplay) for *Father Goose*

7422 Best Writing—Screenplay Based on Material from Another Medium: Edward Anhalt for *Becket*

7423 Best Costume Design/Black & White: Dorothy Jeakins for *The Night of the Iguana*

7424 Best Costume Design/Color: Cecil Beaton for *My Fair Lady*

7425 Best Music/Score Substantially Original: Richard M. Sherman and Robert B. Sherman for *Mary Poppins*

7426 Best Music/Adaptation or Treatment: Andre Previn for *My Fair Lady*

7427 Best Music/Song: Richard M. Sherman and Robert B. Sherman, music and lyrics for "Chim Chim Cheree" from *Mary Poppins*

7428 Best Sound Recording: Warner Brothers Studio Sound Department (George R. Groves, Sound Director) for *My Fair Lady*

7429 Best Special Visual Effects: Peter Ellenshaw, Hamilton Luske and Eustace Lycett for *Mary Poppins*

7430 Best Film Editing: Cotton Warburton for *Mary Poppins*

7431 Best Foreign Language Film: *Yesterday, Today and Tomorrow*—Italy

7432 Best Documentary/Feature: *Jacques Yves-Cousteau's World Without Sun*

7433 Best Documentary/Short Subject: *Nine from Little Rock*

7434 Best Short Subject/Cartoon: *The Pink Phink*

7435 Best Short Subject/Live Action: *Casals Conducts: 1954*

7436 Best Sound Effects: Norman Wanstall for *Goldfinger*

7437 Scientific or Technical/Class I (Academy Statuette): To Petro Vlahos, Wadsworth E. Pohl and Ub Iwerks for the conception and perfection of techniques for Color Travelling Matte Composite Cinematography.

7438 Scientific or Technical/Class II (Academy Plaque): To Sidney P. Solow, Edward H. Reichard, Carl W. Hauge and Job Sanderson of Consolidated Film Laboratories for the design and development of a versatile Automatic 35mm Composite Color Printer. To Pierre Angenieux for the development of a ten-to-one zoom lens for cinematography.

7439 Scientific or Technical/Class III (Certificate of Honorable Mention): To Milton Forman, Richard B. Glickman and Daniel J. Pearlman of ColorTran Industries for advancements in the design and application to motion picture photography of lighting units using quartz iodine lamps. To Stewart Filmscreen Corporation for a seamless translucent Blue Screen for Travelling Matte Color Cinematography. To Anthony Paglia and 20th Century–Fox Studio Mechanical Effects Department for an improved method of producing Explosion Flash Effects for motion pictures. To Edward H. Reichard and Carl W. Hauge of Consolidated Film Industries for the design of a Proximity Cue Detector and its application to motion picture printers. To Edward H. Reichard, Leonard L. Sokolow and Carl W. Hauge of Consolidated Film Laboratories for the design and application to motion picture laboratory practice of a Stroboscopic Scene Tester for color and black-and-white film. To Nelson Tyler for the design and construction of an improved Helicopter Camera System.

7440 Honorary Awards: To William Tuttle for his outstanding make-up achievement in *7 Faces of Dr. Lao*

———————— 1965 ————————

7441 Best Picture: *The Sound of Music*

7442 Best Actor: Lee Marvin in *Cat Ballou*

7443 Best Actress: Julie Christie in *Darling*

7444 Best Director: Robert Wise for *The Sound of Music*

7445 Best Supporting Actor: Martin Balsam in *A Thousand Clowns*

7446 Best Supporting Actress: Shelley Winters in *A Patch of Blue*

7447 Best Art Direction/Color: John Box and Terry Marsh, Set Decoration by Dario Simoni for *Dr. Zhivago*

7448 Best Art Direction/Black & White: Robert Clatworthy, Set Decoration by Joseph Kish for *Ship of Fools*

7449 Best Cinematography/Color: Freddie Young for *Dr. Zhivago*

7450 Best Cinematography/Black & White: Ernest Laszlo for *Ship of Fools*

7451 Best Writing—Story and Screenplay Written Directly for the Screen: Frederick Raphael for *Darling*

7452 Best Writing—Screenplay Based on Material from Another Medium: Robert Bolt for *Dr. Zhivago*

7453 Best Costume Design/Black & White: Julie Harris for *Darling*

7454 Best Costume Design/Color: Phyllis Dalton for *Dr. Zhivago*

7455 Best Music/Score Substantially Original: Maurice Jarre for *Dr. Zhivago*

7456 Best Music/Adaptation or Treatment: Irwin Kostal for *The Sound of Music*

7457 Best Music/Song: Johnny Mandel, music and Paul Francis Webster, lyrics for "The Shadow of Your Smile" from *The Sandpiper*

7458 Best Sound Recording: 20th Century–Fox Studio Sound Department (James P. Corcoran, Sound Director) and Todd-AO Sound Department (Fred Hynes, Sound Director) for *The Sound of Music*

7459 Best Special Visual Effects: John Stears for *Thunderball*

7460 Best Film Editing: William Reynolds for *The Sound of Music*

7461 Best Foreign Language Film: *The Shop on Main Street*—Czechoslovakia

7462 Best Documentary/Feature: *The Eleanor Roosevelt Story*

7463 Best Documentary/Short Subject: *To Be Alive!*

7464 Best Short Subject/Cartoon: *The Dot and the Line*

7465 Best Short Subject/Live Action: *The Chicken*

7466 Best Sound Effects: Tregoweth Brown for *The Great Race*

7467 Scientific or Technical/Class II (Academy Plaque): To Arthur J. Hatch of the Strong Electric Corp., subsidiary of General Precision Equipment Corp., for the design and development of an Air Blown Carbon Arc Projection Lamp. To Stefan Kudelski for the design and development of the Nagra portable ¼" tape recording system for motion picture sound recording.

7468 Jean Hersholt Humanitarian Award: Edmond L. DePatie

7469 Irving G. Thalberg Memorial Award: William Wyler

7470 Honorary Awards: To Bob Hope for unique and distinguished service to our industry and the Academy.

———————— 1966 ————————

7471 Best Picture: *A Man for All Seasons*

7472 Best Actor: Paul Scofield in *A Man for All Seasons*

7473 Best Actress: Elizabeth Taylor in *Who's Afraid of Virginia Woolf?*

7474 Best Director: Fred Zinnemann for *A Man for All Seasons*

7475 Best Supporting Actor: Walter Matthau in *The Fortune Cookie*

7476 **Best Supporting Actress:** Sandy Dennis in *Who's Afraid of Virginia Woolf?*

7477 **Best Art Direction/Color:** Jack Martin Smith and Dale Hennesy, Set Decoration by Walter M. Scott and Stuart A. Reiss for *Fantastic Voyage*

7478 **Best Art Direction/Black & White:** Richard Sylbert, Set Decoration by George James Hopkins for *Who's Afraid of Virginia Woolf?*

7479 **Best Cinematography/Color:** Ted Moore for *A Man for All Seasons*

7480 **Best Cinematography/Black & White:** Haskell Wexler for *Who's Afraid of Virginia Woolf?*

7481 **Best Writing—Story and Screenplay Written Directly for the Screen:** Claude LeLouch (Story) and Pierre Uytterhoeven and Claude LeLouch (Screenplay) for *A Man and a Woman*

7482 **Best Writing—Screenplay Based on Material from Another Medium:** Robert Bolt for *A Man for All Seasons*

7483 **Best Costume Design/Black & White:** Irene Sharaff for *Who's Afraid of Virginia Woolf?*

7484 **Best Costume Design/Color:** Elizabeth Haffenden and Joan Bridge for *A Man for All Seasons*

7485 **Best Music/Original Score:** John Barry for *Born Free*

7486 **Best Music/Adaptation or Treatment:** Ken Thorne for *A Funny Thing Happened on the Way to the Forum*

7487 **Best Music/Song:** John Barry, music and Don Black, lyrics for "Born Free" from *Born Free*

7488 **Best Sound Recording:** Metro-Goldwyn-Mayer Studio Sound Department (Franklin E. Milton, Sound Director) for *Grand Prix*

7489 **Best Special Visual Effects:** Art Cruickshank for *Fantastic Voyage*

7490 **Best Film Editing:** Fredric Steinkamp, Henry Berman, Stewart Linder and Frank Santillo for *Grand Prix*

7491 **Best Foreign Language Film:** *A Man and a Woman*—France

7492 **Best Documentary/Feature:** *The War Game*

7493 **Best Documentary/Short Subject:** *A Year Toward Tomorrow*

7494 **Best Short Subject/Cartoon:** *Herb Alpert and the Tijuana Brass Double Feature*

7495 **Best Short Subject/Live Action:** *Wild Wings*

7496 **Best Sound Effects:** Gordon Daniel for *Grand Prix*

7497 **Scientific or Technical/Class II (Academy Plaque):** To Mitchell Camera Corp. for the design and development of the Mitchell Mark II 35mm Portable Motion Picture Reflex Camera. To Arnold & Richter KG for the design and development of the Arriflex 35mm Portable Reflex Camera.

7498 **Scientific or Technical/Class III (Certificate of Honorable Mention):** To Panavision, Inc., for the design of the Panatran Power Inverter and its application to motion picture camera operation. To Carroll Knudson for the production of a Composer's Manual for Motion Picture Music Synchronization. To Ruby Raskin for the production of Composer's Manual for Motion Picture Synchronization.

7499 **Jean Hersholt Humanitarian Award:** George Bagnall

7500 **Irving G. Thalberg Memorial Award:** Robert Wise

7501 **Honorary Award:** To Y. Frank Freeman for unusual and outstanding service to the Academy during his thirty years in Hollywood. To Yakima Canutt for achievements as a stunt man and for developing safety devices to protect stunt men everywhere.

——————— **1 9 6 7** ———————

7502 **Best Picture:** *In the Heat of the Night*

7503 **Best Actor:** Rod Steiger in *In the Heat of the Night*

7504 **Best Actress:** Katharine Hepburn in *Guess Who's Coming to Dinner*

7505 **Best Director:** Mike Nichols for *The Graduate*

7506 **Best Supporting Actor:** George Kennedy in *Cool Hand Luke*

7507 **Best Supporting Actress:** Estelle Parsons in *Bonnie and Clyde*

7508 **Best Art Direction:** John Truscott and Edward Carrere, Set Decoration by John W. Brown for *Camelot*

7509 **Best Cinematography:** Burnett Guffey for *Bonnie and Clyde*

7510 **Best Writing — Story and Screenplay Written Directly for the Screen:** William Rose for *Guess Who's Coming to Dinner*

7511 **Best Writing — Screenplay Based on Material from Another Medium:** Stirling Silliphant for *In the Heat of the Night*

7512 **Best Costume Design:** John Truscott for *Camelot*

7513 **Best Music/Original Music Score:** Elmer Bernstein for *Thoroughly Modern Millie*

7514 **Best Music/Adaptation or Treatment:** Alfred Newman and Ken Darby for *Camelot*

7515 **Best Music/Song:** "Talk to the Animals" music and lyrics by Leslie Bricusse from *Doctor Doolittle*

7516 **Best Sound Recording:** Samuel Goldwyn Studio Sound Department for *In the Heat of the Night*

7517 **Best Special Visual Effects:** L. B. Abbott for *Doctor Doolittle*

7518 **Best Film Editing:** Hal Ashby for *In the Heat of the Night*

7519 **Best Foreign Language Film:** *Closely Watched Trains* — Czechoslovakia

7520 **Best Documentary/Feature:** *The Anderson Platoon*

7521 **Best Documentary/Short Subject:** *The Redwoods*

7522 **Best Short Subject/Cartoon:** *The Box*

7523 **Best Short Subject/Live Action:** *A Place to Stand*

7524 **Best Sound Effects:** John Poyner for *The Dirty Dozen*

7525 **Scientific or Technical/Class III (Certificate of Honorable Mention):** To the Electro-Optical Division of the Kollmorgen Corp. for the design and development of a series of Motion Picture Projection Lenses. To Panavision, Inc., for a Variable Speed Motor for Motion Picture Cameras. To Fred R. Wilson of Samuel Goldwyn Studio Sound Department for an Audio Level Clamper. To Walden O. Watson and the Universal City Studio Sound Department for new concepts in the design of a Music Scoring Stage.

7526 **Jean Hersholt Humanitarian Award:** Gregory Peck

7527 **Irving G. Thalberg Memorial Award:** Alfred Hitchcock

7528 **Honorary Award:** To Arthur Freed for distinguished service to the Academy and the production of six top-rated Awards telecasts.

———————— **1 9 6 8** ————————

7529 **Best Picture:** *Oliver!*

7530 **Best Actor:** Cliff Robertson in *Charly*

7531 **Best Actress (tie):** Katharine Hepburn in *The Lion in Winter* and Barbra Streisand in *Funny Girl*

7532 **Best Director:** Sir Carol Reed for *Oliver!*

7533 **Best Supporting Actor:** Jack Albertson in *The Subject Was Roses*

7534 **Best Supporting Actress:** Ruth Gordon in *Rosemary's Baby*

7535 **Best Art Direction:** John Box and Terence Marsh, Set Decoration by Vernon Dixon and Ken Muggleston for *Oliver!*

7536 **Best Cinematography:** Pasqualino De Santis for the Franco Zeffirelli production of *Romeo and Juliet*

7537 **Best Writing — Story and Screenplay Written Directly for the Screen:** Mel Brooks for *The Producers*

7538 **Best Writing — Screenplay Based on Material from Another Medium:** James Goldman for *The Lion in Winter*

7539 **Best Costume Design:** Danilo Donati for the Franco Zeffirelli production of *Romeo and Juliet*

7540 **Best Music/Original Score for a Motion Picture (Not a Musical):** John Barry for *The Lion in Winter*

7541 **Best Music/Score for a Musical (Original or Adaptation):** John Green for *Oliver!*

7542 **Best Music/Song:** Michel Legrand, music and Alan and Marilyn Bergman, lyrics for "The Windmills of Your Mind" from *The Thomas Crown Affair*

7543 **Best Sound Recording:** Shepperton Studio Sound Department for *Oliver!*

7544 **Best Special Visual Effects:** Stanley Kubrick for *2001: A Space Odyssey*

7545 **Best Film Editing:** Frank P. Keller for *Bullitt*

7546 **Best Foreign Language Film:** *War and Peace* — Russia

7547 **Best Documentary/Feature:** *Journey Into Self*

7548 **Best Documentary/Short Subject:** *Why Man Creates*

7549 **Best Short Subject/Cartoon:** *Winnie the Pooh and the Blustery Day*

7550 **Best Short Subject/Live Action:** *Robert Kennedy Remembered*

7551 **Scientific or Technical/Class I (Academy Statuette):** To Philip V. Palmquist of Minnesota Mining and Manufacturing Co., Dr. Herbert Meyer of Motion Picture and Television Research Center and Charles D. Staffell of the Rank Organization for the development of a successful embodiment of the reflex background projection system for composite cinematography. To Eastman Kodak Company for the development and introduction of a color reversal intermediate film for motion pictures.

7552 **Scientific or Technical/Class II (Academy Plaque):** To Donald W. Norwood for the design and development of the Norwood Photographic Exposure Meters. To Eastman Kodak Company and Producers Service Company for the development of a new high-speed step-optical reduction printer. To Edmund M. DiGiulio, Niels G. Peterson and Norman S. Hughes of the Cinema Products Company for the design and application of a conversion which makes available the reflex viewing systems for motion picture cameras. To Optical Coating Laboratory, Inc. for the development of an improved anti-reflection coating for photographic and projection lens systems. To Eastman Kodak Company for the introduction of a new high speed motion picture color negative film. To Panavision, Inc. for the conception, design and introduction of a 65mm hand-held motion picture camera. To Todd-AO and Mitchell Camera Company for the design and engineering of the Todd-AO hand-held motion picture camera.

7553 **Scientific or Technical/Class III (Certificate of Honorable Mention):** To Carl W. Hauge and Edward Reichard of Consolidated Film Laboratories and E. Michael Meahl and Roy J. Ridenour of RAMtronics for engineering an automatic exposure control for printing-machine lamps. To Eastman Kodak Company for

a new direct positive film and Consolidated Film Laboratories for the application of this film to the making of post-production work prints.

7554 **Jean Hersholt Humanitarian Award:** Martha Raye

7555 **Honorary Awards:** To John Chambers for his outstanding make-up achievement for *Planet of the Apes.* To Onna White for her outstanding choreography achievement for *Oliver!*

──────── **1 9 6 9** ────────

7556 **Best Picture:** *Midnight Cowboy*

7557 **Best Actor:** John Wayne in *True Grit*

7558 **Best Actress:** Maggie Smith in *The Prime of Miss Jean Brodie*

7559 **Best Director:** John Schlesinger for *Midnight Cowboy*

7560 **Best Supporting Actor:** Gig Young in *They Shoot Horses, Don't They?*

7561 **Best Supporting Actress:** Goldie Hawn in *Cactus Flower*

7562 **Best Art Direction:** John de Cuir, Jack Martin Smith and Herman Blumenthal, Set Decoration by Walter M. Scott, George Hopkins and Raphael Bretton for *Hello, Dolly!*

7563 **Best Cinematography:** Conrad Hall for *Butch Cassidy and the Sundance Kid*

7564 **Best Writing — Story and Screenplay Based on Material Not Previously Published or Produced:** William Goldman for *Butch Cassidy and the Sundance Kid*

7565 **Best Writing — Screenplay Based on Material from Another Medium:** Waldo Salt for *Midnight Cowboy*

7566 **Best Costume Design:** Margaret Furse for *Anne of the Thousand Days*

7567 **Best Music/Original Score for a Motion Picture (Not a Musical):** Burt Bacharach for *Butch Cassidy and the Sundance Kid*

7568 **Best Music/Score for a Musical (Original or Adaptation):** Lenny Hayton and Lionel Newman for *Hello, Dolly!*

7569 **Best Music/Song:** Burt Bacharach, music and Hal David, lyrics for "Raindrops Keep Fallin' on My Head" from *Butch Cassidy and the Sundance Kid*

7570 **Best Sound Recording:** Jack Solomon and Murray Sivack for *Hello, Dolly!*

7571 **Best Special Visual Effects:** Robie Robertson for *Marooned*

7572 **Best Film Editing:** Francoise Bonnot for *Z*

7573 **Best Foreign Language Film:** *Z* — Algeria

7574 **Best Documentary/Feature:** *Arthur Rubinstein — The Love of Life*

7575 **Best Documentary/Short Subject:** *Czechoslovakia 1968*

7576 **Best Short Subject/Cartoon:** *It's Tough to Be a Bird*

7577 **Best Short Subject/Live Action:** *The Magic Machines*

7578 **Scientific or Technical/Class II (Academy Plaque):** To Hazeltine Corp. for the design and development of the Hazeltine Color Film analyzer. To Fouad Said for the design and introduction of the Cinemobile series of equipment trucks for location motion picture production. To Juan de la Cierva and Dynasciences Corp. for the design and development of the Dynalens optical image motion compensator.

7579 **Scientific or Technical/Class III (Certificate of Honorable Mention):** To Popelka of Magna-Tech Electronics Co., Inc., for the development of an Electronically Controlled Looping System. To Fenton Hamilton of Metro-Goldwyn-Mayer Studios for the concept and engineering of a mobile battery-power unit for location lighting. To Panavision, Inc., for the design and development of Panaspeed Motion Picture Camera Motor. To Robert M. Flynn and Russell Hessy of Universal City Studios for a machine gun modification for motion picture photography.

7580 **Jean Hersholt Humanitarian Award:** George Jessel

7581 **Honorary Award:** To Cary Grant for his unique mastery of the art of screen acting with the respect and affection of his colleagues.

——————— **1 9 7 0** ———————

7582 **Best Picture:** *Patton*

7583 **Best Actor:** George C. Scott in *Patton*

7584 **Best Actress:** Glenda Jackson in *Women in Love*

7585 **Best Director:** Franklin J. Schaffner for *Patton*

7586 **Best Supporting Actor:** John Mills in *Ryan's Daughter*

7587 **Best Supporting Actress:** Helen Hayes in *Airport*

7588 **Best Art Direction:** Urie McCleary and Gil Parrondo, Set Decoration by Antonio Mateos for *Patton*

7589 **Best Cinematography:** Freddie Young for *Ryan's Daughter*

7590 **Best Writing — Story and Screenplay Based on Factual Material or Material Not Previously Published or Produced:** Francis Ford Coppola and Edmund H. North for *Patton*

7591 **Best Writing — Screenplay Based on Material from Another Medium:** Ring Lardner, Jr. for *M*A*S*H*

7592 **Best Costume Design:** Nino Novarese for *Cromwell*

7593 **Best Music/Original Score:** Francis Lai for *Love Story*

7594 **Best Music/Original Song Score:** The Beatles for *Let It Be*

7595 **Best Music/Song:** Fred Karlin, music and Robb Royer and James Griffin (a.k.a. Robb Wilson and Arthur James) for "For All We Know" from *Lovers and Other Strangers*

7596 **Best Sound:** Douglas Williams and Don Bassman, 20th Century–Fox for *Patton*

7597 **Best Special Visual Effects:** A. D. Flowers and L. B. Abbott for *Tora! Tora! Tora!*

7598 **Best Film Editing:** Hugh S. Fowler for *Patton*

7599 **Best Foreign Language Film:** *Investigation of a Citizen Above Suspicion* — Italy

7600 **Best Documentary/Feature:** *Woodstock*

7601 **Best Documentary/Short Subject:** *Interviews with My Lai Veterans*

7602 **Best Short Subject/Cartoon:** *Is It Always Right to Be Right?*

7603 **Best Short Subject/Live Action:** *The Resurrection of Broncho Billy*

7604 **Scientific or Technical/Class II (Academy Plaque):** To Leonard Sokolow and Edward H. Reichard of Consolidated Film Laboratories for the concept and engineering of the Color Proofing Printer for motion pictures.

7605 Scientific or Technical/Class III (Academy Citation): To Sylvania Electric Products, Inc., for the development and introduction of a series of compact tungsten halogen lamps for motion picture production. To B. J. Losmandy for the concept, design and application of micro-miniature solid state amplifier modules used in motion picture recording equipment. To Eastman Kodak Co. and Photo Electronics Corp. for the design and engineering of an improved video color analyzer for motion picture laboratories. To Electro-Sound Inc. for the design and introduction of the Series 8000 Sound System for motion picture theaters.

7606 Jean Hersholt Humanitarian Award: Frank Sinatra

7607 Irving G. Thalberg Memorial Award: Ingmar Bergman

7608 Honorary Award: To Lillian Gish for superlative artistry and for distinguished contribution to the progress of motion pictures. To Orson Welles for superlative artistry and versatility in the creation of motion pictures.

———————— **1971** ————————

7609 Best Picture: *The French Connection*

7610 Best Actor: Gene Hackman in *The French Connection*

7611 Best Actress: Jane Fonda in *Klute*

7612 Best Director: William Friedkin for *The French Connection*

7613 Best Supporting Actor: Ben Johnson in *The Last Picture Show*

7614 Best Supporting Actress: Cloris Leachman in *The Last Picture Show*

7615 Best Art Direction: John Box, Ernest Archer, Jack Maxsted and Gil Parrondo, Set Decoration by Vernon Dixon for *Nicholas and Alexandra*

7616 Best Cinematography: Oswald Morris for *Fiddler on the Roof*

7617 Best Writing—Story and Screenplay Based on Factual Material or Material Not Previously Published or Produced: Paddy Chayefsky for *The Hospital*

7618 Best Writing—Screenplay Based on Material from Another Medium: Ernest Tidyman for *The French Connection*

7619 Best Costume Design: Yvonne Blake and Antonio Castillo for *Nicholas and Alexandra*

7620 Best Music/Original Dramatic Score: Michel Legrand for *Summer of '42*

7621 Best Music/Score for a Musical (Original or Adaptation): John Williams for *Fiddler on the Roof*

7622 Best Music/Best Song: "Theme from *Shaft*" by Isaac Hayes from *Shaft*

7623 Sound Recording: Gordon K. McCallum and David Hildyard for *Fiddler on the Roof*

7624 Best Special Visual Effects: Alan Maley, Eustace Lycett and Danny Lee for *Bedknobs and Broomsticks*

7625 Best Film Editing: Jerry Greenberg for *The French Connection*

7626 Best Foreign Language Film: *The Garden of the Finzi-Continis*—Italy

7627 Best Documentary/Feature: *The Hellstrom Chronicle*

7628 Best Documentary/Short Subject: *Sentinels of Silence*

7629 Best Short Subject/Cartoon: *The Crunch Bird*

7630 Best Short Subject/Live Action: *Sentinels of Silence*

7631 Scientific or Technical/Class II (Academy Plaque): To John N. Wilkinson and Optical Radiation Corp. for the development and engineering of a system of xenon lamphouses for motion picture projection.

7632 Scientific or Technical/Class III (Academy Citation): To Thomas Jefferson Hutchinson, James R. Rochester and Fenton Hamilton for the development and introduction of the Sunbrite system of xenon arc lamps for location lighting in motion picture production. To the Photo Research Division of the Kollmorgen Corp. for the development and introduction of the film/lens balanced Three-Color Meter. To Robert D. Auguste and Cinema Products Co. for the development and introduction of a new crystal controlled lightweight motor for the 35mm Arriflex cameras. To Producers Service Corp. and Consolidated Film Laboratories, and Cinema Research

Corp. and Research Products, Inc. for the engineering and implementation of fully automated blow-up motion picture printing systems. To Cinema Products Co. for a control motor to actuate zoom lenses on motion picture cameras.

7633 Honorary Award: To Charles Chaplin for the incalculable effect he has had in making motion pictures the art form of this century.

————— **1972** —————

7634 Best Picture: *The Godfather*
7635 Best Actor: Marlon Brando in *The Godfather*
7636 Best Actress: Liza Minnelli in *Cabaret*
7637 Best Director: Bob Fosse for *Cabaret*
7638 Best Supporting Actor: Joel Grey in *Cabaret*
7639 Best Supporting Actress: Eileen Heckart in *Butterflies Are Free*
7640 Best Art Direction: Rolf Zehetbauer and Jurgen Kiebach, Set Decoration by Herbert Strabel for *Cabaret*
7641 Best Cinematography: Geoffrey Unsworth for *Cabaret*
7642 Best Writing — Story and Screenplay Based on Factual Material Not Previously Published or Produced: Jeremy Larner for *The Candidate*
7643 Best Writing — Screenplay Based on Material from Another Medium: Mario Puzo and Francis Ford Coppola for *The Godfather*
7644 Best Costume Design: Anthony Powell for *Travels with My Aunt*
7645 Best Music/Original Dramatic Score: Charles Chaplin, Raymond Rasch and Larry Russell for *Limelight*
7646 Best Music/Score for a Musical (Original or Adaptation): Ralph Burns for *Cabaret*
7647 Best Music/Song Original for the Picture: Al Kasha and Joel Hirschhorn, music and lyrics for "The Morning After" from *The Poseidon Adventure*
7648 Best Sound: Robert Knudson and David Hildyard for *Cabaret*
7649 Best Film Editing: David Bretherton for *Cabaret*
7650 Best Foreign Language Film: *The Discreet Charm of the Bourgeoisie* — France
7651 Best Documentary/Feature: *Marjoe*
7652 Best Documentary/Short Subject: *This Tiny World*
7653 Best Short Subject/Cartoon: *A Christmas Carol*
7654 Best Short Subject/Live Action: *Norman Rockwell's World . . . An American Dream*
7655 Scientific or Technical/Class II (Academy Plaque): To Joseph E. Bluth for research and development in the field of electronic photography and transfer of videotape to motion picture film. To Edward H. Reichard and Howard T. La-Zare of Consolidated Film Laboratories and Edward Efron of IBM for the engineering of a computerized light valve monitoring system for motion picture printing. To Panavision, Inc. for the development and engineering of the Panaflex motion picture camera.
7656 Scientific or Technical/Class III (Academy Citation): To the Photo Research Division of the Kollmorgen Corporation and the Acme Products Division of PSC Technology, Inc. for the Spectra Gate Photometer for motion picture printers. To Carter Equipment Co., Inc. and RAMtronics for the RAMtronics light-valve photometer for motion picture printers. To David Degenkolb, Harry Larson, Manfred Michelson and Fred Scobey of DeLuxe General, Inc., for the development of a computerized motion picture printer and process control system. To Jiro Mukai and Ryusho Hirose of Canon, Inc. and Wilton R. Holm of AMPTP Motion Picture and Television Research Center for development of the Canon Macro Zoom Lens for motion picture photography. To Philip V. Palmquist and Leonard L. Olson of the 3M Company and Frank P. Clark of AMPTP Motion Picture and Television Research Center for the development of the Nextel simulated blood for motion picture color photography. To E. H. Geissler and G. M. Berggren of Wil-Kin, Inc., for engineering of the Ultra-Vision Motion Picture Theater Projection System.
7657 Special Achievement Award for

Visual Effects: L. B. Abbott and A. D. Flowers for *The Poseidon Adventure*

7658 **Jean Hersholt Humanitarian Award:** Rosalind Russell

7659 **Honorary Award:** To Charles S. Boren, leader for 38 years of the industry's enlightened labor relations and architect of its policy of non-discrimination, with respect and affection of all who work in films. To Edward G. Robinson who achieved greatness as a player, patron of the arts and a dedicated citizen . . . in sum a Renaissance man from his friends in the industry he loves.

—————— **1973** ——————

7660 **Best Picture:** *The Sting*

7661 **Best Actor:** Jack Lemmon in *Save the Tiger*

7662 **Best Actress:** Glenda Jackson in *A Touch of Class*

7663 **Best Director:** George Roy Hill for *The Sting*

7664 **Best Supporting Actor:** John Houseman in *The Paper Chase*

7665 **Best Supporting Actress:** Tatum O'Neal in *Paper Moon*

7666 **Best Art Direction:** Henry Bumstead, Set Decoration by James Payne for *The Sting*

7667 **Best Cinematography:** Sven Nykvist for *Cries and Whispers*

7668 **Best Writing—Story and Screenplay Based on Factual Material or Material Not Previously Published or Produced:** David S. Ward for *The Sting*

7669 **Best Writing—Screenplay Based on Material from Another Medium:** William Peter Blatty for *The Exorcist*

7670 **Best Costume Design:** Edith Head for *The Sting*

7671 **Best Music/Original Dramatic-Score:** Marvin Hamlisch for *The Way We Were*

7672 **Best Music/Scoring—Original Song Score and Adaptation or Scoring—Adaptation:** Marvin Hamlisch for *The Sting*

7673 **Best Music/Song:** Marvin Hamlisch, music and Alan and Marilyn Bergman, lyrics for "The Way We Were" from *The Way We Were*

7674 **Best Sound:** Robert Knudson and Chris Newman for *The Exorcist*

7675 **Best Film Editing:** William Reynolds for *The Sting*

7676 **Best Foreign Language Film:** *Day for Night*—France

7677 **Best Documentary/Feature:** *The Great American Cowboy*

7678 **Best Documentary/Short Subject:** *Princeton: A Search for Answers*

7679 **Best Short Subject/Cartoon:** *Frank Film*

7680 **Best Short Subject/Live Action:** *The Bolero*

7681 **Scientific or Technical/Class II (Academy Plaque):** To Joachim Gerb and Erich Kastner of Arnold & Richter Company for the development and engineering of the Arriflex 35BL motion picture camera. To Magna-Tech Electronics Co., Inc., for the engineering and development of a high-speed re-recording system for motion picture production. To William W. Valliant of PSC Technology Inc., Howard F. Ott of Eastman Kodak Company and Gerry Diebold of the Richmark Camera Service Inc. for the development of a liquid-gate system for motion picture printers. To Harold A. Scheib, Clifford H. Ellis and Roger W. Banks of Research Products Incorporated for the concept and engineering of the Model 2101 optical printer for motion picture optical effects.

7682 **Scientific or Technical/Class III (Academy Citation):** To Roscoe Laboratories, Inc., for the technical advances and the development of a complete system of light-control materials for motion picture photography. To Richard H. Vetter of Todd-AO Corporation for the design of an improved anamorphic focusing system for motion picture photography.

7683 **Jean Hersholt Humanitarian Award:** Lew Wasserman

7684 **Irving G. Thalberg Memorial Award:** Lawrence Weingarten

7685 **Honorary Award:** To Henri Langlois for his devotion to the art of film, his massive contributions to preserving its past and his unswerving faith in its future. To Groucho Marx in recognition of his brilliant creativity and for the unequalled achievements of the Marx Brothers in the art of motion picture comedy.

───────── **1 9 7 4** ─────────

7686 **Best Picture:** *The Godfather Part II*
7687 **Best Actor:** Art Carney in *Harry and Tonto*
7688 **Best Actress:** Ellen Burstyn in *Alice Doesn't Live Here Anymore*
7689 **Best Director:** Francis Ford Coppola for *The Godfather Part II*
7690 **Best Supporting Actor:** Robert De Niro in *The Godfather Part II*
7691 **Best Supporting Actress:** Ingrid Bergman in *Murder on the Orient Express*
7692 **Best Art Direction:** Dean Tavoularis and Angelo Graham, Set Decoration by George R. Nelson for *The Godfather Part II*
7693 **Best Cinematography:** Fred Koenekamp and Joseph Biroc for *The Towering Inferno*
7694 **Best Writing — Original Screenplay:** Robert Towne for *Chinatown*
7695 **Best Writing — Screenplay Adapted from Other Material:** Francis Ford Coppola and Mario Puzo for *The Godfather Part II*
7696 **Best Costume Design:** Theoni V. Aldredge for *The Great Gatsby*
7697 **Best Music/Original Dramatic Score:** Nino Rota and Carmine Coppola for *The Godfather Part II*
7698 **Best Music/Original Song Score and Adaptation or Scoring — Adaptation:** Nelson Riddle for *The Great Gatsby*
7699 **Best Music/Song:** Al Kash and Joel Hirschhorn, music and lyrics for "We May Never Love Like This Again" from *The Towering Inferno*
7700 **Best Visual Effects:** Frank Brendel, Glen Robinson and Albert Whitlock for *Earthquake*
7701 **Best Sound:** Ronald Pierce and Melvin Metcalfe, Sr., for *Earthquake*
7702 **Best Film Editing:** Harold F. Kress and Carl Kress for *The Towering Inferno*
7703 **Best Foreign Language Film:** *Amarcord* — Italy
7704 **Best Documentary/Feature:** *Hearts and Minds*
7705 **Best Documentary/Short Subject:** *Don't*
7706 **Best Short Subject/Cartoon:** *Closed Mondays*

7707 **Best Short Subject/Live Action:** *One-Eyed Men Are Kings*
7708 **Scientific or Technical/Class II (Academy Plaque):** To Joseph D. Kelly of Glen Glenn Sound for the design of new audio control consoles which have advanced the state of the art of sound recording and re-recording for motion picture production. To the Burbank Studios Sound Department for the design of new audio control consoles engineered and constructed by Quad-Eight Sound Corporation. To Samuel Goldwyn Studio Sound Department for the design of new audio control consoles engineered and constructed by the Quad-Eight Sound Corporation. To Quad-Eight Sound Corporation for the engineering and construction of new audio control consoles designed by the Burbank Studios Sound Department and by the Samuel Goldwyn Studio Sound Department. To Walden O. Watson, Richard J. Stumpf, Robert J. Leonard and the Universal City Studios Sound Department for the development and engineering of the Sensurround System for motion picture presentation.
7709 **Scientific or Technical/Class III (Academy Citation):** To Elemack Company for the design and development of their Spyder camera dolly. To Louise Ami of Universal City Studios for the design and construction of a reciprocating camera platform used when photographing special visual effects for motion pictures.
7710 **Jean Hersholt Humanitarian Award:** Arthur B. Krim
7711 **Honorary Award:** To Howard Hawks, a Master American filmmaker, whose creative efforts hold a distinguished place in world cinema. Jean Renoir, a genius who, with grace, responsibility and enviable devotion through silent film, sound film, documentary, feature and television has won the world's admiration.

───────── **1 9 7 5** ─────────

7712 **Best Picture:** *One Flew Over the Cuckoo's Nest*
7713 **Best Actor:** Jack Nicholson in *One Flew Over the Cuckoo's Nest*

7714 **Best Actress:** Louise Fletcher in *One Flew Over the Cuckoo's Nest*

7715 **Best Director:** Milos Forman for *One Flew Over the Cuckoo's Nest*

7716 **Best Supporting Actor:** George Burns in *The Sunshine Boys*

7717 **Best Supporting Actress:** Lee Grant in *Shampoo*

7718 **Best Art Direction:** Ken Adam and Roy Walker, Set Decoration by Vernon Dixon for *Barry Lyndon*

7719 **Best Cinematography:** John Alcott for *Barry Lyndon*

7720 **Best Writing—Original Screenplay:** Frank Pierson for *Dog Day Afternoon*

7721 **Best Writing—Screenplay Adapted from Other Material:** Lawrence Hauben and Bo Goldman for *One Flew Over the Cuckoo's Nest*

7722 **Best Costume Design:** Ulla-Britt Soderlund and Milena Canonero for *Barry Lyndon*

7723 **Best Music/Original Score:** John Williams for *Jaws*

7724 **Best Music/Original Song Score and Adaptation or Scoring—Adaptation:** Leonard Rosenman for *Barry Lyndon*

7725 **Best Music/Song:** Keith Carradine for "I'm Easy" from *Nashville*

7726 **Best Special Effects:** Peter Berkos (Audio), Albert Whitlock and Glen Robinson for *The Hindenburg*

7727 **Best Sound:** Robert L. Hoyt, Roger Heman, Earl Madery and John Carter for *Jaws*

7728 **Best Film Editing:** Verna Fields for *Jaws*

7729 **Best Foreign Language Film:** *Dersu Uzala*—U.S.S.R.

7730 **Best Documentary/Feature:** *The Man Who Skied Down Everest*

7731 **Best Documentary/Short Subject:** *The End of the Game*

7732 **Best Short Subject/Cartoon:** *Great*

7733 **Best Short Subject/Live Action:** *Angel and Big Joe*

7734 **Scientific or Technical/Class II (Academy Plaque):** To Chadwell O'Connor of O'Connor Engineering Laboratories for the concept and engineering of a fluid-damped camera-head for motion picture photography. To William F. Miner of Universal City Studios, Inc., and Westinghouse Electric Corporation for the development and engineering of a solid-state 500-kilowatt, direct-current static rectifier for motion picture lighting.

7735 **Scientific or Technical/Class III (Academy Citation):** To Lawrence W. Butler and Roger Banks for the concept of applying low inertia and stepping electric motors to film transport systems and optical printers for motion picture production. To David J. Degenkolb and Fred Scobey of DeLuxe General Incorporated and John C. Dolan and Richard DuBois of the Akwaklame Company for the development of a technique for silver recovery from photographic wash waters by ion exchange. To Joseph Westheimer for the development of a device to obtain shadowed titles on motion-picture film. To the Carter Equipment Co., Inc. and RAMtronics for the engineering and manufacture of a computerized tape punching system for programming laboratory printing machines. To Hollywood Film Company for the engineering and manufacture of a computerized tape punching system for programming laboratory printing machines. To Bell & Howell for the engineering and manufacture of a computerized tape punching system for programming laboratory printing machines. To Fredrik Schlyter for the design and manufacture of a computerized tape punching system for programming laboratory printing machines.

7736 **Jean Hersholt Humanitarian Award:** Dr. Jules Stein

7737 **Irving G. Thalberg Memorial Award:** Mervyn LeRoy

7738 **Honorary Award:** To Mary Pickford in recognition of her unique contributions to the film industry and the development of film as an artistic medium

———————— **1 9 7 6** ————————

7739 **Best Picture:** *Rocky*

7740 **Best Actor:** Peter Finch in *Network*

7741 **Best Actress:** Faye Dunaway in *Network*

7742 **Best Director:** John G. Avildsen for *Rocky*

7743 **Best Supporting Actor:** Jason Robards in *All the President's Men*

7744 **Best Supporting Actress:** Beatrice Straight in *Network*
7745 **Best Art Direction:** George Jenkins, Set Decoration by George Gaines for *All the President's Men*
7746 **Best Cinematography:** Haskell Wexler for *Bound for Glory*
7747 **Best Writing—Screenplay Written Directly for the Screen—Based on Factual Material or Story Material Not Previously Published or Produced:** Paddy Chayefsky for *Network*
7748 **Best Writing—Screenplay Based on Material from Another Medium:** William Goldman for *All the President's Men*
7749 **Best Costume Design:** Danilo Donati for *Fellini's Casanova*
7750 **Best Music/Original Score:** Jerry Goldsmith for *The Omen*
7751 **Best Music/Original Song Score and Its Adaptation or Adaptation Score:** Leonard Rosenman for *Bound for Glory*
7752 **Best Music/Song:** Barbra Streisand, music and Paul Williams, lyrics for "Evergreen" from *A Star Is Born*
7753 **Best Visual Effects:** Carlo Rambaldi, Glen Robinson and Frank Van Der Veer for *King Kong* and L. B. Abbott, Glen Robinson and Matthew Yuricich for *Logan's Run*
7754 **Best Sound:** Arthur Piantadosi, Les Fresholtz, Dick Alexander and Jim Webb for *All the President's Men*
7755 **Best Film Editing:** Richard Halsey and Scott Conrad for *Rocky*
7756 **Best Foreign Language Film:** *Black and White in Color*—Ivory Coast
7757 **Best Documentary/Feature:** *Harlan County, U.S.A.*
7758 **Best Documentary/Short Subject:** *Number Our Days*
7759 **Best Short Subject/Cartoon:** *Leisure*
7760 **Best Short Subject/Live Action:** *In the Region of Ice*
7761 **Scientific or Technical/Class II (Academy Plaque):** To Consolidated Film Laboratories and the Barneby-Cheney Co. for the development of a system for the recovery of film-cleaning solvent vapors in a motion picture laboratory. To William L. Graham, Manfred G. Michelson, Geoffrey F. Norman and Siegfried Seibert of Technicolor Motion Picture

Corp. for the development and engineering of a continuous, high-speed, color motion picture printing system.
7762 **Scientific or Technical/Class III (Academy Citation):** To Fred Bartscher of Kollmorgen Corp. and Glen Berggren of Schneider Corp. for the design and development of a single lens magnifier for motion picture projection lenses. To Panavision Incorporated for the design and development of super-speed lenses for motion picture photography. To Hiroshi Suzukawa of Canon and Wilton R. Holm of AMPTP Motion Picture and Television Research Center for the design and development of super-speed lenses for motion picture photography. To the Carl Zeiss Co. for the design and development of super-speed lenses for motion picture photography. To the Photo Research Division of the Kollmorgen Corp. for the engineering and manufacture of the Spectra TriColor Meter.
7763 **Irving G. Thalberg Memorial Award:** Pandro S. Berman

——————— **1 9 7 7** ———————

7764 **Best Picture:** *Annie Hall*
7765 **Best Actor:** Richard Dreyfuss in *The Goodbye Girl*
7766 **Best Actress:** Diane Keaton in *Annie Hall*
7767 **Best Director:** Woody Allen for *Annie Hall*
7768 **Best Supporting Actor:** Jason Robards in *Julia*
7769 **Best Supporting Actress:** Vanessa Redgrave in *Julia*
7770 **Best Art Direction:** John Barry, Norman Reynolds and Leslie Dilley, Set Decoration by Roger Christian for *Star Wars*
7771 **Best Cinematography:** Vilmos Zsigmond for *Close Encounters of the Third Kind*
7772 **Best Writing—Screenplay Written Directly for the Screen—Based on Factual Material or Story Material Not Previously Published or Produced:** Woody Allen and Marshall Brickman for *Annie Hall*
7773 **Best Writing—Screenplay Based on Material from Another Medium:** Alvin Sargent for *Julia*

7774 **Best Costume Design:** John Mollo for *Star Wars*

7775 **Best Music/Original Score:** John Williams for *Star Wars*

7776 **Best Music/Original Song Score and Its Adaptation or Adaptation Score:** Jonathan Tunick for *A Little Night Music*

7777 **Best Music/Original Song:** Joseph Brooks, music and lyrics for "You Light Up My Life" from *You Light Up My Life*

7778 **Best Sound Effects Editing:** Frank Warner for *Close Encounters of the Third Kind*

7779 **Best Sound:** Don MacDougall, Ray West, Bob Minkler and Derek Ball for *Star Wars*

7780 **Best Special Visual Effects:** John Stears, John Dykstra, Richard Edlund, Grant McCune and Robert Blalack for *Star Wars*

7781 **Best Film Editing:** Paul Hirsch, Marcia Lucas and Richard Chew for *Star Wars*

7782 **Best Foreign Language Film:** *Madame Rosa*—France

7783 **Best Documentary/Feature:** *Who Are the DeBolts? And Where Did They Get Nineteen Kids?*

7784 **Best Documentary/Short Subject:** *Gravity Is My Enemy*

7785 **Best Short Subject/Cartoon:** *Sand Castle*

7786 **Best Short Subject/Live Action:** *I'll Find a Way*

7787 **Scientific or Technical/Class I (Academy Statuette):** To Garrett Brown and the Cinema Products Co. engineering staff under the supervision of John Jurgens for the invention and development of Steadicam.

7788 **Scientific or Technical/Class II (Academy Plaque):** To Joseph D. Kelly, Emory M. Cohen, Barry K. Henley, Hammond H. Holt and John Agalsoff of Glen Glenn Sound for the concept and development of a post-production audio processing system for motion picture films. To Panavision, Inc. for the concept and engineering of the improvements incorporated in the Panaflex motion picture camera. To N. Paul Kenworthy, Jr. and William R. Latady for the invention and development of the Kenworth Snorkle Camera System for motion picture photography. To John C. Dykstra for the development of a facility uniquely oriented toward visual effects photography. To Alvah J. Miller and Jerry Jeffress for the engineering of the electronic motion control system used in concert for multiple exposure visual effects motion picture photography. To Eastman Kodak Company for the development and introduction of a new duplicating film for motion pictures. To Stefan Kudelski of Nagra Magnetic Recorders, Incorporated, for the engineering of the improvements incorporated in the Nagra 4.2L sound recorder for motion picture production.

7789 **Scientific or Technical/Class III (Academy Citation):** To Ernst F. Nettmann of the Astrovision Division of Continental Camera Systems, Inc., for the engineering of its periscope aerial camera system. To EECO (Electronic Engineering Company of California) for developing a method of interlocking non-sprocketed film and tape media used in motion picture production. To Dr. Bernhard Kühl and Werner Block of OSRAM, GmbH, for the development of the HMI high-efficiency discharge lamp for motion picture lighting. To Panavision, Inc., for the design of Panalite, a camera-mounted controllable light for motion picture photography. To Panavision, Inc., for the engineering of the Panahead gearhead for motion picture cameras. To Piclear, Inc., for originating and developing an attachment to motion picture projectors to improve screen image quality.

7790 **Jean Hersholt Humanitarian Award:** Charlton Heston

7791 **Irving G. Thalberg Memorial Award:** Walter Mirisch

7792 **Honorary Award:** To Margaret Booth for her exceptional contribution to the art of film editing in the motion picture industry.

7793 **Medals of Commendation:** Gordon E. Sawyer and Sidney P. Solow in appreciation for outstanding service and dedication to upholding the high standards of the Academy of Motion Picture Arts and Sciences.

─────── **1 9 7 8** ───────

7794 **Best Picture:** *The Deer Hunter*
7795 **Best Actor:** Jon Voight in *Coming Home*
7796 **Best Actress:** Jane Fonda in *Coming Home*
7797 **Best Director:** Michael Cimino for *The Deer Hunter*
7798 **Best Supporting Actor:** Christopher Walken in *The Deer Hunter*
7799 **Best Supporting Actress:** Maggie Smith in *California Suite*
7800 **Best Art Direction:** Paul Sylbert and Edwin O'Donovan; Set Decoration by George Gaines for *Heaven Can Wait*
7801 **Best Cinematography:** Nestor Almendros for *Days of Heaven*
7802 **Best Costume Design:** Anthony Powell for *Death on the Nile*
7803 **Best Feature Documentary:** *Scared Straight!*
7804 **Best Short Subject Documentary:** *The Flight of the Gossamer Condor*
7805 **Best Film Editing:** Peter Zinner for *The Deer Hunter*
7806 **Best Foreign Language Film:** *Get Out Your Handkerchiefs*—France
7807 **Best Music—Adaptation Score:** Joe Renzetti for *The Buddy Holly Story*
7808 **Best Music—Original Score:** Giorgio Moroder for *Midnight Express*
7809 **Best Music—Original Song:** "Last Dance" from *Thank God It's Friday*, music and lyrics by Paul Jabara
7810 **Best Animated Short Film:** *Special Delivery*—National Film Board of Canada
7811 **Best Live Action Short Film:** *Teenage Father*—Children's Home Society of California
7812 **Best Sound:** Richard Portman, William McCaughey, Aaron Rochin and Darin Knight for *The Deer Hunter*
7813 **Best Writing—Screenplay Based on Material from Another Medium:** Oliver Stone for *Midnight Express*
7814 **Best Writing—Screenplay Written Directly for the Screen:** Story—Nancy Dowd; Screenplay—Waldo Salt and Robert C. Jones for *Coming Home*
7815 **Academy Award of Merit (Academy Statuette):** To Eastman Kodak Company for research and development of a Duplicating Color Film for motion

pictures. To Stefan Kudelski of Nagra Magnetic Recorders, Inc., for the continuing research, design and development of the Nagra Production Sound Recorder for motion pictures. To Panavision, Inc., and its engineering staff under the direction of Robert E. Gottschalk for the concept, design and continuous development of the Panaflex Motion Picture Camera System.
7816 **Scientific and Engineering Award (Academy Plaque):** To Ray M. Dolby, Ioan R. Allen, David P. Robinson, Stephen M. Katz and Philip S. J. Boole of Dolby Laboratories, Inc., for the development and implementation of an improved sound recording and reproducing system for motion picture production and exhibition.
7817 **Technical Achievement Award (Academy Certificate):** To Karl Macher and Glenn M. Berggren of Isco Optische Werke for the development and introduction of the Cinelux-ULTRA lens for 35mm motion picture projection. To David J. Degenkolb, Arthur L. Ford and Fred J. Scobey of DeLuxe General, Inc., for the development of a method to recycle motion picture laboratory photographic wash waters by ion exchange. To Kilchi Sekiguchi of CINE-FI International for the development of CINE-FI Auto Radio Sound System for drive-in theaters. To Leonard Chapman of Leonard Equipment Company for the design and manufacture of a small, mobile, motion picture camera platform known as the Chapman Hustler Dolly. To James L. Fisher of J. L. Fisher, Inc., for the design and manufacture of a small, mobile motion picture camera platform known as the Fisher Model Ten Dolly. To Robert Stindt of Production Grip Equipment Company for the design and manufacture of a small, mobile motion picture camera platform known as the Stindt Dolly.
7818 **Special Achievement Award—Visual Effects:** Les Bowie, Colin Chilvers, Denys Coop, Roy Field, Derek Meddings and Zoran Perisic for *Superman*
7819 **Jean Hersholt Humanitarian Award:** Leo Jaffe
7820 **Honorary Awards:** To Walter Lantz for bringing joy and laughter to

every part of the world through his unique animated motion pictures. To Laurence Olivier for the full body of his work, for the unique achievements of his entire career and his lifetime of contribution to the art of film. To King Vidor for his incomparable achievements as a cinematic creator and innovator. To the Museum of Modern Art Department of Film for the contribution it has made to the public's perception of movies as an art form.

7821 **Medals of Commendation:** To Linwood G. Dunn, Loren L. Ryder and Walden O. Watson in appreciation for outstanding service and dedication in upholding the high standards of the Academy of Motion Picture Arts and Sciences.

———— **1 9 7 9** ————

7822 **Best Picture:** *Kramer vs. Kramer*
7823 **Best Actor:** Dustin Hoffman in *Kramer vs. Kramer*
7824 **Best Actress:** Sally Field in *Norma Rae*
7825 **Best Director:** Robert Benton for *Kramer vs. Kramer*
7826 **Best Supporting Actor:** Melvyn Douglas in *Being There*
7827 **Best Supporting Actress:** Meryl Streep in *Kramer vs. Kramer*
7828 **Best Art Direction:** Philip Rosenberg and Tony Walton; Set Decoration by Edward Stewart and Gary Brink for *All That Jazz*
7829 **Best Cinematography:** Vittorio Storaro for *Apocalypse Now*
7830 **Best Costume Design:** Albert Wolsky for *All That Jazz*
7831 **Best Feature Documentary:** *Best Boy*
7832 **Best Short Subject Documentary:** *Paul Robeson: Tribute to an Artist*
7833 **Best Film Editing:** Alan Heim for *All That Jazz*
7834 **Best Foreign Language Film:** *The Tin Drum* — Federal Republic of Germany
7835 **Best Music — Adaptation Score:** Ralph Burns for *All That Jazz*
7836 **Best Music — Original Score:** Georges Delerue for *A Little Romance*

7837 **Best Music — Original Song:** "It Goes Like It Goes" from *Norma Rae*, music by David Shire, lyrics by Norman Gimbel
7838 **Best Animated Short Film:** *Every Child* — National Film Board of Canada
7839 **Best Live Action Short Film:** *Board and Care*
7840 **Best Sound:** Walter Murch, Mark Berger, Richard Beggs and Nat Boxer for *Apocalypse Now*
7841 **Best Visual Effects:** H. R. Giger, Carlo Rambaldi, Brian Johnson, Nick Allder and Denys Ayling for *Alien*
7842 **Best Writing — Screenplay Based on Material from Another Medium:** Robert Benton for *Kramer vs. Kramer*
7843 **Best Writing — Screenplay Written Directly for the Screen:** Story and screenplay by Steve Tesich for *Breaking Away*
7844 **Academy Award of Merit (Academy Statuette):** To Mark Serrurier for the progressive development of the Moviola from the 1924 invention of his father, Iwan Serrurier, to the present Series 20 sophisticated film editing equipment.
7845 **Scientific and Engineering Award (Academy Plaque):** To Neiman-Tillar Associates for the creative development and to Mini-Micro Systems, Inc., for the design and engineering of an Automated Computer-Controlled Editing Sound System (ACCESS) for motion picture post-production.
7846 **Technical Achievement Award (Academy Certificate):** To Michael V. Chewey, Walter G. Eggers and Allen Hecht of Metro-Goldwyn-Mayer Laboratories for the development of a computer-controlled paper tape programmer system and its applications in the motion picture laboratory. To Irwin Young, Paul Kaufman and Fredrik Schlyter of Du Art Film Laboratories, Inc., for the development of a computer-controlled paper tape programmer system and its applications in the motion picture laboratory. To James S. Stanfield and Paul W. Trester for the development and manufacture of a device for the repair or protection of sprocket holes in motion picture film. To Zoran Perisic of Courier Films Limited for the Zoptic

Special Optical Effects Device for motion picture photography. To A.D. Flowers and Logan R. Frazee for the development of a device to control flight patterns of miniature airplanes during motion picture photography. To Photo Research Division of Kollmorgen Corp. for the development of the Spectra Series II Cine Special Exposure Meter for motion picture photography. To Bruce Lyon and John Lamb for the development of a Video Animation system for testing motion picture animation sequences. To Ross Lowell of Lowell-Light Manufacturing, Inc., for the development of compact lighting equipment for motion picture photography.

7847 **Special Achievement Award – Sound Editing:** Alan Splet for *The Black Stallion*

7848 **Jean Hersholt Humanitarian Award:** Robert Benjamin

7849 **Irving G. Thalberg Memorial Award:** Ray Stark

7850 **Honorary Awards:** To Hal Elias for his dedication and distinguished service to the Academy of Motion Picture Arts and Sciences. To Alec Guinness for advancing the art of screen acting through a host of memorable and distinguished performances.

7851 **Medals of Commendation:** To John O. Aalberg, Charles G. Clarke and John G. Frayne in appreciation for outstanding service and dedication in upholding the high standards of the Academy of Motion Picture Arts and Sciences.

––––––––––– **1 9 8 0** –––––––––––

7852 **Best Picture:** *Ordinary People*
7853 **Best Actor:** Robert de Niro in *Raging Bull*
7854 **Best Actress:** Sissy Spacek in *Coal Miner's Daughter*
7855 **Best Director:** Robert Redford for *Ordinary People*
7856 **Best Supporting Actor:** Timothy Hutton in *Ordinary People*
7857 **Best Supporting Actress:** Mary Steenburgen in *Melvin & Howard*
7858 **Best Art Direction:** Pierre Guffroy and Jack Stephens for *Tess*

7859 **Best Cinematography:** Geoffrey Unsworth and Ghislain Cloquet for *Tess*
7860 **Best Costume Design:** Anthony Powell for *Tess*
7861 **Best Feature Documentary:** *From Mao to Mozart: Isaac Stern in China*
7862 **Best Documentary Short Subject:** *Karl Hess: Toward Liberty*
7863 **Best Film Editing:** Thelma Schoonmaker for *Raging Bull*
7864 **Best Foreign Language Film:** *Moscow Does Not Believe in Tears*
7865 **Best Music – Original Score:** Michael Gore for *Fame*
7866 **Best Music – Original Song:** "Fame" from *Fame*, music by Michael Gore, lyrics by Dean Pitchford
7867 **Best Animated Short Film:** *The Fly* – Budapest
7868 **Best Dramatic Live Action Short Film:** *The Dollar Bottom*
7869 **Best Sound:** Bill Varney, Steve Maslow, Gregg Landaker and Peter Sutton for *The Empire Strikes Back*
7870 **Best Writing – Screenplay Based on Material from Another Medium:** Alvin Sargent for *Ordinary People*
7871 **Best Writing – Screenplay Written Directly for the Screen:** Bo Goldman for *Melvin and Howard*
7872 **Academy Award of Merit (Academy Statuette):** To Linwood G. Dunn, Cecil D. Love and Acme Tool and Manufacturing Co. for the concept, engineering and development of the Acme-Dunn Optical Printer for motion picture special effects.
7873 **Scientific and Engineering Award (Academy Plaque):** To Jean Marie Lavalou, Alain Masseron and David Samuelson of Samuelson Alga Cinema S.A. and Samuelson Film Service Limited for engineering and development of the Louma Camera Crane and remote control system for motion picture production. To Edward B. Krause of Filmline Corp. for the engineering and manufacture of the micro demand drive for continuous motion picture film processors. To Ross Taylor for the concept and development of a system of air guns for propelling objects used in special objects used in motion picture production. To Dr. Bernhard Kühl and Dr. Werner Block

of OSRAM GmbH for the progressive engineering and manufacture of the Osram HMI light source for motion picture color photography. To David A. Grafton for the optical design and engineering of a telecentric anamorphic lens for optical effects printers.

7874 Technical Achievement Award (Academy Certificate): To the Carter Equipment Co. for the development of a continuous contact, total immersion, additive color, motion picture printer. To Hollywood Film Co. for the development of a continuous contact, total immersion, additive color, motion picture printer. To Charles Vaughn and Eugene Nottingham of Cinetron Computer Systems, Inc., for the development of a versatile general purpose computer system for animation and optical effects motion picture photography. To John W. Lang, Walter Hrastnik and Charles J. Watson of Bell and Howell Co. for the development and manufacture of a modular continuous contact motion picture film printer. To Worth Baird of LeVezzi Machine Works, Inc., for the advanced design and manufacture of a film sprocket for motion picture projectors. To Peter A. Regla and Dan Slater of ELICON for the development of a follow-focus system for motion picture optical effects printers and animation stands.

7875 Special Achievement Award— Visual Effects: Brian Johnson, Richard Edlund, Dennis Muren and Bruce Nicholson for *The Empire Strikes Back*

7876 Honorary Awards: To Henry Fonda, the consummate actor, in recognition of his brilliant accomplishments and enduring contribution to the art of motion pictures.

7877 Medal of Commendation: To Fred Hynes in appreciation for outstanding service and dedication in upholding the high standards of the Academy of Motion Picture Arts and Sciences.

——————— **1981** ———————

7878 Best Picture: *Chariots of Fire*
7879 Best Actor: Henry Fonda in *On Golden Pond*
7880 Best Actress: Katharine Hepburn in *On Golden Pond*

7881 Best Director: Warren Beatty for *Reds*
7882 Best Supporting Actor: John Gielgud in *Arthur*
7883 Best Supporting Actress: Maureen Stapleton in *Reds*
7884 Best Art Direction: Norman Reynolds and Leslie Dilley; Set Direction by Michael Ford for *Raiders of the Lost Ark*
7885 Best Cinematography: Vittorio Storaro for *Reds*
7886 Best Costume Design: Milena Canonero for *Chariots of Fire*
7887 Best Feature Documentary: *Genocide*
7888 Best Documentary Short Subject: *Close Harmony*
7889 Best Film Editing: Michael Kahn for *Raiders of the Lost Ark*
7890 Best Foreign Language Film: *Mephisto* — Hungary
7891 Best Make-Up: Rick Baker for *An American Werewolf in London*
7892 Best Music — Original Score: Vangelis for *Chariots of Fire*
7893 Best Music — Best Original Song: "Arthur's Theme (Best That You Can Do)" from *Arthur*, music and lyrics by Burt Bacharach, Carol Bayer Sager, Christopher Cross and Peter Allen
7894 Best Animated Short Film: *Crac*
7895 Best Live Action Short Film: *Violet*
7896 Best Sound: Bill Varney, Steve Maslow, Gregg Landaker and Roy Charman for *Raiders of the Lost Ark*
7897 Best Visual Effects: Richard Edlund, Kit West, Bruce Nicholson and Joe Johnston for *Raiders of the Lost Ark*
7898 Best Writing — Screenplay Based on Material from Another Medium: Ernest Thompson for *On Golden Pond*
7899 Best Writing — Screenplay Written Directly for the Screen: Colin Welland for *Chariots of Fire*
7900 Academy Award of Merit (Academy Statuette): To Fuji Photo Film Co. Limited for the research, development and introduction of a new ultra-high-speed color negative film for motion pictures.
7901 Scientific and Engineering Award (Academy Plaque): To Nelson

Tyler for the progressive development and improvement of the Tyler Helicopter motion picture camera platform. To Leonard Sokolow for the concept and design and Howard T. La Zare for the development of the Consolidated Film Laboratories' Stroboscan motion picture film viewer. To Richard Edlund and Industrial Light and Magic, Inc., for the concept and engineering of a beam-splitter optical composite motion picture printer. To Richard Edlund and Industrial Light and Magic, Inc., for the engineering of the Empire Motion Picture Camera System. To Edward J. Blasko and Dr. Roderick T. Ryan of the Eastman Kodak Co. for the application of the Prostar Microfilm Processor for motion picture title and special effects production.

7902 Technical Achievement (Academy Certificate): To Hal Landaker for the concept and Alan D. Landaker for the engineering of the Burbank Studios' Production Sound Department 24-frame color video system. To Bill Hogan of Ruxton Limited and Richard J. Stumpf and Daniel R. Brewer of Universal City Studios' Production Sound Department for the engineering of a 24-frame color video system. To John DeMuth for the engineering of a 24-frame color video system. To Ernst F. Nettmann of Continental Camera Systems, Inc., for the development of a pitching lens for motion picture photography. To Bill Taylor of Universal City Studios for the concept and specifications for a two format Rotating Head, Aerial Image Optical Printer. To Peter D. Parks of Oxford Scientific Films for the development of the OSF microcosmic zoom device for microscopic photography. To Dr. Louis Stankiewicz and H.L. Blachford for the development of Baryfol sound barrier materials. To Dennis Muren and Stuart Ziff of Industrial Light and Magic, Inc., for the development of a Motion Picture Mover for animation photography.

7903 Special Achievement Award—Sound Effects: Ben Burtt and Richard L. Anderson for *Raiders of the Lost Ark*

7904 Jean Hersholt Humanitarian Award: Danny Kaye

7905 Gordon E. Sawyer Award: Joseph B. Walker

7906 Irving G. Thalberg Award: Albert R. Broccoli

——————— **1 9 8 2** ———————

7907 Best Picture: *Gandhi*
7908 Best Actor: Ben Kingsley in *Gandhi*
7909 Best Actress: Meryl Streep in *Sophie's Choice*
7910 Best Director: Richard Attenborough for *Gandhi*
7911 Best Supporting Actor: Louis Gossett, Jr. in *An Officer and a Gentleman*
7912 Best Supporting Actress: Jessica Lange in *Tootsie*
7913 Best Art Direction: Stuart Craig and Bob Laing, Set Decoration by Michael Seirton for *Gandhi*
7914 Best Cinematography: Billy Williams and Ronnie Taylor for *Gandhi*
7915 Best Costume Design: John Mollo and Bhanu Athaiya for *Gandhi*
7916 Best Feature Documentary: *Just Another Missing Kid*
7917 Best Documentary Short Subject: *If You Love This Planet*
7918 Best Film Editing: John Bloom for *Gandhi*
7919 Best Foreign Language Film: *Volver a Empezar (To Begin Again)*—Spain
7920 Best Make-Up: Saràh Monzani and Michele Burke for *Quest for Fire*
7921 Best Music—Original Score: John Williams for *E.T., the Extra-Terrestrial*
7922 Best Music—Original Song: "Up Where We Belong" from *An Officer and a Gentleman*, music by Jack Nitzsche and Buffy Saint-Marie, lyrics by Will Jennings
7923 Best Music—Original Song Score and Its Adaptation or Adaptation Score: *Victor/Victoria*, song score by Henry Mancini and Leslie Bricusse, adapted by Henry Mancini
7924 Best Animated Short Film: *Tango*—Poland
7925 Best Live Action Short Film: *A Shocking Accident*

7926 **Best Sound:** Robert Knudson, Robert Glass, Don Digirolamo and Gene Cantamessa for *E.T., the Extra-Terrestrial*

7927 **Best Sound Effects Editing:** Charles L. Campbell and Ben Burtt for *E.T., the Extra-Terrestrial*

7928 **Best Visual Effects:** Carlo Rambaldi, Dennis Muren and Kenneth F. Smith for *E.T., the Extra-Terrestrial*

7929 **Best Writing — Screenplay Based on Material from Another Medium:** Costa-Gavras and Donald Stewart for *Missing*

7930 **Best Writing — Screenplay Written Directly for the Screen:** John Briley for *Gandhi*

7931 **Academy Award of Merit (Academy Statuette):** To August Arnold and Erich Kaestner of Arnold & Richter, GmbH for the concept and engineering of the first operational 35mm, hand-held, spinning-mirror reflex motion picture camera.

7932 **Scientific and Engineering Award (Academy Plaque):** To Colin F. Mossman and the Research and Development Group of the Rank Film Laboratories, London, for the engineering and implementation of a 4,000 meter printing system for motion picture laboratories. To Sante Zelli and Salvatore Zelli of Elemack Italia S.r.l., Rome, Italy for the continuing engineering, design and development that has resulted in the Elemack Camera Dolly Systems for motion picture production. To Leonard Chapman for the engineering design, development and manufacture of the PeeWee camera dolly for motion picture production. To Dr. Mohammad S. Nozari of Minnesota Mining and Manufacturing Co. for research and development of the 3M Photogard protective coating for motion picture film. To Brianne Murphy and Donald Schicler of Mitchell Insert Systems, Inc., for the concept, design and manufacture of the MISI Camera Insert Car and Process Trailer. To Jacobus L. Dimmers for the engineering and manufacture of the Teccon Enterprises' magnetic transducer for motion picture sound recording and playback.

7933 **Technical Achievement Award (Academy Certificate):** To Richard W. Deats for the design and manufacture of the "Little Big Crane" for motion picture production. To Constant Tresfou and Adriaan De Rooy of Egripment and to Ed Phillips and Carlos De Mattos of Matthews Studio Equipment, Inc., for the design and manufacture of the "Tulpi Crane" for motion picture production. To Bran Ferren of Associates and Ferren for the design and development of a computerized lighting effect system for motion picture photography. To Christie Electric Corp. and LaVezzi Machine Works, Inc., for the design and manufacture of the Ultramittent film transport and Christie motion picture projectors.

7934 **Jean Hersholt Humanitarian Award:** Walter Mirisch

7935 **Gordon E. Sawyer Award:** John O. Aalberg

7936 **Honorary Award:** Mickey Rooney in recognition of his 60 years of versatility in a variety of memorable film performances.

1983

7937 **Best Picture:** *Terms of Endearment*

7938 **Best Actor:** Robert Duvall in *Tender Mercies*

7939 **Best Actress:** Shirley MacLaine in *Terms of Endearment*

7940 **Best Director:** James L. Brooks for *Terms of Endearment*

7941 **Best Supporting Actor:** Jack Nicholson in *Terms of Endearment*

7942 **Best Supporting Actress:** Linda Hunt in *The Year of Living Dangerously*

7943 **Best Art Direction:** Anna Asp for *Fanny and Alexander*

7944 **Best Cinematography:** Sven Nykvist for *Fanny and Alexander*

7945 **Best Costume Design:** Marik Vos for *Fanny and Alexander*

7946 **Best Feature Documentary:** *He Makes Me Feel Like Dancin'*

7947 **Best Documentary Short Subject:** *Flamenco at 5:15*

7948 **Best Film Editing:** Glenn Farr, Lisa Fruchtman, Stephen A. Roter, Douglas Stewart and Tom Rolf for *The Right Stuff*

7949 **Best Foreign Language Film:** *Fanny and Alexander* — Sweden

7950 **Best Music — Original Score:** Bill Conti for *The Right Stuff*

7951 **Best Music — Original Song:** "Flashdance ... What a Feeling" from *Flashdance*, music by Giorgio Moroder, lyrics by Keith Forsey and Irene Cara

7952 **Best Music — Original Song Score or Adaptation Score:** *Yentl*, song score by Michel Legrand, Alan and Marilyn Bergman

7953 **Best Animated Short Film:** *Sunday in New York*

7954 **Best Live Action Short Film:** *Boys and Girls*

7955 **Best Sound:** Mark Berger, Tom Scott, Randy Thom and David Mac-Millan for *The Right Stuff*

7956 **Best Sound Effects Editing:** Jay Boekelheide for *The Right Stuff*

7957 **Best Writing — Screenplay Based on Material from Another Medium:** James L. Brooks for *Terms of Endearment*

7958 **Best Writing — Screenplay Written Directly for the Screen:** Horton Foote for *Tender Mercies*

7959 **Academy Award of Merit (Academy Statuette):** To Dr. Kurt Karche of OSRAM GmbH for the research and development of xenon short-arc discharge lamps for motion picture projection.

7960 **Scientific and Technical Award (Academy Plaque):** To Jonathan Erland and Roger Dorney of Apogee, Inc., for the engineering and development of a reverse bluescreen traveling matte process for special effects photography. To Gerald L. Turpin of Lightflex International, Ltd., for the design, engineering and development of an on-camera device providing contrast control, sourceless fill light and special effects for motion picture photography. To Gunnar P. Michelson for the engineering and development of an improved, electronic, high-speed, precision light valve for use in motion picture printing machines.

7961 **Technical Achievement Award (Academy Certificate):** To William G. Krokaugger of Mole-Richardson Company for the design and engineering of a portable, 12,000 watt lighting control dimmer for use in motion picture production. To Charles J. Watson, Larry L. Langrehr and John H. Steiner for the development of the BHP electro-mechanical fader for use on continuous motion picture contact printers. To Elizabeth D. De La Mare of De La Mare Engineering, Inc., for the progressive development and continuous research of special effects pyrotechnics originally designed by Glenn W. De La Mare for motion picture production. To Douglas Fries, John Lacey and Michael Sigrist for the design and engineering of a 35mm reflex conversion system for special effects photography. To Jack Cashin of Ultra Stereo Labs, Inc., for the engineering and development of a 4-channel, stereophonic, decoding system for optical motion picture sound track reproduction. To David J. Degenkolb for the design and development of an automated device used in the silver recovery process in motion picture laboratories.

7962 **Special Achievement Award — Visual Effects:** Richard Edlund, Dennis Muren, Ken Ralston and Phil Tippett for *Return of the Jedi*

7963 **Jean Hersholt Humanitarian Award:** M.J. Frankovich

7964 **Gordon E. Sawyer Award:** Dr. John G. Frayne

7965 **Honorary Award:** To Hal Roach in recognition of his unparalleled record of distinguished contributions to the motion picture art form.

─────── **1984** ───────

7966 **Best Picture:** *Amadeus*

7967 **Best Actor:** F. Murray Abraham in *Amadeus*

7968 **Best Actress:** Sally Field in *Places in the Heart*

7969 **Best Director:** Milos Forman for *Amadeus*

7970 **Best Supporting Actor:** Haing S. Ngor in *The Killing Fields*

7971 **Best Supporting Actress:** Peggy Ashcroft in *A Passage to India*

7972 **Best Art Direction:** Patricia Von Brandenstein, Set Decoration by Karel Cerney for *Amadeus*

7973 **Best Cinematography:** Chris Menges for *The Killing Fields*
7974 **Best Costume Design:** Theodor Pistek for *Amadeus*
7975 **Best Feature Documentary:** *The Times of Harvey Milk*
7976 **Best Documentary Short Subject:** *The Stone Carvers*
7977 **Best Film Editing:** Jim Clark for *The Killing Fields*
7978 **Best Foreign Language Film:** *Dangerous Moves* — Switzerland
7979 **Best Make-Up:** Dick Smith and Paul Le Blanc for *Amadeus*
7980 **Best Music — Original Score:** Maurice Jarre for *A Passage to India*
7981 **Best Music — Original Song:** "I Just Called to Say I Love You" from *The Woman in Red*, music and lyrics by Stevie Wonder
7982 **Best Music — Original Song Score:** "Purple Rain" from *Purple Rain*
7983 **Best Animated Short Film:** *Charade*
7984 **Best Live Action Short Film:** *Up*
7985 **Best Sound:** Mark Berger, Tom Scott, Todd Boekelheide and Chris Newman for *Amadeus*
7986 **Best Visual Effects:** Dennis Muren, Michael McAlister, Lorne Peterson and George Gibbs for *Indiana Jones and the Temple of Doom*
7987 **Best Writing — Screenplay Based on Material from Another Medium:** Peter Shaffer for *Amadeus*
7988 **Best Writing — Screenplay Written Directly for the Screen:** Robert Benton for *Places in the Heart*
7989 **Scientific or Technical Award (Academy Plaque):** To Donald A. Anderson and Diana Reiners of 3M Co. for the development of the "Cinetrak" Magnetic Film #350/351 for motion picture sound recording. To Barry M. Stultz, Ruben Avila and Wes Kennedy of Film Processing Corp. for the formulation and application of an improved sound track stripe for 70mm motion picture film, and to John Mosely for the engineering research involved therein. To Kenneth Richter of Richter Cine Equipment for the design and engineering of the R-2 Auto-Collimator for examining image quality at the focal plane of motion picture camera lenses. To Gunther Shaidt

and Rosco Laboratories, Inc., for the development of an improved, non-toxic fluid for creating fog and smoke for motion picture production. To John Whitney, Jr., and Gary Demos of Digital Productions, Inc., for the practical simulation of motion picture photography by means of computer-generated images.
7990 **Technical Achievement Award (Academy Certificate):** To Nat Tiffen of the Tiffen Manufacturing Co. for the production of high-quality, durable, laminated color filters for motion picture photography. To Donald Trumbull, Jonathan Erland, Stephen Fog and Paul Burk of Apogee, Inc., for the design and development of the "Blue Max" high-power, blue-flux projector for traveling matte composite photography. To Jonathan Erland and Robert Bealmear of Apogee, Inc., for an innovative design for front projection screens and an improved method for their construction. To Howard J. Preston of Preston Cinema Systems for the design and development of a variable speed control device with automatic exposure compensation for motion picture cameras.
7991 **Special Achievement Award — Sound Effects Editing:** Kay Rose for *The River*
7992 **Jean Hersholt Humanitarian Award:** David L. Wolper
7993 **Gordon E. Sawyer Award:** Linwood G. Dunn
7994 **Honorary Awards:** To James Stewart for his fifty years of memorable performances, for his high ideals both on and off the screen, with the respect and affection of his colleagues. To the National Endowment for the Arts in recognition of its 20th anniversary and its dedicated commitment to fostering artistic and creative activity and excellence in every area of the arts.

——————— **1985** ———————

7995 **Best Picture:** *Out of Africa*
7996 **Best Actor:** William Hurt in *Kiss of the Spider Woman*
7997 **Best Actress:** Geraldine Page in *The Trip to Bountiful*

7998 Best Director: Sydney Pollack for *Out of Africa*

7999 Best Supporting Actor: Don Ameche in *Cocoon*

8000 Best Supporting Actress: Angelica Huston in *Prizzi's Honor*

8001 Best Art Direction: Stephen Grimes, Set Direction by Josie MacAvin in *Out of Africa*

8002 Best Cinematography: David Watkin for *Out of Africa*

8003 Best Costume Design: Emi Wada for *Ran*

8004 Best Feature Documentary: *Broken Arrow*

8005 Best Documentary Short Subject: *Witness to War: Dr. Charlie Clements*

8006 Best Film Editing: Thom Noble for *Witness*

8007 Best Foreign Language Film: *The Official Story*—Argentina

8008 Best Make-Up: Michael Westmore and Zoltan Elek for *Mask*

8009 Best Music—Original Score: John Barry for *Out of Africa*

8010 Best Music—Original Song: "Say You, Say Me" from *White Nights*, music and lyrics by Lionel Richie

8011 Best Animated Short Film: *Anna & Bella*

8012 Best Live Action Short Film: *Molly's Pilgrim*

8013 Best Sound: Chris Jenkins, Gary Alexander, Larry Stensvold and Peter Handford for *Out of Africa*

8014 Best Visual Effects Editing: Charles L. Campbell and Robert Rutledge for *Back to the Future*

8015 Best Visual Effects: Ken Ralston, Ralph McQuarrie, Scott Farrar and David Berry for *Cocoon*

8016 Best Writing—Screenplay Based on Material from Another Medium: Kurt Luedtke for *Out of Africa*

8017 Best Writing—Screenplay Written Directly for the Screen: William Kelley, Pamela Wallace and Earl W. Wallace for *Witness*

8018 Scientific and Engineering Award (Academy Plaque): To Imax Systems Corporation for a method of filming and exhibiting high-fidelity, large-format, wide-angle motion pictures. To Ernst F. Nettmann of E.F. Nettmann &

Associates for the invention and Ed Phillips and Carlos De Mattos of Matthews Studio Equipment, Inc., for the development of the Cam-Remote for motion picture photography. To Myron Gordon, Joe P. Crookham, Jim Drost and David Crookham of Musco Mobile Lighting, Ltd., for the invention of a method of transporting adjustable, high-intensity luminaires and their application to the motion picture industry.

8019 Technical Achievement (Academy Certificate): To David W. Spencer for the development of an animated Photo Transfer (APT) process. To Harrison & Harrison, optical engineers for the invention and development of the Harrison Diffusion Filters for motion picture photography. To Larry Barton of Cinematography Electronics, Inc., for Precision Speed, Crystal-Controlled Device for motion picture photography. To Alan Landaker of the Burbank Studios for the Mark III Camera Drive for motion picture photography.

8020 Jean Hersholt Humanitarian Award: Charles (Buddy) Rogers

8021 Honorary Awards: To Paul Newman in recognition of his many memorable compelling screen performances and for his personal integrity and dedication to his craft. To Alex North in recognition of his brilliant artistry in the creation of memorable music for a host of distinguished motion pictures.

8022 Medal of Commendation: John H. Whitney, Sr., for cinematic pioneering

——————— **1 9 8 6** ———————

8023 Best Picture: *Platoon*

8024 Best Actor: Paul Newman in *The Color of Money*

8025 Best Actress: Marlee Matlin in *Children of a Lesser God*

8026 Best Director: Oliver Stone for *Platoon*

8027 Best Supporting Actor: Michael Caine in *Hannah and Her Sisters*

8028 Best Supporting Actress: Dianne Wiest in *Hannah and Her Sisters*

8029 Best Art Direction: Gianni Quaranta and Brian Ackland-Snow; Set

Decoration by Brian Savegar and Elio Altamure for *A Room with a View*

8030 **Best Cinematography:** Chris Menges for *The Mission*

8031 **Best Costume Design:** Jenny Beavan and Joe Bright for *A Room with a View*

8032 **Best Feature Documentary:** *Artie Shaw: This Time Is All You've Got* and *Down and Out in America*

8033 **Best Documentary Short Subject:** *Women — For America, for the World*

8034 **Best Film Editing:** Claire Simpson for *Platoon*

8035 **Best Foreign Language Film:** *The Assault* — the Netherlands

8036 **Best Make-Up:** Chris Walas and Stephan Dupuis for *The Fly*

8037 **Best Music — Original Score:** Herbie Hancock for *Round Midnight*

8038 **Best Music — Original Song:** "Take My Breath Away" from *Top Gun*

8039 **Best Animated Short Film:** *A Greek Tragedy*

8040 **Best Live Action Short Film:** *Precious Images*

8041 **Best Sound:** John K. Wilkinson, Richard Rogers, Charles "Bud" Grenzbach and Simon Kaye for *Platoon*

8042 **Best Sound Effects Editing:** Don Sharpe for *Aliens*

8043 **Best Visual Effects:** Robert Skotak, Stan Winston, John Richardson and Suzanne Benson for *Aliens*

8044 **Best Writing — Screenplay Based on Material from Another Medium:** Ruth Prawer Jhabvala for *A Room with a View*

8045 **Best Writing — Screenplay Written Directly for the Screen:** Woody Allen for *Hannah and Her Sisters*

8046 **Scientific and Engineering Award (Academy Plaque):** To Bran Ferren, Charles Harrison and Kenneth Wisner of Associates and Ferren for the concept and design of an advanced optical printer. To Richard Benjamin Grant and Ron Grant of Auricle Control Systems for their invention of the Film Composer's Time Processor. To Anthony D. Bruno and John L. Baptista of Metro-Goldwyn-Mayer Laboratories, Inc., and Manfred G. Michelson and Bruce W. Keller of Technical Film Systems, Inc., for the design and engineering of a Continuous Feed Printer. To Robert Greenberg, Joel Hynek and Eugene Mamut of R/Greenberg Associates, Inc., and Dr. Alfred Thumim, Elan Lipshitz and Darryl A. Armour of the Oxberry Division of Richmark Camera Service, Inc., for the design and development of the RCA/Oxberry Compu-Quad Special Effects Optical Printer. To Professor Fritz Sennheiser of the Sennheiser Electronic Corp. for the invention of an interference tube directional microphone. To Richard Edlund, Gene Whiteman, David Grafton, Mark West, Jerry Jeffress and Bob Wilcox of Boss Film Corp. for the design and development of a Zoom Aerial (ZAP) 65mm Optical Printer. To William L. Fredrick and Hal Needham for the design and development of the Shotmaker Elite camera car and crane.

8047 **Technical Achievement Award (Academy Certificate):** To Lee Electric (Lighting), Ltd., for the design and development of an electronic, flicker-free, discharge lamp control system. To Peter D. Parks of Oxford Scientific Films' Image Quest Division for the development of a live aero-compositor for special effects photography. To Matt Sweeney and Lucinda Strub for the development of an automatic capsule gun for simulating bullet hits for motion picture special effects. To Carl Holmes of Carl E. Holmes Co. and Alexander Bryce of the Burbank Studios for the development of a mobile DC power supply unit for motion picture production photography. To Bran Ferren of Associates and Ferren for the development of a laser synchro-cue system for applications in the motion picture industry. To John L. Baptista of Metro-Goldwyn-Mayer Laboratories, Inc., for the development and installation of a computerized silver recovery operation. To David W. Samuelson for the development of programs incorporated into a pocket computer for motion picture cinematographers, and William B. Pollard for contributing new algorithms on which the programs are based. To Hal Landaker and Alan Landaker of the Burbank

Studios for the development of the Beat System low-frequency cur track for motion picture production sound recording.

8048 **Irving G. Thalberg Memorial Award:** Steven Spielberg

8049 **Honorary Awards:** To Ralph Bellamy for his unique artistry and his distinguished service to the profession of acting.

8050 **Medal of Commendation:** To E. M. (Al) Lewis in appreciation for outstanding service and dedication in upholding the high standards of the Academy of Motion Picture Arts and Sciences.

———————— **1987** ————————

8051 **Best Picture:** *The Last Emperor*

8052 **Best Actor:** Michael Douglas in *Wall Street*

8053 **Best Actress:** Cher in *Moonstruck*

8054 **Best Director:** Bernardo Bertolucci for *The Last Emperor*

8055 **Best Supporting Actor:** Sean Connery in *The Untouchables*

8056 **Best Supporting Actress:** Olympia Dukakis in *Moonstruck*

8057 **Best Art Direction:** Ferdinando Scarfiotti, Set Direction by Bruno Cesari and Osvaldo Desideri for *The Last Emperor*

8058 **Best Cinematography:** Vittorio Storaro for *The Last Emperor*

8059 **Best Costume Design:** James Acheson for *The Last Emperor*

8060 **Best Feature Documentary:** *The Ten-Year Lunch: The Wit and Legend of the Algonquin Round Table*

8061 **Best Short Subject Documentary:** *Young at Heart*

8062 **Best Film Editing:** Gabriella Cristiani for *The Last Emperor*

8063 **Best Foreign Language Film:** *Babette's Feast* — Denmark

8064 **Best Make-Up:** Rick Baker for *Harry and the Hendersons*

8065 **Best Music – Original Score:** Ryuichi Sakamoto, David Byrne and Cong Su for *The Last Emperor*

8066 **Best Music – Original Song:** "(I've Had) the Time of My Life" from *Dirty Dancing*, music by Frankie Previte, John DeNicola and Donald Markowitz, lyrics by Frankie Previte

8067 **Best Animated Short Film:** *The Man Who Planted Trees*

8068 **Best Live Action Short Film:** *Ray's Male Heterosexual Dance Hall*

8069 **Best Sound:** Bill Rowe and Ivan Sharrock for *The Last Emperor*

8070 **Best Visual Effects:** Dennis Muren, William George, Harley Jessup and Kenneth Smith for *Innerspace*

8071 **Best Writing – Screenplay Based on Material from Another Medium:** Mark Peploe and Bernardo Bertolucci for *The Last Emperor*

8072 **Best Writing – Screenplay Written Directly for the Screen:** John Patrick Shanley for *Moonstruck*

8073 **Academy Award of Merit:** To Bernhard Kühl and Werner Block and the OSRAM GmbH Research and Development Department for the invention and the continuing improvement of the Osram HMI light source for motion picture photography.

8074 **Scientific and Engineering Award (Academy Plaque):** To Willi Burth and Kinotone Corp. for the invention and development of the Non-rewind Platter System for motion picture presentations. To Montage Group, Ltd., for the development and Ronald C. Barker and Chester L. Schuler for the invention of the Montage Picture Processor electronic film editing system. To Colin F. Mossman and Rank Film Laboratories Development Group for creating a fully automated, film handling system for improving productivity of high-speed film processing. To Eastman Kodak Co. for the development of Eastman Color High Speed Daylight Negative film 5297/7297. To Eastman Kodak Co. for the development of Eastman Color High Speed SA Negative Film 5295 for blue screen travelling Matte photography. To Fritz Gabriel Bauer for the invention and development of the improved features of the Movican Camera System. Zoran Perisic of Courier Films, Ltd., for the Zoptic dual-zoom front projection system for visual effects photography. To Carl Zeiss Co. for the design and development of a series of superspeed lenses for motion picture photography.

8075 **Technical Achievement Award (Academy Certificate):** To Ioan Allen of

Dolby Laboratories, Inc., for the Cat.43 playback-only noise reduction unit and its practical application to motion picture sound recordings. To John Appolito, Wally Gentleman, William Mesa, Les Paul Robley and Geoffrey H. Williamson for refinements to a dual screen, front projection, image-compositing system. To Jan Jacobsen for the application of a dual screen, front projection system to motion picture special effects photography. To Thaine Morris and David Pier for the development of DSC spark devices for motion picture special effects. To Tadeuz Krzanowski of Industrial Light and Magic, Inc., for the development of a wire rig model support mechanism used to control the movements of miniatures in special effects. To Dan C. Norris and Tim Cook of Norris Film Products for the development of a single-frame exposure system for motion picture photography.

8076 **Special Achievement Award — Sound Effects Editing:** Stephen Flick and John Pospisil for *RoboCop*

8077 **Gordon E. Sawyer Award:** Fred Hynes

8078 **Irving G. Thalberg Memorial Award:** Billy Wilder

──────── **1 9 8 8** ────────

8079 **Best Picture:** *Rain Man*

8080 **Best Actor:** Dustin Hoffman in *Rain Man*

8081 **Best Actress:** Jodie Foster in *The Accused*

8082 **Best Director:** Barry Levinson for *Rain Man*

8083 **Best Supporting Actor:** Kevin Kline in *A Fish Called Wanda*

8084 **Best Supporting Actress:** Geena Davis in *The Accidental Tourist*

8085 **Best Art Direction:** Stuart Craig, Set Decoration by Gerard James for *Dangerous Liaisons*

8086 **Best Cinematography:** Peter Biziou for *Mississippi Burning*

8087 **Best Costume Design:** James Acheson for *Dangerous Liaisons*

8088 **Best Feature Documentary:** *Hotel Terminus: The Life and Times of Klaus Barbie*

8089 **Best Documentary Short Subject:** *You Don't Have to Die*

8090 **Best Film Editing:** Arthur Schmidt for *Who Framed Roger Rabbit?*

8091 **Best Foreign Language Film:** *Pelle the Conqueror* — Denmark

8092 **Best Make-Up:** Ve Neill, Steve La Porte and Robert Short for *Beetlejuice*

8093 **Best Music — Original Score:** Dave Grusin for *The Milagro Beanfield War*

8094 **Best Music — Original Song:** "Let the River Run" from *Working Girl*

8095 **Best Animated Short Film:** *Tin Toy*

8096 **Best Live Action Short Film:** *The Appointments of Dennis Jennings*

8097 **Best Sound:** Les Fresholtz, Dick Alexander, Verne Poore and Willie D. Burton for *Bird*

8098 **Best Sound Effects Editing:** Charles L. Campbell and Louis L. Edemann for *Who Framed Roger Rabbit?*

8099 **Best Visual Effects:** Ken Ralston, Richard Williams, Edward Jones and George Gibbs for *Who Framed Roger Rabbit?*

8100 **Best Writing — Screenplay Based on Material from Another Medium:** Christopher Hampton for *Dangerous Liaisons*

8101 **Best Writing — Screenplay Written Directly for the Screen:** Ronald Bass and Barry Morrow for *Rain Man*

8102 **Academy Award of Merit (Academy Statuette):** To Ray Dolby and Ioan Allen of Dolby Laboratories, Inc., for their continuous contributions to motion picture sound through the research and development programs of Dolby Laboratories.

8103 **Scientific and Engineering Award (Academy Plaque):** To Roy W. Edwards and the engineering staff of Photo-Sonics, Inc., for the design and development of the Photo-Sonics 35mm-ER High-Speed Motion Picture Camera with reflex viewing and video assist. To Arnold & Richter Engineering staff, Otto Blaschek and Arriflex Corp. for the concept and engineering of the Arriflex 35-3 Motion Picture Camera. To Bill Tondreau of Tondreau Systems, Alvah Miller and Paul Johnson of Lynx Robotics,

Peter A. Regla of ELICON, Dan Slater, Bud Elam, Joe Parker and Bill Bryan of Interactive Motion Control and Jerry Jeffress, Ray Feeney, Bill Holland and Kris Brown for their individual contributions and the collective advancements they have brought to the motion picture industry in the field of motion control technology.

8104 Technical Achievement Award (Academy Certificate): To Grant Loucks of Alan Gordon Enterprises Incorporated for the design concept and Geoffrey H. Williamson of Wilcam for the mechanical and electrical engineering of the image 300 35mm High-Speed motion picture camera. To Michael V. Chewey, III for the development of the motion picture industry's first paper tape reader incorporating microscopic technology. To BHP Incorporated, successor to Bell & Howell Professional Equipment Division, for the development of a high-speed reader incorporating microprocessor technology for motion picture laboratories. To Hollywood Film Company for the development of a high-speed reader incorporating microprocessor technology for motion picture laboratories. To Bruce W. Keller and Manfred G. Michelson of Technical Film Systems for the design and development of a high-speed light valve controller and constant current power supply for motion picture laboratories. To Dr. Antal Lisziewicz and Glenn M. Bernggren of ISCO-OPTIC GmbH for the design and development of the Ultra-Star series of motion picture lenses. To James K. Branch of Spectra Cine Incorporated and William L. Blowers and Nasir J. Zaldi for the design and development of the Spectra CineSpot one-degree spotmeter for measuring the brightness of motion picture screens. To Bob Badami, Dick Bernstein and Bill Bernstein of Offbeat Systems for the design and development of the Streamline Scoring System, Mark IV, for motion picture music editing. To Gary Zeller of Zeller International Limited for the development of Zel-Jel fire protection barrier for motion picture stunt work. Emanuel Trilling of Trilling Resources Limited for the development of Stunt-Gel

fire protection barrier for motion picture stunt work. To Paul A. Roos for the invention of a method known as Video Assist, whereby a scene being photographed on motion picture film can be viewed on a monitor and or recorded on video tape.

8105 Special Achievement Award — Animation Direction: Richard Williams for *Who Framed Roger Rabbit?*

8106 Gordon E. Sawyer Award: Gordon Henry Cook

8107 Honorary Awards: To National Film Board of Canada in recognition of its 50th anniversary and its dedicated commitment to originate artistic, creative and technological activity and excellence in every area of film making. To Eastman Kodak Company in recognition of the company's fundamental contributions to the art of motion pictures during the first century of film history.

——————— **1 9 8 9** ———————

8108 Best Picture: *Driving Miss Daisy*

8109 Best Actor: Daniel Day-Lewis in *My Left Foot*

8110 Best Actress: Jessica Tandy in *Driving Miss Daisy*

8111 Best Director: Oliver Stone for *Born on the Fourth of July*

8112 Best Supporting Actor: Denzel Washington in *Glory*

8113 Best Supporting Actress: Brenda Fricker in *My Left Foot*

8114 Best Art Direction: Anton Furst, Set Decoration by Peter Young for *Batman*

8115 Best Cinematography: Freddie Francis for *Glory*

8116 Best Costume Design: Phyllis Dalton for *Henry V*

8117 Best Feature Documentary: *Common Threads: Stories from the Quilt*

8118 Best Documentary Short Subject: *The Johnstown Flood*

8119 Best Film Editing: David Brenner and Joe Hutshing for *Born on the Fourth of July*

8120 Best Foreign Language Film: *Cinema Paradiso* — Italy

8121 Best Make-Up: Manlio Rocchetti, Lynn Barber and Kevin Haney for *Driving Miss Daisy*

8122 **Best Music — Original Score:** Alan Menken for *The Little Mermaid*
8123 **Best Music — Original Song:** "Under the Sea" from *The Little Mermaid*, music by Alan Menken, lyrics by Howard Ashman
8124 **Best Animated Short Film:** *Balance*
8125 **Best Live Action Short Film:** *Work Experience*
8126 **Best Sound:** Donald O. Mitchell, Gregg C. Rudloff, Elliott Tyson and Russell Williams II for *Glory*
8127 **Best Sound Effects Editing:** Ben Burtt and Richard Hymns for *Indiana Jones and the Last Crusade*
8128 **Best Visual Effects:** John Bruno, Dennis Muren, Hoyt Yeatman and Dennis Skotak for *The Abyss*
8129 **Best Writing — Screenplay Based on Material from Another Medium:** Alfred Uhry for *Driving Miss Daisy*
8130 **Best Writing — Screenplay Written Directly for the Screen:** Tom Schulman for *Dead Poets Society*
8131 **Scientific and Engineering Award (Academy Plaque):** To James Ketcham of JSK Engineering for the excellence in engineering and the broad adaptability of the SDA521B Advance/Retard system for magnetic film sound dubbing. To J. Noxon Leavitt for the invention of, and Istec Incorporated for the continuing development of, the Wescam Stabilized Camera System. To Geoffrey H. Williamson of Wilcam Photo Research Incorporated for the design and development and Robert D. Auguste for the electronic design and development of the Wilcam W-7 200 frames-per-second VistaVision rotating mirror reflex camera. To J. L. Fisher of J. L. Fisher Incorporated for the design and manufacture of a small, mobile motion picture camera platform known as the Fisher Model Ten Dolly. To Klaus Resch for the design, Erich Fitz and FGV Schmidle & Fitz for the development of the Super Panther MS-180 Camera Dolly.
8132 **Technical Achievement Award (Academy Certificate):** To Dr. Leo Catozzo for the design and development of the CIR-Catozzo Self-Perforating Adhesive Tape film splicer. To Magna-Tech Electronics Company for the intro-

duction of the first remotely controlled Advance/Retard function for magnetic film sound dubbing.
8133 **Gordon E. Sawyer Award:** Pierre Angenieux
8134 **Jean Hersholt Humanitarian Award:** Howard W. Koch
8135 **Honorary Award:** To Akira Kurosawa for accomplishments that have inspired, delighted, enriched and entertained audiences and influenced filmmakers throughout the world.
8136 **Special Commendation:** The Academy of Motion Picture Arts & Sciences' Board of Governors commends the contributions of the members of the engineering committees of the Society of Motion Picture and Television Engineers (SMPTE), by establishing industry standards, they have greatly contributed to making film a primary form of international communication.

——————— **1 9 9 0** ———————

8137 **Best Picture:** *Dances with Wolves*
8138 **Best Actor:** Jeremy Irons in *Reversal of Fortune*
8139 **Best Actress:** Kathy Bates in *Misery*
8140 **Best Director:** Kevin Costner for *Dances with Wolves*
8141 **Best Supporting Actor:** Joe Pesci in *Goodfellas*
8142 **Best Supporting Actress:** Whoopi Goldberg in *Ghost*
8143 **Best Art Direction:** Richard E. Sylbert, set decoration by Rick Simpson for *Dick Tracy*
8144 **Best Cinematography:** Dean Semler for *Dances with Wolves*
8145 **Best Costume Design:** Franca Squarciapiano for *Cyrano de Bergerac*
8146 **Best Feature Documentary:** *American Dream*
8147 **Best Documentary Short Subject:** *Days of Waiting*
8148 **Best Film Editing:** Neil Travis for *Dances with Wolves*
8149 **Best Foreign Language Film:** *Journey of Hope* — Switzerland
8150 **Best Make-Up:** John Caglione, Jr. and Doug Drexler for *Dick Tracy*
8151 **Best Music — Original Score:** John Barry for *Dances with Wolves*

8152 **Best Music – Original Song:** "Sooner or Later (I Always Get My Man)" from *Dick Tracy*, music and lyrics by Stephen Sondheim

8153 **Best Animated Short Film:** *Creature Comforts*

8154 **Best Live Action Short Film:** *The Lunch Date*

8155 **Best Sound:** Jeffrey Perkins, Bill W. Benton, Greg Watkins and Russell H. Williams II for *Dances with Wolves*

8156 **Best Sound Effects Editing:** Cecelia Hall and George Watters II for *The Hunt for Red October*

8157 **Best Writing – Screenplay Based on Material from Another Source:** Michael Blake for *Dances with Wolves*

8158 **Best Writing – Screenplay Written Directly for the Screen:** Bruce Joel Rubin for *Ghost*

8159 **Academy Award of Merit (Oscar):** To Eastman Kodak Company for the development of T-grain technology and the introduction of EXR color negative films which utilize this technology.

8160 **Scientific and Engineering Award (Academy Plaque):** To Bruce Wilton and Carlos Icinkoff of Mechanical Concepts Incorporated for the development of the Mechanical Concepts Optical Printer Platform. To the Engineering Department of Arnold & Richter for the continued design improvements of the Arriflex BL camera system, culminating in the 35BL-4S model. Fuji Photo Film Company Limited for the development and introduction of the F-Series of color negative films covering the range of film speeds from EI 64 to EI 500. To Manfred G. Michelson of Technical Film Systems Incorporated for the design and development of the first sprocket driven film transport system for color print processors which permits transport speeds in excess of 600 feet per minute. To John W. Lang, Walter Hrastnik and Charles J. Watson of Bell and Howell Company for the development and manufacture of a modular continuous contact motion picture film printer.

8161 **Technical Achievement Award (Academy Certificate):** To William L. Blowers of Belco Associates Incorporated and Thomas F. Denove for the development and manufacture of the Belco/Denove Cinemeter. This digital/analog exposure meter was specifically and uniquely designed for the cinematographer. To Iain Neil for optical design, Takuo Miyagishima for the mechanical design and Panavision Incorporated for the concept and development of the Primo Series of spherical prime lenses for 35mm cinematography. To Christopher S. Gilman and Harvey Hubert, Jr., of the Diligent Dwarves Effects Lab for the development of the Actor Climate System, consisting of heat-transferring undergarments. To Jim Graves of J&G Enterprises for the development of the Cool Suit System, consisting of heat transferring undergarments. To Bengt O. Orhall, Kenneth Lund, Bjorn Selin and Kjell Hogberg of AB-Film Teknik for the development and manufacture of the Mark IV Film subtitling processor, which has increased the speed, simplified the operation and improved the quality of subtitling. To Richard Mule and Pete Romano of HydroImage Incorporated for development of the SeaPar 1200 watt HMI underwater lamp. To Dedo Weigert of Dedo Weigert Film GmbH for the development of the Deolight, a miniature low-voltage tungsten-halogen lighting fixture. To Dr. Fred Kolb, Jr., and Paul Preo for the concept and development of a 35mm projection test film. To Peter Baldwin for the design and Dr. Paul Kiankhooy and the Lightmaker Company for the development of the Lightmaker AC/DC HMI Ballast. To All Union Cinema and Photo Research Institute (NIKFI) for continuously improving and providing 3-D presentations to the Soviet motion picture audiences for the last 25 years.

8162 **Special Achievement Award – Visual Effects:** To Eric Brevig, Rob Bottin, Tim McGovern and Alex Funke for *Total Recall*

8163 **Irving G. Thalberg Memorial Award:** Richard D. Zanuck and David Brown

8164 **Gordon E. Sawyer Award:** Stefan Kudelski

8165 **Honorary Award:** To Sophia Loren, one of the genuine treasures of the world cinema who in a career rich with memorable performances has added permanent lustre to our art form. To Myrna Loy in recognition of her extraordinary qualities both on and off screen with appreciation for a lifetime's worth of indelible performances.

8166 Medals of Commendation: To Roderick T. Ryan, Don Trumbull and Geoffrey H. Williamson in appreciation for outstanding service and dedication in upholding the high standards of the Academy of Motion Picture Arts & Sciences.

1 9 9 1

8167 Best Picture: *The Silence of the Lambs*

8168 Best Actor: Anthony Hopkins in *The Silence of the Lambs*

8169 Best Actress: Jodie Foster in *The Silence of the Lambs*

8170 Best Director: Jonathan Demme for *The Silence of the Lambs*

8171 Best Supporting Actor: Jack Palance in *City Slickers*

8172 Best Supporting Actress: Mercedes Ruehl in *The Fisher King*

8173 Best Art Direction: Dennis Gassner, set decoration by Nancy Haigh for *Bugsy*

8174 Best Cinematography: Robert Richardson for *J.F.K.*

8175 Best Foreign Language Film: *Mediterraneo* — Italy

8176 Best Costume Design: Albert Wolsky for *Bugsy*

8177 Best Documentary Feature: *In the Shadow of the Stars*

8178 Best Documentary Short Subject: *Deadly Deception: General Electric, Nuclear Weapons and Our Environment*

8179 Best Film Editing: Joe Hutshing and Pietro Scalia for *J.F.K.*

8180 Best Make-Up: Stan Winston and Jeff Dawn for *Terminator 2: Judgment Day*

8181 Best Music — Original Score: Alan Menken for *Beauty and the Beast*

8182 Best Music — Original Song: "Beauty and the Beast" from *Beauty and the Beast*, music by Alan Menken, lyrics by Howard Ashman

8183 Best Animated Short Film: *Manipulation*

8184 Best Live Action Short Film: *Session Man*

8185 Best Sound: Tom Johnson, Gary Rydstrom, Gary Summers and Lee Orloff for *Terminator 2: Judgment Day*

8186 Best Sound Effects Editing: Gary Rydstrom and Gloria S. Borders for *Terminator 2: Judgment Day*

8187 Best Visual Effects: Dennis Muren, Stan Winston, Gene Warren, Jr. and Robert Skotak for *Terminator 2: Judgment Day*

8188 Best Writing — Screenplay Based on Material from Another Medium: Ted Tally for *The Silence of the Lamb*s

8189 Best Writing — Screenplay Written Directly for the Screen: Callie Khouri for *Thelma & Louise*

8190 Scientific and Engineering Award (Academy Plaque): To Iain Neil for the optical design, Albert Saiki for the mechanical design, and Panavision Incorporated for the concept and development of the Primo Zoom Lens for 35mm photography. George Thoma for the design, Heinz Feierlein and the engineering department of Sachtler AG for the development and range of fluid head tripods. To Harry J. Baker for the design and development of the first full fluid action tripod head with adjustable degrees of viscous drag. To Guido Cartoni for his pioneering work in developing the technology to achieve selectable and repeatable viscous drag modules in fluid tripod heads. To Ray Feeney, Richard Keeney and Richard J. Lundell for the software development and adaptation of the Solitaire Film Recorder that provides a flexible, cost effective film recording system. To Faz Fazakas, Brian Henson, Dave Housman, Peter Miller and John Stephenson for the development of the Henson Performance Control System. To Mario Celso for his pioneering work in the design, development and manufacture of equipment for carbon arc and xenon power supplies and igniters used in motion picture projection. To Randy Cartwright, David B. Coons, Lem Davis, Thomas Hahn, James Houston, Mark Kimball, Peter Nye, Michael Shantzis, David F. Wolf and the Walt Disney feature animation department for the design and development of the "CAPS" production system for feature film animation. To George Worrall for the design, development and manufacture of the Worrall Geared Camera Head for motion picture production.

8191 Technical Achievement Award (Academy Certificate): To Robert W. Stoker, Jr. for the design and development of a cobweb gun for applying non-toxic cobweb effects on motion picture sets with both safety and ease of operation. To James Doyle for the design and development of the Dry Fogger, which uses liquid nitrogen to produce a safe, dense, low-hanging fog effect. To Dick Cavdek, Steve Hamerski and Otto Nemenz International Incorporated for the opto-mechanical design and development of the Canon/Nemenz Zoom Lens. To Ken Robings and Clairmont Camera for the opto-mechanical design and development of the Canon/Clairmont Camera Zoom Lens. To Century Precision Optics for the opto-mechanical design and development of the Canon/Century Precision Optics Zoom Lens.

8192 Irving G. Thalberg Memorial Award: George Lucas

8193 Gordon E. Sawyer Award: Ray Harryhausen

8194 Academy Honorary Award: To Satyajit Ray, in recognition of his rare mastery of the art of motion pictures, and his profound humanitarian outlook, which has had an indelible influence on filmmakers and audiences throughout the world.

8195 Award of Commendation (Special Plaque): To Pete Comandini, Richard T. Dayton, Donald Hagans and Richard T. Ryan of YCM Laboratories for the creation and development of a motion picture film restoration process using liquid gate and registration correction on a contact printer.

8196 Medal of Commendation: To Richard J. Stumpf and Joseph Westheimer for outstanding service and dedication in upholding the high standards of the Academy of Motion Picture Arts and Sciences.

———— **1992** ————

8197 Best Picture: *Unforgiven*

8198 Best Actor: Al Pacino in *Scent of a Woman*

8199 Best Actress: Emma Thompson in *Howards End*

8200 Best Director: Clint Eastwood for *Unforgiven*

8201 Best Supporting Actor: Gene Hackman in *Unforgiven*

8202 Best Supporting Actress: Marisa Tomei in *My Cousin Vinny*

8203 Best Art Direction: Luciana Arright, Set Decoration by Ian Whittaker for *Howards End*

8204 Best Cinematography: Philippe Rousselot for *A River Runs Through It*

8205 Best Costume Design: Eiko Ishioka for *Bram Stoker's Dracula*

8206 Best Feature Documentary: *The Panama Deception*

8207 Best Documentary Short Subject: *Educating Peter*

8208 Best Film Editing: Joel Cox for *Unforgiven*

8209 Best Foreign Language Film: *Indochine* — France

8210 Best Make-Up: Greg Cannon, Michele Burke and Mathew W. Mungle for *Bram Stoker's Dracula*

8211 Best Music — Original Score: Alan Menken for *Aladdin*

8212 Best Music — Original Song: "A Whole New World" from *Aladdin*, music by Alan Menken, lyrics by Tim Rice

8213 Best Animated Short Film: *Mona Lisa Descending a Staircase*

8214 Best Live Action Short Film: *Omnibus*

8215 Best Sound: Chris Jenkins, Doug Hemphill, Mark Smith and Simon Kaye for *The Last of the Mohicans*

8216 Best Sound Effects Editing: Tom C. McCarthy and David E. Stone for *Bram Stoker's Dracula*

8217 Best Visual Effects: Ken Ralston, Doug Chiang, Doug Smythe and Tom Woodruff, Jr. for *Death Becomes Her*

8218 Best Writing — Screenplay Based on Material Previously Published or Produced: Ruth Prawer Jhabvala for *Howards End*

8219 Best Writing — Screenplay Written Directly for the Screen: Neil Jordan for *The Crying Game*

8220 Academy Award of Merit (Oscar): To Chadwell O'Connor of the

O'Connor Engineering Laboratories for the concept of the fluid-damped camera head for motion picture photography.

8221 Scientific and Engineering Award (Academy Plaque): To Loren Carpenter, Rob Cook, Ed Catmull, Tom Porter, Pat Hanrahan, Tony Apodaca and Darwyn Peachey for the development of "RenderMan" software, which produces images used in motion pictures from 3-D computer descriptions of shape and appearance. To Claus Weidemenn and Robert Orban for the design and Dolby Laboratories for the development of the Dolby Labs "Container." To Ken Bates for the design and development of the Bates Decelerator System for accurately and safely arresting the descent of stunt persons in high freefalls. To Al Mayer for the camera design, Iain Neil and George Kraemer for the optical design, Hans Spirawski and Bill Eslick for the opto-mechanical design and Don Earl for technical support in developing the Panavision System 65 Studio Sync Sound Reflex camera for 65mm motion picture photography. To Douglas Trumbull for the concept, Geoffrey H. Williamson for the movement design, Robert D. Auguste for the electronic design and Edmund M. DiGiulio for the camera system design of the CP-65 Showscan Camera System for 65mm motion picture photography. To Arnold & Richter, Otto Blaschek and the engineering department of ARRI, Austria for the design and development of the Arriflex 765 camera

system for 65mm motion picture photography.

8222 Technical Achievement Award (Academy Certificate): To Ira Tiffen of Tiffen Manufacturing Company for the production of the Ultra Contrast Filter Series for motion picture photography. To Robert R. Burton of Audio Rents Incorporated for the development of the model S-27 4-Band Splitter/Combiner. To Iain Neil for the optical design and Kaz Fudano for the mechanical design of the Panavision Slant Focus Lens for motion picture photography. To Tom Brigham for the original concept and pioneering work and Douglas Smythe and the computer graphics department of Industrial Light & Magic for development and the first implementation in feature motion pictures of the "MORF" system for digital metamorphosis of high resolution images.

8223 Jean Hersholt Humanitarian Award: Audrey Hepburn and Elizabeth Taylor

8224 Gordon E. Sawyer Award: Erich Kaestner

8225 Academy Honorary Award: To Federico Fellini in recognition of his place as one of the screen's master storytellers.

8226 Medal of Commendation: To Petro Valhos in appreciation for outstanding service and dedication in upholding the high standards of the Academy of Motion Picture Arts & Sciences.

Golden Globe Awards for Film

The first Golden Globe Awards were presented in 1944, awarding achievements from 1943. The first ceremonies honored five categories: best picture and best starring and supporting actors and actresses. The original award categories are still honored in addition to other awards, bringing the total now to over two dozen yearly.

The Golden Globe Awards are presented each year by members of the Hollywood Foreign Press Association. At the 13th annual award ceremonies in 1956, the awards were expanded to include television. In addition to the television awards, the Golden Globes now have three best awards: one for drama, one for comedy/musical and one for foreign language film.

Members of the Hollywood Foreign Press Association represent England, Germany, France, Japan, Italy, South Africa, Australia, Argentina, Portugal, Austria, Norway, Sweden and many more. In keeping with the international flavor of the awards, both male and female world film favorites were chosen. This award was presented yearly between 1951 and 1980. First recipients of this award were Jane Wyman (female) and Gregory Peck (male).

Cecil B. DeMille received the best director award in 1953 at the 10th ceremony. In 1952 Cecil B. DeMille was awarded the annual Irving G. Thalberg Memorial Award, presented to any motion picture pioneer regardless of his area of specialization. Today both the best director award is given along with the special individual named for the Cecil B. DeMille Award.

─────── 1 9 4 4 ───────

8227 **Best Motion Picture – Drama:** *The Song of Bernadette*
8228 **Best Motion Picture Actress:** Jennifer Jones in *The Song of Bernadette*
8229 **Best Motion Picture Actor:** Paul Lukas in *Watch on the Rhine*
8230 **Best Supporting Actress:** Katina Paxinou in *For Whom the Bell Tolls*
8231 **Best Supporting Actor:** Akim Tamiroff in *For Whom the Bell Tolls*

─────── 1 9 4 5 ───────

8232 **Best Motion Picture – Drama:** *Going My Way*
8233 **Best Motion Picture Actress:** Ingrid Bergman in *Gaslight*
8234 **Best Motion Picture Actor:** Alexander Knox in *Wilson*
8235 **Best Supporting Actress:** Agnes Moorehead in *Mrs. Parkington*
8236 **Best Supporting Actor:** Barry Fitzgerald in *Going My Way*
8237 **Best Director:** Leo McCarey for *Going My Way*

─────── 1 9 4 6 ───────

8238 **Best Motion Picture – Drama:** *The Lost Weekend*
8239 **Best Motion Picture Actress:** Ingrid Bergman in *Bells of St. Mary's*
8240 **Best Motion Picture Actor:** Ray Milland in *The Lost Weekend*
8241 **Best Supporting Actress:** Angela Lansbury in *The Picture of Dorian Gray*
8242 **Best Supporting Actor:** J. Carroll Naish in *A Medal for Benny*
8243 **Best Director:** Billy Wilder for *The Lost Weekend*
8244 **Best Film Promoting International Goodwill:** *The House I Live In*

─────── 1 9 4 7 ───────

8245 **Best Motion Picture – Drama:** *The Best Years of Our Lives*
8246 **Best Motion Picture Actress:** Rosalind Russell in *Sister Kenny*
8247 **Best Motion Picture Actor:** Gregory Peck in *The Yearling*
8248 **Best Supporting Actress:** Anne Baxter in *The Razor's Edge*

8249 **Best Supporting Actor:** Clifton Webb in *The Razor's Edge*
8250 **Best Motion Picture Director:** Frank Capra for *It's a Wonderful Life*
8251 **Best Film Promoting International Understanding:** *The Last Chance* from Switzerland
8252 **Award for Best Non-Professional Acting:** Harold Russell in *The Best Years of Our Lives*

─────── 1 9 4 8 ───────

8253 **Best Motion Picture – Drama:** *Gentleman's Agreement*
8254 **Best Motion Picture Actress:** Rosalind Russell in *Mourning Becomes Electra*
8255 **Best Motion Picture Actor:** Ronald Coleman in *A Double Life*
8256 **Best Supporting Actress:** Celeste Holm in *Gentleman's Agreement*
8257 **Best Supporting Actor:** Edmund Gwenn in *The Miracle on 34th Street*
8258 **Most Promising Newcomer – Female:** Lois Maxwell in *That Hagen Girl*
8259 **Most Promising Newcomer – Male:** Richard Widmark in *Kiss of Death*
8260 **Best Motion Picture Director:** Elia Kazan for *Gentleman's Agreement*
8261 **Best Screenplay:** George Seaton for *The Miracle on 34th Street*
8262 **Best Motion Picture Score:** Max Steiner for *Life with Father*
8263 **Best Cinematography:** Jack Cardiff for *Black Narcissus*
8264 **Special Award to Best Juvenile Actor:** Dean Stockwell in *Gentleman's Agreement*
8265 **Special Award for Furthering the Influence of the Screen:** Walt Disney for *Bambi*, Hindustani Version

─────── 1 9 4 9 ───────

8266 **Best Motion Picture – Drama:** *Treasure of the Sierra Madre* and *Johnny Belinda*
8267 **Best Motion Picture Actress:** Jane Wyman in *Johnny Belinda*
8268 **Best Motion Picture Actor:** Laurence Olivier in *Hamlet*
8269 **Best Supporting Actress:** Ellen Corby in *I Remember Mama*

8270 Best Supporting Actor: Walter Huston in *Treasure of the Sierra Madre*

8271 Best Motion Picture Director: John Huston for *Treasure of the Sierra Madre*

8272 Best Screenplay: Richard Schweizer for *The Search*

8273 Best Motion Picture Score: Brian Easdale for *The Red Shoes*

8274 Best Cinematography: Gabriel Figueroa for *The Pearl*

8275 Best Film Promoting International Understanding: *The Search*

8276 Special Award to the Best Juvenile Actor: Ivan Jandl in *The Search*

───────── **1950** ─────────

8277 Best Motion Picture – Drama: *All the King's Men*

8278 Best Foreign Film: *The Bicycle Thief* – Italy

8279 Best Motion Picture Actress: Olivia de Havilland in *The Heiress*

8280 Best Motion Picture Actor: Broderick Crawford in *All the King's Men*

8281 Best Supporting Actress: Mercedes McCambridge in *All the King's Men*

8282 Best Supporting Actor: James Whitmore in *Battleground*

8283 Most Promising Newcomer – Female: Mercedes McCambridge in *All the King's Men*

8284 Most Promising Newcomer – Male: Richard Todd in *The Hasty Heart*

8285 Best Motion Picture Director: Robert Rossen for *All the King's Men*

8286 Best Screenplay: Robert Pirosh for *Battleground*

8287 Best Motion Picture Score: Johnny Green for *The Inspector General*

8288 Best Cinematography – Black & White: Frank Planer for *Champion*

8289 Best Cinematography – Color: Walt Disney Studios for *Ichabod and Mr. Toad*

8290 Best Film Promoting International Understanding: *The Hasty Heart*

───────── **1951** ─────────

8291 Best Motion Picture – Drama: *Sunset Boulevard*

8292 Best Motion Picture Actress – Drama: Gloria Swanson in *Sunset Boulevard*

8293 Best Motion Picture Actor – Drama: Jose Ferrer in *Cyrano de Bergerac*

8294 Best Motion Picture Actress – Musical/Comedy: Judy Holliday in *Born Yesterday*

8295 Best Motion Picture Actor – Musical/Comedy: Fred Astaire in *Three Little Words*

8296 Best Supporting Actress: Josephine Hull in *Harvey*

8297 Best Supporting Actor: Edmund Gwenn in *Mister 880*

8298 Best Motion Picture Director: Billy Wilder for *Sunset Boulevard*

8299 Best Screenplay: Joseph L. Mankiewicz for *All About Eve*

8300 Best Motion Picture Score: Franz Waxman for *Sunset Boulevard*

8301 Best Cinematography – Black & White: Frank Planer for *Cyrano de Bergerac*

8302 Best Cinematography – Color: Robert Surtees for *King Solomon's Mines*

8303 Best Film Promoting International Understanding: *Broken Arrow*

8304 World Film Favorite – Female: Jane Wyman

8305 World Film Favorite – Male: Gregory Peck

8306 Most Promising Newcomer: Gene Nelson in *Tea for Two*

───────── **1952** ─────────

8307 Best Motion Picture – Drama: *A Place in the Sun*

8308 Best Motion Picture – Musical/Comedy: *An American in Paris*

8309 Best Motion Picture Actress – Drama: Jane Wyman in *The Blue Veil*

8310 Best Motion Picture Actor – Drama: Fredric March in *Death of a Salesman*

8311 Best Motion Picture Actress – Musical/Comedy: June Allyson in *Too Young to Kiss*

8312 Best Motion Picture Actor – Musical/Comedy: Danny Kaye in *On the Riviera*

8313 Best Supporting Actress: Kim Hunter in *A Streetcar Named Desire*

8314 **Best Supporting Actor:** Peter Ustinov in *Quo Vadis?*

8315 **Most Promising Newcomer— Female:** Pier Angeli in *Teresa*

8316 **Most Promising Newcomer— Male:** Kevin McCarthy in *Death of a Salesman*

8317 **Best Director:** Laslo Benedek for *Death of a Salesman*

8318 **Best Screenplay:** Robert Buckner in *Bright Victory*

8319 **Best Motion Picture Score:** Victor Young for *A September Affair*

8320 **Best Cinematography—Black & White:** Frank Planer for *Death of a Salesman*

8321 **Best Cinematography—Color:** Robert Surtees and William V. Small for *Quo Vadis?*

8322 **Best Film Promoting International Understanding:** *The Day the Earth Stood Still*

8323 **Cecil B. DeMille Award:** Cecil B. DeMille

———— **1953** ————

8324 **Best Motion Picture—Drama:** *The Greatest Show on Earth*

8325 **Best Motion Picture—Musical/ Comedy:** *With a Song in My Heart*

8326 **Best Film Promoting International Understanding:** *Anything Can Happen*

8327 **Best Motion Picture Actress— Drama:** Shirley Booth in *Come Back, Little Sheba*

8328 **Best Motion Picture Actor— Drama:** Gary Cooper in *High Noon*

8329 **Best Motion Picture Actress— Musical/Comedy:** Susan Hayward in *With a Song in My Heart*

8330 **Best Motion Picture Actor— Musical/Comedy:** Donald O'Connor in *Singin' in the Rain*

8331 **Best Supporting Actress:** Katy Jurado in *High Noon*

8332 **Best Supporting Actor:** Millard Mitchell in *My Six Convicts*

8333 **Most Promising Newcomer— Female:** Colette Marchand in *Moulin Rouge*

8334 **Most Promising Newcomer— Male:** Richard Burton in *My Cousin Rachel*

8335 **Best Director:** Cecil B. DeMille for *The Greatest Show on Earth*

8336 **Best Screenplay:** Michael Wilson for *Five Fingers*

8337 **Best Motion Picture Score:** Dimitri Tiomkin for *High Noon*

8338 **Best Motion Picture Cinematography—Black & White:** Floyd Crosby for *High Noon*

8339 **Best Motion Picture Cinematography—Color:** George Barnes and Peverell Marley for *The Greatest Show on Earth*

8340 **Cecil B. DeMille Award:** Walt Disney

8341 **Special Awards for Juvenile Actors:** Brandon De Wilde in *Member of the Wedding* and Frances Kee Teller in *Navajo*

8342 **World Film Favorite—Female:** Susan Hayward

8343 **World Film Favorite—Male:** John Wayne

———— **1954** ————

8344 **Best Motion Picture—Drama:** *The Robe*

8345 **Best Film Promoting International Understanding:** *Little Boy Lost*

8346 **Best Motion Picture Actress— Drama:** Audrey Hepburn in *Roman Holiday*

8347 **Best Motion Picture Actor— Drama:** Spencer Tracy in *The Actress*

8348 **Best Motion Picture Actress— Musical/Comedy:** Ethel Merman in *Call Me Madam*

8349 **Best Motion Picture Actor— Musical/Comedy:** David Niven in *The Moon Is Blue*

8350 **Best Supporting Actress:** Grace Kelly in *Mogambo*

8351 **Best Supporting Actor:** Frank Sinatra in *From Here to Eternity*

8352 **Most Promising Newcomer— Female:** Pat Crowley, Bella Darvi and Barbara Rush

8353 **Most Promising Newcomer— Male:** Hugh O'Brien, Steve Forrest and Richard Egan

8354 **Best Motion Picture Director:** Fred Zinnemann for *From Here to Eternity*

8355 **Best Screenplay:** Helen Deutsch for *Lili*

8356 **Cecil B. DeMille Award:** Darryl F. Zanuck

8357 **World Film Favorite – Female:** Marilyn Monroe

8358 **World Film Favorite – Male:** Robert Taylor and Alan Ladd

8359 **Best Documentary of Historical Interest:** *A Queen Is Crowned*

8360 **Best Western Star:** Guy Madison

8361 **Special Award:** Walt Disney for *The Living Desert*

8362 **Honor Award:** Jack Cummings, producer at MGM for 30 years

———— **1955** ————

8363 **Best Motion Picture – Drama:** *On the Waterfront*

8364 **Best Motion Picture – Musical/Comedy:** *Carmen Jones*

8365 **Best Foreign Films:** *Genevieve* – England; *No Way Back* – Germany; *Twenty-Four Eyes* – Japan; and *La Mujer de Las Camelias* – Argentina

8366 **Best Film Promoting International Understanding:** *Broken Lance*

8367 **Best Motion Picture Actress – Drama:** Grace Kelly in *The Country Girl*

8368 **Best Motion Picture Actor – Drama:** Marlon Brando in *On the Waterfront*

8369 **Best Motion Picture Actress – Musical/Comedy:** Judy Garland in *A Star Is Born*

8370 **Best Motion Picture Actor – Musical/Comedy:** James Mason in *A Star Is Born*

8371 **Best Supporting Actress:** Jan Sterling in *The High and the Mighty*

8372 **Best Supporting Actor:** Edmond O'Brien in *The Barefoot Contessa*

8373 **Most Promising Newcomer – Female:** Shirley MacLaine, Kim Novak and Karen Sharpe

8374 **Most Promising Newcomer – Male:** Joe Adams, George Nader and Jeff Richards

8375 **Best Director:** Elia Kazan for *On the Waterfront*

8376 **Best Screenplay:** Billy Wilder, Samuel Taylor and Ernest Lehman for *Sabrina*

8377 **Best Cinematography – Black & White:** Boris Kaufman for *On the Waterfront*

8378 **Best Cinematography – Color:** Joseph Ruttenberg for *Brigadoon*

8379 **Cecil B. DeMille Award:** Jean Hersholt

8380 **World Film Favorite – Female:** Audrey Hepburn

8381 **World Film Favorite – Male:** Gregory Peck

8382 **Pioneer Award in the Motion Picture Industry:** John Ford

8383 **Pioneer Award for Color on the Screen:** Dr. Herbert Kalmus

8384 **Special Award for Creative Musical Contribution to the Motion Picture:** Dimitri Tiomkin

8385 **Special Award for Experimental Film:** *Anywhere in Our Time* – Germany

———— **1956** ————

8386 **Best Motion Picture – Drama:** *East of Eden*

8387 **Best Motion Picture – Musical/Comedy:** *Guys and Dolls*

8388 **Best Foreign Films:** *Ordet* – Denmark; *Stella* – Greece; *Eyes of Children* – Japan; *Sons, Mothers and a General* – Germany; and *Dangerous Curves* – England

8389 **Best Outdoor Drama:** *Wichita*

8390 **Best Film Promoting International Understanding:** *Love Is a Many-Splendored Thing*

8391 **Best Motion Picture Actress – Drama:** Anna Magnani in *The Rose Tattoo*

8392 **Best Motion Picture Actor – Drama:** Ernest Borgnine in *Marty*

8393 **Best Actress – Musical/Comedy:** Jean Simmons in *Guys and Dolls*

8394 **Best Actor – Musical/Comedy:** Tom Ewell in *Seven Year Itch*

8395 **Best Supporting Actress:** Marisa Pavan in *The Rose Tattoo*

8396 **Best Supporting Actor:** Arthur Kennedy in *Trial*

8397 **Most Promising Newcomer – Female:** Anita Ekberg, Victoria Shaw and Dana Wynter

8398 **Most Promising Newcomer – Male:** Ray Danton and Russ Tamblyn

8399 **Best Motion Picture Director:** Joshua Logan for *Picnic*

8400 **Cecil B. DeMille Award:** Jack Warner

8401 **World Film Favorite — Female:** Grace Kelly

8402 **World Film Favorite — Male:** Marlon Brando

8403 **Hollywood Citizenship Award:** Esther Williams

8404 **Posthumous Award for Best Dramatic Actor:** James Dean

——————— **1957** ———————

8405 **Best Motion Picture — Drama:** *Around the World in 80 Days*

8406 **Best Motion Picture — Musical/Comedy:** *The King and I*

8407 **Best English Language Foreign Film:** *Richard III*

8408 **Best Foreign Language Film:** *The White Reindeer* — Finland; *Before Sundown* — Germany; *The Girls in Black* — Greece; *Roses on the Arm* — Japan; and *War and Peace* — Italy

8409 **Best Film Promoting International Understanding:** *Battle Hymn*

8410 **Best Motion Picture Actress — Drama:** Ingrid Bergman in *Anastasia*

8411 **Best Motion Picture Actor — Drama:** Kirk Douglas in *Lust for Life*

8412 **Best Actress — Musical/Comedy:** Deborah Kerr in *The King and I*

8413 **Best Actor — Musical/Comedy:** Cantinflas in *Around the World in 80 Days*

8414 **Best Supporting Actress:** Eileen Heckart in *The Bad Seed*

8415 **Best Supporting Actor:** Earl Holliman in *The Rainmaker*

8416 **Most Promising Newcomer — Female:** Carroll Baker, Jayne Mansfield and Natalie Wood

8417 **Most Promising Newcomer — Male:** John Kerr, Paul Newman and Anthony Perkins

8418 **Foreign Newcomer Award — Female:** Tania Elg — Finland

8419 **Foreign Newcomer Award — Male:** Jacques Bergerac — France

8420 **Best Motion Picture Director:** Elia Kazan for *Baby Doll*

8421 **Recognition Award for Music in Motion Pictures:** Dimitri Tiomkin

8422 **Cecil B. DeMille Award:** Mervyn LeRoy

8423 **World Film Favorite — Female:** Kim Novak

8424 **World Film Favorite — Male:** James Dean

8425 **Special Award for Advancing the Film Industry:** Edwin Schallert

8426 **Hollywood Citizenship Award:** Ronald Reagan

8427 **Award for Consistent Performance:** Elizabeth Taylor

——————— **1958** ———————

8428 **Best Motion Picture — Drama:** *The Bridge on the River Kwai*

8429 **Best Motion Picture — Musical/Comedy:** *Les Girls*

8430 **Best English Language Foreign Film:** *Woman in a Dressing Gown*

8431 **Best Foreign Language Film:** *Yellow Crow* — Japan; *The Confessions of Felix Krull* — Germany; and *Tizok* — Mexico

8432 **Best Film Promoting International Understanding:** *The Happy Road*

8433 **Best Motion Picture Actress — Drama:** Joanne Woodward in *The Three Faces of Eve*

8434 **Best Motion Picture Actor — Drama:** Alec Guinness in *The Bridge on the River Kwai*

8435 **Best Motion Picture Actress — Musical/Comedy:** Kay Kendall in *Les Girls*

8436 **Best Motion Picture Actor — Musical/Comedy:** Frank Sinatra in *Pal Joey*

8437 **Best Supporting Actress:** Elsa Lanchester in *Witness for the Prosecution*

8438 **Best Supporting Actor:** Red Buttons in *Sayonara*

8439 **Most Promising Newcomer — Female:** Sandra Dee, Carolyn Jones and Diane Varsi

8440 **Most Promising Newcomer — Male:** James Garner, John Saxon and Patrick Wayne

8441 **Best Motion Picture Director:** David Lean for *The Bridge on the River Kwai*

8442 **Special Award for Bettering the Standard of Motion Picture Music:** Hugo Friedhofer

8443 **Cecil B. DeMille Award:** Buddy Adler

8444 **World Film Favorite — Female:** Doris Day

8445 **World Film Favorite – Male:** Tony Curtis

8446 **Best Film Choreography:** Le Roy Prinz

8447 **Best World Entertainment Through Musical Films:** George Sidney

8448 **Most Versatile Actress:** Jean Simmons

8449 **Most Glamorous Actress:** Zsa Zsa Gabor

8450 **Ambassador of Good Will:** Bob Hope

──────── **1 9 5 9** ────────

8451 **Best Motion Picture – Drama:** *The Defiant Ones*

8452 **Best Motion Picture – Comedy:** *Auntie Mame*

8453 **Best Motion Picture – Musical/Comedy:** *Gigi*

8454 **Best English Language Foreign Film:** *A Night to Remember*

8455 **Best Foreign Language Film:** *The Road a Year Long* – Yugoslavia; *The Girl and the River* – France; and *The Girl Rosemarie* – Germany

8456 **Samuel Goldwyn Award:** *Two Eyes, Twelve Hands* – India

8457 **Best Film Promoting International Understanding:** *The Inn of the Sixth Happiness*

8458 **Best Motion Picture Actress – Drama:** Susan Hayward in *I Want to Live!*

8459 **Best Motion Picture Actor – Drama:** David Niven in *Separate Tables*

8460 **Best Motion Picture Actress – Musical/Comedy:** Rosalind Russell in *Auntie Mame*

8461 **Best Motion Picture Actor – Musical/Comedy:** Danny Kaye in *Me and the Colonel*

8462 **Best Supporting Actress:** Hermione Gingold in *Gigi*

8463 **Best Supporting Actor:** Burl Ives in *The Big Country*

8464 **Most Promising Newcomer – Female:** Linda Cristal, Susan Kohner and Tina Louise

8465 **Most Promising Newcomer – Male:** Bradford Dillmann, John Gavin and Efrem Zimbalist, Jr.

8466 **Best Motion Picture Director:** Vincente Minnelli for *Gigi*

8467 **Cecil B. DeMille Award:** Maurice Chevalier

8468 **World Film Favorite – Female:** Deborah Kerr

8469 **World Film Favorite – Male:** Rock Hudson

8470 **Special Award to Best Juvenile:** David Ladd

8471 **Special Award to the Most Versatile Actress:** Shirley MacLaine

──────── **1 9 6 0** ────────

8472 **Best Motion Picture – Drama:** *Ben-Hur*

8473 **Best Motion Picture – Comedy:** *Some Like It Hot*

8474 **Best Motion Picture – Musical:** *Porgy and Bess*

8475 **Best Foreign Films:** *Black Orpheus* – France; *Odd Obsession* – Japan; *The Bridge* – Germany; *Wild Strawberries* – Italy; and *Aren't We Wonderful* – Germany

8476 **Samuel Goldwyn Award:** *Room at the Top*

8477 **Best Film Promoting International Understanding:** *The Diary of Anne Frank*

8478 **Best Motion Picture Actress – Drama:** Elizabeth Taylor in *Suddenly Last Summer*

8479 **Best Motion Picture Actor – Drama:** Anthony Franciosa in *Career*

8480 **Best Motion Picture Actress – Musical/Comedy:** Marilyn Monroe in *Some Like It Hot*

8481 **Best Motion Picture Actor – Musical/Comedy:** Jack Lemmon in *Some Like It Hot*

8482 **Best Supporting Actress:** Susan Kohner in *Imitation of Life*

8483 **Best Supporting Actor:** Stephen Boyd in *Ben-Hur*

8484 **Most Promising Newcomer – Female:** Tuesday Weld, Angie Dickinson, Janet Munro and Stella Stevens

8485 **Most Promising Newcomer – Male:** James Shigeta, Barry Coe, Troy Donahue and George Hamilton

8486 **Best Motion Picture Director:** William Wyler for *Ben-Hur*

8487 **Special Award for Directing the Chariot Race in *Ben-Hur*:** Andrew Marton

8488 Best Motion Picture Score: Ernest Gold for *On the Beach*
8489 Cecil B. DeMille Award: Bing Crosby
8490 World Film Favorite — Female: Doris Day
8491 World Film Favorite — Male: Rock Hudson
8492 Outstanding Merit: *The Nun's Story*
8493 Journalistic Merit Awards: Hedda Hopper and Louella H. Parsons
8494 Special Award to Famous Silent Film Stars: Francis X. Bushman and Ramon Novarro

─────── **1961** ───────

8495 Best Motion Picture — Drama: *Spartacus*
8496 Best Motion Picture — Comedy: *The Apartment*
8497 Best Motion Picture — Musical: *Song Without End*
8498 Best English Language Foreign Film: *The Man with the Green Carnation*
8499 Best Foreign Language Film: *La Vérité* — France and *The Virgin Spring* — Sweden
8500 Best Film Promoting International Understanding: *Hand in Hand*
8501 Best Motion Picture Actress — Drama: Greer Garson in *Sunrise at Campobello*
8502 Best Motion Picture Actor — Drama: Burt Lancaster in *Elmer Gantry*
8503 Best Motion Picture Actress — Musical/Comedy: Shirley MacLaine in *The Apartment*
8504 Best Motion Picture Actor — Musical/Comedy: Jack Lemmon in *The Apartment*
8505 Best Supporting Actress: Janet Leigh in *Psycho*
8506 Best Supporting Actor: Sal Mineo in *Exodus*
8507 Most Promising Newcomer — Female: Ina Balin, Nancy Kwan and Hayley Mills
8508 Most Promising Newcomer — Male: Michael Callan, Mark Damon and Brett Halsey
8509 Best Motion Picture Director: Jack Cardiff for *Sons and Lovers*

8510 Best Motion Picture Score: Dimitri Tiomkin for *The Alamo*
8511 Cecil B. DeMille Award: Fred Astaire
8512 World Film Favorite — Female: Gina Lollobrigida
8513 World Film Favorite — Male: Rock Hudson and Tony Curtis
8514 Special Award for Comedy: Cantinflas
8515 Special Award for Artistic Integrity: Stanley Kramer
8516 Merit Award: *The Sundowners*
8517 Samuel Goldwyn Award: *Never on Sunday* — Greece

─────── **1962** ───────

8518 Best Motion Picture — Drama: *The Guns of Navarone*
8519 Best Motion Picture — Comedy: *A Majority of One*
8520 Best Motion Picture — Musical: *West Side Story*
8521 Best Foreign Language Film: *Two Women* — Italy
8522 Silver Globes: *Animas Tru Jano* — Mexico and *The Good Soldier Schweik* — Germany
8523 Samuel Goldwyn Award for the Best English Film: *The Mark*
8524 Best Film Promoting International Understanding: *A Majority of One*
8525 Best Motion Picture Actress — Drama: Geraldine Page in *Summer and Smoke*
8526 Best Motion Picture Actor — Drama: Maximillian Schell in *Judgment at Nuremberg*
8527 Best Motion Picture Actress — Musical/Comedy: Rosalind Russell in *A Majority of One*
8528 Best Motion Picture Actor — Musical/Comedy: Glenn Ford in *A Pocket Full of Miracles*
8529 Best Supporting Actress: Rita Moreno in *West Side Story*
8530 Best Supporting Actor: George Chakiris in *West Side Story*
8531 Most Promising Newcomer — Female: Christine Kaufmann, Jane Fonda and Ann-Margret
8532 Most Promising Newcomer — Male: Richard Beymer, Bobby Darin and Warren Beatty

8533 **Best Motion Picture Director:** Stanley Kramer for *Judgment at Nuremberg*

8534 **Best Song:** "Town Without Pity" from *Town Without Pity* by Dimitri Tiomkin and Ned Washington

8535 **Best Motion Picture Score:** Dimitri Tiomkin for *Guns of Navarone*

8536 **Cecil B. DeMille Award:** Judy Garland

8537 **World Film Favorite — Female:** Marilyn Monroe

8538 **World Film Favorite — Male:** Charlton Heston

8539 **Special Merit Award:** Samuel Bronston for *El Cid*

8540 **Special Journalistic Merit Award:** Army Archerd — *Daily Variety* and Mike Connolly — *Hollywood Reporter*

——————— **1963** ———————

8541 **Best Motion Picture — Drama:** *Lawrence of Arabia*

8542 **Best Motion Picture — Comedy:** *That Touch of Mink*

8543 **Best Motion Picture — Musical:** *The Music Man*

8544 **Best Foreign Language Films:** *Best of Enemies* — Italy and *Divorce Italian Style* — Italy

8545 **Best Film Promoting International Understanding:** *To Kill a Mockingbird*

8546 **Best Motion Picture Actress — Drama:** Geraldine Page in *Sweet Bird of Youth*

8547 **Best Motion Picture Actor — Drama:** Gregory Peck in *To Kill a Mockingbird*

8548 **Best Motion Picture Actress — Musical/Comedy:** Rosalind Russell in *Gypsy*

8549 **Best Motion Picture Actor — Musical/Comedy:** Marcello Mastroianni in *Divorce Italian Style*

8550 **Best Supporting Actress:** Angela Lansbury in *The Manchurian Candidate*

8551 **Best Supporting Actor:** Omar Sharif in *Lawrence of Arabia*

8552 **Most Promising Newcomer — Female:** Patty Duke, Sue Lyon and Rita Tushingham

8553 **Most Promising Newcomer — Male:** Kier Dullea, Omar Sharif and Terence Stamp

8554 **Best Motion Picture Director:** David Lean for *Lawrence of Arabia*

8555 **Best Motion Picture Score:** Elmer Bernstein for *To Kill a Mockingbird*

8556 **Cecil B. DeMille Award:** Bob Hope

8557 **World Film Favorite — Female:** Doris Day

8558 **World Film Favorite — Male:** Rock Hudson

8559 **Special Award for International Contribution to the Recording World:** Nat "King" Cole

8560 **The Samuel Goldwyn Award:** *Sundays and Cybele* — France

8561 **Cinematography Award — Black & White:** *The Longest Day*

8562 **Cinematography Award — Color:** *Lawrence of Arabia*

——————— **1964** ———————

8563 **Best Motion Picture — Drama:** *The Cardinal*

8564 **Best Motion Picture — Musical/Comedy:** *Tom Jones*

8565 **Best Foreign Language Film:** *Any Number Can Win* — France

8566 **Best Motion Picture Actress — Drama:** Leslie Caron in *The L-Shaped Room*

8567 **Best Motion Picture Actor — Drama:** Sidney Poitier in *Lilies of the Field*

8568 **Best Motion Picture Actress — Musical/Comedy:** Shirley MacLaine in *Irma la Douce*

8569 **Best Motion Picture Actor — Musical/Comedy:** Alberto Sordi in *To Bed or Not to Bed*

8570 **Best Supporting Actress:** Margaret Rutherford in *The V.I.P.s*

8571 **Best Supporting Actor:** John Huston in *The Cardinal*

8572 **Most Promising Newcomer — Female:** Ursula Andress, Tippi Hedren and Elke Sommer

8573 **Most Promising Newcomer — Male:** Albert Finney, Robert Walker and Stathis Giallelis

8574 **Best Motion Picture Director:** Elia Kazan for *America, America*

8575 **Best Motion Picture Promoting International Understanding:** *Lilies of the Field*

8576 **Samuel Goldwyn International Award:** *Yesterday, Today and Tomorrow*

8577 **Cecil B. DeMille Award:** Joseph E. Levine

8578 **World Film Favorite—Female:** Sophia Loren

8579 **World Film Favorite—Male:** Paul Newman

8580 **International Contribution to the Recording World:** Connie Francis

————— **1965** —————

8581 **Best Motion Picture—Drama:** *Becket*

8582 **Best Motion Picture—Musical/Comedy:** *My Fair Lady*

8583 **Best Foreign Language Film:** *Marriage Italian Style*—Italy; *Sallah*—Israel; and *The Girl with the Green Eyes*—England

8584 **Best Motion Picture Actress—Drama:** Anne Bancroft in *The Pumpkin Eater*

8585 **Best Motion Picture Actor—Male:** Peter O'Toole in *Becket*

8586 **Best Motion Picture Actress—Musical/Comedy:** Julie Andrews in *Mary Poppins*

8587 **Best Motion Picture Actor—Musical/Comedy:** Rex Harrison in *My Fair Lady*

8588 **Best Supporting Actress:** Agnes Moorehead in *Hush, Hush, Sweet Charlotte*

8589 **Best Supporting Actor:** Edmond O'Brien in *Seven Days in May*

8590 **Most Promising Newcomer—Female:** Mia Farrow, Celia Kaye and Mary Ann Mobley

8591 **Most Promising Newcomer—Male:** Harve Presnell, George Segal and Chaim Topol

8592 **Best Director:** George Cukor in *My Fair Lady*

8593 **Best Original Score:** Dimitri Tiomkin for *The Fall of the Roman Empire*

8594 **Best Song in a Motion Picture:** "Circus World" from *Circus World* by Dimitri Tiomkin and Ned Washington

8595 **Cecil B. DeMille Award:** James Stewart

8596 **World Film Favorite—Female:** Sophia Loren

8597 **World Film Favorite—Male:** Marcello Mastroianni

————— **1966** —————

8598 **Best Motion Picture—Drama:** *Dr. Zhivago*

8599 **Best Motion Picture—Musical/Comedy:** *The Sound of Music*

8600 **Best English Language Foreign Film:** *Darling*

8601 **Best Foreign Language Film:** *Guilietta of the Spirits*—Italy

8602 **Best Motion Picture Actress—Drama:** Samantha Eggar in *The Collector*

8603 **Best Motion Picture Actor—Drama:** Omar Sharif in *Dr. Zhivago*

8604 **Best Motion Picture Actress—Musical/Comedy:** Julie Andrews in *The Sound of Music*

8605 **Best Motion Picture Actor—Musical/Comedy:** Lee Marvin in *Cat Ballou*

8606 **Best Supporting Actress:** Ruth Gordon in *Inside Daisy Clover*

8607 **Best Supporting Actor:** Oskar Werner in *The Spy Who Came In from the Cold*

8608 **Most Promising Newcomer—Female:** Elizabeth Hartman in *A Patch of Blue*

8609 **Most Promising Newcomer—Male:** Robert Redford in *Inside Daisy Clover*

8610 **Best Director:** David Lean for *Dr. Zhivago*

8611 **Best Screenplay:** Robert Bolt for *Dr. Zhivago*

8612 **Best Original Score:** Maurice Jarre for *Dr. Zhivago*

8613 **Best Original Song in a Motion Picture:** "Forget Domani" from *The Yellow Rolls Royce*

8614 **Cecil B. DeMille Award:** John Wayne

8615 **World Film Favorite—Female:** Natalie Wood

8616 **World Film Favorite—Male:** Paul Newman

————— **1967** —————

8617 **Best Motion Picture—Drama:** *A Man for All Seasons*

8618 **Best Motion Picture – Musical/ Comedy:** *The Russians Are Coming*

8619 **Best English Language Foreign Film:** *Alfie*

8620 **Best Foreign Language Film:** *A Man and a Woman* – France

8621 **Best Motion Picture Actress – Drama:** Anouk Aimee in *A Man and a Woman*

8622 **Best Motion Picture Actor – Drama:** Paul Scofield in *A Man and a Woman*

8623 **Best Motion Picture Actress – Musical/Comedy:** Lynn Redgrave in *Georgy Girl*

8624 **Best Motion Picture Actor – Musical/Comedy:** Alan Arkin in *The Russians Are Coming*

8625 **Best Supporting Actress:** Jocelyn Logarde in *Hawaii*

8626 **Best Supporting Actor:** Richard Attenborough in *The Sand Pebbles*

8627 **Most Promising Newcomer – Female:** Camilla Sparv in *Dead Heat on a Merry-Go-Round*

8628 **Most Promising Newcomer – Male:** James Farentino in *The Pad*

8629 **Best Motion Picture Director:** Fred Zinnemann for *A Man for All Seasons*

8630 **Best Screenplay:** Robert Bolt for *A Man for All Seasons*

8631 **Best Original Score:** Elmer Bernstein for *Hawaii*

8632 **Best Original Song in a Motion Picture:** "Strangers in the Night" from *A Man Could Get Killed*

8633 **Cecil B. DeMille Award:** Charlton Heston

8634 **World Film Favorite – Female:** Julie Andrews

8635 **World Film Favorite – Male:** Steve McQueen

──────── **1 9 6 8** ────────

8636 **Best Motion Picture – Drama:** *In the Heat of the Night*

8637 **Best Motion Picture – Musical/ Comedy:** *The Graduate*

8638 **Best English Language Foreign Film:** *The Fox* – Canada

8639 **Best Foreign Language Film:** *Live for Life* – France

8640 **Best Motion Picture Actress –**
Drama: Dame Edith Evans in *The Whisperers*

8641 **Best Motion Picture Actor – Drama:** Rod Steiger in *In the Heat of the Night*

8642 **Best Motion Picture Actress – Musical/Comedy:** Anne Bancroft in *The Graduate*

8643 **Best Motion Picture Actor – Musical/Comedy:** Richard Harris in *Camelot*

8644 **Best Supporting Actress:** Carol Channing in *Thoroughly Modern Millie*

8645 **Best Supporting Actor:** Richard Attenborough in *Doctor Doolittle*

8646 **Most Promising Newcomer – Female:** Katharine Ross in *The Graduate*

8647 **Most Promising Newcomer – Male:** Dustin Hoffman in *The Graduate*

8648 **Best Motion Picture Director:** Mike Nichols for *The Graduate*

8649 **Best Screenplay:** Stirling Silliphant for *In the Heat of the Night*

8650 **Best Original Score:** Frederick Loewe for *Camelot*

8651 **Best Original Song:** "If Ever I Should Leave You" from *Camelot*

8652 **Cecil B. DeMille Award:** Kirk Douglas

8653 **World Film Favorite – Female:** Julie Andrews

8654 **World Film Favorite – Male:** Paul Newman

──────── **1 9 6 9** ────────

8655 **Best Motion Picture – Drama:** *The Lion in Winter*

8656 **Best Motion Picture – Musical/ Comedy:** *Funny Girl*

8657 **Best English Language Foreign Film:** *Romeo and Juliet*

8658 **Best Foreign Language Film:** *War and Peace* – Russia

8659 **Best Motion Picture Actress – Drama:** Joanne Woodward in *Rachel, Rachel*

8660 **Best Motion Picture Actor – Drama:** Peter O'Toole in *The Lion in Winter*

8661 **Best Motion Picture Actress – Musical/Comedy:** Barbra Streisand in *Funny Girl*

8662 **Best Motion Picture Actor – Musical/Comedy:** Ron Moody in *Oliver!*

8663 **Best Supporting Actress:** Ruth Gordon in *Rosemary's Baby*
8664 **Best Supporting Actor:** Daniel Massey in *Star!*
8665 **Most Promising Newcomer–Female:** Olivia Hussey in *Romeo and Juliet*
8666 **Most Promising Newcomer–Male:** Leonard Whiting in *Romeo and Juliet*
8667 **Best Motion Picture Director:** Paul Newman for *Rachel, Rachel*
8668 **Best Screenplay:** Stirling Silliphant for *Charly*
8669 **Best Original Score:** Alex North for *The Shoes of the Fisherman*
8670 **Best Original Song:** "The Windmills of Your Mind" from *The Thomas Crown Affair*
8671 **Cecil B. DeMille Award:** Gregory Peck
8672 **World Film Favorite–Female:** Sophia Loren
8673 **World Film Favorite–Male:** Sidney Poitier

——————— **1 9 7 0** ———————

8674 **Best Motion Picture–Drama:** *Anne of the Thousand Days*
8675 **Best Motion Picture–Musical/Comedy:** *The Secret of Santa Vittoria*
8676 **Best English Language Foreign Film:** *Oh, What a Lovely War*
8677 **Best Foreign Language Film:** *Z*–Algeria
8678 **Best Motion Picture Actress–Drama:** Genevieve Bujold in *Anne of the Thousand Days*
8679 **Best Motion Picture Actor–Drama:** John Wayne in *True Grit*
8680 **Best Motion Picture Actress–Musical/Comedy:** Patty Duke in *Me, Natalie*
8681 **Best Motion Picture Actor–Musical/Comedy:** Peter O'Toole in *Goodbye, Mr. Chips*
8682 **Best Supporting Actress:** Goldie Hawn in *Cactus Flower*
8683 **Best Supporting Actor:** Gig Young in *They Shoot Horses, Don't They?*
8684 **Most Promising Newcomer–Female:** Ali MacGraw in *Goodbye Columbus*

8685 **Most Promising Newcomer–Male:** Jon Voight in *Midnight Cowboy*
8686 **Best Director–Motion Picture:** Charles Jarrott for *Anne of the Thousand Days*
8687 **Best Screenplay:** John Hale and Bridget Boland for *Anne of the Thousand Days*
8688 **Best Original Score:** Burt Bacharach for *Butch Cassidy and the Sundance Kid*
8689 **Best Original Song:** "Jean" from *The Prime of Miss Jean Brodie*
8690 **Cecil B. DeMille Award:** Joan Crawford
8691 **World Film Favorite–Female:** Barbra Streisand
8692 **World Film Favorite–Male:** Steve McQueen

——————— **1 9 7 1** ———————

8693 **Best Motion Picture–Drama:** *Love Story*
8694 **Best Motion Picture–Musical/Comedy:** *M*A*S*H*
8695 **Best English Language Foreign Film:** *Women in Love*
8696 **Best Foreign Language Film:** *Rider in the Rain*–France
8697 **Best Motion Picture Actress–Drama:** Ali MacGraw in *Love Story*
8698 **Best Motion Picture Actor–Drama:** George C. Scott in *Patton*
8699 **Best Motion Picture Actress–Musical/Comedy:** Carrie Snodgrass in *Diary of a Mad Housewife*
8700 **Best Motion Picture Actor–Musical/Comedy:** Albert Finney in *Scrooge*
8701 **Best Supporting Actress:** Karen Black in *Five Easy Pieces* and Maureen Stapleton in *Airport*
8702 **Best Supporting Actor:** John Mills in *Ryan's Daughter*
8703 **Most Promising Newcomer–Female:** Carrie Snodgrass in *Diary of a Mad Housewife*
8704 **Most Promising Newcomer–Male:** James Earl Jones in *The Great White Hope*
8705 **Best Motion Picture Director:** Arthur Hiller for *Love Story*
8706 **Best Original Score:** Francis Lai for *Love Story*

8707 **Best Original Song:** "Whistling Away the Dark" from *Darling Lili*
8708 **Best Screenplay:** Erich Segal for *Love Story*
8709 **Cecil B. DeMille Award:** Frank Sinatra
8710 **World Film Favorite – Female:** Barbra Streisand
8711 **World Film Favorite – Male:** Clint Eastwood

――――――― **1 9 7 2** ―――――――

8712 **Best Motion Picture – Drama:** *The French Connection*
8713 **Best Motion Picture – Musical/Comedy:** *Fiddler on the Roof*
8714 **Best English Language Foreign Film:** *Sunday, Bloody Sunday*
8715 **Best Foreign Language Film:** *The Policeman* – Israel
8716 **Best Motion Picture Actress – Drama:** Jane Fonda in *Klute*
8717 **Best Motion Picture Actor – Drama:** Gene Hackman in *The French Connection*
8718 **Best Motion Picture Actress – Musical/Comedy:** Twiggy in *The Boy Friend*
8719 **Best Motion Picture Actor – Musical/Comedy:** Chaim Topol in *Fiddler on the Roof*
8720 **Best Motion Picture Supporting Actress:** Ann-Margret in *Carnal Knowledge*
8721 **Best Motion Picture Supporting Actor:** Ben Johnson in *The Last Picture Show*
8722 **Most Promising Newcomer – Female:** Twiggy in *The Boy Friend*
8723 **Most Promising Newcomer – Male:** Desi Arnaz, Jr., in *Red Sky at Morning*
8724 **Best Motion Picture Director:** William Friedkin for *The French Connection*
8725 **Best Screenplay:** Paddy Chayefsky for *The Hospital*
8726 **Best Original Score:** Isaac Hayes for *Shaft*
8727 **Best Original Song:** "Life Is What You Make It" from *Kotch*
8728 **Cecil B. DeMille Award:** Alfred Hitchcock
8729 **World Film Favorite – Female:** Ali MacGraw

8730 **World Film Favorite – Male:** Charles Bronson and Sean Connery

――――――― **1 9 7 3** ―――――――

8731 **Best Motion Picture – Drama:** *The Godfather*
8732 **Best Motion Picture – Musical/Comedy:** *Cabaret*
8733 **Best English Language Foreign Film:** *Young Winston*
8734 **Best Foreign Language Film:** *The Emigrants – Part I* and *The New Land – Part II* – Sweden
8735 **Best Motion Picture Actress – Drama:** Liv Ullman in *The Emigrants*
8736 **Best Motion Picture Actor – Drama:** Marlon Brando in *The Godfather*
8737 **Best Motion Picture Actress – Musical/Comedy:** Liza Minnelli in *Cabaret*
8738 **Best Motion Picture Actor – Musical/Comedy:** Jack Lemmon in *Avanti*
8739 **Best Motion Picture Supporting Actress:** Shelley Winters in *The Poseidon Adventure*
8740 **Best Supporting Actor:** Joel Grey in *Cabaret*
8741 **Most Promising Newcomer – Female:** Diana Ross in *Lady Sings the Blues*
8742 **Most Promising Newcomer – Male:** Edward Albert in *Butterflies Are Free*
8743 **Best Motion Picture Director:** Francis Ford Coppola for *The Godfather*
8744 **Best Screenplay:** Francis Ford Coppola and Mario Puzo for *The Godfather*
8745 **Best Original Score:** Nino Rota for *The Godfather*
8746 **Best Original Song:** "Ben" from *Ben* by Walter Scharf and Don Black
8747 **Best Documentary Film:** *Elvis on Tour* and *Walls of Fire*
8748 **Cecil B. DeMille Award:** Samuel Goldwyn
8749 **World Film Favorite – Female:** Jane Fonda
8750 **World Film Favorite – Male:** Marlon Brando

——————— 1 9 7 4 ———————

8751 **Best Motion Picture — Drama:** *The Exorcist*

8752 **Best Motion Picture — Musical/Comedy:** *American Graffiti*

8753 **Best Foreign Language Film:** *The Pedestrian* — Germany

8754 **Best Motion Picture Actress — Drama:** Marsha Mason in *Cinderella Liberty*

8755 **Best Motion Picture Actor — Drama:** Al Pacino in *Serpico*

8756 **Best Motion Picture Actress — Musical/Comedy:** Glenda Jackson in *A Touch of Class*

8757 **Best Motion Picture Actor — Musical/Comedy:** George Segal in *A Touch of Class*

8758 **Best Motion Picture Supporting Actress:** Linda Blair in *The Exorcist*

8759 **Best Motion Picture Supporting Actor:** John Houseman in *The Paper Chase*

8760 **Most Promising Newcomer — Female:** Tatum O'Neal in *Paper Moon*

8761 **Most Promising Newcomer — Male:** Paul LeMat in *American Graffiti*

8762 **Best Motion Picture Director:** William Friedkin for *The Exorcist*

8763 **Best Screenplay:** William Peter Blatty for *The Exorcist*

8764 **Best Original Score:** Neil Diamond for *Jonathan Livingston Seagull*

8765 **Best Original Song:** "The Way We Were" from *The Way We Were* by Marvin Hamlisch and Marilyn and Alan Bergman

8766 **Best Documentary Film:** *Visions of Eight*

8767 **Cecil B. DeMille Award:** Bette Davis

8768 **World Film Favorite — Female:** Elizabeth Taylor

8769 **World Film Favorite — Male:** Marlon Brando

——————— 1 9 7 5 ———————

8770 **Best Motion Picture — Drama:** *Chinatown*

8771 **Best Motion Picture — Musical/Comedy:** *The Longest Yard*

8772 **Best Foreign Film:** *Scenes from a Marriage* — Sweden

8773 **Best Motion Picture Actress — Drama:** Gena Rowlands in *A Woman Under the Influence*

8774 **Best Motion Picture Actor — Drama:** Jack Nicholson in *Chinatown*

8775 **Best Motion Picture Actress — Musical/Comedy:** Raquel Welch in *The Three Musketeers*

8776 **Best Motion Picture Actor — Musical/Comedy:** Art Carney in *Harry and Tonto*

8777 **Best Motion Picture Supporting Actress:** Karen Black in *The Great Gatsby*

8778 **Best Motion Picture Supporting Actor:** Fred Astaire in *The Towering Inferno*

8779 **Most Promising Newcomer — Female:** Susan Flannery in *The Towering Inferno*

8780 **Most Promising Newcomer — Male:** Joseph Bottoms in *The Dove*

8781 **Best Motion Picture Director:** Roman Polanski in *Chinatown*

8782 **Best Screenplay:** Robert Towne for *Chinatown*

8783 **Best Original Score:** Alan Jay Lerner and Frederick Loewe for *The Little Prince*

8784 **Best Original Song:** "I Feel Love" from *Benji* by Euel and Betty Box

8785 **Best Documentary Film:** *Beautiful People*

8786 **Cecil B. DeMille Award:** Hal B. Wallis

8787 **World Film Favorite — Female:** Barbra Streisand

8788 **World Film Favorite — Male:** Robert Redford

——————— 1 9 7 6 ———————

8789 **Best Motion Picture — Drama:** *One Flew Over the Cuckoo's Nest*

8790 **Best Motion Picture — Musical/Comedy:** *The Sunshine Boys*

8791 **Best Foreign Film:** *Lies My Father Told Me* — Canada

8792 **Best Motion Picture Actress — Drama:** Louise Fletcher in *One Flew Over the Cuckoo's Nest*

8793 **Best Motion Picture Actor — Drama:** Jack Nicholson in *One Flew Over the Cuckoo's Nest*

8794 Best Motion Picture Actress—Musical/Comedy: Ann-Margret in *Tommy*

8795 Best Motion Picture Actor—Musical/Comedy: Walter Matthau in *The Sunshine Boys*

8796 Best Motion Picture Supporting Actress: Brenda Vaccaro in *Once Is Not Enough*

8797 Best Motion Picture Supporting Actor: Richard Benjamin in *The Sunshine Boys*

8798 Best Acting Debut in a Motion Picture—Female: Marilyn Hassett in *The Other Side of the Mountain*

8799 Best Acting Debut in a Motion Picture—Male: Brad Dourif in *One Flew Over the Cuckoo's Nest*

8800 Best Motion Picture Director: Milos Forman for *One Flew Over the Cuckoo's Nest*

8801 Best Screenplay: Lawrence Hauben and Bo Goldman for *One Flew Over the Cuckoo's Nest*

8802 Best Original Score: John Williams for *Jaws*

8803 Best Original Song: "I'm Easy" from *Nashville* music and lyrics by Keith Carradine

8804 Best Documentary Film: *Youthquake*

————— **1977** —————

8805 Best Motion Picture—Drama: *Rocky*

8806 Best Motion Picture—Musical/Comedy: *A Star Is Born*

8807 Best Foreign Film: *Face to Face*—Sweden

8808 Best Documentary: *Altars of the World*

8809 Best Motion Picture Actress—Drama: Faye Dunaway in *Network*

8810 Best Motion Picture Actor—Drama: Peter Finch in *Network*

8811 Best Motion Picture Actress—Musical/Comedy: Barbra Streisand in *A Star Is Born*

8812 Best Motion Picture Actor—Musical/Comedy: Kris Kristofferson in *A Star Is Born*

8813 Best Motion Picture Supporting Actress: Katharine Ross in *Voyage of the Damned*

8814 Best Motion Picture Supporting Actor: Laurence Olivier in *Marathon Man*

8815 Best Acting Debut in a Motion Picture—Female: Jessica Lange in *King Kong*

8816 Best Acting Debut in a Motion Picture—Male: Arnold Schwarzenegger in *Stay Hungry*

8817 Best Motion Picture Director: Sidney Lumet for *Network*

8818 Best Screenplay: Paddy Chayefsky for *Network*

8819 Best Original Score: Paul Williams and Kenny Ascher for *A Star Is Born*

8820 Best Original Song: "Evergreen" from *A Star Is Born*

8821 Cecil B. DeMille Award: Walter Mirisch

8822 World Film Favorite—Female: Sophia Loren

8823 World Film Favorite—Male: Robert Redford

————— **1978** —————

8824 Best Motion Picture—Drama: *The Turning Point*

8825 Best Motion Picture—Musical/Comedy: *The Goodbye Girl*

8826 Best Foreign Film: *A Special Day*—Italy

8827 Best Motion Picture Actress—Drama: Jane Fonda in *Julia*

8828 Best Motion Picture Actor—Drama: Richard Burton in *Equus*

8829 Best Motion Picture Actress—Musical/Comedy: Diane Keaton in *Annie Hall* and Marsha Mason in *The Goodbye Girl*

8830 Best Motion Picture Actor—Musical/Comedy: Richard Dreyfuss in *The Goodbye Girl*

8831 Best Motion Picture Supporting Actress: Vanessa Redgrave in *Julia*

8832 Best Motion Picture Supporting Actor: Peter Firth in *Equus*

8833 Best Motion Picture Director: Herbert Ross for *The Turning Point*

8834 Best Screenplay: Neil Simon for *The Goodbye Girl*

8835 Best Original Score: John Williams for *Star Wars*

8836 Best Original Song: "You Light Up My Life" from *You Light Up My Life*

8837 **Cecil B. DeMille Award:** Red Skelton
8838 **World Film Favorite – Female:** Barbra Streisand
8839 **World Film Favorite – Male:** Robert Redford

———— **1 9 7 9** ————

8840 **Best Motion Picture – Drama:** *Midnight Express*
8841 **Best Motion Picture – Musical/Comedy:** *Heaven Can Wait*
8842 **Best Foreign Film:** *Autumn Sonata* – Sweden
8843 **Best Motion Picture Actress – Drama:** Jane Fonda in *Coming Home*
8844 **Best Motion Picture Actor – Drama:** Jon Voight in *Coming Home*
8845 **Best Motion Picture Actress – Musical/Comedy:** Ellen Burstyn in *Same Time, Next Year* and Maggie Smith in *California Suite*
8846 **Best Motion Picture Actor – Musical/Comedy:** Warren Beatty in *Heaven Can Wait*
8847 **Best Motion Picture Supporting Actress:** Dyan Cannon in *Heaven Can Wait*
8848 **Best Motion Picture Supporting Actor:** John Hurt in *Midnight Express*
8849 **Best Motion Picture Acting Debut – Female:** Irene Miracle in *Midnight Express*
8850 **Best Motion Picture Acting Debut – Male:** Brad Davis in *Midnight Express*
8851 **Best Motion Picture Director:** Michael Cimino for *The Deer Hunter*
8852 **Best Screenplay:** Oliver Stone for *Midnight Express*
8853 **Best Original Score:** Giorgio Moroder for *Midnight Express*
8854 **Best Original Song:** "Last Dance" from *Thank God It's Friday*
8855 **Cecil B. DeMille Award:** Lucille Ball
8856 **World Film Favorite – Female:** Jane Fonda
8857 **World Film Favorite – Male:** John Travolta

———— **1 9 8 0** ————

8858 **Best Motion Picture – Drama:** *Kramer vs. Kramer*

8859 **Best Motion Picture – Musical/Comedy:** *Breaking Away*
8860 **Best Foreign Film:** *La Cage aux Folles* – France/Italy
8861 **Best Motion Picture Actress – Drama:** Sally Field in *Norma Rae*
8862 **Best Motion Picture Actor – Drama:** Dustin Hoffman in *Kramer vs. Kramer*
8863 **Best Motion Picture Actress – Musical/Comedy:** Bette Midler in *The Rose*
8864 **Best Motion Picture Actor – Musical/Comedy:** Peter Sellers in *Being There*
8865 **Best Motion Picture Supporting Actress:** Meryl Streep in *Kramer vs. Kramer*
8866 **Best Motion Picture Supporting Actor:** Melvyn Douglas in *Being There* and Robert Duvall in *Apocalypse Now*
8867 **New Star of the Year in a Motion Picture – Female:** Bette Midler in *The Rose*
8868 **New Star of the Year in a Motion Picture – Male:** Ricky Schroder in *The Champ*
8869 **Best Motion Picture Director:** Francis Coppola for *Apocalypse Now*
8870 **Best Screenplay:** Robert Benton for *Kramer vs. Kramer*
8871 **Best Original Score:** Carmine Coppola and Francis Coppola for *Apocalypse Now*
8872 **Best Original Song:** "The Rose" from *The Rose*
8873 **Cecil B. DeMille Award:** Henry Fonda
8874 **World Film Favorite – Female:** Jane Fonda
8875 **World Film Favorite – Male:** Roger Moore

———— **1 9 8 1** ————

8876 **Best Motion Picture – Drama:** *Ordinary People*
8877 **Best Motion Picture – Musical/Comedy:** *Coal Miner's Daughter*
8878 **Best Foreign Film:** *Tess* – United Kingdom
8879 **Best Motion Picture Actress – Drama:** Mary Tyler Moore in *Ordinary People*
8880 **Best Motion Picture Actor – Drama:** Robert de Niro in *Raging Bull*

8881 **Best Motion Picture Actress –
Musical/Comedy:** Sissy Spacek in *Coal
Miner's Daughter*

8882 **Best Motion Picture Actor –
Musical/Comedy:** Ray Sharkey in *The
Idolmaker*

8883 **Best Motion Picture Actress in a
Supporting Role:** Mary Steenburgen in
Melvin & Howard

8884 **Best Motion Picture Actor in a
Supporting Role:** Timothy Hutton in *Ordinary People*

8885 **New Star of the Year in a Motion
Picture – Female:** Nastassia Kinski in
Tess

8886 **New Star of the Year in a Motion
Picture – Male:** Timothy Hutton in *Ordinary People*

8887 **Best Motion Picture Director:**
Robert Redford for *Ordinary People*

8888 **Best Motion Picture Screenplay:**
William Peter Blatty for *Twinkle,
Twinkle, Killer Kane*

8889 **Best Original Motion Picture
Score:** Dominic Frontiere for *The Stunt
Man*

8890 **Best Original Motion Picture
Song:** "Fame" from *Fame*, music by Michael Gore, lyrics by Dean Pitchford

8891 **Cecil B. DeMille Award:** Gene
Kelly

————— **1 9 8 2** —————

8892 **Best Motion Picture – Drama:**
On Golden Pond

8893 **Best Motion Picture – Musical/
Comedy:** *Arthur*

8894 **Best Foreign Film:** *Chariots of
Fire* – United Kingdom

8895 **Best Motion Picture Actress –
Drama:** Meryl Streep in *The French
Lieutenant's Woman*

8896 **Best Motion Picture Actor –
Drama:** Henry Fonda in *On Golden Pond*

8897 **Best Motion Picture Actress –
Musical/Comedy:** Bernadette Peters in
Pennies from Heaven

8898 **Best Motion Picture Actor – Musical/Comedy:** Dudley Moore in *Arthur*

8899 **Best Motion Picture Supporting
Actress:** Joan Hackett in *Only When I
Laugh*

8900 **Best Motion Picture Director:**
Warren Beatty for *Reds*

8901 **Best Screenplay:** Ernest Thompson for *On Golden Pond*

8902 **Best Original Motion Picture
Song:** "Arthur's Theme (The Best That
You Can Do)" from *Arthur*

8903 **New Star of the Year:** Pia Zadora

8904 **Cecil B. DeMille Award:** Sidney
Poitier

————— **1 9 8 3** —————

8905 **Best Motion Picture – Drama:**
E.T., the Extra-Terrestrial

8906 **Best Motion Picture – Musical/
Comedy:** *Tootsie*

8907 **Best Foreign Film:** *Gandhi* –
United Kingdom/India

8908 **Best Motion Picture Actress and
Actor – Drama:** Meryl Streep in *Sophie's
Choice* and Ben Kingsley in *Gandhi*

8909 **Best Motion Picture Actress and
Actor – Musical/Comedy:** Julie Andrews
in *Victor/Victoria* and Dustin Hoffman
in *Tootsie*

8910 **Best Motion Picture Actress and
Actor in a Supporting Role:** Jessica
Lange in *Tootsie* and Louis Gossett, Jr.
in *An Officer and a Gentleman*

8911 **Best Motion Picture Director:**
Richard Attenborough for *Gandhi*

8912 **Best Motion Picture Screenplay:**
John Briley for *Gandhi*

8913 **Best Original Motion Picture
Score:** John Williams for *E.T., the Extra-Terrestrial*

8914 **Best Original Motion Picture
Song:** "Up Where We Belong" from *An
Officer and a Gentleman*

8915 **New Male and Female Motion
Picture Stars of the Year:** Sandahl
Bergman in *Conan the Barbarian* and
Ben Kingsley in *Gandhi*

8916 **Cecil B. DeMille Award:** Laurence Olivier

————— **1 9 8 4** —————

8917 **Best Motion Picture – Drama:**
Terms of Endearment

8918 **Best Motion Picture – Musical/
Comedy:** *Yentl*

8919 **Best Foreign Film:** *Fanny and
Alexander* – Sweden

8920 **Best Motion Picture Actress –
Drama:** Shirley MacLaine in *Terms of
Endearment*

8921 **Best Motion Picture Actor—Drama:** Tom Courtenay in *The Dresser* and Robert Duvall in *Tender Mercies*

8922 **Best Motion Picture Actress—Musical/Comedy:** Julie Walters in *Educating Rita*

8923 **Best Motion Picture Actor—Musical/Comedy:** Michael Caine in *Educating Rita*

8924 **Best Motion Picture Supporting Actress:** Cher in *Silkwood*

8925 **Best Motion Picture Supporting Actor:** Jack Nicholson in *Terms of Endearment*

8926 **Best Motion Picture Director:** Barbra Streisand for *Yentl*

8927 **Best Motion Picture Screenplay:** James L. Brooks for *Terms of Endearment*

8928 **Original Motion Picture Score:** Giorgio Moroder for *Flashdance*

8929 **Best Original Motion Picture Song:** "Flashdance—What a Feeling" from *Flashdance*, music by Giorgio Moroder, lyrics by Keith Forsey and Irene Cara

8930 **Cecil B. DeMille Award:** Paul Newman

————— **1 9 8 5** —————

8931 **Best Motion Picture—Drama:** *Amadeus*

8932 **Best Motion Picture—Musical/Comedy:** *Romancing the Stone*

8933 **Best Foreign Film:** *A Passage to India*—United Kingdom

8934 **Best Motion Picture Actress—Drama:** Sally Field in *Places in the Heart*

8935 **Best Motion Picture Actor—Drama:** F. Murray Abraham in *Amadeus*

8936 **Best Motion Picture Actress—Musical/Comedy:** Kathleen Turner in *Romancing the Stone*

8937 **Best Motion Picture Actor—Musical/Comedy:** Dudley Moore in *Mickey & Maude*

8938 **Best Motion Picture Actress in a Supporting Role:** Peggy Ashcroft in *A Passage to India*

8939 **Best Motion Picture Actor in a Supporting Role:** Dr. Haing S. Ngor in *The Killing Fields*

8940 **Best Motion Picture Director:** Milos Forman for *Amadeus*

8941 **Best Motion Picture Screenplay:** Peter Shaffer for *Amadeus*

8942 **Best Original Motion Picture Score:** Maurice Jarre for *A Passage to India*

8943 **Best Original Motion Picture Song:** "I Just Called to Say I Love You" from *The Woman in Red*, music and lyrics by Stevie Wonder

8944 **Cecil B. DeMille Award:** Elizabeth Taylor

————— **1 9 8 6** —————

8945 **Best Motion Picture—Drama:** *Out of Africa*

8946 **Best Motion Picture—Musical/Comedy:** *Prizzi's Honor*

8947 **Best Foreign Language Film:** *The Official Story*—Argentina

8948 **Best Motion Picture Actress—Drama:** Whoopi Goldberg in *The Color Purple*

8949 **Best Motion Picture Actor—Drama:** Jon Voight in *Runaway Train*

8950 **Best Motion Picture Actress—Musical/Comedy:** Kathleen Turner in *Prizzi's Honor*

8951 **Best Motion Picture Actor—Musical/Comedy:** Jack Nicholson in *Prizzi's Honor*

8952 **Best Motion Picture Supporting Actress:** Meg Tilly in *Agnes of God*

8953 **Best Motion Picture Supporting Actor:** Klaus Maria Brandauer in *Out of Africa*

8954 **Best Motion Picture Director:** John Huston for *Prizzi's Honor*

8955 **Best Motion Picture Screenplay:** Woody Allen for *The Purple Rose of Cairo*

8956 **Original Motion Picture Score:** John Barry for *Out of Africa*

8957 **Best Original Motion Picture Song:** "Say You, Say Me" from *White Nights*, music and lyrics by Lionel Richie

8958 **Cecil B. DeMille Award:** Barbara Stanwyck

————— **1 9 8 7** —————

8959 **Best Motion Picture—Drama:** *Platoon*

8960 **Best Motion Picture—Musical/Comedy:** *Hannah and Her Sisters*

8961 **Best Foreign Film:** *The Assault*—United Kingdom

8962 **Best Motion Picture Actress**—**Drama:** Marlee Matlin in *Children of a Lesser God*

8963 **Best Motion Picture Actor**—**Drama:** Bob Hoskins in *Mona Lisa*

8964 **Best Motion Picture Actress**—**Musical/Comedy:** Sissy Spacek in *Crimes of the Heart*

8965 **Best Motion Picture Actor**—**Musical/Comedy:** Paul Hogan in *Crocodile Dundee*

8966 **Best Motion Picture Actress in a Supporting Role:** Maggie Smith in *A Room with a View*

8967 **Best Motion Picture Actor in a Supporting Role:** Tom Berenger in *Platoon*

8968 **Best Motion Picture Director:** Oliver Stone for *Platoon*

8969 **Best Motion Picture Screenplay:** Robert Bolt for *The Mission*

8970 **Best Original Motion Picture Score:** Ennio Morricone for *The Mission*

8971 **Best Original Motion Picture Song:** "Take My Breath Away," music by Giorgio Moroder, lyrics by Tom Whitlock

8972 **Cecil B. DeMille Award:** Anthony Quinn

———— **1 9 8 8** ————

8973 **Best Motion Picture**—**Drama:** *The Last Emperor*

8974 **Best Motion Picture**—**Musical/Comedy:** *Hope and Glory*

8975 **Best Foreign Language Film:** *My Life as a Dog*—Sweden

8976 **Best Motion Picture Actress**—**Drama:** Sally Kirkland in *Anna*

8977 **Best Motion Picture Actor**—**Drama:** Michael Douglas in *Wall Street*

8978 **Best Motion Picture Actress**—**Musical/Comedy:** Cher in *Moonstruck*

8979 **Best Motion Picture Actor**—**Musical/Comedy:** Robin Williams in *Good Morning, Vietnam*

8980 **Best Motion Picture Supporting Actress:** Olympia Dukakis in *Moonstruck*

8981 **Best Motion Picture Supporting Actor:** Sean Connery in *The Untouchables*

8982 **Best Motion Picture Director:** Bernardo Bertolucci for *The Last Emperor*

8983 **Best Motion Picture Screenplay:** Mark Peploe and Bernardo Bertolucci for *The Last Emperor*

8984 **Original Motion Picture Score:** Ryuichi Sakamoto, David Byrne and Cong Su for *The Last Emperor*

8985 **Best Original Motion Picture Song:** "(I've Had) the Time of My Life" from *Dirty Dancing*, music and lyrics by Frankie Previte, Donald Markowitz and John DeNicola

8986 **Cecil B. DeMille Award:** Clint Eastwood

———— **1 9 8 9** ————

8987 **Best Motion Picture**—**Drama:** *Rain Man*

8988 **Best Motion Picture**—**Musical/Comedy:** *Working Girl*

8989 **Best Foreign Film:** *Pelle the Conqueror*—Denmark/Sweden

8990 **Best Motion Picture Actress**—**Drama:** Jodie Foster in *The Accused*, Shirley MacLaine in *Madame Sousatzka* and Sigourney Weaver in *Gorillas in the Mist: The Adventures of Diane Fossey*

8991 **Best Motion Picture Actor**—**Drama:** Dustin Hoffman in *Rain Man*

8992 **Best Motion Picture Actress**—**Musical/Comedy:** Melanie Griffith in *Working Girl*

8993 **Best Motion Picture Actor**—**Musical/Comedy:** Tom Hanks in *Big*

8994 **Best Motion Picture Actress in a Supporting Role:** Sigourney Weaver in *Working Girl*

8995 **Best Motion Picture Actor in a Supporting Role:** Martin Landau in *Tucker: The Man and His Dream*

8996 **Best Motion Picture Director:** Clint Eastwood for *Bird*

8997 **Best Motion Picture Screenplay:** Naomi Foner for *Running on Empty*

8998 **Best Original Motion Picture Score:** Maurice Jarre for *Gorillas in the Mist: The Adventures of Diane Fossey*

8999 **Best Original Motion Picture Song:** "Let the River Run" from *Working Girl*, music and lyrics by Carly Simon and "Two Hearts" from *Buster*, music by Lamont Dozier, lyrics by Phil Collins

9000 **Cecil B. DeMille Award:** Doris Day

─────── **1990** ───────

9001 **Best Motion Picture – Drama:** *Born on the Fourth of July*
9002 **Best Motion Picture – Musical/ Comedy:** *Driving Miss Daisy*
9003 **Best Foreign Language Film:** *Cinema Paradiso* – Italy
9004 **Best Motion Picture Actress – Drama:** Michelle Pfeiffer in *The Fabulous Baker Boys*
9005 **Best Motion Picture Actor – Drama:** Tom Cruise in *Born on the Fourth of July*
9006 **Best Motion Picture Actress – Musical/Comedy:** Jessica Tandy in *Driving Miss Daisy*
9007 **Best Motion Picture Actor – Musical/Comedy:** Morgan Freeman in *Driving Miss Daisy*
9008 **Best Motion Picture Supporting Actress:** Julia Roberts in *Steel Magnolias*
9009 **Best Motion Picture Supporting Actor:** Denzel Washington in *Glory*
9010 **Best Motion Picture Director:** Oliver Stone for *Born on the Fourth of July*
9011 **Best Motion Picture Screenplay:** Oliver Stone and Ron Kovic for *Born on the Fourth of July*
9012 **Original Motion Picture Score:** Alan Menken for *The Little Mermaid*
9013 **Best Original Motion Picture Song:** "Under the Sea" from *The Little Mermaid*, music by Alan Menken, lyrics by Howard Ashman
9014 **Cecil B. DeMille Award:** Audrey Hepburn

─────── **1991** ───────

9015 **Best Motion Picture – Drama:** *Dances with Wolves*
9016 **Best Motion Picture – Musical/ Comedy:** *Green Card*
9017 **Best Foreign Film:** *Cyrano de Bergerac* – France
9018 **Best Motion Picture Actress – Drama:** Kathy Bates in *Misery*
9019 **Best Motion Picture Actor – Drama:** Jeremy Irons in *Reversal of Fortune*

9020 **Best Motion Picture Actress – Musical/Comedy:** Julia Roberts in *Pretty Woman*
9021 **Best Motion Picture Actor – Musical/Comedy:** Gerard Depardieu in *Green Card*
9022 **Best Motion Picture Actress in a Supporting Role:** Whoopi Goldberg in *Ghost*
9023 **Best Motion Picture Actor in a Supporting Role:** Bruce Davison in *Longtime Companion*
9024 **Best Motion Picture Director:** Kevin Costner for *Dances with Wolves*
9025 **Best Motion Picture Screenplay:** Michael Blake for *Dances with Wolves*
9026 **Best Original Motion Picture Score:** Ryuichi Sakamoto and Richard Horowitz for *The Sheltering Sky*
9027 **Best Original Motion Picture Song:** "Blaze of Glory" from *Young Guns II*, music and lyrics by Jon Bon Jovi
9028 **Cecil B. DeMille Award:** Jack Lemmon

─────── **1992** ───────

9029 **Best Motion Picture – Drama:** *Bugsy*
9030 **Best Motion Picture – Musical/ Comedy:** *Beauty and the Beast*
9031 **Best Foreign Language Film:** *Europa, Europa* – Germany
9032 **Best Motion Picture Actress – Drama:** Jodie Foster in *The Silence of the Lambs*
9033 **Best Motion Picture Actor – Drama:** Nick Nolte in *The Prince of Tides*
9034 **Best Motion Picture Actress – Musical/Comedy:** Bette Midler in *For the Boys*
9035 **Best Motion Picture Actor – Musical/Comedy:** Robin Williams in *The Fisher King*
9036 **Best Motion Picture Supporting Actress:** Mercedes Ruehl in *The Fisher King*
9037 **Best Motion Picture Supporting Actor:** Jack Palance in *City Slickers*
9038 **Best Motion Picture Director:** Oliver Stone for *JFK*
9039 **Best Motion Picture Screenplay:** Callie Khouri for *Thelma & Louise*
9040 **Original Motion Picture Score:** Alan Menken for *Beauty and the Beast*

9041 **Best Original Motion Picture Song:** "Beauty and the Beast" from *Beauty and the Beast*, music by Alan Menken, lyrics by Howard Ashman

9042 **Cecil B. DeMille Award:** Robert Mitchum

─────── **1 9 9 3** ───────

9043 **Best Motion Picture—Drama:** *Scent of a Woman*

9044 **Best Motion Picture—Musical/Comedy:** *The Player*

9045 **Best Foreign Language Film:** *Indochine*—France

9046 **Best Motion Picture Actress—Drama:** Emma Thompson in *Howards End*

9047 **Best Motion Picture Actor—Drama:** Al Pacino in *Scent of a Woman*

9048 **Best Motion Picture Actress—Musical/Comedy:** Miranda Richardson in *Enchanted April*

9049 **Best Motion Picture Actor—Musical/Comedy:** Tim Robbins in *The Player*

9050 **Best Motion Picture Supporting Actress:** Joan Plowright in *Enchanted April*

9051 **Best Motion Picture Supporting Actor:** Gene Hackman in *Unforgiven*

9052 **Best Motion Picture Director:** Clint Eastwood for *Unforgiven*

9053 **Best Motion Picture Screenplay:** Bo Goldman for *Scent of a Woman*

9054 **Original Motion Picture Score:** Alan Menken for *Aladdin*

9055 **Best Original Motion Picture Song:** "A Whole New World" from *Aladdin*, music by Alan Menken, lyrics by Tim Rice

9056 **Cecil B. DeMille Award:** Robert Mitchum

New York Film Critics' Circle Awards

The New York Drama Critics' Circle has been recognizing achievements in film since 1935. The current committee is made up of film writers and film critics working for New York magazines and newspapers. This includes reviewers from the *New York* magazine, the *Village Voice* newspaper, *Newsday*, *Time* magazine, *Newsweek* magazine, the *Wall Street Journal* and other New York-based publications. The *New York Times* newspaper has long been a member of the Film Critics' Circle but has not voted since 1989.

The awards are presented in December of each year in a ceremony usually held at Sardi's Restaurant. In 1987, a new category for the best new director was added. Different from many other awards systems, the voting uses a system of weighted ballots. Ballots are marked for three films in each category with one, two or three points being awarded for 3rd, 2nd and 1st places respectively.

Since the awards from the New York Film Critics' Circle are announced before the Academy Awards, they frequently are an indicator of the Oscars.

——————— **1 9 3 5** ———————

9057 **Best Picture:** *The Informer*
9058 **Best Actor:** Charles Laughton in *Mutiny on the Bounty* and *Ruggles of Red Gap*
9059 **Best Actress:** Greta Garbo in *Anna Karenina*
9060 **Best Direction:** John Ford for *The Informer*

——————— **1 9 3 6** ———————

9061 **Best Picture:** *Mr. Deeds Goes to Town*
9062 **Best Actor:** Walter Huston in *Dodsworth*
9063 **Best Actress:** Luise Rainer in *The Great Ziegfeld*
9064 **Best Direction:** Rouben Mamoulian for *The Gay Desperado*
9065 **Best Foreign Language Film:** *La Kermesse Héroïque* — France

——————— **1 9 3 7** ———————

9066 **Best Picture:** *The Life of Emile Zola*
9067 **Best Actor:** Paul Muni in *The Life of Emile Zola*
9068 **Best Actress:** Greta Garbo in *Camille*
9069 **Best Direction:** Gregory La Cave for *Stage Door*
9070 **Best Foreign Language Film:** *Mayerling* — France

——————— **1 9 3 8** ———————

9071 **Best Picture:** *The Citadel*
9072 **Best Actor:** James Cagney in *Angels with Dirty Faces*
9073 **Best Actress:** Margaret Sullavan in *Three Comrades*
9074 **Best Direction:** Alfred Hitchcock for *The Lady Vanishes*
9075 **Best Foreign Language Film:** *Grande Illusion* — France

——————— **1 9 3 9** ———————

9076 **Best Picture:** *Wuthering Heights*
9077 **Best Actor:** James Stewart in *Mr. Smith Goes to Washington*
9078 **Best Actress:** Vivien Leigh in *Gone with the Wind*

9079 **Best Direction:** John Ford for *Stagecoach*
9080 **Best Foreign Language Film:** *Harvest* — France

——————— **1 9 4 0** ———————

9081 **Best Picture:** *The Grapes of Wrath*
9082 **Best Actor:** Charles Chaplin in *The Great Dictator*
9083 **Best Actress:** Katharine Hepburn in *The Philadelphia Story*
9084 **Best Direction:** John Ford for *The Grapes of Wrath* and *The Long Voyage Home*
9085 **Best Foreign Language Film:** *The Baker's Wife* — France

——————— **1 9 4 1** ———————

9086 **Best Picture:** *Citizen Kane*
9087 **Best Actor:** Gary Cooper in *Sergeant York*
9088 **Best Actress:** Joan Fontaine in *Suspicion*
9089 **Best Direction:** John Ford for *How Green Was My Valley*

——————— **1 9 4 2** ———————

9090 **Best Picture:** *In Which We Serve*
9091 **Best Actor:** James Cagney in *Yankee Doodle Dandy*
9092 **Best Actress:** Agnes Moorehead in *The Magnificent Ambersons*
9093 **Best Direction:** John Farrow for *Wake Island*

——————— **1 9 4 3** ———————

9094 **Best Picture:** *Watch on the Rhine*
9095 **Best Actor:** Paul Lukas in *Watch on the Rhine*
9096 **Best Actress:** Ida Lupino in *The Hard Way*
9097 **Best Direction:** George Stevens for *The More the Merrier*

——————— **1 9 4 4** ———————

9098 **Best Picture:** *Going My Way*
9099 **Best Actor:** Barry Fitzgerald in *Going My Way*
9100 **Best Actress:** Tallulah Bankhead in *Lifeboat*

9101 **Best Direction:** Leo McCarey for *Going My Way*

——————— **1 9 4 5** ———————

9102 **Best Picture:** *The Lost Weekend*
9103 **Best Actor:** Ray Milland in *The Lost Weekend*
9104 **Best Actress:** Ingrid Bergman in *Spellbound* and *The Bells of St. Mary's*
9105 **Best Direction:** Billy Wilder for *The Lost Weekend*

——————— **1 9 4 6** ———————

9106 **Best Picture:** *The Best Years of Our Lives*
9107 **Best Actor:** Laurence Olivier in *Henry V*
9108 **Best Actress:** Celia Johnson in *Brief Encounter*
9109 **Best Direction:** William Wyler for *The Best Years of Our Lives*
9110 **Best Foreign Language Film:** *Open City* — Italy

——————— **1 9 4 7** ———————

9111 **Best Picture:** *Gentleman's Agreement*
9112 **Best Actor:** William Powell in *Life with Father* and *The Senator Was Indiscreet*
9113 **Best Actress:** Deborah Kerr in *Black Narcissus* and *The Adventuress*
9114 **Best Direction:** Elia Kazan for *Gentleman's Agreement* and *Boomerang*
9115 **Best Foreign Language Film:** *To Live in Peace* — Italy

——————— **1 9 4 8** ———————

9116 **Best Picture:** *Treasure of the Sierra Madre*
9117 **Best Actor:** Laurence Olivier in *Hamlet*
9118 **Best Actress:** Olivia de Havilland in *The Snake Pit*
9119 **Best Direction:** John Huston for *Treasure of the Sierra Madre*
9120 **Best Foreign Language Film:** *Paisan* — Italy

——————— **1 9 4 9** ———————

9121 **Best Picture:** *All the King's Men*
9122 **Best Actor:** Broderick Crawford in *All the King's Men*
9123 **Best Actress:** Olivia de Havilland in *The Heiress*
9124 **Best Direction:** Carol Reed for *The Fallen Idol*
9125 **Best Foreign Language Film:** *The Bicycle Thief* — Italy

——————— **1 9 5 0** ———————

9126 **Best Picture:** *All About Eve*
9127 **Best Actor:** Gregory Peck in *Twelve O'Clock High*
9128 **Best Actress:** Bette Davis in *All About Eve*
9129 **Best Direction:** Joseph L. Mankiewicz for *All About Eve*
9130 **Best Foreign Language Film:** *Ways of Love* — France-Italy

——————— **1 9 5 1** ———————

9131 **Best Picture:** *A Streetcar Named Desire*
9132 **Best Actor:** Arthur Kennedy in *Bright Victory*
9133 **Best Actress:** Vivien Leigh in *A Streetcar Named Desire*
9134 **Best Direction:** Elia Kazan for *A Streetcar Named Desire*
9135 **Best Foreign Language Film:** *Miracle of Milan* — Italy

——————— **1 9 5 2** ———————

9136 **Best Picture:** *High Noon*
9137 **Best Actor:** Ralph Richardson in *Breaking the Sound Barrier*
9138 **Best Actress:** Shirley Booth in *Come Back, Little Sheba*
9139 **Best Direction:** Fred Zinnemann for *High Noon*
9140 **Best Foreign Language Film:** *Forbidden Games* — France

——————— **1 9 5 3** ———————

9141 **Best Picture:** *From Here to Eternity*
9142 **Best Actor:** Burt Lancaster in *From Here to Eternity*

9143 **Best Actress:** Audrey Hepburn in *Roman Holiday*
9144 **Best Direction:** Fred Zinnemann for *From Here to Eternity*
9145 **Best Foreign Language Film:** *Justice Is Done* — France

——————— **1 9 5 4** ———————

9146 **Best Picture:** *On the Waterfront*
9147 **Best Actor:** Marlon Brando in *On the Waterfront*
9148 **Best Actress:** Grace Kelly in *The Country Girl*, *Rear Window* and *Dial M for Murder*
9149 **Best Direction:** Elia Kazan for *On the Waterfront*
9150 **Best Foreign Language Film:** *Gate of Hell* — Japan

——————— **1 9 5 5** ———————

9151 **Best Picture:** *Marty*
9152 **Best Actor:** Ernest Borgnine in *Marty*
9153 **Best Actress:** Anna Magnani in *The Rose Tattoo*
9154 **Best Direction:** David Lean for *Summertime*
9155 **Best Foreign Language Film:** *Diabolique* — France and *Umberto D.* — Italy

——————— **1 9 5 6** ———————

9156 **Best Picture:** *Around the World in 80 Days*
9157 **Best Actor:** Kirk Douglas in *Lust for Life*
9158 **Best Actress:** Ingrid Bergman in *Anastasia*
9159 **Best Direction:** John Huston for *Moby Dick*
9160 **Best Foreign Language Film:** *La Strada* — Italy

——————— **1 9 5 7** ———————

9161 **Best Picture:** *The Bridge on the River Kwai*
9162 **Best Actor:** Alec Guinness in *The Bridge on the River Kwai*
9163 **Best Actress:** Deborah Kerr in *Heaven Knows, Mr. Allison*
9164 **Best Direction:** David Lean for *The Bridge on the River Kwai*

9165 **Best Foreign Language Film:** *Gervaise* — France

——————— **1 9 5 8** ———————

9166 **Best Picture:** *The Defiant Ones*
9167 **Best Actor:** David Niven in *Separate Tables*
9168 **Best Actress:** Susan Hayward in *I Want to Live!*
9169 **Best Direction:** Stanley Kramer for *The Defiant Ones*
9170 **Best Foreign Language Film:** *Mon Oncle* — France
9171 **Best Screenplay Writing:** Nathan E. Douglas and Harold J. Smith for *The Defiant Ones*

——————— **1 9 5 9** ———————

9172 **Best Picture:** *Ben-Hur*
9173 **Best Actor:** James Stewart in *Anatomy of a Murder*
9174 **Best Actress:** Audrey Hepburn in *The Nun's Story*
9175 **Best Direction:** Fred Zinnemann for *The Nun's Story*
9176 **Best Foreign Language Film:** *The 400 Blows* — France
9177 **Best Screenplay Writing:** Wendell Mayes for *Anatomy of a Murder*

——————— **1 9 6 0** ———————

9178 **Best Picture:** *The Apartment* and *Sons and Lovers*
9179 **Best Actor:** Burt Lancaster in *Elmer Gantry*
9180 **Best Actress:** Deborah Kerr in *The Sundowners*
9181 **Best Direction:** Billy Wilder for *The Apartment* and Jack Cardiff for *Sons and Lovers*
9182 **Best Foreign Language Film:** *La Dolce Vita* — Italy
9183 **Best Screenplay Writing:** Billy Wilder and I.A.L. Diamond for *The Apartment*

——————— **1 9 6 1** ———————

9184 **Best Picture:** *West Side Story*
9185 **Best Actor:** Maximillian Schell in *Judgment at Nuremberg*
9186 **Best Actress:** Sophia Loren in *Two Women*

9187 **Best Direction:** Robert Rossen for *The Hustler*
9188 **Best Screenplay Writing:** Abby Mann for *Judgment at Nuremberg*

――――――― **1 9 6 2** ―――――――

No awards made.

――――――― **1 9 6 3** ―――――――

9189 **Best Picture:** *Tom Jones*
9190 **Best Actor:** Albert Finney in *Tom Jones*
9191 **Best Actress:** Patricia Neal in *Hud*
9192 **Best Direction:** Tony Richardson for *Tom Jones*
9193 **Best Foreign Language Film:** *8½* – Italy
9194 **Best Screenplay Writing:** Irving Raveton and Harriet Frank, Jr. for *Hud*

――――――― **1 9 6 4** ―――――――

9195 **Best Picture:** *My Fair Lady*
9196 **Best Actor:** Rex Harrison in *My Fair Lady*
9197 **Best Actress:** Kim Stanley in *Séance on a Wet Afternoon*
9198 **Best Direction:** Stanley Kubrick for *Dr. Strangelove*
9199 **Best Foreign Language Film:** *That Man from Rio* – France
9200 **Best Screenplay Writing:** Harold Pinter for *The Servant*
9201 **Special Award:** *To Be Alive!* film at Johnson Wax pavilion at New York World's Fair

――――――― **1 9 6 5** ―――――――

9202 **Best Picture:** *Darling*
9203 **Best Actor:** Oskar Werner in *Ship of Fools*
9204 **Best Actress:** Julie Christie in *Darling*
9205 **Best Direction:** John Schlesinger for *Darling*
9206 **Best Foreign Language Film:** *Juliet of the Spirits* – Italy

――――――― **1 9 6 6** ―――――――

9207 **Best Picture:** *A Man for All Seasons*

9208 **Best Actor:** Paul Scofield in *A Man for All Seasons*
9209 **Best Actress:** Elizabeth Taylor in *Who's Afraid of Virginia Woolf?* and Lynn Redgrave in *Georgy Girl*
9210 **Best Direction:** Fred Zinnemann for *A Man for All Seasons*
9211 **Best Foreign Language Film:** *The Shop on Main Street* – Czechoslovakia
9212 **Best Screenplay Writing:** Robert Bolt for *A Man for All Seasons*

――――――― **1 9 6 7** ―――――――

9213 **Best Picture:** *In the Heat of the Night*
9214 **Best Actor:** Rod Steiger in *In the Heat of the Night*
9215 **Best Actress:** Dame Edith Evans in *The Whisperers*
9216 **Best Direction:** Mike Nichols for *The Graduate*
9217 **Best Foreign Language Film:** *La Guerre Est Finie* – France
9218 **Best Screenplay Writing:** David Newman and Robert Benton for *Bonnie and Clyde*

――――――― **1 9 6 8** ―――――――

9219 **Best Picture:** *The Lion in Winter*
9220 **Best Actor:** Alan Arkin in *The Heart Is a Lonely Hunter*
9221 **Best Actress:** Joanne Woodward in *Rachel, Rachel*
9222 **Best Direction:** Paul Newman for *Rachel, Rachel*
9223 **Best Foreign Language Film:** *War and Peace* – Russia
9224 **Best Screenplay Writing:** Lorenzo Semple, Jr., for *Pretty Poison*

――――――― **1 9 6 9** ―――――――

9225 **Best Picture:** *Z*
9226 **Best Actor:** Jon Voight in *Midnight Cowboy*
9227 **Best Actress:** Jane Fonda in *They Shoot Horses, Don't They?*
9228 **Best Direction:** Costa-Gavras for *Z*
9229 **Best Screenplay Writing:** Paul Mazursky and Larry Tucker for *Bob & Carol & Ted & Alice*

──────── **1 9 7 0** ────────

9230 **Best Picture:** *Five Easy Pieces*
9231 **Best Actor:** George C. Scott in *Patton*
9232 **Best Actress:** Glenda Jackson in *Women in Love*
9233 **Best Direction:** Bob Rafelson for *Five Easy Pieces*
9234 **Best Screenplay Writing:** Eric Rohmer for *Ma Nuit Chez Maude*

──────── **1 9 7 1** ────────

9235 **Best Picture:** *A Clockwork Orange*
9236 **Best Actor:** Gene Hackman in *French Connection*
9237 **Best Actress:** Jane Fonda in *Klute*
9238 **Best Direction:** Stanley Kubrick for *A Clockwork Orange*
9239 **Best Screenplay Writing:** Penelope Gilliatt for *Sunday, Bloody Sunday* and Larry McMurtry and Peter Bogdanovich for *The Last Picture Show*

──────── **1 9 7 2** ────────

9240 **Best Picture:** *Cries and Whispers*
9241 **Best Actor:** Laurence Olivier in *Sleuth*
9242 **Best Actress:** Liv Ullman in *Cries and Whispers*
9243 **Best Direction:** Ingmar Bergman for *Cries and Whispers*
9244 **Best Screenplay Writing:** Ingmar Bergman for *Cries and Whispers*
9245 **Best Supporting Actor:** Robert Duvall in *The Godfather*
9246 **Best Supporting Actress:** Jeannie Berlin in *The Heartbreak Kid*
9247 **Special Award:** *The Sorrow and the Pity*—documentary from France

──────── **1 9 7 3** ────────

9248 **Best Picture:** *Day for Night*
9249 **Best Actor:** Marlon Brando in *The Godfather*
9250 **Best Actress:** Joanne Woodward in *Summer Wishes, Winter Dreams*
9251 **Best Direction:** François Truffaut for *Day for Night*
9252 **Best Screenplay Writing:** George

Lucas, Gloria Katz and Willard Huyck for *American Graffiti*
9253 **Best Supporting Actor:** Robert De Niro in *Mean Streets*
9254 **Best Supporting Actress:** Valentina Cortese in *Day for Night*

──────── **1 9 7 4** ────────

9255 **Best Picture:** *Amarcord*
9256 **Best Actor:** Jack Nicholson in *Chinatown*
9257 **Best Actress:** Liv Ullman in *Scenes from a Marriage*
9258 **Best Direction:** Federico Fellini for *Amarcord*
9259 **Best Screenplay Writing:** Ingmar Bergman for *Scenes from a Marriage*
9260 **Best Supporting Actor:** Charles Boyer in *Stavisky*
9261 **Best Supporting Actress:** Valerie Perrine in *Lenny*

──────── **1 9 7 5** ────────

9262 **Best Picture:** *Nashville*
9263 **Best Actor:** Jack Nicholson in *One Flew Over the Cuckoo's Nest*
9264 **Best Actress:** Isabelle Adjani in *The Story of Adele H*
9265 **Best Direction:** Robert Altman for *Nashville*
9266 **Best Screenplay Writing:** François Truffaut, Jean Gruault and Suzanne Schiffman for *The Story of Adele H*
9267 **Best Supporting Actor:** Alan Arkin in *Hearts of the West*
9268 **Best Supporting Actress:** Lily Tomlin in *Nashville*

──────── **1 9 7 6** ────────

9269 **Best Picture:** *All the President's Men*
9270 **Best Actor:** Robert de Niro in *Taxi Driver*
9271 **Best Actress:** Liv Ullman in *Face to Face*
9272 **Best Direction:** Alan J. Pakula for *All the President's Men*
9273 **Best Screenplay Writing:** Paddy Chayefsky for *Network*
9274 **Best Supporting Actor:** Jason Robards, Jr., in *All the President's Men*

9275 **Best Supporting Actress:** Talia Shire in *Rocky*

──────── **1 9 7 7** ────────

9276 **Best Picture:** *Annie Hall*
9277 **Best Actor:** Sir John Gielgud in *Providence*
9278 **Best Actress:** Diane Keaton in *Annie Hall*
9279 **Best Direction:** Woody Allen for *Annie Hall*
9280 **Best Screenplay Writing:** Woody Allen and Marshall Brickman for *Annie Hall*
9281 **Best Supporting Actor:** Maximillian Schell in *Julia*
9282 **Best Supporting Actress:** Sissy Spacek in *Three Women*

──────── **1 9 7 8** ────────

9283 **Best Picture:** *The Deer Hunter*
9284 **Best Foreign Film:** *Bread & Chocolate* — Italy
9285 **Best Actress:** Ingrid Bergman in *Autumn Sonata*
9286 **Best Actor:** Jon Voight in *Coming Home*
9287 **Best Director:** Terrence Malick for *Days of Heaven*
9288 **Best Supporting Actor:** Christopher Walken in *The Deer Hunter*
9289 **Best Supporting Actress:** Maureen Stapleton in *Interiors*
9290 **Best Screenplay:** Paul Mazursky for *An Unmarried Woman*

──────── **1 9 7 9** ────────

9291 **Best Picture:** *Breaking Away*
9292 **Best Actor:** Dustin Hoffman in *Kramer vs. Kramer* and *Agatha*
9293 **Best Actress:** Sally Field in *Norma Rae*
9294 **Best Director:** Woody Allen for *Manhattan* and Robert Benton for *Kramer vs. Kramer*
9295 **Best Supporting Actor:** Frederic Forrest in *Apocalypse Now* and *The Rose*
9296 **Best Supporting Actress:** Meryl Streep in *Kramer vs. Kramer, The Seduction of Joe Tynan* and *Manhattan*
9297 **Best Cinematography:** Caleb Deschanel for *The Black Stallion* and *Being There*

9298 **Best Screenplay:** Steve Tesich for *Breaking Away*

──────── **1 9 8 0** ────────

9299 **Best Film:** *Ordinary People*
9300 **Best Actor:** Robert De Niro in *Raging Bull*
9301 **Best Actress:** Sissy Spacek in *Coal Miner's Daughter*
9302 **Best Director:** Jonathan Demme for *Melvin & Howard*
9303 **Best Screenplay:** Bo Goldman for *Melvin & Howard*
9304 **Best Supporting Actress:** Mary Steenburgen in *Melvin & Howard*
9305 **Best Supporting Actor:** Joe Pesci in *Raging Bull*
9306 **Best Foreign Film:** *Mon Oncle d'Amérique* — France
9307 **Best Documentary:** *Best Boy*
9308 **Best Cinematography:** Ghislain Cloquet and Geoffrey Unsworth for *Tess*

──────── **1 9 8 1** ────────

9309 **Best Film:** *Reds*
9310 **Best Actor:** Burt Lancaster in *Atlantic City*
9311 **Best Actress:** Glenda Jackson in *Stevie*
9312 **Best Supporting Actress:** Mona Washbourne in *Stevie*
9313 **Best Supporting Actor:** John Gielgud in *Arthur*
9314 **Best Director:** Sidney Lumet for *Prince of the City*
9315 **Best Screenwriting:** John Guare for *Atlantic City*
9316 **Best Cinematography:** *Chariots of Fire*
9317 **Best Foreign Film:** *Pixote* — Brazil

──────── **1 9 8 2** ────────

9318 **Best Picture:** *Gandhi*
9319 **Best Actor:** Ben Kingsley in *Gandhi*
9320 **Best Actress:** Meryl Streep in *Sophie's Choice*
9321 **Best Director:** Sydney Pollack for *Tootsie*
9322 **Best Screenplay:** Larry Gelbart and Murray Schisgal for *Tootsie*

9323 **Best Supporting Actress:** Jessica Lange in *Tootsie*

9324 **Best Supporting Actor:** John Lithgow in *The World According to Garp*

9325 **Best Cinematography:** Nestor Almendros for *Sophie's Choice*

9326 **Best Foreign Film:** *Time Stands Still* — Hungary

——————— **1 9 8 3** ———————

9327 **Best Picture:** *Terms of Endearment*

9328 **Best Foreign Film:** *Fanny and Alexander* — Sweden

9329 **Best Director:** Ingmar Bergman for *Fanny and Alexander*

9330 **Best Actress:** Shirley MacLaine in *Terms of Endearment*

9331 **Best Actor:** Robert Duvall in *Tender Mercies*

9332 **Best Supporting Actor:** Jack Nicholson in *Terms of Endearment*

9333 **Best Supporting Actress:** Linda Hunt in *The Year of Living Dangerously*

9334 **Best Screenplay:** Bill Forsyth for *Local Hero*

9335 **Best Cinematography:** Gordon Willis for *Zelig*

——————— **1 9 8 4** ———————

9336 **Best Picture:** *A Passage to India*

9337 **Best Director:** David Lean for *A Passage to India*

9338 **Best Actress:** Peggy Ashcroft in *A Passage to India*

9339 **Best Actor:** Steve Martin in *All of Me*

9340 **Best Supporting Actress:** Christine Lahti in *Swing Shift*

9341 **Best Supporting Actor:** Sir Ralph Richardson in *Greystoke*

9342 **Best Screenplay:** Robert Benton for *Places in the Heart*

9343 **Best Cinematography:** Chris Menges for *The Killing Fields*

9344 **Best Foreign Film:** *Sunday in the Country*

9345 **Best Documentary:** *The Life and Times of Harvey Milk*

——————— **1 9 8 5** ———————

9346 **Best Picture:** *Prizzi's Honor*

9347 **Best Director:** John Huston for *Prizzi's Honor*

9348 **Best Actress:** Norma Aleandro in *The Official Story*

9349 **Best Actor:** Jack Nicholson in *Prizzi's Honor*

9350 **Best Supporting Actress:** Angelica Huston in *Prizzi's Honor*

9351 **Best Supporting Actor:** Klaus Maria Brandauer in *Out of Africa*

9352 **Best Screenplay:** Woody Allen for *The Purple Rose of Cairo*

9353 **Best Cinematography:** David Watkin for *Out of Africa*

9354 **Best Foreign Film:** *Ran*

9355 **Best Documentary:** *Shoah*

——————— **1 9 8 6** ———————

9356 **Best Picture:** *Hannah and Her Sisters*

9357 **Best Director:** Woody Allen for *Hannah and Her Sisters*

9358 **Best Actress:** Sissy Spacek in *Crimes of the Heart*

9359 **Best Actor:** Bob Hoskins in *Mona Lisa*

9360 **Best Supporting Actress:** Diane Wiest in *Hannah and Her Sisters*

9361 **Best Supporting Actor:** Daniel Day Lewis in *A Room with a View*

9362 **Best Screenplay:** *My Beautiful Laundrette*

9363 **Best Cinematography:** *A Room with a View*

9364 **Best Foreign Film:** *The Decline of the American Empire*

9365 **Best Documentary:** *Marlene*

——————— **1 9 8 7** ———————

9366 **Best Picture:** *Broadcast News*

9367 **Best Director:** James L. Brooks for *Broadcast News*

9368 **Best Actress:** Holly Hunter in *Broadcast News*

9369 **Best Actor:** Jack Nicholson in *Broadcast News, Ironweed* and *The Witches of Eastwick*

9370 **Best Supporting Actress:** Vanessa Redgrave in *Prick Up Your Ears*

9371 **Best Supporting Actor:** Morgan Freeman in *Street Smart*

9372 **Best Screenplay:** James L. Brooks for *Broadcast News*

─────── **1 9 8 8** ───────

9373 **Best Picture:** *Accidental Tourist*
9374 **Best Director:** Chris Menges for *A World Apart*
9375 **Best Actress:** Meryl Streep in *A Cry in the Dark*
9376 **Best Actor:** Jeremy Irons in *Dead Ringers*
9377 **Best Supporting Actress:** Diane Venora in *Bird*
9378 **Best Supporting Actor:** Dean Stockwell in *Tucker: The Man and His Dream* and *Married to the Mob*
9379 **Best Screenplay:** *Bull Durham*
9380 **Best Cinematography:** Henri Alekan for *Wings of Desire*
9381 **Best Foreign Film:** *Women on the Verge of a Nervous Breakdown*
9382 **Best Documentary:** *Thin Blue Line*

─────── **1 9 8 9** ───────

9383 **Best Picture:** *My Left Foot*
9384 **Best Director:** Paul Mazursky for *Enemies, a Love Story*
9385 **Best Actress:** Michelle Pfeiffer in *The Fabulous Baker Boys*
9386 **Best Actor:** Daniel Day Lewis in *My Left Foot*
9387 **Best Supporting Actress:** Lena Olin in *Enemies, a Love Story*
9388 **Best Supporting Actor:** Alan Alda in *Crimes and Misdemeanors*
9389 **Best Screenplay:** Gus Van Sandt, Jr., and Daniel Yost for *Drugstore Cowboy*
9390 **Best Cinematography:** Ernest Dickerson for *Do the Right Thing*
9391 **Best Foreign Film:** *Story of Women*
9392 **Best Documentary:** *Roger and Me*
9393 **Best New Director:** Kenneth Branagh for *Henry V*

─────── **1 9 9 0** ───────

9394 **Best Picture:** *Goodfellas*
9395 **Best Actor:** Robert de Niro in *Awakenings* and *Goodfellas*
9396 **Best Actress:** Joanne Woodward in *Mr. and Mrs. Bridge*
9397 **Best Director:** Martin Scorsese for *Goodfellas*
9398 **Best Supporting Actor:** Bruce Davison in *Longtime Companion*
9399 **Best Supporting Actress:** Jennifer Jason Leigh in *Miami Blues* and *Last Exit to Brooklyn*
9400 **Best Screenplay:** Ruth Prawer Jhabvala for *Mr. and Mrs. Bridge*
9401 **Best Foreign Film:** *The Nasty Girl*
9402 **Best Cinematography:** Vittorio Storaro for *The Sheltering Sky*
9403 **Best New Director:** Whit Stillman for *Metropolitan*
9404 **Special Award:** Bruce Goldstein and Karen Cooper, programmers at the New York Theatre Film Forum

─────── **1 9 9 1** ───────

9405 **Best Picture:** *Silence of the Lambs*
9406 **Best Director:** Jonathan Demme for *Silence of the Lambs*
9407 **Best Actor:** Anthony Hopkins in *Silence of the Lambs*
9408 **Best Actress:** Jodie Foster in *Silence of the Lambs*
9409 **Best Supporting Actor:** Samuel Jackson in *Jungle Fever*
9410 **Best Supporting Actress:** Judy Davis in *Barton Fink* and *Naked Lunch*
9411 **Best Screenplay:** David Cronenberg for *Naked Lunch*
9412 **Best Foreign Film:** *Europa, Europa* – Germany
9413 **Best Cinematography:** Roger Deakins for *Barton Fink*
9414 **Best Documentary:** *Paris Is Burning*
9415 **Best First Time Director:** John Singleton for *Boyz N the Hood*

─────── **1 9 9 2** ───────

9416 **Best Picture:** *The Player*
9417 **Best Director:** Robert Altman for *The Player*
9418 **Best Actress:** Emma Thompson in *Howards End*
9419 **Best Actor:** Denzel Washington in *Malcolm X*
9420 **Best Supporting Actress:** Miranda Richardson in *The Crying Game, Damage* and *Enchanted April*

9421 **Best Supporting Actor:** Gene Hackman in *Unforgiven*

9422 **Best Screenplay:** *The Crying Game*

9423 **Best Cinematography:** Jean Lerine for *The Player*

9424 **Best Foreign Film:** *Raise the Red Lantern*

9425 **Best Documentary:** *Brothers Keeper*

9426 **Best New Director:** Allison Anders for *Gas Food Lodging*

———————— **1 9 9 3** ————————

9427 **Best Picture:** *Schindler's List*

9428 **Best Actor:** David Thewlis in *Naked*

9429 **Best Actress:** Holly Hunter in *The Piano*

9430 **Best Direction:** Jane Campion for *The Piano*

9431 **Best Screenplay Writing:** Jane Campion for *The Piano*

9432 **Best Supporting Actor:** Ralph Fiennes in *Schindler's List*

9433 **Best Supporting Actress:** Gong Li in *Farewell My Concubine*

9434 **Best Cinematography:** Janusz Kaminski for *Schindler's List*

9435 **Best Foreign Language Film:** *Farewell My Concubine*

9436 **Best Documentary:** *Visions of Light*

Part Four

THEATRE

The Antoinette Perry (Tony) Awards

Antoinette Perry died in 1946 following many years of service as chairwoman of the board and secretary of the American Theatre Wing. A member of the men's executive committee for the American Theatre Wing suggested that the Wing initiate a series of awards for theatrical excellence in memory of Antoinette Perry.

The first awards were given on Easter Sunday in 1947. They consisted of a scroll along with either a cigarette lighter or a compact. The familiar silver medallion did not make its first appearance for another two years.

In 1967 the Wing authorized the League of American Theatres to plan and carry out the award ceremonies and present the awards. For almost 20 years the ceremonies had been held in the ballroom of a New York hotel. The League, recognizing them as an important vehicle advertising New York theatres, moved the ceremonies to a Broadway theatre.

The Tony Awards represent a high point in the history of award presentations. Each show is tightly planned and produced. A lot of waiting for recipients to come to stage is eliminated by seating nominees on the aisle.

When arriving at the podium, an unofficial policy is followed — keeping the acceptance speech brief. This helps to keep the awards presentations professional.

Throughout the years, the categories have changed with new ones replacing older ones no longer applicable. This allows the awards to recognize the various achievements of each season. It also allows the viewer to see some of the best of that year's productions.

--------- **1947** ---------

9437 **Dramatic Actor:** Jose Ferrer in *Cyrano de Bergerac* and Fredric March in *Years Ago*

9438 **Dramatic Actress:** Ingrid Bergman in *Joan of Lorraine* and Helen Hayes in *Happy Birthday*

9439 **Supporting or Featured Dramatic Actress:** Patricia Neal in *Another Part of the Forest*

9440 **Supporting or Featured Musical Actor:** David Wayne in *Finian's Rainbow*

9441 **Director:** Elia Kazan for *All My Sons*

9442 **Costumes:** David Ffolkes for *Henry VIII* and Lucinda Ballard for *Happy Birthday, Another Part of the Forest, Street Scene, John Loves Mary,* and *The Chocolate Soldier*

9443 **Choreographers:** Agnes DeMille for *Brigadoon* and Michael Kidd for *Finian's Rainbow*

9444 **Special Awards:** Dora Chamberlain, Mr. and Mrs. Ira Katzenberg, Jules Leventhal, Burns Mantle, P. A. MacDonald, Arthur Miller, Vincent Sardi, Sr. and Kurt Weill

--------- **1948** ---------

9445 **Dramatic Actor:** Henry Fonda in *Mister Roberts*, Paul Kelly in *Command Decision* and Basil Rathbone in *The Heiress*

9446 **Dramatic Actress:** Judith Anderson in *Medea*, Katharine Cornell in *Antony and Cleopatra* and Jessica Tandy in *A Streetcar Named Desire*

9447 **Musical Actor:** Paul Hartman in *Angel in the Wings*

9448 **Musical Actress:** Grace Hartman in *Angel in the Wings*

9449 **Play:** *Mister Roberts* by Thomas Heggen and Joshua Logan/based on the novel by Thomas Heggen

9450 **Producer:** Leland Hayward for *Mister Roberts*

9451 **Authors:** Thomas Heggen and Joshua Logan for *Mister Roberts*

9452 **Costumes:** Mary Percy Schenck for *The Heiress*

9453 **Scenic Designer:** Horace Armistead for *The Medium*

9454 **Choreographer:** Jerome Robbins for *High Button Shoes*

9455 **Stage Technicians:** George Gebhardt and George Pierce

9456 **Special Awards:** Vera Allen, Paul Beisman, Joe E. Brown, Robert Dowling, Experimental Theatre, Incorporated, Rosamond Gilder, June Lockhart, Mary Martin, Robert Porterfield and James Whitmore

--------- **1949** ---------

9457 **Dramatic Actor:** Rex Harrison in *Anne of the Thousand Days*

9458 **Dramatic Actress:** Martita Hunt in *The Madwoman of Chaillot*

9459 **Supporting or Featured Dramatic Actor:** Arthur Kennedy in *Death of a Salesman*

9460 **Supporting or Featured Dramatic Actress:** Shirley Booth in *Goodbye, My Fancy*

9461 **Musical Actor:** Ray Bolger in *Where's Charley?*

9462 **Musical Actress:** Nanette Fabray in *Love Life*

9463 **Play:** *Death of a Salesman* by Arthur Miller

9464 **Dramatic Producers:** Kermit Bloomgarden and Walter Fried for *Death of a Salesman*

9465 **Author:** Arthur Miller for *Death of a Salesman*

9466 **Musical:** *Kiss Me Kate* music and lyrics by Cole Porter, book by Bella and Samuel Spewack

9467 **Musical Producers:** Saint-Subber and Lemuel Ayers for *Kiss Me Kate*

9468 **Musical Authors:** Bella and Samuel Spewack for *Kiss Me Kate*

9469 **Composer and Lyricist:** Cole Porter for *Kiss Me Kate*

9470 **Costumes:** Lemuel Ayers for *Kiss Me Kate*

9471 **Scenic Designer:** Jo Mielziner for *Sleepy Hollow, Summer and Smoke, Anne of the Thousand Days, Death of a Salesman* and *South Pacific*

9472 **Choreographer:** Gower Champion for *Lend an Ear*

9473 **Conductor and Musical Director:** Max Meth for *As the Girls Go*

────────── **1 9 5 0** ──────────

9474 Dramatic Actor: Sidney Blackmer in *Come Back, Little Sheba*
9475 Dramatic Actress: Shirley Booth in *Come Back, Little Sheba*
9476 Musical Actor: Ezio Pinza in *South Pacific*
9477 Musical Actress: Mary Martin in *South Pacific*
9478 Supporting or Featured Musical Actor: Myron McCormick in *South Pacific*
9479 Supporting or Featured Musical Actress: Juanita Hall in *South Pacific*
9480 Play: *The Cocktail Party* by T. S. Eliot
9481 Dramatic Producer: Gilbert Miller for *The Cocktail Party*
9482 Dramatic Author: T. S. Eliot for *The Cocktail Party*
9483 Director: Joshua Logan for *South Pacific*
9484 Musical: *South Pacific*, music by Richard Rodgers, lyrics by Oscar Hammerstein II, book by Oscar Hammerstein II and Joshua Logan
9485 Musical Producers: Richard Rodgers, Oscar Hammerstein II, Leland Hayward and Joshua Logan for *South Pacific*
9486 Musical Authors: Oscar Hammerstein II and Joshua Logan for *South Pacific*
9487 Composer: Richard Rodgers for *South Pacific*
9488 Costumes: Aline Bernstein for *Regina*
9489 Scenic Designer: Jo Mielziner for *The Innocents*
9490 Choreographer: Helen Tamiris for *Touch and Go*
9491 Conductor and Musical Director: Maurice Abravanel for *Regina*
9492 Stage Technician: Joe Lynn, master propertyman for *Miss Liberty*
9493 Special Awards: Maurice Evans, Mrs. Eleanor Roosevelt presented a special award to a volunteer worker of the American Theatre Wing's hospital program.

────────── **1 9 5 1** ──────────

9494 Dramatic Actor: Claude Rains in *Darkness at Noon*

9495 Dramatic Actress: Uta Hagen in *The Country Girl*
9496 Supporting or Featured Dramatic Actor: Eli Wallach in *The Rose Tattoo*
9497 Supporting or Featured Dramatic Actress: Maureen Stapleton in *The Rose Tattoo*
9498 Musical Actor: Robert Alda in *Guys and Dolls*
9499 Musical Actress: Ethel Merman in *Call Me Madam*
9500 Supporting or Featured Musical Actor: Russell Nype in *Call Me Madam*
9501 Supporting or Featured Musical Actress: Isabel Bigley in *Call Me Madam*
9502 Play: *The Rose Tattoo* by Tennessee Williams
9503 Dramatic Producer: Cheryl Crawford for *The Rose Tattoo*
9504 Dramatic Author: Tennessee Williams for *The Rose Tattoo*
9505 Director: George S. Kaufman for *Guys and Dolls*
9506 Musical: *Guys and Dolls*, music and lyrics by Frank Loesser, book by Jo Swerling and Abe Burrows
9507 Musical Producers: Cy Feuer and Ernest H. Martin for *Guys and Dolls*
9508 Musical Authors: Jo Swerling and Abe Burrows for *Guys and Dolls*
9509 Composer and Lyricist: Frank Loesser for *Guys and Dolls*
9510 Costumes: Miles White for *Bless You All*
9511 Scenic Designer: Boris Aronson for *The Rose Tattoo*, *The Country Girl* and *Season in the Sun*
9512 Choreographer: Michael Kidd for *Guys and Dolls*
9513 Conductor and Musical Director: Lehman Engel for *The Consul*
9514 Stage Technician: Richard Raven for *The Autumn Garden*
9515 Special Award: Ruth Green

────────── **1 9 5 2** ──────────

9516 Dramatic Actor: Jose Ferrer in *The Shrike*
9517 Dramatic Actress: Julie Harris in *I Am a Camera*
9518 Musical Actor: Phil Silvers in *Top Banana*

9519 **Musical Actress:** Gertrude Lawrence in *The King & I*

9520 **Supporting or Featured Dramatic Actor:** John Cromwell in *Point of No Return*

9521 **Supporting or Featured Dramatic Actress:** Marian Winters in *I Am a Camera*

9522 **Supporting or Featured Musical Actor:** Yul Brynner in *The King & I*

9523 **Supporting or Featured Musical Actress:** Helen Gallagher in *Pal Joey*

9524 **Play:** *The Fourposter* by Jan de Hartog

9525 **Musical:** *The King & I*, book and lyrics by Oscar Hammerstein II and Richard Rodgers

9526 **Director:** Jose Ferrer for *The Shrike, The Fourposter* and *Stalag 17*

9527 **Costumes:** Irene Sharaff for *The King & I*

9528 **Scenic Designer:** Jo Mielziner for *The King & I*

9529 **Choreographer:** Robert Alton for *Pal Joey*

9530 **Conductor and Musical Director:** Max Meth for *Pal Joey*

9531 **Stage Technician:** Peter Feller, master carpenter for *Call Me Madam*

9532 **Special Awards:** Edward Kook, Judy Garland and Charles Boyer

─────── **1953** ───────

9533 **Dramatic Actor:** Tom Ewell in *The Seven Year Itch*

9534 **Dramatic Actress:** Shirley Booth in *Time of the Cuckoo*

9535 **Supporting or Featured Dramatic Actor:** John Williams for *Dial M for Murder*

9536 **Supporting or Featured Dramatic Actress:** Beatrice Straight in *The Crucible*

9537 **Musical Actor:** Thomas Mitchell in *Hazel Flagg*

9538 **Musical Actress:** Rosalind Russell in *Wonderful Town*

9539 **Supporting or Featured Musical Actor:** Hiram Sherman in *Two's Company*

9540 **Supporting or Featured Musical Actress:** Sheila Bond in *Wish You Were Here*

9541 **Play:** *The Crucible* by Arthur Miller

9542 **Dramatic Producer:** Kermit Bloomgarden for *The Crucible*

9543 **Dramatic Author:** Arthur Miller for *The Crucible*

9544 **Director:** Joshua Logan for *Picnic*

9545 **Musical:** *Wonderful Town*, book by Joseph Fields and Jerome Chodorov, music by Leonard Bernstein, lyrics by Betty Comden and Adolph Green

9546 **Musical Producer:** Robert Fryer for *Wonderful Town*

9547 **Musical Authors:** Joseph Fields and Jerome Chodorov for *Wonderful Town*

9548 **Composer:** Leonard Bernstein for *Wonderful Town*

9549 **Costume Designer:** Miles White for *Hazel Flagg*

9550 **Scenic Designer:** Raoul Pene du Bois for *Wonderful Town*

9551 **Choreographer:** Donald Saddler for *Wonderful Town*

9552 **Conductor and Musical Director:** Lehman Engel for *Wonderful Town* and the Gilbert and Sullivan season

9553 **Stage Technician:** Abe Kurnit for *Wish You Were Here*

9554 **Special Awards:** Beatrice Lillie, Danny Kaye and Equity Community Theatre

─────── **1954** ───────

9555 **Dramatic Actor:** David Wayne in *The Teahouse of the August Moon*

9556 **Dramatic Actress:** Audrey Hepburn in *Ondine*

9557 **Musical Actor:** Alfred Drake in *Kismet*

9558 **Musical Actress:** Dolores Gray in *Carnival in Flanders*

9559 **Supporting or Featured Dramatic Actor:** John Kerr in *Tea and Sympathy*

9560 **Supporting or Featured Dramatic Actress:** Jo Van Fleet in *The Trip to Bountiful*

9561 **Supporting or Featured Musical Actor:** Harry Belafonte in *John Murray Anderson's Almanac*

9562 **Supporting or Featured Musical Actress:** Gwen Verdon in *Can-Can*

9563 **Play:** *The Teahouse of the August Moon* by John Patrick

9564 **Dramatic Producer:** Maurice Evans and George Schaefer for *The Teahouse of the August Moon*

9565 **Dramatic Author:** John Patrick for *The Teahouse of the August Moon*

9566 **Director:** Alfred Lunt for *Ondine*

9567 **Musical:** *Kismet*, book by Charles Lederer and Luther Davis, music by Alexander Borodin, adapted and with lyrics by Robert Wright and George Forrest

9568 **Musical Producer:** Charles Lederer for *Kismet*

9569 **Musical Author:** Charles Lederer and Luther Davis for *Kismet*

9570 **Composer:** Alexander Borodin for *Kismet*

9571 **Costume Designer:** Richard Whorf for *Ondine*

9572 **Scenic Designer:** Peter Larkin for *Ondine* and *The Teahouse of the August Moon*

9573 **Choreographer:** Michael Kidd for *Can-Can*

9574 **Musical Conductor:** Louis Adrian for *Kismet*

9575 **Stage Technician:** John Davis for *Picnic*

—————— **1 9 5 5** ——————

9576 **Dramatic Actor:** Alfred Lunt in *Quadrille*

9577 **Dramatic Actress:** Nancy Kelly for *The Bad Seed*

9578 **Supporting or Featured Dramatic Actor:** Francis L. Sullivan in *Witness for the Prosecution*

9579 **Supporting or Featured Dramatic Actress:** Patricia Jessel in *Witness for the Prosecution*

9580 **Musical Actor:** Walter Slezak in *Fanny*

9581 **Musical Actress:** Mary Martin in *Peter Pan*

9582 **Supporting or Featured Musical Actor:** Cyril Ritchard in *Peter Pan*

9583 **Supporting or Featured Musical Actress:** Carol Haney in *The Pajama Game*

9584 **Play:** *The Desperate Hours* by Joseph Hayes

9585 **Dramatic Producers:** Howard Erskine and Joseph Hayes for *The Desperate Hours*

9586 **Dramatic Author:** Joseph Hayes for *The Desperate Hours*

9587 **Director:** Robert Montgomery for *The Desperate Hours*

9588 **Musical:** *The Pajama Game*, book by George Abbott and Richard Bissell, music and lyrics by Richard Adler and Jerry Ross

9589 **Musical Producers:** Frederick Brisson, Robert Griffith and Harold S. Prince for *The Pajama Game*

9590 **Musical Authors:** George Abbott and Richard Bissell for *The Pajama Game*

9591 **Composer and Lyricist:** Richard Adler and Jerry Ross for *The Pajama Game*

9592 **Costume Designer:** Cecil Beaton for *Quadrille*

9593 **Scenic Designer:** Oliver Messel for *House of Flowers*

9594 **Choreographer:** Bob Fosse for *The Pajama Game*

9595 **Conductor and Musical Director:** Thomas Schippers for *The Saint of Bleecker Street*

9596 **Stage Technician:** Richard Rodda for *Peter Pan*

9597 **Special Award:** Proscenium Productions

—————— **1 9 5 6** ——————

9598 **Dramatic Actor:** Paul Muni in *Inherit the Wind*

9599 **Dramatic Actress:** Julie Harris in *The Lark*

9600 **Musical Actor:** Ray Walston in *Damn Yankees*

9601 **Musical Actress:** Gwen Verdon in *Damn Yankees*

9602 **Supporting or Featured Dramatic Actor:** Ed Begley in *Inherit the Wind*

9603 **Supporting or Featured Dramatic Actress:** Una Merkel in *The Ponder Heart*

9604 **Supporting or Featured Musical Actor:** Russ Brown in *Damn Yankees*

9605 **Supporting or Featured Musical Actress:** Lotte Lenya in *The Threepenny Opera*

9606 **Play:** *The Diary of Anne Frank* by Frances Goodrich and Albert Hackett, produced by Kermit Bloomgarden

9607 **Director:** Tyrone Guthrie for *The Matchmaker, Six Characters in Search of an Author* and *Tamburlaine the Great*

9608 **Dramatic Authors:** Frances Goodrich and Albert Hackett for *The Diary of Anne Frank*

9609 **Dramatic Producer:** Kermit Bloomgarden for *The Diary of Anne Frank*

9610 **Musical:** *Damn Yankees* by George Abbott and Douglass Wallop, music by Richard Adler and Jerry Ross, produced by Frederick Brisson, Robert Griffith, Harold S. Prince in association with Albert B. Taylor

9611 **Musical Authors:** George Abbott and Douglass Wallop for *Damn Yankees*

9612 **Musical Producers:** Frederick Brisson, Robert Griffith, Harold S. Prince in association with Albert B. Taylor for *Damn Yankees*

9613 **Composer and Lyricist:** Richard Adler and Jerry Ross for *Damn Yankees*

9614 **Conductor and Musical Director:** Hal Hastings for *Damn Yankees*

9615 **Scenic Designer:** Peter Larkin for *Inherit the Wind* and *No Time for Sergeants*

9616 **Costume Designer:** Alvin Colt for *The Lark, Phoenix '55* and *Pipe Dream*

9617 **Choreographer:** Bob Fosse for *Damn Yankees*

9618 **Stage Technician:** Harry Green, electrician and sound technician for *Middle of the Night* and *Damn Yankees*

9619 **Special Awards:** *The Threepenny Opera* and the Theatre Collection of the New York Public Library

——————— **1957** ———————

9620 **Dramatic Actor:** Fredric March in *Long Day's Journey Into Night*

9621 **Dramatic Actress:** Margaret Leighton in *Separate Tables*

9622 **Supporting or Featured Dramatic Actor:** Frank Conroy in *The Potting Shed*

9623 **Supporting or Featured Dramatic Actress:** Peggy Cass in *Auntie Mame*

9624 **Musical Actor:** Rex Harrison in *My Fair Lady*

9625 **Musical Actress:** Judy Holliday in *Bells Are Ringing*

9626 **Supporting or Featured Musical Actor:** Sydney Chaplin in *Bells Are Ringing*

9627 **Supporting or Featured Musical Actress:** Edith Adams in *Li'l Abner*

9628 **Play:** *Long Day's Journey Into Night* by Eugene O'Neill, produced by Leigh Connell, Theodore Mann and Jose Quintero

9629 **Dramatic Producer:** Leigh Connell, Theodore Mann and Jose Quintero for *Long Day's Journey Into Night*

9630 **Dramatic Author:** Eugene O'Neill for *Long Day's Journey Into Night*

9631 **Director:** Moss Hart for *My Fair Lady*

9632 **Musical:** *My Fair Lady*, book and lyrics by Alan Jay Lerner, music by Frederick Loewe, produced by Herman Levin

9633 **Musical Producer:** Herman Levin for *My Fair Lady*

9634 **Musical Author:** Alan Jay Lerner for *My Fair Lady*

9635 **Composer:** Frederick Loewe for *My Fair Lady*

9636 **Conductor and Musical Director:** Franz Allers for *My Fair Lady*

9637 **Scenic Designer:** Oliver Smith for *A Clearing in the Woods, Candide, Auntie Mame, My Fair Lady, Eugenia* and *A Visit to a Small Planet*

9638 **Costume Designer:** Cecil Beaton for *Little Glass Clock* and *My Fair Lady*

9639 **Choreographer:** Michael Kidd for *Li'l Abner*

9640 **Stage Technician:** Howard McDonald (posthumous), carpenter for *Major Barbara*

9641 **Special Awards:** American Shakespeare Festival, Jean Louis Barrault — French Repertory, Robert Russell Bennett, William Hammerstein and Paul Shyre

——————— **1958** ———————

9642 **Dramatic Actor:** Ralph Bellamy in *Sunrise at Campobello*

9643 **Dramatic Actress:** Helen Hayes in *Time Remembered*

9644 **Musical Actor:** Robert Preston in *The Music Man*

9645 **Musical Actress:** Gwen Verdon in *New Girl in Town* and Thelma Ritter *New Girl in Town*

9646 **Supporting or Featured Dramatic Actor:** Henry Jones in *Sunrise at Campobello*

9647 **Supporting or Featured Dramatic Actress:** Anne Bancroft in *Two for the Seesaw*

9648 **Supporting or Featured Musical Actor:** David Burns in *The Music Man*

9649 **Supporting or Featured Musical Actress:** Barbara Cook in *The Music Man*

9650 **Play:** *Sunrise at Campobello* by Dore Schary

9651 **Dramatic Director:** Vincent J. Donehue for *Sunrise at Campobello*

9652 **Dramatic Author:** Dore Schary for *Sunrise at Campobello*

9653 **Musical:** *The Music Man*, book by Meredith Willson and Frank Lacey, music and lyrics by Meredith Willson

9654 **Musical Author:** Meredith Willson and Frank Lacey for *The Music Man*

9655 **Musical Producer:** Kermit Bloomgarden, Herbert Greene, Frank Productions for *The Music Man*

9656 **Composer and Lyricist:** Meredith Willson for *The Music Man*

9657 **Conductor and Musical Director:** Herbert Greene for *The Music Man*

9658 **Scenic Designer:** Oliver Smith for *West Side Story*

9659 **Costume Designer:** Motley for *The First Gentleman*

9660 **Choreographer:** Jerome Robbins for *West Side Story*

9661 **Stage Technician:** Harry Romar for *Time Remembered*

9662 **Special Awards:** New York Shakespeare Festival and Mrs. Martin Beck

──────── 1 9 5 9 ────────

9663 **Dramatic Actor:** Jason Robards, Jr., in *The Disenchanted*

9664 **Dramatic Actress:** Gertrude Berg in *A Majority of One*

9665 **Supporting or Featured Dramatic Actor:** Charlie Ruggles in *The Pleasure of His Company*

9666 **Supporting or Featured Dramatic Actress:** Julie Newmar in *The Marriage-Go-Round*

9667 **Musical Actor:** Richard Kiley in *Redhead*

9668 **Musical Actress:** Gwen Verdon in *Redhead*

9669 **Supporting or Featured Musical Actor:** Russell Nype in *Goldilocks* and the cast of *La Plume de Ma Tante*

9670 **Supporting or Featured Musical Actress:** Pat Stanley in *Goldilocks* and the cast of *La Plume de Ma Tante*

9671 **Play:** *J. B.* by Archibald MacLeish, produced by Alfred de Ligare, Jr.

9672 **Dramatic Producer:** Alfred de Ligare, Jr. for *J. B.*

9673 **Dramatic Author:** Archibald MacLeish for *J. B.*

9674 **Director:** Elia Kazan for *J. B.*

9675 **Musical:** *Redhead* by Herbert and Dorothy Fields, Sidney Sheldon and David Shaw, music by Albert Hague, lyrics by Dorothy Fields

9676 **Musical Producer:** Robert Fryer and Lawrence Carr for *Redhead*

9677 **Musical Author:** Herbert and Dorothy Fields, Sidney Sheldon and David Shaw for *Redhead*

9678 **Composer:** Albert Hague for *Redhead*

9679 **Conductor and Musical Director:** Salvatore Dell'Isola for *Flower Drum Song*

9680 **Scenic Designer:** Donald Oenslager for *A Majority of One*

9681 **Costume Designer:** Rouben Ter-Arutunian for *Redhead*

9682 **Choreographer:** Bob Fosse for *Redhead*

9683 **Stage Technician:** Sam Knapp for *The Music Man*

9684 **Special Awards:** John Gielgud and Howard Lindsay and Russell Crouse

──────── 1 9 6 0 ────────

9685 **Dramatic Actor:** Melvyn Douglas in *The Best Man*

9686 **Dramatic Actress:** Anne Bancroft in *The Miracle Worker*

9687 **Supporting or Featured Dramatic Actor:** Roddy McDowall in *The Fighting Cock*

9688 **Supporting or Featured Dramatic Actress:** Anne Revere in *Toys in the Attic*

9689 **Musical Actor:** Jackie Gleason in *Take Me Along*

9690 **Musical Actress:** Mary Martin in *The Sound of Music*

9691 **Supporting or Featured Musical Actor:** Tom Bosley in *Fiorello!*

9692 **Supporting or Featured Musical Actress:** Patricia Neway in *The Sound of Music*

9693 **Play:** *The Miracle Worker* by William Gibson, produced by Fred Coe

9694 **Dramatic Producer:** Fred Coe for *The Miracle Worker*

9695 **Dramatic Author:** William Gibson for *The Miracle Worker*

9696 **Dramatic Director:** Arthur Penn for *The Miracle Worker*

9697 **Musical:** *Fiorello!* by Jerome Weidman and George Abbott, lyrics by Sheldon Harnick, music by Jerry Bock, produced by Robert E. Griffith and Harold S. Prince and *The Sound of Music* by Howard Lindsay and Russell Crouse, lyrics by Oscar Hammerstein II, music by Richard Rodgers, produced by Leland Hayward, Richard Halliday, Rodgers and Hammerstein

9698 **Musical Producers:** Robert E. Griffith and Harold S. Prince for *Fiorello!* and Leland Hayward and Richard Halliday for *The Sound of Music*

9699 **Musical Authors:** Jerome Weidman and George Abbott for *Fiorello!* and Howard Lindsay and Russell Crouse for *The Sound of Music*

9700 **Musical Director:** George Abbott for *Fiorello!*

9701 **Composers:** Jerry Bock for *Fiorello!* and Richard Rodgers for *The Sound of Music*

9702 **Conductor and Musical Director:** Frederick Dvonch for *The Sound of Music*

9703 **Dramatic Scenic Designer:** Howard Bay for *Toys in the Attic*

9704 **Musical Scenic Director:** Oliver Smith for *The Sound of Music*

9705 **Costume Designer:** Cecil Beaton for *Saratoga*

9706 **Choreographer:** Michael Kidd for *Destry Rides Again*

9707 **Stage Technician:** John Walters, chief carpenter for *The Miracle Worker*

9708 **Special Awards:** John D. Rockefeller III and James Thurber and Burgess Meredith for *A Thurber Carnival*

——————— **1961** ———————

9709 **Dramatic Actor:** Zero Mostel in *Rhinoceros*

9710 **Dramatic Actress:** Joan Plowright in *A Taste of Honey*

9711 **Supporting or Featured Dramatic Actor:** Martin Gabel in *Big Fish, Little Fish*

9712 **Supporting or Featured Dramatic Actress:** Colleen Dewhurst in *All the Way Home*

9713 **Musical Actor:** Richard Burton in *Camelot*

9714 **Musical Actress:** Elizabeth Seal in *Irma la Douce*

9715 **Supporting or Featured Musical Actor:** Dick Van Dyke in *Bye, Bye Birdie*

9716 **Supporting or Featured Musical Actress:** Tammy Grimes in *The Unsinkable Molly Brown*

9717 **Play:** *Becket* by Jean Anouilh, translated by Lucienne Hill, produced by David Merrick

9718 **Dramatic Producer:** David Merrick for *Becket*

9719 **Dramatic Author:** Jean Anouilh for *Becket*

9720 **Dramatic Director:** Sir John Gielgud for *Big Fish, Little Fish*

9721 **Musical:** *Bye, Bye Birdie*, book by Michael Stewart, music by Charles Strouse, lyrics by Lee Adams, produced by Edwin Padula in association with L. Slade Brown

9722 **Musical Producer:** Edwin Padula for *Bye, Bye Birdie*

9723 **Musical Author:** Michael Stewart for *Bye, Bye Birdie*

9724 **Conductor and Musical Director:** Franz Allers for *Camelot*

9725 **Dramatic Scenic Designer:** Oliver Smith for *Becket*

9726 **Dramatic Costume Designer:** Motley for *Becket*

9727 **Musical Costume Designer:** Adrian and Tony Duquette for *Camelot*

9728 **Choreographer:** Gower Champion for *Bye, Bye Birdie*

9729 **Stage Technician:** Teddy Van Bemmal for *Becket*

9730 **Special Awards:** David Merrick and the Theatre Guild

——————— **1 9 6 2** ———————

9731 Dramatic Actor: Paul Scofield in *A Man for All Seasons*

9732 Dramatic Actress: Margaret Leighton in *Night of the Iguana*

9733 Supporting or Featured Dramatic Actor: Walter Matthau in *A Shot in the Dark*

9734 Supporting or Featured Dramatic Actress: Elizabeth Ashley in *Take Her, She's Mine*

9735 Musical Actor: Robert Morse in *How to Succeed in Business Without Really Trying*

9736 Musical Actress: Anna Maria Alberghetti in *Carnival* and Diahann Carroll in *No Strings*

9737 Supporting or Featured Musical Actor: Charles Nelson Reilly in *How to Succeed in Business Without Really Trying*

9738 Supporting or Featured Musical Actress: Phyllis Newman in *Subways Are for Sleeping*

9739 Play: *A Man for All Seasons* by Robert Bolt, produced by Robert Whitehead and Roger L. Stevens

9740 Dramatic Producer: Robert Whitehead and Roger L. Stevens for *A Man for All Seasons*

9741 Dramatic Author: Robert Bolt for *A Man for All Seasons*

9742 Dramatic Director: Noel Willman for *A Man for All Seasons*

9743 Musical: *How to Succeed in Business Without Really Trying*, book by Abe Burrows, Jack Weinstock and Willie Gilbert, music and lyrics by Frank Loesser, produced by Cy Feuer and Ernest Martin

9744 Musical Producers: Cy Feuer and Ernest Martin for *How to Succeed in Business Without Really Trying*

9745 Musical Authors: Abe Burrows, Jack Weinstock and Willie Gilbert for *How to Succeed in Business Without Really Trying*

9746 Musical Director: Abe Burrows for *How to Succeed in Business Without Really Trying*

9747 Composer: Richard Rodgers for *No Strings*

9748 Conductor and Musical Director: Elliott Lawrence for *How to Succeed in Business Without Really Trying*

9749 Scenic Designer: Will Steven Armstrong for *Carnival*

9750 Costume Designer: Lucinda Ballard for *The Gay Life*

9751 Choreographer: Agnes DeMille for *Kwamina* and Joe Layton for *No Strings*

9752 Stage Technician: Michael Burns for *A Man for All Seasons*

9753 Special Awards: Brooks Atkinson, Franco Zeffirelli, Richard Rodgers. Richard Rodgers also received the Tony for "No Strings"

——————— **1 9 6 3** ———————

9754 Dramatic Actor: Arthur Hill in *Who's Afraid of Virginia Woolf?*

9755 Dramatic Actress: Uta Hagen in *Who's Afraid of Virginia Woolf?*

9756 Supporting or Featured Dramatic Actor: Alan Arkin in *Enter Laughing*

9757 Supporting or Featured Dramatic Actress: Sandy Dennis in *A Thousand Clowns*

9758 Musical Actor: Zero Mostel in *A Funny Thing Happened on the Way to the Forum*

9759 Musical Actress: Vivien Leigh in *Tovaricha Douce*

9760 Supporting or Featured Musical Actor: David Burns in *A Funny Thing Happened on the Way to the Forum*

9761 Supporting or Featured Musical Actress: Anna Quayle in *Stop the World—I Want to Get Off*

9762 Play: *Who's Afraid of Virginia Woolf?* by Edward Albee, produced by Theatre 1963, Richard Barr and Clinton Wilder

9763 Dramatic Producers: Richard Barr and Clinton Wilder, Theatre 1963 for *Who's Afraid of Virginia Woolf?*

9764 Dramatic Director: Alan Schneider for *Who's Afraid of Virginia Woolf?*

9765 Musical: *A Funny Thing Happened on the Way to the Forum*, book by Burt Shevelove and Larry Gelbart, music and lyrics by Stephen Sondheim, produced by Harold Prince

9766 Musical Authors: Burt Shevelove and Larry Gelbart for *A Funny Thing Happened on the Way to the Forum*

9767 **Musical Producer:** Harold Prince for *A Funny Thing Happened on the Way to the Forum*

9768 **Musical Director:** George Abbott for *A Funny Thing Happened on the Way to the Forum*

9769 **Composer and Lyricist:** Lionel Bart for *Oliver!*

9770 **Conductor and Musical Director:** Donald Pippin for *Oliver!*

9771 **Scenic Designer:** Sean Kenny for *Oliver!*

9772 **Costume Designer:** Anthony Powell for *School for Scandal*

9773 **Choreographer:** Bob Fosse for *Little Me*

9774 **Stage Technician:** Solly Pernick for *Mr. President*

9775 **Special Awards:** W. McNeil Lowry, Irving Berlin, Alan Bennett, Peter Cook, Jonathan Miller and Dudley Moore

——————— **1964** ———————

9776 **Dramatic Actor:** Alec Guinness in *Dylan*

9777 **Dramatic Actress:** Sandy Dennis in *Any Wednesday*

9778 **Supporting or Featured Dramatic Actor:** Hume Cronyn in *Hamlet*

9779 **Supporting or Featured Dramatic Actress:** Barbara Loden in *After the Fall*

9780 **Musical Actor:** Bert Lahr in *Foxy*

9781 **Musical Actress:** Carol Channing in *Hello, Dolly!*

9782 **Supporting or Featured Musical Actor:** Jack Cassidy in *She Loves Me*

9783 **Supporting or Featured Musical Actress:** Tessie O'Shea in *The Girl Who Came to Supper*

9784 **Play:** *Luther* by John Osborne, produced by David Merrick

9785 **Dramatic Producer:** Herman Shumlin for *The Deputy*

9786 **Dramatic Author:** John Osborne for *Luther*

9787 **Dramatic Director:** Mike Nichols for *Barefoot in the Park*

9788 **Musical:** *Hello, Dolly!*, book by Michael Stewart, music and lyrics by Jerry Herman, produced by David Merrick

9789 **Musical Author:** Michael Stewart for *Hello, Dolly!*

9790 **Musical Producer:** David Merrick for *Hello, Dolly!*

9791 **Musical Director:** Gower Champion for *Hello, Dolly!*

9792 **Composer and Lyricist:** Jerry Herman for *Hello, Dolly!*

9793 **Conductor and Musical Director:** Shepard Coleman for *Hello, Dolly!*

9794 **Scenic Designer:** Oliver Smith for *Hello, Dolly!*

9795 **Costume Designer:** Freddy Wittop for *Hello, Dolly!*

9796 **Choreographer:** Gower Champion for *Hello, Dolly!*

9797 **Special Awards:** Eva Le Gallienne

——————— **1965** ———————

9798 **Dramatic Actor:** Walter Matthau in *The Odd Couple*

9799 **Dramatic Actress:** Irene Worth in *Tiny Alice*

9800 **Supporting or Featured Dramatic Actor:** Jack Albertson in *The Subject Was Roses*

9801 **Supporting or Featured Dramatic Actress:** Alice Ghostley in *The Sign in Sidney Brustein's Window*

9802 **Musical Actor:** Zero Mostel in *Fiddler on the Roof*

9803 **Musical Actress:** Liza Minnelli in *Flora, the Red Menace*

9804 **Supporting or Featured Musical Actor:** Victor Spinetti in *Oh, What a Lovely War*

9805 **Supporting or Featured Musical Actress:** Maria Karnilova in *Fiddler on the Roof*

9806 **Play:** *The Subject Was Roses* by Frank Gilroy, produced by Edgar Lansbury

9807 **Dramatic Producer:** Claire Nichtern for *Luv*

9808 **Dramatic Director:** Mike Nichols for *Luv* and *The Odd Couple*

9809 **Dramatic Author:** Neil Simon for *The Odd Couple*

9810 **Musical:** *Fiddler on the Roof*, book by Joseph Stein, music by Jerry Bock, lyrics by Sheldon Harnick, produced by Harold Prince

9811 **Musical Author:** Joseph Stein for *Fiddler on the Roof*

9812 **Musical Producer:** Harold Prince for *Fiddler on the Roof*

9813 **Musical Director:** Jerome Robbins for *Fiddler on the Roof*

9814 **Composer and Lyricist:** Jerry Bock and Sheldon Harnick for *Fiddler on the Roof*

9815 **Scenic Designer:** Oliver Smith for *Baker Street*, *Luv* and *The Odd Couple*

9816 **Costume Designer:** Patricia Zipprodt for *Fiddler on the Roof*

9817 **Choreographer:** Jerome Robbins for *Fiddler on the Roof*

9818 **Special Awards:** Gilbert Miller and Oliver Smith

——————— **1 9 6 6** ———————

9819 **Dramatic Actor:** Hal Holbrook in *Mark Twain Tonight!*

9820 **Dramatic Actress:** Rosemary Harris for *The Lion in Winter*

9821 **Supporting or Featured Dramatic Actor:** Patrick Magee in *Marat/Sade*

9822 **Supporting or Featured Dramatic Actress:** Zoe Caldwell in *Slapstick Tragedy*

9823 **Musical Actor:** Richard Kiley in *Man of La Mancha*

9824 **Musical Actress:** Angela Lansbury in *Mame*

9825 **Supporting or Featured Musical Actor:** Frankie Michaels in *Mame*

9826 **Supporting or Featured Musical Actress:** Beatrice Arthur in *Mame*

9827 **Play:** *Marat/Sade* by Peter Weiss, English version by Geoffrey Skelton, produced by the David Merrick Arts Foundation

9828 **Dramatic Director:** Peter Brook for *Marat/Sade*

9829 **Musical:** *Man of La Mancha*, book by Dale Wasserman, music by Mitch Leigh, lyrics by Joe Darion, produced by Albert W. Selden and Hal James

9830 **Musical Director:** Albert Marre for *Man of La Mancha*

9831 **Composer and Lyricist:** Mitch Leigh and Joe Darion for *Man of La Mancha*

9832 **Scenic Designer:** Howard Bay for *Man of La Mancha*

9833 **Costume Designer:** Gunilla Palmstierna-Weiss for *Marat/Sade*

9834 **Choreographer:** Bob Fosse for *Sweet Charity*

——————— **1 9 6 7** ———————

9835 **Dramatic Actor:** Paul Rogers in *The Homecoming*

9836 **Dramatic Actress:** Beryl Reid in *The Killing of Sister George*

9837 **Supporting or Featured Dramatic Actor:** Ian Holm in *The Homecoming*

9838 **Supporting or Featured Dramatic Actress:** Marian Seldes in *A Delicate Balance*

9839 **Musical Actor:** Robert Preston in *I Do! I Do!*

9840 **Musical Actress:** Barbara Harris in *The Apple Tree*

9841 **Supporting or Featured Musical Actor:** Joel Grey in *Cabaret*

9842 **Supporting or Featured Musical Actress:** Peg Murray in *Cabaret*

9843 **Play:** *The Homecoming* by Harold Pinter, produced by Alexander H. Cohen

9844 **Dramatic Director:** Peter Hall for *The Homecoming*

9845 **Musical:** *Cabaret*, book by Joe Masteroff, music by John Kander, lyrics by Fred Ebb, produced by Harold Prince in association with Ruth Mitchell

9846 **Musical Director:** Harold Prince for *Cabaret*

9847 **Composer and Lyricist:** John Kander and Fred Ebb for *Cabaret*

9848 **Scene Designer:** Boris Aronson for *Cabaret*

9849 **Choreographer:** Ronald Field for *Cabaret*

9850 **Costume Designer:** Patricia Zipprodt for *Cabaret*

——————— **1 9 6 8** ———————

9851 **Dramatic Actor:** Martin Balsam in *You Know I Can't Hear You When the Water's Running*

9852 **Dramatic Actress:** Zoe Caldwell in *The Prime of Miss Jean Brodie*

9853 **Supporting or Featured Dramatic Actor:** James Patterson in *The Birthday Party*

9854 **Supporting or Featured Dramatic Actress:** Zena Walker in *Joe Egg*

9855 **Musical Actor:** Robert Goulet in *The Happy Time*

9856 **Musical Actress:** Patricia Routledge in *Darling of the Day* and Leslie Uggams in *Hallelujah, Baby!*

9857 **Supporting or Featured Musical Actor:** Hiram Sherman in *How Now, Dow Jones*

9858 **Supporting or Featured Musical Actress:** Lillian Hayman in *Hallelujah, Baby!*

9859 **Play:** *Rosenkrantz and Guildenstern Are Dead* by Tom Stoppard, produced by the David Merrick Arts Foundation

9860 **Dramatic Producer:** David Merrick Arts Foundation for *Rosenkrantz and Guildenstern Are Dead*

9861 **Dramatic Director:** Mike Nichols for *Plaza Suite*

9862 **Musical:** *Hallelujah, Baby!*, book by Arthur Laurents, music by Jule Styne, lyrics by Betty Comden and Adolph Green, produced by Albert Selden, Hal James, Jane C. Nusbaum and Harry Rigby

9863 **Musical Producer:** Albert Selden, Hal James, Jane C. Nusbaum and Harry Rigby for *Hallelujah, Baby!*

9864 **Musical Director:** Gower Champion for *The Happy Time*

9865 **Composer and Lyricist:** Jule Styne, Betty Comden and Adolph Green for *Hallelujah, Baby!*

9866 **Scenic Designer:** Desmond Heeley for *Rosenkrantz and Guildenstern Are Dead*

9867 **Costume Designer:** Desmond Heeley for *Rosenkrantz and Guildenstern Are Dead*

9868 **Choreographer:** Gower Champion for *The Happy Time*

9869 **Special Award:** Audrey Hepburn, Carol Channing, Pearl Bailey, David Merrick, Maurice Chevalier, APA-Phoenix Theatre and Marlene Dietrich

--------------- **1 9 6 9** ---------------

9870 **Dramatic Actor:** James Earl Jones in *The Great White Hope*

9871 **Dramatic Actress:** Julie Harris in *Forty Carats*

9872 **Supporting or Featured Dramatic Actor:** Al Pacino in *Does a Tiger Wear a Necktie?*

9873 **Supporting or Featured Dramatic Actress:** Jane Alexander in *The Great White Hope*

9874 **Musical Actor:** Jerry Orbach in *Promises, Promises*

9875 **Musical Actress:** Angela Lansbury in *Dear World*

9876 **Supporting or Featured Musical Actor:** Ronald Holgate in *1776*

9877 **Supporting or Featured Musical Actress:** Marian Mercer in *Promises, Promises*

9878 **Play:** *The Great White Hope* by Howard Sackler, produced by Herman Levin

9879 **Dramatic Director:** Peter Dews for *Hadrian VII*

9880 **Musical:** *1776*, book by Peter Stone, music and lyrics by Sherman Edwards, produced by Stuart Ostrow

9881 **Musical Director:** Peter Hunt for *1776*

9882 **Scenic Designer:** Boris Aronson for *Zorba*

9883 **Costume Designer:** Loudon Sainthill for *Canterbury Tales*

9884 **Choreographer:** Joe Layton for *George M!*

9885 **Special Awards:** The National Theatre Company of Great Britain, the Negro Ensemble Company, Rex Harrison, Leonard Bernstein and Carol Burnett

--------------- **1 9 7 0** ---------------

9886 **Dramatic Actor:** Fritz Weaver in *Child's Play*

9887 **Dramatic Actress:** Tammy Grimes in *Private Lives* (Revival)

9888 **Supporting or Featured Dramatic Actor:** Ken Howard in *Child's Play*

9889 **Supporting or Featured Dramatic Actress:** Blythe Danner in *Butterflies Are Free*

9890 **Musical Actor:** Cleavon Little in *Purlie*

9891 **Musical Actress:** Lauren Bacall in *Applause*

9892 **Supporting or Featured Musical Actress:** Melba Moore in *Purlie*

9893 **Supporting or Featured Musical Actor:** René Auberjonois in *Coco*

9894 **Play:** *Borstal Boy* by Frank McMahon, produced by Michael McAloney, Burton C. Kaiser

9895 **Dramatic Director:** Joseph Hardy for *Child's Play*

9896 **Musical:** *Applause*, book by Betty Comden and Adolph Green, music by Charles Strouse, lyrics by Lee Adams, produced by Joseph Kipness and Lawrence Kasha

9897 **Musical Director:** Ron Field for *Applause*

9898 **Scenic Designer:** Jo Mielziner for *Child's Play*

9899 **Costume Designer:** Cecil Beaton for *Coco*

9900 **Choreographer:** Ron Field for *Applause*

9901 **Lighting Designer:** Jo Mielziner for *Child's Play*

9902 **Special Awards:** Noel Coward, the New York Shakespeare Festival, Barbra Streisand, Alfred Lunt and Lynn Fontanne

——————— **1 9 7 1** ———————

9903 **Dramatic Actor:** Brian Bedford in *The School for Wives*

9904 **Dramatic Actress:** Maureen Stapleton in *Gingerbread Lady*

9905 **Supporting or Featured Dramatic Actor:** Paul Sand in *Story Theatre*

9906 **Supporting or Featured Dramatic Actress:** Rae Allen in *And Miss Reardon Drinks a Little*

9907 **Musical Actor:** Hal Linden in *The Rothchilds*

9908 **Musical Actress:** Helen Gallagher in *No, No, Nanette*

9909 **Supporting or Featured Musical Actor:** Keene Curtis in *The Rothchilds*

9910 **Supporting or Featured Musical Actress:** Patsy Kelly in *No, No, Nanette*

9911 **Play:** *Sleuth* by Anthony Shaffer, produced by Helen Bonfils, Morton Gottlieb and Michael White

9912 **Dramatic Producer:** Helen Bonfils, Morton Gottlieb and Michael White for *Sleuth*

9913 **Dramatic Director:** Peter Brook for *A Midsummer Night's Dream*

9914 **Musical:** *Company* produced by Harold Prince

9915 **Musical Producer:** Harold Prince for *Company*

9916 **Musical Director:** Harold Prince for *Company*

9917 **Musical Book:** George Furth for *Company*

9918 **Musical Lyrics:** Stephen Sondheim for *Company*

9919 **Musical Score:** Stephen Sondheim for *Company*

9920 **Scenic Designer:** Boris Aronson for *Company*

9921 **Costume Designer:** Raoul Pene du Bois for *No, No, Nanette*

9922 **Choreographer:** Donald Saddler for *No, No, Nanette*

9923 **Lighting Designer:** H. R. Poindexter for *Story Theatre*

9924 **Special Awards:** Elliot Norton, Ingram Ash, *Playbill* and Roger L. Stevens

——————— **1 9 7 2** ———————

9925 **Dramatic Actor:** Cliff Gorman in *Lenny*

9926 **Dramatic Actress:** Sada Thompson in *Twigs*

9927 **Supporting or Featured Dramatic Actor:** Vincent Gardenia in *The Prisoner of Second Avenue*

9928 **Supporting or Featured Dramatic Actress:** Elizabeth Wilson in *Sticks and Bones*

9929 **Musical Actor:** Phil Silvers in *A Funny Thing Happened on the Way to the Forum* (Revival)

9930 **Musical Actress:** Alexis Smith in *Follies*

9931 **Supporting or Featured Musical Actor:** Larry Blyden in *A Funny Thing Happened on the Way to the Forum* (revival)

9932 **Supporting or Featured Musical Actress:** Linda Hopkins in *Inner City*

9933 **Play:** *Sticks and Bones* by David Rabe, produced by the New York Shakespeare Festival — Joseph Papp

9934 **Dramatic Director:** Mike Nichols for *The Prisoner of Second Avenue*

9935 **Musical:** *Two Gentlemen of Verona* produced by the New York Shakespeare Festival — Joseph Papp

9936 **Musical Director:** Harold Prince and Michael Bennett for *Follies*

9937 **Musical Book:** *Two Gentlemen of Verona* by John Guare and Mel Shapiro

9938 **Score:** *Follies* composed by and lyrics by Stephen Sondheim

9939 **Scenic Director:** Boris Aronson for *Follies*

9940 **Costume Designer:** Florence Klotz for *Follies*

9941 **Choreographer:** Michael Bennett for *Follies*

9942 **Lighting Director:** Tharon Musser for *Follies*

9943 **Special Awards:** The Theatre Guild–American Theatre Society, Richard Rodgers, *Fiddler on the Roof* and Ethel Merman

──────── **1 9 7 3** ────────

9944 **Dramatic Actor:** Alan Bates in *Butley*

9945 **Dramatic Actress:** Julie Harris in *The Last of Mrs. Lincoln*

9946 **Supporting or Featured Dramatic Actor:** John Lithgow in *The Changing Room*

9947 **Supporting or Featured Dramatic Actress:** Leora Dana in *The Last of Mrs. Lincoln*

9948 **Musical Actor:** Ben Vereen in *Pippin*

9949 **Musical Actress:** Glynis Johns in *A Little Night Music*

9950 **Supporting or Featured Musical Actor:** George S. Irving in *Irene*

9951 **Supporting or Featured Musical Actress:** Patricia Elliot in *A Little Night Music*

9952 **Play:** *That Championship Season* by Jason Miller, produced by the New York Shakespeare Festival — Joseph Papp

9953 **Dramatic Director:** A. J. Antoon for *That Championship Season*

9954 **Musical:** *A Little Night Music* produced by Harold Prince

9955 **Musical Director:** Bob Fosse for *Pippin*

9956 **Musical Book:** *A Little Night Music* by Hugh Wheeler

9957 **Musical Score:** *A Little Night Music*, book and lyrics by Stephen Sondheim

9958 **Scenic Designer:** Tony Walton for *Pippin*

9959 **Costume Designer:** Florence Klotz for *A Little Night Music*

9960 **Choreographer:** Bob Fosse for *Pippin*

9961 **Lighting Designer:** Jules Fisher for *Pippin*

9962 **Special Awards:** John Lindsay, Actors' Fund of America and the Shubert Organization

──────── **1 9 7 4** ────────

9963 **Dramatic Actor:** Michael Moriarty in *Find Your Way Home*

9964 **Dramatic Actress:** Colleen Dewhurst in *A Moon for the Misbegotten*

9965 **Supporting or Featured Dramatic Actor:** Ed Flanders in *A Moon for the Misbegotten*

9966 **Supporting or Featured Dramatic Actress:** Frances Sternhagen in *The Good Doctor*

9967 **Musical Actor:** Christopher Plummer in *Cyrano*

9968 **Musical Actress:** Virginia Capers in *Raisin*

9969 **Supporting or Featured Musical Actor:** Tommy Tune in *Seesaw*

9970 **Supporting or Featured Musical Actress:** Janie Sell in *Over Here!*

9971 **Play:** *The River Niger* by Joseph A. Walker, produced by the Negro Ensemble Company, Inc.

9972 **Dramatic Director:** Jose Quintero for *A Moon for the Misbegotten*

9973 **Musical:** *Raisin* produced by Robert Nemiroff

9974 **Musical Director:** Harold Prince for *Candide*

9975 **Musical Book:** *Candide* by Hugh Wheeler

9976 **Score:** *Gigi*, music by Frederick Loewe, lyrics by Alan Jay Lerner

9977 **Scenic Director:** Franne and Eugene Lee for *Candide*

9978 **Costume Designer:** Franne Lee for *Candide*

9979 **Choreographer:** Michael Bennett for *Seesaw*

9980 **Lighting Director:** Jules Fisher for *Ulysses in Nighttown*

9981 **Special Awards:** Liza Minnelli, Bette Midler, *A Moon for the Misbegotten*, Actor's Equity Association, Theatre Development Fund, John F. Wharton, *Candide*, Harold Friedlander, Peter Cook and Dudley Moore in *Good Evening*

—————— **1975** ——————

9982 Dramatic Actor: John Kani and Winston Ntshona in *Sizwe Banzi Is Dead* and *The Island*

9983 Dramatic Actress: Ellen Burstyn in *Same Time, Next Year*

9984 Supporting or Featured Dramatic Actor: Frank Langella in *Seascape*

9985 Supporting or Featured Dramatic Actress: Rita Moreno in *The Ritz*

9986 Musical Actor: John Cullum in *Shenandoah*

9987 Musical Actress: Angela Lansbury in *Gypsy*

9988 Supporting or Featured Musical Actor: Ted Ross in *The Wiz*

9989 Supporting or Featured Musical Actress: Dee Dee Bridgewater in *The Wiz*

9990 Play: *Equus* by Peter Shaffer, produced by Kermit Bloomgarden and Doris Cole Abrahams

9991 Dramatic Director: John Dexter for *Equus*

9992 Musical: *The Wiz* produced by Ken Harper

9993 Musical Director: Geoffrey Holder for *The Wiz*

9994 Musical Book: *Shenandoah* by James Lee Barrett, Peter Udell and Philip Rose

9995 Score: *The Wiz*, music and lyrics by Charlie Smalls

9996 Scenic Designer: Carl Toms for *Sherlock Holmes*

9997 Costume Designer: Geoffrey Holder for *The Wiz*

9998 Choreographer: George Faison for *The Wiz*

9999 Lighting Designer: Neil Peter Jampolis for *Sherlock Holmes*

10000 Special Awards: Neil Simon and Al Hirschfeld

—————— **1976** ——————

10001 Dramatic Actor: John Wood in *Travesties*

10002 Dramatic Actress: Irene Worth in *Sweet Bird of Youth*

10003 Supporting or Featured Dramatic Actor: Edward Herrmann in *Mrs. Warren's Profession*

10004 Supporting or Featured Dramatic Actress: Shirley Knight in *Kennedy's Children*

10005 Musical Actor: George Rose in *My Fair Lady*

10006 Musical Actress: Donna McKechnie in *A Chorus Line*

10007 Supporting or Featured Musical Actor: Sammy Williams in *A Chorus Line*

10008 Supporting or Featured Musical Actress: Carole Bishop in *A Chorus Line*

10009 Play: *Travesties* by Tom Stoppard, produced by David Merrick, Doris Cole Abrahams and Barry Fredrik in association with S. Spencer Davids and Eddie Kulukundis

10010 Dramatic Director: Ellis Rabb for *The Royal Family*

10011 Musical: *A Chorus Line* produced by Joseph Papp, New York Shakespeare Festival

10012 Musical Director: Michael Bennett for *A Chorus Line*

10013 Musical Book: *A Chorus Line* by James Kirkwood and Nicholas Dante

10014 Score: *A Chorus Line*, music by Marvin Hamlisch, lyrics by Edward Kleban

10015 Scenic Designer: Boris Aronson for *Pacific Overtures*

10016 Costume Designer: Florence Klotz for *Pacific Overtures*

10017 Choreographer: Michael Bennett and Bob Avian for *A Chorus Line*

10018 Lighting Designer: Tharon Musser for *A Chorus Line*

10019 Special Awards: Mathilde Pincus — *Circle in the Square*, Thomas H. Fitzgerald — *The Arena Stage* and Richard Burton — *Equus*

—————— **1977** ——————

10020 Dramatic Actor: Al Pacino in *The Basic Training of Pavlo Hummel*

10021 Dramatic Actress: Julie Harris in *The Belle of Amherst*

10022 Supporting or Featured Dramatic Actor: Jonathan Pryce in *Comedians*

10023 Supporting or Featured Dramatic Actress: Tarzana Beverley in *For Colored Girls Who Have Considered Suicide/When the Rainbow Is Enuf*

10024 Musical Actor: Barry Bostwick in *The Robber Bridegroom*

10025 **Musical Actress:** Dorothy Loudon in *Annie*

10026 **Supporting or Featured Musical Actor:** Lenny Baker in *I Love My Wife*

10027 **Supporting or Featured Musical Actress:** Delores Hall in *Your Arm's Too Short to Box with God*

10028 **Play:** *The Shadow Box* by Michael Cristofer, produced by Allan Francis, Ken Marsolais, Lester Osterman and Leonard Soloway

10029 **Dramatic Director:** Gordon Davidson for *The Shadow Box*

10030 **Musical:** *Annie* produced by Lewis Allen, Mike Nichols, Irwin Meyer and Stephen R. Friedman

10031 **Musical Director:** Gene Saks for *I Love My Wife*

10032 **Musical Book:** *Annie* by Thomas Meehan

10033 **Score:** *Annie* music by Charles Strouse, lyrics by Martin Charnin

10034 **Scenic Designer:** David Mitchell for *Annie*

10035 **Costume Designer:** Theoni V. Aldredge for *Annie* and Santo Loquasto for *The Cherry Orchard*

10036 **Choreographer:** Peter Genaro for *Annie*

10037 **Most Innovative Production of a Revival:** *Porgy and Bess* produced by Sherwin M. Goldman and the Houston Grand Opera

10038 **Special Awards:** Lily Tomlin, Barry Manilow, Diana Ross, National Theatre for the Deaf, Mark Taper Forum and Equity Library Theatre

---- **1 9 7 8** ----

10039 **Dramatic Actor:** Barnard Hughes in *Da*

10040 **Dramatic Actress:** Jessica Tandy in *The Gin Game*

10041 **Supporting or Featured Dramatic Actor:** Lester Rawlins in *Da*

10042 **Supporting or Featured Dramatic Actress:** Ann Wedgeworth in *Chapter Two*

10043 **Musical Actor:** John Cullum in *On the Twentieth Century*

10044 **Musical Actress:** Liza Minnelli in *The Act*

10045 **Supporting or Featured Musical Actor:** Kevin Kline in *On the Twentieth Century*

10046 **Supporting or Featured Musical Actress:** Nell Carter in *Ain't Misbehavin'*

10047 **Play:** *Da* by Hugh Leonard, produced by Lester Osterman, Marilyn Strauss and Marc Howard

10048 **Dramatic Director:** Melvin Bernhardt in *Da*

10049 **Musical:** *Ain't Misbehavin'* produced by Emanuel Azenberg, Dasha Epstein, the Shubert Organization and Columbia Pictures

10050 **Musical Director:** Richard Maltby, Jr. for *Ain't Misbehavin'*

10051 **Musical Book:** *On the Twentieth Century* by Betty Comden and Adolph Green

10052 **Score:** *On the Twentieth Century* music by Cy Coleman, lyrics by Betty Comden and Adolph Green

10053 **Scenic Designer:** Robin Wagner for *On the Twentieth Century*

10054 **Costume Designer:** Edward Gorey for *Dracula*

10055 **Choreographer:** Bob Fosse for *Dancin'*

10056 **Lighting Designer:** Jules Fisher for *Dancin'*

10057 **Most Innovative Production of a Revival:** *Dracula* produced by Jujamcyn Theaters, Elizabeth McCann, John Wulp, Victor Lurie, Nelle Nugent and Max Weitzenhoffer

10058 **Special Award:** The Long Wharf Theatre

---- **1 9 7 9** ----

10059 **Dramatic Actor:** Tom Conti in *Whose Life Is It Anyway?*

10060 **Dramatic Actress:** Constance Cummings in *Wings* and Carole Shelley in *The Elephant Man*

10061 **Supporting or Featured Dramatic Actor:** Michael Gough in *Bedroom Farce*

10062 **Supporting or Featured Dramatic Actress:** Joan Hickson in *Bedroom Farce*

10063 **Musical Actor:** Len Cariou in *Sweeney Todd*

10064 **Musical Actress:** Angela Lansbury in *Sweeney Todd*

10065 **Supporting or Featured Musical Actor:** Henderson Forsythe in *The Best Little Whorehouse in Texas*

10066 **Supporting or Featured Musical Actress:** Carlin Glynn in *The Best Little Whorehouse in Texas*

10067 **Play:** *The Elephant Man* by Bernard Pomerance, produced by Richmond Crinkley, Elizabeth I. McCann and Nelle Nugent

10068 **Dramatic Director:** Jack Hofsiss for *The Elephant Man*

10069 **Musical:** *Sweeney Todd* produced by Richard Barr, Charles Woodward, Robert Fryer, Mary Lea Johnson and Martin Richards

10070 **Musical Director:** Harold Prince for *Sweeney Todd*

10071 **Musical Book:** *Sweeney Todd* by Hugh Wheeler

10072 **Score:** *Sweeney Todd* music by Stephen Sondheim, lyrics by Stephen Sondheim

10073 **Scenic Designer:** Eugene Lee for *Sweeney Todd*

10074 **Costume Designer:** Franne Lee for *Sweeney Todd*

10075 **Choreographer:** Michael Bennett and Bob Avian for *Ballroom*

10076 **Lighting Designer:** Roger Morgan for *The Crucifer of Blood*

10077 **Special Awards:** Henry Fonda, Walter F. Diehl, Eugene O'Neill Memorial Theatre and American Conservatory Theatre

———— **1980** ————

10078 **Dramatic Actor:** John Rubenstein in *Children of a Lesser God*

10079 **Dramatic Actress:** Phyllis Frelich in *Children of a Lesser God*

10080 **Supporting or Featured Dramatic Actor:** David Rounds in *Morning's at Seven*

10081 **Supporting or Featured Dramatic Actress:** Dinah Manoff in *I Ought to Be in Pictures*

10082 **Musical Actor:** Jim Dale in *Barnum*

10083 **Musical Actress:** Patti Lupone in *Evita*

10084 **Supporting or Featured Musical Actor:** Mandy Patinkin in *Evita*

10085 **Supporting or Featured Musical Actress:** Priscilla Lopez in *A Day in Hollywood/A Night in the Ukraine*

10086 **Play:** *Children of a Lesser God* by Mark Medoff, produced by Emanuel Azenberg, the Shubert Organization, Mrs. Dasha Epstein and Ron Dante

10087 **Dramatic Director:** Vivian Matalon for *Morning's at Seven*

10088 **Musical:** *Evita* produced by Robert Stigwood

10089 **Musical Director:** Harold Prince for *Evita*

10090 **Musical Book:** *Evita* by Tim Rice

10091 **Score:** *Evita* music by Andrew Lloyd Webber, lyrics by Tim Rice

10092 **Scenic Designer:** John Lee Beatty for *Talley's Folly* and David Mitchell for *Barnum*

10093 **Costume Designer:** Theoni V. Aldredge for *Barnum*

10094 **Choreographer:** Tommy Tune and Thommie Walsh for *A Day in Hollywood/A Night in the Ukraine*

10095 **Lighting Designer:** David Hersey for *Evita*

10096 **Reproduction (Play or Musical):** *Morning's at Seven*

10097 **Special Award:** Mary Tyler Moore, Actor's Theatre of Louisville and Godspeed Opera House

———— **1981** ————

10098 **Dramatic Actor:** Ian McKellen in *Amadeus*

10099 **Dramatic Actress:** Jane Lapotaire in *Piaf*

10100 **Supporting or Featured Dramatic Actor:** Brian Backer in *The Floating Light Bulb*

10101 **Supporting or Featured Dramatic Actress:** Swoosie Kurtz in *Fifth of July*

10102 **Musical Actor:** Kevin Kline in *The Pirates of Penzance*

10103 **Musical Actress:** Lauren Bacall in *Woman of the Year*

10104 **Supporting or Featured Musical Actor:** Hinton Battle in *Sophisticated Ladies*

10105 **Supporting or Featured Musical Actress:** Marilyn Cooper in *Woman of the Year*

10106 **Play:** *Amadeus* by Peter Shaffer,

produced by the Shubert Organization, Elizabeth I. McCann, Nelle Nugent and Roger S. Berlind

10107 **Dramatic Director:** Peter Hall for *Amadeus*

10108 **Musical:** *42nd Street* produced by David Merrick

10109 **Musical Director:** Wilford Leach for *The Pirates of Penzance*

10110 **Musical Book:** *Woman of the Year* by Peter Stone

10111 **Score:** *Woman of the Year* music by John Kander, lyrics by Fred Ebb

10112 **Scenic Designer:** John Bury for *Amadeus*

10113 **Costume Designer:** Willa Kim for *Sophisticated Ladies*

10114 **Choreographer:** Gower Champion for *42nd Street*

10115 **Lighting Designer:** John Bury for *Amadeus*

10116 **Reproduction (Play or Musical):** *The Pirates of Penzance*

10117 **Special Awards:** Lena Horne and Trinity Square Repertory Company

———————— **1982** ————————

10118 **Dramatic Actor:** Roger Rees in *The Life and Adventures of Nicholas Nickleby*

10119 **Dramatic Actress:** Zoe Caldwell in *Medea*

10120 **Supporting or Featured Dramatic Actor:** Zakes Mokae in *Master Harold—And the Boys*

10121 **Supporting or Featured Dramatic Actress:** Amanda Plummer in *Agnes of God*

10122 **Musical Actor:** Ben Harney in *Dreamgirls*

10123 **Musical Actress:** Jennifer Holliday in *Dreamgirls*

10124 **Supporting or Featured Musical Actor:** Cleavant Derricks in *Dreamgirls*

10125 **Supporting or Featured Musical Actress:** Liliane Montevecchi in *Nine*

10126 **Play:** *The Life and Adventures of Nicholas Nickleby* by David Edgar, produced by James M. Nederlander, the Shubert Organization, Elizabeth I. McCann and Nelle Nugent

10127 **Dramatic Director:** Trevor Nunn and John Caird for *The Life and Adventures of Nicholas Nickleby*

10128 **Musical:** *Nine* produced by Michel Stuart, Harvey J. Claris, Roger S. Berlind, James M. Nederlander, Francine LeFrak and Kenneth D. Greenblatt

10129 **Musical Director:** Tommy Tune for *Nine*

10130 **Musical Book:** *Dreamgirls* by Tom Eyen

10131 **Score:** *Nine* music by Maury Yeston, lyrics by Maury Yeston

10132 **Scenic Designer:** John Napier and Dermot Hayes for *The Life and Adventures of Nicholas Nickleby*

10133 **Costume Designer:** William Ivey Long for *Nine*

10134 **Choreographer:** Michael Bennett and Michael Peters for *Dreamgirls*

10135 **Lighting Designer:** Tharon Musser for *Dreamgirls*

10136 **Reproduction (Play or Musical):** *Othello*

10137 **Special Award:** The Guthrie Theatre and The Actor's Fund of America

———————— **1983** ————————

10138 **Dramatic Actor:** Harvey Fierstein in *Torch Song Trilogy*

10139 **Dramatic Actress:** Jessica Tandy in *Foxfire*

10140 **Supporting or Featured Dramatic Actor:** Matthew Broderick in *Brighton Beach Memoirs*

10141 **Supporting or Featured Dramatic Actress:** Judith Ivey in *Steaming July*

10142 **Musical Actor:** Tommy Tune in *My One and Only*

10143 **Musical Actress:** Natalia Makarova in *On Your Toes*

10144 **Supporting or Featured Musical Actor:** Charles "Honi" Coles in *My One and Only*

10145 **Supporting or Featured Musical Actress:** Betty Buckley in *Cats*

10146 **Play:** *Torch Song Trilogy* by Harvey Fierstein, produced by Kenneth Waissman, Martin Markinson, Lawrence Lane, John Glines, Donald Tick, and BetMar

10147 **Dramatic Director:** Gene Saks for *Brighton Beach Memoirs*

10148 **Musical:** *Cats* produced by Cameron Mackintosh

10149 **Musical Director:** Trevor Nunn for *Cats*

10150 **Musical Book:** *Cats* by T. S. Eliot

10151 **Score:** *Cats* music by Andrew Lloyd Webber, lyrics by T. S. Eliot

10152 **Scenic Designer:** Ming Cho Lee for *K2*

10153 **Costume Designer:** John Napier for *Cats*

10154 **Choreographer:** Tommy Tune and Thommie Walsh for *My One and Only*

10155 **Lighting Designer:** David Hersey for *Cats*

10156 **Reproduction (Play or Musical):** *On Your Toes*

10157 **Special Awards:** The Theatre Collection of the Museum of the City of New York, accepting: Dr. Mary C. Henderson — Oregon Shakespeare Festival Association, accepting: Mr. Jerry Turner, Mr. William W. Patton

─────────── **1 9 8 4** ───────────

10158 **Dramatic Actor:** Jeremy Irons in *The Real Thing*

10159 **Dramatic Actress:** Glenn Close in *The Real Thing*

10160 **Supporting or Featured Dramatic Actor:** Joe Mantegna in *Glengarry Glen Ross*

10161 **Supporting or Featured Dramatic Actress:** Christine Baranski in *The Real Thing*

10162 **Musical Actor:** George Hearn in *La Cage aux Folles*

10163 **Musical Actress:** Chita Rivera in *The Rink*

10164 **Supporting or Featured Musical Actor:** Hinton Battle in *The Tap Dance Kid*

10165 **Supporting or Featured Musical Actress:** Lila Kadrova in *Zorba*

10166 **Play:** *The Real Thing* by Tom Stoppard, produced by Emanuel Azenberg, the Shubert Organization, Icarus Productions, Byron Goldman, Ivan Bloch, Roger Berlind and Michael Codron

10167 **Dramatic Director:** Mike Nichols for *The Real Thing*

10168 **Musical:** *La Cage aux Folles* produced by Allan Carr, Kenneth D. Greenblatt, Marvin A. Krauss, Stewart F. Lane, James M. Nederlander, Martin Richards, Barry Brown and Fritz Holt

10169 **Musical Director:** Arthur Laurents for *La Cage aux Folles*

10170 **Musical Book:** *La Cage aux Folles* by Harvey Fierstein

10171 **Score:** *La Cage aux Folles* music by Jerry Herman, lyrics by Jerry Herman

10172 **Scenic Designer:** Tony Straiges for *Sunday in the Park with George*

10173 **Costume Designer:** Theoni V. Aldredge for *La Cage aux Folles*

10174 **Choreographer:** Danny Daniels for *The Tap Dance Kid*

10175 **Lighting Designer:** Richard Nelson for *Sunday in the Park with George*

10176 **Reproduction (Play or Musical):** *Death of a Salesman*

10177 **Special Award:** San Diego Old Globe Theatre, "La Tragédie de Carmen," Al Hirschfeld (Brooks Atkinson Award) and Peter Feller

─────────── **1 9 8 5** ───────────

10178 **Dramatic Actor:** Derek Jacobi in *Much Ado About Nothing*

10179 **Dramatic Actress:** Stockard Channing in *Joe Egg*

10180 **Supporting or Featured Dramatic Actor:** Barry Miller in *Biloxi Blues*

10181 **Supporting or Featured Dramatic Actress:** Judith Ivey in *Hurlyburly*

10182 **Supporting or Featured Musical Actor:** Ron Richardson in *Big River*

10183 **Supporting or Featured Musical Actress:** Lailani Jones in *Grind*

10184 **Play:** *Biloxi Blues* by Neil Simon, produced by Emanuel Azenberg, Center Theatre Group/Ahmanson Theatre, Los Angeles

10185 **Dramatic Director:** Gene Saks for *Biloxi Blues*

10186 **Musical:** *Big River* produced by Rocco Landesman, Heidi Landesman, Rick Steiner, M. Anthony Fisher and Dodger Productions

10187 **Musical Director:** Des McAnuff for *Big River*

10188 **Musical Book:** *Big River* by William Hauptman

10189 **Score:** *Big River* by Roger Miller

10190 **Scenic Designer:** Heidi Landesman for *Big River*
10191 **Costume Designer:** Florence Klotz for *Grind*
10192 **Lighting Designer:** Richard Riddell for *Big River*
10193 **Reproduction (Play or Musical):** *Joe Egg*
10194 **Special Awards:** Yul Brynner, Edwin Lester, New York State Council on the Arts and Steppenwolf Theatre

———————— **1986** ————————

10195 **Dramatic Actor:** Judd Hirsch in *I'm Not Rappaport*
10196 **Dramatic Actress:** Lily Tomlin in *The Search for Signs of Intelligent Life in the Universe*
10197 **Supporting or Featured Dramatic Actor:** John Mahoney in *The House of Blue Leaves*
10198 **Supporting or Featured Dramatic Actress:** Swoosie Kurtz in *The House of Blue Leaves*
10199 **Musical Actor:** George Rose in *The Mystery of Edwin Drood*
10200 **Musical Actress:** Bernadette Peters in *Song & Dance*
10201 **Supporting or Featured Musical Actor:** Michael Rupert in *Sweet Charity*
10202 **Supporting or Featured Musical Actress:** Bebe Neuwirth in *Sweet Charity*
10203 **Play:** *I'm Not Rappaport* by Herb Gardner, produced by James Walsh, Lewis Allen and Martin Heinfling
10204 **Dramatic Director:** Jerry Zaks for *The House of Blue Leaves*
10205 **Musical:** *The Mystery of Edwin Drood* produced by Joseph Papp
10206 **Musical Director:** Wilford Leach for *The Mystery of Edwin Drood*
10207 **Musical Book:** *The Mystery of Edwin Drood* by Rupert Holmes
10208 **Score:** *The Mystery of Edwin Drood* by Rupert Holmes
10209 **Scenic Designer:** Tony Walton for *The House of Blue Leaves*
10210 **Costume Designer:** Patricia Zipprodt for *Sweet Charity*
10211 **Choreographer:** Bob Fosse for *Big Deal*
10212 **Lighting Designer:** Pat Collins for *I'm Not Rappaport*

10213 **Reproduction (Play or Musical):** *Sweet Charity*
10214 **Special Award:** American Repertory Theater

———————— **1987** ————————

10215 **Dramatic Actor:** James Earl Jones in *Fences*
10216 **Dramatic Actress:** Linda Lavin in *Broadway Bound*
10217 **Supporting or Featured Dramatic Actor:** John Randolph in *Broadway Bound*
10218 **Supporting or Featured Dramatic Actress:** Mary Alice in *Fences*
10219 **Musical Actor:** Robert Lindsay in *Me and My Girl*
10220 **Musical Actress:** Maryann Plunkett in *Me and My Girl*
10221 **Supporting or Featured Musical Actor:** Michael Maguire in *Les Misérables*
10222 **Supporting or Featured Musical Actress:** Frances Ruffelle in *Les Misérables*
10223 **Play:** *Fences* by August Wilson, produced by Carole Shorenstein Hays and the Yale Repertory Theater
10224 **Dramatic Director:** Lloyd Richards for *Fences*
10225 **Musical:** *Les Misérables* produced by Cameron Mackintosh
10226 **Musical Director:** Trevor Nunn and John Caird for *Les Misérables*
10227 **Musical Book:** *Les Misérables* by Alain Boublil and Claude-Michel Schönberg
10228 **Score:** *Les Misérables* music by Claude-Michel Schonberg, lyrics by Herbert Kretzmer and Alain Boublil
10229 **Scenic Designer:** John Napier for *Les Misérables*
10230 **Costume Designer:** John Napier for *Starlight Express*
10231 **Choreographer:** Gillian Gregory for *Me and My Girl*
10232 **Lighting Designer:** David Hersey for *Les Misérables*
10233 **Best Revival:** *All My Sons* produced by Jay H. Fuchs, Steven Warnick and Charles Patsos
10234 **Special Awards:** George Abbott, Jackie Mason and the San Francisco Mime Troupe

———————— **1 9 8 8** ————————

10235 **Dramatic Actor:** Ron Silver in *Speed-the-Plow*

10236 **Dramatic Actress:** Joan Allen in *Burn This*

10237 **Supporting or Featured Dramatic Actor:** B. D. Wong in *M. Butterfly*

10238 **Supporting or Featured Dramatic Actress:** L. Scott Caldwell in *Joe Turner's Come and Gone*

10239 **Musical Actor:** Michael Crawford in *The Phantom of the Opera*

10240 **Musical Actress:** Joanna Gleason in *Into the Woods*

10241 **Supporting or Featured Musical Actor:** Bill McCutcheon in *Anything Goes*

10242 **Supporting or Featured Musical Actress:** Judy Kaye in *The Phantom of the Opera*

10243 **Play:** *M. Butterfly* by David Henry Hwang, produced by Stuart Ostrow and David Geffen

10244 **Dramatic Director:** John Dexter for *M. Butterfly*

10245 **Musical:** *The Phantom of the Opera* produced by Cameron Mackintosh, the Really Useful Theatre Company, Incorporated

10246 **Musical Director:** Harold Prince for *The Phantom of the Opera*

10247 **Musical Book:** *Into the Woods* by James Lapine

10248 **Score:** *Into the Woods* music and lyrics by Stephen Sondheim

10249 **Scenic Designer:** Maria Bjornson for *The Phantom of the Opera*

10250 **Costume Designer:** Maria Bjornson for *The Phantom of the Opera*

10251 **Choreographer:** Michael Smuin for *Anything Goes*

10252 **Lighting Designer:** Andrew Bridge for *The Phantom of the Opera*

10253 **Revival (Play or Musical):** *Anything Goes* produced by Lincoln Center Theater, Gregory Mosher and Bernard Gersten

10254 **Special Award:** Brooklyn Academy of Music and South Coast Repertory of Costa Mesa, California

———————— **1 9 8 9** ————————

10255 **Dramatic Actor:** Philip Bosco in *Lend Me a Tenor*

10256 **Dramatic Actress:** Pauline Collins in *Shirley Valentine*

10257 **Supporting or Featured Dramatic Actor:** Boyd Gaines in *The Heidi Chronicles*

10258 **Supporting or Featured Dramatic Actress:** Christine Baranski in *Rumors*

10259 **Musical Actor:** Jason Alexander in *Jerome Robbins' Broadway*

10260 **Musical Actress:** Ruth Brown in *Black and Blue*

10261 **Supporting or Featured Musical Actor:** Scott Wise in *Jerome Robbins' Broadway*

10262 **Supporting or Featured Musical Actress:** Debbie Shapiro in *Jerome Robbins' Broadway*

10263 **Play:** *The Heidi Chronicles* by Wendy Wasserstein, produced by the Shubert Organization, Suntory International Corporation, James Walsh and Playwrights Horizon

10264 **Dramatic Director:** Jerry Zaks for *Lend Me a Tenor*

10265 **Musical:** *Jerome Robbins' Broadway* produced by the Shubert Organization, Roger Berlind, Suntory International Corporation, Byron Goldman and Emanuel Azenberg

10266 **Musical Director:** Jerome Robbins for *Jerome Robbins' Broadway*

10267 **Scenic Designer:** Santo Loquasto for *Cafe Crown*

10268 **Costume Designer:** Claudio Segovia and Hector Orezzoli for *Black and Blue*

10269 **Choreographer:** Cholly Atkins, Henry LeTang, Frankie Manning and Fayard Nicholas for *Black and Blue*

10270 **Lighting Designer:** Jennifer Tipton for *Jerome Robbins' Broadway*

10271 **Best Revival:** *Ah, Wilderness!* produced by Ken Marsolais, Alexander H. Cohen, the Kennedy Center for the Performing Arts, Yale Repertory Theater, Richard Norton, Irma Oestreicher and Elizabeth D. White and *Our Town* produced by Lincoln Center Theater, Gregory Mosher and Bernard Gersten

10272 **Special Award:** Hartford Stage Company

———————— **1 9 9 0** ————————

10273 **Dramatic Actor:** Robert Morse in *Tru*

10274 **Dramatic Actress:** Maggie Smith in *Lettice and Lovage*

10275 **Supporting or Featured Dramatic Actor:** Charles Durning in *Cat on a Hot Tin Roof*

10276 **Supporting or Featured Dramatic Actress:** Margaret Tyzack in *Lettice and Lovage*

10277 **Musical Actor:** James Naughton in *City of Angels*

10278 **Musical Actress:** Tyne Daly in *Gypsy*

10279 **Supporting or Featured Musical Actor:** Michael Jeter in *Grand Hotel, the Musical*

10280 **Supporting or Featured Musical Actress:** Randy Graff in *City of Angels*

10281 **Play:** *The Grapes of Wrath* by Frank Galati, produced by the Shubert Organization, Steppenwolf Theatre Company, Suntory International Corporation and Jujamcyn Theaters

10282 **Dramatic Director:** Frank Galati for *The Grapes of Wrath*

10283 **Musical:** *City of Angels* produced by Nick Vanoff, Roger Berlind, Jujamcyn Theaters, Suntory International Corporation and the Shubert Organization

10284 **Musical Director:** Tommy Tune for *Grand Hotel, the Musical*

10285 **Musical Book:** *City of Angels* by Larry Gelbart

10286 **Musical Score:** *City of Angels* music by Cy Coleman, lyrics by David Zippel

10287 **Scenic Designer:** Robin Wagner for *City of Angels*

10288 **Costume Designer:** Santo Loquasto for *Grand Hotel, the Musical*

10289 **Choreographer:** Tommy Tune for *Grand Hotel, the Musical*

10290 **Lighting Designer:** Jules Fisher for *Grand Hotel, the Musical*

10291 **Revival:** *Gypsy* produced by Barry and Fran Weissler, Kathy Levin and Barry Brown

10292 **Special Award:** Seattle Repertory Company

10293 **Tony Honor:** Alfred Drake for excellence in the theatre

————— **1991** —————

10294 **Dramatic Actor:** Nigel Hawthorne in *Shadowlands*

10295 **Dramatic Actress:** Mercedes Ruehl in *Lost in Yonkers*

10296 **Supporting or Featured Dramatic Actor:** Kevin Spacey in *Lost in Yonkers*

10297 **Supporting or Featured Dramatic Actress:** Irene Worth in *Lost in Yonkers*

10298 **Musical Actor:** Jonathan Pryce in *Miss Saigon*

10299 **Musical Actress:** Lea Salonga in *Miss Saigon*

10300 **Supporting or Featured Musical Actor:** Hinton Battle in *Miss Saigon*

10301 **Supporting or Featured Musical Actress:** Daisy Eagan in *The Secret Garden*

10302 **Play:** *Lost in Yonkers* by Neil Simon, produced by Emanuel Azenberg

10303 **Dramatic Director:** Jerry Zaks for *Six Degrees of Separation*

10304 **Musical:** *The Will Rogers Follies* produced by Pierre Cossette, Martin Richards, Sam Crothers, James M. Nederlander, Stewart F. Lane, Max Weitzenhoffer and Japan Satellite Broadcasting, Incorporated

10305 **Musical Director:** Tommy Tune for *The Will Rogers Follies*

10306 **Musical Book:** *The Secret Garden* by Marsha Norman

10307 **Musical Score:** *The Will Rogers Follies* music by Cy Coleman, lyrics by Betty Comden and Adolph Green

10308 **Scenic Designer:** Heidi Landesman for *The Secret Garden*

10309 **Costume Designer:** Willa Kim for *The Will Rogers Follies*

10310 **Choreographer:** Tommy Tune for *The Will Rogers Follies*

10311 **Lighting Designer:** Jules Fisher for *The Will Rogers Follies*

10312 **Best Revival:** *Fiddler on the Roof* produced by Barry and Fran Weissler and the Pace Theatrical Group

10313 **Special Award:** Yale Repertory Theater

10314 **Tony Honor:** Father George Moore

————— **1992** —————

10315 **Dramatic Actor:** Judd Hirsch in *Conversations with My Father*

10316 **Dramatic Actress:** Glenn Close in *Death and the Maiden*

10317 **Supporting or Featured Dramatic Actor:** Larry Fishburne in *Two Trains Running*

10318 **Supporting or Featured Dramatic Actress:** Brid Brennan in *Dancing at Lughnasa*

10319 **Musical Actor:** Gregory Hines in *Jelly's Last Jam*

10320 **Musical Actress:** Faith Prince in *Guys and Dolls*

10321 **Supporting or Featured Musical Actor:** Scott Waara in *The Most Happy Fella*

10322 **Supporting or Featured Musical Actress:** Tonya Pinkins in *Jelly's Last Jam*

10323 **Play:** *Dancing at Lughnasa* by Brian Friel, produced by Noel Pearson, Bill Kenwright and Joseph Harris

10324 **Dramatic Director:** Patrick Mason for *Dancing at Lughnasa*

10325 **Musical:** *Crazy for You* produced by Roger Horchow and Elizabeth Williams

10326 **Musical Director:** Jerry Zaks for *Guys and Dolls*

10327 **Musical Book:** *Falsettos* by William Finn and James Lapine

10328 **Musical Score:** *Falsettos* music and lyrics by William Finn

10329 **Scenic Designer:** Tony Walton for *Guys and Dolls*

10330 **Costume Designer:** William Ivey Long for *Crazy for You*

10331 **Choreographer:** Susan Stroman for *Crazy for You*

10332 **Lighting Designer:** Jules Fisher for *Jelly's Last Jam*

10333 **Revival:** *Guys and Dolls* produced by Dodger Productions, Roger Berlind, Jujamcyn Theaters/TV Asahi, Kardana Productions and the John F. Kennedy Center for the Performing Arts

10334 **Special Award:** The Goodman Theatre of Chicago

10335 **Tony Honor:** *The Fantasticks*

———— **1993** ————

10336 **Dramatic Actor:** Ron Liebman in *Angels in America: Millennium Approaches*

10337 **Dramatic Actress:** Madeline Kahn in *The Sisters Rosensweig*

10338 **Supporting or Featured Dramatic Actor:** Stephen Spinella in *Angels in America: Millennium Approaches*

10339 **Supporting or Featured Dramatic Actress:** Debra Monk in *Redwood Curtain*

10340 **Musical Actor:** Brent Carver in *Kiss of the Spider Woman, the Musical*

10341 **Musical Actress:** Chita Rivera in *Kiss of the Spider Woman, the Musical*

10342 **Supporting or Featured Musical Actor:** Anthony Cerveris in *Kiss of the Spider Woman, the Musical*

10343 **Supporting or Featured Musical Actress:** Andrea Martin in *My Favorite Year*

10344 **Play:** *Angels in America: Millennium Approaches* by Tony Kushner, produced by Jujamcyn Theaters, Mark Taper Forum/Gordon Davidson, Margo Lion, Susan Quint Gallin, Jon B. Platt, the Baruch-Frankel-Viertel Group, Frederick Zollo and Herb Alpert

10345 **Dramatic Director:** George C. Wolfe for *Angels in America: Millennium Approaches*

10346 **Musical:** *Kiss of the Spider Woman, the Musical* produced by the Live Entertainment Corporation of Canada/Garth Drabinsky

10347 **Musical Director:** Des McAnuff for *The Who's Tommy*

10348 **Musical Book:** *Kiss of the Spider Woman, the Musical* by Terrence McNally

10349 **Musical Score:** *Kiss of the Spider Woman, the Musical* music by John Kander, lyrics by Fred Ebb and *The Who's Tommy* music by Pete Townshend, lyrics by Pete Townshend

10350 **Scenic Designer:** John Arnone for *The Who's Tommy*

10351 **Costume Designer:** Florence Klotz for *Kiss of the Spider Woman, the Musical*

10352 **Choreographer:** Wayne Cilento for *The Who's Tommy*

10353 **Lighting Designer:** Chris Parry for *The Who's Tommy*

10354 **Best Revival:** *Anna Christie* produced by Roundtable Theatre Company and Todd Haimes

10355 **Special Awards:** *Oklahoma* —50th Anniversary and the La Jolla Playhouse

10356 **Tony Honors:** IATSE and Broadway Cares/Equity Fights AIDS

Pulitzer Prize for Drama

Joseph Pulitzer died in 1911. In his will he left $2 million to Columbia University. A graduate school of journalism was to be established with $1.5 million. The remaining $.5 million was an endowment to establish prizes.

The early Pulitzer award recipients in drama were chosen by the prize board which was chaired by the president of Columbia University. His prudish mind was easily offended and because it was, he prevented worthy plays from being honored. This prompted other theatre organizations to honor plays they felt were being ignored.

Famous playwrights were honored, but not always for their best work. Eugene O'Neill received the Pulitzer in 1920 for *Beyond the Horizon*, in 1922 for *Anna Christie* and finally in 1957 for *Long Days Journey Into Night*. Tennessee Williams received the 1948 Pulitzer Prize for drama with his play *A Streetcar Named Desire*.

But today plays by these men which are looked at as classics of the American stage were never honored. Eugene O'Neill wrote *The Iceman Cometh* and Tennessee Williams wrote *Cat on a Hot Tin Roof* and neither play was honored with a Pulitzer. Because these and other deserving plays were overlooked for Pulitzer prizes, organizations like the Tony Awards were created.

─────── **1 9 1 7** ───────

No award given.

─────── **1 9 1 8** ───────

10357 *Why Marry?* by Jesse Lynch Williams

─────── **1 9 1 9** ───────

No award given

─────── **1 9 2 0** ───────

10358 *Beyond the Horizon* by Eugene O'Neill

─────── **1 9 2 1** ───────

10359 *Miss Lulu Bett* by Zona Gale

─────── **1 9 2 2** ───────

10360 *Anna Christie* by Eugene O'Neill

─────── **1 9 2 3** ───────

10361 *Icebound* by Owen Davis

─────── **1 9 2 4** ───────

10362 *Hell-Bent for Heaven* by Hatcher Hughes

─────── **1 9 2 5** ───────

10363 *They Knew What They Wanted* by Sidney Howard

─────── **1 9 2 6** ───────

10364 *Craig's Wife* by George Kelly

─────── **1 9 2 7** ───────

10365 *In Abraham's Bosom* by Paul Green

─────── **1 9 2 8** ───────

10366 *Strange Interlude* by Eugene O'Neill

─────── **1 9 2 9** ───────

10367 *Street Scene* by Elmer L. Rice

─────── **1 9 3 0** ───────

10368 *The Green Pastures* by Marc Connelly

─────── **1 9 3 1** ───────

10369 *Alison's House* by Susan Glaspell

─────── **1 9 3 2** ───────

10370 *Of Thee I Sing* by George S. Kaufman, Ira Gershwin and Morris Ryskind

─────── **1 9 3 3** ───────

10371 *Both Your Houses* by Maxwell Anderson

─────── **1 9 3 4** ───────

10372 *Men in White* by Sidney Kingsley

─────── **1 9 3 5** ───────

10373 *The Old Maid* by Zoe Akins

─────── **1 9 3 6** ───────

10374 *Idiot's Delight* by Robert E. Sherwood

─────── **1 9 3 7** ───────

10375 *You Can't Take It with You* by Moss Hart and George S. Kaufman

─────── **1 9 3 8** ───────

10376 *Our Town* by Thornton Wilder

─────── **1 9 3 9** ───────

10377 *Abe Lincoln in Illinois* by Robert E. Sherwood

─────── **1 9 4 0** ───────

10378 *The Time of Your Life* by William Saroyan

——————— **1 9 4 1** ———————

10379 *There Shall Be No Night* by Robert E. Sherwood

——————— **1 9 4 2** ———————

No award given

——————— **1 9 4 3** ———————

10380 *The Skin of Our Teeth* by Thornton Wilder

——————— **1 9 4 4** ———————

10381 Special award: *Oklahoma!* by Richard Rodgers and Oscar Hammerstein II

——————— **1 9 4 5** ———————

10382 *Harvey* by Mary Chase

——————— **1 9 4 6** ———————

10383 *State of the Union* by Russell Crouse and Howard Lindsay

——————— **1 9 4 7** ———————

No award given

——————— **1 9 4 8** ———————

10384 *A Streetcar Named Desire* by Tennessee Williams

——————— **1 9 4 9** ———————

10385 *Death of a Salesman* by Arthur Miller

——————— **1 9 5 0** ———————

10386 *South Pacific* by Richard Rodgers, Oscar Hammerstein II and Joshua Logan

——————— **1 9 5 1** ———————

No award given

——————— **1 9 5 2** ———————

10387 *The Shrike* by Joseph Kramm

——————— **1 9 5 3** ———————

10388 *Picnic* by William Inge

——————— **1 9 5 4** ———————

10389 *The Teahouse of the August Moon* by John Patrick

——————— **1 9 5 5** ———————

10390 *Cat on a Hot Tin Roof* by Tennessee Williams

——————— **1 9 5 6** ———————

10391 *Diary of Anne Frank* by Albert Hackett and Frances Goodrich

——————— **1 9 5 7** ———————

10392 *Long Day's Journey Into Night* by Eugene O'Neill

——————— **1 9 5 8** ———————

10393 *Look Homeward, Angel* by Ketti Frings

——————— **1 9 5 9** ———————

10394 *J. B.* by Archibald MacLeish

——————— **1 9 6 0** ———————

10395 *Fiorello!* by Jerome Weidman and George Abbott, music by Jerry Bock and lyrics by Sheldon Harnick

——————— **1 9 6 1** ———————

10396 *All the Way Home* by Tad Mosel

——————— **1 9 6 2** ———————

10397 *How to Succeed in Business Without Really Trying* by Frank Loesser and Abe Burrows

——————— **1 9 6 3** ———————

No award given

——————— **1 9 6 4** ———————

No award given

————— **1 9 6 5** —————

10398 *The Subject Was Roses* by Frank Gilroy

————— **1 9 6 6** —————

No award given

————— **1 9 6 7** —————

10399 *A Delicate Balance* by Edward Albee

————— **1 9 6 8** —————

No award given

————— **1 9 6 9** —————

10400 *The Great White Hope* by Howard Sackler

————— **1 9 7 0** —————

10401 *No Place to Be Somebody* by Charles Gordone

————— **1 9 7 1** —————

10402 *The Effect of Gamma Rays on Man-in-the-Moon Marigolds* by Paul Zindel

————— **1 9 7 2** —————

No award given

————— **1 9 7 3** —————

10403 *That Championship Season* by Jason Miller

————— **1 9 7 4** —————

No award given

————— **1 9 7 5** —————

10404 *Seascape* by Edward Albee

————— **1 9 7 6** —————

10405 *A Chorus Line* conceived, choreographed and directed by Michael Bennett; book by James Kirkwood and Nicholas Dante; music by Marvin Hamlisch; lyrics by Edward Kleban

————— **1 9 7 7** —————

10406 *The Shadow Box* by Michael Cristofer

————— **1 9 7 8** —————

10407 *The Gin Game* by Donald L. Coburn

————— **1 9 7 9** —————

10408 *Buried Child* by Sam Shepard

————— **1 9 8 0** —————

10409 *Talley's Folly* by Lanford Wilson

————— **1 9 8 1** —————

10410 *Crimes of the Heart* by Beth Henley

————— **1 9 8 2** —————

10411 *A Soldier's Play* by Charles Fuller

————— **1 9 8 3** —————

10412 *'Night Mother* by Jason Miller

————— **1 9 8 4** —————

10413 *Glengarry Glen Ross* by David Mamet

————— **1 9 8 5** —————

10414 *Sunday in the Park with George* Music and Lyrics by Stephen Sondheim, book by James Lapine

————— **1 9 8 6** —————

No award given

————— **1 9 8 7** —————

10415 *Fences* by August Wilson

——————— **1 9 8 8** ———————

10416 *Driving Miss Daisy* by Alfred Uhry

——————— **1 9 8 9** ———————

10417 *The Heidi Chronicles* by Wendy Wasserstein

——————— **1 9 9 0** ———————

10418 *The Piano Lesson* by August Wilson

——————— **1 9 9 1** ———————

10419 *Lost in Yonkers* by Neil Simon

——————— **1 9 9 2** ———————

10420 *The Kentucky Cycle* by Robert Schenkkan

——————— **1 9 9 3** ———————

10421 *Angels in America: Millennium Approaches* by Tony Kushner

Off Broadway Drama Awards (Obies)

The newest of the four theatrical awards to be listed in this book, these drama awards are limited in scope to the Off Broadway stage. The oldest theatrical award, the Pulitzer, began in 1917 and honored any play written either in the United States or abroad. The next award to be given was that of the New York Drama Critics' Circle, begun to honor plays which the critics felt were being overlooked by the Pulitzer Prize for Drama. The Tony Awards also honored plays which the New York theatrical producers felt were being overlooked but the plays under consideration were limited to those appearing on Broadway.

In 1956 the New York newspaper *The Village Voice* decided to remedy that situation by presenting awards to New York plays limited to those being staged in Off Broadway theatres. Many of the playwrights, performers, directors and plays went on to be highly successful. Winner of best director at the first award ceremony was Jose Quintero for Eugene O'Neill's *The Iceman Cometh*.

O'Neill went on to win the 1957 Tony Award for *Long Day's Journey Into Night*. Jose Quintero went on to win not only the Tony for that play but for the 1974 production of *A Moon for the Misbegotten*. Also the Off Broadway plays themselves have received recognition and been made into successful movies. *Six Degrees of Separation* was honored in 1991 by the Obies and was made into a 1994 movie. *Driving Miss Daisy* was staged Off Broadway in 1987 and went on to be filmed and win an Oscar for Jessica Tandy at the 1989 Academy Award ceremonies.

369

—————— **1956** ——————

10422 **Best Play/Best New American Play:** *Absalom* by Lionel Abel

10423 **Best Musical:** *Three Penny Opera* by Bertolt Brecht and Kurt Weill, adapted by Marc Blitzstein

10424 **Best Production:** *Uncle Vanya* at the Fourth Street Theatre

10425 **Best Actress:** Julie Bovasso in *The Maids*

10426 **Best Actor:** Jason Robards, Jr. in *The Iceman Cometh* and George Voskovec in *Uncle Vanya*

10427 **Best Director:** Jose Quintero for *The Iceman Cometh*

10428 **Distinguished Sets, Lighting or Costumes:** Klaus Holm and Alvin Colt

10429 **Distinguished Performances by Actresses:** Peggy McKay, Shirlee Emmons, Frances Sternhagen and Nancy Wickwire

10430 **Distinguished Performances by Actors:** Gerald Hiken, Alan Ansara, Roberts Blossom and Addison Powell

10431 **Special Citations and Awards which do not fit into other categories:** The Phoenix Theatre, the Shakespeare Workshop Theatre, the Tempo Playhouse

—————— **1957** ——————

10432 **Best Play/Best New American Play:** *A House Remembered* by Louis A. Lippe

10433 **Best Actress:** Colleen Dewhurst in *The Taming of the Shrew*, *The Eagle Has Two Heads* and *Camille*

10434 **Best Director:** Gene Frankel for *Volpone*

10435 **Distinguished Performances by Actresses:** Marguerite Lenert, Betty Miller and Jutta Wolf

10436 **Distinguished Performances by Actors:** Thayer David, Michael Kane and Arthur Malet

10437 **Best Production:** *Exiles* by the Renata Theatre

10438 **Best Actor:** William Smithers in *The Sea Gull*

10439 **Special Citations and Awards which do not fit into other categories:** Paul Shyre

—————— **1958** ——————

10440 **Best Play/Best New American Play:** *Endgame* by Samuel Beckett

10441 **Distinguished Plays:** *The Brothers Karamazov* by Boris Tumarin and Jack Sydow (Best Adaptation) *The Crucible* by Arthur Miller, directed by Word Baker (Best Revival), *Comic Strip* by George Panetta (Best Comedy) and *Guest of the Nation* by Neil McKenzie (Best One Act Play)

10442 **Best Actress:** Anne Meacham in *Garden District*

10443 **Best Actor:** George C. Scott in *Richard III*, *As You Like It* and *Children of Darkness*

10444 **Best Director:** Stuart Vaughan for the New York Shakespeare Festival

10445 **Distinguished Sets, Lighting or Costumes:** David Hays, Will Steven Armstrong and Nikola Cernovich

10446 **Best Music:** David Amram

10447 **Distinguished Performances by Actresses:** Tammy Grimes, Grania O'Malley and Nydia Westman

10448 **Distinguished Performance by Actors:** Leonardo Cimino, Jack Cannon, Robert Geiringer and Michael Higgins

10449 **Special Citations and Awards which do not fit into other categories:** The Phoenix Theatre, the Theatre Club and Lucille Lortel

—————— **1959** ——————

10450 **Best Play/Best New American Play:** *The Quare Fellow* by Samuel Beckett

10451 **Best Musical:** *A Party with Betty Comden and Adolph Green*

10452 **Best Revue:** *Diversions* by Steven Vinaver

10453 **Best Production:** *Ivanov* by Daniel Hineck and Harlan Quist

10454 **Best Actress:** Kathleen Maguire in *The Time of the Cuckoo*

10455 **Best Actor:** Alfredo Ryder in *I Rise in Flame, Cried the Phoenix*

10456 **Best Director:** William Ball for *Ivanov* (foreign play) and Jack Ragotzy, Arthur Laurents for the cycle (American plays)

10457 **Distinguished Performance by Actresses:** Rosina Fernhoff, Anne Fielding and Nancy Wickwire

10458 **Distinguished Performances by Actors:** Zero Mostel, Lester Rawlins and Harold Scott

10459 **Distinguished Sets, Lighting or Costumes:** David Hays, Will Steven Armstrong, Nikola Cernovich

10460 **Special Citations and Awards which do not fit into other categories:** Hal Holbrook

––––––– **1 9 6 0** –––––––

10461 **Best Play/Best New American Play:** *The Connection* by Jack Gelber

10462 **Best Foreign Play:** *The Balcony* by Jean Genet

10463 **Distinguished Play:** *Krapp's Last Tape* by Samuel Beckett, *The Prodigal* by Jack Richardson and *The Zoo Story* by Edward Albee

10464 **Best Production:** *The Connection* by Julian Beck and Judith Malina

10465 **Best Actress:** Eileen Brennan in *Little Mary Sunshine*

10466 **Best Actor:** Warren Finnerty in *The Connection*

10467 **Best Director:** Gene Frankel for *Machinal*

10468 **Distinguished Sets, Lighting or Costumes:** David Hays

10469 **Distinguished Performances by Actresses:** Patricia Falkenhain, Elisa Loti and Nancy Marchand

10470 **Distinguished Performances by Actors:** William Daniels, Donald Davis, Vincent Gardenia, John Heffernan and Jock Livingston

10471 **Special Citations and Awards which do not fit into other categories:** Brooks Atkinson

––––––– **1 9 6 1** –––––––

10472 **Best Play/Best New American Play:** *The Blacks* by Jean Genet

10473 **Best Off Off Broadway Production:** *The Premise* produced and directed by Theodore Flicker

10474 **Best Production:** *Hedda Gabler* produced and directed by David Ross

10475 **Best Actress:** Anne Meacham in *Hedda Gabler*

10476 **Best Actor:** Khigh Dheigh in *In the Jungle of Cities*

10477 **Best Music:** Teiji Ito

10478 **Best Director:** Gerald A. Freedman for *The Taming of the Shrew*

10479 **Distinguished Performances by Actresses:** Joan Hackett, Gerry Jedd and Surya Kumari

10480 **Distinguished Performances by Actors:** Godfrey M. Cambridge, James Coco and Lester Rawlins

10481 **Special Citations and Awards which do not fit in other categories:** Bernard Frechtman

––––––– **1 9 6 2** –––––––

10482 **Best Play/Best New American Play:** *Who'll Save the Plowboy?* by Frank D. Gilroy

10483 **Best Foreign Play:** *Happy Days* by Samuel Beckett

10484 **Best Musical:** *Fly Blackbird* by C. Jackson, James Hatch and Jerome Eskow

10485 **Best Actress:** Barbara Harris in *Oh Dad, Poor Dad, Mama's Hung You in the Closet and I'm Feelin' So Sad*

10486 **Best Actor:** James Earl Jones in *Clandestine in the Morning Line, The Apple* and *Moon on a Rainbow Shawl*

10487 **Best Director:** John Wulp for *Red Eye of Love*

10488 **Distinguished Sets, Lighting or Costumes:** Norris Houghton

10489 **Distinguished Performances by Actresses:** Sudie Bond, Vinnette Carrol, Rosemary Harris and Ruth White

10490 **Distinguished Performances by Actors:** Clayton Corzatte, Geoff Garland, Gerald O'Laughlin and Paul Roebling

10491 **Special Citations and Awards which do not fit into other categories:** Ellis Rabb for *The Hostage*

––––––– **1 9 6 3** –––––––

10492 **Best Production:** *Six Characters in Search of an Author* by the Martinique Theater and *The Boys from Syracuse* (musical) by the Theater Four

10493 **Best Actress:** Colleen Dewhurst in *Desire Under the Elms*

10494 **Best Actor:** George C. Scott in *Desire Under the Elms*

10495 **Best Director:** Alan Schneider for Pinter plays

10496 **Distinguished Performances by Actresses:** Jacqueline Brooks, Olympia Dukakis, Anne Jackson and Madeline Sherwood

10497 **Distinguished Performances by Actors:** Joseph Chaikin, Michael O'Sullivan, James Patterson and Eli Wallach

10498 **Special Citations and Awards which do not fit into other categories:** Jean Erdman *The Second City*

──────── **1 9 6 4** ────────

10499 **Best Play/Best New American Play:** *Play* by Samuel Beckett and *Dutchman* by Leroi Jones

10500 **Distinguished Play:** *Home Movies* by Rosalyn Drexler and *Funny House of a Negro* by Adrienne Kennedy

10501 **Best Production:** *The Brig* by the Living Theatre and *What Happened* (musical) by the Theater Four

10502 **Best Performances:** Gloria Foster in *In White America*

10503 **Best Music:** Al Carmines

10504 **Best Director:** Judith Malina for *The Brig*

10505 **Distinguished Direction:** Lawrence Kornfeld

10506 **Distinguished Sets, Lighting or Costumes:** Julian Beck

10507 **Distinguished Performances by Actresses:** Joyce Ebert, Lee Grant, Estelle Parsons, Diana Sands and Marian Seldes

10508 **Distinguished Performances by Actors:** Philip Bruns, David Hurst, Taylor Mead, Hack Warden and Ronald Weyand

10509 **Special Citations and Awards which do not fit in other categories:** Judson Memorial Church

──────── **1 9 6 5** ────────

10510 **Best Play/Best New American Play:** *The Old Glory* by Robert Lowell

10511 **Distinguished Play:** *Promenade* and *The Successful Life of Three* by Maria Irene Fornes

10512 **Best Production:** *The Cradle Will Rock* (musical) by the Theater Four

10513 **Distinguished Performances, both Male and Female:** Roscoe Lee Browne, Frank Langella and Lester Rawlins in *The Old Glory*

10514 **Best Director:** Ulu Grosbard for *A View from the Bridge*

10515 **Distinguished Sets, Lighting or Costumes:** Willa Kim

10516 **Distinguished Performances by Actresses:** Margaret De Priest, Rosemary Harris, Frances Sternhagen and Sada Thompson

10517 **Distinguished Performances by Actors:** Brian Bedford, Roberts Blossom, Dean Dittman, Joseph Chaikin, Robert Duvall and James Earl Jones

10518 **Special Citations and Awards which do not fit into other categories:** The Paper Bag Players, Caffe Cino and Cafe la Mama

──────── **1 9 6 6** ────────

10519 **Best Play/Best New American Play:** *The Journey of the Fifth Horse* by Ronald Ribman

10520 **Distinguished Play:** *Good Day* by Emanuel Peluso and *Chicago, Icarus's Mother* and *Red Cross* by Sam Shepard

10521 **Best Actress:** Jane White in *Coriolanus* and *Love's Labor's Lost*

10522 **Best Actor:** Dustin Hoffman in *The Journey of the Fifth Horse*

10523 **Distinguished Direction:** Remy Charlip and Jacques Levy

10524 **Distinguished Sets, Lighting or Costumes:** Lindsey Decker and Ed Wittstein

10525 **Distinguished Performances by Actresses:** Clarice Blackburn, Marie-Claire Charba, Gloria Foster, Sharon Gaines and Florence Tarlow

10526 **Distinguished Performances by Actors:** Frank Langella, Michael Lipton, Kevin O'Connor, Jess Osuna and Douglas Turner

10527 **Special Citations and Awards which do not fit in other categories:** Joseph H. Dunn, H. M. Koutakas, Peter Schumann, Theater for Ideas and Theater in the Street

──────── **1 9 6 7** ────────

10528 **Distinguished Play:** *Futz* by Rochelle Owens and *La Turista* by Sam Shepard

10529 **Distinguished Foreign Play:** *Eh?* by Henry Livings

10530 **Best Actor:** Seth Allen in *Futz*

10531 **Best Director:** Tom O'Horgan for *Futz*

10532 **Distinguished Sets, Lighting or Costumes:** John Dodd

10533 **Distinguished Performances by Actresses:** Bette Henritze

10534 **Distinguished Performances by Actors:** Tom Aldredge, Robert Bonnard, Alvin Epstein, Neil Flanagan, Stacy Keach, Terry Kiser, Eddie McCarty, Robert Salvio and Rip Torn

10535 **Special Citations and Awards which do not fit into other categories:** La Mama Troupe, the Open Theater, Tom Sankey, the Second Story Players and Jeff Weiss

——————— **1 9 6 8** ———————

10536 **Best Foreign Play:** *The Memorandum* by Vaclav Havel

10537 **Best Musical:** *In Circles* by Gertrude Stein and Al Carmines

10538 **Distinguished Play:** *Muzeeka* by John Guare, *The Indian Wants the Bronx* by Israel Horvitz and *Melodrama Play* and *Forensic and the Navigators* by Sam Shepard

10539 **Best Actress:** Billie Dixon in *The Beard*

10540 **Best Actor:** Al Pacino in *The Indian Wants the Bronx*

10541 **Best Director:** Michael A. Schultz for *Song of the Lusitanian Bogey*

10542 **Distinguished Direction:** John Hancock and Rip Torn

10543 **Distinguished Sets, Lighting or Costumes:** Robert La Vigna

10544 **Distinguished Performances by Actresses:** Jean David, Mari Gorman and Peggy Pope

10545 **Distinguished Performances by Actors:** John Cazale, James Coco, Cliff Gorman, Moses Gunn and Roy R. Schneider

10546 **Special Citations and Awards which do not fit into other categories:** The Fortune Society, the Negro Ensemble Company, the San Francisco Mime Troupe and El Teatro Campesino

——————— **1 9 6 9** ———————

An altered format awarded Obies for distinguished achievement instead of awards for specific categories.

10547 The Living Theatre for *Frankenstein*

10548 Jeff Weiss for *The International Wrestling Match*

10549 Julie Bovasso for *Gloria and Esperanza*

10550 Judith Malina and Julian Beck for *Antigone*

10551 Israel Horvitz for *The Honest-to-God Schnozzola*

10552 Jules Feiffer for *Little Murders*

10553 Ronald Tavel for *The Boy on the Straight Back Chair*

10554 Nathan George and Ron O'Neal for *No Place to Be Somebody*

10555 Arlene Rothlein for *The Poor Little Match Girl*

10556 Theater Genesis for sustained excellence

10557 The Open Theater for *The Serpent*

10558 Om Theater for *Riot*

10559 The Performance Group for *Dionysus in '69*

——————— **1 9 7 0** ———————

10560 **Best Play/Best New American Play:** *The Effect of Gamma Rays on Man-in-the-Moon Marigolds* by Paul Zindel and *Approaching Simone* by Megan Terry

10561 **Best Foreign Play:** *What the Butler Saw* by Joe Orton

10562 **Best Musical:** *The Last Sweet Days of Isaac* by Gretchen Cryer and Nancy Ford and *The Me Nobody Knows* by Robert Livingston, Gary William Friedman and Will Holt

10563 **Distinguished Play:** *The Deer Kill* by Murray Mednick and *The Increased Difficulty of Concentration* by Vaclav Havel

10564 **Best Performances:** Sada Thompson in *The Effect of Gamma Rays on Man-in-the-Moon Marigolds*

10565 **Distinguished Direction:** Alan Arkin, Melvin Bernhardt, Maxine Klein and Gilbert Moses

10566 **Distinguished Performances by Actresses:** Rue McClanahan, Roberta Maxwell, Fredericka Weber and Pamela Payton-Wright

10567 Distinguished Performances by Actors: Beeson Carroll, Vincent Gardenia, Harold Gould, Anthony Holland, Lee Kissman, Ron Liebman and Austin Pendleton

10568 Special Citations and Awards which do not fit into other categories: The Chelsea Theater Center, Gardner Compton and Emile Ardolino for *Elephant Steps*, Andre Gregory, the Ridiculous Theater Company and the Theater of the Ridiculous

——————— **1 9 7 1** ———————

10569 Best Play/Best New American Play: *House of Blue Leaves* by John Guare

10570 Distinguished Playwriting: *The Fabulous Miss Marie* and *In New England Winter* by Ed Bullins; and *Basic Training of Pavlo Hummel* by David Rabe

10571 Distinguished Foreign Play: *Boseman and Lena* by Athol Fugard, *AC/DC* by Heathcote Williams and *Dream on Monkey Mountain* by Derek Walcott

10572 Distinguished Production: *The Trial of the Catonsville Nine*

10573 Best Actor: Jack MacGowran in *Beckett*

10574 Best Actress: Ruby Dee in *Boesman and Lena*

10575 Distinguished Sets, Lighting or Costumes: John Scheffer

10576 Distinguished Direction: John Berry, Jeff Bleckner, Gordon Davidson, John Hirsch and Larry Kornfeld

10577 Distinguished Performances by Actresses: Susan Batson, Margaret Braidwood and Joan Macintosh

10578 Distinguished Performances by Actors: Hector Elizondo, Donald Ewer, Sonny Jim, Stacy Keach, Harris Laskaway, William Schallert and James Woods

10579 Special Citations and Awards which do not fit into other categories: *Orlando Furioso* and Kirk Kirksey

——————— **1 9 7 2** ———————

10580 Best Production: *The Mutation Show* by the Open Theater

10581 Distinguished Direction: Wilford Leach and John Braswell, Mel Shapiro, Michael Smith and Tom Sydorick

10582 Distinguished Sets, Lighting or Costumes: Video Free America for visual effects

10583 Music: Micki Grant and Elizabeth Swados

10584 Distinguished Performances by Actresses: Salome Bey, Marilyn Chris, Jeanne Hepple, Marilyn Sokol, Kathleen Widdoes and Elizabeth Wilson

10585 Distinguished Performances by Actors: Maurice Blanc, Alex Bradford, Ron Faber, Danny Sewall and Ed Zang

10586 Special Citations and Awards which do not fit into other categories: Charles Stanley, Meredith Monk, the Theater of Latin America and Free the Army

——————— **1 9 7 3** ———————

10587 Best Play/Best New American Play: *Hot L Baltimore* by Lanford Wilson and *The River Niger* by Joseph A. Walker

10588 Distinguished Play: *The Tooth of Crime* by Sam Shepard, *Big Foot* by Ronald Tavel and *What If I Had Turned Up Heads?* by J. E. Gaines

10589 Distinguished Foreign Play: *Not I* by Samuel Beckett and *Kasper* by Peter Handke

10590 Distinguished Direction: Jack Gelber, William E. Latham and Marshall W. Mason

10591 Distinguished Performances by Actresses: Mari Gorman, Lola Pashalinski, Alice Playton, Roxie Roker and Jessica Tandy

10592 Distinguished Performances by Actors: Hume Cronyn, James Hilbrandt, Stacy Keach, Christopher Lloyd, Charles Ludlam, Douglas Turner Wood and Sam Waterston

10593 Special Citations and Awards which do not fit into other categories: Richard Foreman, the San Francisco Mime Troupe, the City Center Acting Company and Workshop of the Player's Art

──────── **1 9 7 4** ────────

10594 Best Play/Best New American Play: *Short Eyes* by Miguel Pinero
10595 Best Foreign Play: *The Contractor* by David Storey
10596 Distinguished Play: *Bad Habits* by Terrence McNally, *When You Comin' Back, Red Ryder?* by Mark Medoff and *The Great McDaddy* by Paul Carter Harrison
10597 Distinguished Performances both Male and Female: Barbara Barrie in *The Killdeer*, Joseph Buloff in *Hard to Be a Jew*, Kevin Conway in *When You Comin' Back, Red Ryder?*, Conchita Ferrell in *The Sea Horse*, Loretta Greene in *The Sirens*, Barbara Montgomery in *My Sister, My Sister*, Zipora Spaizman in *Stepnyu* and Elizabeth Sturges in *When You Comin' Back, Red Ryder?*
10598 Distinguished Direction: Marvin Felix Camillo, Robert Drivas, David Licht, John Pasquin and Harold Prince
10599 Distinguished Sets, Lighting or Costumes: Theoni Aldredge, Holmes Easley and Christopher Thomas
10600 Music: Bill Elliott
10601 Special Citations and Awards which do not fit into other categories: Peter Schumann's Bread & Puppet Theater, the Brooklyn Academy of Music, CSC Repertory Company and Robert Wilson

──────── **1 9 7 5** ────────

10602 Best Play/Best New American Play: *The First Breeze of Summer* by Leslie Lee
10603 Distinguished Plays: *The Taking of Miss Janie* by Ed Bullins, *The Mound Builders* by Lanford Wilson, *Our Late Night* by Wallace Shawn and *Action* by Sam Shepard
10604 Distinguished Performances, both Male and Female: Reyno in *The First Breeze of Summer,* Moses Gunn in *The First Breeze of Summer,* Dick Latessa in *Philemon*, Kevin McCarthy in *Harry Outside*, Stephen D. Newman in *Polly*, Christopher Walken in *Kid Champion*, Ian Trigger in *The True History of Squire Jonathan*, Cara Duff-McCormick in *Craig's Wife*, Priscilla Smith in *Trilogy*, Tanya Berezin in *The Mound*

Builders and Tovah Feldsuh in *Yentl the Yeshiva Boy*
10605 Distinguished Direction: Lawrence Kornfeld for *Listen to Me*, Marshall W. Mason for *Battle of Angels* and *The Mound Builders* and Gilbert Moses for *The Taking of Miss Janie*
10606 Distinguished Sets, Lighting or Costumes: Robert U. Taylor for *Polly* and John Lee Beatty for *Down by the River...*, *Battle of Angels* and *The Mound Builders*
10607 Special Citations and Awards which do not fit into other categories: Andre Serban for *Trilogy*, the Royal Shakespeare Company for *Summerfolk*, Charles Ludlam for *Professor Bedlam's Punch and Judy Show*, the Henry Street Settlement, Charles Pierce, Mabou Mines
10608 Sustained Achievement: Special 20-year Obies to: Judith Malina and Julian Beck, Ted Mann and the Circle in the Square, Joseph Papp, Ellen Stewart and *The Fantasticks*

──────── **1 9 7 6** ────────

10609 Best New Play: *Sexual Perversity in Chicago* and especially *American Buffalo* by David Mamet
10610 Best Production: *Rhoda in Potatoland* by Richard Foreman
10611 Distinguished Performances, both Male and Female: Robert Christian in *Blood Knot*, Pamela Payton-Wright in *Jesse and the Bandit Queen,* Priscilla Smith in *The Good Woman of Setzuan*, David Warrilow in *The Lost Ones*, June Gable in *Comedy of Errors*, Sammy Williams in *A Chorus Line*, Priscilla Lopez in *A Chorus Line*, Joyce Aaron in *Acrobatics*, Mike Kellin in *American Buffalo*, Roberts Blossom in *Ice Age*, Crystal Field in *Day Old Bread*, Tony LoBianco in *Yankees 3, Detroit 0*, T. Miratti in *The Shortchanged Revue* and Kate Manheim in *Rhoda in Potatoland*
10612 Distinguished Direction: Marshall W. Mason for *Knock Knock* and *Serenading Louie* and JoAnne Akalaitis for *Cascando*
10613 Distinguished Sets, Lighting or Costumes: Donald Brooks for *The Tempest*

10614 **Music:** Philip Glass
10615 **Special Citations and Awards which do not fit into other categories:** Ralph Lee for *The Halloween Parade*, Morton Lichter and Gordon Rogoff for *Old-Timers' Sexual Symphony*, Santo Loquasto for sets and costumes for *Comedy of Errors*, Meredith Monk for *Quarry*, Edward Bond for *Bingo* at the Yale Repertory Theater, Neil Flanagan for outstanding contribution to Off Off Broadway, *Chile! Chile!* special documentary theater award and the creators of *A Chorus Line*

———— **1977** ————

10616 **Best Play/Best New American Play:** *Curse of the Starving Class* by Sam Shepard
10617 **Distinguished Production:** *The Club*, *For Colored Girls Who Have Considered Suicide/When the Rainbow Is Enuf* and *Dressed Like an Egg*
10618 **Distinguished Performances, both Male and Female:** Danny Aiello in *Gemini*, Martin Balsam in *Cold Storage*, Lucinda Childs in *Einstein on the Beach*, James Coco in *The Transfiguration of Benno Blimpie*, Anne DeSalvo in *Gemini*, John Heard in *G. R. Point*, Jo Henderson in *Ladyhouse Blues*, William Hurt in *My Life*, Joseph Maher in *Savages*, Roberta Maxwell in *Ashes*, Brian Murray in *Ashes*, Lola Pashalinski in *Der Ring Gott Farblonjet*, Marian Seldes in *Isadora Duncan Sleeps with the Russian Navy* and Margaret Wright in *A Manoir*
10619 **Distinguished Plays:** *G.R. Point* by David Berry, *Fefu and Her Friends* by Maria Irene Fornes, *Domino Courts* by William Hauptman, *Gemini* and *The Transformation of Benno Blimpie* by Albert Innaurato and *Ashes* by David Rudkin
10620 **Distinguished Direction:** Melvin Bernhardt for *Children* and Gordon Davidson for *Savages*
10621 **Special Citations and Awards which do not fit into other categories:** Barbara Garson for *The Dinosaur Door*, Manhattan Theater Club for sustained excellence, the New York Street Theater Caravan for sustained excellence,

Theater for the New City for sustained excellence, Philip Glass for music for *Einstein on the Beach*, Ping Chong for *Humboldt's Current*, creators of the Nightclub Cantata, Charles Ludlam for design of *Der Ring Gott Farblonjet*, Carole Oditz for costumes for *Crazy Locomotive,* Douglas Schmidt for set of *Crazy Locomotive* and Burl Hass for lighting for *Crazy Locomotive*, Henry Millman for set for *Domino Courts* and Edward M. Greenberg for lighting for *Domino Courts*
10622 **Sustained Achievement:** Joseph Chaikin

———— **1978** ————

10623 **Best Play:** *Shaggy Dog Animation* by Lee Breuer
10624 **Distinguished Direction:** Robert Allan Ackerman for *Prayer for My Daughter*, Thomas Bullard for *Statements After an Arrest Under the Immorality Act* and Elizabeth Swados for *Runaways*
10625 **Distinguished Performances, both Male and Female:** Richard Bauer in *Landscape of the Body* and *The Dybbuk*, Nell Carter in *Ain't Misbehavin'*, Alma Cuervo in *Uncommon Women*, Swoosie Kurtz in *Uncommon Women*, Kaiulani Lee in *Safe House*, Bruce Myers in *The Dybbuk* and Lee S. Wilkof in *The Present Time*
10626 **Distinguished Sets, Lighting or Costumes:** Garland Wright and John Arnone for *K* and Robert Yodice for *Museum*
10627 **Special Citations:** *Ain't Misbehavin'*, Eric Bentley, Joseph Dunn and Ira Koljonen for *Preface*, James Lapine for *Photograph*, Jerry Mayer for *Taud Show*, Stuart Sherman, Winston Tong and Squat
10628 **Lifetime Achievement:** Peter Schumann's Bread & Puppet Theater

———— **1979** ————

10629 **Best Play:** *Josephine* (adaptation of Franz Kafka short story) by Michael McClure
10630 **Distinguished Performances, both Male and Female:** Joseph Buloff in

The Price, Constance Cummings in *Wings,* Fred Gwynne in *Grand Magic,* Judd Hirsch in *Talley's Folly,* Marcell Rosenblatt in *Vienna Notes,* Meryl Streep in *Taken in Marriage,* Elizabeth Wilson in *Taken in Marriage,* Mary Alice Nongogoand in *Julius Caesar* and Philip Anglim in *The Elephant Man*

10631 Distinguished Direction: Maria Irene Fornes for *Eyes on the Harem* and Jack Hollis for *The Elephant Man*

10632 Distinguished Sets, Lighting or Costumes: Theater X for *Fierce Longing* and Jennifer Tipton Public Theater

10633 Distinguished Plays: Rosalyn Drexler for *The Writer's Opera,* Susan Miller for *Nasty Rumors and Final Remarks,* Richard Nelson for *Vienna Notes,* Bernard Pomerance for *The Elephant Man* and Sam Shepard for *Burned Child*

10634 Special Citations: The French Department at NYU for its Samuel Beckett festival, the Negro Ensemble Company for sustained excellence of ensemble acting, Tadeusz Kantor for *The Dead Class,* JoAnne Akalaitis, Ellen McElduff and David Warrilow for *Southern Exposure* and Gordon Chater, Richard Wherett and Steve J. Spears for *The Elocution of Benjamin*

10635 Sustained Achievement: Al Carmines

───────── **1 9 8 0** ─────────

10636 Playwriting: Lee Breuer script and direction for *A Prelude to Death in Venice,* Christopher Durang for *Sister Mary Ignatius Explains It All for You,* Romulus Linney for *Tennessee,* Roland Muldoon script and performance for *Full Confessions of a Socialist* and Jeff Weiss script and performance for *That's How the Rent Gets Paid (Part Three)*

10637 Performance: Michael Burrell in *Hess,* Michael Cristofer in *Chinchilla,* Lindsay Crouse in *Reunion,* Elizabeth Franz in *Sister Mary Ignatius Explains It All for You,* Morgan Freeman in *Mother Courage* and *Coriolanus,* John Heard in *Othello* and *Split,* Michael Higgins in *Reunion,* Madeline Le Roux in *La Justice,* John Polito for performances with Dodger Theater Company and the

BAM Theater Company, Bill Raymond in *A Prelude to Death in Venice,* Dianne Wiest in *The Art of Dining* and Hattie Winston in *Mother Courage* and *The Michigan*

10638 Direction: A.J. Antoon for *The Art of Dining,* Edward Cornell for *Johnny on a Spot* and Elizabeth LeCompte for *Point Judith*

10639 Design: Ruth Maleczech and Julie Archer for the design of *Vanishing Pictures,* Sally Jacobs for the designs of *Conference of the Birds,* Beverly Emmons for distinguished lighting design and Laura Crow for costumes for *Mary Stuart*

10640 Special Citations: The Flying Karamazov Brothers, the actors of Le Centre International de Creations Theatricales for outstanding ensemble performances, Ellen Stewart and La Mama E.T.C. for contribution to the American theater by the importation of foreign companies, David Jones and Richard Nelson for innovative programming at the BAM Theater Company and Ntozake Shange for her adaptation of *Mother Courage.*

───────── **1 9 8 1** ─────────

10641 Best Play: David Henry Hwang for *FOB*

10642 Best Production: Emily Mann for *Still Life*

10643 Playwriting: Charles Fuller for *Zooman and the Sign,* Amlie Gray for *How I Got That Story* and Lon Jenkins script and direction for *Limbo Tales*

10644 Performances: Christopher Walken in *The Sea Gull,* Meryl Streep in *Alice in Concert,* John Spencer in *Still Life,* Michele Shay in *Meetings,* William Sadler in *Limbo Tales,* Timothy Near in *Still Life,* Mary McDonnel in *Still Life,* John Lane in *FOB* and *The Dance* and *The Railroad,* Kevin Kline in *The Pirates of Penzance,* Mary Beth Hurt in *Crimes of the Heart,* Bob Guston in *How I Got That Story* and Giancarlo Esposito in *Zooman and the Sign*

10645 Direction: Melvin Bernhardt for *Crimes of the Heart,* Wilford Leach for *The Pirates of Penzance* and Toby Robertson for *Pericles*

10646 **Design:** Manuel Lutgambaret and Douglas Ball for *Request Concert*, Jim Meeda for sustained excellence in set design, Dennis Parichy for sustained excellence in lighting design and Bioslips costume design for *Lust in Space*

10647 **Special Citations:** JoAnne Akalaitis and Mabou Mines for *Dead End Kids*, Joseph Chaikin and the Winter Project for *Tourists and Refugees,* Bill Irwin for his inspired clowning, Bruce Myers for *A Dybbuk for Two People* and Repertoire Espanol

10648 **Sustained Achievement:** Negro Ensemble Company

─────── **1 9 8 2** ───────

10649 **Best New American Play:** *Metamorphosis in Miniature* and *Mr. Dead and Mrs. Free*

10650 **Best Theater Piece:** *Wielopole Wielopole* by Tadeusz Kantor

10651 **Distinguished Playwriting:** *Cloud 9* by Caryl Churchill, *Stops and Virgins* by Robert Auletta

10652 **Distinguished Direction:** Tommy Tune for *Cloud 9*

10653 **Distinguished Design:** Jim Clayburgh for sustained excellence in set design and Arden Fingerhut for sustained excellence in lighting design

10654 **Distinguished Performances:** Irene Worth in *The Chalk Garden*, Josef Sommer in *Lydie Breeze*, Carole Shelley in *Twelve Dreams*, Kevin O'Connor in *Chucky's Hunch*, *Birdbath* and *Crossing the Crab Nebula*, Kevin McMillan in *Weekends Like Other People*, E. Katherine Kerr in *Cloud 9*, Michael Gross in *No End of Blame*, Christine Estabrook in *Pastorale*, Ray Dooley in *Peer Gynt*, James Barbosa in *Soon Jack November* and Kevin Bacon in *Forty Deuce* and *Poor Little Lambs*

10655 **Distinguished Ensemble Performances:** Lisa Banes, Brenda Currin, Elizabeth McGovern and Beverly May in *My Sister in This House*, Adolph Caesar, Larry Riley and Denzel Washington in *A Soldier's Play*

10656 **Sustained Achievement:** Maria Irene Fornes

10657 **Special Citations:** La Mama: 20th anniversary celebration, Harvey Fierstein for *Torch Song Trilogy* and the Theater Communications Group

─────── **1 9 8 3** ───────

10658 **Performance:** Glenn Close in *The Singular Life of Albert Nobbs*, Ruth Maleczech in *Hair*, John Malkovich in *True West*, John Daniels in *Johnny Got His Gun*, Donald Moffatt in *Painting Churches*, Gary Wise in *The Tooth of Crime*, Christine Baranski in *A Midsummer Night's Dream* and Spear Aruba in *Yellow Fever*

10659 **Ensemble Performance:** Director Kenneth Frankel and the cast of *Quartermain's Terms*, director Max Sufford Clark and the Royal Court cast of *Top Girls* and the New York Shakespeare Festival cast of *Top Girls*

10660 **Playwriting:** Caryl Churchill for *Top Girls*, John Howe distinguished playwriting, Harry Kondoleon—most promising young playwright and David Mamet for *Edmond*

10661 **Directing:** Gregory Mosher for *Edmond* and Gary Sinise for *True West*

10662 **Design:** Heidi Landesman for *A Midsummer Night's Dream* and *Painting Churches*

10663 **Special Citations:** The Big Apple Circus, Ethyl Eichelberger for *Lucrezia Borgia*, Michael Moschen, Fred Garbo and Bob Berky for *Foolsfire*, the Zagreb Theater Company for *The Liberation of Shopje*, the musical production of *The Mother of Us All*, the musical performance of *Poopie Nongena*, Dramatists Play Service for its commitment to new work, Performing Arts Journal publications and Theater Development Fund for its Off-Off Broadway voucher program

10664 **Sustained Achievement:** Lanford Wilson, Marshall Mason and the Circle Repertory Company

─────── **1 9 8 4** ───────

10665 **Best New American Play:** Sam Shepard for *Fool for Love*

10666 **Best Musical:** Lee Breuer and Bob Telsch for *Gospel at Colonus*

10667 **Direction:** JoAnne Akalaitis for *Through the Leaves*, Maria Irene Fornes for *The Danube*, *Sarita* and *Mud*, Lawrence Sacharow for *Five of Us* and Sam Shepard for *Fool for Love*

10668 **Performance:** F. Murray Abraham in *Uncle Vanya*, Kathy Baker in *Fool for Love*, Sheila Dabney in *Sarita*, Morgan Freeman in *Gospel at Colonus*, George Guidall in *Cinders*, Ed Harris in *Fool for Love*, Richard Jordan in *A Private View*, Ruth Maleczech in *Through the Leaves*, Stephen McHattie for *Mensch Meier*, Frederick Neumann in *Through the Leaves*, Will Patton in *Fool for Love* and Dianne Wiest in *Serenading Louie* and *Other Places*

10669 **Playwriting:** Samuel Beckett for *Ohio Impromptu*, *What Where*, *Catastrophe* and *Rocket*, Maria Irene Fornes for *The Danube*, *Sarita* and *Mud*, Vaclav Havel for *A Private View*, Lon Jenkins for *Five of Us*, Franz Xaver Kroetz for *Through the Leaves* and *Mensch Meier* and Ted Tally for *Terra Nova*

10670 **Design:** Adrianne Lobel set design for *The Vampires* and *All Night Long*, Bill Stabile set design for *Spookhouse*, *Damned Manon* and *Sacree Sandre* and Douglas Stein for *Through the Leaves*

10671 **Special Citations:** Percy Ntwa, Mbongeni Ngema and Barney Simon for their production of *Woza Albert*, International Theater Institute of the U.S., Inc., Pamela Reed for sustained excellence of performance, Anne and Jules Weiss for their tireless devotion to Off and Off Off Broadway and Richard Peaslee for his musical score for *The Garden of Earthly Delights*

10672 **Sustained Achievement:** Music-Theater Group/Lenox Arts Center

———— **1985** ————

10673 **Best Play:** Maria Irene Fornes for *The Conduct of Life*

10674 **Direction:** John Malkovich for *Balm in Gilead*, Barbara Vann for *Bound to Rise* and Jerry Zaks for *The Foreigner* and *The Marriage of Bette and Boo*

10675 **Performance:** Dennis Boutsikaris in *The Nest of the Woodgrouse*, Frances Foster in *Sustained Excellence*, Jonathan Hadary in *As Is*, Anthony

Heald in *Henry V*, *The Foreigner* and *Digby*, Laurie Metcalf in *Balm in Gilead*, John Turtorru in *Danny in the Deep Blue Sea* and Ron Vawter in *Sustained Excellence*

10676 **Playwriting:** Christopher Durang for *The Marriage of Bette and Boo*, Rosalyn Drexler for *Transients Welcome* and William M. Hoffman for *As Is*

10677 **Design:** Judy Dearing for costume design, Victor En Yu Tan for lighting design and Loren Sherman for set design

10678 **Ensemble Performance:** Charles Ludlam and Everett Quinton for *The Mystery of Irma Vep* and the cast of *The Marriage of Bette and Boo*

10679 **Music:** Peter Gordon for *Othello* and Max Roach for *Shepardsets*

10680 **Special Citations:** The Asia Society, Penn and Teller, Julie Taymor, Spalding Gray for *Swimming to Cambodia*, The Roy Hart Theater for *Pagliacci* and *An Evening with Ekkard Schall*

10681 **Sustained Achievement:** Meredith Monk

———— **1986** ————

10682 **Best Performance:** Swoosie Kurtz in *The House of Blue Leaves*

10683 **Sustained Excellence in Performance:** Edward Herrmann and Kevin Kline

10684 **For Performance:** Elizabeth Welch in *A Time to Start Living*, Tom Cayler in *A Matter of Life and Death*, Dylan Baker in *Not About Heroes*, Kathryn Pogson in *Aunt Dan and Lemon*, Jill Eikenberry in *Lemon Sky* and *Life Under Water*, Josef Sommer in *Largo Desolato*, Elizabeth Wilson in *Anteroom*, Farley Granger in *Talley & Son*, Helen Stenborg in *Talley & Son* and Norma Aleandro in *About Love and Other Stories About Love*

10685 **Distinguished Playwriting:** Wallace Shawn for *Aunt Dan and Lemon*

10686 **Playwriting:** Eric Bogosian for *Drinking in America*, Martha Clarke for *Vienna: Lusthaus*, John Jesurun for *Deep Sleep*, Tadeusz Kantor for *Let the Artist Die* and Lee Nagrin for *Bird/Bear*

10687 **Direction:** Richard Foreman for *Largo Desolato*

10688 **Costume Design:** Rita Ryack
10689 **Lighting Design:** Paul Gallo
10690 **Set Design:** Edward T. Gianfrancesco
10691 **Music:** Teiji Ito
10692 **Sustained Achievement:** Mabou Mines

─────── **1 9 8 7** ───────

10693 **Best New American Play:** Richard Foreman for *The Cure* and *Film Is Evil, Radio Is Good*
10694 **Direction:** Garland Wright for *On the Verge*
10695 **Sustained Excellence in Direction:** Carole Rothman
10696 **Performance:** Morgan Freeman in *Driving Miss Daisy*, Dana Ivey in *Driving Miss Daisy*, John Kelly in *Pass the Blutwurst, Bitte*, Laura Hicks in *On the Verge*, Robin Bartlett in *The Early Girl*, Rob Besserer in *The Hunger Artist*, Anthony Holland in *The Hunger Artist*, Clarice Taylor in *Moms*, Bill Raymond in *Cold Harbor* and Geina Mhlophe in *Born in the USA*
10697 **Sustained Excellence of Performance:** Philip Bosco, Blackeyed-Susan and Andrew Jackness
10698 **Sustained Excellence of Lighting Design:** James F. Ingalls
10699 **Set and Costume Design:** Robert Israel for *The Hunger Artist*
10700 **Lighting Design:** Paul Gallo for *The Hunger Artist*
10701 **Awards Also Presented to:** Judith Malina for *The Living Theater Retrospect*, the Woza Afrika Foundation, Dario Fo and Frances Rame, The Non-Traditional Casting Project, La Mama Great Jones Repertory Company for its revival of *Fragments of a Greek Trilogy*
10702 **Sustained Achievement:** Charles Ludlam and the Ridiculous Theater Company

─────── **1 9 8 8** ───────

10703 **Best New Play:** Caryl Churchill for *Serious Money* and Maria Irene Fornes for *Abingdon Square*
10704 **Direction:** Anne Bogart for *No Plays No Poetry...*, Peter Brook for *The Mahabharata* and Julie Taymor for *Juan Darien*
10705 **Performance:** Larry Bazell in *The Signal Season of Dummy Hoy*, Kathy Bates in *Frankie & Johnny in the Clair de Lune*, Yvonne Bryceland in *The Road to Mecca*, Victor Garber in *Wenceslas Square*, Amy Irving in *The Road to Mecca*, Erland Josephson in *The Cherry Orchard*, Gordana Rashovich in *A Shayna Maidel*, John Seitz in *Abingdon Square*, Peggy Shaw in *Dress Suits to Hire*, Tina Shepard in *The Three Lives of Lucie Cabrol* and Lauren Tom in *American Notes*
10706 **Sustained Excellence in Performance:** George Bartenieff and Roberts Blossom
10707 **Sustained Excellence of Stage Design:** Eva Buchmuller
10708 **Sustained Excellence of Scenic Design:** Huck Snyder
10709 **Sustained Excellence of Stage Combat Choreography:** B.H. Barry
10710 **Music:** Elliot Goldenthal for *Juan Darien*
10711 **Sustained Achievement:** Richard Foreman
10712 **Also Awarded:** Christopher Reeve for his courageous work on behalf of Chilean artists

─────── **1 9 8 9** ───────

10713 **Performance:** Mark Blum in *Gus and Al*, Naill Buggy in *Aristocrats*, William Converse-Roberts in *Love's Labor's Lost*, Fyvush Finkel in *Cafe Crown*, Gloria Foster in *The Forbidden City*, Paul Hecht in *Enrico IV*, Nancy Marchand in *The Cocktail Hour*, Tim McDonnell in *Diary of a Madman*, Will Patton in *What Did He See?*, Lonny Price in *The Immigrant*, Everett Quinton in *A Tale of Two Cities*, Rocco Sisto in *The Winter's Tale* and Kathy Najimy and Mo Gaffney in *The Kathy and Mo Show*
10714 **Direction:** Ingmar Bergman for *Hamlet* and Peter Stein for *Falstaff*
10715 **Sustained Excellence of Direction:** Rene Buch
10716 **Sustained Excellence of Set Design:** Donald Eastman
10717 **Sustained Excellence of Costume Design:** Gabriel Berry and Susan Young

10718 **Sustained Achievement:** Irene Worth

10719 **Citations:** Leo Bassi for *Nero's Last Folly*, Dance Theater Workshop, the Dramatists Guild for Young Playwrights Festival, Janie Geiser for *Stories from Here*, Rachel Rosenthal for *Rachel's Brain*, Tamamatsu Yoshida for *The Warrior Ant* and Paul Zaloom for *The House of Horror*

———— **1 9 9 0** ————

10720 **Direction:** Liz Diamond for *Imperceptible Mutabilities in the Third Kingdom*, Norman Rene for *Prelude to a Kiss*, Jim Simpson for *Bad Penny* and George C. Wolfe for *Spunk*

10721 **Design:** Daniel Moses Schreier for sustained sound design and George Taypin for sustained excellence in set design

10722 **Special Citations:** Eric Bogosian for *Sex, Drugs, Rock & Roll*, Dan Hurlin for *A Cool Million*, Joseph Papp for his courageous stand against censorship and the San Francisco Mime Troupe for *Seeing Double*

10723 **Performance:** Alec Baldwin in *Prelude to a Kiss*, Elzbieta Czyzewska in *Crowbar*, Karen Evans-Kandel, Ruth Maleczech, Greg Mehrten and Isabell Monk in *Lear*, Marcia Jean Kurtz in *The Loman Family Picnic* and *When She Danced*, Stephen Mellor in *Terminal Hip*, Jean Stapleton in *Mountain Language* and *The Birthday Party*, Pamala Tyson in *Imperceptible Mutabilities in the Third Kingdom*, Courtney B. Vance in *My Children! My Africa!*, Danitra Vance in *Spunk*, Lillias White in *Romance in Hard Times*

10724 **Sustained Achievement:** Mary Schultz for sustained excellence

———— **1 9 9 1** ————

10725 **Best New Play:** Wallace Shawn for *The Fever*

10726 **Performance:** Eileen Atkins in *A Room of One's Own*, Stockard Channing in *Six Degrees of Separation*, Joan Copeland in *The American Plan*, Angela Coathbain in *The Good Times Are Kill-*ing Me, Tony Goldwyn in *The Sum of Us*, Jan Leslie Harding in *Sincerity Forever*, John Leguizamo in *Mambo Mouth*, Michael Lombard in *What's Wrong with This Picture?*, Jodie Markell in *Machinal*, Anne Pitosiak in *Pygmalion*, Ron Rifkin in *The Substance of Fire*, Kathleen Widdoes in *Tower of Evil*, Betty Bourne, Preeless Pearl, Peggy Shaw and Lois Weaver, Ensemble performances in *Belle Reprieve*

10727 **Direction:** Lisa Peterson for *Light Shining in Buckinghamshire* and Michael Groff for *Handkerchief*

10728 **Design:** John Gromada for sound design of *Machinal*

10729 **Playwriting:** John Guare for *Six Degrees of Separation* and Mac Wellman for *Sincerity Forever*

10730 **Sustained Achievement:** Frances Aronson for lighting design, Mark Beard for set design, William Ivey for costume design

10731 **Special Citations:** Blue Man Group, John Kelly for *For Love of a Poet*, BACA Downtown, New York Theatre Workshop, New York Shakespeare Festival 1990-91 season, Lori E. Seid for stage management, Theatre of New York City for *Stop the War: A Festival for Peace in the Middle East*

———— **1 9 9 2** ————

10732 **Best New American Play:** *Sight Unseen* by Donald Marguiles, *Sally's Rape* by Robbie McCauley and *The Baltimore Waltz* by Paula Vogel

10733 **Direction:** Anne Bogart for *The Baltimore Waltz* and Mark Wing-Davy for *Mad Forest*

10734 **Performance:** Dennis Boutsikaris in *Sight Unseen*, Laura Esterman in *Marvin's Room*, Deborah Hedwall in *Sight Unseen*, Cherry Jones in *The Baltimore Waltz*, James McDaniel in *Before It Hits Home*, S. Epatha Merkerson in *I'm Not Stupid*, Roger Rees in *End of the Day* and Lynn Thigpen in *Boseman and Lena*

10735 **Sustained Excellence of Performance:** Larry Bryggman, Randy Danson, Cordelia Gonzales and Nathan Lane

10736 **Sustained Excellence of Playwriting:** Neal Bell and Romulus Linney

10737 **Sustained Excellence of Set Design:** John Arnone

10738 **Sustained Excellence of Sets and Costumes:** Marina Draghici

10739 **Special Citations:** Gerard Allessandrini for *Forbidden Broadway*, the New York International Festival of the Arts for presenting the works of Ingmar Bergman, Tadeusz Kantor and Eimuntas Nekrosius, the Public Theatre for the conception and design of *'Tis a Pity She's a Whore*, David Gordon for *The Mysteries* and *What's So Funny?*, Anna Deavere Smith for *Fires in the Mirror*, Ron Vawter for *Roy Cohn/Jack Smith* and Jeff Weiss for *Hot Keys*

10740 **Sustained Achievement:** Athol Fugard

———————— **1 9 9 3** ————————

10741 **Performance:** Jane Alexander in *The Sisters Rosensweig*, Frances Conroy in *The Last Yankee*, David Drake in *The Night Larry Kramer Kissed Me*, Giancarlo Esposito in *Distant Fires*, Geoffrey C. Ewing in *Ali*, Hallie Foote in *The Roads to Home*, Edward Hibbert in *Jeffrey*, Bill Irwin in *Texts for Nothing*, Robert Klein in *The Sisters Rosensweig*, John Cameron Mitchell in *The Destiny of Me* and Linda Stephens in *Wings*

10742 **Sustained Excellence of Performance:** Miriam Colon and Ellen Parker

10743 **Direction:** Christopher Ashley for *Jeffrey*, Michael Maggio for *Wings* and Frederick Zollo for *Aven'U Boys*

10744 **Sustained Excellence of Set Design:** Loy Arcenas

10745 **Sustained Excellence of Lighting Design:** Howard Thies

10746 **Playwriting:** Harry Kondoleon for *The Houseguests*, Larry Kramer for *The Destiny of Me*, Jose Rivera for *Marisol* and Paul Rudnick for *Jeffrey*

10747 **Citations:** Cirque du Soleil, Betty Corwin of the New York Public Library Archives, the Ensemble Studio Theatre for the One-Act Play Marathon, The International Festival of Puppet Theatre, Ariane Mnouchkine for *Les Atrides* and *Serious Fun!*

10748 **Sustained Achievement:** JoAnne Akalaitis

New York Drama Critics' Circle Awards

The current New York Drama Critics' Circle was formed during the season 1934 to 1935. This organization of drama critics revived the award created by a previous group which had ceased to functon. Drama critics were frustrated with existing award programs and felt that they represented a too narrow and conservative viewpoint. New York Drama Critics' Circle Awards were created to correct this. In order to correct the situation, the membership was limited to first or second reviewers of the drama scene in New York.

Drama critics come from daily newspapers in New York, weekly newspapers and some New York–based magazines (i.e., *The New Yorker*). Only print reviewers are allowed membership; no broadcast reviewers are allowed. Membership in the New York Drama Critics' Circle is by invitation and election only.

The only obligatory statuette awarded is in the Best Play category. If the best play is foreign, a Best American Play is named. If the best play is American, a Best Foreign Play is named. Decisions on all other awards given are up to the judgment of the members of the New York Drama Critics' Circle. Occasional special awards are given. Recipients of these special awards cannot be runners-up from another category. Only original entrants may be given special awards.

The plays selected are not limited to the Broadway stage as are the Tony Awards. Nor are they limited to Off Broadway plays as are the Obie Awards. Any play on the New York stage is eligible.

──────── **1936** ────────

10749 **Best American Play:** *Winterset* by Maxwell Anderson

──────── **1937** ────────

10750 **Best American Play:** *High Tor* by Maxwell Anderson

──────── **1938** ────────

10751 **Best American Play:** *Of Mice and Men* by John Steinbeck
10752 **Best Foreign Play:** *Shadow and Substance* by Paul Vincent Carroll

──────── **1939** ────────

10753 **Best Foreign Play:** *The White Steed* by Paul Vincent Carroll

──────── **1940** ────────

10754 **Best American Play:** *The Time of Your Life* by William Saroyan

──────── **1941** ────────

10755 **Best American Play:** *Watch on the Rhine* by Lillian Hellman
10756 **Best Foreign Play:** *The Corn Is Green* by Emlyn Williams

──────── **1942** ────────

10757 **Best Foreign Play:** *Blithe Spirit* by Noel Coward

──────── **1943** ────────

10758 **Best American Play:** *The Patriots* by Sidney Kingsley

──────── **1944** ────────

10759 **Best Foreign Play:** *Jacobowski and the Colonel* by Franz Werfel and S.N. Behrman

──────── **1945** ────────

10760 **Best American Play:** *The Glass Menagerie* by Tennessee Williams

──────── **1946** ────────

10761 **Best Musical:** *Carousel* by Richard Rodgers and Oscar Hammerstein II

──────── **1947** ────────

10762 **Best American Play:** *All My Sons* by Arthur Miller
10763 **Best Foreign Play:** *No Exit* by Jean-Paul Sartre
10764 **Best Musical:** *Brigadoon* by Alan Jay Lerner and Frederick Loewe

──────── **1948** ────────

10765 **Best American Play:** *A Streetcar Named Desire* by Tennessee Williams
10766 **Best Foreign Play:** *The Winslow Boy* by Terence Rattigan

──────── **1949** ────────

10767 **Best American Play:** *Death of a Salesman* by Arthur Miller
10768 **Best Foreign Play:** *The Madwoman of Chaillot* by Maurice Valency
10769 **Best Musical:** *South Pacific* by Richard Rodgers, Oscar Hammerstein II and Joshua Logan

──────── **1950** ────────

10770 **Best American Play:** *The Member of the Wedding* by Carson McCullers
10771 **Best Foreign Play:** *The Cocktail Party* by T. S. Eliot
10772 **Best Musical:** *The Consul* by Gian-Carlo Menotti

──────── **1951** ────────

10773 **Best American Play:** *Darkness at Noon* by Sidney Kingsley
10774 **Best Foreign Play:** *The Lady's Not for Burning* by Christopher Fry
10775 **Best Musical:** *Guys and Dolls* by Jo Swerling, Abe Burrows and Frank Loesser

──────── **1952** ────────

10776 **Best American Play:** *I Am a Camera* by John van Druten

10777 Best Foreign Play: *Venus Observed* by Christopher Fry
10778 Best Musical: *Pal Joey* by Richard Rodgers and Lorenz Hart
10779 Special Citation: *Don Juan in Hell* by George Bernard Shaw

——————— **1 9 5 3** ———————

10780 Best American Play: *Picnic* by William Inge
10781 Best Foreign Play: *The Love of Four Colonels* by Peter Ustinov
10782 Best Musical: *Wonderful Town* by Joseph Fields, Jerome Chodorov, Betty Comden and Adolph Green

——————— **1 9 5 4** ———————

10783 Best American Play: *Teahouse of the August Moon* by John Patrick
10784 Best Foreign Play: *Ondine* by Maurice Valency
10785 Best Musical: John LaTouche and Jerome Moross for *The Golden Apple*

——————— **1 9 5 5** ———————

10786 Best American Play: *Cat on a Hot Tin Roof* by Tennessee Williams
10787 Best Foreign Play: *Witness for the Prosecution* by Agatha Christie
10788 Best Musical: *The Saint of Bleecker Street* by Gian-Carlo Menotti

——————— **1 9 5 6** ———————

10789 Best American Play: *The Diary of Anne Frank* by Frances Goodrich and Albert Hackett
10790 Best Foreign Play: *Tiger at the Gates* by Christopher Fry
10791 Best Musical: *My Fair Lady* by Alan Jay Lerner and Frederick Loewe

——————— **1 9 5 7** ———————

10792 Best American Play: *Long Day's Journey Into Night* by Eugene O'Neill
10793 Best Foreign Play: *Waltz of the Torreadors* by Jean Anouilh
10794 Best Musical: *The Most Happy Fella* by Frank Loesser

——————— **1 9 5 8** ———————

10795 Best American Play: *Look Homeward, Angel* by Ketti Frings
10796 Best Foreign Play: *Look Back in Anger* by John Osborne
10797 Best Musical: Meredith Willson for *The Music Man*

——————— **1 9 5 9** ———————

10798 Best American Play: *A Raisin in the Sun* by Lorraine Hansberry
10799 Best Foreign Play: *The Visit* by Friedrich Dürrenmatt
10800 Best Musical: *La Plume de Ma Tante* by Robert Dhery, Gerald Calvi and Ross Parker

——————— **1 9 6 0** ———————

10801 Best American Play: *Toys in the Attic* by Lillian Hellman
10802 Best Foreign Play: *Five Finger Exercise* by Peter Schaffer
10803 Best Musical: George Abbott, Jerome Weidman, Sheldon Harnick and Jerry Bock for *Fiorello!*

——————— **1 9 6 1** ———————

10804 Best American Play: *All the Way Home* by Tad Mosel
10805 Best Foreign Play: *A Taste of Honey* by Shelagh Delaney
10806 Best Musical: Michael Stewart and Bob Merrill for *Carnival!*

——————— **1 9 6 2** ———————

10807 Best American Play: *The Night of the Iguana* by Tennessee Williams
10808 Best Foreign Play: *A Man for All Seasons* by Robert Bolt
10809 Best Musical: Abe Burrows, Jack Weinstock, Willie Gilbert and Frank Loesser for *How to Succeed in Business Without Really Trying*

——————— **1 9 6 3** ———————

10810 Best Play Regardless of Category: *Who's Afraid of Virginia Woolf?* by Edward Albee
10811 Special Citation: *Beyond the Fringe* written by the performers

─────── **1 9 6 4** ───────

10812 Best Play Regardless of Category: *Luther* by John Osborne
10813 Best Musical: *Hello, Dolly!* by Jerry Herman
10814 Special Citation: *The Trojan Women* by Euripides

─────── **1 9 6 5** ───────

10815 Best Play Regardless of Category: *The Subject Was Roses* by Frank Gilroy
10816 Best Musical: *Fiddler on the Roof* by Joseph Stein, Jerry Bock and Sheldon Harnick

─────── **1 9 6 6** ───────

10817 Best Play Regardless of Category: *The Persecution and Assassination of Marat as Performed by the Inmates of the Asylum of Charenton Under the Direction of the Marquis de Sade* by Peter Weiss
10818 Best Musical: Dale Wasserman, Mitch Leigh and Joe Darion for *Man of La Mancha*

─────── **1 9 6 7** ───────

10819 Best Play Regardless of Category: *The Homecoming* by Harold Pinter
10820 Best Musical: *Cabaret* by John Kander, Fred Ebb, Joe Masteroff, John van Druten and Christopher Isherwood

─────── **1 9 6 8** ───────

10821 Best Play Regardless of Category: *Rosenkrantz and Guildenstern Are Dead* by Tom Stoppard
10822 Best Musical: *Your Own Thing* by Donald Driver, Hal Hester and Danny Apolimar

─────── **1 9 6 9** ───────

10823 Best Play Regardless of Category: *The Great White Hope* by Howard Sackler
10824 Best Musical: *1776* by Sherman Edwards and Peter Stone

─────── **1 9 7 0** ───────

10825 Best American Play: *The Effect of Gamma Rays on Man-in-the-Moon Marigolds* by Paul Zindel
10826 Best Play Regardless of Category: *Borstal Boy* by Frank McMahon
10827 Best Musical: Stephen Sondheim and George Furth for *Company*

─────── **1 9 7 1** ───────

10828 Best American Play: *The House of Blue Leaves* by John Guare
10829 Best Play Regardless of Category: *Home* by David Storey
10830 Best Musical: Stephen Sondheim and James Goldman for *Follies*

─────── **1 9 7 2** ───────

10831 Best Play Regardless of Category: *That Championship Season* by Jason Miller
10832 Best Foreign Play: *The Screens* by Jean Genet
10833 Best Musical: Galt MacDermott and John Guare for *Two Gentlemen of Verona*
10834 Special Citation: To *Sticks and Bones* by David Rabe and *Old Times* by Harold Pinter

─────── **1 9 7 3** ───────

10835 Best American Play: *Hot L Baltimore* by Lanford Wilson
10836 Best Play Regardless of Category: *The Changing Room* by David Storey
10837 Best Musical: Hugh Wheeler and Stephen Sondheim for *A Little Night Music*

─────── **1 9 7 4** ───────

10838 Best American Play: *Short Eyes* by Miguel Pinero
10839 Best Play Regardless of Category: *The Contractor* by David Storey
10840 Best Musical: *Candide* by Hugh Wheeler, Leonard Bernstein, Richard Wilbur, Stephen Sondheim and John LaTouche

—————— **1975** ——————

10841 **Best American Play:** *The Taking of Miss Janie* by Ed Bullins
10842 **Best Play Regardless of Category:** *Equus* by Peter Shaffer
10843 **Best Musical:** Michael Bennett, choreographer and director; James Kirkwood and Nicholas Dante, book; Marvin Hamlisch, music; and Edward Kleban, lyrics for *A Chorus Line*

—————— **1976** ——————

10844 **Best American Play:** *Streamers* by David Rabe
10845 **Best Play Regardless of Category:** *Travesties* by Tom Stoppard
10846 **Best Musical:** Stephen Sondheim, music and lyrics; Jerome Weidman, book; and Hugh Wheeler, additional material for *Pacific Overtures*

—————— **1977** ——————

10847 **Best American Play:** *American Buffalo* by David Mamet
10848 **Best Play Regardless of Category:** *Otherwise Engaged* by Simon Gray
10849 **Best Musical:** Charles Strouse, music; Martin Charnin, lyrics; Thomas Meehan, book; and Mike Nichols, producer for *Annie*

—————— **1978** ——————

10850 **Best Musical:** *Ain't Misbehavin'* by Fats Waller
10851 **Best Play Regardless of Category:** *Da* by Hugh Leonard

—————— **1979** ——————

10852 **Best Play Regardless of Category:** *The Elephant Man* by Bernard Pomerance
10853 **Best Musical:** *Sweeney Todd, the Demon Barber of Fleet Street* by Christopher Bond, Hugh Wheeler and Stephen Sondheim

—————— **1980** ——————

10854 **Best Foreign Play:** *Betrayal* by Harold Pinter

10855 **Best Play Regardless of Category:** *Talley's Folly* by Lanford Wilson
10856 **Best Musical:** *Evita* by Andrew Lloyd Webber and Tim Rice
10857 **Special Citation:** To Peter Brook's Le Centre International de Créations Théatricales for its repertory

—————— **1981** ——————

10858 **Best Play Regardless of Category:** *A Lesson from Aloes* by Athol Fugard
10859 **Best American Play:** *Crimes of the Heart* by Beth Henley
10860 **Special Citations:** To *Lena Horne: The Lady and Her Music* and the New York Shakespeare Festival production of *The Pirates of Penzance* by W.S. Gilbert and Arthur Sullivan

—————— **1982** ——————

10861 **Best Play Regardless of Category:** *The Life and Adventures of Nicholas Nickleby* by Charles Dickens, David Edgar and Stephen Oliver
10862 **Best American Play:** *A Soldier's Play* by Charles Fuller

—————— **1983** ——————

10863 **Best Play Regardless of Category:** *Brighton Beach Memoirs* by Neil Simon
10864 **Best Foreign Play:** *Plenty* by David Hare
10865 **Best Musical:** *Little Shop of Horrors* by Howard Ashman and Alan Menken
10866 **Special Citation:** To the Young Playwrights Festival

—————— **1984** ——————

10867 **Best American Play:** *Glengarry Glen Ross* by David Mamet
10868 **Best Play Regardless of Category:** *The Real Thing* by Tom Stoppard
10869 **Best Musical:** *Sunday in the Park with George* by James Lapine and Stephen Sondheim
10870 **Special Citation:** To Samuel Beckett for his body of work

——————— 1 9 8 5 ———————

10871 **Best Play Regardless of Category:** *Ma Rainey's Black Bottom* by August Wilson

——————— 1 9 8 6 ———————

10872 **Best Play Regardless of Category:** *A Lie of the Mind* by Sam Shepard
10873 **Best Foreign Play:** *Benefactors* by Michael Frayn
10874 **Special Citation:** To *The Search for Signs of Intelligent Life in the Universe* by Jane Wagner

——————— 1 9 8 7 ———————

10875 **Best Play Regardless of Category:** *Fences* by August Wilson
10876 **Best Foreign Play:** *Les Liaisons Dangereuses* by Choderlos de Laelos and Christopher Hampton
10877 **Best Musical:** *Les Misérables* by Victor Hugo, Alain Boublil, Claude-Michel Schönberg and Herbert Kretzmer

——————— 1 9 8 8 ———————

10878 **Best Play Regardless of Category:** *Joe Turner's Come and Gone* by August Wilson
10879 **Best Foreign Play:** *The Road to Mecca* by Athol Fugard
10880 **Best Musical:** *Into the Woods* by James Lapine and Stephen Sondheim

——————— 1 9 8 9 ———————

10881 **Best Play Regardless of Category:** *The Heidi Chronicles* by Wendy Wasserstein
10882 **Best Foreign Play:** *Aristocrats* by Brian Friel
10883 **Special Citation:** To Bill Irwin for *Largely New York*

——————— 1 9 9 0 ———————

10884 **Best Foreign Play:** *Privates on Parade* by Peter Nichols and Denis King
10885 **Best Play Regardless of Category:** *The Piano Lesson* by August Wilson
10886 **Best Musical:** *City of Angels* by Larry Gelbart, Cy Coleman and David Zippel

——————— 1 9 9 1 ———————

10887 **Best Play Regardless of Category:** *Six Degrees of Separation* by John Guare
10888 **Best Foreign Play:** *Our Country's Good* by Timberlake Wertenbaker
10889 **Best Musical:** *Will Rogers Follies*, book by Peter Stone
10890 **Special Citation:** To Eileen Atkins for her portrayal of Virginia Woolf in *A Room of One's Own*

——————— 1 9 9 2 ———————

10891 **Best Play Regardless of Category:** *Dancing at Lughnasa* by Brian Friel
10892 **Best American Play:** *Two Trains Running* by August Wilson

——————— 1 9 9 3 ———————

10893 **Best Play Regardless of Category:** *Angels in America: Millennium Approaches* by Tony Kushner
10894 **Best Foreign Play:** *Someone Who'll Watch Over Me* by Frank McGuinness
10895 **Best Musical:** *Kiss of the Spider Woman — The Musical* by Terrence McNally, music by John Kander and Fred Ebb

Index of Names and Organizations

Index of Titles